OXFORD HISTORY OF
ENGLISH LITERATURE

Edited by

F. P. WILSON *and* BONAMY DOBRÉE

THE OXFORD HISTORY OF
ENGLISH LITERATURE

Edited by

F. P. WILSON *and* BONAMY DOBRÉE

EIGHT
MODERN WRITERS

BY

J. I. M. STEWART

OXFORD
AT THE CLARENDON PRESS

© *Oxford University Press 1963*

FIRST PUBLISHED 1963
REPRINTED, WITH CORRECTIONS, 1964

PRINTED IN GREAT BRITAIN

TO MY WIFE

PREFACE

IN *Victorian England: Portrait of an Age* G. M. Young writes:

To a foreigner, the age through which we ourselves have been living is the age of Galsworthy, Wells, and Shaw; before them of Wilde. Something, doubtless, beside literary enjoyment guides his taste.

It is Young's point that the foreigner, in exalting these writers, is showing a 'malicious preference for what is most critical and most subversive' of England in the heyday of her imperialism. Here is 'an echo of that passionate jealousy of England which for a generation was the most widely diffused emotion in Europe'. And Young adds (for he has been reviewing the history of Anglo-Irish relations): 'Two Irishmen in a list of four. It is something to be thought of.'

From this volume I have excluded living writers, and have then attempted a record of the eight who seem to me of unchallengeable importance in the period. Wilde is not among these: nevertheless there are three Irishmen, since to Shaw I have added Yeats and Joyce. So again there is 'something to be thought of'. Moreover I include in James an American, in Conrad a Pole, and in Kipling an Indian-born writer who remained to some extent an explorer rather than a native of England. But I do not think that Young's 'malicious preference' has been at work in me, a Scot, to produce this incidence. It is a fact of literary history of which we must make what we can.

My inclusions and exclusions are best not defended: let them be shot at by anybody who is interested. I will only say that, unlike the jealous foreigner, I have let nothing 'beside literary enjoyment' guide my taste. It would be rash to suggest that the chosen eight will eventually prove to be the only great writers of their age. As the mists of near-contemporaneity disperse, other peaks must appear. But I think it likely that these eight will remain important landmarks when literary historians come to a fuller survey of the terrain. Meantime they afford a scale against which a good deal can be measured in a tentative way. What I have attempted is a volume that may serve as a companion to a first fairly extensive reading in them. The introductory chapter merely sketches in a general background in the light of this purpose.

I am grateful to the General Editors, Professor F. P. Wilson and Professor Bonamy Dobrée, for a great deal of help and patience; to Mr. Rayner Heppenstall for detailed and valuable criticism of the whole work; and to Mr. J. A. Burrow, Mr. C. H. Collie, and Mr. Howell Daniels for equally valuable criticism of individual chapters. Mr. Daniels has put me further in his debt by providing the bibliographies of Hardy, James, Conrad, Yeats, and Lawrence. In the introductory chapter I have reproduced the substance of the Garnett Sedgewick Memorial Lecture given in the University of British Columbia in 1961; in the chapter on Hardy some paragraphs from a paper which appeared in *Essays and Studies* for 1948; and in the chapter on Joyce parts of a pamphlet published in 1957 in the series *Writers and their Work*. For permission to quote substantially from copyright material I am grateful to the Trustees of the Hardy Estate, Messrs. Macmillan and Company, and the Macmillan Company of New York (Thomas Hardy's *Collected Poems*); to the Public Trustee and the Society of Authors (Bernard Shaw's *Man and Superman* and *Major Barbara*); to Mrs. George Bambridge, Messrs. A. P. Watt & Son, Messrs. Methuen & Company, the Macmillan Company of Canada, and Messrs. Doubleday & Company (Rudyard Kipling's *The Seven Seas, Plain Tales from the Hills, Puck of Pook's Hill*, and 'In Partibus'); to Mrs. W. B. Yeats, Messrs. A. P. Watt & Son, Messrs. Macmillan & Company, and the Macmillan Company of New York (W. B. Yeats's *Collected Poems*); to Messrs. Jonathan Cape Ltd., the Viking Press, and the Society of Authors (James Joyce's *Chamber Music, Pomes Penyeach*, and *A Portrait of the Artist as a Young Man*); to Messrs. Laurence Pollinger Ltd., the Viking Press, and the Estate of the late Mrs. Frieda Lawrence (D. H. Lawrence's *Collected Poems, The Rainbow, Women in Love, Kangaroo*, and *The Captain's Doll*); and to the Society of Authors, Messrs. Jonathan Cape Ltd., and Messrs. Holt, Rinehart & Winston (A. E. Housman's 'With rue my heart is laden').

J. I. M. S.

Christ Church, Oxford
30 September 1962

CONTENTS

I · INTRODUCTION

I

THE present volume, some convenient backward glances apart, begins at 1880. It is the year of an old-fashioned novel, *The Trumpet Major*, and of a novel not so old-fashioned, *Washington Square*. George Eliot died. Flaubert died. Maupassant published *Boule de suif*, Zola *Nana*, and Dostoevski *The Brothers Karamazov*. But literary history, like the neo-classical dramatists, observes the *liaison des scènes*; we never arrive at a cleared stage. So here is only the suggestion of a changed balance. If we look in 1880 for a single definitive event we may find it not in imaginative literature but in the appearance in England of the American Henry George's *Progress and Poverty*. In 1871 *The Times* had judged it possible to 'look at the present with undisturbed satisfaction'. But as the decade advanced it became clear that rising production was not bringing rising prosperity. Prices sank, and by 1879 the spectre of general unemployment had declared itself. Britain was facing perplexities of which no very sufficient analysis was available. Along with the products of her industrial revolution she had inevitably sold its techniques, and her customers were already becoming her competitors. A new economic imperialism was to be the answer worked out rapidly and vigorously in face of this exigency. But the vastly increased complexity and the radically changing tensions in the social structure as a whole were seen by some far to transcend the sphere of classical economics. From George's book may be dated a new sort of involvement of the speculative and imaginative intelligence in the largest social questions. A literature of protest or outcry, such as Mrs. Gaskell's or Charles Kingsley's, was not enough; nor did pietistic solutions—the gospel of a change of heart—hold water. Political science must be mastered in the interest of political morality, and the resultant findings be brought home to the people alike by rational persuasion and the resources of art. The London Democratic

Federation was founded in 1881 and the Fabian Society and the Socialist League in 1884. *News from Nowhere* was published in 1890. *Widowers' Houses* was played in 1892.

Britain's second empire, like her industrial revolution, was made possible by science; its instruments were the submarine telegraph, fire power, and the reliability of steam. But science, as well as liberating vast material forces, assaulted the mind. This is the grand commonplace of every disquisition on the age, and we may glance at it by moving on a little and considering the year 1888. It is only necessary to listen with half an ear at this point in order to hear history turning with a faint creak on its hinge.

In 1888 Matthew Arnold dies. T. S. Eliot is born. Arnold's niece, Mrs. Humphry Ward, publishes *Robert Elsmere*—in this emulating her other Arnold uncle, William, who in *Oakfield* (1853) had produced a religious novel turning on the temptations of Indian army life. And Elsmere was only the first of a line of clergymen with whose interwoven doctrinal and domestic difficulties Mrs. Ward edified and entertained her public; as late as 1911 we find Elsmere's daughter marrying another of these unfortunate men in *The Case of Richard Meynell*. Throughout the age literature and religion come variously together, and in the process there is perhaps a progression to be observed. In 1848 a finer mind than Mrs. Ward's had judged fiction a fitting medium for the discussion of a priestly vocation, and the result was Newman's *Loss and Gain*. *Adam Bede* appeared in 1859, and Arnold's *Literature and Dogma* fourteen years later. Kipling's 'Recessional' was printed in *The Times* on 17 July 1897. Mr. Eliot was to have *Thoughts after Lambeth* in 1931 and to expound his views on modern heresy to an American audience a little later. When we consider, against George Eliot's achievement and Arnold's, what Mr. Gladstone and other eminent persons were prepared to applaud in Mrs. Ward, we must suspect a seeping away of the intellectual energies of the time from areas where they had hitherto been intensively at play. When we notice that the Deity addressed in Kipling's striking poem is as patently a trope of rhetoric as He is in equally striking poems of Hardy's, and when we mark the tone of Mr. Eliot's theological discourses and their general odd-man-out effect, we are made sharply aware of something already sufficiently evident: the progressive dominance of purely secular assumptions throughout the age, and the surprising facility with which men were able to persuade themselves that they could make do with these. Samuel Butler's *The Way of All Flesh*, begun in 1873 and left in a drawer like a time-bomb until 1903, is significant here. It cannot be called a less serious book than *Adam Bede*. Yet it seems to celebrate the achieving of a confident and cheerful irreverence inconceivable in the most assured agnostic of the mid-Victorian period. It rings out Clough and Hardy as absolutely as it rings out Canon Butler himself. It rings in Shaw and Wells.

This movement into an age of science and rationalism is something so large as to be difficult to keep in clear focus; we stare through it without reading the signs, as we do through an advertisement in too brutally sprawled a type. It comes home to us most effectively if we try to consider its impact upon whatever may be our own familiar environment and particular concern. Oxford undergraduates, turning over family letters, may find themselves surprised by the topics upon which their great-grandfathers thought it interesting to correspond in vacations. They may reflect, when tramping their laboratories, that in Newman's prime the pursuit of experimental philosophy in their University was confined to a cellar in Balliol and a small building in Christ Church's back yard. And when disposed to ascribe vaguely to 'the influence of science' a certain aridity in the methods by which they are now invited to study literature, they may usefully consider that this is only indirectly true. The multitude of persons whose acute minds now afflict them in textbooks and journals have in fact nothing scientific about them but are theologians *manqués*. A hundred years ago they would have been planning themselves a reputation not from some dissection of Donne or Yeats but from a well-conceived pamphlet on Pelagianism or a history of liturgical lights.

2

Butler has somewhere a witticism about the amount of doubt that lived in the honest faith of his contemporaries. Yet we now incline to admire the Victorians just because of the truth in the gibe; they did well, we feel, not too quickly to throw up the sponge, but to remain fighting in the ring until the bell went. Nevertheless, because the world in which we live is perpetually changing, at times rapidly and disturbingly changing, our guesses about that world must be perpetually changing too. Literature and the arts are among our means of guessing, and for this reason any literature and art will be of inferior quality and interest which has not been created at some growing-point of its time. The period of our present study, more perhaps than some others, affords the spectacle of a good deal of aesthetic waste thus occasioned. We are conscious of writers of talent and sensibility who do not really command our attention, since they have either ignored the challenge of their age or met it in an inadequate manner.

Robert Bridges is perhaps the finest artist that we have to characterize in this way. The earlier of his *Shorter Poems*, in particular, hold an authentic lyric power, and even much later he can make us pause and admire:

> Open for me the gates of delight,
> The gates of the garden of man's desire;
> Where spirits touch'd by heavenly fire
>   Have planted the trees of life.—
> Their branches in beauty are spread,
>   Their fruit divine
> To the nations is given for bread,
>   And crush'd into wine.

But what—we find ourselves asking—is wrong? What underlies our feeling that the counters have worn a little too smooth? We answer that the poet has elected to write out of a phase of imaginative experience that is no longer actual, but historical. And yet what is to seek in Bridges is precisely an historical sense. Had he seen his time accurately in relation to other times he would not have thought to write, as he did in *The Testament of Beauty* (1929), a long philosophical poem, nor would he have proposed to recommend this archaic contrivance by clothing it in elaborate metrical innovation. Still, what is wrong in Bridges is almost balanced by what is right. If one wants to see this particular sort of wrongness in chemical purity one has to turn to William Watson.

This we need not do now. But a contemporary of Watson's, James Barrie, was a writer of more considerable talent which won wide acclaim, and it is worth pausing to consider why his name suggests today not so much plays to see and novels to read as a case to consider. His work represents, we may think, very much that sustained and uncontrolled exhibition of a morbid personality which Mr. Eliot was at one time disposed to see as the mainspring of Hardy. With Barrie the process takes the form— very different from any imaginable in the author of *Jude the Obscure*—of exploiting any convention that can be used to assert the wholesomeness and sweetness of the general situation. The Victorian cult of childhood was tough on children, and the Victorian attitude to women was a stain upon the age. But at least these things had to be, and for reasons—too ramifying to be entered upon—having nothing to do with any individual's psychopathology. Barrie is still feebly involved with them; he is an instance of an artist perpetuating bad and obsolete guesses for his own ease and for the ease of lazy minds and time-lagged sensibilities. He entered the London theatre, we have to note, in the same year as Shaw.

'Escape literature' has become a common term, and it suggests itself here. A wise circumspection is not invariably, perhaps, observed in its use. Thus the sense in which it may be applied to Stevenson, a compatriot of Barrie's and his senior by a decade, is not an easy one. Stevenson in himself represents an escape; he is one of the very few persons artistically endowed who in a whole hundred years and more have escaped the direr consequences of being born north of the Tweed. He was an invalid, and his best writing—which is superb—lay in the field of romance. Heroes and heroines and villains are its mainstays; and this shows at once, we may be told, that it is idle stuff. Yet escape is of a special, and perhaps precious, quality when it is into an ideal world. Stevenson follows Scott. He hands on to innumerable popular writers a tradition in which it is important that a gentleman should know just when to draw his sword or punch a gangster on the jaw. If gentlemen are no longer put to making these calculations—except, indeed, in conditions of mass slaughter—it is perhaps the gentlemen who are doing the escaping, after all.

But Stevenson as well as being a romancer was an aesthete. He wrote a delicate prose. His hair depended upon his shoulders and he wore a velvet jacket—dangerous manifestations for which, it may here be recorded, Edinburgh parents and school-masters were looking out with anxiety many years after his death. That death took place in 1894, which was the year of Pater's death too. If, as Yeats reminds us in writing of the

Rhymers, not everybody in the nineties wore velvet, it was no
doubt Pater who was the chastening impulse. The prophet of
a subfusc decadence, he ran to a huge moustache but would
not have ventured upon flowing locks. We deprecate Henry
James's description of him as a 'faint, embarrassed figure'—
yet we can ourselves hardly think of him without smiling, so
infinitely incapable of experiences appears this high priest of
experience at its extreme. The aesthetes and decadents of the
age are not, perhaps, too absolutely to be fathered on him; yet
with him they have in common the stance less of escapists than
of men whom something has eluded. With a greater effort of
the intelligence and the will, we feel, they might at least in part
have escaped escapism, as Morris did; and Johnson, Dowson, and
Beardsley need not have been left clutching mere simulacra in
Holy Church, fleshly fulfilment, an art that was only for art. In
Yeats they nourished for a brief space the giant of a later time;
awkwardly among them was John Davidson, a man of heroic
integrity and potentially of poetic mark; Max Beerbohm, who
contrived to give an air of wit to the statement that he belonged
to the Beardsley period, carried forward from that period an
indifférent pose which was drastically to delimit the reach of
a formidably fused critical and comic talent. It is no accident
that Beerbohm's prime aversion was Kipling, for it was Kipling
who, by the mere spectacle of a man who had caught hold of
something, was first to cast the Beardsley period into perspective. But of course it was not the Beardsley period at all. It was
the Wilde period. That Wilde dominated so large a segment of
the eighties and nineties may in fact be their measure. Yet his
is certainly a figure that cannot be passed by.

                                    3

    Whistler, from whom Wilde in a sense stole the aesthetic
show, was to declare that the 'esurient Oscar' had 'the courage
of the opinions . . . of others!' However this may be, Wilde's
possessing plain courage is a cardinal fact about him as a man—
is the only personal fact, perhaps, worth recording. He was
lured to the United States as a cock-shy. In a full awareness of
this, and upon being asked at a customs barrier whether he
had anything to declare, he answered, 'Nothing but my genius!'
It was extremely flamboyant and even a little vulgar, and he

was to be vulgar and flamboyant enough throughout his career. If his character was courageous it was weak, and success did no good to it. But there was something large about him as well as something bloated; something generous in intellect as well as flashing in wit. And yet nearly all his assaults upon the art— or Art—that he so sincerely (if again flamboyantly) exalted were failures or at least operations of little account; and it has lately become clear that his letters are to be, with his legend, his best monument. Yeats's prose, at least, was for a time not less silly and over-scented than Wilde's. Yet Yeats was to achieve the stature of a major English poet, whereas Wilde was done for long before his overt fate overtook him. Why? We may say, if in an insular mood, that his excellent education unfortunately enabled him to make more of the contemporary French decadence than Yeats could manage. But we do better to note—if we are to continue what is only an insubstantial comparison— that Yeats had Sligo and Rosses whereas Wilde had only his bizarre mother's *salon* in Merrion Square. To have nothing to hold on to is even more fatal to large talents than to small, and Wilde suffered from his hour more even than did the minor members of Yeats's 'Tragic Generation'. Unlike James, who had both dinner parties and an absorbed interest in the survival of moral ideas in an affluent society, he had the dinner parties only. By the time he wrote *The Soul of Man under Socialism* (1891) there had been too many of them for him not to fail, not just to fail, in the serious consideration of a substantial subject. The essay is said to have been bad for the parties—Wilde came to be disliked by the fashionable society that cultivated him—and the parties were bad for the essay and everything else. His situation has been expressed with characteristic colour by G. K. Chesterton at the end of *The Victorian Age in Literature* (1913): 'Anselm would have despised a civic crown, but he would not have despised a relic. Voltaire would have despised a relic, but he would not have despised a vote. We hardly find them both despised till we come to the age of Oscar Wilde.'

Wilde, in fact, is the first distinguished tenant of Heartbreak House—and Chesterton will be found to have provided the metaphor in the very year that Shaw began the play. According to Chesterton, too, it was Shaw who, along with Kipling, least ineffectively explored means of breaking out: socialism and imperialism were real forces, together totally destructive of the

Victorian compromise, to the interests of which it was possible
for the imagination to harness itself, gaining release by having
again a load to draw. There is strength in this analysis; much
writing of importance in the new century can be placed in terms
of it. It fails only in not taking due account of a certain virtue
in the age not to be classed as of a disruptive sort. We are here
obliged to take a further glance at social history.

4

There is a real grimness in the eighties and nineties, and at
the turn of the century things look bad. We have noted the
underlying economic dilemma. It was breeding, beneath the
surface of national life, problems more urgent than a Fabian
policy seemed likely to master. And on the surface, the polite
surface, there glittered a most impolite and vulgar opulence
the perfect memorial to which is Sargent's series of portraits
and portrait groups in the Tate Gallery. It is the age of cigars
and diamonds; of the incursion of Levantine persons into the
hunting field and the manor; of the digging out, within the
shadow of Rheims Cathedral, of vaster and vaster caverns for
the storage of millions and millions more bottles of champagne.
Yet this age discovered for itself a real strength—formidable
indeed if not particularly glorious—in a certain obstinate
social cohesion. Visiting foreigners, we are told, are constantly
staggered by the rigid class-stratifications to be found in these
islands. They will concede, if well informed, the process whereby a governing class perpetually recruits itself, with prudence
and cunning, from people of gathering substance coming up
from below. It seems to be less obvious to them that a converse
form of assimilation must exist; that the thing can be managed
at all only on a basis of give-and-take. Typically, the boys who
move from some small provincial and commercial prosperity
through public schools into a new ambience have insisted on
taking a good deal along with them; they impose as well as
accept; and the impositions are themselves accepted. Similar
processes occur at the other social frontiers, so that the English
class-system perpetually exists and is perpetually changing. The
change may be more apparent now at one point and now at
another, and its incidence may not be the same in different
geographical regions. Middle-aged people bred in the Home

Counties, and brought up to note a mysterious absoluteness in the gap between the upper-middle and lower-middle classes, have to modify their picture if they move north, just as they have to modify it if—resisting outrage and bewilderment—they allow some credence to the younger social novelists of the present generation. It seems hardly within the genius of the British people that this process should have any stop. And it has produced in our own century large areas of confidence, of common assumption, of openness, of ability to get along on working assumptions, such as the troubled souls of the Victorians could scarcely have looked forward to. All this is not to be proclaimed as any very notable achievement of spiritual health. But it did, in the immediate period to which we now come, produce a confident, widely available, open, and empirically proceeding literature of far-reaching social relevance. There are in that literature peaks from which the view is scarcely reassuring. At the same time it is a literature of a breadth and a modestly rich productivity unexampled in our history: a terrain through which we could wander, harvesting and gleaning, for a very long time.

5

We may again pause for a moment at a single year. It is 1904. We are Edwardians now—and the Victorian age, in departing, seems obligingly to have taken most of its anxieties in its baggage. The solvents glimpsed and dreaded by our grandfathers have flooded in and done their work, yet the large and liberal fabric of modern European civilization triumphantly stands.

For it is not in Britain alone that cohesive forces appear to be in control. In Germany *Buddenbrooks* has been published, but it is hard to catch any real sense that the *Burgerzeit* is in decline. In France Proust has been translating Ruskin; presently he will enter Dr. Sollier's clinic for neurotics, but will see no reason to stop there for very long, since to a contrived seclusion of his own all society will repair should he choose to require it. In Russia, indeed, it is the very year in which the axes are heard in *The Cherry Orchard,* and Chekhov himself dies as if upon their stroke. But when a young contemporary of his, Ivan Pavlov, is awarded a Nobel prize it occurs to none of his compatriots to take the matter amiss. Europe is like a great country-house.

Its drawing-room, as Henry James points out, is the Piazza San Marco in Venice.

In London they are going to *Peter Pan*—and although *Die Traumdeutung* has been these four years on the library shelves of Vienna nobody in the Duke of York's Theatre is much disturbed by the Freudian character of the *Boy Who Would Not Grow Up*. They are going, too, to *John Bull's Other Island*, in which—however much its author may be a revolutionary politician and economist—the tedious Irish Question has been delightfully laughed away. The year has indeed been ushered in upon a graver note, for the first part of *The Dynasts* appeared in time to be a Christmas present among lovers of poetry. *The Trumpet Major* is now twenty-four years old, and Hardy has abandoned the antique form of fiction he so long commanded. But *The Trumpet Major* is a Napoleonic tale, and over the intervening decades Hardy has been cherishing an epoch well remembered by old people when he was a boy. Now, freshening up on the detail from an unassuming *History of Europe*, and consulting his own bleak sense of what everybody is soon to be calling the human situation, he contrives a monistic epic-drama for the age of disenchantment in which he believes he lives. But the material is much of it legendary or even familiar, most of the verse is of the comfortable sub-Shakespearian sort, and the sustaining moral feeling—*pace* Mr. Eliot—is straight out of Sunday School. *The Dynasts* is a work of magnificent breadth and elevation. But we do not really pause over it as upon something sharply new. Over anything in the way of poetry, for some reason, we are not going to do *that* for a good many years.

What we may pause over in 1904 is the fact that it produced both *Nostromo* and *The Golden Bowl*. The collocation arrests us as declaring that the English novel, which came of age with *Middlemarch*, has now reached a full maturity and become the predominant literary form of the new century. There will still be people who don't read novels except at the seaside or in railway trains. But they will no longer be able, quite honestly, to give themselves airs. For after only a short time-lag English prose fiction has come abreast of French and Russian. It must now carry, as it has never very notably carried before, a large part of the burden of the exploratory imaginative consciousness of its age. To name *Nostromo* and *The Golden Bowl* in this context is to ascribe to these novels not merely a quality of artistic consideration hitherto infrequent in their kind but also something of the character of prophecy. In its due place, this will appear. But for the moment we are to consider the typical productions of the Edwardian and Georgian age—the productions of what Virginia Woolf, who herself rode so gallantly at the stiffest fences, called 'the thick dull middle class of letters . . . not the aristocracy'.

6

At the head of those who wrote prose fiction chiefly grounded in social life and social criticism stands H. G. Wells. His basic endowment as a novelist was scarcely generous, since he had only a moderate interest in men and women. Mr. Montgomery Belgion has written a witty and destructive essay in which Wells is depicted as incapable of believing in the reality of his fellow-beings, except in the restricted sense of their forming part of the environment of Wells—an environment the sole business of which is to be 'tamed'. Thus the environment, on the whole, went in for monogamy; Wells, on the whole, did not; so anything, clearly, would vastly mend the world that should 'tame' the environment in this regard.

That here is a mainspring of Wells's enormous productivity is no doubt true, but the analysis is defective if it leaves to his credit no more than a series of brilliant scientific romances and a few novels interesting to pupil teachers and shop boys because written from the inside by a clever plebeian who had sold Manchester wares and struggled in a Board school or commercial academy. There is far more to Wells than that. He fulfilled one of the wholly legitimate functions of literature more vigorously and abundantly, perhaps, than it had ever been fulfilled in English before. 'The end of our foundation is the knowledge of causes, and secret motions of things; and the enlarging of the bounds of human empire, to the effecting of all things possible.' No Jacobean boy can have got a greater thrill from Bacon's words than did a generation of Georgians from Wells's untiring dramatizings of certain areas of their own impatience and their own aspiration. There was, conceivably, not much wisdom to be gained from him. But there was a great deal of exhilaration— the wine, of all wines, keenest on the palate of youth. And upon youth—not literary youth merely, but youth substantially and at large—no writer was to have a comparable influence until

George Orwell. And there was not to be a great deal that was exhilarating about him.

George Gissing, Wells's senior by nine years, is at an opposite pole here. His novels, which taken together form a considerable artistic achievement, are nearly all dismal records of the genteel urban poverty which constituted the environment of their author. Wells was Gissing's friend, crossed Europe with a bad cold to attend him at his death-bed, and commemorated the occasion with the words: 'So ended all that flimsy inordinate stir of grey matter that was George Gissing. He was a pessimistic writer.' This obituary curiosity brings us back to the oddity of the English class structure. Wells could not forgive Gissing for being so stupid as to wear himself out in clinging to gentility when, even socially, he could have got much farther through a free and efficiently planned employment of his talent.

More satisfactory to Wells's mind was Arnold Bennett, a cheerfully objective enthusiast for life, who, Wells records, 'had a through ticket and a time-table'. We are now inclined to think of Bennett's time-table as containing a single demarcated hour for serious literary accomplishment, and the result to be *The Old Wives' Tale*. Bennett certainly ended in a total subservience to the cheapest conception of success in his profession. Yet almost as little as Wells is he to be written off as negligible. Having acquired, if somewhat superficially, the canons of French naturalism, he applied them to aspects of English provincial life intimately known to him, with results a good deal more authentic than those achieved by interested observers from other social orbits—the earlier George Moore, for example —although these had perhaps pondered more maturely the aims and intellectual background of the literary kind to which they were contributing.

John Galsworthy, the last of the more prominent novelists whose activities spanned the First World War, has less of the vitality that Bennett so abundantly possessed; he has less, too, of the artistry that was Bennett's only in a very moderate degree. He came rather late to fiction, the art of which he appears to have studied with the set design of employing it to present a reasoned criticism of society. Having mastered, as he supposed, the rules, he steadily and skilfully stuck to them. He does, that is to say, faithfully present his strictures in scenic or dramatized form; there are no diatribes and little that is really boring in his large panorama of upper-middle-class life through the later nineteenth and earlier twentieth centuries. But his work has no bite, and the final judgement on *The Forsyte Saga* (1922) must reside in the fact that it quickly came to be found in every Forsyte home in the land. There is a parody by Max Beerbohm in *A Christmas Garland* (1912) which rather cruelly renders what is now the only fascination of Galsworthy's work: its exhibition of a humane and honourable and talented English gentleman believing himself to be achieving in fiction a searching criticism of modern English society in works which must have been entirely acceptable and unsurprising to, say, his fellow-Harrovian, Lord Baldwin. About his writing there is a not displeasing air of the amateur; one feels before it, as before that of Sir Charles Snow upon whom his mantle was to fall, that here is a very able man who could do other things as well as he is doing this—and that he is indeed doing this quite surprisingly well for one who so clearly has no particular occasion to be doing this at all. Galsworthy would have made a good barrister, which is what he started out to be. He would have disliked *Lady Chatterley's Lover*, but his dispassionateness would have enabled him to defend it in court with ability. Lawrence, who contrived to regard *The Forsyte Saga* as eminently obscene, would have had no power to see and advance a case for it.

Over against the amateurism of Galsworthy—his slight air of having borrowed literature as a charity organizer borrows a garden or a park—may be placed the extreme professionalism of Mr. Somerset Maugham. It is a professionalism guarded by a Gallic sense of the dignity of letters, but at the same time allowing for a large complaisance in the following of public taste. This has appeared very clearly in the theatre, where Maugham carried on from Jones and Pinero the tradition of the efficient theatrical piece at a decent level of intelligence and literary craft. That 'the drama's laws, the drama's patrons give' was a proposition first enunciated by a sensible man, and another sensible man, Bernard Shaw, was far from neglecting it. Most of the drama of our period continues to be written in a spirit of the frankest accommodation to the box-office—until the poets, indeed, beaten back in their inept assaults upon the theatre in the later Victorian age, take fresh courage from Ireland, and renew the attack in the age of Eliot. Shaw was a propagandist for the realistic Ibsen, although nothing of his own is quintessentially Ibsenite. William Archer, Ibsen's translator, was equally a propagandist for a serious 'prose' theatre in general, and he left a sort of testament in *The Old Drama and the New* (1923). In attempts at the thing itself there is not a great deal of success to record. But John Drinkwater's historical plays are of some note, and *The Voysey Inheritance* (1905) and *Waste* (1907) suggest that Harley Granville-Barker, had he not found it so hard to satisfy himself (he recast almost every sentence of *Waste* twenty years after its first composition), might have taken as high a place in dramatic writing as he took in dramatic production and dramatic criticism.

7

Poetry in the war years and those immediately preceding them we generally think of in terms first of Masefield—vigorous, prolific, and a sort of metrical equivalent of the exoteric Conrad —and second of a largish group of smallish writers, happily gathered conveniently into faggots by Edward Marsh in the volumes of *Georgian Poetry* (1912–22). The Georgian poets, thus defined, in fact included a writer of unique vision in Walter de la Mare, a genius in D. H. Lawrence, and a dark horse in Robert Graves. Marsh himself was to declare in an epilogue that he had 'tried to choose no verse but such as, in Wordsworth's phrase:

> The high and tender Muses shall accept
> With gracious smile, deliberately pleased.'

By Wordsworth's own most authentic poetry, perhaps, Muses thus disposed would have been a good deal put out, as they would have been put out by Swinburne or Hopkins or Hardy. Lasses like these were bred for Shropshire Lads. Nevertheless, Marsh on his own principles chose well. The Georgians are variously delightful, and it has been accurately said that they revived a lyrical impulse in a not very lyrical age. But once more we are aware of amateurism, of justice lurking in the joke that here were week-end poets. They lacked that radical passion for their medium and its regular purification which marks the dedicated artist. It is here that the group known for a time as Imagists is of some importance, and it is here that Mr. Ezra Pound is very important indeed. Pound, for the double reason that he is alive and an American citizen, must be substantively beyond the purview of the present volume. But its latter course, at least, is haunted by his strident voice. Even more than Eliot, he is its seminal intelligence at the highest levels. The Imagists got nowhere very far. It is significant that one of their theorists, T. E. Hulme—like another theorist after him, Mr. William Empson—produced what may be called a little set of laboratory poems to prove that the theory was right. But they had the professional instinct. And this was something rather un-English at the time.

For here was England full of good-quality novelists, playwrights, and poets—much as it was full of good-quality goods in good-quality shops. But it seemed no age of masterpieces. In particular the Novel—as we have seen, the predominant form—appeared to have enjoyed its efflorescence. Hardy had given it up, Conrad's power over it was in a decline, James's last great book we hailed in passing the year 1904. There was only Lawrence—and Lawrence's concern with fiction James at least would have judged very amateurish indeed; he had saluted it as giving us, higgledy-piggledy, 'a nearer view of commoner things'. The discovery of the age had been that it could remain not wholly insensitive, not without a widely diffused pleasure in things of the mind and imagination, while sunk in materialism, only just not resigned to social injustice, public-school religion, finance-capital politics, and Burlington House art. Against all this—it may be put—there was only Captain Shotover's voice. But Captain Shotover drank too much rum and was plainly mad. Besides, he had been created by Bernard Shaw. Then came the German Kaiser and his war. On the war it was Shaw's main feeling that he could of course talk common sense about it. Without doubt he could. But the war stunned James—James who, in the matters of our concern in this book, had been the Master of his age.

These final notes on the time are not offered as prelude to any historical or even aesthetic generalization. They are merely designed to point the perplexities that attend any attempt to talk about backgrounds. Europe had been in conflagration and was still in places smouldering. Much frivolity and elegant fiddling had promptly followed—1921, for example, producing *Crome Yellow*, *Héloïse and Abélard*, and *Queen Victoria*. But 1922 proved to be an *annus mirabilis* almost without parallel in English literature.

8

It will be found a year of some note, for that matter, in France. But in England the thing is more surprising. Yeats was fifty-seven, and *Later Poems* was a reasonable title for a gathering which, although it went back to *The Wind Among the Reeds* of 1899, came down to *The Wild Swans at Coole* (1917) and *Michael Robartes and the Dancer* (1921). Certainly the volume would have made evident to any perceptive reader the large authority and mounting excitement that were to set Yeats's actual later poems, as yet a lustre and more ahead, among the peaks of English poetry. But 1922 did not merely presage a great achievement. It saw the publication of *The Waste Land* and of *Ulysses*.

Short though the perspective still be, we can already say with confidence that these are both works of the first importance in English literary history. Scholars will pivot an era upon them as infallibly as they do upon *The Shepheardes Calender* or *Lyrical Ballads*. Both are Janus-faced: innovatory and forward-looking in one aspect, reaching deep into the past in another. They bear this mark of stature: that instantly upon their appearance anything that can be seen in any relationship to them is changed. Mr. E. M. Forster disliked *Ulysses*, and judged it to be Joyce's intention to 'cover the universe with mud'. He certainly let it exert no influence upon *A Passage to India*. Yet when *A Passage to India*—itself a great novel—came out in 1924 it was inescapably not the same book as it would have been if there had been no 1922. Authentic works of art bear upon each other in this way.

As for overt influences, they may be briefly instanced. Virginia Woolf did not like *Ulysses* either. Still less did she like Mr. Eliot's admiring it. 'And Tom, great Tom, thinks this on a par with *War and Peace*! An illiterate, underbred book it seems to me.' Yet *Jacob's Room* (1922) was written before the appearance of *Ulysses*, and *Mrs. Dalloway* (1925) shortly after. Whether consciously or not, *Mrs. Dalloway* owes much to *Ulysses*, the debt extending to a precise architectonic conception. And *Mrs. Dalloway* is a necessary stepping-stone to *To the Lighthouse* (1927), in which Mrs. Woolf herself rises to a great novel.

Dame Edith Sitwell was born in the year before Mr. Eliot, and she was before him in writing brilliantly polished light verse. She was well behind him in moving away from it. In the year following *The Waste Land* she published *Bucolic Comedies*,

so that we all at that time, when we had had enough of Madame
Sosostris and the Phoenician Sailor, would turn to chanting
about Lily O'Grady, silly and shady, and her decorative if obscure connexion with Calliope, Io, Pomona, Antiope, Echo, and
Clio. Yet Dame Edith's verse has developed subsequently in
a way that might earn her the title, were it not an absurd one,
of the Little Yeats. She has passed, that is to say, from one sort
of poetry, maintained well into maturity, to another sort of
poetry of vastly greater scope and reverberation. And a poem
like 'The Shadow of Cain' (1947) shows clearly that it is to
a world of feeling largely created by Mr. Eliot that much of
this transformation must be due. Dame Edith is established,
as a consequence, as the greatest English woman poet after
Emily Brontë. Her art has so grown that it is she who has
written least inadequately of

> the Cloud in the Heavens shaped like the hand
> Of Man

on the most ominous of recorded dates in human history, the
sixth of August 1945.

In literary chronicles eras have to close. Ours closes then. In
1915, when Flanders was mud and blood, Hardy, already
brooding on *The Dynasts*, wrote a poem which he called 'In
Time of "The Breaking of Nations" ':

> Only a man harrowing clods
>   In a slow silent walk
> With an old horse that stumbles and nods
>   Half asleep as they stalk.
>
> Only thin smoke without flame
>   From the heaps of couch-grass:
> Yet this will go onward the same
>   Though Dynasties pass.
>
> Yonder a maid and her wight
>   Come whispering by:
> War's annals will fade into night
>   Ere their story die.

In the 1960's this sombrely consolatory reflection of Hardy's
is no longer valid, since the Dynasties are likely to vaporize
man and horse, maid and wight, before passing on to vaporize
each other. 'There are no longer problems of the spirit,' William

Faulkner said when he received the Nobel Prize for literature in 1950. 'There is only the question: When will I be blown up?' And having thus acknowledged the tragedy of our time to lie in 'a general and universal physical fear', Faulkner stated what he conceived to be the young writer's task:

> He must teach himself that the basest of all things is to be afraid; and, teaching himself that, forget it for ever, leaving no room in his workshop for anything but the old verities and truths of the heart....
>
> Until he relearns these things, he will write as though he stood among and watched the end of man.

II · HARDY

THOMAS HARDY was born in 1840 in the parish of Stinsford, Dorset. His father was a master mason, but a family tradition asserted that the Hardys had been gentry in an earlier time. The boy was emotional, intellectually precocious, and like his father a lover of music. His mother was ambitious that he should be lettered, and when the dream of a clerical career faded and he was apprenticed to an architect in Dorchester he faithfully continued the classical studies he had begun, rising at six or at four to read Virgil and Homer. He thus became, like his own Clym Yeobright, 'a real perusing man'. Hardy is more of a scholar than his homespun style, his habitual awkwardness of expression, might suggest.

His early years were passed partly in the country and partly in a country town, so that he gained a broad view of rural society. In old age he said that he had been far from darkening the picture and that, had he told the truth about village life, 'no one would have stood it'. This was no doubt true. When in *Jude the Obscure* he eventually wrote in a tone admitting notice of a hedge under which 'girls had given themselves to lovers who would not turn their heads to look at them by the next harvest', and of his hero's introduction to his future wife as being by way of a slap from a pig's pizzle, the outcry against the book was immediate. From the first he had been attentive to the grimmer aspects of the world about him. He could recall from boyhood 'horrible scenes at public floggings'. Another early reminiscence, recorded in the third person, has the sharp visual effect which he regularly commands in his fiction:

One summer morning at Bockhampton, just before he sat down to breakfast, he remembered that a man was to be hanged at eight o'clock at Dorchester. He took up the big brass telescope that had been handed on in the family, and hastened to a hill on the heath a quarter of a mile from the house, whence he looked towards the town. The sun behind his back shone straight on the white stone façade of the gaol, the gallows upon it, and the form of the murderer in white fustian, the executioner and officials in dark clothing and the crowd below being invisible at this distance of nearly three miles. At the moment of his placing the glass to his eye the white figure dropped downwards, and the faint note of the town clock struck eight. . . . He seemed alone on the heath with the hanged man, and crept homeward wishing he had not been so curious.

Aware that life is grim, he contrived to be pleased that it is often macabre. To hold a candle at an autopsy, to spend the greater part of a day at a lunatic asylum 'interested in the pathos of the cases', to be shown by Lord Portsmouth 'a bridge over which bastards were thrown and drowned', to find himself by chance 'looking through a slit' at the coffin of Lord Warwick who had once invited him on a visit and to murmur 'Here I am at last, and here are you to receive me!', to know the story of the doctor who, even when married, kept a dead baby 'on his mantelpiece in a large glass jar': these were among Hardy's pleasures. He was an agnostic with a fondness for arranging friends' funerals and choosing appropriate hymns; and in his last years he was always likely to propose to visitors a walk to Stinsford to view 'the various graves'. Hardy's was a Gothic imagination.

His training was for some years in the architecture of the Gothic revival. But when he came to London to pursue his profession he found himself drawn to writing, and experimented in both verse and prose. Then he fell in love, and authorship took on a new aspect. For some years he wrote fiction pertinaciously, and eventually gained both a competence and his bride. Here is one explanation of his subsequent attitude to his novels. He looked upon this choice within the literary field as one persisted in to gain an end aside from art, and an end which brought disillusion and pain. His later life calls for little description. Living as a countryman still, he retained great simplicity both of manners and of mind. Artistic sophistication did not come easily to him, and his judgements upon some of his contemporaries are scarcely those of a critical intelligence. Meredith he seems to have been content virtually to dismiss. Henry James, although less unreadable, he declared to be occupied with subjects 'one could be interested in at moments when there is nothing larger to think of'—and as a man James

owned 'a ponderously warm manner of saying nothing in
infinite sentences'. Such popular commonplace is disconcerting.
Mr. Allen Tate supposes that Hardy must have become 'a somewhat complacent and tiresome old gentleman'. He certainly
had some temptation to the oracular, attracting as he did the
sort of reverence reserved by the English for octogenarians of
eminence. But if he became a legend he remained alert; he was
courteous to the curious, cordially welcoming to young writers
and eager to question them on the state of literature, resigned
even to the professors who came from America and Japan in
order to ask 'all sorts of questions about one's private life'.
After all, had not *Tess of the D'Urbervilles* been translated into
Japanese? But only half of it, the second Mrs. Hardy would
explain. For in Japan it is held virtuous in a girl to sell herself
to assist her family, and upon this view there would be no tragedy
in Tess's living with Alec d'Urberville. And Hardy, anxious to
acquit these far-off translators of any discourtesy, would point
out that the book in its entirety was rather long for the Japanese.
'They like literary works to be very short', he said.

When Hardy died in 1928 part of his remains was buried in
Westminster Abbey. Those who were present on that rainy
afternoon will not forget an awe and queerness in the occasion:
the unexpected size of the crowd, the eminence and odd assort-
ment of the pall-bearers, the knowledge that his having two
simultaneous funerals (for at the same hour they were burying
his heart among the 'various graves' at Stinsford) would have
pleased the anecdotal Hardy in the shades. There was the problem, too, of the fitness of what was being done—of 'the enact-
ment in question', as he would have called it. 'I have been
looking for God 50 years', he once wrote, 'and I think that if he
had existed I should have discovered him.' But at the end of
a career given to 'infinite trying to reconcile a scientific view of
life with the emotional and spiritual' he believed in the enduring
necessity of something which he wished to call religion. This
might be preserved, he believed, by rational reform within the
Church of England. In his last years he seems to have persuaded
himself that, even for professional theologians, Christianity
might come to mean simply the 'emotional morality and altru-
ism that was taught by Jesus Christ'. When the new Prayer
Book appeared he was bitterly disappointed and from that time
lost all hopes of seeing the church representative of modern

thinking minds. Of his dilemma, so characteristic of his age, a few of his sayings about himself are revealing. He said that he would have preferred to be a cathedral organist to anything else in the world. And he said that he had 'tried to spread over art the latest illumination of the time'.

That this illumination only makes more visible a great darkness overshadowing the human theatre is the discovery which constitutes the ironic plight of the Late Victorian age—an age, in G. M. Young's words, 'carried beyond sight of its old landmarks, and gazing doubtfully down an illimitable vista, of cosmic changes endlessly proceeding, and ephemeral suffering endlessly to be renewed'. Hardy's distinction lies in his command over a territory upon which this disenchanted vision can play with peculiarly mordant effect. Wessex is an older world than that of the Late Victorians; to step into it is to step into an otherwise vanished England. It can be viewed as a world before the Fall, before that second expulsion from Paradise which science has decreed. Certainly it is pre-Darwinian country. Disturbing anatomical investigation is unknown there—unless a local doctor, more out of whim than zeal, lays dark plans against an old woman's skull. Should a young astronomer set up a telescope upon a tower nobody will feel his horizons threatened—for is it not confidently known that the sky and the earth are the same even in 'the distant kingdom of Bath'? The Wessex knaps and heaths and valleys, which bear upon their face the gravure of epoch upon epoch of human history, are the home of men often deeply read in traditional human wisdom and yet born to an Arcadian innocence about humanity's actual place in nature's scheme. And it is among them, Hardy writes, 'that happiness will find her last refuge on earth, since it is among them that a perfect insight into the conditions of existence will be longest postponed'. Here then the irony lies. We watch people who, by almost every standard, live harder and narrower lives than we; yet knowing less they may hope more; and yet again, and just because of this, the awakening of the sensitive and ill-fated among them must be bitter indeed.

The struggle between an intellect subdued to determinism and an imagination nourished upon the Christian assertion of spiritual and moral order wrought Hardy to poetry. He regarded himself as primarily a poet, and he was accustomed to declare that he wrote prose for money. Quite as much as Trollope he was what is now called a commercial novelist, and one particularly concerned to secure the profitable serial publication of his books. 'The truth is', he wrote in his thirty-fifth year, 'that I am willing, and indeed anxious, to give up any points which may be desirable in a story when read as a whole, for the sake of others which shall please those who read it in numbers.' Ten years later his novel-writing was still 'mere journeywork'; he was conscious of having recklessly damaged *The Mayor of Casterbridge* by cramming a striking incident into almost every week's part; and when *Tess of the D'Urbervilles* was finished in a somewhat different temper he yet bowdlerized it for serial publication with a thoroughness that turned the story to nonsense. It had been 'a hand-to-mouth matter—writing serials', he said, looking back over his career; he had never cared very much about writing novels and seldom read any novels now; he could not understand how Tennyson came to take the 'downward step' of reading novels in his later years. Clearly, Hardy did not wish to rate highly what was still regarded as among the less elevated literary forms. Into the novel of the time George Eliot had decanted abundant seriousness and Meredith abundant intellectual sophistication. But the English novelists as a body had not yet learnt from French and Russian masters to march upon the commanding heights of literature. An eminent novelist might be also a critic, a wit, a man of the world, even a philosopher, but on the strength of his fiction he was likely to give himself no great airs. He was producing books which the cultivated 'took up', 'glanced through', or 'turned over', and upon which the larger public by which he lived exercised a grotesque moral censorship. Hardy knew that he made concessions to prudery ('I don't quite like the suggestion of the very close embrace in the London churchyard', Leslie Stephen as editor of the *Cornhill* once wrote to him). He knew that he purveyed sensational stories and that he continued to write while his imagination slept. He can hardly have been unaware that his style was often bad with the badness of the magazines. All this inclined him to depreciate his novels, and it is not altogether surprising that, thinking as he did, he was to end his career as little skilled in almost everything belonging to the craft of prose fiction as when he began. His simplicity of mind extended itself over his artistry and almost certainly impaired it on the critical side. Thus he could write: 'If novelists were a little less in the dark about the appearance of their own works, what productions they might bring forth! But they are much in the position of the man inside the hobbyhorse at a Christmas masque, and have no consciousness of the absurdity of its trot, at times, in the spectator's eyes.' This holds of some of Hardy's finest work. He must always have been a little baffled at not being able to retire from the completed book, as from an architectural performance, and survey it at a single *coup d'œil*.

But although the conditions under which he wrote, together with his critical *naïveté* before the problems of prose, are in part responsible for the unequal quality of his work, we cannot be sure that they much hampered his genius. The novels abound in oddly ironic situations organized upon a basis of coincidence and intricate accident, and these might appear to be the mere issue of his need to achieve popular sensation. But we find the same elements again and again in his verse, where he was certainly uninfluenced by considerations of vulgar appeal. It is not easy to say just what makes the right vehicle for a writer of powerful and original impulse, or where lie the canons of artistry essential to him. Had Dickens listened to better-educated people on the sins of polysyllabic humour and exaggerated pathos his powers might have been frozen at their marvellous source. Hardy's English, although cumbersome and worn, linked itself with that of romancers potent with him since childhood. Had he abandoned his open communications with these, and like Pater schooled himself by writing words on paper lozenges and studying their every possible arrangement, he might have finished few novels and certainly would never have written the final paragraph of *The Woodlanders*. And this too is to be noticed: not only did Hardy revise his old novels with an elaborate care little suggestive of indifference or disdain; he also came to them at the start in an artist's way, and felt about them as an artist when they were finished. 'It is what I might have deserved', he wrote of some compliment paid to him by Coventry Patmore, 'if my novels had been exact transcripts of their original irradiated conception, before any attempt at working out that glorious dream had been made—and the impossibility of getting it on paper had been brought home to me.'

Hardy, then, was a countryman of simple birth, upon the forming of whose ambitions the knowledge of a gentle strain may have had its effect. Growing up in an age in which man's sense of the universe was radically changing, and himself of a temper to be affected both intellectually and emotionally by this change in its widest reach, he chose for long to express himself in popular literary forms, and was more content than many lesser contemporaries with old-fashioned conveyances and stand-bys. He involved broadly delineated characters in artificial plots designed to achieve effects of sensation and surprise. Yet he made these common fables the vehicle of high emotion and the instrument of a controlling tragic purpose. His view of life was sombre, at times indeed darkened beyond any easy acceptance. But he relieved the severity of his pictures in three principal ways. He interposed rustic characters conceived indeed in terms of a worn comic convention but vivified through his feeling for their speech—a feeling which enabled him to suggest effects, at once quaint and convincing, of an immemorial choric wisdom. He constantly interwove, through imagery and description, his own sense of the beauty and deep composing power of nature. He showed our aspirations as being of more account than our appetites, and the fidelity of noble men and noble women as being stronger than the grave. This is the portrait of Hardy. So far as it goes, it is the portrait too of Shakespeare.

2

He first attempted a sweeping satire upon polite society, which was to have been called *The Poor Man and the Lady*. But George Meredith, acting as a publisher's reader, persuaded him to scrap this in favour of a novel with more plot. The result was *Desperate Remedies* (1871), a tale of intrigue much in the manner of Wilkie Collins. It seems a far cry from such territory to the Hintocks or Egdon Heath; yet Hardy has here come at once upon fruitful ground. Coincidence regularly working to thicken a plot or increase a plight, and catastrophe springing unexpectedly from seemingly trivial things, are devices making greatly for the ease of pedestrian fictions. But Hardy was to use them imaginatively. He liked them, just as he liked complicated groining or a good gargoyle. 'A strange concurrence of phenomena now confronts us', he announces at one point, with a relish it is impossible not to feel. For the rest, his first published novel chiefly presages troubles to come. He cannot make his educated people carry their education lightly, and when they try to bring a play of mind to bear upon their situations they talk like prigs or lecturers. A related weakness is his manner of bringing in literary or artistic allusions. When a character looks down into a rainwater-butt we are told that 'the reflection from the smooth stagnant surface tinged his face with the greenish shades of Correggio's nudes'. We must connect Hardy's love of paintings with his marked pictorial power, evidence of which this novel already shows. But Correggio's nudes come in with an awkwardness that he never outgrew. When he was revising the serialized *Mayor of Casterbridge* for its appearance in volume form he thought to increase the literary standing of so majestic a tragedy by dropping in just such knick-knackery as this. Again, we must notice how heavily his patient prose may tread. Suspense and early morning do not chill a man; they 'cause a sensation of chilliness to pervade his frame'. There is no book of Hardy's without these flaws. Tears are 'an access of eye-moisture' in *Jude the Obscure*.

Desperate Remedies won some praise but was condemned by the *Spectator* on moral grounds, so that Hardy began his novelist's career as he was to end it. Adverse notice discouraged him and he now acted on a hint very different from Meredith's to cultivate plot. John Morley, to whom *The Poor Man and the Lady* was shown, had praised the strength and freshness of some rural scenes, and these Hardy made the basis of *Under the Greenwood Tree* (1872), in which he comes into all that part of his kingdom which knows more of sunshine than shadow. This book, which owes something to the Dorset scholar-poet William Barnes, balances a general view of rustic life with the delicately sketched wooing by Dick the tranter's son of one slightly above him socially, the schoolmistress Fancy Day, 'just husband-high'. With the Mellstock choir, and particularly in their scene of expostulation with the vicar, Hardy arrives at his mature comedy. There is Shakespearian quality in the picture of Thomas Leaf, Thomas Leaf's attitude to himself, and his fellows' attitude to him. Yet in the interest of his idyll Hardy has here almost excluded what was already the characteristic colouring of his mind. The novel bears as its sub-title *A Rural Painting of the Dutch School*—a fancy possibly suggested by matter at the beginning of the second part of *Adam Bede*. But it is rather—to draw more precisely upon this favourite field of his imagery—a J. F. Millet, making its placid statement in a gallery presently to be hung with the sad and compassionate art of a Josef Israëls.

A Pair of Blue Eyes (1873), which may be regarded as a last apprentice piece, opens as another story of a young man's love for a socially superior girl. For his framework Hardy returns to the linked coincidences of *Desperate Remedies*, at the same time trying to extend his command of character and find scope for his developing tragic sense. Elfride Swancourt, the daughter of a snobbish clergyman, finds herself in love with a young architect of humble birth, Stephen Smith. Agreeing to a secret marriage, she accompanies him to London, loses heart, and travels home overnight. Smith goes to India and presently there turns up as Elfride's suitor his old friend and mentor, Henry Knight. She comes to respond to Knight's love with a maturer passion, but soon it appears that 'inbred in him was an invincible objection to be any but the first comer in a woman's heart'. So strong is this unfortunate taste for 'untried lips' that Elfride has to cheat and is soon exposed.

'Elfride, we must bid good-bye to compliment,' said Knight: 'we must do without politeness now. Look in my face, and as you believe in God above, tell me truly one thing more. Were you away alone with him?'

'Yes.'

'Did you return home the same day on which you left it?'

'No.'

The word fell like a bolt, and the very land and sky seemed to suffer. Knight turned aside. . . . 'You must forget me,' he said. 'We shall not marry, Elfride.'

Elfride's monosyllabic and quite misleading reply in face of the staring implication of Knight's second question is disastrous and strains our credulity. Yet the stroke belongs with the whole system of the book. Again and again the event goes ingeniously against the heroine and has, in the words of Hardy as he characteristically underlines his own formula, 'a virtue in the accident of its juncture far beyond any it intrinsically exhibited'. The effect is as of poor Elfride's playing desperately for happiness and fulfilment against some supernal master-strategist who deploys forces slender in themselves with unerring skill. And at the end this dark power directs its malevolent fun elsewhere. Knight and Smith meet by accident. Each discovers how he has wronged Elfride, and each decides to seek her out.

They find themselves on the same train and with it they notice that there travels a 'sombre van'. It proves to hold Elfride's body, and they learn how she had married a nobleman whose motherless children were fond of her, and how her husband's devotion was powerless to prevent her dying of a broken heart. The place at which her end is finally revealed to her former lovers is an inn called the Welcome Home.

This novel poses a central problem in Hardy. Nothing disturbed him more than the charge that he saw the power behind the universe as an imbecile jester. He had schooled himself in determinism—which, however, he modified to give scope to tragedy, holding that the individual will has its measure of freedom during certain moments of equilibrium in that universal Will within which it is comprised. Where he could be read in another sense—so he often said—it was merely as a result of his employing some trope of rhetoric natural to the excited imagination. But why, believing this, does Hardy so often seem to play against his characters with loaded dice? 'My art', he wrote, 'is to intensify the expression of things, as is done by Crivelli, Bellini, &c., so that the heart and inner meaning is made vividly visible.' He judged that each of us inclines to take an unwarrantably rosy view of his own individual destiny, and that from this comes a general tendency to minimize the extent to which mere brute circumstance, nature's neutrality and indifference, negates the sum of human effort, falsifies our calculations, and betrays our hopes. 'To intensify the expression of things', therefore, so as to make vividly visible 'the heart and inner meaning' of the underlying human situation to us who will avert our gaze if we can, the writer must sharply step up the incidence upon human destiny of the mere blind recalcitrance of the universe. In *A Pair of Blue Eyes* the method is pushed so far that we wonder—not for the last time—whether the writer is not obeying some other prompting than this of artistic calculation. And the book has further weaknesses. Knight, the 'reviewer and essayist', is a dummy. Yet Hardy achieves something with him by a strikingly imaginative expedient. The scene in which this chilly man's life is in peril on a cliff and he is saved with a rope made from Elfride's clothes (incidentally a good place in which to study the reach, power, and yet obstinately continuing awkwardness of Hardy's kindled prose) unites the couple in an intensely shared emotional experience, and is more

effective than much laboured writing in pushing the more
attractive Smith out of the picture. Indeed if anything in the
book might prepare us for what is now immediately to come
it would be this. As Knight clings desperately to the rock,
counting the seconds, and sees before him the fossilized remains
of 'one of the early crustaceans called Trilobites', with the result
that his succeeding moments become a vision of aeons of geological time, we feel that the mind of his creator too is opening
upon some larger scene; that here is the first stepping of Hardy's
imagination towards the vast theatre of his maturer art.

3

We arrive, as by this steep slope, upon the broad plateau of
Hardy's prose comprising *Far from the Madding Crowd* (1874),
The Return of the Native (1878), *The Mayor of Casterbridge* (1886),
and *The Woodlanders* (1887)—a plateau beyond which rise the
stark peaks of *Tess of the D'Urbervilles* (1891) and *Jude the
Obscure* (1896). The first four all preserve some amenity which
the other two—more particularly the last—abandon. There are
readers who from the sombre ground of Hardy's central achievement look back with regret upon the sunlight of *Under the Greenwood Tree*. But that sombre ground itself shows as half paradisic
when viewed from amid the inky shadows of Flintcomb-Ash or
Aldbrickham.

Far from the Madding Crowd tells the story of Bathsheba Ever-
dene, an independent farmer, and of the tragic passion which,
through a thoughtless prank, she inspires in her neighbour, the
reserved and lonely Boldwood. Eventually she marries Sergeant
Troy, a libertine, and loves him only the more as his faithless-
ness is revealed to her. But a time comes when Troy is believed
drowned; Boldwood's consuming passion is rekindled by hope
and for the second time tortured by doubtful promises until,
just as he believes that his desire is to be gratified, Troy reappears, claims his wife, and is shot dead by his now insane
rival. All this time Bathsheba has had another faithful lover in
Gabriel Oak, her first suitor, whom undeserved misfortune has
reduced to the position of her shepherd. In the end these two
are married, and the novel has a subdued and tranquil close.
What raises it above the commonplace of Victorian fiction is
the way in which its episodes of passion and violence are so

implicated with the life of the fields that they take their place
as only one aspect of a universe elsewhere deeply ordered and
composed. The seasons bring their tasks: lambing, dipping,
shearing, haymaking, thatching the ricks; and each is made the
setting of some turn in the action, so that the fable—worn
though it is and irritated by much subsidiary complication of
a conventional sort—seems to take on the inevitability of these
ageless cycles. The story unfolds in a long sequence of vivid
pictures. Two of these—that in which, at a touch on a dark
lantern, Sergeant Troy, brilliant in brass and scarlet, springs
fatally into existence before Bathsheba; and that other, curiously prelusive of the art of D. H. Lawrence, in which Troy,
with a striking symbolism of physical surrender and possession,
subjects Bathsheba to a species of ordeal by sword-play—are
perhaps only more celebrated, and not more nearly consummate, than numerous others. In this power to make us *see*, in
observation of and control over a wide diversity of natural
things, and in the perfection of the rustic chorus which meets
in the malthouse, *Far from the Madding Crowd* is a sudden glory
in Hardy's writing. All the variety of nature is painted, and
against it conscious beings who, in spite of the harsh conditions
nature imposes, achieve an equilibrium amid its stresses, and
find purpose and direction within a culture having something of
its own immemorial majesty: a culture of which the great barn
described in the twenty-second chapter is one of Hardy's most
finely evocative symbols.

It is the fertility of nature that is everywhere felt in *Far from
the Madding Crowd*. The human story, although affording the
spectacle of much tragic waste, ends upon a note of fruition.
In *The Return of the Native* a similar ending is heavy with a new
irony; and it is largely from a changed vision of the face of
nature that the darkened picture comes. Eustacia Vye rebels
against her environment—narrow, barren, and inimical—and
in the end she is broken 'by the cruel obstructiveness of all
about her'. Clym Yeobright returns within the influence of the
environment, but disregards it. As a result he has no grip on its
actual situations and no understanding of how its influence on
others is ruthlessly shaping his own destiny. Both are defeated
by Egdon Heath. This desolate region, Hardy tells us, 'it is
pleasant to dream . . . may be the heath of that traditionary
King of Wessex—Lear'. The description of it with which the

book opens again instances the overwhelming total effect that
he can achieve with prose consistently vulnerable in detail. We
are made aware of the heath simultaneously under two aspects.
Egdon is Nature in its otherness, closed to Mind. Its nightly
roll into darkness, its unchanged state through aeons which
show the neighbouring Roman road as but of yesterday, its
natural affinity with night, storm, and all ungenial things: these
make it typify the vast neutral unregarding universe that forms
the theatre of our destiny—so that Yeobright at the crisis of his
tragedy looks out and sees 'only the imperturbable countenance
of the heath, which, having defied the cataclysmal onsets of
centuries, reduced to insignificance by its seamed and antique
features the wildest turmoil of a single man'. But at the same
time the heath, 'slighted and enduring' and with 'a lonely face,
suggesting tragical possibilities', itself symbolizes the human
situation as progressively perceived by modern man. It thus
awaits recognition and acceptance by anyone coming to see
that a joyous and confident attitude to life 'grows less and less
possible as we uncover the defects of natural laws', or who
admits, in a phrase of Hardy's elsewhere, 'the chronic melancholy which is taking hold of the civilized races with the decline
of belief in a beneficent power'. It is only to man in some pristine ignorance of his place in the universe that Egdon is alien
as a natural scene; 'to a more recently learnt emotion' it is
beautiful because expressive of the new disenchantment. To be
reconciled to his heath—we may suppose Hardy as saying—is
Lear's final wisdom. And yet what makes Egdon so moving is
not merely the reach of its symbolism but also the particularity
and concreteness with which, again and again, the symbol is
rendered. In one instance of Hardy's power here—the description of the sound made by the nocturnal wind scouring the
mummied heath bells of the past summer—we find an example
of the subtle way in which he blends his people with their
region. 'Throughout the blowing of these plaintive November
winds that note bore a great resemblance to the ruins of human
song which remain to the throat of four-score and ten. It was
a worn whisper, dry and papery.' Only a little before we have
been listening to just such ruins of human song from Granfer
Cantle.

There are those who judge the proem on Egdon Heath to be
heavy and portentous work. We must at least acknowledge that

it has prompted a good deal of writing against which these charges may be confidently made. It is not to the advantage of one of the greatest of modern novels, for instance, that Mr. E. M. Forster has taken the Egdon route to the Marabar caves in *A Passage to India*. Moreover we do not feel, as we do before D. H. Lawrence's evocations of the Australian bush in *Kangaroo*, that we are in the presence of the sheer thing itself, miraculously unveiled. From Egdon we are receiving what Hardy gives. Here is the proper theatre for the action that is to follow, but we must accept a certain sense of unrefined theatrical bustle, of banging and hammering, as the bleak properties are assembled and shoved into place. Yet all this fits in with the large dramatic simplicity of what is proposed.

There is once more a rustic chorus. Its members sometimes by a clownish ineptitude give a luckless turn to the action, but more commonly dispose themselves agreeably for the purposes of comic relief. Slightly above them are certain subsidiary personages of the fable proper. These suffer mild trial and are awarded mild happiness. Then comes the heroine—the heroine and the two lovers between whom she fatally moves. Eustacia Vye is at the start a disturbingly theatrical creation. Her maternal grandfather had a cousin in the peerage; her lips form 'the curve so well known in the arts of design as the cimarecta, or ogee'; 'in a dim light, and with a slight rearrangement of her hair'—reservations as gravely absurd as Hardy anywhere achieves—'her general figure might have stood for that of either of the higher female deities'. Bourbon roses, rubies, tropical midnights, the lotus-eaters, the march in *Athalie*, Tartarus, Richter, Phaeacia's isle, Saul, Jacob, David, Pontius Pilate, Héloïse, and Cleopatra are all piled up before us as Eustacia takes the stage—yet she steps clear of this huddled ineptitude and commands our acceptance of her reality at once. Romantic, sensual and ignorant, and living with a neglectful grandfather on the lonely heath, she has admitted the advances of Wildeve, a professional engineer who has for no very pressing reason come down to keeping a public house. Wildeve reluctantly marries another girl to whom he has pledged himself. But by this time there has occurred the event from which the novel takes its title. Clym Yeobright, a young man of semi-genteel origins and not previously known to Eustacia, has returned home from a long stay in Paris, where it is understood that he has made a successful career in the jewellery trade. An escape to Paris represents for Eustacia the acme of imagined happiness. But when she marries Yeobright it is to find that he cannot be deflected from a high-minded if nebulous proposal to remain on Egdon and there start some system of rural education. Yeobright, in fact, is idealistic, gentle, melancholic, and—we must feel—entirely a bore. The incompatibility of the marriage is exacerbated by misunderstanding and coldness between Eustacia and his mother, to whom he is devoted. His application to study during his honeymoon precipitates a grave disease of the eyes, and it appears that he is going to be willing to end his and his wife's days in a hut, supporting himself by furze-cutting, the most humble of rural employments. The death of Yeobright's mother, for which Eustacia bears some oblique responsibility, makes matters worse. Eventually, fretted and humiliated, Eustacia thinks to flee to Paris, almost certainly under Wildeve's protection. The attempt to carry out this plan, upon a night on which Egdon Heath is excelling itself in inclemency, leads to her and Wildeve's death, and Yeobright finds 'his vocation in the career of an itinerant open-air preacher and lecturer on morally unimpeachable subjects'.

The Return of the Native is potentially a tragedy of great simplicity. Nothing is necessary to its catastrophe except the characters and their environment in its largest and least accidental play upon them. To this even the austerest art might be willing to add some ironic twist of fate. But Hardy, as nearly always, goes beyond this. Chance holds another field-day throughout the action. We are left at the end wondering again whether the argument from Crivelli and Bellini is really a valid contribution to the aesthetic of fiction and not rather the ingenious rationalizing of a constitutional morbidity. When an unlucky run of trivial events leads Mrs. Yeobright to think that her son and his wife have closed their door against her, the impression is powerful enough; the story at its cardinal point here turns effectively on this strong single hinge. But nothing more is gained when the unfortunate old lady is bitten by an adder on the way home. Strokes of this kind can only weaken each other when made to jostle within the covers of a single book. Sometimes Hardy appears to be led to them by a delight in bizarre visual effect, as when much misunderstanding is made to follow upon a dicing match conducted by the light of glow-worms.

Sometimes stock devices appear to be operating almost by rote, as when a letter miscarries or there is misunderstanding over the place fixed for a wedding. Sometimes an irony seems simply too good to be missed, as when a devoted small boy thinks to enliven Eustacia with a bonfire and so produces the signal for a rendezvous which proves fatal to her. These ingenuities persist to the end. Since Eustacia has earlier admitted thoughts of suicide, we are likely to believe that she has drowned herself. But attentive reading shows that she has become disoriented in the darkness through mistaking for a window in Wildeve's inn the lamp of a gig which happens to have been moved to a sheltered position a quarter of a mile away. Eustacia, we may conclude, has been following a false light. But at least she dies through the incidence of mere chance. In face of all this it is possible to feel that crass casualty absorbs a disabling amount of Hardy's interest and energy in the book. The interplay of character is in general vigorous enough. Yet in major places it tends to become both melodramatic and perfunctory. It is as if Hardy is hurrying by in the persuasion that simple human conflict is not his primary concern.

It is at least the single burden of *The Return of the Native* that the universe is careless of the needs and desires of the tiny individual existences it includes within itself. The scale upon which Hardy draws his pictures enforces this. The characters are seldom other than minute figures creeping across great spaces under a vast overarching sky. In the next novel of the group effects of this sort virtually disappear, never again to preponderate in Hardy's prose. *The Mayor of Casterbridge* presents something quite new: a figure of heroic proportions. Henchard, the Mayor, is the most powerful, as he is also the most original, character in the novels. His tragedy, in both its weakness and its strength, is more nearly Shakespearian than is anything else of the kind in Hardy. The plot is artificial and full of sensational incidents. Much that is crucial for both the action and the growth of the sentiment is perfunctorily treated. Often the author is evidently casting about for fresh matter with which to assuage a greedy and artistically careless magazine public. Indeed, for that public he was here writing more deliberately than usual, so that what the completed manuscript required was not the customary bowdlerizing for serial purposes but variously 'improving' for its eventual publication in volume form. It is astonishing that a book so written, in which the very staple of the prose cries out: 'Good enough for the *Graphic*', should yet so completely declare the strong hand of genius. There is again an improbably large measure of bad luck—yet we seem to be waiting less for the next stroke of ingenuity than for the next beat of the pulse of fate. And this pulse beats through Henchard himself. He is one subverted from within, and this by way of what is large in him. But if in the main Henchard himself monopolizes Hardy's imaginative vigour, and round about him there is much that is arbitrary and much that is sluggish, the novel has its felicities as well as its power. The town of Casterbridge is finely realized. And we may notice how the pity and terror of Henchard's death has set over against it the pathos of his wife's, as that is given to us in Mrs. Cuxsom's lament—a passage illustrating Hardy's strikingly transformed verbal sensibility in such places:

'And she was as white as marble-stone,' said Mrs. Cuxsom. 'And likewise such a thoughtful woman, too—ah, poor soul—that a' minded every little thing that wanted tending. "Yes," says she, "when I'm gone, and my last breath's blowed, look in the top drawer o' the chest in the back room by the window, and you'll find all my coffin clothes; a piece of flannel—that's to put under me, and the little piece is to put under my head; and my new stockings for my feet— they are folded alongside, and all my other things. And there's four ounce pennies, the heaviest I could find, a-tied up in bits of linen, for weights—two for my right eye and two for my left," she said. "And when you've used 'em, and my eyes don't open no more, bury the pennies, good souls, and don't ye go spending 'em, for I shouldn't like it. And open the windows as soon as I am carried out, and make it as cheerful as you can for Elizabeth-Jane."'

'Ah, poor heart!'

'Well, and Martha did it, and buried the ounce pennies in the garden. But if ye'll believe words, that man, Christopher Coney, went and dug 'em up, and spent 'em at the Three Mariners. "Faith," he said, "why should death rob life o' fourpence? Death's not of such good report that we should respect 'en to that extent," says he.'

"Twas a cannibal deed!' deprecated her listeners. . . .

'Well, poor soul; she's helpless to hinder that or anything now,' answered Mother Cuxsom. 'And all her shining keys will be took from her, and her cupboards opened; and little things a' didn't wish seen, anybody will see; and her wishes and ways will all be as nothing!'

'Why should death rob life o' fourpence?' The same thing was said by a statelier personage than Christopher Coney:

> What was unreasonably committed to the ground is reasonably resumed from it: Let Monuments and rich Fabricks, not Riches, adorn mens ashes. The commerce of the living is not to be transferred unto the dead: It is no injustice to take that which none complaines to lose, and no man is wronged where no man is possessor.

It may not be Sir Thomas Browne who is the better English stylist here.

The last novel of the plateau, *The Woodlanders*, returns to the method of spreading interest over a group of characters, and of implicating them, this time subtly rather than powerfully, with a natural scene. But it has its place in the unfolding of Hardy's art, since it is the story of an unhappy marriage promoted by snobbery and perpetuated by convention. Melbury, the prosperous timber-merchant of the Hintocks, educates his daughter Grace as a lady. Although she is really pledged to the simple and staunch Giles Winterborne, Melbury encourages her to listen to social prompting rather than natural feeling and marry Fitzpiers, the shoddy representative of an ancient family. Her husband misconducts himself and she finally runs away, taking refuge in the single-roomed hut to which Winterborne has been reduced through misfortune. In an anxious observance of sexual propriety Winterborne, who is ill, spends several inclement nights virtually in the open, and to the risk in this her own anxieties blind her. As a result he dies. Grace is reconciled to her husband, although it is clear she will be unhappy, and from this socially approved but in fact debasing compromise the book passes to close upon the sublime figure of the peasant girl Marty South, mourning by the grave of Winterborne whom she has passionately and selflessly loved. All these woodland folk are star-crossed still and there is the invariable heightened series of ill chances and disastrous coincidences. Nevertheless Hardy throws an altogether new emphasis upon two forces the power of which he has frequently shown already. These are the keen sense of social distinction possessed by countrymen, and their ready acceptance, as a condition of any secure social standing, of the letter of man-made moral law. Up till now he has been mainly concerned with the Potter and the pot. Now, and while not abandoning his usual role of advocate for the pot in some more than supernal court, he is becoming increasingly conscious that pots, big and little, regularly treat one another with a merciless intolerance. It is a discovery likely to lead a determinist into logical confusion. And indeed what may be called Hardy's theory of the human situation, although it continues to be asserted rigidly and to an increasingly diagrammatic effect in all his succeeding major writing, no longer comes to us as representing the true centre of his feeling. We read on in a perplexity perhaps most nearly resolved by Mr. R. P. Blackmur when he remarks that Hardy is the great example of a sensibility violated by ideas.

4

It is at this point that Hardy's minor novels are best mentioned. In *The Hand of Ethelberta* (1876) he tried to extend his range to polite comedy in a story cleverly calculated to discount his social inexperience. Ethelberta, a butler's daughter, has become a fashionable widow whose task is to keep her head above water while assisting a family whose existence she must conceal. What is good is her resourcefulness, and a deftness of plot which came easily to Hardy. But the territory is not truly his; it is to be far more entertainingly commanded by the young H. G. Wells. Moreover Ethelberta's story is too long drawn out. This is true also of *A Laodicean* (1881), written during illness and in the reading as in the writing less a novel than a treadmill—Hardy's only unredeemed failure during a lifetime in the grim trade of making a living out of books. *The Trumpet-Major* (1880) is a small substantial success because, in turning to the Napoleonic period which he was coming to know so well, he keeps within his own range both of society and of tone and feeling. Here blended with the idyllic light of *Under the Greenwood Tree* is a subdued illumination from his own authentic temper. Irony is basic to the story, since John Loveday, in rescuing his brother Bob from the undesirable Matilda, unwittingly loses to him the woman he loves, Anne Garland; and from this loss passes, a gallant and gentle figure, to death in battle. There are other sombre touches, as the end of the miserly uncle Benjy—whose body when found 'was little more than a light empty husk, dry and fleshless as that of a dead heron found on a moor in January'. Again, the heroine is perhaps too keenly observed to be quite comfortable in an idyll. Her shame-fastness is no more than the socially necessary counterpoise to an unsleeping sexuality. She is the work of one at once suscep-tible and perceptive before the charm of women. In another setting she could embody the full dangerousness and fatality of her kind as Hardy sees it. In all the novels except *The Mayor of Casterbridge* his chief interest is in his women. They are the common instrument by which the universal Will, the blind onward drive of life, thwarts or destroys the hopes and purposes of individual men. At the same time they are themselves, in the singleness of their service, conscious or unconscious, to the same thrust of creation, peculiarly representative of the helplessness of humanity before the commands of fate. All this colours the pretty picture of Anne Garland and her lovers.

The two remaining books here, *Two on a Tower* (1882) and *The Well-Beloved* (1897, but published in a serial version five years earlier), stand apart from the rest of Hardy's prose. The first designs, according to the preface, 'to set the emotional history of two infinitesimal lives against the stupendous back-ground of the stellar universe', and it begins very well, although not quite to this plan. The whole episode of Lady Constantine's falling in love with the rural astronomer Swithin St. Cleeve is delightfully done. The young Swithin himself might easily be a lifeless prig, but is saved by the well-rendered mingling of his rustic and gentle components. 'Swithin', we are told, 'did not observe the tender reproach in Viviette's eyes when he showed by his tale his decided notion that the prime use of dark nights lay in their furtherance of practical astronomy.' This is the book's conflict in a sentence, and it is possible that the theme of the rival attractions of study and courtship, of the stars and of a woman's eyes, was suggested to Hardy by the situation and imagery of *Love's Labour's Lost*, a play which he had studied for the purpose of introducing a scene of amateur theatricals into *A Laodicean*, the immediately preceding novel. *Two on a Tower* goes a little deeper than the ironic comedy of a county Venus and a scientifically preoccupied Adonis. Lady Constan-tine's is eventually a tragic love. Yet the artistic expression of her tragedy largely founders in conventional intrigue. Tiresome complications encumber the book's design. These, while most obviously the product of a determination to write so many thousand words, are also prompted by the writer's anxiety to introduce as little immorality as possible into his narrative: thus the need for Lady Constantine to believe herself married to her lover before yielding to him occasions some unlikely incidents in the depths of Africa. It will be found that other of Hardy's novels creak in places for similar reasons of propriety.

The Well-Beloved is about a man who has to confess to the woman he would marry that he was the suitor too of her mother and her grandmother. It is on record as appealing to Proust both as having 'the touch of the grotesque which is an essential part of all great works' and as attempting something in his own kind. But to embody so artificial a conception in a substantial work of realistic fiction was an uncritical venture. Hardy, who delighted in anecdotes of this sort, made several of them the basis of a number of his short stories. These, again, hold in the main more of his eccentricity than of his genius. Where successful they are best described as bizarre, and when unsuccessful they must be admitted melodramatic and morbid.

5

It is upon Hardy's last two novels that opinion most sharply divides. Their power is undeniable; some special urgency of feeling has plainly attended their composition; at the same time there appears to sound through them the voice of a man who can no longer conceal impatience with large aspects of his craft. But this last impression, although we may be encouraged in it by the very moderate estimation in which we know Hardy to have held prose fiction, is conceivably mistaken. Hardy is least an artist, is most inside the hobbyhorse, when he takes from his ideas the largest licence to narrow and intensify his response to experience. He seems to have been unaware that *Jude the Obscure*, in particular, is less a novel than an outcry, and he was surprised and hurt by reactions to the book which we may still find comprehensible today.

Gerard Manley Hopkins declared that Hardy in his prose rises only to his great strokes and does not, like such an altogether smaller man as Stevenson, write continuously well. This is to say that his genius engages itself fully only with those parts of the novels that have the pitch of poetry. And by poetry here we really mean a full play of sensibility, largely expressed in an observant and creative compassion, which in Hardy tends to be inhibited rather than released by what is most emphatic in the intellectual persuasions with which he has equipped himself. Certainly when he applies his philosophy of the raw deal persistently through the minor conduct of an intricate realistic fiction—as he does with a mounting compulsiveness in both the final novels—the effect, although formidable and unforgettable, is often uninspired, dismal, and obscurely but fatally lacking in the final integrity of art. Almost overwhelming emotion has gone into these books, but it has come out again simply as an overwhelming emotion that Thomas Hardy feels, and feels that we ought to be made to feel. One heroic figure apart, the emotion tends to by-pass the characters. If Madame Tussaud had theological designs upon us, and fitted up an Inferno supplemented by a loudspeaker commentary directed at us from the ceiling, the effect might remind us of these at once moving and imaginatively insufficient productions. It comes down to this: that Hardy, intuitively and as an artist, was able to give his people dimensions, a destiny and a spiritual significance to which his philosophy does not entitle them. To try to *feel* exclusively in terms of that philosophy, to strain the eye upon Schopenhauer and Spencer while closing the ear to the whispering of earth, to subdue an historical to a contemporary sense, to arraign rather than to remark and reflect: these are all impulses that detract from Hardy's power over a realized creation. For they lead to a generalized and undiscriminating pessimism—such as he was always, indeed, hot to deny—in the darkness of which the notion of artistic achievement must for the time be almost without meaning. The last novels have their places of commanding eminence. But there is much in them which is artistically perfunctory beyond almost anything in the earlier Hardy, and which disappoints or offends us by being at once so harshly stated and so little 'done'. From this defect, it is true, the books do not fail to gain a certain positive flavour, so that misgiving soon attends us if we embark on comprehensive censure. Dr. Leavis has said that Hardy in his verse makes a style out of stylelessness. It is possible to feel that in the last novels he makes a queer sort of aesthetic out of artistic neglect. This holds more of *Jude* than of *Tess*. Indeed the two books are by no means commensurate. *Tess* has some claim to be Hardy's *Lear*. *Jude* is certainly his *Timon*.

Tess Durbeyfield, a peasant girl set in a dangerous situation

by her desire to aid an improvident family, is more or less forcibly seduced by Alec d'Urberville, a pretender to the ancient
lineage which is actually hers. She becomes his mistress for a
short time and then breaks away. Her illegitimate child dies
and she makes a new start, eventually finding a prospect of
happiness in her passionate love of Angel Clare, the idealistic
and speciously emancipated younger son of a clergyman. Her
confession to him miscarries; and when on her wedding night,
and after receiving a similar confession from him, she tells her
story, he rejects her and goes off to South America. Then his
silence constitutes a more and more evident desertion against
which she long, and through bitter misfortunes, hopes in vain.
Broken-hearted at last, and once more urged by her family's
need, she returns to d'Urberville. And finally, upon her husband's eventually turning up with belated feelings of forgiveness,
she kills d'Urberville with a knife intended for the dissection
of a cold ham. Things have gone against her all the time, as
they have against most of her creator's heroines. Tess, like
the wretch once spied through the young Hardy's telescope, is
hanged.

Jude Fawley's story is rather bleaker, and certainly much
more ingeniously calamitous. A little orphaned baker's boy in
a Wessex hamlet, he is first introduced to us being thrashed
by a farmer who has hired him to scare away the rooks, and
who fails to appreciate the motive prompting the child to invite
the birds to feed instead. But Jude as well as being tender-
hearted is serious and intelligent. Having seen a smear of light
on the night horizon, and believing it to be the city of Christminster (which is Oxford), he is fired by the ambition of learning. Towards this he struggles, tenaciously and in isolation, for
years. He has taught himself a surprising amount of Latin and
Greek when he is unfortunately trapped into marriage by a low,
indeed an almost improbably vile, young woman called Arabella. In his resulting unhappiness he makes some ominous
experiments with beer before his wife—providentially, we might
foolishly suppose—throws him over and departs to Australia.
Jude makes his way to Christminster, finds employment as a
stonemason, and communes with the shades of departed scholars
—their living successors being wholly uninterested in him.
Then he meets a cousin, Sue Bridehead, and falls in love
with her. It is a bad choice, if only because the cousins have

a common ancestry in persons disposed to suicide and all marital unluckiness. Sue, who is in part a real Hardy heroine and in part a New Woman out of Ibsen, works in a shop selling liturgical objects—an employment from which she finds relief in reading Gibbon, notably 'the chapter dealing with the reign of Julian the Apostate', and in hiding in her room two large and naked plaster casts of Venus and Apollo. But these last do not promise in her what they might, since the chief sign of her hereditary neurotic constitution is a pathological frigidity. It is clear that we are heading for misery. She marries a decent schoolmaster, but later takes refuge from him in a cupboard, and upon being discovered there at once makes him a speech verbatim out of her reading in J. S. Mill. Arabella returns, and there is a fatal occasion upon which Jude succumbs to her 'midnight contiguity'. There are divorces, conscientious refusals of the bondage of the marriage laws, and Hardy's usual muddled appointments and missed trains. Jude proves to have a son by Arabella, an unnatural child known as Little Father Time. At the climax of the story Little Father Time hangs himself—again in a cupboard—having first hanged two other children, unrealized to the point of namelessness, whom Jude has eventually had by Sue. Jude, whose piety initially vied with his learning, is now bitterly agnostic. Sue, the former collector of heathen divinities, has embraced a narrow and morbid Christianity. Jude takes to drink and dies in a general debility. Sue returns in physical loathing to the embraces of her former husband the schoolmaster. A multitude of small heavy ironies accompany the march of this desperate narrative, as does a running commentary upon the wickedness of English sexual conventions and the brutal exclusiveness of the English higher educational system. Continually as we read, we have a startled sense of things that a great and gentle spirit has been bottling up.

What marks these novels is, in the first place, an increase in that concern with human institutions already found in *The Woodlanders*. The regardlessness of the universe towards that which has tragically come to consciousness within it is now seen as miniatured in the regardlessness of society towards the individual. Men collectively and for their material ease have decreed ordinances against which they see with complacency individuals break themselves and bleed; and to these ordinances they have baselessly ascribed supernatural sanction—so that

Tess, carrying her illegitimate child among scenes declaring the naturalness of procreation, must yet be burdened by a conviction that she has transgressed more than a man-made law. And of society's disregard of what is valuable in an individual other individuals are constantly the instruments. When Tess slips a letter under Angel's door and it goes beneath the carpet we are aware that the nature of things is at play upon her directly. But when she attempts to visit her parents-in-law, who in fact would receive her kindly, and turns back discouraged upon overhearing the conversation of Angel's brothers, we feel that had these young men but had hearts of charity, and been unblinkered by a narrow morality, Tess would not have gone to the gallows. Thus the grim report that Hardy brings back from the universe at large, he now finds that he must bring back only too often from the human individual. And once attention is thus centred upon the blindness of men—beings whom our every habit of mind obliges us to consider capable of moral choice—it is easy to read blindness as malevolence. So it is then tempting to conclude that the pervasiveness of this malevolence reflects, after all, some larger malignity in the constitution of the universe—a universe hitherto regularly claimed by the intellect as neutral, and sometimes claimed by the feelings as in a mute accord, even, with the sentient creation. Under the weight of their misfortunes Jude and Sue would 'sit silent, more bodeful of the direct antagonism of things than of their insensate and stolid obstructiveness'. In other words they cease to evince chiefly the 'scientific' consciousness hitherto professed by Hardy, which sees misfortune as proceeding from necessity. Instead they evince a consciousness which, in one of Hardy's essentially emotional temperament, is likely to erupt in any phase of exceptional strain: a consciousness, virtually Manichaean, of triumphantly hostile intention everywhere operative; 'things' comprehending both a large inclination of the cosmos and the entrenched human prejudices of Christminster. It is to Hardy, we are very aware, as well as to Jude and Sue, that 'affliction makes opposing forces loom anthropomorphous'.

Thus although Hardy claims still to multiply fate's booby-traps simply to enforce upon us, who are comfortable moles, the consequences of nature's mere indifference, actually he is now doing so partly by way of relieving his own irrational sense—

itself perhaps a psychological end-product of 'rationalism'—of a vast malevolence working against us. In theory there is no evil in his universe, only mechanism at jar with the sad accident of consciousness. But this must be an unstable persuasion in one of Hardy's depth of feeling, and in *Tess of the D'Urbervilles* and *Jude the Obscure* primitive ways of taking experience break through the skin of his nineteenth-century thinking as never before. Had the irruption been pervasive and decisive, a new sort of coherence might have emerged in his work. But in fact we have only a confusion in the presence of which there can be outcry powerful enough, but little of the serenity of art.

But these are courageous and uncompromising books. Grotesquely though he scribbled over the manuscript of *Tess* in coloured ink in order to produce copy suitable for a magazine, Hardy was yet for the first time in published work conceding virtually nothing. In this there is possibly the influence of Ibsen, the English productions of whose plays he was at this time regularly attending and finding congenial. Of *Tess* and *Jude* he might have said—drawing upon his description of *Hedda Gabler*—that he was concerned 'to depict human beings, human emotions, and human destinies, upon a groundwork of certain of the social conditions and principles of the present day'. And plainly the books are a revolt against that notion of the novelist as a socially acceptable entertainer with which he had always temporized so far. In particular he obeyed his new and darker sense by renouncing all use of the patina which time sets on the face of sorrow. In prose *Tess* and *Jude* are his only serious dealings with the here-and-now world of his maturity, and *Jude* is his only major novel denuded of solace from 'antique works and ways of labour in woods and fields'. Moreover while *Tess*, like *The Mayor of Casterbridge*, is dominated by a single figure, *Jude*, like the majority of the novels, is concerned rather with a group of figures in interaction. It is as if Hardy felt that in *Tess* he had not got far enough away from literary convention and the lure of art. Tess herself has great stature, and may have seemed to him to render a final impression more in the grand manner of tragedy than his present sense of the mere desperation of the human situation warranted. Jude is—with large and uncongenial labour, we feel—made precisely life-size. His ambition—although Hardy puts into it so much intense personal feeling—is a very ordinary mingling of genuine desire for knowledge with muddled determination to get on. He must have a good brain but he is certainly not allowed to charm us with his brilliance. And the whole course of life in which he and the other characters are involved—its carnal or unconsidered marriages, its divorces and drab reunitings and physical incompatibilities, its shifting aims and abrasive material struggles, its disappointments drowned in beer—is something closer to the texture of average modern living than Hardy had before achieved. Yet this is incongruously shot through with a species of wild and morbid poetry. It is from an actual poem, significantly enough—'Midnight on the Great Western' in *Moments of Vision*—that Little Father Time enters the story to an effect the extravagance of which Hardy seems to be totally blind to. Little Father Time has his moments; he supposes the colleges of Christminster to be jails; but his final deed has no more substance than last night's nightmare, and in the whole book it is perhaps this small epitome of woe that chiefly gives the game away. We are having foisted on us as human life a puppet show that is *not* human life; and this is something which neither tragedy nor comedy—and far less anything bearing the credentials of realistic fiction—ought to be. *Jude* is thus a book far harder to take than its predecessor. *Tess*—it was declared by a reviewer—'except during a few hours spent with cows, has not a gleam of sunshine anywhere'. *Jude* omits even the cows. Perhaps Mr. John Holloway is thinking of this when he remarks, at the end of an excellent study, that in Hardy's final novel 'all rectifying solidities have dropped out of sight'.

6

Hardy had always written poetry. Now at fifty-eight he published *Wessex Poems* (1898) and this, although poorly received, was shortly followed by *Poems of the Past and Present* (1902). At sixty-three came the first part of *The Dynasts* (1903) amid bewilderment which clarified itself into substantial recognition only with the appearance of the third and final part five years later. *Time's Laughingstocks* (1909) followed. Hardy was seventy-four when he published *Satires of Circumstance* (1914), the volume containing by far his finest lyrics. And at this date half of his lyrical poetry was yet to come in *Moments of Vision* (1917), *Late Lyrics and Earlier* (1922), *Human Shows, Far Phantasies* (1925), and

Winter Words (1928). For this last book he wrote in a projected preface: 'So far as I am aware, I happen to be the only English poet who has brought out a new volume of verse on his . . . birthday.' But he died before he was able to insert 'eighty-eighth' and fate thus prevented perhaps the only boast ever proposed by his pen. At this time he mentioned too what, looking back, was the only ambition he could remember: 'to have some poem or poems in a good anthology like the Golden Treasury'. And indeed his humility was entire. It is said that when from his position at the head of English letters he sent poems to the London *Mercury* he would accompany them with an offer of amendment or withdrawal if they were not suitable, and shortly before his death he took particular pleasure in a letter of acceptance from the editor of *The Times*.

The immediate occasion of Hardy's turning away from prose was the hostility that greeted *Jude*. His notebook for 1896 records the opinion that it might be in verse that he could express most freely ideas and emotions unacceptable to the public. He adds that if Galileo had used verse the Inquisition might have let him alone. But it must have been the nature as much as the reception of *Jude* that was decisive. However opaque the hide of the hobbyhorse, Hardy can scarcely have failed to gain some dim uncomfortable vision of his book as essentially a perfunctory though still powerful fictional disguising of an obsessive sense of sexual and educational deprivation. At least what is authentically imaginative there calls out for liberation from a form at once too constricting and too diffuse. When he declared that 'you could get the whole of a novel into three pages of verse' the rash generalization had its validity for his own work. All through the novels we best remember places at which the poet takes over. 'He requires', Arthur Symons says, 'a certain amount of emotion to shake off the lethargy natural to his style.' This preponderating reliance upon feeling made the lyric a natural unit of utterance. Yet Hardy lacked much that a poet is the better for possessing, and a sense of this might well have made him, so modest as he was, pause on the threshold of poetry had he not been saved by the very simplicity of his mind. The following note, made in 1902, expresses the sum of his thought:

Poetry. There is a latent music in the sincere utterance of deep emotion, however expressed, which fills the place of the actual word-music in rhythmic phraseology on thinner emotive subjects, or on subjects with next to none at all. And supposing a total poetic effect to be represented by a unit, its component fractions may be either, say:

Emotion three-quarters, plus Expression one quarter, or
Emotion one quarter, plus Expression three-quarters.

This suggested conception seems to me to be the only one which explains all cases, including those instances of verse that apparently infringe all rules, and yet bring unreasoned convictions that they are poetry.

Hardy does not pause to inquire whether the more or less of 'utterance' be not in fact the more or less of 'expression'. He might have confounded poetry with effusion had he not known instinctively that utterance is achieved only in proportion to the control which the poet possesses over the evocative and condensing powers of language, and that the more emotional pressure there be the greater is the need of rigorously confining form. For a weakness in the first of these commands he tried to compensate in various ways, notably by neologism which is often a sort of privative telegraphese, and by a strong, concrete, and generally familiar imagery. But it was on a discipline of structure that he chiefly relied. Like Donne he knew the importance of drawing his pains through rhyme's vexation. He unremittingly presses his matter into the intricate crevasses of one or another severe stanzaic form of his own devising. A great part of the effectiveness of his technique comes from his ability to obey rules of verse-making as intricate and arbitrary as, say, Swinburne's, while yet achieving strong spare statement and the impression of a mind forming and turning its thought precisely as it is initially prompted to do. Two short poems will make these characteristics and virtues clear:

ACCORDING TO THE MIGHTY WORKING

When moiling seems at cease
　In the vague void of night-time,
　And heaven's wide roomage stormless
　Between the dusk and light-time,
　And fear at last is formless,
We call the allurement Peace.

Peace, this hid riot, Change,
　This revel of quick-cued mumming,

This never truly being,
This evermore becoming,
This spinner's wheel onfleeing
Outside perception's range.

ONCE AT SWANAGE

The spray sprang up across the cusps of the moon,
And all its light loomed green
As a witch-flame's weirdsome sheen
At the minute of an incantation scene;
And it greened our gaze—that night at demilune.

Roaring high and roaring low was the sea
Behind the headland shores:
It symboled the slamming of doors,
Or a regiment hurrying over hollow floors. . . .
And there we two stood, hands clasped; I and she!

These are poems disposing at once of the notion that when
Hardy turned to verse he was mistaken about what it was really
given him to do. We may sometimes find his poetry too prosaic,
but never—unless when he lucklessly requires the fairies to provide a jewelled and silver-lined golden casket for the dust of
Shelley's skylark—too poetic. Absurdities may be garnered
from his large output of verse:

Is the fair woman who carried that sunshade
A skeleton just as her property is?—

but there is no English poet since Wordsworth whose pedes-
trianisms are so frequently satisfactory to the habituated ear,
bringing 'unreasoned convictions that they are poetry'.

Again like Donne, Hardy was fortunate in being able with
some justification to regard as exhausted a whole tradition of
poetry in which he could himself scarcely have excelled.

As one that for a weary space has lain
Lull'd by the songs of Circe and her wine
In gardens near the pale of Proserpine,
Where that Aeaean isle forgets the main,
And only the low lutes of love complain,
And only shadows of wan lovers pine.

To this tune Hardy's many wan lovers were never to pine.
Just as he judged Egdon Heath rather than the vineyards and

myrtle-gardens of south Europe to be congruous with a modern sensibility, so too he considered that the modern poet had better work in iron than in gold. He wished, he told Edmund Gosse, to avoid the jewelled line. It is not recorded whether Gosse inquired if it had courted him. In a sense Hardy is in all this deftly exploiting his own blank places. George Moore declared that Hardy 'popularised pessimism and coaxed his readers into drinking from an old tin pot a beverage that had hitherto only been offered to them in golden and jewelled goblets'. Two years before *Wessex Poems* it had been so offered by A. E. Housman:

> With rue my heart is laden
> For golden friends I had,
> For many a rose-lipt maiden
> And many a lightfoot lad.
>
> By brooks too broad for leaping
> The lightfoot boys are laid;
> The rose-lipt girls are sleeping
> In fields where roses fade.

From Housman's goblet we receive, in that first experience of poetry to which so much must be allowed, something that from Hardy we shall seldom get. Yet it is in Hardy's plain pewter that the finer consonance with his theme and with his age rests:

> You did not walk with me
> Of late to the hill-top tree
> By the gated ways,
> As in earlier days;
> You were weak and lame,
> So you never came,
> And I went alone, and I did not mind,
> Not thinking of you as left behind.
>
> I walked up there to-day
> Just in the former way;
> Surveyed around
> The familiar ground
> By myself again:
> What difference, then?
> Only that underlying sense
> Of the look of a room on returning thence.

Housman's technique is contrived with some pretension to give us what we are obliged to think of as the voice of poetry. Hardy's gives us his own voice and experience—his own and therefore ours.

In several technical ways, as for example in his care to preserve a sufficient relationship with the natural rhetoric of speech, Hardy is a forward-looking poet. Browning's was the most important literary influence upon his verse, but it was an influence exercised over one already firmly wedded to the lucidity of hymns and ballads. (There is a shred of connexion between Hardy and Kipling in this.) Hardy is always clear. To be obscure, he said, as some of the younger poets were, was not fair to the reader; Herbert Spencer had pointed out that the energy devoted to discovering the meaning of what one reads is spent at the cost of what might have been given to appreciating it. And whereas it is recorded of Meredith that when friends sought elucidations of his poems he would turn from any specific point with laughter and supply only the general statement that in poetry his aim was concentration and suggestion, Hardy on the contrary would draw up his chair and at once accept the onus of explanation. Here he is at a remove from Browning—to whom he comes close, however, in matters of diction, dramatic method, love of concrete situation, and effective exploitation of the grotesque. And Browning had influence over more than Hardy's technical accomplishment, since he represented for the younger man a grand enigma of the age. In the regard of each poet the stars were a dust blown through the same immensities; for each the fossils told the same story in the rocks. And yet—Hardy said—Browning showed a 'robustious, swaggering' cheerfulness 'worthy of a dissenting grocer', while he himself, writing as he believed in the full stream of his time, was constrained to be more consistently sombre than almost any previous English poet. Was Browning's attitude at bottom 'cowardly and insincere'? Could it conceivably be a mere bait thrown out to catch the public?

On Hardy's perplexity here there is one obvious comment to be made. Individual temper is quite as important as any *Zeitgeist* in determining responses to experience. Men are in general little willing to acknowledge the extent to which their reading of the universe proceeds from the innermost recesses of their personality and from private histories which have been in substantial degree chosen under pressure from the same

obscure source. To Hardy the sorrow which he saw writ large
over all sublunary things seemed matter of objective fact. But
Browning, denying this, was an objective fact too, and Browning teased him to the end. When in his eightieth year Hardy
attended a service in Exeter Cathedral, the anthem put 'Abt
Vogler' into his mind, and it was now he felt he would have
liked above all things to be a cathedral organist. But he went
away and wrote a poem which records, in something like Browning's anapaests, the story of a lady organist whose unconventional
morals bring her into disfavour; who gains the permission of
her pious employers to continue the work she loves by accepting
drastically reduced terms; and who, when even this shrewd
bargain eventually fails, is left thinking out a sensational suicide
in the face of the congregation.

Compared with much that surrounds it, 'The Chapel-
Organist' is a tolerably cheerful poem. For Hardy was now
writing to please himself, and in doing so he cut yet further
the already meagre ration of fulfilled and happy living which
he had allowed to the consumers of his novels. But the effect of
the poetry comes not merely from this rejection of all softening
circumstance but also from the writer's new freedom to do one
thing at a time. Just as each of Dickens's novels is a sort of
Christmas hamper so is each of Hardy's a Pandora's box;
variousness and profusion are the traditional expectations, and
at the rifling touch out tumble all kinds of puddings and pies,
jokes and surprises from the one, as every conceivable kind of
misfortune from the other. But in Hardy's poems the lid opens
and closes upon some single form of sorrow, disengaged from its
thronging fellows, and the effect is the more poignant and the
stronger. Yet although many of the poems are notably pure in
kind, isolating after an almost scientific fashion the several areas
of Hardy's experience in order to explore them fully, it is of
only passing usefulness to split into categories work that is
finally so single. Each kind of verse—philosophic, narrative,
dramatic, or lyrical—builds up its own total impression, and
all these impressions then enter into our experience of one or
another single poem. It is perhaps this organic quality of
Hardy's poetry that gives so extraordinary a fullness of life to
verse in which the predominant vision is of man as

> but a thing of flesh and bone
> Speeding on to its cleft in the clay.

7

Of the kinds in so far as they may be distinguished, the most immediately striking is the philosophic or cosmic. It is signifi-cant that the greater number of poems of this sort come com-paratively early (notably in *Poems of the Past and Present*) for they represent less Hardy's achieved poetry than a preliminary statement of the climate into which that poetry must consent to be born. The poet makes the grand tour of the universe, and in doing so talks with a good many august entities and personages: Crass Casualty, Time, Doom, the Mother, Death, Nature, and, finally, God—whose funeral he attends at a date specifically given as between the years 1908 and 1910. Every-where he receives the same report of a cosmos 'lightless on every side', where the intellect must acknowledge as futile any hope of 'heart to heart returning after dust to dust'. Nature labours mindlessly and her production of sentient beings has been the most luckless of conceivable accidents. God, always 'a forced device', is now seen to dwindle day by day 'Beneath the deicide eyes of seers'. To the question 'Who or what shall fill his place?' the poet can but respond 'No answerer I'. He sees only two infinitesimal glints of light. Since the Mindless Mover has for-tuitously produced minds it is possible that there may be some more comprehensive development of the same sort in the future, so that cheerfully disposed persons may declare:

> By some still close-cowled mystery
> We have reached feeling faster than he,
> But he will overtake us anon,
>   If the world goes on.

Similarly, in his old age, Hardy notes the vague new feeling of hitherto unapprehended modes of duration generated by talk of the 'fourth dimension'. Everything may not after all be defaced by the fell hand of Time in quite the simple way we have supposed. There may be some hope in that.

This is the ground bass of Hardy's poetry, and those poems that have little more cannot be other than bleak—the more so because they are never magniloquent. Again we may compare with Housman:

> Ay, look: high heaven and earth ail from the prime foundation;
> All thoughts to rive the heart are here, and all are vain:

Horror and scorn and hate and fear and indignation—
Oh why did I awake? when shall I sleep again?

Hardy's is quite another manner:

A time there was—as one may guess
And as, indeed, earth's testimonies tell—
Before the birth of consciousness,
When all went well . . .

But the disease of feeling germed,
And primal rightness took the tinct of wrong;
Ere nescience shall be reaffirmed
How long, how long?

It is only occasionally, as in the sonnet 'At a Lunar Eclipse',
that Hardy allows himself any gesture, any magnificence of
phrase in these confrontations of mechanism, of 'the grimness
of the general situation'. And this is artful. While actually saying
a good deal, he contrives to suggest that he is holding his tongue
—which would be perhaps the least inadequate manner of
meeting the universe he discerns. In *Moments of Vision*, in
another lunar poem, there is indeed a hint given to the poet
that absolute silence might be best. The moon, after witnessing
some painful suicide, peers in upon him at his desk

curious to look
Into the blinkered mind
Of one who wants to write a book
In a world of such a kind.

In the end Hardy did decide to say no more. The resolve is
chronicled in about his nine-hundredth poem.

All this is bleak enough, and as a vein of inspiration might
soon have been exhausted. But Hardy's vision, although pervasively conditioned by the far vistas so daunting to his age,
was savingly active nearer home. He wished to be remembered
as one with the habit of noticing familiar things:

When the Present has latched its postern behind my tremulous stay,
And the May month flaps its glad green leaves like wings,
Delicate-filmed as new-spun silk, will the neighbours say,
'He was a man who used to notice such things'?

He was at once alert and compassionate; in neither sense did
he think the less of people for being without his own sombre
extension of view; he was ceaselessly moved to sympathetic

participation in 'all the vast various moils that mean a world
alive'. The very keenness of his observation is sometimes a disability. It seizes the smallest irony—

> And the hoarse auctioneer is dead,
> Who 'Going—going!' so often said—

and perhaps attracts too much of the attention of the poet to
specific precipitating occasions. The 'Satires of Circumstance
in Fifteen Glimpses', of which he thought so highly as to let
them supply the title for an important volume, are certainly
mordant, but they are the work of one who, for the time, has
let himself go about biting on too little. The second is called
'In Church':

> 'And now to God the Father', he ends,
> And his voice thrills up to the topmost tiles:
> Each listener chokes as he bows and bends,
> And emotion pervades the crowded aisles.
> Then the preacher glides to the vestry-door,
> And shuts it, and thinks he is seen no more.
>
> The door swings softly ajar meanwhile,
> And a pupil of his in the Bible class,
> Who adores him as one without gloss or guile,
> Sees her idol stand with a satisfied smile
> And re-enact at the vestry-glass
> Each pulpit gesture in deft dumb-show
> That had moved the congregation so.

We feel something almost small-minded in the poet's sitting
down to versify such a 'glimpse' as this, and remember the
bombardment with petty ironies which troubled our progress
through *Jude the Obscure*. Most of the narrative and anecdotal
poems are much better; and they are at their best when the
matter is of a simplicity answering to that simple sense of
the human plight from which all their poignancy derives. 'The
Dance at the Phoenix', 'The Slow Nature', 'A Trampwoman's
Tragedy' (his own favourite), and 'A Sunday Morning Tragedy'
are examples. But others are little more than versified tales of
ingenuity. Thus in 'The Contretemps' the narrator, about to
board the Jersey boat with another man's wife, embraces in
the dark the wrong woman, one who in her turn is proposing
to elope with another woman's husband. A frequent formula is
that of some disillusioning encounter at the end of a pilgrimage

of love or affection. In 'The Whipper-In' a son returns to the
father with whom he had quarrelled and is rejoiced to catch
a glimpse of his red coat through a hedge—only to be told

> though that is his coat, 'tis now
> The scarecrow of a rick;
> You'll see when you get nearer—
> 'Tis spread out on a stick.

The whipper-in no longer needs a coat. In 'The Supplanter' a
man makes a journey to the grave of his beloved but on arrival
finds the cemetery closed and its keeper giving a party to
celebrate his daughter's twentieth birthday. 'He drops his
wreath, and enters in'—with lamentable results vigorously
worked out in the remainder of the poem. In 'The Dame of
Athelhall' a woman fleeing with her lover is seized with remorse,
says good-bye to him for ever, and returns to the house of her
husband, whom she straightway overhears telling a friend that
her flight has been for the best and that he can himself now
take his 'new true bride'. These ironic quenchings of expectation
sometimes have the grimly humorous note that Hardy loved
in an anecdote—as in the verses beginning

> 'Ah, are you digging on my grave
> My loved one?—planting rue?'

and ending with an apology on the part of a favourite dog, who
has forgotten that it is above his mistress's body that he has
been providently burying a titbit.

Many of these poems are much better than is suggested by
their bare bones. Hardy's overmastering sense that 'Sportsman
Time but rears his brood to kill' no doubt prompts him to consider somewhat too curiously *intra sepulchrum*, 'where the worms
waggle under the grass', and his mortuary verse stretches from
the Burns-like fun of 'The Levelled Churchyard' through the
rather shocking humour of 'Unrealised' and the sedate little
surprise of 'Paying Calls' to the grim 'The Six Boards', the
eerily beautiful 'Voices from Things Growing in a Churchyard',
and the sombre 'In Death Divided':

> I shall rot here, with those whom in their day
> You never knew,
> And alien ones who, ere they chilled to clay,
> Met not my view,
> Will in your distant grave-place ever neighbour you.

> No shade of pinnacle or tree or tower,
>> While earth endures,
> Will fall on my mound and within the hour
>> Steal on to yours;
> One robin never haunt our two green covertures.

With this poem we have come to other country. It may be compared with Landor:

> Mild is the parting year, and sweet
>> The odour of the falling spray;
> Life passes on more rudely fleet,
>> And balmless is its closing day.

> I wait its close, I court its gloom,
>> But mourn that never must there fall
> Or on my breast or on my tomb
>> The tear that would have sooth'd it all.

There is still something of the difference between Hardy and Housman, the difference between a poetry that is as life itself and a poetry of which the first care is to interpose between us and life some special and secluded virtue of its own. Nevertheless as Hardy's verse becomes more directly touched by intense personal experience its accent grows, in fact, less idiosyncratic, and his lyrics from a private world are a vindication of that simple aesthetic of a 'latent music in the sincere utterance of deep emotion'. 'At an Inn', a poem giving, in John Freeman's phrase, 'the naked uncompanioned body of sorrow', instances in its first stanza the transition from uncertainty to certainty of statement:

> When we as strangers sought
>> Their catering care,
> Veiled smiles bespoke their thought
>> Of what we were.
> They warmed as they opined
>> Us more than friends—
> That we had all resigned
>> For love's dear ends.

> And that swift sympathy
>> With living love
> Which quicks the world—maybe
>> The spheres above,

Made them our ministers,
      Moved them to say,
'Ah, God, that bliss like theirs
      Would flush our day!'

And we were left alone
      As Love's own pair;
Yet never the love-light shone
      Between us there!
But that which chilled the breath
      Of afternoon,
And palsied unto death
      The pane-fly's tune.

The kiss their zeal foretold,
      And now deemed come,
Came not: within his hold
      Love lingered numb.
Why cast he on our port
      A bloom not ours?
Why shaped us for his sport
      In after-hours?

As we seemed we were not
      That day afar,
And now we seem not what
      We aching are.
O severing sea and land,
      O laws of men,
Ere death, once let us stand
      As we stood then!

'The Statue and the Bust', with its subdued allegory of the
springs of artistic creation, of all Browning's poems haunted
Hardy most. And although the incident in 'At an Inn' is no
doubt dramatic and personative (as Hardy declared the bulk
of his writing in this kind to be) it is surely touched into being
by some enduring personal predicament. Much of the poetry
left to be considered is of love frustrated by temperament or
fate, or of nostalgic moods in which 'it seemed a thing for weep-
ing . . . that Now, not Then, held reign'. But we are always in
the presence of something larger than one man's bad luck. The
lost chance, the deprivation, the secret and inexplicable wound
become, just as do the ironies of circumstance in the narrative
poems, symbols of some primal wryness in the universe:

Rain on the windows, creaking doors,
  With blasts that besom the green,
And I am here, and you are there,
  And a hundred miles between!

O were it but the weather, Dear,
  O were it but the miles
That summed up all our severance,
  There might be room for smiles.

But that thwart thing betwixt us twain,
  Which nothing cleaves or clears,
Is more than distance, Dear, or rain,
  And longer than the years!

On a biographical level we may come to know about the
'thwart thing', reading of it perhaps in 'The Interloper' and
'A Procession of Dead Days'. But if it is a personal disaster it
is also something of a different order—something perceived
with equal urgency by another mind which stands peculiarly
apart in 'Victoria's formal middle time', that of Newman. It is
'some terrible aboriginal calamity' and at the sight of its farthest operation, as upon the starved robin at the window, Hardy
flings open his heart in the same love and pity, confronting all
and asking nothing, as quickens his most domestically motivated
poems. He passes as it were straight through his particular
moment of experience to its ground, there to rest for the time in
the only ease the tragic sense of life really admits, that of some
achieved exploration of reality.

But it is notable that when Hardy, in the 'Apology' to *Late
Lyrics and Earlier*, came to define his purpose in poetry, he said
a little more than this, declaring that he attempted 'the exploration of reality, and its frank recognition stage by stage along the
survey, with an eye to the best consummation possible: briefly,
evolutionary meliorism'. This has been dismissed as something
not actually working in the poems. But at least he had the
impulse to challenge life; to wring from it whatever values
were still viable in the chill climate that his temperament and
scientific determinism had combined to create. Three of his
most celebrated poems, 'The Impercipient', 'The Darkling
Thrush', and 'The Oxen', show his still reverent regard for one
reading of life which did not pass this test. Had the feather in
'A Sign-Seeker' fallen he would have realized as quickly as any

man its weight, and his rejoicing would have been unflawed.
He is alert for whatever emotional fulfilment he judged the
human condition to allow, and he finds it most abundantly in
the wide comity of sorrow which his sympathetic imagination
opens up to him. But he finds it too—and more positively—in
that very love of man and woman from which he has constantly
discerned so much tragedy and disaster to spring. The poet
asserts the magic of love's moment quite as abundantly as he
records fatal occasions upon which that moment is let slip. He
asserts the power of the moment to carry far across the tide of
time. Even while he renders its evanescence, its frailty, and the
cruel ironies it may prelude, he acknowledges it as the potent
seed from which grow into their own independence the qualities
of fidelity, tenderness, and pity that give dignity and meaning
to human life. The centre of achievement here is in the twenty-
one *Poems of 1912–13*, threnodies in which a poet older than the
Milton of *Samson Agonistes* gives us as great love poetry as any
written in English during the first half of the twentieth century.
Memory is the gift of sorrow, and the measure of a loss is what
it recalls of the remembered thing when first bestowed. From
the utmost simplicities of bereavement and its first regrets—

> How she would have loved
> A party to-day! . . .

Woman much missed, how you call to me, call to me,
Saying that now you are not as you were
When you had changed from the one who was all to me,
But as at first, when our day was fair . . .
Summer gave us sweets, but autumn wrought division—

the poet turns to recall his courtship of the woman now dead:

Yes: I have re-entered your olden haunts at last;
Through the years, through the dead scenes I have tracked you.

And the evocations as they rise up are so precise and so overwhelmingly real as to be an assertion of a very lordship of the
years. He sees, 'distinctly yet':

> Myself and a girlish form benighted
>   In dry March weather. We climb the road
> Beside a chaise. We had just alighted
>   To ease the sturdy pony's load
>   When he sighed and slowed.

What we did as we climbed, and what we talked of
  Matters not much, nor to what it led,—
Something that life will not be balked of
  Without rude reason till hope is dead,
    And feeling fled.

It filled but a minute. But was there ever
  A time of such quality, since or before,
In that hill's story? To one mind never,
  Though it has been climbed, foot-swift, foot-sore,
    By thousands more.

Primaeval rocks form the road's steep border,
  And much have they faced there, first and last,
Of the transitory in Earth's long order;
  But what they record in colour and cast
    Is—that we two passed.

And to me, though Time's unflinching rigour,
  In mindless rote, has ruled from sight
The substance now, one phantom figure
  Remains on the slope, as when that night
    Saw us alight.

In these poems with their simplicity of statement and complexity
of evocation—for what they intimate is something beyond corruption grasped in the contemplation of more kinds of death
than one—there is a new certainty in the poet's accent:

They say he sees as an instant thing
    More clear than to-day,
    A sweet soft scene
    That once was in play
    By that briny green;
    Yes, notes alway
    Warm, real, and keen,
    What his back years bring—
A phantom of his own figuring . . .

A ghost-girl-rider. And though, toil-tried,
    He withers daily,
    Time touches her not,
    But she still rides gaily
    In his rapt thought
    On that shagged and shaly
    Atlantic spot,
    And as when first eyed
Draws rein and sings to the swing of the tide.

The sad old man—he of Augustus John's profound portrait—making his way to one among the 'various graves' at Stinsford is a figure we can vividly see. But this last stanza is something other than a sad old man's writing. Here there has indeed come unsolicited to Hardy poetry's voice, so that the lines carry beyond themselves—beyond even their effect of a splendid taunt hurled at oblivion by the imagination.

8

Hardy would have wished his reputation to rest finally upon his longest-considered and most ambitious work. If by constitution he was one exceptionally sensitive to 'sounds of insult, shame, and wrong' he was also one for whom early association had rendered inescapably stirring and romantic the echo of 'trumpets blown for wars'. Out of this divided feeling came *The Dynasts*, his 'epic-drama of the war with Napoleon, in three parts, nineteen acts, and one hundred and thirty scenes'. When he was a boy Napoleon's campaigns, especially his threatened invasion of the south of England, hung in that region between living memory and popular legend which Scott's best writing shows as particularly appealing to the historical imagination. The appeal was enhanced for Hardy by his claim to kinship with that Thomas Masterman Hardy who had been Nelson's flag-captain at Trafalgar. As early as 1870 he went to Chelsea Hospital to talk with veterans of Waterloo, and six years later he visited the battlefield. From this time onwards his notebooks witness the growth of a conception upon the fringes of which stand *The Trumpet-Major* and numerous short poems and stories. The notion of a series of ballads 'forming altogether an Iliad of Europe from 1789 to 1815' early gave way to a preference for some dramatic form and to the problems of disposing this upon the large canvas that the size of his spectacle would require. He faced in particular one crucial issue. The work was to acknowledge 'the wide prevalence of the Monistic theory of the Universe' and thus to constitute 'the modern expression of a modern outlook'. How in a vast drama that must necessarily deal with 'a world alive' was Hardy to render his overmastering sense of 'Life's impulsion by Incognizance'? 'Write a history of human automatism', he essays in one note, and in another: 'Mode for a historical Drama. Action mostly automatic; reflex movement, etc. Not the result of what is called *motive*, though always ostensibly so, even to the actors' own consciousness.' The crux lay there. If upon the characters themselves was laid the full burden of expounding the system of determinism by which they were bound, the drama would perish and the possibility of its greatest irony be lost. 'A spectral tone must be adopted', he notes in 1889, and adds somewhat vaguely: 'Royal Ghosts'. But some time earlier than this he had seen much more: 'The human race to be shown as one great network or tissue which quivers in every part when one point is shaken, like a spider's web if touched. Abstract realisms to be in the form of Spirits, Spectral Figures, etc.' Here was his method. First there must be an overworld of abstract intelligences sufficiently diversified to provide interpretation and comment in a form which had itself substantial dramatic colouring. Secondly there must be the power to realize the human scene when distanced to the point at which its mass-automatism is revealed; the power to see what from the overworld would be seen.

There is a passage in Ruskin's *Stones of Venice*, beginning 'Let us for a moment try to raise ourselves even above the level of the birds' flight', and evoking 'Italy and Spain, laid like pieces of a golden pavement into the sea-blue', from which Hardy may have drawn a hint for his extraordinary aerial visions. But Ruskin's is in the comparison a static, and Hardy's a kinetic, imagination. When in 1879 Hardy viewed the Lord Mayor's Show 'from the upper windows of *Good Words* in Ludgate Hill' he had jotted down:

As the crowd grows denser it loses its character of an aggregate of countless units, and becomes an organic whole, a molluscous black creature having nothing in common with humanity, that takes the shape of the streets along which it has lain itself, and throws out horrid excrescences and limbs into neighbouring alleys; a creature whose voice exudes from its scaly coat, and who has an eye in every pore of its body. The balconies, stands, and railway-bridge are occupied by small detached shapes of the same tissue, but of gentler motion, as if they were the spawn of the monster in their midst.

In *The War of the Worlds* (1898) H. G. Wells was to achieve something of this effect in describing the fleeing millions of London as they would have appeared to a balloonist: 'a huge

map, and in the southward *blotted* . . . as if some monstrous pen
had flung ink upon the chart'. But Hardy, in his evocation of
the allied forces closing in upon France after the ruin of the
Grand Army, evokes an even finer scene in this manner:

At first nothing—not even the river itself—seems to move in the
panorama. But anon certain strange dark patches in the landscape,
flexuous and riband-shaped, are discerned to be moving slowly.
Only one movable object on earth is large enough to be conspicuous
herefrom, and that is an army. The moving shapes are armies.

The nearest, almost beneath us, is defiling across the river by a
bridge of boats, near the junction of the Rhine and the Neckar,
where the oval town of Mannheim, standing in the fork between the
two rivers, has from here the look of a human head in a cleft stick.
Martial music from many bands strikes up as the crossing is effected,
and the undulating columns twinkle as if they were scaly serpents. . . .

Many miles to the left, down-stream, near the little town of
Caube, another army is seen to be simultaneously crossing the pale
current, its arms and accoutrements twinkling in like manner. . . .
Turning now to the right, far away by Basel (beyond which the
Swiss mountains close the scene), a still larger train of war-geared
humanity, two hundred thousand strong, is discernible. It has already
crossed the water, which is much narrower here, and has advanced
several miles westward, where its ductile mass of greyness and
glitter is beheld parting into six columns, that march on in flexuous
courses of varying direction. . . .

All these dark and grey columns, converging westward by sure
degrees, advance without opposition. They glide on as if by gravita-
tion, in fluid figures, dictated by the conformation of the country,
like water from a burst reservoir; mostly snake-shaped, but occasionally with batrachian and saurian outlines. In spite of the immensity
of this human mechanism on its surface, the winter landscape wears
an impassive look, as if nothing were happening.

Evening closes in, and the Dumb Show is obscured.

9

In a 'fore scene' the Phantom Intelligences of the overworld
discuss the unconscious operation of the Immanent Will and
resolve to observe its present working upon earth. Then 'the
nether sky opens, and Europe is disclosed', first remotely and
later to a nearer view, so that 'the peoples, distressed by events
which they did not cause, are seen writhing, crawling, heaving,
and vibrating in their various cities and nationalities'. After

a further and momentary vision of all this as a single organic process, constituting 'the anatomy of the Will', the fore scene closes and we are upon a ridge in Wessex from which two travellers marvel that they can see almost half across the channel, discuss the danger of invasion, engage in a political dispute, and listen to the marching song of a company of soldiers. Where this first scene is merely representative, the second and third scenes are specifically historical, presenting respectively the French Minister of Marine reading a directive from Napoleon and a major debate in the House of Commons. The fourth scene is a dumb show displaying the French army of invasion at Boulogne, the fifth gives the talk in an aristocratic London drawing-room, and the sixth the spectacle in Milan Cathedral upon the coronation of Napoleon. The second act opens with a conversation between Nelson and Collingwood, and passes first to the French Admiral Villeneuve writing a minute to Napoleon and then to Napoleon dictating orders to a secretary while awaiting news at Boulogne. Upon this follows a short scene of familiar dialogue in a crowd during the holding of a review by George III, and a somewhat longer scene, described in a footnote as 'traditionary', of rustic humour in which a false alarm of invasion agitates the inhabitants of Egdon Heath. Hardy is careful to actualize the mundane action by stressing whenever possible well-documented historical episodes, and by setting over against his overworld an answering background of simple people and common occasions. To anchor his fable in solid fact was essential if it was not to be washed away by great tides of that supernal commentary into which a large part of his imaginative energy would inevitably be drawn. The great majority of the scenes belong to formal history, and the highlights are commonly set battle-pieces. The first part rises to the twin crises of Trafalgar and Austerlitz. The second deals largely with the Peninsular Campaign. The third opens with Napoleon's advance upon Moscow and ends with the last of the Hundred Days. Upon these tremendous occasions the philosophic contemplator of 'the peoples . . . in their various cities and nationalities' fires his cannon and directs his charges with great zest. Had Hardy as a boy not rejoiced with those who could remember the first trouncings of Boney in popular song, *The Dynasts* would be considerably less alive than it is.

But its life had to come too from the power and variety of its language. Here the main burden is borne by blank verse. The form was new to Hardy, and his command of it is sometimes said to be quite inadequate to the task proposed. But what he could wring from it with some success was what, in fact, he chiefly required: a concise medium for all that middle part of his subject—largely matter of statecraft and strategy—in which force and momentum must be more apposite than any rhetorical elevation. A parliamentary debate rendered in prose even as rounded and full as Burke's or Sheridan's would have set a tone incompatible with the total imaginative statement at which he aimed. But the low-keyed verse which he employs gives such a passage at once requisite dignity and a brisk pace:

> I thank you, gentlemen, unfeignedly.
> But—no man has saved England, let me say:
> England has saved herself, by her exertions:
> She will, I trust, save Europe by her example!

We are tempted to say of this, as of much else in the kind, that the poet shows sufficient confidence in the digestive power of his medium. Yet his blank verse nearly always remains his own. Effects of pastiche, when admitted, may be naïve but are not unpleasing:

> Besides poor Scott, my lord, and Charles Adair,
> Lieutenant Ram, and Whipple, captain's clerk,
> There's Smith, and Palmer, midshipmen, just killed,
> And fifty odd of seamen and marines. . . .

>   the captain's woman there,
> Desperate for life, climbed from the gunroom port
> Upon the rudder-chains; stripped herself stark,
> And swam for the Pickle's boat. Our men in charge,
> Seeing her great breasts bulging on the brine,
> Sang out, 'A mermaid 'tis!' . . .

> Ay; where is Nelson? Faith, by this late time
> He may be sodden; churned in Biscay swirls;
> Or blown to polar bears by boreal gales;
> Or sleeping amorously in some calm cave
> On the Canaries' or Atlantis' shore
> Upon the bosom of his Dido dear.

But on the whole it is blank verse most effective when even its elevations are subdued, as in Nelson's

He who is with himself dissatisfied,
Though all the world find satisfaction in him,
Is like a rainbow-coloured bird gone blind,
That gives delight it shares not. Happiness?
It's the philosopher's stone no alchemy
Shall light on in this world I am weary of.—
Smiling I'd pass to my long home to-morrow
Could I with honour, and my country's gain . . .

or Napoleon's final

Great men are meteors that consume themselves
To light the earth. This is my burnt-out hour.

Certainly Hardy here held no reserves of power with which
to equip his Intelligences. Where these speak in blank verse
their language is distinguished from that of the mundane
characters chiefly by an abstract vocabulary, vaguely scientific
in its associations, which at times approaches a jargon. This in
itself would not have rendered successful what was in fact the
most ticklish part of the design. The Intelligences must above
all else have largeness, and yet the field of comment which
entities so circumstanced may be made to cover is not wide.
When the Spirit of the Years has announced that

like a knitter drowsed,
Whose fingers play in skilled unmindfulness,
The Will has woven with an absent heed
Since life first was; and ever will so weave

and the Spirit of the Pities has deplored 'the intolerable antilogy
of making figments feel', they have really had their say. The
success with which Hardy draws out, diversifies, and deepens
this matter is largely due to his old command over a wide
variety of lyric measures, now marshalled in the service of the
several disembodied choruses attendant upon the scene. At the
meeting of Napoleon and Marie-Louise the Ironic Spirits chant
to aerial music:

First 'twas a finished coquette,
And now it's a raw ingénue.—
Blonde instead of brunette,
An old wife doffed for a new.
She'll bring him a baby,
As quickly as maybe,
And that's what he wants her to do,
Hoo-hoo!
And that's what he wants her to do!

And from this the kind ranges through the rapid but weighted recitative of the Recording Angel and the Rumours to the superb evocation by the Years of the fate of the dumb creatures upon the field of Waterloo—

> The snail draws in at the terrible tread,
> But in vain; he is crushed by the felloe-rim—

and the pregnant colloquy interpolated upon the scene portraying the madness of George III. The king, helpless in the hands of physicians whose ministrations are a torment to him, is complimented on having won a 'glorious victory' at Albuera, and a perception of the mockery latent in this drives him to violence:

SPIRIT OF THE PITIES

> Something within me aches to pray
> To some Great Heart, to take away
> This evil day, this evil day!

CHORUS IRONIC

> Ha-ha! That's good. Thou'lt pray to It:—
> But where do Its compassions sit?
> Yea, where abides the heart of It?

> Is it where sky-fires flame and flit,
> Or solar craters spew and spit,
> Or ultra-stellar night-webs knit?

> What is Its shape? Man's counterfeit?
> That turns in some far sphere unlit
> The Wheel which drives the Infinite?

SPIRIT OF THE PITIES

> Mock on, mock on! Yet I'll go pray
> To some Great Heart, who haply may
> Charm mortal miseries away!

The King's Paroxysm continues. The attendants hold him.

In this, the drama's most intensely realized and appalling spectacle, Hardy employs a mingling of verse and prose, and in general he had far too well considered the deploying in *The Dynasts* of all his available powers to forget the author of the opening chapter of *The Return of the Native*. He uses prose in scenes of lowered tension, whether vulgar or polite, humorous or ironic. He uses it too to command powerful effects of realism and pathos, as in the description of the deserters from Sir John Moore's army in their cellar. But above all in the descriptive settings, whether they have the form of expanded stage-directions or of the disposition of a dumb show, his prose has unflagging power. It is as if in these packed, precise, and dynamic miniatures the writer were making atonement for many diffuse and clumsy sentences once dispatched to the circulating libraries. They are both vivid in themselves and faithfully approximated to the disembodied vision posited—this largely through the use of a technique which has sometimes been described as prelusive of the cinema. Good examples are the first swoop down upon Europe, and the answering withdrawal above Milan Cathedral hard upon the pompous show of Napoleon's coronation there:

The point of view recedes, the whole fabric smalling into distance and becoming like a rare, delicately carved alabaster ornament. The city itself sinks to miniature, the Alps show afar as a white corrugation, the Adriatic and the Gulf of Genoa appear on this and on that hand, with Italy between them, till clouds cover the panorama.

With this and with the many evocations of royal progresses and marching armies we feel somewhat as men before the egg of Columbus. Now similar omelets can be scrambled in every studio —and the sound-track too is familiar with such expressionist devices as that whereby we are told after a scene in a London drawing-room that 'the confused tongues of the assembly waste away into distance, till they are heard but as the babblings of the sea from a high cliff', so that we have momentarily evoked for us the barrier standing between this receding spectacle and the power of Napoleon to which we are hurried in the next. Yet remarkable as are these aeronautical feats they are exceeded by the terrifying and equally hallucinatory realism of the pictures of the French in retreat from Moscow amid obliterating snows, or by such a detailed description of carnage as that at Albuera, where, after 'the birds in the wood, unaware that this day is to be different from every other day they have known there, are heard singing their overtures with their usual serenity', there is a remorseless evocation of the battle, closing upon heaps of corpses 'which steam with their own warmth as the spring rain falls gently upon them'.

In examining *The Dynasts* critics seldom pay much attention to the dramatist's portrayal of human character and its unfolding in action. They sometimes assert that the human characters are deliberately dwarfed, and even that what is stiff and threadbare about the blank verse is happily calculated to give an impression of that helpless puppetry which Napoleon alone among them explicitly acknowledges but which the whole philosophic conception of the drama postulates. And here certainly we would seem to touch the crucial difficulty by which Hardy was confronted, that of finding elbow-room within the logic of his myth for some sufficient impression of actual human struggle, with its attendant assumption of free will, in default of which the drama would perish still-born. Yet in practice this problem tended to present itself the other way round. The titanic clash of the nations and their leaders had to be so rendered that, with all its excitement and suspense, there should yet hang before it some semi-transparent gauze of the myth's weaving. And Hardy achieves this by exploiting our sense of the nature of dramatic illusion, whereby there may coexist in our consciousness impressions of the free agency of the persons appearing before us and of their moving unintermittently under an exterior compulsion. He had been aware of something of the sort in the Christmas mummers of his childhood, with 'the curiously hypnotizing impressiveness of their automatic style, that of persons who spoke by no will of their own'. When Max Beerbohm declared that Hardy's death of Nelson recalled to him a peep-show version of the occasion familiar to his boyhood he was putting his finger near the pulse of the machine. And the consequent need subtly to flatten or attenuate character to something like a consciously preserved theatrical role was convenient to Hardy, who had never succeeded in making wholly lifelike the behaviour of persons at all exalted in the social scale. But as creations of the theatre—that cosmic theatre in which we peer over the shoulders of the Intelligences vocal in their stalls—he manages them adequately enough. It is the final particular in which he here brilliantly uses to the full precisely what it was his to use.

Hardy's largest achievement is fittingly a work of the historical imagination. If his future is secure it is chiefly because he brought to the contemplation of human life so abundant a sense of the past. Standing upon Rainbarrow, a wayfarer on the *Via Iceniana*, or scanning the unchanged down which had once been the mere mount or margin to King George and fifteen thousand men, he appears to have the very spirit of history at his side. Time, he believed, breaks counterfeits, and that in two senses. The intellect advances with the centuries upon truths which, if we are by no means the happier for knowing them, are truths still. And what in human conduct is least inadequate to the human plight we best learn from bending upon familiar and immediate things a mind which has long acknowledged the deepening power of historical reflection. 'My contemplations are of Time', says Yeats, 'that has transfigured me.' Of that transfiguration Hardy is sufficiently aware:

> Time, to make me grieve,
> Part steals, lets part abide;
> And shakes this fragile frame at eve
> With throbbings of noontide.

But in another sense too time transfigures Hardy. It sets fleetingly upon his face as he looks forward the glint of an uncertain hope; and as he looks backward, constant compassion and a noble pride. Were it not for this, the final word upon his work might well be taken from his own last poem:

> Why load men's minds with more to bear
> That bear already ails to spare?

As it is, his books do not leave us in despair, but rather acknowledging, in the words of Lionel Johnson, 'a sense of awe, in the presence of a landscape filled with immemorial signs of age; a sense of tranquillity in the presence of human toil, so bound up and associated with the venerable needs of human life'.

III · JAMES

HENRY JAMES was born in New York City in 1843—not, like his elder brother William, in an hotel, but nevertheless into the condition, as he said, of nothing less than an hotel child. His father, inheriting a sufficient fortune from commercial sources, lived in detachment from practical affairs, concerned to evolve a private religious system of a Swedenborgian cast, and relying for the education of his children now on a rapid succession of native governesses, tutors, and academies, and now upon prolonged, leisurely, and random European travel. An interesting comparison may be drawn between James's early environment as described in *A Small Boy and Others* (1913) and that of a somewhat later American expatriate, Logan Pearsall Smith, recorded in *Unforgotten Years* (1938). The Pearsall Smiths were given not to religious speculation but to pietistic fervour, and the magnet of their lives was certain great aristocratic houses in England where a kindred enthusiasm obtained. But as their tenets were narrower than those of the Jameses so were their notions about their children less liberal. Young Logan, unlike young Henry, had to fight his way out of that family warehouse or counting-house which was regarded as the natural apprenticeship to life of young Americans even of the most substantial mercantile class. But the nostalgia for the culture and the social forms of the Old World was common to both families.

Upon James himself this nostalgia appears to have operated virtually from infancy. It is to 'the sense of Europe' that he declares his very earliest consciousness to have awakened. He regarded with awe schoolfellows who 'enjoyed the pre-eminence of being European'. He believed himself to have retained a visual memory of Paris experienced at the age of sixteen months. And he owned to a 'prompt distaste, a strange precocity of criticism, for so much aridity' as the American scene too often

F

presented in comparison. That he had been bred in an 'unformed and unseasoned society' and that the world of his childhood had been 'very young indeed, young with its own juvenility, as well as with ours', are convictions no doubt founded in fact. But in the strength with which the boy set his heart far away we must see the concurrence of a family sentiment and a personal plight. The large lack of interest of the Jameses in the common pursuits of their fellow citizens made them decisively a clan—a cousinship, James records, living 'by pure serenity, sociability and loquacity'. Isolated within this group by his birth, James was also in some degree insulated from it by his temperament. Alone of the family he found the sociability and loquacity difficult. William, the future philosopher, sixteen months his senior, was in everything dazzlingly ahead; his resolute onslaughts upon sundry fields of knowledge emphasized by contrast 'the loose ways, the strange process of waste, through which nature and fortune may deal on occasion with those whose faculty for application is all and only in their imagination and their sensibility'. Henry himself seemed fit only for 'the so far from showy practice of wondering and dawdling and gaping'. Recalling the freedom he was allowed in the beguiling streets of New York, he was to distinguish the reason thus:

What I look back to as my infant licence can only have had for its ground some timely conviction on the part of my elders that the only form of riot or revel ever known to me would be that of the visiting mind. Wasn't I myself for that matter even at that time all acutely and yet resignedly, even quite fatalistically, aware of what to think of this? I at any rate watch the small boy dawdle and gape again, I smell the cold dusty paint and iron as the rails of the Eighteenth Street corner rub his contemplative nose, and, feeling him foredoomed, withhold from him no grain of my sympathy. . . . For there was the very pattern and measure of all he was to demand: just to *be* somewhere—almost anywhere would do—and somehow receive an impression or an accession, feel a relation or a vibration.

'Almost anywhere would do'—but Europe was known to be 'vast and various and dense', and to its vibrations James had clearly attuned himself in fancy long before his actual expatriation began. That his precocious 'sense of Europe' was in fact his sense of an ideal world is the cardinal biographical fact about him. Here is the key to his entire artistic development. The European actuality in which he was so to submerge himself was essentially no more than the vehicle or the medium of an art always itself instinctively ideal.

In 1861, and shortly after returning with his family from five years of almost continuous travel abroad, James's sense of predestined confinement to a contemplative role was enhanced by his suffering a disabling accident. The nature of this is unknown. But as he was a lifelong celibate it has been conjectured that he exploited the mishap to escape pursuits which were intolerable to him on other and nervous grounds. Mental as well as physical illness had its place in the annals of his family, and he himself in later life was to go through at least one period of severe neurotic disturbance. But whenever individuals or families evoke curiosity distresses of this sort are likely to be brought to light. There is no reason to suppose they happen less often among the obscure, and troubles endemic in modern civilization are unlikely to yield much to criticism. When James as a young man left America virtually for good, he took with him a sane and capacious intellect, a progressively strengthening habit of fruitful and keenly relished social intercourse, and a counterbalancing devotion, necessarily lonely, to the service of a major art. Upon any liberal reckoning, his was a full and fortunate life. The greater part of his adult years were lived, comfortably and judiciously, in London or at Rye in Sussex. The First World War, indeed, came to him as a staggering shock, and there is a classic place in which he expresses the utter bewilderment of his sort of liberal consciousness before it:

The plunge of civilization into this abyss of blood and darkness . . . is a thing that so gives away the whole long age during which we have supposed the world to be, with whatever abatement, gradually bettering, that to have to take it all now for what the treacherous years were all the while really making for and meaning is too tragic for any words.

But at least he was sure of where his convictions lay. In 1915, when his countrymen were not yet fighting, he thought it proper to become a British subject. He died in the following year, shortly after receiving the Order of Merit from King George the Fifth.

2

'It's a complex fate, being an American', James wrote to Charles Eliot Norton in 1872, 'and one of the responsibilities it

entails is fighting against a superstitious valuation of Europe.'
Critics have argued that the fight was at once gratuitous and
fatal; that James, failing to find in the Old World any reality
corresponding to his childhood's fantasy, struggled on amid
increasing bewilderments until his sense of human values
gradually decomposed. He would have done better to remain
with and celebrate his own people.

Yet James is what he knew himself to be: a representative and
not a renegade American. He stands as the supreme historian
of the colonial situation—a fact clear to anyone who has lived
for a term of years in a 'new' country passing through a phase of
feeling and development approximating to that in the United
States a hundred years ago. For there people both simple and
cultivated are aware of two systems of roots. To be bred within
a certain social structure and to a certain face of nature, and to
be implicated, less perceptibly but no less profoundly, with distant people and an older way of life: this is a complicated state
of affairs, and one fruitful of problems not easily resolved.
Moreover, particular expressions of religious or political intolerance, such as drive men across the seas and into exile, may
be less enduring than the sense of that exile; and this can prompt
in whole classes and generations a poignant if submerged sense
of banishment needlessly prolonged. James is the heir to such
feelings on the eastern seaboard of the North American continent; he is the artist who undertakes the burden of exploring
their consequences. At the same time he is something more, and
if in the end his American pilgrims are not rigidly American
nor his European vistas verifiable in Baedeker, this is less because
the international theme is too much for him than because his
creative faculty has the instinct to transcend it.

Nevertheless the difficulty of his *donnée* set its mark upon
James's mind and art. Discerning a deep ethical cleavage between those cultures the relationship of which he had made his
prime concern, he was regularly beset by conflicting readings
of conduct and character. It has been maintained that this
problem of judgement and allegiance produces a pervasive
ambiguity in the novels. James grew less and less able to make
up his mind on people and systems, and fell into a way of leaving
vital matters open to alternative interpretations. He was thus
increasingly ignorant of what his characters were up to or worth.
Finally he declined into exploiting the mysteries of a superb

technique in order to divert attention from his shortcomings—
shortcomings which had their origin in his inability to choose
between American and European points of view.

We shall find much in our reading which makes this a criticism to be reckoned with. Broadly speaking, James sees Americans as good and Europeans as beautiful; and his art in its
ideal aspect is the quest of a synthesis through an imagined
order. Yet he never seems to be certain where to stop admiring
a life lived in terms not of moral ideas but of style. Is not a
high style, an aristocratic style, itself a sufficient morality?
The answer, coming low but resonant from the farthest recesses
of his creation, is an uncompromising No. Yet we are a little
prompted to feel that James would at times have his cake
and eat it. He seems vulgarly or at least naïvely lavish in approval of futile ways of life, sterile conceptions of breeding, highly
polished social disciplines, even while aiming to celebrate virtues
of a very different order. Thus in *The Golden Bowl* the Ververs
defer to a world with which we are convinced that moral natures
so strong and pure as theirs ought to be impatient. And James
himself abides the same judgement. His best writing deals
essentially with matters of ethical concern, and the finest thing
about his finest characters is the justness of their moral perceptions. Yet so unremittingly is this filtered to us through the
trivialities of an artificial social intercourse—the preservation of
which is with his characters as a first rule of life—that the clear
stream of James's high gravity dwindles to a silver thread which
the eye, alarmed by the seemingly pervasive aridity of the
scene, may well miss altogether. H. G. Wells, after likening
James to 'a magnificent but painful hippopotamus resolved at
any cost upon picking up a pea which has got into a corner of
its den', deplored that his characters should display minds of
large calibre and fine discrimination regularly focused upon
some petty residuum of human interest. And Wells concluded
that, although 'a very important figure in the literary world of
that time', James unfortunately 'had no idea of the possible use
of the novel as a help to conduct'. Wells's own novels are lavish
in the provision of both conduct and misconduct, and they
evince the most patent designs upon the reader as a social being.
With James reticence is an inflexible canon. Often his characters cling to it fanatically when we feel that a vigorous Wellsian
showdown would wonderfully clear the air. His conclusions

upon life and conduct have to be distilled from his writing rather than picked up from its surface.

It is not perhaps simply to reticence that there must be attributed another potentially disturbing aspect of James's work. André Gide declared James's heroes to be 'only winged busts'. Mr. E. M. Forster, rather less cautiously, has pronounced that 'maimed creatures can alone breathe' in his pages. It is certainly true that a disembodied intelligence might read through the novels without discovering that, here on earth, bodies do exist. The conventions of his period must have allowed James to view without undue alarm the blank spaces which temperamental disinclination or disability thus left upon his page. But to readers habituated to a franker fiction they are disconcerting— for some reason more disconcerting than similar lacunas in other Victorian authors. James is so much occupied with individual emotional experience, so curious in the shades of personal relationship, and above all so skilled in exposing the play of consciousness in his characters, that the uncertain existence of a basic dynamic is bewildering. His men perhaps more than his women are liable to be felt as only moieties of humanity. As individuals they are displeasingly, and in the mass they are implausibly, deficient in simple masculinity. To watch some of James's fictions in their unfolding is rather like watching a complex working model in a museum of technology. The pistons drive and the wheels go round precisely as in the real thing. But the steam isn't there, and we feel obscurely cheated by the knowledge that a trickle of ingeniously applied electricity is in fact the motive power of the exhibition. James, like Thackeray before him, was disposed to attribute something of his circumscription here to the taboos of English and American society. He was to declare of more than one of his books that had he been writing for a French public he would have handled his problems of sexual relationship differently. But although his masters, after the native Hawthorne, were the French writers of his own and the preceding generation, he was never, as *French Poets and Novelists* (1878) already reveals, at home with certain aspects of their naturalism. His uncompromising fastidiousness and puritanism in these regards should be recognized from the start as sharply channelling his genius. There are things that do not happen to his characters when happen they should: doors that do not open; barriers that fail to go down. No apple is ever eaten in James's garden. Perhaps to this rather than to the necessity of dissimulating a hopeless indecision between the balanced carrots of America and Europe is due much of the fabulous elaboration of his later technique.

3

James begins with essays exploring the sufficiently remote world of contemporary French literature. The same period finds him, in his own phrase, 'bumping about, to acquire skill, in the shallow waters and sandy coves of the "short story"'. He is also discovering themes. Some of his earliest tales, such as 'The Romance of Certain Old Clothes', take over from Hawthorne and Poe an exploitation of the supernatural which he will subtilize later. Others are already of the international situation. They mark the contrast between 'the latent preparedness of the American mind even for the most characteristic features of English life' and the answering English disposition to think of the United States 'as of some fabled planet, alien to the British orbit, lately proclaimed to have the admixture of atmospheric gases required to support animal life'. Talent for evoking the spirit of place, such as was to inform the series of books beginning with *Transatlantic Sketches* (1875) and concluding with *Italian Hours* (1909), fortifies such an essentially romantic story as 'The Passionate Pilgrim'. 'The long grey battered public face of the colleges' of Oxford, with the 'plain perpendicular of the so mildly conventual fronts', are descriptions finely precise; and there is resource in the comparison of the invisible corporate existence of the university amid these colleges to 'the medieval mystical presence of the Empire in the old States of Germany'. 'The Madonna of the Future', with similar pictures of Florence, is a more deliberate study in the romantic attitude. Theobald, the painter who leaves the beginnings of his great work unsketched on the canvas while his model grows imperceptibly into an old woman, is the first of James's portrayals of artistic temperament. More successful in itself, and even more significant for the future, is 'Madame de Mauves', the story of an American woman whom some inflexible inner principle forbids to break with her dissipated French husband. Looking back on this heroine after many years, James discerned that 'she muffled her charming head in the lightest finest vaguest tissue of romance and put twenty questions by'. In her predicament, and in thus drawing her life from a compulsion enigmatical even to herself, she is the forerunner of one of James's major creations, Isabel Archer.

In the first novel, *Watch and Ward* (serialized 1871), the young Bostonian Roger Lawrence resembles later heroes in having little to do except call upon ladies at tea-time or take a short turn in the park. Owning 'a timid but strenuous desire to fathom the depths of matrimony', he adopts a twelve-year-old ward with the covert intention of thus gaining a bride. For long Nora Lambert causes anxiety. Is she going to be pretty? Is she interesting? James's dimmest men commonly have exacting standards, and if perceptive may pick princesses in disguise. For Nora the magic wand is a period of residence in Rome. There, 'fed by the sources of esthetic delight, her nature had risen calmly to its allotted level'. But when Lawrence's plan is at length revealed to her she receives it 'staring, open-mouthed, pale as death, with her poor young face blank with horror'. In the young James's treatment of this aspect of the story there is a surprising intuitive command of the psychology of sex, frequently pointed by a choice of incident or imagery the erotic significance of which ripples alarmingly beneath the thinnest skin of urbane unconsciousness:

Roger caught himself wondering whether, at the worst, a little precursory love-making would do any harm. The ground might be gently tickled to receive his own sowing; the petals of the young girl's nature, playfully forced apart, would leave the golden heart of the flower but the more accessible to his own vertical rays.

It is the more curious in the writing of one who was to behave with such massive circumspection in sketching the field of direct sexual encounter. There is on record a judgement of James's that *Tess of the D'Urbervilles* is 'vile': 'The pretence of "sexuality" is only equalled by the absence of it.' In maturity he himself was to guard very warily against any similar charge.

Less convincing than Nora Lambert's immediate reaction to the discovery of her guardian's intention is her immediate flight to the protection of a disreputable male cousin. Her blindness here, like Isabel Archer's in *The Portrait of a Lady*, recalls the old melodramatic convention of the invisibility of the villain. James's greatest novels are to be about betrayal—

a theme which, if the due concentration of art is to be bestowed
on it, perhaps requires that this hoary make-believe should walk.
Certainly one often expects from the quick sensibility of his
women more of intuitive appraisal than they manage. A truth
surely discoverable in a glance, in a touch or the absence of a
touch, they will arrive at only through a volume of polite conversation. The disability is of a piece with their whole world.
A more instinctive perception of worth and sincerity on the
part of, say, Milly Theale in *The Wings of the Dove*, would be in
James's air a lightning flash bringing the whole elaborately pro-
pelled machine to a stop. But Nora's flight, if it be implausibly
motivated, is powerfully felt. To be a lady and unescorted in
the streets, to have to jostle with quite poor people and find a
cup of tea in an ungenteel shop: this to the young James is
fully as terrible as it is. He renders it very well. And although
the book dries quickly out into shallows, Nora Lambert is alive
and gains our sympathy. Moreover her story embodies what
is to be one of James's recurrent situations: that in which
one character makes himself responsible for the initiation or
development of another, with unpredictable results. Here
indeed is the basis of the succeeding and much richer novel,
Roderick Hudson (1875).

Hudson is a young sculptor of genius who is picked up from
his New England town and brought to Rome by the wealthy
and cultivated Rowland Mallet. The book's theme is essentially the incompleteness of each of these men. Mallet feels that
he is himself something of an artist, but one without the faculty
of expression. This Hudson abundantly has, but he in turn
fatally lacks all refinement of moral perception. It is Mallet who
discerns in Mary Garland, Hudson's plain and provincial
fiancée, a great beauty of the spirit. Hudson callously borrows
Mary's money to pursue the fascinating Christina Light, and
when Christina is constrained to marry Prince Casamassima he
chooses to die virtually by his own hand. In this portrait of an
artist compelled to throw himself open to experience however
fatal, and rebelling against the wardenship of his cautious and
inhibited, yet sensitive and morally far more perceptive, friend,
we may fancy a projection of some conflict within the author.
We may even judge it significant that it is Hudson who dies and
Mallet—so essentially a 'visiting mind'—who lives on to become,
many years later, the Lambert Strether of *The Ambassadors*.

And so with the women. Mary, sensuously unschooled and un-appealing, conscious of the armour of her own high and severe morality, awakens to new potentialities of warmth and grace in the presence of answering heights of mature civilization first glimpsed in Rome. Christina, a product of that civilization at its most artificial, appealing supremely to the aesthetic sense, accompanied always by her milk-white poodle Stentorello (a creature as emblematical as Una's lamb), is shown as vindi-cating still an uncertain but genuine largeness and generosity of impulse even amid corruption. These two, admirable as characters realistically conceived, have plainly a representative and almost symbolical function. They are like two mistresses between whom James himself must waver. And each has descendants in his later work. Mary's ethical sensibility, her innocence, her vulnerability, her underlying strength—which, to James's thinking, represents the spiritual heritage of the old America: of all this Maggie Verver in *The Golden Bowl* is to be the supreme exemplar. And there, correspondingly, Charlotte Stant descends from Christina—the American so europeanized as virtually to be Europe: its high style, its exquisite intricate surface, its unscrupulousness shot with magnanimity. Yet *Roderick Hudson* is interesting not merely, or even chiefly, for what it presages, whether here or in its technique of presenta-tion by means of a single exploratory consciousness. Unskilfully constructed and proportioned, it has characters recalling Dickens in vitality and Meredith in brilliance.

Of that innocence abroad which is to give James so much of his material *Roderick Hudson* exhibits several pristine varieties. The gallery is augmented in *The American* (1877). There is Mr. Leavenworth, who commissions from Hudson a pure white allegorical representation of Culture, designed to stand out against the morocco and gilt library of the large residential structure which he is erecting on the banks of the Ohio. There is the clerical Mr. Babcock, holidaying at the expense of his congregation, and vastly worried lest they should not get a fair return in the breadth of their pastor's artistic cultivation. Both these are overgone by Hudson's mother, whose bewilderment before the eternal city is at once pathetic and amusing, and by Tom Tristram in *The American*, who touches the comical sublime. 'I don't call this Paris!' he cries in the *Salon carré* of the Louvre. 'Do you know General Packard? Do you know C. P. Hatch?

Do you know Miss Kitty Upjohn?' This gregarious pilgrim is
to be met with still.

Yet the innocence of those of his invading countrymen in
whom James is chiefly interested is sharply qualified. In *The
American* the symbolically named Christopher Newman, that
inverted Columbus whose simplicity is to be betrayed by the
aristocratic French family to whose daughter he aspires, displays, it is true, an ignorance uncompromisingly vast. Haunting
picture-galleries, he is capable of 'gazing with culpable serenity
at inferior productions'. He even mistakes the Marquis de
Bellegarde for a major-domo. Nevertheless he claims truly to
have the instincts if not the forms of an old civilization. James
is evidently concerned to assert through him, even at some
sacrifice of plausibility, both the continuity of Western culture
submerged in American life and the thesis that pioneer conditions create aristocratic attitudes in a generation. On his
first visit to the Bellegarde mansion Newman remarks affably,
just as Mr. Leavenworth would do, 'Your house is of a very fine
style of architecture', and he is barely prevented from accepting
a malicious invitation to make a grand tour of it. Yet he is not
in the least a rough diamond. Pitched into the streets at fourteen, and for long concerned only with amassing a huge fortune
out of the manufacture of wash-tubs, he is never made uneasy
by his new surroundings even when at sea in them. Before the
complexities of hitherto unapprehended personal relationships
he is seldom without the power of concise and lucid speech. If
the international situation is to expose itself with economy, its
typical figures—'dispossessed princes and wandering heirs'—
must move about with less superficial friction and more
articulateness than sheer realism could venture on.

It was of the essence of James's conception in *The American*
that his hero should be intolerably wronged by 'persons pretending to represent the highest possible civilization', and that
some sinister disclosure should offer the slighted hero a revenge
which at the last moment he would put by. James came to feel
that he had mismanaged this. 'The real note of policy in forlorn
aristocracies', he wrote, is the 'accommodation of the theory of
a noble indifference to the practice of a deep avidity.' Instead
of deciding that Newman was impossible, and thereupon
banishing Madame de Cintré to a convent, the de Bellegardes
would in real life have swallowed the American and his millions

without a scruple and been nasty after the wedding rather than before it. But the real weakness of the book—again not unremarked by James—lies elsewhere. The wrong done to Newman can be deep, 'violent and insolent, like all great strokes of evil', only if something more than his vanity and sense of property is involved. And we shall acquiesce in this interpretation only if we apprehend between Madame de Cintré and himself a genuine and reciprocal passionate relationship. The spectacle of an aristocratic French widow of some maturity abjectly bowing to a family decree is an uninformed and novelette-like device decisively negating this effect. And yet more fatal is the manner in which it pleases James to set Newman about his wooing. Were we first to meet Romeo drinking tea with a match-making old matron of Verona, and being persuaded by her to take a look at the Capulets' girl, would Romeo, sigh as he might thereafter, ever quite recover in our regard? 'It was too strange and too mocking to be real', we are told of Newman's betrayal; 'it was like a page torn out of some superannuated unreadable book, with no context in his own experience.' Just so young Troilus felt as he lingered out the hours on Troy's walls and watched the lights being kindled, one by one, in the tents of the Achaians. A story of love made and severed must be romantic other than in the sense actually claimed by James for this book. It is only if the experience of love is regarded as transcendent and transforming that its destruction or decay becomes fully poignant. In *The American* James has rather blundered into this archetypal story. If Christopher Newman— a character in himself brilliantly realized—was to be the particular innocent beguiled, betrayed, and cruelly wronged, it ought not perhaps to have been over a lady.

James was to find in the innocence of his countrymen a subject of steadily increasing complexity. Yet it remained his instinct not to sever contact with what has proved, in the issue, an indestructible element of transatlantic mythology. Americans are unsophisticated but good; Europeans—and, even more, Americans when europeanized—are polished, but unreliable and possibly depraved. This theme in some of its simpler variations may be distinguished in a further group of writings rounding off the first phase of his career.

In 'Four Meetings' the narrator is introduced in a little New England town to Caroline Spencer, a schoolmistress who

is saving and studying in order to fulfil the one intense desire
of her lonely life: foreign travel. 'I have a faith that I shall go.
I have a cousin in Europe!' she says in the earlier and simpler
text of the story. The second meeting with Miss Spencer is in
Le Havre. Newly landed, she is full of delight and wonder. But
the cousin is on the spot to meet her—an American art student
from Paris, whom the narrator sees at once to be a vulgar
wastrel, corrupted to the shoddiest Bohemianism. By the third
meeting, later that day, Miss Spencer, believing a cock-and-
bull story of his having married a countess whose father has
disowned her, has parted with all her money to her cousin and
is preparing to go home. 'I am very sure', she bravely declares,
'I shall see something of this dear old Europe yet.' At the fourth
meeting we are back in New England. The cousin is dead, and
the 'countess', a low Parisienne, has arrived to batten on Miss
Spencer, whom she treats with insolence and ingratitude. 'As
I went past the Baptist church'—the story ends—'I reflected
that poor Miss Spencer had been right in her presentiment that
she should still see something of that dear old Europe.' This tale
is tragic as well as pathetic, because its heroine is innocent in
two senses. She cannot tell an artist from an impostor, or a
countess from a trollop—just as Newman cannot tell a marquis
from a major-domo. But this alone would not have been fatal.
She is also innocent as having unimpaired moral standards.
Convinced that her cousin is in need as a result of a love-match,
she conceives it her duty to give him all she has. Believing later
that his widow has a claim on her, she receives her and waits on
her. What has made Miss Spencer vulnerable is a virtue. She
carries it to Europe and Europe betrays her.

    'An International Episode' is high comedy, and perhaps the
first of James's works to suggest how reasonable was his later
obstinate and ill-starred attempt upon the theatre; a play of
Wilde's set beside this short story will appear no more formally
distinguished and of a far less substantial wit. When Mr. Percy
Beaumont visits the United States on somewhat nebulous legal
business he is accompanied by his kinsman Lord Lambeth—
Lord Lambeth making the trip (as he ingenuously explains to
those American citizens who entertain him) for a lark. When
the charming, as also serious and intellectual, Bessie Alden
proves full of curiosity about the status, possessions, and legis-
lative responsibilities of a duke's son, Mr. Beaumont (who is

very clever) sees only one possible interpretation. He acts promptly and has Lord Lambeth's family find a pretext for summoning the young man home. Soon Miss Alden sets out for Europe. She looks forward to renewing her acquaintance with Lord Lambeth. It has to be explained to her that American hospitality is not always very substantially returned by the English aristocracy, and that if unwary she may be suspected of hunting a title. And this, although Miss Alden can barely make sense of it, proves to be true. Lord Lambeth's family take alarm again and behave in a freezing manner. Eventually Lord Lambeth proposes marriage. Miss Alden likes him, and has been doing her best to like him more. But the plain fact is that the young man is rather stupid, very ignorant, and almost wholly idle. Miss Alden has been obliged to comment to him with disfavour on the circumstance that persons of distinction in learning or the arts are absent from his social ambience. He appears to have no sense of his 'position' as she conceives it: one in which great privileges imply corresponding burdens of public duty. So Miss Alden turns Lord Lambeth down. She is concerned, we may say, to show the flag. There can, to her sense, be no reality in the idea of her belonging to a vulgar category. It is not in her to be haunted by the sense of a vulgar imputation. Coming to Europe, she will not relinquish—rather she will assert—the standards of what is, in fact, a purer society. Thus when her sister represents to her the impropriety of going about London in a hansom-cab with a highly respectable young countryman—a thing blameless in Boston, but here not done— Miss Alden will have nothing of it. 'Why', she asks, 'should I suffer the restrictions of a society of which I enjoy none of the privileges?' The same question is asked—implicitly—by a far less articulate and much more famous heroine of James's, Daisy Miller.

The story (1879) to which this ill-fated girl gives her name was the only widely popular work that James ever achieved. In his own country, indeed, it was something of a *succès de scandale*, being vigorously denounced as an insult to American girlhood. This was unreasonable. Daisy, far more fanatically than Miss Alden, is determined to show the flag. Wandering about Europe with an absurd mother and a horrid little brother in whom James's conception of the 'hotel child' finds alarming expression, she is almost singular among her creator's women in being

underbred, completely uncultivated, and devoid even of the
elements of natural taste. This constitutes her pathos. Her
operative principles might be colloquially expressed as a passion
for dating and an imperviousness to the remotest suggestion of
petting. Daisy's mother is disappointed by Rome; she has been
led to expect something different; but far from her is the thought
that her daughter should conduct herself otherwise there than
in New York. And in New York during the previous winter, as
Daisy is delighted to point out, she had been given seventeen
dinners, 'and three of them were by gentlemen'. So in Rome
the enviable girl picks up gentlemen as she likes, goes round
with them, scolds them—and would be most cruelly hurt and
shocked by any imputation against her delicacy. The American
community, anxiously and crudely conforming to continental
canons in these matters, more and more disapproves. Daisy is
eventually ostracized. But she too is one for whom, for long, a
vulgar imputation can mean nothing. When the full weight of
the censure she has incurred does come home to her she puts her
chin up and goes right ahead. Finally she engages in an inspection of the Colosseum in moonlight, accompanied by an Italian
admirer. Here she is observed by a young American who has
hitherto had the sensibility to understand her innocence. But
this excursion seems to him so shocking that he concludes
Daisy's morals to be definitively impaired. She must be 'a young
lady whom a gentleman need no longer be at pains to respect'.
So he says something disrespectful, and this atrocity has a
startling result. Daisy crumples, returns to her hotel, and in
a few days is dead. James seems eventually to have found too
much poetry in *Daisy Miller*, and in the preface to the New
York edition he puts a finely precise formulation of this criticism
into the mouth of a friend.

In *The Europeans* (1878) it is the Old World that comes to
explore the New. A europeanized brother and sister return to
visit their relations in Massachusetts. Felix, an urbanely gay
artist, is disinterested. Eugenia, having contracted in Germany
a dubious morganatic marriage, has specific ends in view. But
Mr. Acton, although the man of the world in the semi-rural
society depicted, discreetly withdraws himself from the influence
of her charms upon discovering that she is prone to prevarication. Felix rescues a restless female cousin from a duty-ridden
Unitarian pastor, who proves a much better match for the

cousin's sister. Eugenia has to decide that this provincial continent is unappreciative of superior women, and she returns to
Europe defeated. It was perhaps James's intention, in resuming
the study of his countrymen on their own ground, to fortify his
exhibition of their innocence with overtones of an irony which
—at least in their private inspection of the Boston world—his
own family had always abundantly possessed. The attitude of
the Wentworths is somewhat narrowly prudential. They are
as aware as Mr. Leavenworth of the importance of their moral
tone. 'The doctrine, as it may almost be called, of the oppressive
gravity of mistakes was one of the most cherished traditions of
the Wentworth family.' When Felix first meets his cousins he
supposes that they must be under the influence of 'some melancholy memory or some depressing expectation'. But this is a
misinterpretation:

To consider an event, crudely and baldly, in the light of the
pleasure it might bring them was an intellectual exercise with which
Felix Young's American cousins were almost wholly unacquainted,
and which they scarcely supposed to be largely pursued in any
section of human society. The arrival of Felix and his sister was a
satisfaction, but it was a singularly joyless and inelastic satisfaction.

Nevertheless the whole charm of the book proceeds from its
realization that here, in New England, is 'a rigidity that had no
illiberal meaning'. 'It's primitive; it's patriarchal; it's the *ton* of
the golden age', Felix exclaims in what is no bad description of
a quiet, highly bred Puritanism. The Wentworths own indeed
a wholly instrumental culture. Nothing may be received for its
own sake. Everything must be handled cautiously in the interest of whatever ethical improvement can be extracted from it.
Yet the spectacle of their peering from behind this system of
life, apprehensive, bewildered, and fascinated, at the strangers of
their own kin who have come amongst them is extremely pleasing.

James's return to the European scene in *Confidence* (1880) is
unpropitious. Designed like its predecessor to be light, this novel
is empty; if *The Europeans* is a soufflé, *Confidence* is a laboriously
inflated, carefully symmetrical, yet never effectively airborne,
balloon. 'Highly civilized young Americans, born to an easy
fortune and a tranquil destiny', pursue about the watering-
places of the Continent a sequence of events which few will
remember save as insignificantly subserving a bleakly formal
conception. All the relationships turn tiresomely inside out and

back again. James's artistry has been caught—as with far more success it will be caught later—by the conception of pattern, and he has not paused to feel or render his characters interesting. We learn that the hero 'had made several lively excursions into medieval history', and that his principal friend, being interested in science, 'had distributed money very freely among the investigating classes'. Early in the book we come fatally to feel that the very mild intrinsic interest which the cautious matrimonial advances and retreats of these idle young men may have is not likely to justify the ritual fuss made over them. In *The Europeans* the thin and conventional treatment of amative processes is immaterial, our interest being caught in the comedy of two cultures which James so brilliantly commands. In *Confidence* there is not, beneath the dilute drawing-room wooing, enough of the weight and tug of human appetite to give substance or impetus to the fiction. A critic handed this ominously sterile book upon publication might well have declared the talent developing through *Roderick Hudson* and *The American* to have come prematurely to its death-bed. Such a judgement would have been disproved in the following year by the appearance of James's first unchallengeable masterpiece.

4

The Portrait of a Lady (1881) reflects perhaps the deepest experience in James's life, the death in 1870 of his cousin Minny Temple, 'radiant and rare, extinguished in her first youth'. James is unprepared, indeed, to evoke one actually dying of consumption as his cousin died. That has to await a later and deeper book. Rather it is the general truth about Minny that he isolates and dramatizes in the story of Isabel Archer. A girl who lingeringly perishes on the threshold of a life for which she is apt and eager has above all things been cheated, betrayed. And Isabel's fate, even though not mortal, is betrayal in the hardest sense. Instead of sentence of death she meets Madame Merle and Gilbert Osmond. Only for her successor Milly Theale is a worse fate reserved—Milly who must harbour at once in the sickroom of her palace the Dark Angel and in its outer chambers Merton Densher and Kate Croy.

On a lawn before the mellow Gardencourt an aged and finely simple American banker, Mr. Touchett, is entertaining

a young nobleman to tea. Lord Warburton has 'the air of a
happy temperament fertilised by a high civilisation', but Mr.
Touchett is no more impressed by him than an American
gentleman—particularly after thirty years in England—should
be. A third figure on the lawn is Mr. Touchett's son Ralph—an
invalid little likely, it will appear, long to survive his ailing
father. Both Lord Warburton and Ralph are unmarried, and
Mr. Touchett's wife is an eccentric person whose wanderings
admit of small commerce with her husband and son. It is known
however that this lady is presently to arrive with an orphan niece
from America. There is some kindly but light-hearted speculation on the unknown girl, and Mr. Touchett, whose sense of
humour remains native, warns Lord Warburton that he is not
to marry her. Whereupon the gentlemen look up and Isabel
Archer is advancing upon them. Mrs. Touchett has arrived at
Gardencourt, retired to her apartments, and left her protégée to
her own devices. Isabel is unsophisticated but well-read, charming yet decidedly independent; and all three gentlemen are
delighted with her. She is eager for knowledge, for life, and for
the pursuit of high if somewhat undefined ideals. Before coming
to Europe she has declined the addresses of a formidable young
captain of industry called Caspar Goodwood. Isabel looks like
being hard to woo, largely because she has such a good conceit
of herself. 'Sometimes she went so far as to wish that she might
find herself some day in a difficult position, so that she should
have the pleasure of being as heroic as the occasion demanded.
. . . She was always planning out her development, desiring her
perfection, observing her progress.' The genuineness of this
romantic largeness of aspiration is soon put to a stiff test. She
receives a proposal from Lord Warburton and declines it. 'She
couldn't marry Lord Warburton; the idea failed to support any
enlightened prejudice in favour of the free exploration of life
that she had hitherto entertained.'

Two things now happen to this intransigent girl. She makes
friends with an old familiar of Mrs. Touchett's, Madame Merle.
The moment of her coming into a drawing-room and finding
this strange woman at the piano has a masterly ominousness, is
indefinably fateful and sinister. Madame Merle, 'rare, superior
and pre-eminent', deceives Isabel plausibly enough, since she
is in fact a highly evolved symbol of the world. But it is possible
to feel that James himself, here as elsewhere, gives to a brilliant

social surface something in excess of its just due. Remorseless with his figures of evil in the end, he yet treats their rarity, superiority, and pre-eminence ambiguously—at once as qualities and appearances—so that we apprehend too insistent an invitation to admire men and women as if they were paintings or curios or fine furniture. A related problem is raised by Isabel's second acquisition. Mr. Touchett dies, and it appears that he has been persuaded by his son to leave her a fortune. Great riches fascinated James, and of his three major heroines each is more fabulously wealthy than the last. Yet to each of them her wealth is a calamity. 'You've too many graceful illusions. Your newly-acquired thousands will shut you up more and more to the society of a few selfish and heartless people who will be interested in keeping them up.' The words are prophetic, but they are spoken to Isabel by a character who is a figure of fun. Although wealth does constitute in the great novels just such a prison, for James life outside that prison has no imaginative—as it had no personal—appeal. His most admired people are willing prisoners within those material splendours which for him are sufficient symbols of high civilization; they subscribe to that way of life; saints or angels though they be, their first thought is always for the observance of its strictest social forms. If this troubles us here, it will trouble us again.

Isabel with her fortune departs under Mrs. Touchett's protection for the Continent, and for the moment we leave her for another point of view. In his modestly exquisite Florentine apartments a middle-aged widower, Gilbert Osmond, is in conversation with two nuns responsible for the education of his fifteen-year-old daughter Pansy, a monument of horrifying docility, brought up presumably upon religious principles and indubitably to please her father. As Osmond's satisfaction is almost exclusively in minor works of art, it is fortunate that Pansy is just that—doubly a work of art, indeed, since both James and the nuns have notably triumphed in the making of her. Her mother is in fact Madame Merle, who presently appears with a proposal to obtain a fortune for this unacknowledged child by marrying her new friend, Isabel, to her former lover, Osmond. And Isabel falls into the trap. Osmond is a sterile dilettante, and one less concerned to achieve fine tastes and perceptions than to have these, and other superiorities, acknowledged by the very world from which he claims to live aloof.

But Isabel in her inexperience accepts him as she has accepted Madame Merle:

For the moment she only said to herself that this 'new relation' would perhaps prove her very most distinguished. Madame Merle had had that note of rarity, but what quite other power it immediately gained when sounded by a man! It was not so much what he said and did, but rather what he withheld, that marked him for her as by one of those signs of the highly curious that he was showing her on the underside of old plates and in the corner of sixteenth-century drawings.

To put her burdensome fortune to the beneficient use of buying Osmond more old plates is, in a sense, splendidly and heroically romantic. Isabel has refused an English peer; she now gives her hand and fortune to a poor gentleman modestly cultivating life's finer vibrations:

'I've a few good things', Mr. Osmond allowed; 'indeed I've nothing very bad. . . . The events of my life have been absolutely unperceived by any one save myself; getting an old silver crucifix at a bargain (I've never bought anything dear, of course), or discovering, as I once did, a sketch by Correggio.'

To this sort of thing a generous girl from Albany might well hearken with respect and awe. But it was a different matter—how different, we may wonder if James himself knows—to marry it. 'There had been nothing very delicate', we are told in the earlier text of the novel, 'in inheriting seventy thousand pounds, and she hoped he might use her fortune in a way that might make her think better of it.' But Isabel's was a decision about giving away herself as well as her money, and James's tinkering with this passage suggests his suspicion that delicacy and indelicacy have got awkwardly mixed up. Osmond, at least, contrives the appearance of 'stirred senses and deep intentions'; the marriage takes place; and only after an interval of some years is the narrative resumed. Isabel has been disillusioned; she knows her husband for what he is. And this he cannot forgive. He hates her.

The book has its further crises. There is a moment when Isabel comes upon Osmond and Madame Merle unaware; her husband is sitting, Madame Merle is standing; an obscure intimation of the truth comes to her. Eventually she learns everything—the sum of her betrayal. Lord Warburton turns up

and takes it into his head that he wants to marry Pansy. Isabel
sees that the attraction is still really herself, and sends him away.
This missing of a magnificent match for their daughter disappoints Osmond and Madame Merle bitterly. Ralph Touchett
proves to be dying at Gardencourt, and Osmond's malignity is
now such that he forbids Isabel to go to him. Isabel goes, is
present at his death-bed, has once more to resist Caspar Goodwood in what is the novel's only glimpse of physical passion,
and then returns to her husband. Behind her is a period of
incredulous terror as she has taken the measure of her dwelling;
before her is renunciation. Ardent for the free exploration of
life, she will be ground in the mill of the conventional. 'Constantly present to her mind', we are told, 'were all the traditionary decencies and sanctities of marriage.' 'I can't publish
my mistake', she says to a friend who has learnt the truth. 'I
don't think that's decent. I'd much rather die.' And so the
door of her own splendid Roman palace slams upon her as
fatally and finally as did that of the Carmelite convent upon
Madame de Cintré in *The American*. We may reflect that, two
years before the publication of *The Portrait of a Lady*, another
door had closed with a reverberation heard across the length of
Europe—the door slammed by Nora Helmer in Ibsen's *A Doll's
House*. But Nora is on the outside; and Torvald Helmer, a much
less nasty person than Gilbert Osmond, is left to digest his
marital insufficiencies in solitude.

The subject of *The Portrait of a Lady* is Isabel's illusion of
freedom, where actually her whole course of life is determined.
Suddenly granted wealth and seeming independence, she
thinks that she is laying hold on life. But really her cultural
heritage—including the simple fact that she *is* a lady—is laying
hold on her, and that heritage takes her back to Osmond in the
end. James would appear to approve as well as chronicle his
heroine's renunciation. He may even be charged with evoking
a quasi-religious sanction for what is in fact an instance of
transcendentalized good form. For amid all the cheats and
corruptions of European society by which, fondly and romantically admiring, his Americans are prone to be let down, there is
one principle which their maturer experience will endorse as
valid. It is the principle of keeping up appearances, of placing
public decorum above private impulse. Beyond almost everything else, James and James's initiates prize that sort of breeding

which enables a man or woman to preserve good formal
manners despite every urgency of passion or emotion which may
be assailing them. Nor is it hard to distinguish how James
comes by this allegiance. When he condemned the large and
impeccable art of Flaubert on the ground that it lacks moral
dignity, he was naming his own ultimate value. But moral dignity appeared to him something fully viable only in the nourishing and sustaining medium of high civilization. And for James,
as Sir Herbert Read has said, civilization meant 'a perfectly
definite historical phenomenon'. It was what tradition and all
the fine accumulations of time had given to the cultivated classes
of western society in his own day. He was extremely sensitive to
the material tokens by which this tradition asserted itself—
although not perhaps so sensitive to them in detail and as individual works of art as aware of them in the gross as massively
accumulated symbols of the idea. Hence his preoccupation with
and deference towards grand or beautiful things and their
owners. It seldom occurred to him that the attitude of the effective proprietors of these supremely significant objects could be
one of vast inattention. He imagined—perhaps we must say in
every sense—an aristocracy of culture so conscious of its tradition on the aesthetic side that its main business became that of
living aesthetically up to it. These wonderful beings are intensely
conscious that their wardenship of the tradition is a matter of
sustained aesthetic perceptiveness in the fields alike of connoisseurship and conduct. The idea of style dominates the living
of James's characters as much as it dominates that collecting of
objets d'art with which they are, to our seeming, often so finically
concerned. Hence the transcendentalizing of the idea of good
form. It is not in itself moral dignity. But it is the touchstone of
that perfected civility without which moral dignity is impossible.
The idea does not permit Isabel to break even a quite common
old plate over Osmond's head. It does not permit her to say,
'Gilbert, I sometimes think—extravagant though it seems—
that you are even more ridiculous than you are small and
mean'. And, not permitting this, it cannot permit her openly to
turn away from him.

5

'It is not well', an American critic of James has written, 'for
the artist to turn cosmopolitan, for the flavour of the fruit comes
from the soil and sunshine of its native fields.' In testing the thesis

that James's expatriation was an artistic disaster, we must give particular attention to the next group of his novels. *Washington Square* (1881) has a purely American setting, and is among the most finished of his productions. Dr. Sloper, a fashionable New York physician, is left a widower with one daughter, Catherine, whose strength and delicacy of feeling he fails to appreciate, since he is unable to forgive her for being plain, dull, and virtually unmarriageable. A considerable heiress, she is presently caught in the toils of a plausible fortune-hunter, Morris Townsend. Dr. Sloper successfully fights the threatened match, but with so little consideration for his daughter's feelings that she is eventually left, cruelly disillusioned by the revelation of Townsend's mercenary nature, without the resource of any intimate human relationship. Seventeen years later Townsend reappears and forces himself into her presence, knowing that the death of her father has put her in command of an independent fortune. She dismisses him absolutely and without hesitation. James has perfectly subdued his writing to this simple theme. The book is native in its substance, but shows a fine harmony of matter and style learnt from foreign masters—perhaps as much from Flaubert, whom James detested, as from Turgenev, whom he revered. To Turgenev may be owing, too, something of the mastery with which the small group of characters is developed. Dr. Sloper is at once highly representative—the type of the parent in a fatal relationship to his child—and a unique human being. The same consideration holds of Catherine's aunt, Mrs. Penniman, a provincial Pandarus in petticoats, but without shrewdness or humour, delivered over hopelessly to a debased, fatuous, and faintly but pervasively prurient romanticism. Yet, with all this, the novel is neither rich nor promising. Its people are alive, but life does not pulse in it or them. If we can imagine the Wentworths in *The Europeans* studied in a tranquillity and to a depth made feasible by the absence of their disturbing transatlantic cousins; if we can imagine *Watch and Ward* rewritten by a James who has matured his art at the feet of its masters, we are near the measure of *Washington Square*. It is a masterpiece which we read with admiration but without anxiety, and for what we soon perceive it to be: a tale of faded pathos, a chronicle of passive suffering finely controlled, as the book itself is finely controlled.

Comparing *Washington Square* with another story of a thwarted

marriage, Christopher Newman's in *The American*, we are likely
to feel at first, indeed, that the advantage lies with the all-
American book. It is not merely that its art is more mature.
A pervasive uneasiness seems to be purged from James's writing
when his eye is bent upon New York. Here he has an assured
command of his social scene, whereas in the international novels
we have a constant sense of characters conspiring with their
creator to keep up a high style, like women on the walls of
a Royal Academy exhibition, anxiously holding poses of un-
accustomed stateliness and grace. Yet while it is good for a
novelist to be poised before a spectacle it is yet better for him to
be moved. His most precious stock-in-trade is not what he best
knows but what he most intensely responds to. It is perhaps
desirable, as conducive to both family and national piety, that
our imagination and emotions should be principally stirred by
the old folks at home; but among artists this is by no means
universally the fact. Hardy's imagination kindled almost exclusively after this fashion. But to his contemporary Meredith
the old folks were commonly no more than an embarrassing
accident to be concealed when filling up census forms. James
would, conceivably, have been most appropriately domesticated
with the Wentworths and the Slopers and the people presently
to be encountered in *The Bostonians*. But it was elsewhere that
his pulse quickened and his thoughts grew. The flavour of the
fruit does come, no doubt, from the soil and sunshine of its
native fields. But an artist is not a vegetable, nor is a biologically
benign climate necessarily what he requires. Rather he requires
whatever sun, although perhaps unfamiliar and bewildering,
casts for him the most dramatic light upon the human comedy.
For some writers a back yard, a front parlour, may be the most
moving theatre upon which human destiny displays itself.
James's people meet their moments in the Colosseum or the
Sistine Chapel. Or, like Newman, they pass within the 'grossly-
imaged' portals of Notre-Dame and settle their account while
listening to the 'far-away bells chiming off into space, at long
intervals, the big bronze syllables of the Word'. Newman finds,
all unconsciously, what is for him the right setting for the great
creative act of his life. In this he is almost a symbol of James
himself, whose mind kindled to its fullest creation only in the
presence of the immemorial and the august. 'This romanticisa-
tion of European culture', it has been declared, 'worked to his

undoing, for it constrained the artist to a lifelong pursuit of intangible realities that existed only in his imagination.' Poor James—or poor Shelley! Ideal constructions, vividly realized and powerfully charged with emotion, hold some prominence in the great art of the world. James's vision of Europe may be as queer as El Greco's of the Saints, but we shall be foolish to mind this provided it is as exciting and as beautiful.

The American, then, is a product of less artistic skill but deeper artistic excitement than *Washington Square*. A somewhat different but equally significant comparison presents itself in the two immediately succeeding novels, *The Bostonians* and *The Princess Casamassima* (alike published in 1886). Both these treat of public issues, and examine phases and movements of social conscience. *The Bostonians* is recognizably the same sort of novel as *Felix Holt* or *Alton Locke* or *Ann Veronica*. If *The Princess Casamassima* takes something of its inspiration, conceivably, from *Le Rouge et le Noir*, it looks forward to *Jude the Obscure* and *The Secret Agent*. James, in fact, did not turn massively upon the inner consciousness without deliberate and sustained trial of something else, and now he appears to be attempting a balanced development in his fiction of the inner and the outer life. He was disappointed by the reception of these two books, both of which had an adverse effect upon such reputation as he had achieved. Their failure may have prompted him to take his own road to an elaborate psychological fiction, to his vast explorations of a consciousness which he may be said almost to have invented for the purpose, as mathematicians invent multi-dimensional geometries.

The Bostonians is all-American, and a most brilliant novel. It may be the measure of James's determination to be robust that the book has its climax in a brawl. Nor is its heroine a girl of the privileged and sheltered sort common in James. Verena Tarrant has been brought up to exploit her charming personality and odd flair for natural rhetoric upon public platforms. From activities of this sort, vaguely 'inspirational', she is caught up by the intense and possessive Olive Chancellor into a movement of militant feminism, until eventually rescued by a reactionary young man from the South, Basil Ransom. We do in the end become much concerned that Ransom should get his girl, since this issue of the affair represents at least simple health, whereas the relationship aimed at by Olive Chancellor is a morbid one. It is characteristic of James that he can give a subtle and full-scale representation of sexual deviation without batting an eyelid or admitting for a moment that he is not as profoundly unconscious of the actual mechanisms at work as are the self-deluded characters involved in it. The novel has a background in delusion, and affords a mordant and amusing panorama of the near-lunatic fringe of an earnest, intellectual, and culturally unfurnished society. James judged his subject 'strong and good, with a large rich interest', and he substantiates this claim in what is nevertheless again not a genial book. His mind is far too capacious and just to miss either the heroism or the pathos of his theme, but his overriding attitude is described not unfairly by Miss Rebecca West as 'nagging hostility to political effort'. He is appalled by a society apparently unable to cultivate privacy, a society in which the people have rights but the person has none. Had Matthew Arnold, instead of *Culture and Anarchy*, written a novel about reformers anxious to secure us the right to marry our deceased wife's sister, and about the Reverend William Cattle, and about the British College of Health in the New Road, the flavour might have been not unlike that of *The Bostonians*.

The Bostonians is admirably constructed, at once finely of a piece and richly diversified, luminous, lucid, pointed, effective. Compared with it, *The Princess Casamassima* appears almost chaotic. James's notebooks show the whole course of *The Bostonians* to have been clear to him before he set pen to paper, but of *The Princess Casamassima* we learn chiefly that much was vague to him as he wrote and that, plunging in rather wildly, he landed himself with a diversity of characters difficult to reduce to order. It was not often that a book caught him, as it were, unawares. Here, it seems that we have something like a sudden precipitation of impressions stored up during lonely prowlings in just such London streets as were to constitute the imaginative world of a very different novelist, George Gissing. The hero, Hyacinth Robinson, *déclassé*, neither of one blood nor another, a 'trapped spectator', is discernibly a remote imaginative projection of elements in James's own situation in his early London days. And the glimmer of Hyacinth seems to have hurried James into a creative process, for him, quite unusually phantasmagoric and improvised. Hyacinth's mother was a French work-girl; his father he believes to be an English lord; the

Princess Casamassima who takes him up is of course none other than Christina Light of *Roderick Hudson*. The groundwork of the book is the class-war—in the days when the class-war was known as the social question and was debated by respectable artisans in secret societies presided over by *émigrés* of the year '48, and was moreover a subject of passing curiosity among benevolent aristocratic ladies given to slumming. James was scarcely well qualified to depict the English working man in incipient insurgence. His endeavour to collect in his current notebook suitably plebeian phrases with which to embellish their talk does not get beyond two or three efforts, of which the most striking is ''Ere today, somewhere else tomorrow: that's '*is* motto'. There is nothing so powerful in the book as its first episode, in which the child Hyacinth is marked for life by the visit he is made to pay to a dying woman—his mother, as he later discovers— imprisoned for the murder of his father. But if the latter course of the book lacks coherence, it has an interior life that *The Bostonians* lacks. For James has returned to the theme, the predicament, in the face of which his imagination stirs. Mature civilization and an observer in an ambiguous relation to it: that is the basis of *The Princess Casamassima*. Hyacinth, because he belongs and doesn't belong, because he admires and despises, is torn asunder in the end. He cannot harmonize the findings of his moral sensibility (which demands that social justice come first) with the findings of his aesthetic and imaginative sensibility (which asserts the primacy of grandeur, of style, of the rich superimpositions of centuries of undisturbed privilege). And this surely is James's dilemma. He too, because of his betwixt-and-between position, owns both an ethical absolutism and an aesthetic absolutism. In terms of the social question the conflict of loyalties is insoluble. Perhaps it kills James the social novelist just as it kills Hyacinth Robinson the social assassin. Much of James's later writing is an effort to escape from his dilemma by taking it up in terms of the inner life of the individual and inquiring repeatedly whether, at their highest level, the aesthetic and the moral sanction be not one; whether to live fully in the light of the one conception is not to fulfil the demands of the other as well.

6

The effort to embody in his work a strong element of panoramic social fiction is continued by James in *The Tragic Muse*

(1890), a long, initially vigorous, and in the end strangely inert novel. Nick Dormer sacrifices to his ambition as a painter both his expected political career and his marriage to a politically minded lady. His friend Peter Sherringham, interested from the vantage-ground of a similar social position in the art of the theatre, resigns his more intimate interest in Miriam Rooth when it becomes evident that her career as a tragic actress is paramount with her. Not since *Confidence*—and never before on such a scale—had James demanded sustained interest in the amatory fortunes of two young men irremediably lacking in radical masculinity. And the book's implicit claim to explore, against a realistic and finely particularized background of English society, considerable depths and complexities of emotional life makes the central failure the more disastrous. It is as a renewing of the interest in artistic temperament first canvassed in *Roderick Hudson* and 'The Madonna of the Future', and as a pointer to a growing preoccupation of James's at this time, that *The Tragic Muse* has its chief significance. The first circumstance makes apposite here the mention of a group of related short stories. The second necessitates notice, however brief, of James's curious involvement in theatrical ambitions and enterprise.

In 'The Author of Beltraffio' the wife of Mark Ambient, an 'aesthetic' novelist given wholly to the pursuit of beauty, so fears his future influence upon their small son that she deliberately lets the child die. The violence of this conception—of which the notebooks show James to have been sufficiently aware— would seem to indicate the continued urgency within himself of the conflict first dramatized in *Roderick Hudson*, and at the same time to point forward to a phase of some morbidity through which his work is presently to pass. 'The Lesson of the Master' is of maturer quality, and in effect brilliantly argues abnegation as the way of art; its theme is to be echoed by W. B. Yeats when he declares in *Estrangement* that he has known more men destroyed by the desire to have wife and child and to keep them in comfort than by drink and harlots. Henry St. George, a leader of the profession of letters whose prolific writing has declined from its first high excellence, plants the blame with great eloquence on his delightful but distracting wife and children. On the death of Mrs. St. George he gives up writing and marries again, pleased that he is thereby preserving a younger writer of great promise from making the same match in defiance of the axiom that the artist must be dedicated 'to intellectual, not to personal passion'. This story is more celebrated than pleasing. St. George's subjection to his first wife is ridiculous, and his presentation of his plight to the younger writer scarcely the sanctified confidence that James would seem to suppose. Better is the ironic comedy of 'The Death of the Lion'. Here Neil Paraday, a writer of equal genius, is so lionized as the consequence of a belated *succès d'estime* that he fails to survive a fashionable house-party at which everybody exploits him and nobody has read his books. Women, including an absentee wife, are again decidedly the prime agents of artistic shipwreck. And James seems to take for granted an abject obedience to society's call. Paraday 'filled his lungs, for the most part, with the comedy of his queer fate' and fatally visited a chilly duke on a wet day, leaving the unique manuscript in which he had abundantly sketched what would have been his masterpiece to vanish in transmission from Lady Augusta Minch's maid to Lord Dorimont's man. In 'The Next Time' Ray Limbert, another author of high talent, is constrained by marital and parental responsibilities to write in a popular manner. But the harder he strives to be really vulgar 'next time' the more esoterically distinguished does the result prove to be. He is hopelessly isolated in a world in which 'even twaddle cunningly calculated was far above people's heads'. This ungenial situation finally kills him. 'The Coxon Fund' sets the Coleridge-like Frank Saltram amid a different sequence of embarrassments stemming from the same conflict of the artistic temper and acquisitive society; financial independence is fatal to Saltram when it eventually comes, and 'the very day he found himself able to publish he wholly ceased to produce'. In 'The Figure in the Carpet' yet another eminent novelist, Hugh Vereker, discloses to a young admirer that criticism has entirely missed the one element of quintessential significance in his entire *œuvre*. After prodigious efforts another young critic penetrates to the truth, but a series of fatalities prevents its ever being given to the world. In this story the theme of esoteric artistic revelation is oddly implicated with that of sexual consummation, and aesthetic passion is confounded with frenzied curiosity. It was published in 1896 and may be described as James's closest approach to the mere *chic* of its melancholy decade. 'The Great Good Place' tells how George Dane, an author whose abundant success has filled his days with harassing social duties to a point of complete nervous exhaustion, dreams of an establishment designed for the relief of such conditions and embodying the more agreeable features of a monastery, a clinic, a country-house, and a luxury hotel. In 'The Velvet Glove', one of James's last short stories, John Berridge, an author recently risen to great fame, is pursued by a lady of dazzling beauty—but only in the hope (it transpires) that he will write a preface for her latest worthless and pseudonymous novel. The paradox here is driven home. The lady is a princess. She and her lover appear to Berridge as Olympians, persons commanding 'life in irreflective joy and at the highest thinkable level of prepared security and unconscious insolence'. Thus Berridge himself, although become a person of celebrity in polished society, is in something like the position of the small Henry James, his nose to the cold dusty paint and iron of the Eighteenth Street corner. The princess—as he urges upon her—need 'only live' in order to *be* the Romance that *he* must perpetually strive to capture with his pen. Yet what his art achieves upon a basis of exclusion and deprivation her rich and vivid personal life leaves her utterly short of when she too attempts to write. And art is sanative. His informed allegiance to it enables him to reject her proposal with dignity and kindliness; her debasement of it has led her to something low and silly in personal conduct.

These stories taken together constitute both an amusing analysis of the dilemma of the artist in society and a splendid assertion of the arduousness of art. Yet they cannot be felt as themselves the product of a high artistic confidence. We are shown a succession of gifted men taking for granted a narrow conception of human society; they are perpetually before us in white ties, which they sport with all the submissiveness of a cowed felon being led away in a halter. Moreover—and even amid this atmosphere of the *salon*—what may be called the monastic theory of art is pressed hard. James's artists are never buffeted into art, but seem artists by magic. They are represented as offering us a noble wine from the broad vineyards of their contemplative habit, and it is a wine, it seems, unfortified by any drop of the hard spirit of experience. For the artist, involvement in life is represented as almost exclusively abrasive. But artists who subscribe wholeheartedly to this doctrine may find themselves awkwardly placed. There is in the Ashmolean

Museum in Oxford a cartoon by Sir Max Beerbohm sufficiently exhibiting the dangers of the monastic fallacy. James is at a keyhole.

In these years he was also in the theatre—and was there eventually to be betrayed into a posture of almost equal embarrassment. What he sought was popular success; what he achieved was to stand bewildered on the stage at the conclusion of his *Guy Domville* (1895) and hear the applause of well-wishers in the stalls drowned by booing and hissing from the gallery. It was painful, but a revelation. James had been thinking of literary reputation in what was, in fact, an out-moded way; and we must understand the force of this if we are not to be disconcerted by the odd impurity of his intermittent dramatic aspirations—which sustained him, we can only note, through the completing, at one time or another, of twelve plays in all. Today the notion that the greatest writers of an age are likely to be the most widely acclaimed and handsomely rewarded will provoke a smile from every instructed schoolboy, and authors of austere intentions and high integrity must recoil in alarm when any but the most meagre royalty statement reaches them from a publisher. The James of the short stories at which we have been glancing already understood the implacable advance of this bleak climate. But the James who toiled after theatrical reputation looked back to an earlier time—one in which lack of general acclaim could scarcely be accounted for distinction and might well be felt as a humiliation. Writing to a friend after the failure of *Guy Domville* he declared that he 'had fallen on evil days—every sign or symbol of one's being in the least *wanted*, anywhere or by anyone, having so utterly failed'. He was a little to comfort himself with the persuasion that from his unsuccessful struggle with the stage he had carried away a command of fresh techniques applicable to the novel. And to the novel he turned back. An entry in his current notebook marks the occasion with unusual emotion:

I take up my *own* old pen again—the pen of all my old unforgettable efforts and sacred struggles. To myself—today—I need say no more. Large and full and high the future still opens. It is now indeed that I may do the work of my life. And I will. I have only to *face* my problems. But all that is of the ineffable—too deep and pure for any utterance. Shrouded in sacred silence let it rest.

7

He seems now to have renounced for the time any thought of popular success. Whether or not he had indeed gained from the theatre, as he believed, a technique of scenic presentation making for economy and unity, it is certain that his writing was to become increasingly difficult as he evolved an elaborate verbal instrument for the expression of increasingly absorbing and even obsessive ethical concerns. In *The Spoils of Poynton* (1897) there is much to amuse, but it is a novel, nevertheless, underlying which is all the rigidity of a morality. The aesthetic sensibility of Mrs. Gereth has enabled her to create at Poynton an incomparable treasure-house of beautiful pieces finely composed, and this she would preserve from the dire threat of a philistine daughter-in-law in Mona Brigstock. The Brigstocks are impossible, their own house being filled with 'gimcracks that might have been keepsakes for maid-servants and nondescript conveniences that might have been prizes for the blind'. Mrs. Gereth forms her own plot for defeating these terrible people. But the book's heroine, Fleda Vetch, while possessing instinctively all her patroness's feeling for 'things', owns too a standard of personal honour so high that she must renounce Owen Gereth when his mother contrives that Owen should turn to her from Mona. She must renounce him even although she loves him and he would willingly be rescued from his atrocious betrothed. Fleda is thus wrecked upon, and wrecks, Mrs. Gereth's plan for the safeguarding of her treasures. These finally go up in flame, and with them perishes the mainspring of their former mistress's existence. Owen marries Mona, whom he has come to detest, and Fleda is left with nothing but the citadel of her own integrity. The growth of this short book, so significant for James's final development, may be followed in considerable detail in the notebooks.

What Maisie Knew (1897) and *The Awkward Age* (1899) initiate that final phase of James's writing which is surely his greatest, but in the assimilating of which even apt and practised readers have constantly to contend with indigestible elaborations and a brilliance of treatment which does not always seem to shed any very full light on the matter in hand. *What Maisie Knew* employs a supple but at the same time highly subtilized and complex prose to filter much involved adult depravity through the innocent but perceptive consciousness of the heroine, a small girl at once pathetically isolated and tragically involved. *The Awkward Age*, which presents a slightly older girl living in a social set scarcely more attractive, is similarly at a first reading chiefly remarkable as a *tour de force*. It is dramatized to a point at which the text is virtually that of a play with percurrent stage-directions of exquisite precision. In its structure it has all the virtuosity, as in its whole body it has something of the oppressive airlessness, of a Nicolas Poussin. Yet if we emerge gasping, it is probably with a strong inclination to plunge in again. It may be otherwise with *The Sacred Fount* (1901). At least those who maintain that James is now losing contact with significant human experience and sinking into the laboured exercise of a sterile artifice may point with some confidence to a work seemingly both prompted by and designed to anatomize a morbid sexuality, but presented with so nightmarish an obliquity of statement as to be—like the related but vastly more popular and effective short story 'The Turn of the Screw'—insusceptible of any assured interpretation.

It must be a question whether the unfavourable view of James's later development taken by some critics has not in fact been furthered by the series of prefaces provided by the author for the collected edition of 1907–9. These prefaces, indeed, have been described as a profound aesthetic revelation. Yet there is something disproportionate, even false, in the obtrusiveness of their concern with technique. The firm moral accent which in the novels themselves is seldom lost may pass unremarked by a reader of these ponderous but elusive discourses upon the craft of James's fictions. Such of his working notebooks as have been preserved often better represent the actual bent of his creating mind. Thus the single extant note of substance for *The Awkward Age*, although brief, makes clear James's radical absorption in the problems of conduct he proposes to explore. From the preface, on the other hand, one would conclude his concern to be almost exclusively with the book's rarefied mechanics, and there is preserved no sense of the tragedy which it in fact achieves. As *maître* the older James, never apparently fully assured of himself as artist, was prone to exhibitionism. As moralist he maintained a deep personal reticence. It is what his finest characters are apt to do.

8

The Ambassadors (1903), for which James wrote an elaborate sketch or 'scenario' of 20,000 words, was designed for serial publication, and in its own fashion it bears as clear an impress of this as does *The Mayor of Casterbridge*. It was elaborated, like so many of James's works, from a casual anecdote—one from which he gained 'the little idea of the figure of an elderly man who hasn't "lived" ' and who becomes sorrowfully aware of the fact 'in the presence of some great human spectacle, some great organisation for the Immediate, the Agreeable, for curiosity, and experiment and perception, for Enjoyment, in a word'. Thus was born Lambert Strether. He is a widower from New England, sent to Europe as the ambassador of Mrs. Newsome, the philanthropic and generally superior widow of a manufacturer of some highly successful but anonymous object of domestic utility. Strether's task is to bring home, alike to sound mercantile pursuits and sound American marriage, Mrs. Newsome's errant son Chad, who is reluctant to leave Paris and must therefore be presumed in the grip of vice. Strether finds Chad unexpectedly assimilated to the most refined civilization of the place. And for this an unexpected sort of woman has been responsible: Madame de Vionnet, an exquisite flower of the same high order, living with her equally charming daughter in separation from an impossible but authentically aristocratic husband. Bit by bit (serial part by serial part, in fact) Strether has to change ground. First when supposing in his innocence that here can be only a virtuous attachment, and even later when he has discovered that they are in fact lovers, he stands by Chad and Madame de Vionnet. In the end he has to stand by the lady alone, insisting that Chad stick to his mistress or be ashamed of himself. But we know that the young man, beneath all his polish far less sensitive and perceptive than the elderly ambassador, will presently tire of his liaison, pack up, and go home to the life his mother designs for him.

In several aspects *The Ambassadors* seems to admit those charges of triviality and snobbery which have frequently been brought against it. The concrete exemplifications of Chad Newsome's improvement are scarcely impressive—he has learnt, we are told, how to make a presentation and to enter a box at the theatre—and of his mistress James's care for the 'infinite tact

and delicacy of presentation' has produced a portrait decidedly
lacking in bone. Strether, however, is a different matter. Nothing
comes to us other than through the single centre of consciousness represented by his mind. And the picture of that mind in
steady transformation, in constant growth, is itself a growing-
point in prose fiction. Strether's is a mind regularly knowing a
little more than it has yet formulated, so that we watch a subtle
interplay of ignorance and knowledge, doubt and certainty,
acknowledgement and unacknowledgement. Of this there is a
consummate instance near the end of the book, when in the
course of a solitary ramble by the Seine he comes upon Chad
and Madame de Vionnet in circumstances showing them unmistakably as lovers. The result is not merely or precisely—as
one critic would have it—'his long-delayed perception of their
real relationship'. As Strether recognizes the pair in the boat,
and sees that they have recognized him and are debating
whether they can dissimulate and row on, 'it was', we are told,
'a sharp fantastic crisis that had popped up as if in a dream, and
it had had only to last the few seconds to make him feel it as
quite horrible'. But he has already, lurkingly yet absolutely,
known the mere fact. What now comes to him as horrible is
something different. The necessarily clandestine nature of the
relationship, abruptly demonstrated, speaks to him of its finite-
ness and mortality. As one stage in his disillusionment is confirmed another comes hoveringly into view. In this scene too
there is a fineness of contrivance that proceeds from the object
of Strether's excursion:

He had taken the train a few days after this from a station—as well
as *to* a station—selected almost at random; such days, whatever
should happen, were numbered, and he had gone forth under the
impulse—artless enough, no doubt—to give the whole of one of
them to that French ruralism, with its cool special green, into which
he had hitherto looked only through the little oblong window of the
picture-frame. It had been as yet for the most part but a land of
fancy for him—the background of fiction, the medium of art, the
nursery of letters; practically as distant as Greece, but practically
also well-nigh as consecrated. Romance could weave itself, for
Strether's sense, out of elements mild enough; and even after what
he had, as he felt, lately 'been through' he could thrill a little at the
chance of seeing something somewhere that would remind him of a
certain small Lambinet that had charmed him, long years before,
at a Boston dealer's and that he had quite absurdly never forgotten.

The solitary expedition is a success. Strether finds his Lambinet,
glimpsing it from the train and 'getting out as securely as if to
keep an appointment'. The picture is before him and he walks
straight into it—free of the artist's golden world, the brazen put
behind him for the day. And the thing is marvellously kept up.
He walks on and on through his picture and at evening sits
down in an inn garden bordering the river to await his dinner
in peace:

> Strether sat there and, though hungry, felt at peace; the confidence
> that had so gathered for him deepened with the lap of the water,
> the ripple of the surface, the rustle of the reeds on the opposite
> bank, the faint diffused coolness and the slight rock of a couple of
> small boats attached to a rough landing-place hard by. The valley
> on the farther side was all copper-green level and glazed pearly sky,
> a sky hatched across with screens of trimmed trees, which looked
> flat, like espaliers; and though the rest of the village straggled away
> in the near quarter the view had an emptiness that made one of the
> boats suggestive. Such a river set one afloat almost before one could
> take up the oars—the idle play of which would be moreover the
> aid to the full impression. This perception went so far as to bring
> him to his feet; but that movement, in turn, made him feel afresh
> that he was tired, and while he leaned against a post and continued
> to look out he saw something that gave him a sharper arrest.
>
> What he saw was exactly the right thing—a boat advancing round
> the bend and containing a man who held the paddles and a lady,
> at the stern, with a pink parasol. It was suddenly as if these figures,
> or something like them, had been wanted in the picture, had been
> wanted more or less all day, and had now drifted into sight, with the
> slow current, on purpose to fill up the measure. They came slowly,
> floating down . . . .

But what has been 'wanting in the picture'—wanting to complete a world exquisitely ideal—turns out to be the actual:
Madame de Vionnet and Chad, borne on a stream suddenly
symbolical of the fact that all things flow; that the ideal, as soon
as it embodies itself in the flesh and in fleshly striving, must
have its bourne and term. Lambinet has vanished and the
lovers are telling an elderly and embarrassed pilgrim from
Woolett this and that futile and degrading fib.

This scene is one of the novelist's high felicities. Nevertheless
in his whole handling of Chad Newsome's story it is possible to
feel a nervous as well as an artistic reticence. From any consummated love-affair James was constitutionally disposed to shy

aside; and although he does in fact in his later work hold considerable traffic in irregular relationships, they are commonly intimated with a deviousness approaching fuss. Equally to be remarked is a sort of subterraneous cunning that lies deep beneath his artistry and appears bent, whenever possible, on letting the male characters off. An infinite apprehensiveness of approach, remorseless testings against one or another demand of a fastidious sensibility—and the situation breaks down, renunciation is accepted or (as we may suspect) achieved. In the next-written novel, *The Wings of the Dove*, there is but one carnal act recorded, and at the end of the story inescapable cogencies —both deeply moral and deeply aesthetic—forbid its ever being repeated. *The Golden Bowl* is to carry the whole predisposition yet further, and a retrospective view from that final elevation must reveal a startling number of male characters whom we would scarcely, if men, wish to resemble, or, if women, plan to have about the house. But James's art distils itself from his necessities, and nowhere more triumphantly than at this point in his career, in a novel in which far more is risked than in *The Ambassadors*, and of which the achievement is much larger if a little less perfect. *The Ambassadors* is surely the finest novel of high comedy in the language. Its successor is a book in which a similar comedy is set at play against a tragic background.

The basis of *The Wings of the Dove* (1902) is a story which many readers find shocking and incredible. Kate Croy and Merton Densher, a young English couple who are in love but without the means to marry comfortably, form a design upon Milly Theale, an American girl of immense wealth and exquisite sensibility whom they know to be suffering from a mortal disease. Densher is to conquer her affections and marry her, so that her wealth may come to the lovers when she presently dies. In the end it is she who conquers him. The discovery of the truth is mortal to her, but she leaves Densher a fortune and he realizes that something has happened which makes it impossible that he should profit by such generosity for the purpose proposed. From the ugly plot against the dying girl James finally educes tragedy. Here is a terrifying vision of the power of evil to lurk, infect, enormously waste, and destroy; but a vision too of the redemptive process which evil evokes and by which it is defeated. For James the Christian religion appears to have meant little more than cathedrals and mild social convenience;

it certainly figures most frequently as a means of withdrawing unwanted members of a house-party from his scene on a Sunday morning, and it seldom plays much part on the occasion of more definitive exits. Yet here, it must be felt, is Christian, not pagan, writing; tragedy, like Shakespeare's, concerned less with happiness and misery than with grace.

The structure of *The Wings of the Dove* dissatisfied its author as notably evidencing a regular weakness, 'the inveterate displacement of his general centre'. The middle of the novel is 'makeshift' and the latter half 'false and deformed':

> This whole corner of the picture bristles with 'dodges' . . . for disguising the reduced scale of the exhibition, for foreshortening at any cost, for imparting to patches the value of presences, for dressing objects in an *air* as of the dimensions they can't possibly have.

This is a regular pattern in James's view of himself. As he works, he is so possessed with the riches of his subject that he is induced to 'overtreat' its earlier stages and so has to make a disagreeably huddled progress at the close. Mr. Edmund Wilson, one of his acutest critics, declines to take this quite at its face value. The foreshortening and the dodges, he suggests, are

> evidently due to James's increasing incapacity for dealing directly with scenes of emotion rather than to the esoteric motives he alleges. And so his curious, constant complaint that he is unable to do certain things because there is no longer space within the prescribed limits of the story is certainly only another hollow excuse: he never seems to be aware of the amount of space he is wasting through the roundabout locutions or quite gratuitous verbiage with which he habitually pads out his sentences—and which is itself a form of staving off his main problems.

It is true that a sort of fending-off action became habitual with James, and sometimes he can be caught as quite simply hating to call a spade a spade. He seems to have supposed that fastidious people don't—and so Densher must turn on not the electric light but 'the white light of convenience'. On the whole however his dealings with the concrete world can be vindicated as finely economical. In the later books this is often achieved through a technique of impressionism. The evocation of Matcham, a great country-house, is here a minor example: 'Once more things melted together—the beauty and the history and the facility and the splendid midsummer glow.' Quite as much as to Kate Croy, material things spoke to James—but spoke principally of the lives with which they were implicated or had been implicated. In the previous book Madame de Vionnet and the order for which she stands are given to us largely in terms of her house and its contents. Even this is done atmospherically. The statements are at once generalized and precise. Or certain broad appearances are suggested, with here and there a congruous specific object sharply lit. In *The Wings of the Dove* there is a companion piece. For Strether we have Densher, and for the first floor in the rue de Bellechasse we have 'the tall rich heavy house at Lancaster Gate':

It was the language of the house itself that spoke to him, writing out for him with surpassing breadth and freedom the associations and conceptions, the ideals and possibilities of the mistress. Never, he felt sure, had he seen so many things so unanimously ugly— operatively, ominously so cruel. . . . He couldn't describe and dismiss them collectively, call them either mid-Victorian or Early—not being certain they were rangeable under one rubric. It was only manifest they were splendid and were furthermore conclusively British. They constituted an order and abounded in rare material— precious woods, metals, stuffs, stones. He had never dreamed of anything so fringed and scalloped, so buttoned and corded, drawn everywhere so tight and curled everywhere so thick. He had never dreamed of so much gilt and glass, so much satin and plush, so much rosewood and marble and malachite. But it was above all the solid forms, the wasted finish, the misguided cost, the general attestation of morality and money, a good conscience and a big balance. These things finally represented for him a portentous negation of his own world of thought—of which, for that matter, in presence of them, he became as for the first time hopelessly aware. They revealed it to him by their merciless difference.

This with its appearance of evocation at leisure is economical, all the same. But more economical still—and major instances of the same power and technique for making a setting dramatic —are certain of the Venetian passages: for example that giving us the Palazzo Leporelli—a Veronese with Milly enthroned; and that in which the sea storm rises and the Piazza San Marco, the 'great social saloon, a smooth-floored, blue-roofed chamber of amenity', shows like 'a great drawing-room, the drawing-room of Europe, profaned and bewildered by some reverse of fortune'.

James is a master of the concisely evocative use of language, and his verbiage has on the whole its chief haven in his characters' talk. He had early formed a tiresome idea of polite conversation, which he supposed to consist in the unflagging endeavour of each participant supremely to stretch the wits of interlocutors by constant recourse to oblique, allusive, and provocatively ambiguous forms of utterance. In the most intimate relationships people must be with each other above all things verbally stimulating. Talk must be encounter, fence, combat—or it must be ballet, classical ballet, but improvised as the dance proceeds. This, which can so fatigue us, seems never to fatigue James. Yet he was perhaps aware of the strained effect which this technique of conversation by shade and nuance and intimation creates, and therefore cultivated a compensatory virtuosity of imagery—imagery often making clear and actual for us colloquies the logical development of which may be somewhat tenuous or elusive. Much, for example, is added to our sense of the reality of Milly's early consultations with Sir Luke Strett by the brilliantly touched-in 'So crystal-clean the great empty cup of attention that he set between them on the table'.

There is a sense in which *The Wings of the Dove* abundantly requires all its richness of facture. Initially conceived as a work of minor compass, it continues through all its elaboration to bear the mark of this intention, and its essential constituents are at times perceptibly thinly spread. Dealing as it does with the international situation, moving as it does about Europe (and that not without glances at America), and turning moreover upon social as well as personal exigencies, it might easily have taken the form of something like a panoramic novel, exploiting a wide diversity of subsidiary persons and contributory occasions. Instead of this it has both a cast and a scenic organization comparable with a play. The effect is at times of a few people being kept rather exactingly on the floor. They are discernibly puffing and blowing, if the truth be told, by the time the curtain falls. There are places in which we feel that the intrigue is being too closely worked, and that the grand strategy alike of James's novel and Kate Croy's plot withdraws behind the elaboration of its tactical manœuvre. Points of very minor significance are elucidated with the same portentous caution and subtlety as matters of the greatest moment. In Max Beerbohm's *A Christmas Garland* there is a little parody, 'The Mote in the Middle

Distance', in which this tendency is exquisitely travestied.
James's later works indeed are pervasively vulnerable to the
parodist; give them only a small twist and they must appear
extremely strange performances, drastic abstractions from common and recognizable human experience. Mr. E. M. Forster
has expressed this view forcibly:

The characters, besides being few in number, are constructed on
very stingy lines. They are incapable of fun, of rapid motion, of
carnality, and of nine-tenths of heroism. Their clothes will not take
off, the diseases that ravage them are anonymous, like the sources
of their income, their servants are noiseless or resemble themselves,
no social explanation of the world we know is possible for them, for
there are no stupid people in their world, no barriers of language,
and no poor. Even their sensations are limited. They can land in
Europe and look at works of art and at each other, but that is all.
. . . They remind one of the exquisite deformities who haunted
Egyptian art in the reign of Akhnaton—huge heads and tiny legs,
but nevertheless charming. In the following reign they disappear.

But if there is much in James's idiosyncrasy that may be ridiculed there is far more in his craft that must be admired. What
particularly astonishes in *The Wings of the Dove* is the manipulation of the 'point of view'. In *The Ambassadors* this is constant.
From start to finish we watch, not so much one mind indeed,
as the play of chosen occasions upon one mind, so that it is
a mind at once open to us and yet keeping its certain inviolate
places—and furthermore periodically part-veiled from us whenever Strether takes on a speaking part. But if *The Ambassadors*
is a complex engine in this regard, *The Wings of the Dove* is far
more so, since its method allows for finely calculated transitions
from one centre of consciousness to another. James works, as
he says in the preface, on 'an elastic but a definite system'. His
main point of concern, in raising his fable from pictorial to
dramatic pitch by revealing now this and now that interior
theatre, must have been in the right fading in and out of the
doomed Milly Theale's consciousness. If Milly is (as Mr.
Edmund Wilson says) 'quite real at the core of the cloudy
integument with which James has swathed her about', the
reason must lie at least partly in the fact that James boldly
and in central places 'goes behind' with her. If we had not
earlier had her consciousness, as he says, 'full blown', it is likely
that she would be too cloudy by a long way, nor would there

be possible the wonderful effect of her proud lonely withdrawal from us as disease increases its hold. She no longer 'comes down', nor may we any longer pay our occasional visits to the high chamber of her secret thought. Yet the main point about Milly's consciousness is that we never penetrate direct into its farther recesses. Only occasionally does some ominous murmur from these carry to places of more public audience. When Milly sits on her alpine height and looks down upon the kingdoms of the earth we must stand back—must stand back with the devoted Mrs. Stringham and guess. What of Milly's consciousness we have is, that is to say, its surface—its surface, like Strether's, as of an exquisitely sensitive reagent to immediate experience. It is possible that we are given too little of the deeper Milly, asked to take her a shade too much on trust, and are conscious as a result that the creating of her is very much a triumph of the Master's conjuring. But she is a peak of that conjuring, and one of those rare characters, presences, call them what we will, that are larger than their containing book. She remains in our minds—to quote Mr. Wilson once more—'as a personality independent of the novel, the kind of personality, deeply felt, invested with poetic beauty and unmistakably individualized, which only the creators of the first rank can give life to'.

9

The Golden Bowl (1904), James's last major performance, is of all his works the most prodigious and enigmatical. Others may be teasing or invite description in terms of paradox. *The Awkward Age* is at once fascinating and almost unreadable, unquestionably tedious and undeniably an absorbing masterpiece. But we are acquainted with other novels like that: *Clarissa*, for instance, or *Ulysses*. And at the end of *The Awkward Age* we are not left in any haunting uncertainty about the book's very meaning. With *The Golden Bowl* we are. It is James's *Hamlet* —and like *Hamlet* is perhaps most honestly explored from the standpoint of an acknowledged intellectual irritation.

Adam Verver is an American millionaire. His fortune is of his own making and now he has no further business concerns but moves about Europe, a widower in early middle-age, collecting works of art. For he has a wonderful plan. He is going to present his native place, American City, with a whole

museum of the world's masterpieces. It is an activity which
many of the great robber barons of industrial America pursued,
but Mr. Verver is distinguished by having himself the finest and
surest taste. Loving and understanding art, he goes about buying it and storing it 'in masses . . . in Paris, in Italy, in Spain, in
warehouses, vaults, banks, safes, wonderful secret places', so
that one day his tremendous museum may suddenly open up
upon what we feel may be a rather bewildered community.
The beginning of the story, however, finds the Ververs established in a fashionable part of London, 'where Mr. Verver had
pitched a tent suggesting that of Alexander furnished with the
spoils of Darius'. Although so passionately attached to art,
Adam Verver appears to have no contact with artists; he gives
enormous sums for the works of those who are dead, but shows
no interest in any who are still engaged in the difficult business
of keeping themselves alive. His social world such as it is (for
he is a very shy man) is simply the best that dollars can buy at
the time. But the grand postulate of the story is his innocence,
and the fact of his moral sensibility as exactly matching his
aesthetic. With life's major issues he has the happiness of being
able to deal as if they were exquisitely fragile collector's pieces,
never doing other than feel his way into a situation with the
delicacy and caution of a creature virtually consisting of
antennae.

From Italy and for his daughter this surprising industrialist
makes a new purchase, Prince Amerigo. It is made a sort of
joke among the characters that the Prince is part of the Verver
collection—for having popes among his ancestors and a cardinal
as a great-uncle he has decidedly the requisite high authenticities.
But at the same time we are to suppose that Maggie Verver,
a creature of the same refined nervous constitution as the father
to whom she is devoted, is in love with her Prince, and that
the Prince as he goes forward to the marriage is wholesomely
attracted by his bride as well as by the untold wealth she brings
along with her. Mr. Verver is now a little lonely and Maggie
sees that there must be another purchase; she decides upon
a certain Charlotte Stant, a former school-fellow now conveniently impoverished. Unfortunately Charlotte has previously
been Prince Amerigo's mistress, and she still has a talent for
the relationship which she is unlikely to let fust in her unused.
Since, after their respective marriages, father and daughter

remain almost completely absorbed in each other, the former lovers are thrown much together. Presently they are committing adultery. But to this ugly word the novel never has recourse, and some early reviewers were cautious enough to take the story as turning upon a merely spiritual infidelity. Certainly James does not intend this. He is draping his table-legs in petticoats, not maintaining the table to be defying nature and floating in air. And indeed the whole book may be declared built up on keeping things nameless; the elder Mr. Newsome's small object of domestic utility and Milly Theale's disease announce the principle of which *The Golden Bowl* is the grand treatment. But if we are by no means conducted into the inner chambers of this liaison we are abundantly entertained in its outer corridors and anterooms. The Prince and Charlotte are not, one judges, very nice people, but at least they have an abundance of nice feelings. The return to their guilty passion is made through a labyrinth of delicately ambiguous impulses and over miles of studiously difficult conversation. It is as if they are conscious of having to be as superb, sublime, and magnificent as the other characters frequently declare them to be. Eventually Maggie discovers the truth and, through much torment of mind, contrives to play a waiting game. The Prince finds out that she has found out, and she finally wins him back simply by ignoring her own knowledge, by giving no sign. Thus Maggie and her father—who has also come to know—triumph in the end. They triumph without a single open reference, even between themselves, to the actual facts of the case.

Many people are unable to read this novel without feeling somewhat at odds with its author. The wickedness of Kate Croy's plan was in its proposal to violate a personality by treating it as an instrument, a means to an end. Prince Amerigo is used in very much the same way by the Ververs, and of Charlotte Stant too the Ververs think essentially as a means—a means to readjusting Adam Verver to the changed situation brought about by his daughter's marriage. It is easy to feel the consummated physical passion of Charlotte and her former lover, even if we find the couple unendearing, as more wholesome than either of the book's legal marriages. But the end proves such a judgement to be dead against James's intention. Mr. Verver, although not an old man, is unable, we are specifically told, to give his wife children—a circumstance which the evident high degree of his psychical concentration upon his daughter may a little help to explain. He knows that Charlotte has married him for money and that she has lived in his own house in covert adultery with his own daughter's husband. And he simply carries her off to America to continue living as his wife. As between this couple at least, there is no question of confession, repentance, reconciliation, forgiveness. It is simply a matter of keeping up social appearances and the old queer canon of reticence—a sort of second-hand aristocratic code that is part of the Verver collection. It is simply this and a certain element of punishment. Adam Verver can still presumably 'take' his native America. But for Charlotte—long expatriate—it appears to be envisaged as a penal settlement.

It is not surprising that there are admirers of *The Wings of the Dove* who yet regard its successor as evincing a sudden winter of the novelist's genius, a winter in which little survives other than his most tiresome idiosyncrasies, limited judgements, and questionable convictions. Something like this view was taken, for example, by Miss Rebecca West in one of the first and ablest appraisals of the whole body of James's work:

He ceased, as time went on, to pay any attention to the emotional values of his stories; it is one of the strangest things about *The Golden Bowl* that the frame on which there hangs the most elaborate integument of suggestion and exposition ever woven by the mind of man is an ugly and incompletely invented story about some people who are sexually mad. . . . Although it is plain that people who buy 'made-up' marriages are more awful than the admittedly awful people who buy 'made-up' ties, they are presented to one as vibrating exquisitely to every fine chord of life, as thinking about each other with the anxious subtlety of lovers, as so steeped in a sense of one another that they invent a sea of poetic phrases, beautiful images, discerning metaphors that break on the reader's mind like the unceasing surf. . . . And to cap it all these people are not even human, for their thoughts concerning their relationships are so impassioned and so elaborate that they can never have had either energy or time for the consideration of anything else in the world. A race of creatures so inveterately specialist as Maggie Verver could never have attained man's mastery over environment, but would still be specialising on the cocoa-nut or some such simple form of diet.

Decidedly *The Golden Bowl* is not good as a novel.

The last point here—the 'inveterate specialisation' of the people,

the manner in which they are sealed off from all the common
traffic of the world like exotic fish in a tank—is the occasion
of an odd anecdote told by Edith Wharton:

> One result of the application of his theories puzzled and troubled
> me. His latest novels, for all their profound moral beauty, seemed to
> me more and more lacking in atmosphere, more and more severed
> from that thick nourishing human air in which we all live and move.
> . . . Preoccupied by this, I one day said to him: 'What was your idea
> in suspending the four principal characters in *The Golden Bowl* in
> the void? What sort of life did they lead when they were not watch-
> ing each other, and fencing with each other? Why have you stripped
> them of all the *human fringes* we necessarily trail after us through life?'
> He looked at me in surprise, and I saw at once that the surprise
> was painful, and wished I had not spoken. I had assumed that his
> system was a deliberate one, carefully thought out, and had been
> genuinely anxious to hear his reasons. But after a pause of reflection
> he answered in a disturbed voice: 'My dear—I didn't know I had!'

This is an interesting story, but it is unnecessary to conclude
from it that the 'void' in which James suspends his characters
is without significance, and it has indeed been interpreted as
representing the disappearance from the modern world of any
sort of tolerably supporting order upon which the sensitive individual may repose. It is certainly arguable that *The Golden
Bowl*, like most of James's later work, veers towards myth; that
'the strangely insulated, shut-off life of the actors' seems to
be exhibited, with some notion of representative significance,
against the background of a 'great historical and geographical
tradition'; and that the irony of spiritual desperation amid
material abundance which is the core of Maggie's position may
have some wide if obscure reference to the plight of the individual caught up in modern acquisitive society. Yet it is to be
doubted whether we shall interpret this novel with any success
on the lines applicable, say, to Dreiser's *An American Tragedy*,
or by maintaining—as Mr. Stephen Spender has done—that
the 'wickedness of the characters lies primarily in their situation'
and that 'the evil . . . is simply the evil of their modern world'.
For James 'evil' decidedly did not mean 'the malaise of our
time', 'the unsolved riddle of social injustice', or anything of the
sort. And of what was actually cardinal in his design it is possible that we may learn something by considering the genesis
of the work.

Progressively absorbed as he was in problems of form, James seems to have been attracted to his story in the first place largely because it presented an interesting pattern. 'The whole situation', he wrote in the first of the two notes preserved to us, 'works in a kind of inevitable rotary way. . . . A necessary basis for all this'—he means for the symmetrical unfolding of his design—'must have been an intense and exceptional degree of attachment between the father and daughter.' Here, in fact we might hazard, is something required by the plot, and in which the author is not proposing to be interested for its own sake. The position is rather like that in which, according to Professor E. E. Stoll, we often find ourselves in regard to Shakespeare. Matter into which we ourselves want to read psychological significance the dramatist is accepting without psychological inquiry, simply for the sake of the action he must develop. There *has* to be an unusual degree of attachment; James creates it with a will—and then, pleased with his success, proceeds to declare the thing beautiful without very much thinking. That we may manage to pity, but certainly not to admire, remains something of which his busy pattern-hunting mind simply remains ignorant.

This way of taking the matter gives us something unsatisfactory indeed, but not an unsatisfactoriness at the heart of the novel. And it is only after we have distinguished how much of the book is being proposed to us—often, no doubt, fondly—as a wholly agreeable superficial *décor*, that we shall have much chance of penetrating to its recesses. That in the *décor* may lurk symbolic depths which James was unaware of is likely enough. But this need not complicate our inquiry.

'The *subject*', a further note declares, 'is really the pathetic simplicity and good faith of the father and daughter in their abandonment.' Here again the proposal is to present persons to be wholly approved, and there is no reason to doubt that James viewed himself as holding to this throughout all the elaboration of the novel. When he introduced the theme of wealth it was almost certainly without any conscious intention of impairing or even complicating this primary response to the Ververs which he is going to solicit from us. Neither Mr. Verver's vast fortune nor his high connoisseurship is required in the basic fable. Although so massively fed into the novel, they are without designed largeness of implication. These things are going to set off the essential pathos and simplicity of the father

and daughter; they are going to make the predatory aspect of
the Prince and Charlotte more plausible; and they are going to
serve for general magnificence. James has no notion that we
respect opulence less than he does—and we are, no doubt,
entitled to feel that this is grossly imperceptive of him. He has
no inkling that our satisfaction with the Verver spectacle has,
like the Bowl, its flaw. Christopher Newman in *The American*
is an odd self-made man; Adam Verver is an incredible one,
violating *decorum* in the old sense, since the character imputed
to him is unrepresentative, and its unrepresentativeness unexplained. Christopher Newman's proposed use of his small pile
appears rather futile; Adam Verver's use of his millions is
enormously so. He hires 'the noble privacy of Fawns' and this
ostentation attracts designing ladies with whom he can't cope.
He has switched from acquiring money to acquiring 'early
Florentine religious subjects' from impoverished noblemen, or
Oriental tiles from Mr. Gutermann-Seuss of Brighton. 'It was
all, at bottom, in him', we are told, 'the aesthetic principle,
planted where it could burn with a cold, still flame.' And
having thus evidently read Pater, Mr. Verver conceives himself 'as equal somehow . . . to the great seers, the invokers and
encouragers of beauty—and he didn't after all perhaps dangle so
far below the great producers and creators'. We may find this
staggering, but James is far from offering it to us other than
with a straight face. The manner of life of Mr. Verver and his
daughter—a fine cultivation of the private life and a public
trafficking, for the ultimate benefit of society, in beautiful
things—represents for James a programme of which they are
very far from needing to feel ashamed. To us the book may seem
to close upon a future for Maggie and her Prince that is likely
to be appallingly empty—however many more *principini* may
arrive on the scene. But this judgement is certainly not being
asked of us; its very possibility appears as unexpected as was
Edith Wharton's question. All this region of the book, then, is
within the field of James's mere idiosyncrasy: his confessed
ability to 'stand a lot of gold', his approval of unlimited leisure,
of complete disregard of speculative or public interests and
responsibilities provided the loss there be gain in the field of
personal relations, of 'the finer discrimination, the deeper sincerity' among an *élite*. We must therefore simply try not to find
distraction and a barrier in matters where James is supposing

common ground and an agreeable unanimity of view. And he
is being rather bland, facile, complacent about all this because it
is remote from the core of his design. Here, so far, is no more than
a pleasing and at the same time dramatically effective setting
for his actual drama. In what is that actual drama to consist?

At its inception it was to be nothing very portentous.
'Dramatic, ironic, . . . compact, *charpenté*, living, touching,
amusing'—these are the epithets with which James at first
defines his project. And perhaps the influence of this tone—of
this 'compositional key', as he liked to say—a little persists in
the novel, to our further confusion of response. But eventually
the drama does become portentous. James had, and knew that
he had, a tragic imagination. He saw life as savage and sinister.
And he proposed to conduct into the presence of this vision,
and set fighting for very survival there, one initially pictured
as owning all the innocence and ignorance of paradise. This
was to be Maggie Verver's assignment—an assignment with
evil, a confrontation with what is below, and just below, civilized
decency. The Prince, although he is himself the agent in
bringing her to this place, is the character in the book who has
the maturest understanding of it. He understands, by birth-
right, this basis of the human situation. 'Everything's terrible,
cara, in the heart of man.' There is a treachery at the core of life,
and it is something other and greater than the agents through
whom it operates. It is a beast crouched in the jungle with
incredible cunning, and one never knows when it may spring.
The most confident words that our moments of joy can utter
may be charged with the irony of its tautened muscles. 'I'm
going to see in Charlotte', Maggie says, '. . . more than I've
ever seen.' Society of course has ways of trying to cope, and the
choric Mrs. Assingham knows all about them. 'The forms are
two-thirds of conduct' and 'What is morality but high intelligence?' She picks up the flawed Bowl and smashes it. And of
all this Maggie realizes the deep immemorial wisdom. The
decorum of appearances must be kept; cry aloud and the
jungle will be howling round you.

> Only at a dread of dark
> Quaver . . .

Meredith's wisdom is James's here. To cling to the surface of
civilization, to preserve the appearance of decency and grace

—yes, to hush things up—these are disciplines good in themselves. Yet it is not here that the final assertion of the book is
designed to lie. How could it be, with the ink scarcely dry upon
The Wings of the Dove? The high correlation, indeed, between
the moral and the aesthetic sensibility, between fine behaviour
and fine feeling, is valuable to us in our worst hour. But
Maggie is to be displayed as having, in the last crisis, another
and immeasurably more powerful resource, selfless love. The
depths that do veritably lie in *The Golden Bowl* are proved by the
emotional pitch to which the story in its crucial places does, and
mysteriously, rise. When these places come we know that the
characters, despite every absurdity and tiresomeness with which
the author's advancing oddity has draped them, are quite real
underneath; are indeed representatively enjoying and suffering human beings. They may be, as somebody has said, rather
presences than persons for a good part of their course—'presences
gliding through the shadow and shimmer of late Turneresque
landscapes'—and they may baffle us by seeming to claim for
sundry minor facets of their being applause which we find small
inclination to give. But they are real in the end because the
world of good and evil in which they finally discover themselves
is real. They are real because James, often in this last phase at
sea in the directing of our superficial sympathies, has a high
command over the farther reaches of moral experience.

10

With *The Golden Bowl* the major phase of James's career closed,
but he remained despite intermittent illness and nervous depression miscellaneously productive throughout the succeeding decade. A visit to America in 1904–5 produced one of
his most remarkable later short stories, 'The Jolly Corner'; a
volume of travel-sketches, *The American Scene* (1907), which is
rich alike in documentary and personal interest; at least part
of the impulse to construct his two volumes of memoirs, *A Small
Boy and Others* (1913) and *Notes of a Son and Brother* (1914); and
the setting for a new novel, brilliant in inception but quickly
losing impetus, the first three books of which, together with some
notes on the projected whole, were published posthumously
as *The Ivory Tower* (1917). James's most important final labours
however were the prefaces and revisions undertaken for the

New York edition of his works (1907–9). Of the prefaces something has already been said. The extensive revisions in which he involved himself both at this time and on earlier occasions testify to the lifelong passion with which he devoted himself to the craft of fiction.

IV · SHAW

GEORGE BERNARD SHAW was born in Dublin in 1856, nine years before his fellow-townsman Yeats and twenty-six before his fellow-townsman Joyce. Yeats's Ireland was not yet discernible. 'My business in life', Shaw was to write, 'could not be transacted . . . out of an experience confined to Ireland. . . . There was no Gaelic League in those days, nor any sense that Ireland had in herself the seed of culture.' Joyce's Dublin, however, was already there. 'A certain flippant futile derision and belittlement that confuses the noble and serious with the base and ludicrous seems to me peculiar to Dublin.' Shaw, whom many were to accuse of just this proclivity, left Dublin rather earlier in youth than Joyce was to do, and since he travelled very light in point of emotional attachments he left it much more effectively. Being disabled from academic accomplishment by the discovery—inconvenient in a schoolboy —that 'pressing people to learn things they do not want to know is as unwholesome and disastrous as feeding them on saw-dust', he had found himself at sixteen in the position of a land agent's junior clerk. His employers were more satisfied with him than he was with them. At twenty he departed to London, determined to write; and in London or near it he continued to live until his death seventy-four years later. His background, although Protestant, was not unlike Joyce's: connexions ranging from persons of social consequence to persons of only vestigial gentility; drink; much music, mainly operatic; family penury implacably advancing year by year. But the Shaw household appears to have been distinguished from the Joyce household and most others by an entire absence of any warmth of feeling between its members. Shaw was a Stephen Dedalus undistracted by the claims of affection or the impulse to rebel. When, in later life, he claimed to be 'a treacherous brute in matters of pure affection' it was to the 'frightful self-sufficiency' induced by this domestic peculiarity that he pointed as a cause. The only relation about whom he liked to talk was his uncle William, who had believed himself to be the Holy Ghost and whose death from heart-failure was precipitated by a gallant attempt to decapitate or strangle himself with a carpet bag. Bertrand Russell records the 'unutterable boredom' with which Mrs. Bernard Shaw would listen to the reiteration of this extravagant anecdote. At least it well illustrated Shaw's general proposition that 'if you cannot get rid of the family skeleton, you may as well make it dance'.

His mother sang. Her devotion to her art was such that when her singing-master departed for London she soon followed, taking her daughters with her. Shaw joined her on his own arrival in 1876, and on her earnings, together with a pound a week remitted by her husband from Dublin, the household contrived to live for many years. Yet mother and son seldom had meals together and never took any interest in each other's affairs—until, indeed, he attended her cremation, an event which he describes in a letter with some reasonable emotion and a blaze of wit. Shaw read in the British Museum, interested himself in politics, became an active Socialist, and entered upon what was to be a long and brilliant career as a public speaker. He wrote, with something like Trollope's regularity of performance, five novels which found no publisher. He had arrived in London only six years after the death of Dickens, and his adoptive countrymen were not yet ripe for fiction which was, in substance, already Shavian. At the same time they might have judged stilted and old-fashioned a style that draws upon the eighteenth century. Whether by luck or cunning, Shaw at the end of the nineteenth century was indeed not much touched by the influence of antecedent nineteenth-century prose, so many esteemed monuments of which are so variously bad. His writing has Augustan purity, sharpened and quickened by the practice of debate. This alone would make something admirable. Shaw was in a position to add to it a play of wit unexcelled in the English language. The first decade of his endeavours to entertain the British public on the strength of these endowments was recompensed, he liked to declare, at the rate of just over ten shillings a year.

His earliest success was as a critic on the *Saturday Review*, to which he was recruited in 1895 under the editorship of Frank

Harris. He had previously found some work both as a book reviewer and as an art critic, and the informal training of his boyhood had enabled him to write fluently and knowledgeably on music in the *Star* where, moreover, his exuberance of entertaining digression makes his notices entirely agreeable to the tone-deaf. But it was in the *Saturday Review* that he found himself. He was an admirable judge of the theatre, and the more effective for being incorruptible. As a critic who was also a playwright, he stood in a morally delicate relationship to the powerful actor-managers of the time, and he never sold them options on works that he had reason to suppose them without any intention to produce. His dealings with the complex world of the London stage fall outside the scope of a brief account of him as a dramatist. But they are well documented and make amusing reading.

Shaw believed the great discovery of his adolescence to have been of the existence within him of moral passion. Of less exalted passion he appears to have had very little. Once or twice he had love made to him in a definitive manner. But he regarded this intimate experience largely as a matter of acquiring information. Long correspondences with Ellen Terry and Mrs. Patrick Campbell suggest that the role of lover came most easily to him at a remove comfortably bridged by the penny post. It is perhaps significant that the correspondence with Mrs. Campbell has itself been dramatized for production on the public stage. The result is diverting but not wholly pleasing.

When just over forty, and after having suffered a severe illness, Shaw married an Irish lady. She combined good family with advanced views, 'cleverness and character', green eyes, and a private fortune which he was fond of insisting to be round the million mark. About the same time his plays had their first successes, and began to earn money which his own skilled management was eventually going to turn into one of the most valuable literary properties of the age. He now abandoned all suggestion of Bohemianism in his manner of life. And although he remained high in the intellectual councils of the Fabian Society and other progressive bodies, his underlying convictions began to undergo radical change. At the same time he devoted less energy to oratory and more to his true profession. *Caesar and Cleopatra*, his first carefully perfected play, was completed in 1898. Nevertheless, like D. H. Lawrence after him, he retained a poor view of the business of being an artist, declaring himself to be, in company with Shelley, 'a social reformer and doctrinaire first, last, and all the time'.

The remainder of Shaw's long life was not eventful. At his death he took pleasure in emphasizing its prosperous, bourgeois, curiously unaesthetic tone by proposing to the British nation as a place of pilgrimage his extremely commonplace house with its extremely commonplace contents. Yet to every controversial subject and in every pronouncement he applied almost to the end the master formula: 'Find the right thing to say, and then say it with the utmost levity.' In critical times his method was felt by many, rightly or wrongly, as an unseasonable clowning; thus, his 'Common Sense About the War', printed in the *New Statesman* in November 1914, suggested to H. G. Wells 'an idiot child laughing in a hospital'. He consistently employed arts of showmanship that are not commonly held becoming in a writer unquestionably eminent. Even those whose debt to Shaw goes beyond that to any other writer may find their idol's insistence on Shaw a little irksome when they sit down to re-read him in the thirty-six volumes of his Collected Works.

2

It is sometimes asserted that Shaw set no great store by his profession as a playwright; that the plays themselves are no more than cleverly and amusingly dramatized illustrations of the doctrines of his prefaces; and that the prefaces are emerging as superior to the plays. But at least it was Shaw's determination that the plays should make their way that brought the prefaces into being at all. English managers fought shy of his work, and he saw that if this state of affairs were not to continue his plays must be read and discussed. But printed plays had a very restricted currency, and he resolved to make his own more attractive to the reader in two ways: by expanding the meagre stage-directions of convention into vivid sketches alike of setting, character, and 'business', and by writing substantial introductory essays which should hold out to the prospective purchaser the bait of something more than he would get in the theatre, if and when the play was produced. The prefaces were written to sell Shaw's plays, even if the plays were written (as, to a varying extent, they certainly were) to sell Shaw's ideas. The

effective basis of all his writing is the debating-hall. But whereas
the prefaces seem to come to us frankly and overwhelmingly
from one corner of the platform, the plays are artistically contrived to give the illusion of the entire cut-and-thrust of the
occasion, together with fair play all round. Shaw's statement
that for art's sake alone he 'would not face the toil of writing
a single sentence' is simply untrue, for the art of the plays is
elaborated not to give us something more persuasive than the
prefaces but simply something more delightful. This does not
mean that the plays have nothing of a preacher's designs upon
us. Every one of them patently has.

These designs were not in themselves out of the way. They
were grounded in all those advanced commonplaces of the age
(then, no doubt, outrages still to the conservative majority)
which belonged to the tradition of Bentham and Mill. Shaw
began by believing that, for the practical purposes of securing
an ordered life for men in society, sufficient truth lies ready to
the hand of educated and reasonable persons, and that this
truth can be successfully recommended to the generality by
exposition and argument. To this end a writer or speaker must
employ all those resources of rhetoric which conduce, in Shaw's
own phrase, to sheer 'effectiveness of statement': defined terms,
clear senses, sustained lucidity, vivid analogy, and an appeal
directed or appearing to be directed not to the emotions but to
the intelligence. Here lay the road of ordered progress in a
democratic country—a progress constantly impeded by forces
which a first faithful scrutiny distinguishes as selfish, hypo-
critical, or even malign, but which analysis will show to be our
common responsibility, since in fact they are the simple product of inefficiencies and stupidities in which we have all acquiesced. These are the leading ideas with which Shaw set out to
establish himself as a playwright in the new European theatre
of Ibsen.

The beginnings of a modern realistic drama in England are
commonly dated from T. W. Robertson's *Caste* in 1867. Certainly when Shaw approached the stage something like Robertson's tradition was being continued by Arthur Pinero and
Henry Arthur Jones—with Jones perhaps a little less indisposed
than Pinero to break away from that still obstinately surviving
convention of an artificial plot which was in fact, under modern
conditions, incompatible with the realistic idea. The arrival of

Ibsen was of decisive importance, and it may be dated from 1889, when *A Doll's House* was played in the translation of William Archer. Two years later J. T. Grein founded the Independent Theatre Society and produced *Ghosts*. Shaw, who was about to publish his *Quintessence of Ibsenism*, proposed to Grein that he should complete for him an abortive play which Shaw had begun in collaboration with Archer some years previously. The result was *Widowers' Houses*, of which Grein contrived two performances in 1892.

Shaw's preface gives a brisk description of how he rehandled this joint venture when he took it over entirely from Archer:

Laying violent hands on his thoroughly planned scheme for a sympathetically romantic 'well made play' of the type then in vogue, I perversely distorted it into a grotesquely realistic exposure of slum landlordism, municipal jobbery, and the pecuniary and matrimonial ties between them and the pleasant people of 'independent' incomes who imagine that such sordid matters do not touch their own lives. The result was revoltingly incongruous. . . . The farcical trivialities in which I followed the fashion of the times . . . became silly and irritating beyond all endurance when intruded upon a subject of such depth, reality, and force as that into which I had plunged my drama.

These self-strictures, abundantly verifiable in the first edition of *Widowers' Houses*, are still to some extent applicable to the final form of the play as printed in *Plays: Pleasant and Unpleasant* (1898). The uncertainty of Shaw's start, like the Laodicean quality in the seriousness of Pinero and Jones, is an index of the contemporary impoverishment of the English stage, and of the confusion into which it was thrown by the new voice from Norway. But about Shaw himself the incongruities in *Widowers' Houses* are yet more informative. Those 'farcical trivialities', 'tomfooleries', and 'silly pleasantries' which he condemns in the early form of his play are in fact the first expression of his authentic dramatic genius. In the first speech in the definitive text an English tourist in Germany proposes to 'do' Frankfurt, where, in addition to a zoo, 'there is a very graceful female statue in the private house of a nobleman', and on the next day Nuremberg, which has the 'finest collection of instruments of torture in the world'. A minute later, scandalized by the relaxed behaviour of a travelling-companion, he declares that 'it may not matter before the natives; but the people who came on

board the steamer at Bonn are English'. And the fact that his
companion has brought only a Norfolk jacket prompts him to
the unanswerable inquiry: 'How are they to know that you
are well connected if you do not shew it by your manners?'
This is in the common tradition of English light social satire.
Almost the whole of the first act, with its tourists authenticating
the merits of their churches in Baedeker and making wary
reconnaissances into each other's social standing, might be
dramatized out of E. M. Forster. The social scene, indeed, lies
a little farther back than in *A Room with a View*. Sartorius the
slum landlord, to whose daughter Blanche the well-connected
Dr. Trench has taken his sudden fancy, arouses no suspicion in
Trench's conventional friend Cokane as a consequence of anything in his manners or bearing; what defines him is the way he
makes his living, and not the extent to which he reveals himself
as having been, or not been, at a permissible school.

But it is not merely the steady amusingness of the first act, as
of much of what follows, which seems at odds with Shaw's main
intention in *Widowers' Houses*. The action must clearly pivot on
the effect upon Trench, and so upon Blanche, of Trench's discovery first of the horrible social evil upon which the girl's
father prospers, and second of the fact that his own income
owns the same tainted source. Elementary dramatic calculation
would seem to require that the lovers should be presented in
a preponderantly sympathetic light. But in fact Trench is helpless, sheepish, and conceited, and Blanche is a disingenuous
girl, out to catch her man by every device of calculated impul-
siveness and false pathos: all these qualities, lest we should miss
them in the dialogue, are rammed home in italic print as we go
along. Both characters are subsequently developed in terms of
a sort of doctrinaire anti-romanticism. Trench's revolt of conscience is an abortive and undignified affair; Blanche's refusal
of him when he gives in is neurotic, petulant, and in key with
the surprising episode in which she is exhibited torturing the
parlourmaid; in their final reconciliation she is merely a shrew
and he feebly and passively libidinous. There is no attempt to
hold a balance between all this frailty and absurdity on the one
hand and any genuine capacity for suffering on the other. Thus
the misery in Sartorius's slums has no power to boomerang on
Sartorius's villa. Shaw has dissipated the central dramatic irony
of his conception in pointlessly ramifying sub-ironic comedy.

He ends up as far from Ibsen as Pinero does in *The Second Mrs. Tanqueray*.

Widowers' Houses betrays uncertainty of intention by admitting inapposite matter in the treatment of a serious theme. Shaw's second play, *The Philanderer*, shows a similar weakness. Offered to Grein in 1893 but not publicly produced until 1905, it is written not in Ibsen's manner but in ridicule of current Ibsenite affectations, with much of its action taking place in an extravagantly conceived Ibsen club, membership of which is restricted to unwomanly women and unmanly men. The characters are well adapted to this almost burlesque purpose, but from the start Shaw is proposing for them a sober representative function which they are quite unfitted to sustain. They typify, his preface tells us, 'the intellectually and artistically conscious classes in modern society'; and we are assured that the scene with which the play opens, the atmosphere in which it proceeds, and the marriage with which it ends are as authentic to these classes as they are unpleasant. This, we must feel, is really to have the characters half-inside Ibsen after all—and very incongruously, since they are equally half-inside English Restoration comedy. Charteris, the Philanderer, indefatigably witty through a variety of manœuvres designed to rid him of a cast mistress (or flirt), is a remote descendant of Etherege's Dorimant, and the theme of sexual relationship as open to scientific experiment, productive of witty debate, and inevitably troubled by the irruptions of simple human nature, evidently belongs to the same tradition. But the characters are neither solid enough for the one kind of drama nor entertainingly wicked enough for the other, and a pervasive lack of definition is made apparent in the single point that we are left unable to decide just what philandering is, and suspecting that Shaw has not decided either. What wears best in the play is its extraneous fun: notably the plight of Dr. Paramore when he receives shattering proof (secured by an Italian who has been feeding beef and alcohol to a camel) that Paramore's Disease does not exist, and that his most interesting patients, far from being at their last gasp, are perfectly healthy people. One of them, Colonel Craven, indignant at having been sentenced to death 'on the strength of three dogs and an infernal monkey', and complaining that he has been induced to do 'a lot of serious thinking and reading and extra church going' which now turns out to have been a waste of time, comes to us, as we begin to re-read the plays, with the effect of the first notes in a familiar and delectable symphony. And the whole comedy, although it may survive, in Max Beerbohm's image, more as a matter of sticks than of rockets, is closer to the line of Shaw's true development than is the far stronger and more startling play which immediately succeeded it.

3

Mrs. Warren's Profession, again written for the Independent Theatre Society, proved so difficult to steer past the censorship that it achieved only technical copyright representation until 1902, when the Stage Society managed two restricted performances. Shaw describes it in his preface as representing a return to the vein he had worked in *Widowers' Houses*, and as being upon 'a social subject of tremendous force'. The operative word is 'social'. He is concerned to show prostitution, as he was concerned to show the slums, in its aspect as an economically determined disorder. He calls us into his theatre, indeed, that we may be guilty people sitting at a play. But what we are to acknowledge is not an evil in man's heart. It is a 'defective social organisation' for which the remedy lies ready to man's hand. This emphasis dictates the primary contrast drawn between Mrs. Warren and her daughter Vivie. In character they are not dissimilar. Each has grit and strong practical sense. But Vivie has been to Newnham and owns a trained mind, capable of standing back from and analysing sentiment; she has tied with the third wrangler and can earn a living as an actuary tomorrow. Her mother as a girl belonged to no such tiny minority; she had to accept that 'the only way for a woman to provide for herself decently is for her to be good to some man that can afford to be good to her'. Grasping this early, Mrs. Warren has risen rapidly in her profession; in fact we are asked a little to stretch our imaginations and to believe that in her forties she has become the manager and part-owner of successful brothels all over the Continent. This is the revelation that awaits Vivie, and it is certainly more shattering than any that could break upon the daughter of a mere slum landlord like Sartorius. But there is a possibility yet more dire. Mrs. Warren in the early stages of her career has necessarily been abundantly promiscuous. Some of her old male friends are still around her now. Vivie may find herself being wooed by a half-brother, or even by her own father.

This time, we feel, the Ibsenite has really provided himself with the quintessential material of an Ibsen play. What may result is melodrama, and what ought to result is tragedy. But that Shaw—as one of his biographers declares—never planned a play in advance seems an assertion quite untenable in face of the opening of *Mrs. Warren's Profession*. He does look ahead —and his initial impulse is immediately to secure himself against the possibility of having any substantial tragic effect on his hands later on. No more than in *Widowers' Houses* has he the instinct to deal in anything of the sort. The first action of Vivie, fresh from Newnham, is to give the feebly romantic Praed a paralysing handshake, declare her intention to 'do some law, with one eye on the Stock Exchange', and add that, when tired of working, she likes 'a comfortable chair, a cigar, a little whisky, and a novel with a good detective story in it'. We might be back with *The Philanderer* and listening to one of the young ladies of the Ibsen club. Vivie has typed herself as briskly as Hotchkiss in *Getting Married* is going to do when he whips out a visiting card inscribed 'The Celebrated Coward'. And Shaw at once proceeds to a further precaution against our later responding to his people with sympathetic concern rather than with interest. Frank Gardner, the son of an absurd and formerly licentious clergyman who may or may not be Vivie's father, begins, as soon as he steps on the stage, to vindicate the initial stage direction which calls him an 'entirely good-for-nothing young fellow'. He is further described as possessing 'agreeably disrespectful manners', and in his exemplification of this trait he is in fact establishing an important Shavian type. For Shaw —as Beerbohm observes—is fond of 'alternately impudent and whining young men . . . all of them as destitute of hearts as they are of manners, and all of them endowed with an equal measure of chilly sensuality'. Vivie has from the first a disenchanted view of Frank, who in a perfectly good-natured way is after any money she may have, and she has little difficulty in deciding that their dubiously fraternal relationship brings him as close as she wants him. Fortunately or unfortunately, all that she has to withdraw from in arriving at this attitude appears to be a patch or two of spooning and baby-talk not remotely approximated to the rest of her character. In her mother's old friend and partner Sir George Crofts there is an effective exhibition of lust. In Vivie herself, before she realizes that her mother and Crofts are in active business still, there is an exhibition of compassion which is the more moving through having as its background the general hardness and severity of her disposition. But we leave her as we have been carefully invited to find her, and when she buries herself luxuriously in her actuarial calculations as the curtain falls we are conscious that she has experienced horror and a sense of contamination, indeed, but not that she has seen the destruction of anything that she has a disposition to value and respond to.

Yet as soon as we have acquiesced in its radical and deliberate abnegation of tragic effect we shall acknowledge *Mrs. Warren's Profession* as an original and memorable play. The latter part of the second act, in which Vivie's icy and head-on counter-attack upon her mother's attempted assumption of authority precipitates revelation, is a passage of concentrated dramatic exposition such as Shaw is never to excel. 'Who are you? What are you?' Vivie demands, and is almost immediately brought hard up against the whole problem of moral responsibility. She protests: 'People are always blaming their circumstances for what they are. I don't believe in circumstances. The people who get on in this world are the people who get up and look for the circumstances they want, and, if they can't find them, make them.' But Mrs. Warren has herself got on in the world, and precisely by adopting this programme. Together with her sister Liz (now leading a highly respectable retired life in Winchester, close to the cathedral) she rebelled against one form of the ruthless exploitation of girls (a third sister had died from the effects of a twelve-hour day in a white-lead factory, although she had 'only expected to get her hands a little paralyzed') and accepted another kind of exploitation in which there was some future for a girl who kept her head and formed habits of industry and thrift. A brothel is a much better-conducted place than a factory or a scullery: 'None of our girls were ever treated as I was treated in the scullery of that temperance place.' On the other hand the profession is not to be set in a glamorous light: 'It's not work that any woman would do for pleasure, goodness knows.' There is even something at fault about the system that produces it:

Of course it's worth while to a poor girl, if she can resist temptation and is good-looking and well conducted and sensible. It's far better than any other employment open to her. I always thought that oughtn't to be. It c a n ' t be right, Vivie, that there shouldn't be better opportunities for women. I stick to that: it's wrong. But it's so, right or wrong; and a girl must make the best of it.

To Vivie's inquiry as to whether she does not feel ashamed, she replies on the same easy level:

Well, of course, dearie, it's only good manners to be ashamed of it: it's expected from a woman. Women have to pretend to feel a great deal that they don't feel. . . . What's the use in such hypocrisy? If people arrange the world that way for women, there's no good pretending that it's arranged the other way. I never was a bit ashamed really. I consider that I had a right to be proud that we managed everything so respectably.

But all this reasonableness in Mrs. Warren is far from meaning that she is not deeply corrupted. Now a prosperous woman, she continues to run her brothels because they bring in money, and money is something that she likes. 'And what else is there for me to do? The life suits me: I'm fit for it and not for anything else. If I didn't do it somebody else would; so I don't do any real harm by it.' Shakespeare's Pompey Bum could not produce better logic than this, and Mrs. Warren like Pompey is funny in her wickedness. At the same time she is very adequately horrifying—as in the passage near the end of the play in which she addresses to her daughter, all unconsciously, what must have been her stock speech for procuring girls for her establishments.

4

Shaw followed his three unpleasant or 'propaganda' plays with four pleasant ones: *Arms and the Man, Candida, You Never Can Tell,* and *The Man of Destiny* (rightly subtitled 'A Trifle'). All were designed to be viable in the West End theatre; all rely upon a light and witty presentation of more or less discreetly chosen heterodoxies, whether sentimental, moral, or merely theatrical; and the first, at least, has very little substance.

Arms and the Man (1894) belongs to the same year as Anthony Hope's *The Prisoner of Zenda.* It presents a Bulgaria into which such a novel could be introduced with great acceptance, since it represents the more polite inhabitants as having begun to

acquire, together with some material tokens of western civilization, the stock western romantic attitudes to both war and love.
Bluntschli, who is filling in time as a mercenary soldier until
he inherits his father's hotels in Switzerland, has other ideas—
asserting, for example, that soldiers are quite often frightened,
and that during an engagement chocolate is likely to be more
useful than cartridges. Shaw wrote more amusing plays, but
no play that is so merely amusing. Yet there was a considerable
disposition to regard it as shocking or even disgraceful. The
Prince of Wales, although perhaps unacquainted with Thomas
Rymer's censure of the dramatic character of Iago as violating
the *decorum* of the soldier, was outraged on similar grounds, and
gravely supposed that the author must be mad.[1]

Candida is more important both in itself and for English
theatrical history. It had only provincial performance (1895)
until 1904, when Harley Granville-Barker persuaded J. E.
Vedrenne, then managing the Royal Court Theatre, to present
it in half a dozen matinee performances, with Granville-Barker
himself in the part of Marchbanks. The enterprise met with
modest success, and Vedrenne and Granville-Barker were
encouraged to enter into a partnership. This lasted until the
summer of 1907, and asserted, both in choice of plays and in
methods of production, standards for which playgoers had
hitherto been obliged to cross the Channel. In *Candida* itself
there was much that was calculated to please the simplest
Victorian sentiment for 'domestic drama'. Charles Wyndham,
who as a popular actor of the time must have been well up in
such feelings, is reported as moved to tears by Shaw's reading
of the final scene. Here Candida vindicates our expectations
of one in whom 'amused maternal indulgence' is the habitual
expression by sending packing in a kindly way the eighteen-
year-old poet who has declared himself in love with her, and by
forgiving, equally kindly, the clerical husband whose insensitive-
ness and lack of inner security have betrayed him into handling
the situation ineptly. The play is deftly built upon paradoxes
which come well within the scope of theatrical representation
and which lead to a denouement of perfect dramatic elegance.
James Morell, the tirelessly active Christian Socialist incumbent
of a north-east London parish, appears a strong man and is in

[1] As Yeats told this story, it was the Duke of Edinburgh who was outraged,
and the Prince of Wales was 'very pleasant'.

fact 'a great baby'. He can labour honestly to secure happiness for others, but it is on the unexpressed and unconscious condition that happiness is adequately laid on for himself. Eugene Marchbanks, the poet, is immature, emotional, hysterical, and cowardly, but there is ready to come to birth in him that power of renouncing personal happiness in the interest of impersonal purpose which is always to be, for Shaw, the mark of strength and greatness. Candida, ironically admitting a sort of auction between the men, listens to her husband desperately clinging to his public sense of himself and offering his strength for her defence and his authority and position for her dignity. Marchbanks offers his weakness, his desolation, his heart's need. Candida is deceived by neither bid, and when she says 'I give myself to the weaker of the two' it is Marchbanks who understands what she means.

Shaw has a much better knowledge of clergymen—or at least of accomplished platform-speakers in elevated causes—than he has of poets. Morell is entirely convincing within the conventions of the play; he is always limited, sometimes absurd, never contemptible. Marchbanks is patchy. A swift sensitiveness of response to others and an understanding of the workings of their emotions are not, it seems, sufficient endowment for a stage poet, and Shaw provides his Shelleyan youth with an outfit of poetical sentiments and with chunks of poetical prose neither of which have worn at all well. We must think it strange that one who began his career as professional critic of one art after another, and ended it as himself the greatest living exponent of a major artistic form, should be almost uniformly unconvincing in the presentation of artists of any sort. It is perhaps because he never very effectively made up his mind about the nature of artistic creation. One of his conclusions here appears to be that the artist describes new countries but is himself no colonist. Later, when Shaw comes to occupy himself with theories of evolution, he makes this persuasion play its part in his picture of the workings of sexual selection. It is possible to interpret Candida's choice as already foreshadowing this. If there is something of a special puzzle in her having a father so extremely vulgar as the entertaining Mr. Burgess, she is at least his true daughter in being wholly philistine. This appears the more clearly because she does, with all her compassionateness, so beautifully live up to her name. Her talk makes it patent that

Marchbanks's poetry is as much 'moonshine' to her as Morell's speech-making is harmless vanity. She pets Marchbanks in his character as a forlorn boy, but in his poethood he is at once meaningless to her and dangerous. In sticking to her husband she is both obeying her dominant maternal instinct and remaining with a reliable man, whose children will go to more reliable schools than Eton and there learn reliable ways—only taking a little time off from cricket, perhaps, to read by a river's side the verses of mighty poets in their misery dead. Between woman as *magna mater* and man as artist there is a conflict of creative modes. The idea lies only in the hinterland of *Candida*, but eventually Shaw enunciates it clearly enough. It is to become obsessional with the great English writer of the succeeding generation, D. H. Lawrence.

We tend to remember *Candida* as a more or less serious play in the course of which we have been lavishly refreshed with wit. *You Never Can Tell* (written 1895–6, produced 1899) leaves the memory only of something gloriously funny. But it has its own serious element, the necessary extrication of which from the general hilariousness of the piece makes a tricky problem in production. Confronted with mere print, however, we can with adequate gravity exhibit Gloria Clandon as a transitional figure between Vivie Warren and the heroine of *Man and Superman*, Ann Whitefield. Although her background is not Newnham but Madeira, Gloria has been so effectively indoctrinated with the new feminism by her mother, the celebrated authoress of *Twentieth Century Children*, that not Vivie herself could have been more icily unresponsive to the advances of an enterprising dentist. 'Let me say at once, Mr. Valentine, that pretty speeches make very sickly conversation. Pray let us be friends, if we are to be friends, in a sensible and wholesome way. . . . I do not think the conditions of marriage at present are such as any self-respecting woman can accept.' Even the outrageous suggestion that she is a feminine prig she receives 'with elaborate calm, sitting up like a High-school-mistress posing to be photographed'. But when the dentist—who regards himself with some justification as skilled in 'the duel of sex'—at last scores a hit, it is to discover in Gloria, after she has experienced a brief bewilderment and shame, a duellist of sex who can plainly take him on left-handed. Valentine understands both the technique of romantic love-making and how to adapt that technique to the special case of the New Woman. At the same time, like Vivie's Frank Gardner, he is a conscious and confessed fortune-hunter taking licence from the tradition of Gilbertian comedy. But he is also in love—and finding himself in the grip of an insensate and depersonalizing biological process is only less terrifying than finding that Gloria is in its grip too. A generation nursed on *The Rainbow* is scarcely likely to find this, or any of its derivatives in later Shaw, precisely strong meat—or any sort of wonderful banishing of nonsense about how sex really takes us. But, as with a great deal else in Shaw, the waning of our sense of revelation admits a livelier sense of the vivacity with which the thing is done, so that with the passing of the years the play has probably gained in unity of tone. Its materials are quite conventional: the disconcerting and disconcerted long-lost father, the younger children as *enfants terribles*, the rapid farcical ending with music, dancing, and false noses, the comic waiter pottering in and out. But Philip Clandon, at least, is endowed with a wit so sparkling that he remains far the most agreeable of Shaw's exercises in juvenile impudence, and the unfailingly tactful William, whose favourite aphorism gives the play its title, is the adequate Divine Providence of this wholly comic world.

5

The Devil's Disciple (completed in 1897 and produced in New York in the same year) is a different sort of ingenious transmutation of a popular theatrical kind. Set in New Hampshire during the War of Independence, it presents the familiar spectacle of the black sheep of a family discovering in himself, at a moment of crisis, an unsuspected capacity for heroic action. Richard Dudgeon is a man in embittered revolt against not the English but the puritanism, in large part degenerate and horrible, in which he has been brought up. He has just witnessed the hanging as a rebel of his reprobate uncle Peter, and on this occasion has sent to his dying father the message that 'he would stand by his wicked uncle, and stand against his good parents, in this world and the next'. On coming home to take up his patrimony he is treated as wholly of the Devil's dominion, and he accepts the character with *panache*. But when the English troops arrive and he is seized in mistake for the minister, Anthony Anderson, whom they propose to hang, he conceals

his true identity and does his best to ensure that Anderson shall
escape. His arrest takes place in the presence of Anderson's
young wife Judith, who makes the conventional romantic
assumption that Dudgeon must be in love with her. Dudgeon's
blank disavowal of anything of the sort is the point at which the
play parts company with popular melodrama. He puts forward
a public motive:

> RICHARD. . . . They are determined to cow us by making an
> example of somebody on that gallows to-day. Well, let us cow them
> by showing that we can stand by one another to the death. That
> is the only force that can send Burgoyne back across the Atlantic and
> make America a nation.
>
> JUDITH (*impatiently*). Oh, what does all that matter?
>
> RICHARD (*laughing*). True: what does it matter? what does any-
> thing matter? You see, men have these strange notions, Mrs.
> Anderson; and women see the folly of them.

But the truth lies deeper than this, and Dudgeon presently
discovers and declares it:

> If I said—to please you—that I did what I did ever so little for
> your sake, I lied as men always lie to women. You know how much
> I have lived with worthless men—aye, and worthless women too.
> Well, they could all rise to some sort of goodness and kindness when
> they were in love (*the word love comes from him with true Puritan scorn*).
> That has taught me to set very little store by the goodness that only
> comes out red hot. What I did last night, I did in cold blood, caring
> not half so much for your husband or (*ruthlessly*) for you (*she droops,
> stricken*) as I do for myself. I had no motive and no interest: all I can
> tell you is that when it came to the point whether I would take
> my neck out of the noose and put another man's into it, I could not
> do it. I don't know why not: I see myself as a fool for my pains;
> but I could not and I cannot.

Judith has no understanding of all this, and when she sums it up
as meaning simply that he does not love her, he is revolted.
Meanwhile his action has stirred Anderson to exchange his
Bible for his pistols. The tables are in consequence turned upon
the English at the eleventh hour. Their capitulation is in sight
and they have to let Dudgeon—now condemned in his true
identity—stand down from the gallows. In the last stages of the
play the tone is skilfully changed through the prominence given
to the English General Burgoyne, who conducts the whole
affair with urbane wit. Anxious to get the distasteful routine

execution over, he has murmured 'We must not detain Mr. Dudgeon'. And when Anderson rushes in at the first stroke of twelve, thanking God that he is in time, Burgoyne glances at his watch and says that it has been in ample time, since he would never dream of hanging any gentleman by an American clock.

It was part of Shaw's showmanship to invite from time to time debate as to whether his plays were not better than Shakespeare's. That they are in some regards very like Shakespeare's is apparent even in *The Devil's Disciple*, although it is not an important work. The characters are closely related to the popular theatrical stereotypes of the age. They step in and out of their merely conventional shells, often without much psychological coherence or plausibility, in the interest of the quite new designs and purposes which the dramatist is pursuing. And similarly with the situations. These are nearly all familiar in the vulgar theatre, and are again exploited in the creating of something highly individual. This individuality is that of a contemplative spirit. There is a current of thought beneath the sparkling surface of the play which never diffuses itself away in the individual action but flows on to break surface in later work where, in turn, other at first imperceptible currents begin to run. Richard Dudgeon stands beneath the gibbet throughout a scene which is a theatrically brilliant compost of seemingly incompatible tragic and comic effects. But the point of dramatic growth lies in Dudgeon's character and motive. We see that the anti-romantic is himself a romantic leaning over backwards; that this posture and temperament are not the best calculated for effective action; and that Parson Anderson is likely to be our best man in a tight place. But we also see a man performing a good deed in a manner that is mysteriously gratuitous. Dudgeon acts spontaneously from a nature which has developed under certain absolute imperatives. And thus although he is a vital being to whom the prospect of death is an agony, his decision cannot properly be called the issue of moral struggle. In fact we are being invited to agree that virtue is a possession rather than an achievement.

This proposition, although it would seem unpromising for drama, is at once carried straight through by Shaw to a far greater play. *Caesar and Cleopatra*, not professionally produced until 1906, was completed in 1898.

6

Shaw's Caesar is clearly designed, in the first place, to stand in strong dramatic—or extra-dramatic—contrast to Shakespeare's Antony. Shakespeare sets beside Cleopatra a romantic voluptuary, ready to sacrifice an empire to her. Shaw provides her with what Hamlet sought: a man who is not passion's slave —and one willing, during a difficult campaign, to give what time he can to her sadly neglected moral and political education. It cannot, it seems, be maintained that there is much historical warrant for this view of the situation. Although Shaw believed himself to have discovered the lineaments of his hero in Mommsen, and defended him in controversy with all the dexterity one might expect, a Caesar who almost forgets to say good-bye to his little pupil before departing for Rome is not easy to reconcile with one who in fact caused the lady to be transported thither and provided with an establishment in his own palace. In Shaw's play Caesar's susceptibility to the charm of women has become, like some of his actions in Gaul, no more than a momentary and disturbing memory. And if he remains recognizably the conqueror of legend, aloof as Shakespeare's Caesar when he declares himself 'constant as the northern star', he is, too, Shakespeare's Brutus when he takes his instrument from the sleeping Lucius. Magnanimity is difficult to exhibit on a stage; in the chill wind of dramatic history there rattle the skeletons of innumerable perished tragedies of admiration. It is astonishing that Shaw, starting from the postulate that greatness of mind, when it has simply happened in an individual, cannot unhappen or be troubled, and is in fact the equivalent of 'enchanted sword, superequine horse and magical invulnerability', should be wholly successful in giving his Caesar the stature he designs for him.

And it is done without poetry. In the first scene (as in performance it became), where Caesar, believing himself alone, greets the Sphinx as like himself a stranger to the race of men, the actor has to contend with that uncertainty of accent which is so often evident when Shaw attempts elevation of style. But comedy can be itself a sort of poetry:

CAESAR. . . . . Sphinx, Sphinx: I have climbed mountains at night to hear in the distance the stealthy footfall of the winds that chase your sands in forbidden play—our invisible children, O Sphinx, laughing in whispers. My way hither was the way of destiny; for I am he of whose genius you are the symbol: part brute, part woman, and part god—nothing of man in me at all. Have I read your riddle, Sphinx?

THE GIRL (*who has wakened, and peeped cautiously from her nest to see who is speaking*). Old gentleman.

CAESAR (*starting violently, and clutching his sword*). Immortal gods!

THE GIRL. Old gentleman: don't run away.

CAESAR (*stupefied*). 'Old gentleman: don't run away'!!! This! to Julius Caesar!

Cleopatra—thus revealed snuggled up against her favourite small Sphinx in the desert—rapidly displays an imperfect sense of the responsibilities of queenship. Being descended from the Nile, she is entitled to do what she likes, so she looks forward to terrifying the nurse who has terrified her, to poisoning the slaves and seeing them wriggle, and—later, this, when the full possibilities of royalty have come home to her—to a succession of handsome lovers whom she will eventually cause to be whipped to death. Caesar is one whom the thought of vengeance fills with horror and who is incapable of resentment. 'O thou foolish Egyptian,' he says to Pothinus, 'what have I to do with resentment? Do I resent the wind when it chills me, or the night when it makes me stumble in the darkness?' But although he is so remote from this potentially vicious child, he interrupts her fantasies to wonder, sensibly and kindly, why she is not at home and in bed. Cleopatra, who has probably never encountered a preponderantly rational being before, is soon enormously impressed, and later gets great satisfaction from playing Caesar to her own court.

But Caesar has no illusions about his success as an educator. When Cleopatra contrives the treacherous assassination of a prisoner whom he regards as a guest, he is angry but not surprised, and her attempt to justify herself educes from him one of the central speeches of the play:

CLEOPATRA (*vehemently*). Listen to me, Caesar. If one man in all Alexandria can be found to say that I did wrong, I swear to have myself crucified on the door of the palace by my own slaves.

CAESAR. If one man in all the world can be found, now or forever, to know that you did wrong, that man will have either to conquer the world as I have, or be crucified by it. (*The uproar in the streets again reaches them.*) Do you hear? These knockers at your gate are also believers in vengeance and in stabbing. You have slain their leader: it is right that they shall slay you. . . . And then in the name of that right (*he emphasizes the word with great scorn*) shall I not slay them for murdering their Queen, and be slain in my turn by their countrymen as the invader of their fatherland? Can Rome do less then than slay these slayers, too, to shew the world how Rome avenges her sons and her honor. And so, to the end of history, murder shall breed murder, always in the name of right and honor and peace, until the gods are tired of blood and create a race that can understand.

Caesar speaks in the same accent when the great library of Alexandria goes up in flames; to the agonized scholar's 'What is burning there is the memory of mankind' he replies 'A shameful memory. Let it burn.' And when asked, because he has made a realistic appreciation of a difficult military situation, 'Does Caesar despair?' he answers 'He who has never hoped can never despair.' That speeches of this sort carry themselves triumphantly in the theatre in the middle of constant hilarity is an index of the almost entire success with which Shaw has created his Caesar on his lonely eminence. The trick is performed by never for a moment letting the eminence appear a pedestal. Caesar moves about freely and without a trace of stiffness; among the things he is incapable of resenting we must number the finding himself amid such a crush of persons framed entirely for our amusement. Shaw, who sometimes subscribed to the fancy that nature, after a time-lag, copies the creations of art, was to persuade himself in old age that one or two real Caesars were appearing in this earthly theatre. But in truth the gods were not yet tired of blood, and no new race had been created.

Cleopatra, sorry to lose Caesar but glad he will not be coming back, is left awaiting the arrival of Mark Antony. She is a less wholly undesirable queen than when we first met her, but she remains an unimpressive testimony to the powers of education. The next play, *Captain Brassbound's Conversion* (1900), might almost be intended to redress a balance here, since it accords the voice of reason, or of reasonableness, the triumph commemorated in its title. The simplest of Shaw's comic moralities, it takes its origin from the observation that 'a tranquil woman can go on sewing longer than an angry man can go on fuming'. Its setting is lifted with unashamed efficiency from a travel

book by Cunninghame Graham. An English judge, on holiday
with his sister-in-law Lady Cicely Waynflete in Morocco,
employs as escort a certain Captain Brassbound, who is in fact
a pirate or smuggler. Brassbound proves, moreover, to be the
judge's nephew, determined to hand over the travellers to
fanatical tribesmen in order to avenge an injustice which he
believes to have been done to his mother. But Lady Cicely is a
woman who combines unshakeable aristocratic self-confidence
with so much spontaneous kindliness, practical good-sense,
and—what is the salt of the character—unfailing guile and
unscrupulousness, that in no time she is running Brassbound's
crew and Brassbound himself on improved hygienic and moral
principles respectively. In the last act an American gunboat
turns up, so that it is now the pirates who are in a tight place.
Lady Cicely is as competent at baffling the nonsense called
justice as she has been at baffling the equal nonsense calling
itself revenge, and after a brief romantic passage between
Brassbound and herself—perhaps more conformable to theatrical
expectation than to the logic of the play—the characters go
their several ways.

Nothing of this turning melodrama to comedy, and comedy
to sermon, holds anything very fresh in itself, and we begin
to be aware of areas of Shaw's dramaturgy that are constructed
on frugal principles. The Cockney pirates will be reproduced
in the banditti of *Man and Superman*; and Brassbound, appearing
before the American officers suddenly resplendent in the clothes
of an ambassador, repeats out of *Widowers' Houses* an effect
which will be again repeated in *Pygmalion*. The strength of the
play lies in the function of the wit. The characters are endowed
with a form of repartee which, in addition to its power to disconcert an interlocutor and set his behaviour and sentiments in
a ridiculous light, progressively reveals in the speaker himself
a configuration of traits at once unexpected and plausible.
Everything that is funny appears to become informative as well.
This limited but authentic psychological basis of the entertainment lends it a vitality which summary description scarcely
suggests.

7

Man and Superman (1905) belongs, like the *Futurist Manifesto*
of which Marinetti was to deliver himself a few years later, to

the first great age of the motor-car. Such action as the play possesses turns upon a flight and pursuit across Europe in two of these exciting new conveyances. In the second act the curtain actually rises upon a 'thousand pound' automobile broken down in the centre of the stage, and falls as the same vehicle, with motility restored, 'plunges forward' into the wings. In the first act, contrastingly, it has risen upon a study 'handsomely and solidly furnished' with busts of John Bright and Mr. Herbert Spencer, enlarged photographs of Huxley and George Eliot, and autotypes of allegories by Mr. G. F. Watts. A stage-direction tells us that on the 'threshold of a drama of ideas' an accurate sense of period is essential, and that Roebuck Ramsden, the owner of these artistic treasures, was born in 1839. In one aspect *Man and Superman* is concerned with prophesying change in terms of the largest of time-scales, and is in fact a prologue to *Back to Methuselah*. But in another aspect it is designed to exhibit revolutions in attitude and sentiment conceived of as actually having occurred within a generation: the generation between Ramsden, 'a Unitarian and Free Trader from his boyhood and an Evolutionist from the publication of *The Origin of Species*', and Jack Tanner, the Socialist intellectual and author of the—to Ramsden—scandalous and abominable *Revolutionist's Handbook*.

Tanner is an ideologue and a chatterbox, but also 'a sensitive susceptible, exaggerative earnest man'. Ann Whitefield, who owns an answering vitality unaccompanied by the slightest interest in abstract ideas, has contrived to be made the ward of Tanner and Ramsden jointly. From the start she has marked down Tanner as her husband. Tanner, although he never tires of denouncing the monstrous duplicity of Ann's professions of submissiveness to the wishes alike of her lately deceased father and of her entirely negative mother (which she has a genius for inventing on the spot), is for long unaware of her real design. He maintains a cocksure insistence that Ann will marry his friend Octavius Robinson, who is desperately and romantically in love with her. We are asked to believe that Octavius—Ann's Ricky-ticky-tavy—is a poet. In fact he is throughout the play the merest sentimental cipher, unendowed even with the conventional poeticizing vein of Marchbanks in *Candida*. Tanner's first bravura speeches—and these form the recurrent highlights of the play—are devoted to enforcing upon Octavius his theory

of the implacable hostility which must subsist between woman
and artist. A woman takes care of any man only as a soldier
takes care of his rifle or a musician of his violin. 'The whole
purpose of Nature embodied in a woman' is to enslave a man:

OCTAVIUS. What matter, if the slavery makes us happy?

TANNER. No matter at all if you have no purpose of your own,
and are, like most men, a mere breadwinner. But you, Tavy, are an
artist: that is, you have a purpose as absorbing and as unscrupulous
as a woman's purpose.

OCTAVIUS. Not unscrupulous.

TANNER. Quite unscrupulous. The true artist will let his wife
starve, his children go barefoot, his mother drudge for his living at
seventy, sooner than work at anything but his art. To women he is
half vivisector, half vampire. He gets into intimate relations with
them to study them, to strip the mask of convention from them, to
surprise their inmost secrets, knowing that they have the power to
rouse his deepest creative energies, to rescue him from his cold
reason, to make him see visions and dream dreams, to inspire him,
as he calls it. . . . In the rage of that creation he is as ruthless as the
woman, as dangerous to her as she to him, and as horribly fascinating. Of all human struggles there is none so treacherous and remorseless as the struggle between the artist man and the mother woman.
Which shall use up the other? that is the issue between them. And
it is all the deadlier because, in your romanticist cant, they love one
another.

In the middle of the first act this predominant theme is
brilliantly diversified by another. Violet, the unmarried sister
of Octavius, is discovered as having visited an obstetrician.
There is general horror and indignation, coupled with demands
that the 'scoundrel' be found and forced to marry her. It is a
fine rhetorical chance for Tanner:

TANNER. . . . What would you not give, Tavy, to turn it into a
railway accident, with all her bones broken, or something equally
respectable and deserving of sympathy?

OCTAVIUS. Don't be brutal, Jack.

TANNER. Brutal! Good Heavens, man, what are you crying for?
Here is a woman whom we all supposed to be making bad water
color sketches, practising Grieg and Brahms, gadding about to
concerts and parties, wasting her life and her money. We suddenly
learn that she has turned from these sillinesses to the fulfilment of
her highest purpose and greatest function—to increase, multiply
and replenish the earth. And instead of admiring her courage and

rejoicing in her instinct; instead of crowning the completed womanhood and raising the triumphal strain of 'Unto us a child is born:
unto us a son is given', here you are—you who have been as merry
as grigs in your mourning for the dead—all pulling long faces and
looking as ashamed and disgraced as if the girl had committed the
vilest of crimes.

RAMSDEN (*roaring with rage*). I will not have these abominations
uttered in my house . . . .

OCTAVIUS. But who is the man? He can make reparation by
marrying her; and he shall, or he shall answer for it to me . . . .

TANNER. So we are to marry your sister to a damned scoundrel by
way of reforming her character! On my soul, I think you are all mad.

But presently the tables are turned upon Tanner. When he
offers Violet his public congratulations on her action, she feels
more insulted than by all the reproaches of her family, and
announces that she has in fact contracted a marriage which she
has reasons for keeping private for a time. Tanner has jumped
to conclusions like the rest. In the later course of the action we
discover that Violet's husband is a young American totally
dependent on a self-made Irish immigrant father who is determined that he shall marry a woman with a title. Violet's competent handling of this situation is adequately tied in to the
later development of the comedy. At the moment we learn that
Ann, who has been behaving in face of the situation as a model
of pained, shocked, and embarrassed modesty, in fact has been
in Violet's confidence throughout. But not even this revelation
of Ann's exquisite disingenuousness makes any impression on
the enamoured Octavius.

The second act is scarcely equal to the first. It 'dates'—less
because of the thousand-pound automobile than because of the
automobile's chauffeur, 'Enry Straker, the New Man. Tanner's
conversation with this employee from Sherbrooke Road Board
School and the Polytechnic is theatrically reminiscent of an
Elizabethan courtier engaged in back-chat with the Fool, and
Straker as a 'very momentous social phenomenon' comes home
to us now with a slightly off-target effect. But it is Straker at least
who first grasps the true intentions of Ann. And when Ann over-
reaches herself in mendacious stratagems to secure Tanner's
company, it suddenly flashes on Tanner that he is indeed himself 'the marked down victim, the destined prey'. He bundles
Straker into the car and drives hard for Dover. Ann, who knows

that 'the only really simple thing is to go straight for what you want and grab it', gets her way in Granada in the last act. She amuses us by practising her arts of prevarication to the full, tenderly and regretfully informing Octavius that her mother is determined that she shall marry Tanner and that it is clear from her father's will that he had the same intention. And to Octavius's expostulation that she is not bound always to sacrifice herself to the wishes of her parents she replies with the sublime: 'My father loved me. My mother loves me. Surely their wishes are a better guide than my own selfishness.' Her final victory, however, has to be by way of direct assault. Tanner, his back to the wall, acknowledges that he is in the grip of the Life Force. He cries out that he will not marry her; she cries out that he will. She has concentrated all her allure and is at a last gasp of exhaustion and agony. But she has a perfect sense of timing. Reaching this extremity just as the rest of the party return to the scene, she announces that she has promised to marry Tanner, and then falls down in a faint. There is nothing for Tanner to do but make one of his virtuoso speeches announcing that the marriage will take place in a registry office, and that all wedding presents will be sold and the proceeds devoted to distributing free copies of the *Revolutionist's Handbook*. Ann, who has made a rapid recovery, has the last word but one:

VIOLET (*with intense conviction*). You are a brute, Jack.

ANN (*looking at him with fond pride and caressing his arm*). Never mind her, dear. Go on talking.

TANNER. Talking!

Universal laughter.

We have to go back to *The Way of the World* for anything in high comedy quite comparable to Jack Tanner and Ann White-field. Roebuck Ramsden, who prides himself that he was an advanced man before Tanner was born, and upon whose entirely illiberal and obscurantist horizons there does just convincingly glimmer a twilight of good feeling and good sense, is a dramatic creation of similar quality. Of these and the other admirably assorted and balanced characters one would be inclined to say that the single care is to provide us with un-commonly intelligent and outstandingly witty entertainment. It is only in the long and excrescent third act (first produced in 1907) that the play becomes decidedly more a 'drama of ideas' than any normal English theatrical audience can readily digest. Here Tanner and Straker, while crossing the Sierra Nevada, are captured by a band of comico-philosophic robbers led by a certain Mendoza, who has taken to this way of life after being a waiter at the Savoy Hotel. Some rather perfunctory fun is extracted from the conflicting political persuasions of his followers. Then everybody goes to sleep. The music of Mozart's *Don Giovanni* introduces a long dream sequence in which Tanner has become his ancestor Don Juan Tenorio, Ann has become Doña Ana de Ulloa, and Ramsden has become her father the Commander as represented in his statue. Then—this time to the music of Gounod—Mendoza reappears as the Devil and presides over a long debate in Hell. It is perhaps the operatic rather than the intellectual boundaries of drama that are being explored. The arguments of the Devil, and still more those of Juan, are advanced through a series of elaborately built-up set speeches which seem designed less to induce reflection than the demand that this particular piece of virtuosity be repeated *da capo* and at once. When Juan tells the Devil that the Devil's friends are the dullest dogs he knows, he elaborates his judgement in this way:

They are not beautiful: they are only decorated. They are not clean: they are only shaved and starched. They are not dignified: they are only fashionably dressed. They are not educated: they are only college passmen. They are not religious: they are only pew-renters. They are not moral: they are only conventional. They are not virtuous: they are only cowardly. They are not even vicious: they are only 'frail'. They are not artistic: they are only lascivious. They are not prosperous: they are only rich. They are not loyal: they are only servile; not dutiful, only sheepish; not public spirited, only patriotic; not courageous, only quarrelsome; not determined, only obstinate; not masterful, only domineering; not self-controlled, only obtuse; not self-respecting, only vain; not kind, only sentimental; not social, only gregarious; not considerate, only polite; not intelligent, only opinionated; not progressive, only factious; not imaginative, only superstitious; not just, only vindictive; not generous, only propitiatory; not disciplined, only cowed; and not truthful at all—liars every one of them, to the very backbone of their souls.

When Mr. Esmé Percy delivered himself of this speech it was hard not to believe that his voice was soaring above a whole

aims as at present'. And from this Tanner passes on to sweeping eugenic proposals:

> The great central purpose of breeding the race, ay, breeding it to heights now deemed superhuman: that purpose which is now hidden in a mephitic cloud of love and romance and prudery and fastidiousness, will break through into clear sunlight as a purpose no longer to be confused with the gratification of personal fancies.

The fact that 'the sex relation is not a personal or friendly relation at all', but rather something contrived by Nature on a scruff-of-the-neck basis, we have already seen as taking unawares Gloria Clandon and her dentist in *You Never Can Tell*. The climax of *Man and Superman* is designed to enforce the same lesson; and what Don Juan is saying now has again relevance to the comedy proper. In his preface—which takes the form of an 'Epistle Dedicatory to Arthur Bingham Walkley'—Shaw makes the point explicitly, writing of Tanner and Ann:

> The woman's need of him to enable her to carry on Nature's most urgent work, does not prevail against him until his resistance gathers her energy to a climax at which she dares to throw away her customary exploitations of the conventional affectionate and dutiful poses, and claim him by natural right for a purpose that far transcends their mortal personal purposes.

In all this we may feel an element of confusion—or at least a tenuousness of connexion between Shaw the comic dramatist and Shaw the proponent of the Life Force. The 'Epistle Dedicatory' passes from an elevated consideration of 'the struggle of Life to become divinely conscious of itself' to the more practical point that 'democracy, the last refuge of cheap misgovernment, will ruin us if our citizens are ill bred':

> I do not know whether you have any illusions left on the subject of education, progress, and so forth. I have none. . . . The certainty that acquirements are negligible as elements in practical heredity has demolished the hopes of the educationists as well as the terrors of the degeneracy mongers; and we know now that there is no hereditary 'governing class' any more than a hereditary hooliganism. We must either breed political capacity or be ruined. . . . Promiscuous breeding has produced a weakness of character that is too timid to face the full stringency of a thoroughly competitive struggle for existence and too lazy and petty to organise the commonwealth co-operatively.

It seems not very certain whether the coming together of Tanner and Ann represents 'promiscuous breeding' still, or whether the manner of that coming together gives us an assurance that the Life Force itself is here adequately pursuing 'the great central purpose of breeding the race'. The drift of thought in both the play and the 'Epistle' would suggest that Tanner, as a 'philosophic man', should be directed in his mating by some competent planning authority and then left alone to pursue those higher speculative and creative activities with which domesticity and romantic involvement alike interfere. We can only be sure that Ann Whitefield would be perfectly content that, in the face of such problems, Tanner should go on talking. And he does, indeed, go on talking outside the bounds of the play. In *The Revolutionist's Handbook*, printed as an appendix, we hear his very voice telling us that the Holy Ghost is now the sole survivor of the Trinity, that marriage as an indispensable condition of mating must delay the advent of the Superman, that we do ill to be governed by a mob of grown-up Eton boys, that we connive at the lascivious clamour of the flagellomaniac and tear birds to pieces to decorate our women's hats. In *Maxims for Revolutionists*, which is appended in turn to *The Revolutionist's Handbook*, we get more of the same thing—perhaps with a stronger suggestion of matter weeded out of the dialogue. And the 'Epistle Dedicatory' has at least one passage so authentic to Tanner that it is sometimes quoted as from the play:

This is the true joy in life, the being used for a purpose recognized by yourself as a mighty one; the being thoroughly worn out before you are thrown on the scrap heap; the being a force of Nature instead of a feverish selfish little clod of ailments and grievances complaining that the world will not devote itself to making you happy. And also the only real tragedy in life is the being used by personally minded men for purposes which you recognize to be base. All the rest is at worst mere misfortune or mortality: this alone is misery, slavery, hell on earth . . . .

The Superman, the Devil says, is as old as Prometheus. And the accent of this suggests to us how much, at bottom, the typical Shavian *persona* is a Promethean and romantic figure.

8

Shaw calls the central part of *Man and Superman* 'a Shavio-Socratic dialogue', but he is perhaps recognizing it as more

Shavian than Socratic when he adds that he has no illusions 'as to the permanence of those forms of thought (call them opinions) by which I strive to communicate my bent to my fellows'.

To younger men they are already outmoded; for though they have no more lost their logic than an eighteenth-century pastel has lost its drawing or its color, yet, like the pastel, they grow indefinably shabby, and will grow shabbier until they cease to count at all, when my books will either perish, or, if the world is still poor enough to want them, will have to stand, with Bunyan's, by quite amorphous qualities of temper and energy.

Temper and energy are what remain freshest in *John Bull's Other Island* (1904). The background of Anglo-Irish relations against which the tenuous action of this play moves has faded into history. And comparison with a few pages of Joyce's *Dubliners* will make it immediately clear that Shaw's characters, thus left unsupported by extraneous interest, own very little of nature. The central figure, Tom Broadbent, is a purely theatrical creation. His conception is brilliant: he is the stage Englishman pitched to the key of those innumerable stage Irishmen who have for generations laboured so hard for the diversion of London audiences in their theatres. Broadbent was intended in the first instance as entertainment for Irishmen, the play having been written at the request of Yeats for the Abbey Theatre in Dublin. Broadbent made his début nevertheless at the Court, where he constituted Shaw's first substantial popular success. His character being ludicrously compounded of obtuseness, sentimentality, moral self-satisfaction, and material self-interest, it was with understandable ironic delight that his creator thus saw him being taken to the hearts of Englishmen as a whimsical exaggeration of all their most estimable and endearing qualities. Over against Broadbent is set his business partner, the long-expatriate Irishman Larry Doyle. Doyle is a disillusioned man whose thwarted imaginative nature is so warily and bitterly repressed when the two visit his home in Rosscullen that he not only rejects any involvement in its local affairs but is obstinately negative towards Nora Reilly, who has been waiting for him since their youth. Broadbent, although incapable of seeing anything as it actually is, has a self-confidence that carries all before it. He becomes engaged to Nora and then goes on to the more important business of establishing himself as parliamentary candidate for the constituency. His notions of ingratiating himself

with the electors are exquisitely inept, as when he thinks to deliver a pig to a farmer in his motor-car and becomes involved
in an accident which is at once horrifying and extravagantly
funny. But it is the author as well as Broadbent who sacrifices
Nora to this political fantasy, and the play has less of orthodox
dramatic structure than anything Shaw had yet written. Yet at
least it is endlessly resourceful in the exhibition of those basic
incongruities of temperament with which it sets out to amuse.
When Doyle compresses his whole predicament into the wish
that he could find a country to live in where the facts are not
brutal and the dreams not unreal, Broadbent sympathetically
agrees that things indeed look black, but points out that there
will be a great change after the next election. Samuel Johnson,
who judged Congreve to have formed 'a peculiar idea of comic
excellence' in giving prominence to 'unexpected answers', would
have found *John Bull's Other Island* very peculiar indeed.

If the play has a point of growth—and one linking it to what
was immediately to follow—this lies in the character of Father
Keegan, in whom, for the first time, a religious consciousness is
explored. Father Keegan, long ago, has had the ill-luck to be
called to the death-bed of an elderly Hindoo, and to have there
made a discovery which has necessitated his being unfrocked
and declared mad:

KEEGAN. . . . This man did not complain of his misfortunes. They
were brought upon him, he said, by sins committed in a former
existence. Then, without a word of comfort from me, he died with
a clear-eyed resignation that my most earnest exhortations have
rarely produced in a Christian, and left me sitting there by his
bedside with the mystery of this world suddenly revealed to me.

BROADBENT. That is a remarkable tribute to the liberty of conscience enjoyed by the subjects of our Indian Empire.

LARRY. No doubt; but may we venture to ask what is the mystery
of this world?

KEEGAN. This world, sir, is very clearly a place of torment and
penance, a place where the fool flourishes and the good and wise
are hated and persecuted, a place where men and women torture
one another in the name of love; where children are scourged and
enslaved in the name of parental duty and education; where the
weak in body are poisoned and mutilated in the name of healing,
and the weak in character are put to the horrible torture of
imprisonment, not for hours but for years, in the name of justice.
It is a place where the hardest toil is a welcome refuge from the

horror and tedium of pleasure, and where charity and good works are done only for hire to ransom the souls of the spoiler and the sybarite. Now, sir, there is only one place of horror and torment known to my religion; and that place is hell. Therefore it is plain to me that this earth of ours must be hell, and that we are all here, as the Indian revealed to me—perhaps he was sent to reveal it to me—to expiate crimes committed by us in a former existence. . . .

BROADBENT. Your idea is a very clever one, Mr. Keegan: really most brilliant: *I* should never have thought of it. But it seems to me —if I may say so—that you are overlooking the fact that, of the evils you describe, some are absolutely necessary for the preservation of society, and others are encouraged only when the Tories are in office.

In the third act of *Man and Superman* we have already been shown a hell offering 'the horror and tedium of pleasure'. And here, as there, we are being taken outside the boundaries of comedy, so that we have a slightly jarring sense when we are returned to Broadbent's anticlimactic invoking of the Tories. But in characters like Father Keegan—he is first revealed to us in unashamedly Franciscan colloquy with a grasshopper—Shaw is never in fact to lose interest. More authentically an artist than a prophet, he nevertheless presents, paradoxically, a surer grip of the religious than of the artistic character.

Yet Shaw's susceptibility to religious emotion, and his skill in giving it dramatic embodiment, does not much affect his adherence to the rationalistic and pragmatic tenets of his age. Religion is a good thing, and 'perhaps the most stupendous fact in the whole world-situation' is simply that 'at present there is not a single credible established religion'. Our 'sanguinary popular creed' requires to be purified and rationalized —and a great deal in our social practices honestly squared with its essentials—before 'the great teachers of the world' will cease to scoff at it. These are persuasions which might plausibly have been ascribed to that notably advanced Victorian, the Roebuck Ramsden of *Man and Superman*. In fact they are expressed by Shaw himself at the end of the preface to *Major Barbara* (1905), another comedy making an implicit claim to serious intentions.

9

Lady Britomart is discovered at the opening of the play taking counsel—if it can be called that—with her son Stephen as she faces a family crisis. Her manner of treating him, which is in blank contradiction to her command that he realize he is a grown-up man while she is only a woman, is extremely amusing in itself without for a moment impeding a brilliantly rapid and lucid exposition. Stephen's sisters are getting married and both will need money. The main recommendation of Sarah's young man, Charles Lomax, is that he will one day be a millionaire, but for some years he will have only a small allowance. Yet this engagement has at least been conventionally arrived at, whereas with Barbara it has been otherwise:

And what about Barbara? I thought Barbara was going to make the most brilliant career of all of you. And what does she do? Joins the Salvation Army; discharges her maid; lives on a pound a week; and walks in one evening with a professor of Greek whom she has picked up in the street, and who pretends to be a Salvationist, and actually plays the big drum for her in public because he has fallen head over ears in love with her.

This somewhat disingenuous scholar, Adolphus Cusins, Lady Britomart has decided to approve. 'We are Whigs', she says, 'and believe in liberty. Let snobbish people say what they please: Barbara shall marry, not the man they like, but the man *I* like.' She has no illusions, however, about either Lomax's power to earn money or Cusins's quiet willingness to spend it. Therefore the children's father has had to be called in, and is due to arrive at any moment. This is a shock to Stephen, since Andrew Undershaft is a parent upon whom he has never set eyes—and since, being the largest armament manufacturer in Europe, he must be regarded as in trade. But there is another peculiarity about him which Lady Britomart now reveals:

Be a good boy, Stephen, and listen to me patiently. The Undershafts are descended from a foundling in the parish of St. Andrew Undershaft in the city. That was long ago, in the reign of James the First. Well, this foundling was adopted by an armorer and gunmaker. In the course of time the foundling succeeded to the business; and from some notion of gratitude, or some vow or something, he adopted another foundling, and left the business to him. And that foundling did the same. Ever since that, the cannon business has always been left to an adopted foundling named Andrew Undershaft.

This gives us what is to be the Gilbertian framework of the play, and at the same time the reason why Lady Britomart separated from her husband. It is true that the Antonine emperors all adopted their successors. But she is a daughter of the Earl of Stevenage; the Stevenages are as good as the Antonines; and therefore it was outrageous of her husband to want to cling to the old tradition still.

Barbara is interested in her father's arrival. He has a soul to be saved like anybody else. And he is immediately interested in her; Blood and Fire, the motto of the Salvation Army, might be his own. And when Lomax, shocked, says 'But not your sort of blood and fire, you know', he replies 'My sort of blood cleanses: my sort of fire purifies'. We are left at the end of the first act wondering whether this view of the aerial battleship and the disappearing rampart gun is to be vindicated as more than a flight of rhetoric. But father and daughter have made a compact. Undershaft is to visit Barbara's Salvation Army Shelter, and then she and the family are to visit his armament works. The second act, which presents the first of these visits, marks the coming to full maturity of Shaw's dramatic talent. It shows, in a setting of skilfully realized minor characters, Barbara first in the confident exercise of her religious vocation and then in despair as she is driven to realize that the Army must rely for its very existence upon the charity of concerns such as Bodger's Distillery, the evil effects of whose enterprise it has been her whole effort to fight. Of this realization her father is the cunning architect, since he has designs upon her as a convert to his own religion, the nature of which begins to define itself in a colloquy with Cusins:

CUSINS. You know, I do not admit that I am imposing on Barbara. I am quite genuinely interested in the views of the Salvation Army. The fact is, I am a sort of collector of religions; and the curious thing is that I find I can believe them all. By the way, have you any religion?

UNDERSHAFT. Yes.

CUSINS. Anything out of the common?

UNDERSHAFT. Only that there are two things necessary to Salvation.

CUSINS (*disappointed, but polite*) Ah, the Church Catechism. Charles Lomax also belongs to the Established Church.

UNDERSHAFT. The two things are—

CUSINS. Baptism and—

UNDERSHAFT. No. Money and gunpowder.

CUSINS (*surprised, but interested*) That is the general opinion of our governing classes. The novelty is in hearing any man confess it.

UNDERSHAFT. Just so.

CUSINS. Excuse me: is there any place in your religion for honor, justice, truth, love, mercy and so forth?

UNDERSHAFT. Yes: they are the graces and luxuries of a rich, strong, and safe life.

CUSINS. Suppose one is forced to choose between them and money or gunpowder?

UNDERSHAFT. Choose money and gunpowder; for without enough of both you cannot afford the others.

CUSINS. That is your religion?

UNDERSHAFT. Yes.

The cadence of this reply makes a full close in the conversation.

Undershaft presently proposes a compact:

I am a millionaire; you are a poet; Barbara is a savior of souls. What have we three to do with the common mob of slaves and idolaters? . . . We three must stand together above the common people: how else can we help their children to climb up beside us? Barbara must belong to us, not to the Salvation Army.

Undershaft is simultaneously advancing a mystique of power—by which he means control over everybody else—and a benevolent proposal eventually to make everybody else powerful. This looks like contradiction and nonsense. It becomes reasonable only if watered down to the less striking proposition that it will be to the general advantage to satisfy the material needs of men on as broad a social basis as possible. Such an aspiration is perhaps a religion of sorts, but in the pursuance of it an arms manufacturer appears to be in no special position of advantage. The logic of the play demands that, in the third act, both Barbara and Cusins should be persuaded that he is. Cusins, indeed, is no great problem. He has admitted that he can believe anything, and his temperament is freakish to the point of instability. At the moment of Barbara's utmost despair he has thrown himself so irresponsibly into an ironic Dionysiac masquerade that we retain very little interest in him: nothing, surely, is odder than the extraneous information that his character was felt by Shaw to bear some relation to that of the Greek scholar Gilbert Murray. Barbara is another matter. Her relationship to Cusins does indeed a little disconcert us. It involves that sort of relapse upon baby-talk which we remember in Vivie Warren. But Shaw has created her—and it has to be reiterated that he possesses in an unexpected degree the power to do this—as a person of authentic religious bent. 'It is through religion alone

that we can win Barbara', Undershaft has clear-sightedly told
Cusins. What, then, do Undershaft's religious credentials, so to
speak, eventually prove to be?

The third act addresses itself to the answer, and there is
perhaps no better place in which to examine the degree of
intellectual coherence lying behind a typical Shavian 'drama
of ideas'. The scene is the armament works, to which everybody
has repaired, and which everybody is surprised to find not
a sulphurous hell but a spacious garden city, equipped with
schools, libraries, nursing homes, and—among other religious
edifices—a William Morris Labor Church. Lady Britomart,
with a *naïveté* we should not have expected in her, is so enchanted
by the thought that 'all that plate and linen, all that furniture
and those houses and orchards and gardens belong to us' that
she makes what proves to be an inspired suggestion. Barbara,
after all, has rights as well as Stephen. These will be done justice
to if her future husband, Cusins, succeeds to the inheritance.
Undershaft—again a little surprisingly in one who must be
a good judge of men—says that he would ask nothing better,
if only Cusins were a foundling. And Cusins at once turns out
to be the next best thing: an Australian whose mother was his
father's deceased wife's sister. Upon this absurdity Undershaft
declares him to be eligible. Cusins drives a hard provisional
bargain—and then declares that the real tug of war is still to
come. There is a moral question, 'an abyss of moral horror
between me and your accursed aerial battleships'. This introduces, between Undershaft, Cusins, and Barbara, the last and
crucial debate in the play. Undershaft begins by propounding
the true faith of an armourer: to give arms to all men who offer
an honest price for them. Earlier, when Stephen has got on a
high horse as a future legislator, his father, in a typical Shavian
bravura speech, has declared that he, Andrew Undershaft, is
the effective government of England. 'No, my friend: you will
do what pays us. You will make war when it suits us, and keep
peace when it doesn't.' But now he declares that, in some deeper
sense, he has no power of his own; and he startles Barbara,
who has known selflessness, by adding 'enigmatically' that what
drives his great concern is a will of which he is but a part. And
Barbara admits her own predicament:

BARBARA. . . . . I stood on the rock I thought eternal; and without
a word of warning it reeled and crumbled under me. I was safe

with an infinite wisdom watching me, an army marching to Salvation with me; and in a moment, at a stroke of your pen in a cheque book, I stood alone; and the heavens were empty . . . .

UNDERSHAFT. Come, come, my daughter! don't make too much of your little tinpot tragedy. What do we do here when we spend years of work and thought and thousands of pounds of solid cash on a new gun or an aerial battleship that turns out just a hairsbreadth wrong after all? Scrap it. Scrap it without wasting another hour or another pound on it. Well, you have made for yourself something that you call a morality or a religion or what not. It doesn't fit the facts. Well, scrap it. Scrap it and get one that does fit. That is what is wrong with the world at present. It scraps its obsolete steam engines and dynamos; but it won't scrap its old prejudices and its old moralities and its old religions and its old political constitutions. What's the result? In machinery it does very well; but in morals and religion and politics it is working at a loss that brings it nearer bankruptcy every year. Don't persist in that folly. If your old religion broke down yesterday, get a newer and a better one for tomorrow.

BARBARA. Oh how gladly I would take a better one to my soul! But you offer me a worse one. (*Turning on him with sudden vehemence*). Justify yourself: shew me some light through the darkness of this dreadful place, with its beautifully clean workshops, and respectable workmen, and model homes.

UNDERSHAFT. Cleanliness and respectability do not need justification, Barbara: they justify themselves. I see no darkness here, no dreadfulness. In your Salvation shelter I saw poverty, misery, cold and hunger. You gave them bread and treacle and dreams of heaven. I give from thirty shillings a week to twelve thousand a year. They find their own dreams; but I look after the drainage.

BARBARA. And their souls?

UNDERSHAFT. I save their souls just as I saved yours.

Souls are saved, he goes on to assert, by being saved from the crime of poverty—poverty which is the worst of all crimes, since when subject to it no spirit can soar: 'It is cheap work converting starving men with a Bible in one hand and a slice of bread in the other. I will undertake to convert West Ham to Mahometanism on the same terms. Try your hand on my men: their souls are hungry because their bodies are full.' Shaw is now exploiting to the full the rapid serial nature of dramatic representation. In reading, we may pause to weigh a paradox like this; in the theatre we are swept on by Undershaft's rhetoric. He would rather be a thief than a pauper, rather a murderer than a slave. But this, even as it flies, we should catch as an astonishing statement for one speculative thinker and moralist to put in the mouth of another. For what Undershaft is saying is this: that it is preferable to do an evil deed than to exist in a state in which the doing or suffering of evil deeds is hard to avoid. That this is, as he at once explicitly claims, the 'more moral' course is a contention so demonstrably untenable that we must hold suspect what he goes on to say in justification of his specific trade:

Poverty and slavery have stood up for centuries to your sermons and leading articles: they will not stand up to my machine guns.... Your pious mob fills up ballot papers and imagines it is governing its masters; but the ballot paper that really governs is the paper that has a bullet wrapped up in it. ... When you vote, you only change the names of the cabinet. When you shoot, you pull down governments, inaugurate new epochs, abolish old orders and set up new. Is that historically true, Mr. Learned Man, or is it not?

Cusins has to admit the historical truth. Yet the validity of the argument seems to depend on the ownership of the machine guns and the direction of the bullets; and we have already learned that it is part of Undershaft's code to sell anything to anybody. Unless we are to take his 'Whatever can blow men up can blow society up' as an assertion of the desirability of universal disruption, there is really no plausibility in the contention that the manufacture and indiscriminate distribution of arms is a beneficent activity at all. When Cusins says that he hates war, Undershaft replies 'Hatred is the coward's revenge for being intimidated. Dare you make war on war? Here are the means'—and points to an artillery shell. It is difficult to follow this, but Cusins is finally convinced by it:

As a teacher of Greek I gave the intellectual man weapons against the common man. I now want to give the common man weapons against the intellectual man. I love the common people. I want to arm them against the lawyer, the doctor, the priest, the literary man, the professor, the artist, and the politician, who, once in authority, are the most dangerous, disastrous, and tyrannical of all the fools, rascals, and impostors. I want a democratic power strong enough to force the intellectual oligarchy to use its genius for the general good or else perish.

Cusin's love of the common people is a new discovery, and it is puzzling to find an intelligent man apparently believing that the manufacture of highly efficient weapons by a vast capitalist concern is much calculated to advance popular causes. With Barbara at the end of the play we are on somewhat surer ground—although her recovery of faith has not the moving and convincing quality of her earlier loss of it. She decides that 'turning our backs on Bodger and Undershaft is turning our backs on life' and she sees in the large community created by her father the opportunity for her old work under new, and more honest, conditions: –

My father shall never throw it in my teeth again that my converts were bribed with bread. (*She is transfigured.*) I have got rid of the bribe of bread. I have got rid of the bribe of heaven. Let God's work be done for its own sake: the work he had to create us to do because it cannot be done except by living men and women. When I die, let him be in my debt, not I in his; and let me forgive him as becomes a woman of my rank.

It is with some abruptness that Barbara has in fact stumbled upon the idea of the Life Force. And although, as she embraces her 'dear little Dolly boy' in the person of Cusins, she cries out 'Glory Hallelujah', there remains about the sort of salvation to be preached to her new charges a vagueness which would not go down well with her old colleagues in the West Ham Shelter.

In *Man and Superman* we have had heaven defined as the effort to bring heaven about. It is the quintessentially instrumentalist philosophy behind this that gives the thought in *Major Barbara* any coherence it has. At about the time of his writing the play Shaw wrote too a preface for his hitherto unpublished second novel, *The Irrational Knot*. On page 10 of this he declares that 'Money is indeed the most important thing in the world; and all sound and successful personal and national morality should have this fact for its basis'. Three pages later he records that, being as a young man free of the whole world of art, he had found the world of artificial greatness founded on money to be 'repugnant and contemptible'. The first of these statements is about money as a means and the second is about money as an end. To rejoice in money when you can rejoice in Titian and Beethoven and Shelley is fatuous and disgusting. On the other hand money is the supremely important thing because, rightly handled, it is the supreme instrument in securing social reform—and social reform is an important part of the job of bringing heaven about. And in *Major Barbara*, as almost everywhere in Shaw, it is in its aspect as a means that one or another attitude or persuasion is important. Things come up for spot judgement according as to whether they will or will not influence other things in a desirable direction. Undershaft's philosophy, Cusins's apologia, Barbara's decision: all these are found upon analysis to reflect this habit of mind.

At the end of the preface to *The Irrational Knot* Shaw declares that the novel should be 'regarded as an early attempt on the part of the Life Force to write *A Doll's House* in English by the instrumentality of a very immature writer aged 24', and exhorts us to 'realize that though the Life Force supplies us with its own purpose, it has no other brains to work with than those it has painfully and imperfectly evolved in our heads'. The peculiar Providence that lays this heavy burden on humanity is to be further explored in a later serious phase of Shaw's dramaturgy. But what follows immediately upon *Major Barbara* is a period of comparative relaxation, lasting until the years immediately before the First World War, in which Shaw produces two or three supremely good light comedies together with much miscellaneous dramatic writing of no great importance. None of this requires more than brief examination.

10

Shaw's plays frequently seem to take their origin from a frugal and astute retrospective glance over previous work in search of promising material. *Major Barbara* uses as a springboard for its action that theme of a father making the acquaintance of his grown-up children which had proved effective in *You Never Can Tell*. *The Doctor's Dilemma* (1906), if it may be said in general to implement Cusins's desire to arm the common people against the 'fools, rascals, and imposters' constituting the professional classes, gets its specific cue from the only permanently amusing element in *The Philanderer*: the vagaries of medical science in relation to the unfortunate individual patient. But Shaw's satire upon the doctors is enchantingly good-humoured and equitable; they are 'fools, rascals, and impostors' only in a Shavian and saving sense; and when one of them cries out in a moment of despairing frankness 'We're not a profession: we're a conspiracy' it is in a context that leaves our sympathy, although not perhaps our confidence, unimpaired. The doctors do their best for Dubedat, the painter who is dying of consumption. Indeed they do better for him than does Shaw. They have to decide, in effect, whether in face of some not wholly plausible limitation of technical resources they save the life of Dubedat or of someone else. Dubedat has boundless talent—but when he dines with the doctors he borrows money all round, steals a cigarette case, explores the possibility of selling the charms of his wife, and is unmasked as a bigamist. This paradox of the morally imbecile genius destroys itself in the making. Neither Henry James's Roderick Hudson nor Joyce Cary's Gully Jimson leaves us quite so indisposed to believe in the reality of the powers attributed to him as does Dubedat. When, just before his death, he is wheeled into his studio, 'feebly folds his hands and utters his creed' to the effect that he believes 'in Michael Angelo, Velasquez, and Rembrandt; in the might of design, the mystery of color, the redemption of all things by Beauty' and so forth, we are left simply with the other, and recurrent, paradox that an artist so authentic as Bernard Shaw should completely fail in the presentation of an artist. There is a point at which Dubedat, as if aware of his own imaginative nullity, solicits our laughter by declaring that he doesn't believe in morality, since he is a disciple of Bernard Shaw. There could be no clearer sign that Shaw found Dubedat boring. But he cannot so have found the doctors. They constitute, as a conversation piece, a work of art far ahead of anything that Dubedat could do.

The Shewing-up of Blanco Posnet (first produced by Lady Gregory and Yeats at the Abbey Theatre in 1909) is a light variation on the theme of *The Devil's Disciple*. Blanco is a horse-thief who gives up his chance of escape from his pursuers as a consequence of surrendering the stolen animal to a woman with a sick child. In performing this decent action he surprises himself out of his senses, and hits with striking rapidity upon the doctrine of the Life Force:

Yah! What about the croup? It was early days when He made the croup, I guess. It was the best He could think of then; but when it turned out wrong on His hands He made you and me to fight the croup for him. You bet He didn't make us for nothing; and He wouldn't have made us at all if He could have done His work without us.

In England the play ran into trouble with the Lord Chamberlain, who would permit public performance only if all mention of the existence of God were removed from the text. On this absurdity and the theme of censorship in general Shaw wrote one of his most pungent prefaces. *Getting Married* (1908) and *Misalliance* (1910) are long discussion plays, and each is provided with a long preface. The first deals (and 'deals' is the entirely faithful word) with marriage. There is a bishop who is writing a book on the history of marriage, his daughter whose wedding-day it is, and an array of characters, major and minor, who stand in almost every conceivable relation to the marital state. The comic waiter has returned from *You Never Can Tell*; he is married to a perfect wife and mother—which is why, he explains, all his children have run away from home. Later he introduces his sister-in-law Mrs. George, who provides a mediumistic séance, somewhat too patently designed to give a fillip to the latter part of the play. When Reginald, a prospective divorcee, is prompted to exclaim to his reluctant supplanter 'You damned scoundrel, how dare you throw my wife over like that before my face?' the key of plausible travesty to which the whole piece is pitched is characteristically struck. *Misalliance* is about parents and children, and to the anatomy of this theme we have an almost immediate impression that there has been summoned a whole company of Shavian stereotypes. Hypatia Tarleton, who hates 'talk, talk, talk', possesses 'boundless energy and audacity held in leash', and, with entire ruthlessness and unflawed hypocrisy, abandons her fiancé to hunt a more attractive male, is a disagreeable cousin of Ann Whitefield. Her brother Johnny, who asks seriously 'Has it ever occurred to you that a man with an open mind must be a bit of a scoundrel?' is in a somewhat similar relationship to Tom Broadbent ('You can draw a line', he also says, 'and make other chaps toe it. That's what I call morality'). The clerk Gunner, proposing to avenge his mother's dishonour and hiding with a revolver in a turkish bath, is an epigone of Brassbound's. Jack Tanner's motor-car has become an aeroplane, and Lina Szczepanowska, the *femme fatale* and female contortionist who falls out of it through the glass of Mr. Tarleton's conservatory, is a deliberately bizarre invention with the same limited theatrical effectiveness as the clairvoyant Mrs. George. The play's central figure, the elder John Tarleton, has greater dramatic vitality—this despite his tiresome habit of perpetually recommending to us the reading of his favourite authors ('The superman's an idea. I believe in ideas. Read Whatshisname'). As a drama of ideas *Misalliance* appears designed to advance the notion that the relationship of parents and children is embarrassing, that 'no child should know its own father', and that in a thousand years it will probably be distinctly bad form to own to any such knowledge. We may feel that Tanner was on the same ground, but more surely and robustly, when he told poor Mrs. Whitefield that 'the tables of consanguinity have a natural basis in a natural repugnance'. The short *Overruled* (1912) carries echoes from as far back as *The Philanderer*, and rehearses some of the material of *Getting Married* within a symmetrical and highly artificial framework presenting two men prosecuting abortive flirtations each with the other's wife and each in ignorance of the other's proceeding. *Fanny's First Play* (1911) applies the same effective if unrefined formula to a different situation. A young engaged couple, severally and unbeknown to each other or to their highly respectable shop-keeping families, are sent to jail for disorderly behaviour. The girl emerges from this experience with much the better credit. In the end she abjures her inadequate lover and decides to marry her father's footman, who is called Juggins and has been revealed as the disguised brother of a duke. This light and rapid comedy is provided with an induction which explains the title. Fanny is a clever girl from Cambridge, the daughter of the highly cultivated and fastidious Count O'Dowda, a gentleman clinging to the graces of a vanished age. Learning that his daughter has written a play, the Count arranges for a private production, which the leading dramatic critics of the day are invited to attend. The play pains him very much. But the critics, although unimpressed, discuss in an epilogue the possibility of its being by Granville-Barker, Barrie, Pinero, or Bernard Shaw. All this fun has become rather faded. Shaw is here far behind the Molière of *La Critique de l'École des Femmes*.

In *Androcles and the Lion* (1913) he may be described as at least equally far behind Corneille's *Polyeucte*. Of the Christian martyrs who escape death in the Colosseum at the pantomime close of this play only the aristocratic Roman lady Lavinia is presented with much conviction. And the noble speech in which she justifies her resolution to die is rather protestant than Christian;

she cannot, on her conscience, offer even a little pinch of incense before an altar set up, as she conceives it, to the worship of terror and darkness and cruelty and greed. The thesis is expanded in a note at the end of the piece:

> I have represented one of the Roman persecutions of the early Christians, not as the conflict of a false theology with a true, but as what all such persecutions essentially are: an attempt to suppress a propaganda that seemed to threaten the interests involved in the established law and order, organized and maintained in the name of religion and justice by politicians who are pure opportunist Have-and-Holders. People who are shewn by their inner light the possibility of a better world based on the demand of the spirit for a nobler and more abundant life, not for themselves at the expense of others, but for everybody, are naturally dreaded and therefore hated by the Have-and-Holders. . . . Therefore my martyrs are the martyrs of all time, and my persecutors the persecutors of all time.

But the comic lion (with which Androcles waltzes rapturously about the stage hard upon the slaughter, by the lapsed Christian Ferrovius, of six gladiators and a man with a whip) is a sufficient indication that the play has no ambition to match this serious if familiar theme. The long preface, essentially an attempt to demonstrate that Christ was a thwarted Fabian, is among the most imaginatively limited of Shaw's performances.

II

Pygmalion (1913) is another matter: Shaw's superb farewell to high comedy. None of the plays has shown more vitality. It has made the best of the Shaw films, and as a musical comedy has enjoyed record-breaking runs. Eliza Doolittle, the Cockney flower-girl whom the whim of an eccentric phonetician recreates as a lady able to hold her own in society, may seem to be related only tenuously to her original in legend. In one sense she is the very antithesis of Galatea, since she starts a child of nature and ends an artefact. Nor is Higgins ever allowed to acknowledge to himself that he might fall in love with her. But another sense runs counter to this. Eliza's transformation is more than from common girl to lady. Higgins begins with what is to him no more than a new piece of studio material or laboratory equipment, and eventually has to acknowledge his creation as an enjoying and suffering woman. The play thus comes to move, in a manner unusual with Shaw, at more levels than one. 'You have no idea', Higgins tells his mother, 'how frightfully interesting it is to take a human being and change her into a quite different human being by creating a new speech for her. It's filling up the deepest gulf that separates class from class and soul from soul.' This has—particularly, perhaps, in England—its social truth and comic potentiality. The third act, in which Eliza is exhibited at a polite tea-party at the half-way stage of having acquired upper-class articulations while preserving a distinctly lower-class conversational range, has a reasonable claim to be reckoned the most amusing in English drama, and it is not in the least impaired by the comparatively muted impact which low expletives are likely to achieve in drawing-rooms today. The social truth is deepened with Eliza's own perception that 'really and truly, apart from the things anyone can pick up (the dressing and the proper way of speaking, and so on), the difference between a lady and a flower girl is not how she behaves, but how she's treated'.

It is in the fourth act, however, that the play touches depth. Higgins has brought off his bet; he has had enough of the game; and he makes no scruple of announcing to his friend Colonel Pickering in Eliza's presence that 'It was a silly notion: the whole thing has been a bore'. To Eliza, Higgins has always been a boor as well as a tyrant. But Pickering has consistently behaved towards her as it is pleasant to think a gentleman would. The moral lesson now driven home—that it is inhuman to treat any human being as a means to an end—is achieved by a technique which, if found in Shakespeare, would be described as that of episodic intensification. Pickering is for a time not quite Pickering, and Higgins is more impossibly Higgins than before. The fifth act, which presents Eliza's come-back by way of a successful bid for independence, is by comparison uncertain and ineffective. It instances the extreme difficulty of writing a classical comedy without recourse to a conventional close. Instead of a preface, *Pygmalion* has a prose epilogue designed to persuade us of the propriety and indeed inevitability of Eliza's marrying not Higgins but Freddy Eynsford Hill, the lightly sketched 'silly ass' character of the play. They set up a flower-shop, we are told, and eventually make a success of it after completing some necessary studies at the London School of Economics. This conclusion, Shaw asserts,

is so obvious that it 'would hardly need telling if our imaginations were not so enfeebled by their lazy dependence on the
ready-mades and reach-me-downs of the ragshop in which
Romance keeps its stock of "happy endings" to misfit all stories'.
It has to be observed, however, that Shaw himself admirably
exploits in the subsidiary parts of his play a good deal that is
ready-made—although the prefabrication, indeed, has taken
place in the Shavian factory. Those who deprecate the arrival
of Richard III at Bosworth Field on a live horse and who are
unimpressed by Jack Tanner's expensive car may judge jejune
the London taxicab which here jerks on and off the stage in the
first act. And Eliza's father the dustman, although his fortuitous
elevation from a comfortable place among the undeserving
poor presents a brilliantly grotesque parallel to his daughter's
situation, owes his moment of chief theatrical effectiveness to
a device echoed from as far back as *Widowers' Houses*.

12

Heartbreak House, begun in 1913, concludes with an incident
suggested to Shaw by a Zeppelin raid near his own home two
years later. It was published in 1919, with a preface in which
Shaw explains that he withheld it from the theatre during the
war as a matter of loyalty. 'The art of the dramatic poet knows
no patriotism . . . cares not whether Germany or England
perish', and there are therefore times when it must be silent.
But this was not perhaps the sole reason for postponement. The
play, which began even more than commonly as improvisation,
came to occupy a special place in Shaw's regard. He tinkered
with it a good deal, and eventually showed a most unusual
reluctance to part with it, read it aloud, or comment upon it
in any way. The first production was in New York in 1920.

In considering the structure of *Heartbreak House* we have to
bear in mind that much of what is ramshackle in it is a matter
of deliberate effect. Nevertheless the circumstances of its composition have left one probably undesigned confusion. The
background is neither clearly peace nor war. Early on there is
a casual reference to 'tanks', a word first applied to armoured
vehicles in December 1915. There is no other suggestion,
whether explicit or implicit, of war. The air raid at the end of
the play is foreseen by none of the characters, even though it

has been preluded by 'a sort of splendid drumming in the sky'.
On the other hand, it has been foreseen—off-stage—by the
police, who have telephoned to threaten prosecution if the
lights are not extinguished in Captain Shotover's house. Sir
Desmond MacCarthy, whose collected theatrical notices still
constitute the only consistently intelligent artistic discussion
of Shaw, finds in his own reading of these discrepancies the
serious weakness in the play:

It purports to be a picture of the upper-class intelligentsia of
England during the first world war; of an English country-house
group corresponding in futility to Chekhov's characters in *The
Cherry Orchard* and *Uncle Vanya*, I repeat, in wartime. And there lies
the flaw. As a picture of behaviour and talk in an English country
house during the summer of nineteen-fifteen or sixteen or seventeen,
or whenever the action is supposed to take place, the play has no
relation to reality. Whatever cogency it might have had as an
exposure of the fecklessness of the cultured upper-class in England
before the war, at the time when the characters and situations were
conceived by the dramatist, has been falsified by his post-dating
it in order to exhibit Nemesis in the form of falling bombs.

In fact, *Heartbreak House* must be received as a pre-war play,
and the air raid—although the dramatist gives us no help here
—only as a symbolical adumbration of the actual course of
events.

The influence of Tchekov, which is substantial but not radical,
was emphasized by Shaw himself. He gave his play the sub-
title of 'a Fantasia in the Russian manner on English themes',
and wrote:

HEARTBREAK HOUSE is not merely the name of the play which
follows this preface. It is cultured, leisured Europe before the war.
. . . A Russian playwright, Tchekov, had produced four fascinating
dramatic studies of Heartbreak House, of which three, The Cherry
Orchard, Uncle Vanya, and The Seagull, had been performed in
England. . . . We stared and said, 'How Russian!' They did not
strike me in that way. Just as Ibsen's intensely Norwegian plays
exactly fitted every middle and professional class suburb in Europe,
these intensely Russian plays fitted all the country houses in Europe
in which the pleasures of music, art, literature, and the theatre had
supplanted hunting, shooting, fishing, flirting, eating, and drinking.
The same nice people, the same utter futility.

Actually, the inhabitants of Shaw's Heartbreak House display little active interest in the arts, and quite a lot in flirting—and this, indeed, is equally true of the majority of the people in Serebrakoff's house, or in Mme Ranevsky's or Andrey Prosorov's. With an obviousness somewhat surprising in so mature, idiosyncratic, and confident a playwright, Shaw has sent his people to school with Tchekov's in a number of ways. They are preoccupied with the analysis of emotion, mostly in terms of self-reference, and the men weep at least as readily as the women. They indulge in eccentricities of behaviour—like Lopakhin when he sticks his head through a door and moos, or Gaev as he wanders in and out immersed in his imaginary game of billiards. Their talk is often inconsequent, and is occasionally built up into odd choric effects. They are irked by a vast boredom inherent in their own sophistication and lack of social function, just as Tchekov's characters are irked by the tedium and cultural poverty of provincial life. Ellie Dunn's disillusionment in love—the only substantial hinge upon which *Heartbreak House* turns—is a cruder and theatrically sharper equivalent of a type of frustration equally cardinal in all Tchekov's major plays. But Shaw's characters never echo Tchekov's where one might most expect them to do so: in asserting the solace of work and the likelihood of man's eventually achieving a society less unhappy than our own. And in fact the two worlds are really very different. The 'atmosphere' from which Shaw once declared that his play had generated itself is not the nostalgic and elegiac atmosphere of *The Cherry Orchard*. Rather it is apocalyptic. Captain Shotover is eighty-eight and mad. His two daughters have an aspect in which they are fiends. Boss Mangan, the business man driven to a frenzy by Heartbreak House, proposes to strip himself naked. 'Poor wretch!' Hector Hushabye exclaims at the end of the second act—and adds, as 'he lifts his fists in invocation to heaven': 'Fall. Fall and crush'. These reverberations from *King Lear* are not insignificant. For *Heartbreak House* is the play in which Shaw confronts, for the first time in his imaginative writing, the small extent of his faith in man. What lies just beneath the play's surface is despair. It is thus in intention, or impulsion, radically different from almost all the rest of his work. But this new and irruptive Shaw does not, in fact, rise clear of the habituated comic writer. The play is lengthened out, and its unity of tone impaired, by farcical episodes. One of these, that of the detected burglar, has the air of a small prefabricated Shavian joke tipped inconsequently into the action.

The precipitating occasion of the action may also be judged inappositely farcical. Ellie Dunn, the daughter of the idealistic and unsuccessful Mazzini Dunn, has fallen in love with the romantically fascinating Marcus Darnley, whose recitals of his own heroic and surprising exploits have had the effect of making Othello's wooing of Desdemona her favourite place in Shakespeare. When, however, Ellie arrives on a visit to her friend Mrs. Hushabye, a lady presiding over her father Captain Shotover's household, she discovers that 'Marcus Darnley' is in fact her friend's husband Hector—who, as well as being authentically a courageous man, is a pathological liar and a deceiver of women. The consequence of Ellie's disillusionment is not wholly convincing. She feels that her heart is broken, and is turned instantaneously from an ingenuous and affectionate girl into a woman who believes that her only salvation lies in being as hard as nails. She is even prepared to marry Mangan, the clumsily unscrupulous business man who has deliberately ruined her father, once she has ensured by her utterly contemptuous treatment of him that she will have the upper hand in the deal. We have to go back to *Mrs. Warren's Profession* for an understanding of the situation. Ellie has become a Vivie Warren—but one viewed by a creator now far more perceptive of what is really likely to result from the hard-as-nails gospel. Ellie's assertion that money is the prerequisite of salvation is something which she has inherited by way of the early Shaw from Samuel Butler. Shotover, who is the mature Shaw, is concerned to preserve her from taking this limited paradox at its face value. Shotover himself has no easy or hopeful alternative to suggest. He knows himself to be an old mad mystic, keeping a senile dreaming at bay through the unreliable agency of rum, and constrained by his final view of the human situation to devote the remnants of his skill as an inventor to crazy projects of universal annihilation. But he fights for Ellie—and always with the sharp pregnant utterance which sets him apart from the general run of Shaw's unquenchably loquacious characters:

ELLIE. Does nothing ever disturb you, Captain Shotover?

CAPTAIN SHOTOVER. I've stood on the bridge for eighteen hours in a typhoon. Life here is stormier; but I can stand it.

ELLIE. Do you think I ought to marry Mr Mangan?

CAPTAIN SHOTOVER (*never looking up*). One rock is as good as another to be wrecked on.

ELLIE. I am not in love with him.

CAPTAIN SHOTOVER. Who said you were?

ELLIE. You are not surprised?

CAPTAIN SHOTOVER. Surprised! At my age!

ELLIE. It seems to me quite fair. He wants me for one thing: I want him for another.

CAPTAIN SHOTOVER. Money?

ELLIE. Yes. . . .

CAPTAIN SHOTOVER. If you're marrying for business, you can't be too businesslike.

ELLIE. Why do women always want other women's husbands?

CAPTAIN SHOTOVER. Why do horse-thieves prefer a horse that is broken-in to one that is wild?

ELLIE (*with a short laugh*). I suppose so. What a vile world it is!

CAPTAIN SHOTOVER. It doesn't concern me. I'm nearly out of it.

ELLIE. And I'm only just beginning.

CAPTAIN SHOTOVER. Yes; so look ahead.

ELLIE. Well, I think I am being very prudent.

CAPTAIN SHOTOVER. I didn't say prudent. I said look ahead.

ELLIE. What's the difference? . . . Oh, you are very old-fashioned, Captain. Does any modern girl believe that the legal and illegal ways of getting money are the honest and dishonest ways? Mangan robbed my father and my father's friends. I should rob all the money back from Mangan if the police would let me. As they won't, I must get it back by marrying him.

CAPTAIN SHOTOVER. I can't argue: I'm too old: my mind is made up and finished. All I can tell you is that, old-fashioned or new-fashioned, if you sell yourself, you deal your soul a blow that all the books and pictures and concerts and scenery in the world won't heal (*he gets up suddenly and makes for the pantry*) . . . It confuses me to be answered. It discourages me. I cannot bear men and women. I have to run away. I must run away now (*he tries to*).

But Shotover is not in fact routed. He wins Ellie by recalling the code of his own youth:

I sit here working out my old ideas as a means of destroying my fellow-creatures. I see my daughters and their men leading foolish lives of romance and sentiment and snobbery. I see you, the younger generation, turning from their romance and sentiment and snobbery to money and comfort and hard common sense. I was ten times happier on the bridge in the typhoon, or frozen into Arctic ice for months in darkness, than you or they have ever been. You are looking for a rich husband. At your age I looked for hardship, danger, horror, and death, that I might feel the life in me more intensely. I did not let the fear of death govern my life; and my reward was, I had my life. You are going to let the fear of poverty govern your life; and your reward will be that you will eat, but you will not live.

His conception of strength is one that has earlier been asserted by Caesar. And Ellie, unlike Cleopatra, comes to understand it:

> ELLIE. . . . I feel so happy with you. (*She takes his hand, almost unconsciously, and pats it.*) I thought I should never feel happy again.
> CAPTAIN SHOTOVER. Why?
> ELLIE. Don't you know?
> CAPTAIN SHOTOVER. No.
> ELLIE. Heartbreak. I fell in love with Hector, and didn't know he was married.
> CAPTAIN SHOTOVER. Heartbreak? Are you one of those who are so sufficient to themselves that they are only happy when they are stripped of everything, even of hope?
> ELLIE (*gripping the hand*). It seems so; for I feel now as if there was nothing I could not do, because I want nothing.
> CAPTAIN SHOTOVER. That's the only real strength. That's genius. That's better than rum.

In most of what comes after this we are likely to have a sense of Shaw as casting about for some means of continuing and concluding his play. The note of desperation returns, and is made vivid in Shotover's image of England as a drifting ship, with the captain in his bunk drinking bottled ditch-water, and the crew gambling in the forecastle. He advises the posturing but intelligent Hector Hushabye to learn his business as an Englishman, and when asked what that business is he replies: 'Navigation. Learn it and live; or leave it and be damned.' It is only a moment later that the first exploding bomb is heard. Hushabye with a fatuous bravado runs about the house turning on all the lights. Mangan and the burglar are killed. Ellie, although she has learnt so much wisdom from her sage, agrees with Mrs. Hushabye that it has been a glorious experience. The play ends with her 'radiant' at the prospect of the raiders returning on the following night. It is a slightly uncertain final curtain. And we feel—as we do with some of the other plays— that it might with advantage have fallen just a little earlier.

13

'To be in hell is to drift: to be in heaven is to steer.' Don Juan's aphorism in *Man and Superman* might stand as epigraph to the later play—and indeed Captain Shotover's master-image seems directly derived from it. Why modern man has stopped steering—with all those consequences in futility and nihilism which Heartbreak House and the Europe it represents evince—is expounded in a section of the preface which points directly forward to the ambitious project upon which Shaw is presently to advance: the 'metabiological Pentateuch', *Back to Methuselah* (published 1921, produced first in New York 1922). Modern scientific determinism is at the root of the trouble—and particularly its assertion of 'that lifeless method of evolution which its investigators called Natural Selection'. It is this 'pseudo-science as disastrous as the blackest Calvinism' that has paralysed us by insisting that 'mind, choice, purpose, conscience, will, and so forth' are mere figment and illusion. But it is equally Shaw himself, we may feel, who is being driven to see cherished beliefs as illusory. His faith in man as he is has suffered further contraction and he is persuaded that, for all that the conscious human intellect can do, the ship must drift still. If the superman is to be achieved it will not be through eugenic breeding. Only in some far more profoundly creative act, to be conceived of as a striving at the unconscious roots of Life itself, is there any hope of a real bettering of the human condition. And Shaw's conception of the nature of that bettering is also undergoing change. *The Intelligent Woman's Guide to Socialism and Capitalism* (1928) is an elaborate and devoted work from which it is clear that the practical Fabian long remained alive in him; and its 'Peroration', indeed, remains perhaps the finest prose passage in his writings. But at the same time Shaw is losing interest in the old view—still implied by Ellie Dunn— that it is the business of the human being to enjoy refined and rational pleasures, the necessary basis for which is plenty of money all round. This loss of interest in an old postulate appears particularly in the dropping of any sort of aesthetic delectation from Shaw's picture of an evolved human society. *Back to Methuselah* convinces us how little congruous with the true bent of his mind was his début as a critic of music and painting. What he plumps for in the end is something he calls contemplation.

What his contemplators are to contemplate is obscure. It is certainly not God. Perhaps it is relevant to this problem that a great many of the books about Shaw are crammed with photographs of Shaw, and that a number of these represent Shaw contemplating paintings and busts of Shaw. There is certainly something basically narcissistic in the far-off, divine event to which creation, as he conceives it, moves.

The doctrine of creative evolution is not readily adaptable to the entertainment of theatre-goers in New York or London, and the interest of *Back to Methuselah* lies more in Shaw's resourcefulness here than in the work's 'metabiological' burden. He spins out his theme into five short plays. *In the Beginning* shows Adam and Eve in the Garden, conscious both that immortality would be intolerable to them and that Life must go on. The Serpent teaches them the secret of sexual reproduction, which their parent Lilith has made possible by willing herself into two. This is the first distinguishable act of Creative Evolution: 'You imagine what you desire; you will what you imagine; and at last you create what you will.' Progress, advanced ideas, and adventures begin with Cain, who judges his parents out of date and invents warfare and slavery. Eve sees that all this is childish, that already most of her grandchildren are dying before they have sense enough to know how to live. Enoch was still a mere child at eighty, and humanity will have to accept a different life-span if human achievement is to count for anything.

In *The Gospel of the Brothers Barnabas* Eve's conviction is rekindled in the minds of a philosopher and a biologist in the early nineteen-twenties. It is clear to Franklyn and Conrad Barnabas that 'the political and social problems raised by our civilization cannot be solved by mere human mushrooms' and that the term of human life must be extended to at least three centuries. And this is something which they believe may soon simply happen—not gradually, but by one of those jumps which the new science of Creative Evolution has shown to be the true means of Life's development. Most of the amusement in this play—and it is unflaggingly concerned to amuse—comes from the keen but inept interest in the brothers' ideas displayed by two Liberal politicians, Lubin and Joyce Burge, who are in fact extravagant lampoons upon Asquith and Lloyd George. When they discover that the proposal does not turn upon the discovery of a pill or nostrum, and that the Barnabases simply

believe that by spreading the knowledge and conviction of
what is required they may conjure up, apparently at an unconscious level, the act of will which alone is needed, they lose
interest in the new idea as being not at all likely to influence
a General Election. It is two minor characters in this play,
a parlourmaid and an undistinguished young clergyman, who
turn up as the first—and, we are made to feel, quite involuntary
—long-livers in *The Thing Happens*, set in the year 2170 A.D.
The effective government of England has now devolved upon
Chinese and negro civil servants. The politicians of the time,
from whom most of the fun is again extracted, are cast in a
convention of near-imbecility which allows some illusion that
the long-livers are indeed already the possessors of a more than
human wisdom. It is in the fourth play, *Tragedy of an Elderly
Gentleman*, that Shaw runs into real difficulty. How is he to
depict this new wisdom when it has had a further eight centuries in which to mature itself? It can be done only by continuing to exhibit it as setting the old follies in their place. We
are therefore asked to believe that the British Empire, which is
still an affair of short-livers, has dispatched its Prime Minister
and others from its capital in Baghdad to consult an Oracle
maintained by the long-livers of Britain on the south shore of
Galway Bay in Ireland. Such visitors, it appears, can just
support the society of natives who have not yet advanced beyond
their first century, but if they encounter the seniors of these
they are likely to die of discouragement. It is the tragedy of the
elderly gentleman (who is the father-in-law of the visiting
Prime Minister, Mr. Badger Bluebin) that a glimmer of rationality makes him unable to contemplate the horror of returning
to Baghdad, while at the same time he is a mere infant entirely
unfitted to remain in the new society. We are at least left in no
doubt of the validity of this latter proposition, since his fatuity
has been laid bare for us at disastrous length. The stripling long-
livers who bear the brunt of dealing with the visitors would even
command our sympathy, were they not condemned by their
own roles to a wholly disagreeable assiduity in snubbing and
squashing. This is a bad patch in *Back to Methuselah*. Shaw must
have required all the confidence of which he was so largely
possessed to move on from it to his final consideration of the
terrestrial situation in 31920 A.D. The concluding play is called
As Far As Thought Can Reach.

What Shaw in fact achieves in response to this challenge is a
remarkable triumph of imaginative drama. The curtain rises
on 'a dainty little classic temple' and on youths and maidens
dancing to the music of flute players. 'There are no children.'
But in fact these dancers are the infants of the new order,
hatched full-grown from the egg (for mankind has become
oviparous), and enjoying for a space of three or four years the
nursery games of love-making and the arts. Later they will have
to accept maturity in a life of contemplation which, physical
accident aside, will stretch into eternity. But if these babies
present an idealized image of our own stage of development
as the dramatist sees it, another and more faithful one is
offered us in the two automata constructed by the infant
scientist Pygmalion. These describe themselves as Ozymandias
and Cleopatra-Semiramis, and they expatiate in a pompous
rhetoric making clear that they represent, in fact, humanity as
scientific determinism conceives it, 'the children of Cause and
Effect'. They then quarrel; Pygmalion intervenes; the female
automaton bites him, so that he immediately dies. Two Ancients
enter and examine the automata—which cease to function
while mouthing dying speeches reminiscent of poetic drama,
and are then removed and destroyed 'with the rest of the laboratory refuse'. The incident provides the Ancients with some
occasion to address the babies on serious philosophical themes,
explaining that it is the ultimate task of Spirit to free itself from
Matter, so that finally there shall be only Thought, which will
be Life Eternal. Darkness falls. The ghosts of Adam, Eve, Cain,
and the Serpent appear and speak. Lilith becomes visible and
questions them. They answer according to their natures, and
fade. Lilith pronounces an epilogue beginning 'They have
accepted the burden of eternal life' and ending 'It is enough
that there is a beyond'. The Ancients are themselves infants.
Nature, judging that they have done well so far, watches and
forbears. On this bleak and serious doctrine the whole work
closes.

14

Back to Methuselah displays a writer in his middle sixties who
is still unable with any certainty to bring together within an
artistic unity his two most powerful impulses: those which
render apposite enough the title *Bernard Shaw: Playboy and*

Prophet given by Mr. Archibald Henderson to one of his monu-
mental biographies. The seriousness of Lilith is really not
reconcilable with the absurdity of Lubin and Burge, and Shaw's
Pentateuch leaves us with the apprehension that the old formula
'Find the right thing to say, and then say it with the utmost
levity' may have brought its author to a dead end. That Shaw
had some sense of this himself perhaps appears in what he now
attempted.

Saint Joan (1923) achieves a unique and almost perfect integration of high comic powers with strong convictions. The
result is certainly his outstanding play, conceivably the finest
and most moving English drama since *The Winter's Tale* or
The Tempest. It owns that sure mark of greatness: a stature
that remains intact after every consideration has been given to
evident and undeniable imperfections. A preserved admiration
for it amid the changed literary fashions of the mid-twentieth
century may fairly be set, along with a similarly preserved
admiration for the poetry and prose of Hardy and the short
stories of Kipling, among the touchstones of a good and catholic
literary taste.

There is, at the simplest, a new tact in the use of laughter.
Two instances of this occur at the end of the first scene. Robert
de Baudricourt, the military squire who eventually agrees to
send Joan to the Dauphin, is a man of the commonest clay,
disguising behind aggressive bluster a decided weakness of will.
When Joan, receiving his grudging permission to go forward,
cried out 'Oh, squire! Your head is all circled with light, like
a saint's', the dramatic effect—which is of the sudden and
overwhelming order of Miranda's 'Oh brave new world'—is
enhanced alike by the antecedent comedy of his character and
by the immediate touch of genius in the stage-direction telling
us that he has 'looked up for his halo rather apprehensively'.
There is the same fusion of our laughter with deep emotion
in the moment upon which the scene closes—a moment which
looks forward to the Archbishop's definition of a miracle as an
event which creates faith, while at the same time knitting perfectly with the comedy of the 'three Barbary hens and the black'
upon which the action has opened:

*Robert, still very doubtful whether he has not been made a fool of by a
crazy female, and a social inferior to boot, scratches his head and slowly comes
back from the door.*

The steward runs in with a basket.
STEWARD. Sir, sir—
ROBERT. What now?
STEWARD. The hens are laying like mad, sir. Five dozen eggs!
ROBERT (*stiffens convulsively; crosses himself; and forms with his pale lips the words*) Christ in heaven! (*Aloud but breathless*) She did come from God.

Or, again, there is the handling of John de Stogumber, the Earl of Warwick's chaplain, whose charge against Joan is that she 'denies to England her legitimate conquests, given her by God because of her peculiar fitness to rule over less civilized races for their own good' and who takes it as self-evident that the Archangel Michael talks in English if he talks at all. We have had this character before in the Britannus of *Caesar and Cleopatra*, and are constrained to admit that farcical anachronism could no farther go. But when, in the end, it is de Stogumber who is chosen by the dramatist to bring before us the physical horror of Joan's end, the joke is not dropped but transmuted in the one point of comfort the wretched man can see: 'She asked for a cross. A soldier gave her two sticks tied together. Thank God he was an Englishman! I might have done it; but I did not: I am a coward, a mad dog, a fool. But he was an Englishman too.'

Neither in minor matters of this sort nor in the play as a whole is it an essentially historical imagination that is at work. 'There is a new spirit rising in men', the Archbishop says in the second scene; 'we are at the dawning of a wider epoch.' And in the fourth scene Warwick and the Bishop of Beauvais look forward apprehensively to dangers for which they coin the names Protestantism and Nationalism. These characters carry, of course, the burden of making intelligible to us what could scarcely in actual fact be intelligible to themselves, and Shaw has both achieved this with a brilliant lucidity in the play and cogently defended in his preface its dramatic propriety. Even so, we are rather sharply aware that his interest is not in the pressure and density of an actual historical situation. Rather it is in Joan in her most representative quality as one of those who have been—in the words used at her canonization—endowed with heroic virtues and favoured with private revelations. To some extent at least Shaw the disciple of Butler has given place to Shaw the disciple of Bunyan. He shows no inclination, indeed, to the truths of revealed religion. Joan's voices do not come, as she supposes them to do, from a God in any sense acceptable to believing Christians. They simply represent, the preface tells us, the 'pressure upon her of the driving force that is behind evolution'. The evolution is very much that of Samuel Butler and the brothers Barnabas still. The preface speaks of 'the fountain of inspiration which is continually flowing in the universe' and of 'the eternal soul in Nature'. It condemns the 'rationalist' view that 'new ideas cannot come otherwise than by conscious ratiocination'. And it asserts that 'no official organisation of mortal men . . . can keep pace with the private judgment of persons of genius'. This is the crux. The spirit bloweth where it listeth. It is the parlourmaid and not the statesman or philosopher who first lives for three hundred years; it is the ignorant country girl and not the learned and humane Inquisitor whom the Life Force categorically commands. 'The voices come first', Joan says, 'and I find the reasons after.' Joan's faith in her voices is the obverse of Shaw's deepening scepticism before human institutions. Of these institutions he takes the medieval Catholic Church as supremely representative. For that Church as he sees it he contrives the effect of a wonderfully fair hearing. There is a transcendent instance of this immediately before Joan is brought in for trial. Ladvenu, a young Dominican, asks: 'But is there any great harm in the girl's heresy? Is it not merely her simplicity? Many saints have said as much as Joan.' The Inquisitor replies that heresy begins with people who are to all appearance better than their neighbours. And his speech is perhaps the finest—as it is certainly one of the longest—in all the plays.

Yet Shaw's final antagonism to the Church's point of view is absolute. There can be no blessing on councils, synods, and assemblies—unless indeed they have the grace to receive that wisdom which comes into the world only through the channel of the inspired individual. In Shaw's decline this persuasion led him into a strangely uncritical approbation of the new absolutisms rising in Europe. If it leads him first to his finest play, he has his heroine to thank for it. He has been a playwright for thirty years—and now, at the end of a long line of brilliant inventions, there stands at last a real human being. A young woman whose intervention in the dynastic struggles of the fifteenth century is to be received as a manifestation of the

Life Force, urging ever higher the human race at large, seems a conception of dubious dramatic promise, and one could have had, before the event, very little assurance that Shaw's Maid would not be of the same order as Schiller's or Mark Twain's. In fact, she is a major dramatic achievement. Nor does she simply rise clear of the persons, events, and profuse speechifyings surrounding her. Rather she raises them to her own plane, and is thus literally the making of the play. She is a Shavian heroine —distinguishably, one may say, the creation of the writer who discerned in the Helena of *All's Well* one of the finest of Shakespeare's women. At the same time she is the true sister of Catherine of Siena and Theresa of Avila. And this is perhaps Shaw's work rather than history's.

Saint Joan was followed by a six-year silence. *The Apple Cart*, produced in 1929 just before Shaw's seventy-third birthday, is the first of a number of plays, mainly political extravaganzas, of declining power. It shows King Magnus, an able and disinterested constitutional monarch, outmanœuvring a Cabinet rendered in the convention of travesty first exploited in *The Gospel of the Brothers Barnabas*—the Prime Minister Proteus being a lampoon upon the Labour leader Ramsay MacDonald which echoes the lampooning in the earlier play of MacDonald's Liberal predecessors.

Yet the comparative weakness of this and later plays scarcely consists in Shaw's having nothing new to say. He is very adequately aware of the emerging social and political contexts amid which the twentieth century is coming of age. *Too True to be Good* (1932) is a rambling fable which ends surprisingly and powerfully upon a figure who is certainly Shaw himself confronting his own obsolescence in a world of post-war bright young things, and still quenchlessly talking and perorating as fog rises and thickens around him. *On the Rocks* (1933) displays an almost sprightly determination to keep abreast or ahead of the time by chronicling the advance of fascism and the breakdown of parliamentary government in England. *The Simpleton of the Unexpected Isles* (1935) advances yet farther and presents the Day of Judgement. Nor are the surface qualities of Shaw's wit markedly in eclipse in this last phase. What is lacking is rather the old compulsion constantly to deploy the wit in the interest of effective encounter. It was in this that his true power lay from the first, and it is this that made him the most influential writer of his age. Undoubtedly the width of his appeal has adversely affected his subsequent reputation with some who take a restricted view of the nature and function of imaginative literature. But many of his plays can scarcely prove other than lastingly delightful, since they are the product of vigorous intelligence joined to inexhaustible comic invention.

V · CONRAD

JOSEPH CONRAD, quite as much as Henry James, invites speculation on the theme of exile. He was born in 1857 in one of the southern provinces of Poland; he died in 1924 at Bishopsbourne in Kent, and is buried at Canterbury. His father, Apollo Korzeniowski, was a country gentleman of melancholic and mystical temperament, unable to administer even a small estate successfully, and with some inclination to literary pursuits. From these he was diverted by a patriotic fervour which, being uncontrolled by any practical sagacity, led to his prosecution by the Tsarist authorities, and dispatch into exile at Vologda in Russia. Apollo's wife chose to share his privations, her health gave way, and she died in 1865. During the following four years the boy led a lonely and dismal life with his father, whose anxieties were now concentrated upon his education. Restive and lethargic under instruction, Conrad early became an avid reader of romances, Captain Marryat's among them. It is recorded that he wrote plays and declared that he would become a great writer. When he was twelve his father died. He was placed in the charge of an amiable if somewhat lavishly admonitory uncle, and within two or three years he was demanding to be allowed to go to sea. His thought had thus turned to the one profession which must inevitably take him out of Poland. His uncle at first opposed the plan. But the boy, being the son of a political convict, was liable to long service as a ranker in the Russian army. This may have been a factor in his eventually getting his way. Before his seventeenth birthday he was in the Mediterranean, his family's proposal being that he should make his career in the French merchant navy. At first he was unsettled and improvident. He may have engaged in gun-running for the Carlists; there was an obscurer occasion upon which he was wounded as the consequence either of a duel or of attempted suicide. But in 1878 he joined an

English ship and addressed himself to the sobrieties of his profession. Eight years after that again he received his Master Mariner's certificate and became a naturalized British subject.

This is a strange background for a great English novelist. It has been maintained that Conrad as he came to maturity acknowledged or half-acknowledged something shameful in having left Poland, and that much of his writing is generated in the haunting persuasion that he had betrayed his manhood even before he grew into it. There is only a limited critical interest in the thesis that all his work is an allegory of desertion and expiation. Yet he is undoubtedly an artist in whose creations the echo of some deep inner conflict is constantly heard. His last work of unimpaired quality, *The Shadow-Line* (1917), illustrates this. A directly autobiographical narrative based upon Conrad's first experience of command when, in 1888, he was given the barque *Otago* at Bangkok, it carries the sub-title 'A Confession' and turns upon one of the superstitions of the sea. The young captain finds that his predecessor, a disreputable and sinister character, has died on the ship, which now appears to be under a curse. 'All the immense forces of the world' seem to be ranged supernaturally against it on this, its immediately succeeding voyage. It is becalmed; the crew go down with fever almost to the last man; the stock of quinine has vanished from its bottles. The chief mate declares, as the ship vainly tries to struggle south, that the old captain, buried somewhere ahead, bars the way and will never let them past. There follows trial upon trial to the limit of human endurance, and the ship eventually makes port with only the young captain himself on his feet. For the narrator it is the story of an ordeal, an initiation. Will he pass? That is the essential question, and it gives us the first and simplest interest in Conrad's world. We come upon rather deeper matter with the figure of Ransome, the calm, devoted steward whose weak heart puts him in immediate danger of death whenever, in the crisis, he resolutely sets a hand to a rope—and who, when all is over, is savagely determined to be paid off: 'For an instant he was another being. And I saw under the worth and the comeliness of the man the humble reality of things. Life was a boon to him—this precarious hard life—and he was thoroughly alarmed about himself.' An intransigent standard of personal honour, and the answering need to acknowledge 'the humble reality of things': these stand over against each other here.

The Shadow-Line has indeed a private resonance. We can sense in it, as Mr. Guerard points out, a muted dramatizing of that 'living through and throwing off of an immobilizing neurotic depression' which constituted the rhythm of Conrad's personal life; and of which, he himself wrote to Edward Garnett, the severity was such that in a lunatic asylum it would be called madness. Yet *The Shadow-Line* comes to us in the main as a dealing in straight heroic values—the simpler of *les valeurs idéales* to the celebration of which he once declared that all his gifts were dedicated. Much of the effect of his writing derives from his bringing to these elemental issues all the reach of a subtle as well as a powerful literary art. Heroes stretched to breaking-point under the double burden of a merciless nature unleashed against them and a remorseless doubt or self-distrust mining from within; and others, no longer heroes, because they have broken under the strain: this is no esoteric formula; and its effects come to us magnificently, with little need for explanatory words. But in the finest of all the short stories, 'The Secret Sharer', written in 1909, there is something more problematical. Here again there is a first command, and the young captain's lurking fear receives explicit statement: 'I wondered how far I should turn out faithful to that ideal conception of one's own personality every man sets up for himself secretly.' What happens as a consequence of this strung-up resolve to acknowledge only an ideal self is something like a dissociation of personality—or the story is an allegory of this. Out of the sea in the dead of night comes Leggatt, the murderer, the captain's other self, 'exactly the same' but guilty, to be accepted, to be hidden from the world, to be so hidden dressed in a sleeping-suit, the very garb of the unacknowledged or night side of life according to the symbolism of dreams; and finally to depart, as he came, into the mysterious sea under the towering enigmatical shadow of Koh-ring—the secret sharer, the other self admitted, entertained, honourably voided, discharged as a result of the superhuman assertion of the braced will that has taken the ship and all its souls under the very gate of Erebus.

This is a highly charged story, of great psychological as well as literary interest. Indeed the threat to a willed and achieved personality constituted by the possible eruption of a subliminal self is a theme for which Conrad finds symbolical expression in some of his most memorable places. And his account of how he began writing, first given in *Some Reminiscences* (1912), is significant as conveying a related sense of hidden identity. He is in his thirty-second year, and experiencing the deep indolence of a sailor during a spell ashore. One morning he has the breakfast-table cleared early, without at all knowing why. For a little time he stands looking out of the window. And then the 'inexplicable event', as he called it, occurs. He sits down and begins to write his first novel:

It was not the outcome of a need—the famous need of self-expression which artists find in their search for motives. The necessity which impelled me was a hidden, obscure necessity, a completely masked and unaccountable phenomenon. . . . Till I began to write that novel I had written nothing but letters, and not very many of these. I never made a note of a fact, of an impression or of an anecdote in my life. The conception of a planned book was entirely outside my mental range when I sat down to write; the ambition of being an author had never turned up amongst these gracious imaginary existences one creates fondly for oneself at times in the stillness and immobility of a day-dream: yet it stands clear as the sun at noonday that from the moment I had done blackening over the first manuscript page of 'Almayer's Folly' . . . from the moment I had, in the simplicity of my heart and the amazing ignorance of my mind, written that page the die was cast. Never had Rubicon been more blindly forded, without invocation to the gods, without fear of men.

Conrad liked to emphasize our ignorance of definitive moments when they come. But here is something more: a remarkable evocation of the rising into conscious expression of another secret sharer. Nor is its impressiveness much qualified by the discovery that it does a little stretch the facts: Conrad having, for example, already tried his luck as a writer by entering a short story for a competition in *Tit-Bits*. He would have been superhuman had he added a footnote recording this unassuming attempt.

The novel thus begun was not to be published until he was thirty-seven. His late start may be accounted for partly in terms of his linguistic situation. French he knew in his nursery and spoke with perfection. English he never heard until he went to sea, and throughout his life his command of its intonations was so imperfect that his talk was virtually unintelligible except to his intimates. Yet he is a very notable, if an obstinately

uncertain, English stylist. He never makes us feel, as Hardy
can do, that he is triumphing in spite of an inadequate control of language. Hardy has perceptions that are both larger
and more precise than Conrad's, but to express them he grabs
words by handfuls, forcing them by the sheer weight of his
emotion more or less effectively into his service. It is always
something of a rape of language. Conrad is the most studious
of lovers. His wooing of the whole body of the English language
is a process holding, for the spectator, a mingling of tedium and
fascination. The affair has its over-sultry moments, its occasional
extravagance of pose. Yet there can be no doubt of the depth
and complexity of response which the pertinacious lover elicits.
Conrad is never afraid of rhetoric or of a prose approaching the
frontiers of poetry. His elaborately extended cadences, subtly
gratifying the ear even while again and again cheating it of
an expected pause, carry a large part of the burden of his
constitutional melancholy. At the same time they form a kind
of rhythmic correlative of that unintermitted striving to gain a
longitude, to match the gale, which is his grand symbol for
what we do best to address our lives to. It is recorded that he was
fond of Jeremy Taylor—and from Taylor and other seventeenth-
century writers he may have learned more directly than an
Englishman would find it easy to do, simply because he was
less aware of the dangers of archaism, fine writing, and pastiche.
A larger and older eloquence than that of the Victorian age
sounds often in his prose—for example, when he celebrates the
sailors of the *Narcissus*:

Men hard to manage, but easy to inspire; voiceless men—but
men enough to scorn in their hearts the sentimental voices that
bewailed the hardness of their fate. It was a fate unique and their
own; the capacity to bear it appeared to them the privilege of the
chosen! Their generation lived inarticulate and indispensable,
without knowing the sweetness of affections or the refuge of a home
—and died free from the dark menace of a narrow grave. They were
the everlasting children of the mysterious sea.

2

The book that began to get itself written, slowly and painfully, on the morning upon which Conrad felt so oddly
impelled to have the table cleared, was *Almayer's Folly* (1895).

It was based, as nearly all Conrad's writing was to be, upon personal experience. Almayer had been a trader—possibly Eurasian—on a station some forty miles up a Bornean river: a misfit the contortions of whose personality in the face of failure had made him a byword among the islands. It was conceivably in his aspect as an exile that he had lurked in Conrad's mind for years before his surprising appearance on paper. 'Why'—Conrad makes him cry—'I have been trying to get out of this infernal place for twenty years, and I can't. You hear, man! I can't, and never shall! Never!' He is represented as married to a Malay woman with no taste for white men's ways. She is a mere savage from whom he turns away to concentrate his affection upon his daughter Nina, whom he brings home after an education in a European family in the Dutch colonial capital to live with him on his steadily more impoverished trading station. For Nina he endlessly elaborates grandiose and feckless plans. When she too turns to the darkness of native life and runs away with the young Malay, Dain, Almayer's hold on himself slips entirely, and he dies in opium and squalor. To this story is added a great deal of intrigue between Europeans, natives, and Arabs up and down the river. It is not a novel that commands its people or paints any memorable picture of human actions and passions. Conrad had voyaged among the islands but had no intimate knowledge of their inhabitants, whom he interprets in terms of the conventions of European fiction. The conflict of race in Nina and the growth of her love for Dain are unconvincing. Although Almayer himself is less easily forgotten he is not held in so sharp a focus as one would expect upon the theory that he is a character in whom Conrad discerned a kinship with himself. Yet neither this novel nor its immediate successor, *An Outcast of the Islands* (1896), should be ignored even in a short view of Conrad's work. In them he learns to command the spirit of place.

The Pantai, Almayer's river, is something really seen and sensed, for Conrad is already brilliantly resourceful in evoking the background of his fiction. And if it refuses to stay as background, if it bears down upon us with far more confidence in its own concrete reality than the characters yet contrive to evince, this has an appropriateness that is evident enough. The constant advance and closing in of forest and river, as if to swallow and dissolve in their violent chiaroscuro the human beings who have momentarily hacked themselves out breathing-space and elbow-room amid these savage proliferations, is congruous with the whole mood and theme of the fiction. One comes quickly to feel that Conrad could get a great deal from a glimpse of any natural scene. He felt exotic places more powerfully and precisely than he felt exotic peoples. What governs and animates this and all his early writing is his emotional response not to his actors but to their backcloth. So uncertain are his people, so questionable as we read seems the inner life he would attribute to them, that the final impression of the early books is of some powerful act of scene-setting, on a stage where the tentatively rehearsing players have as yet scarcely projected themselves into their parts. He seems to begin as a creator of *décor*, or at least at an extreme of the romantic exploitation of landscape as a state of the soul. His technique is partly that of attributing sentience to inanimate things, and partly a sort of half-way house to such an attribution through the nature of his constant similes. The first novel opens with Almayer leaning on the balustrade of his veranda at sunset, gazing down the river that flows, 'indifferent and hurried', before his eyes. He watches a drifting tree. 'The tree swung slowly round, amid the hiss and foam of the water, and soon getting free of the obstruction began to move down stream again, rolling slowly over, raising upwards a long, denuded branch, like a hand lifted in mute appeal to heaven against the river's brutal and unnecessary violence.' There is much more simile than metaphor in all the early prose. It is strong and telling, but frequently we feel that it is being hunted for. We recall that Conrad is teaching himself to write—and in a foreign language.

Here indeed is the simple explanation of the primacy given to the backcloth over the actors: the backcloth keeps conveniently still for study. Or better (since it can be so terrifyingly dynamic) it is perpetually doing the same impressive things over and over again. What, besides the slowly growing manuscript of his novel, did Conrad carry about the world with him during those years of apprenticeship to writing? It was, he records, 'the hallucination of the Eastern Archipelago'. Here was his infinitely patient first model. In 'Karain', a short story written in 1897, he speaks of 'the scenic landscape that intruded upon the reality of our lives by its motionless fantasy of outline and colour'. It is just this that intrudes upon the people in the novels. It was in this business of elaborating at his leisure a technique for describing, or rather for evoking, a manageable because immobile world that Conrad first absorbed himself. 'And green islets scattered through the calm of noonday lie upon the level of a polished sea, like a handful of emeralds on a buckler of steel.' 'The light and heat fell upon the settlement, the clearings, and the river as if flung down by an angry hand.' It has been called his adjectival phase. Certainly it is the steady, considered feeding-in of adjectives that gives his early prose its slow laboured movement, its melancholy drag, its odd effect of being perpetually on the edge of losing momentum and music while seldom in fact doing so. But already he is powerfully exploiting this first grip on the language in the interest of a vision or at least of a temperament. Even the early Conrad is not a mere stylist. Yet he does seem to begin rather from an urge to write than from a compulsion to express a predicament. Moreover the play of temperament as it becomes progressively prominent does not notably yield to any single and simple interpretation. The Conrad over-world, with its vast vague gestures, its inscrutabilities, mysteries, illusions, and despairs, is something of considerable complexity. And it is first distilled for us not from Almayer's situation as an exile, or anything of the sort, but rather from the permanent forms of exotic nature, recalled with hallucinatory clearness, in which Conrad found tractable material when embarking upon the formidable career of man of letters in a language not his own.

His first talent then—akin to that of another sailor, Pierre Loti, from whom he may have learned—was for taking experience in terms of impressionism. But from the first, too, he had the instinct, if not the ability, to exploit this talent to ends that are dramatic and not simply pictorial. In the Malayan stories the natural scene is given, somewhat laboriously, a choric role. It is obliged industriously to point and comment upon human affairs. Essentially not very far from Hardy's vast neutral unregarding universe, it is less impressive because more insistently stage-managed. At times it may be felt as almost comically subservient in the promptness with which it skips into the right part of the picture, moans when it can most effectively moan, exudes warm breaths or cold breaths at the appropriate moment, disposes its dawns and its sunsets with an obliging sense of what will be congruous with the situation immediately in hand. Conrad acquires quite early an almost dangerous facility in the creation of atmosphere.

In *The Nigger of the 'Narcissus'* (1898) what is potentially theatrical in this expertness is controlled by the combined weight and simplicity of the task primarily in hand: a picture of the merchant seaman's life, and a celebration of his virtue into which there is only very lightly touched any notice of situations or predicaments with which those virtues are inadequate to deal. *The Nigger of the 'Narcissus'* is not without symbolic implication of that largely involuntary sort which can readily be magnified by a sophisticated interpretative criticism. But essentially it is again heroic in kind. The long description of the struggle with the storm, the great moment of the righting of the ship, must rank as among the finest expressions of the heroic life to be found in English. A preface to the story, written within a few months of its completion but not printed along with it for many years, makes a fitting commentary, since it is the finest of his discussions of the aesthetic of fiction. 'Youth', written in the following year, is a short story with a similar marine setting, but carrying both lyrical and elegiac suggestion. Substantially, and within the bounds of artistic contrivance, an autobiographical record, it was characterized by Conrad as a feat of memory purely, with a significance beginning and ending with itself. A young officer—the Marlow who is to relate so many of Conrad's tales—finds himself in charge of one of the open boats of a cargo steamer which has to be abandoned. His whole experience, culminating in his first sight of Asia thus achieved under his own command, is like a strong wine to him:

> I did not know how good a man I was till then. I remember the drawn faces, the dejected figures of my two men, and I remember my youth and the feeling that will never come back any more—the feeling that I could last for ever, outlast the sea, the earth, and all men; the deceitful feeling that lures us on to joys, to perils, to love, to vain effort—to death; the triumphant conviction of strength, the heat of life in the handful of dust, the glow in the heart that with every year grows dim, grows cold, grows small, and expires—and expires, too soon, too soon—before life itself.

In this with its heavy epizeuxis Conrad's devoted courting of the eloquence of his adopted language is evident enough. But the mood evoked is comprehensible and finite; and putting it it on paper, he says, was merely a matter of 'simple colouring'.

3

It was otherwise with 'Heart of Darkness', written in 1899. The autobiographical basis of this is in maturer experience, a voyage up the Congo, undertaken in 1890, which appears to have had a profound effect upon his imagination and indeed his personality. Before it, he told Edward Garnett, he had been 'just a mere animal'. And in the story he was concerned, he recorded, with 'experience pushed a little (and only very little) beyond the actual facts of the case. . . . That sombre theme had to be given a sinister resonance, a tonality of its own, a continued vibration that, I hoped, would hang in the air and dwell on the ear after the last note had been struck'. To this end he marshals all his developed resources of atmospheric writing, and achieves a masterpiece which is at once overpowering and enigmatical.

The story is narrated by Marlow to a company gathered on a yawl near Gravesend, waiting for the turn of the tide, so that we are told: 'The sea-reach of the Thames stretched before us like the beginning of an interminable waterway'—as in fact it is. 'The venerable stream' is evoked in all its immemorial associations—and then Marlow's voice breaks as it were the silence in which we are contemplating the spectacle. This also, he says, has been one of the dark places of the earth, and he sketches its effect upon some young Roman legionary:

He has to live in the midst of the incomprehensible, which is also detestable. And it has a fascination, too, that goes to work upon him. The fascination of the abomination—you know, imagine the growing regrets, the longing to escape, the powerless disgust, the surrender, the hate.

Marlow goes on to tell the story of Kurtz. We learn how Marlow, commissioned to command a river steamer far up the Congo, crawls towards the equator in a French coasting steamer. The tropics thrust out at him, with increasing force, intimations of their power to disintegrate and corrupt the standards and the very consciousness of culture:

Once, I remember, we came upon a man-of-war anchored off the coast. There wasn't even a shed there, and she was shelling the bush. It appears the French had one of their wars going on there-abouts. Her ensign dropped limp like a rag; the muzzles of the long six-inch guns stuck out all over the low hull; the greasy, slimy swell swung her up lazily and let her down, swaying her thin masts. In the empty immensity of earth, sky, and water, there she was, incomprehensible, firing into a continent.

Then comes the voyage up the river and Marlow's arrival at the trading station. A crazy railway is being built. Mercilessly exploited native labourers are dying of disease or starvation in utter neglect. In the heart of this savage wilderness there is being carried on a ghastly and futile travesty of a developing material civilization. This is the environment within which Kurtz is discovered. He stands at the end of an ascending series of corrupting nightmares—and his reputation is that of a prodigy of benevolence and enlightenment, an isolated civilizing genius in charge of an upper station. He is abhorred and feared by his fellow-traders, who intrigue and slander and hate each other in their mad scramble for ivory, and who have in fact succeeded in isolating him for months in the hope that the climate will kill him. The first section of the story ends with Marlow curious 'to see whether this man, who had come out equipped with moral ideas of some sort, would climb to the top after all and how he would set about his work when there'.

But Kurtz has become depraved and perverted beyond description—this while still able to awe with a hollow eloquence full of the loftiest moral idealism the simple young Russian who is his only white associate. The first intimation of the state of the case is the weird and passionate behaviour of the natives when they believe that Kurtz is to be taken away from them. These negroes—simply glimpsed in the grip of their inexplicable emotions, or heard in a loud cry as of infinite desolation soaring slowly in the opaque air—are altogether more convincing than the Malays within whose skin Conrad had supposed he could insert himself in the Islands novels and stories. Kurtz has become a god, the centre and recipient of unspeakable rites. Mortally ill, he is brought on board ship. He escapes on hands and knees, crawling painfully back to the darkness that has enslaved him. Then he is secured again and the steamer sails with him:

The brown current ran swiftly out of the heart of darkness, bearing us down towards the sea. . . . Kurtz discoursed. A voice! a voice! It rang deep to the very last. It survived his strength to hide in the magnificent folds of eloquence the barren darkness of his heart. . . . The shade of the original Kurtz frequented the bedside of the hollow sham, whose fate it was to be buried presently in the mould of primeval earth.

Somewhere the uncorrupted man lurks in Kurtz, a judging presence. And he acknowledges the horror with his last breath:

> Anything approaching the change that came over his features I have never seen before, and hope never to see again. . . . It was as though a veil had been rent. I saw on that ivory face the expression of sombre pride, of ruthless power, of craven terror—of an intense and hopeless despair. Did he live his life again in every detail of desire, temptation, and surrender during that supreme moment of complete knowledge? He cried in a whisper at some image, at some vision—he cried out twice, a cry that was no more than a breath—
> 'The horror! The horror!'
> I blew the candle out and left the cabin. . . .

Marlow returns to the mean and predatory scoundrels (the pilgrims, as he calls them in irony) whom it is his business to ferry up and down the nightmare river:

> I blew the candle out and left the cabin. The pilgrims were dining in the mess-room, and I took my place opposite the manager, who lifted his eyes to give me a questioning glance, which I successfully ignored. He leaned back, serene, with that peculiar smile of his sealing the unexpressed depths of his meanness. A continuous shower of small flies streamed upon the lamp, upon the cloth, upon our hands and faces. Suddenly the manager's boy put his insolent black head in the doorway, and said in a tone of scathing contempt—
> 'Mistah Kurtz—he dead.'

The story concludes with a brief epilogue in which Marlow tells of his being constrained to visit the woman to whom Kurtz had been betrothed. She is utterly trusting and believing, living under the spell still of his hollow, easily eloquent idealism. She insists on knowing what were his last words. And Marlow says that Kurtz died pronouncing her name.

> Marlow ceased, and sat apart, indistinct and silent, in the pose of a meditating Buddha. Nobody moved for a time. 'We have lost the first of the ebb', said the Director, suddenly. I raised my head. The offing was barred by a black bank of clouds, and the tranquil waterway leading to the uttermost ends of the earth flowed sombre under an overcast sky—seemed to lead into the heart of an immense darkness.

This dreadful tale has been variously interpreted and valued.
It has been viewed as essentially about Marlow, who represents
the simple virtues of honesty, courage, pity, and fidelity, and
who in Kurtz meets not only intimations of an evil before which
these are no resource but also an individual with whom he is
horrified to feel some obscure shadow of identity. His own code
is a sufficient armour against the plain scoundrels among whom
he finds himself, but is wholly vulnerable when confronted
by the darkness of Kurtz, with whom, inexplicably, he has
to acknowledge a link. This reading finds some support in the
text, but is far from rendering lucid the conception of evil
which Conrad is endeavouring to convey. Another estimate
regards the story as valid in all its concrete exemplifications of
corruption, but vitiated by a portentous insistence that the
profundity and significance of Marlow's revelation lies in an
unmapped hinterland of sinister suggestion. Certainly we may
rather sharply feel that Conrad has gone all out to create the
'resonance' of which his preface speaks, and that he has achieved
this at the cost of failing to make Kurtz any very convincing
individual creation.

There is perhaps an illuminating contrast to be made here
with Captain MacWhirr in 'Typhoon' (1903), a keenly and
triumphantly realized figure free of any metaphysical penumbra. Kurtz, as soon as we a little disengage him from his
brilliantly macabre ambience, is nothing like so actual. And
another comparison suggests itself. 'Heart of Darkness' has
marked affinities with James's 'The Turn of the Screw'. Both
stories invite us to stand appalled before not simply evil but
some unspeakable and inexpressible quintessence of it. The
writers make a bogy of vice, a great to-do over never quite
contriving or daring to lift the curtain on its naked gigantic
form. Evil thus posed is not often very successfully domesticated
in England; it is among the things they order better in France.
Mr. Graham Greene, who has learned both from France and
Conrad, has grasped this fact, and never proposes to make our
flesh creep as Conrad and James in these stories do.

Kurtz may be described as the logical consequence for any
man of admitting a breach in those defences which the guarding
of personal integrity constantly requires. The line of human
heads with which his station had been embellished only showed,
Marlow reflects, 'that there was something wanting in him—

some small matter which, when the pressing need arose, could not be found'. Or—as it is elsewhere put—'his nerves went wrong'. There are several other tales of this period—notably 'Falk' and 'The End of the Tether'—which turn upon this theme. And it makes, if with a somewhat less lurid colouring, the basis of *Lord Jim* (1900).

Lord Jim may be regarded as another tale within the group, expanded to novel-length by the addition of a disproportionate epilogue which is itself a sort of throw-back to Almayer's world. But the structural *naïveté*—if it be that—is not incompatible with a thematic complexity, perhaps intuitively achieved, which makes *Lord Jim* as far from a simple exotic romance as anything that Conrad achieved. The first part tells how a young ship's officer, romantic, sensitive, and wholesome, loses his nerve in a moment of danger and is disgraced. In the second part he is shown rehabilitating himself as a figure of authority and integrity in a native state. But his past catches up with him in the form of a crew of desperadoes who know his story and claim his help in the name of a kinship in moral failure. He responds to this perverse point of honour with a strained chivalry the consequences of which are mortal to him. *Lord Jim* may be taken as what Conrad himself called it: 'a free and wandering tale' centred in a 'simple and sensitive character'. It is doubtless in this aspect that it has become the most widely read of his works. Yet the attitude informing the book is not itself simple. To an English reader there is likely to seem something excessive, even obsessed, in the concept of honour upon which it turns. Thus it has been declared that Conrad here makes just the sort of fuss about honour that D. H. Lawrence perpetually does about sex; that Jim is less a good man gone wrong than a compulsive neurotic; and that the novelist must be indicted as having written a morbid book. Conrad appears to represent Jim's loss as absolute. Honour is conceived almost as a physical possession, say a pocket-watch: at a lurch of the ship it drops into the sea and is gone for good. Or it is like one of the senses. The searing blade passes, blindness follows, and there is nothing whatever to be done about it. Yet the doubts which the absoluteness of Conrad's conception must raise are deliberately made to stir in the book itself—and notably in the mind of Marlow, who eventually enters it as narrator:

I was made to look at the convention that lurks in all truth and

on the essential sincerity of falsehood. He appealed to all sides at
once—to the side turned perpetually to the light of day, and to that
side of us which, like the other hemisphere of the moon, exists
stealthily in perpetual darkness, with only a fearful ashy light falling
at times on the edge. He swayed me. I own to it, I own up.

Marlow acknowledges something of Jim in himself, just as he
had done of Kurtz, and it has been maintained that we see him
in a bewilderment and insecurity which is not artistically contrived to illuminate the theme of the novel, but is rather an
undesigned spill-over from some muddle in which Conrad
stands himself. Appraisal of this sort appears to lead back,
whether profitably or not, to argument on the psychogenesis of
Conrad's work in his ambivalent attitude to his own past. Jim
deserts his ship as it threatens to go down, and the jump cuts
him off for ever from his own ideal and untried conception of
himself. And as the young Jim jumps, so had jumped the young
Conrad. 'I verily believe', he wrote in *Some Reminiscences*, 'mine
was the only case of a boy of my nationality and antecedents
taking a, so to speak, standing jump out of his racial surroundings and associations.' Conrad, it is true, always maintained a
rational and controlled attitude to his early history and to any
charge of apostasy brought against him by Poles. Yet on visiting
Poland late in life he is said to have betrayed some sense of
guilt and a fear of being slighted. More than he quite consciously knew, he may indeed have remained a man banished
from those 'vast brown spaces of earth', fruitful beneath the
toil of generations of his kin, which he had exchanged for the
unanswering immensities of the unharvested sea. Certainly of
his own country he was to write with a moving eloquence—
'that country which demands to be loved as no other country
has ever been loved, with the mournful affection one bears to
the unforgotten dead'.

Yet the power over us of Conrad's response to the sense of
exile, potent in this novel, certainly does not proceed simply
from our recognition of an underlying special situation, a
complex of feeling unique and set apart as the consequence of
a specific political and moral background's having been at play
upon a strongly individual mind. It is the grand characteristic
of Conrad's art that, wherever it takes us, the scene universalizes
itself even as that art begins to speak. The deck of the *Narcissus*,
the nightmare reaches of the upper Congo, Jim's Patusan, the

remote republic of Costaguana, the stuffy little kitchen behind
Mr. Verloc's disreputable shop: they all take larger dimension
while we watch. Here always is the terrestrial universe as, in
our moments of clearest awareness, we know it to be: over-
shadowed by guilt, a place of exile into which we have been
betrayed, where we must live by the sweat of our brow, by
hard toil upon the frozen ropes as the dark seas drive higher—
by this and by what assertion of continuing human dignity we
can wring from this. Conrad does speak, perhaps, from a heart
of exile. But the story of a Fall and of a Paradise lost to us is, of
all our myths, perhaps the one most immemorially central to
the human imagination. One of the reasons why Conrad's art
is so powerful may indeed lie in this: that the circumstances of
his youth and the force of his genius moved him again and again
to its poignant re-creation.

4

It is in *Nostromo* (1904) that his genius achieves its most
vigorous and abundant, if not perhaps its most subtle, expression. This is one of the great English novels, and the circumstances of its composition are remarkably interesting. Conrad,
as we have seen, had become a novelist suddenly and as if upon
the irruption of another personality, a personality impelled to
creation. But he always found writing painful and difficult.
He was among those who agonize themselves over a sentence or
a word—as also among those who 'go dry', who intermittently
have to face an apparent total surcease of inventive power,
staring at the blank sheet for days on end. The extra strains and
fatigues pressing upon one in his linguistic situation must have
been a factor here. Day by day he faced much intellectual
labour which in a native Englishman would have been replaced
by intuitive processes. But side by side with the impression of
agonized effort which the record reveals stands the strong
suggestion of another Conrad who, virtually regardless of this,
came and went at the desk. The superb artist who, in *Nostromo*,
appears and takes charge is substantially dissociated from the
striving Conrad and the diurnal man. The latter was in poor
trim. In exchanging the sea for the English countryside, a wife,
and two sons, he had been far from steering into halcyon
weather. His temperament was growing increasingly sombre.

It is very possible that through some involutional process the burden of his earliest, tragic environment was coming to weigh upon him more heavily, producing intractable endogenous depression, a deepening of the disposition to see *tout en noir* which he had so often revealed in his letters. So far he had enjoyed no popular success, and constant practical anxieties added to his troubles. There are spells when his biography makes quite harrowing reading, and his minor fiction is often tortured and cruel without being very good. *Nostromo* matches all this in being a sombre book, and one still profoundly concerned with self-distrust and self-betrayal. But at the same time it has all the order in variety, all the serenity subsuming turmoil, of the highest art.

Begun when he was forty-six and finished two years later (which was twenty years before his death), *Nostromo* was destined to remain his richest imaginative creation. In *Some Reminiscences* he has left an account of his fight for it:

All I know is that, for twenty months, neglecting the common joys of life that fall to the lot of the humblest on this earth, I had, like the prophet of old, 'wrestled with the Lord' for my creation, for the headlands of the coast, for the darkness of the Placid Gulf, the light on the snows, the clouds on the sky, and for the breath of life that had to be blown into the shapes of men and women, of Latin and Saxon, of Jew and Gentile. These are, perhaps, strong words, but it is difficult to characterize otherwise the intimacy and the strain of a creative effort in which mind and will and conscience are engaged to the full, hour after hour, day after day, away from the world, and to the exclusion of all that makes life really lovable and gentle—something for which a material parallel can only be found in the everlasting sombre stress of the westward winter passage round Cape Horn. For that too is the wrestling of men with the might of their Creator, in a great isolation from the world, without the amenities and consolations of life, a lonely struggle under a sense of over-matched littleness, for no reward that could be adequate, but for the mere winning of a longitude. . . . A long, long and desperate fray. Long! I suppose I went to bed sometimes, and got up the same number of times. Yes, I suppose I slept, and ate the food put before me, and talked connectedly to my household on suitable occasions. But I had never been aware of the even flow of daily life, made easy and noiseless for me by a silent, watchful, tireless affection. Indeed, it seemed to me that I had been sitting at that table surrounded by the litter of a desperate fray for days and nights on end.

In imagination Conrad sojourned in Costaguana two years. How long had he spent in any actual corresponding place? 'I am dying', he wrote to Cunninghame Graham, 'over that cursed *Nostromo* thing. All my memories of Central America seem to slip away. I just had a glimpse 25 years ago,—a short glance. That is not enough *pour bâtir un roman dessus*. And yet one must live.' It is probable that Cunninghame Graham answered the implicit appeal by putting some relevant reading in Conrad's way. But at least the novelist's first-hand acquaintance with any part of the American continent was sketchy. And at first he seems not to have realized the weight and dimensions that the book was going to have, referring to it as 'a story belonging to the "Karain" class of tales'—a strange description as coming from one embarking upon what is for us a finely integrated and elaborately patterned long novel. But Conrad appears to have been convinced throughout that it was a hand-to-mouth affair. To H. G. Wells he writes, apparently when about a third of the way through: 'I, my dear Wells, am absolutely out of my mind with the worry and apprehension of my work. I go on as one would cycle over a precipice along a 14-inch plank. If I falter I am lost.' Later he wrote to John Galsworthy:

The book is, this moment, half done, and I feel half dead and wholly imbecile. . . . I didn't write to you because, upon my word, I am ashamed to write to anybody. I feel myself strangely growing into a sort of outcast. A mental and moral outcast. I hear nothing— think of nothing—I reflect upon nothing—I cut myself off—and with all that I can just only keep going, or rather keep on lagging from one wretched story to another—and always deeper in the mire.

During the final month, he told William Rothenstein, he worked virtually night and day, going to bed at three and sitting down again at nine. 'All the time at it, with the tenacity of despair.' It had been, he confided to Edward Garnett, 'a dangerous illness'. Conrad was always, indeed, complaining of unbearable strain. 'Je vois tout avec un tel découragement. . . . Mes nerfs sont tout à fait détraqués.' 'Une espèce de torpeur intellectuelle . . . m'oppresse.' 'Je suis en train de lutter avec Chap. XI; une lutte à mort Vous savez!' 'Twelve pages written and I sit before them every morning, day after day, for the last two months and cannot add a sentence, add a word! I am paralysed.' 'It is ghastly.' 'I sit down for eight hours every day—

and the sitting down is all.' 'I can't eat—I dream—nightmares
—and scare my wife.' Throughout his career there can be no
doubt of the extremity of his distresses. A man alike by temperamental inclination and early training formal, controlled, and
elaborately courteous, he would tip over into hysterical rages
during which he would chatter and scream like a monkey.
But the agony of *Nostromo* would appear to have exceeded
all. So here then is a curious and suggestive spectacle: Conrad
stumbling, groping forward, desperate and arid, through what is,
in fact, a complex and majestic artistic whole. It would seem that
a process felt as blindfolded inch-by-inch fumbling around and
forward may issue in a work particularly notable for its imaginative confidence and for the richness and subtlety of interplay
between its various parts. The inward and invisible artist
appears to have been authoritatively at work throughout, and
the agony and constantly baffled and bewildered toil of the
conscious man shows as an uncomfortable by-product rather
than as an effective agent in the accomplishing of the creative
task. Whether Conrad knew that he had produced a triumphant
thing is not clear. He was depressed by the consciousness that,
with the public, *Nostromo* was 'the blackest possible frost'. And
to Cunninghame Graham he declared that it made him feel a
'fraud'. But this is in a context of apology for not being, like his
correspondent, an authority on South America.

The germ of the novel was in a 'vagrant anecdote completely
destitute of valuable details' which he claimed to have heard
when in the Gulf of Mexico in 1875 or 1876, and which he
certainly read in an obscure volume of nautical reminiscences,
On Many Seas, published in 1897. It told of the single-handed
theft of a lighter laden with silver during a South American
revolution. Conrad came to identify the thief in his own mind
with a certain 'modern and unlawful wanderer with his own
legend of loves, dangers, and bloodshed', Dominic Cervoni, of
whom he gives an account in the reticently autobiographical
The Mirror of the Sea (1906), and upon whom he based several
characters. For the central action he found a background
in revolution and counter-revolution, in political tyranny and
political idealism. Once more Poland is in his mind. He tells
how he remembered his first love, 'an uncompromising Puritan
of patriotism with no taint of the slightest worldliness in her
thoughts', and associated her with the Antonia Avellanos of the

novel. He remembered too his own levity in the presence of her political passion, and from this aspect of himself perhaps grew the Martin Decoud who was to say good-bye to Antonia even as he himself had once said good-bye to her original. But this gives no more than a few elements in the preliminary chemistry of the book.

In the corrupt state of Costaguana Charles Gould has inherited a silver-mine from a father whom the rapacity of successive governments had broken and in effect killed; and to Costaguana he brings his English bride, being determined that the mine shall be the instrument of the country's regeneration, and so of an achievement he owes to his father's memory. He is a romantic at heart, clinging to this ideal conception of himself as vindicating his family's name. Eventually he takes a gamble, backing a liberal régime in which there seems to be some hope of better public order for the country. But this régime is overthrown by a military coup, and it appears certain that in a matter of hours Sulaco, the province in which the mine lies, will be in the power of a reactionary general and his ruffianly army. The town rabble is out of hand. The gentry— remnants of a Spanish-American aristocracy, elevated in political and moral feeling but impoverished and unpractical —have barricaded themselves in their club and are drawing up high-sounding proclamations. It is determined that a great store of silver must be got out to sea, where it may be picked up and taken to safety by a European steamer. This task, like every other requiring resolution and daring, is given to a man of the people, commonly called Nostromo, the Capataz de Carga- dores. He is one for whom the value of life consists in personal prestige—and made incorruptible, we are told, by his enormous vanity, 'that finest form of egotism which can take on the aspect of every virtue'. Together with Martin Decoud, a europeanized young Costaguanan aristocrat, he contrives to secrete the treasure on an island. Decoud remains there in hiding. Nos- tromo returns to the mainland, where his courage is made further use of in a mission which soon transforms the military situation, enabling Sulaco to secede on its own terms from the rest of Costaguana, and to enter upon a period of growing material prosperity and political stability. Meanwhile solitude —so often an ordeal in Conrad—has been too much for Decoud and he has committed suicide in circumstances making it appear likely that the silver was lost at sea. Nostromo, persuaded that he has been treated as no more than a convenient tool by his employers, yields to the temptation to keep quiet about the treasure; and he secretly enriches himself from it over a period of years. The necessity of maintaining access to the silver is in part responsible for involving him in a love intrigue which results in his violent death.

Nostromo is described in its sub-title as a 'tale'—*A Tale of the Seaboard*—and at the level of a narrative of adventure it is as absorbing as *Treasure Island*. Conrad's work has often a deceptive outwardness, and here it may be some time before we realize how powerfully the rich complexity of material is organized around the consideration of a single idea: the influence upon society and upon individuals of those 'material interests' in which Charles Gould has pinned his faith:

What is wanted here is law, good faith, order, security. Anyone can declaim about these things, but I pin my faith to material interests. Only let the material interests once get a firm footing, and they are bound to impose the conditions on which alone they can continue to exist. That's how your money-making is justified here in the face of lawlessness and disorder. It is justified because the security which it demands must be shared with an oppressed people. A better justice will come afterwards. That's your ray of hope.

And indeed prosperity and the outward face of justice come to Sulaco with the eventual triumph of the silver. Old Captain Mitchell, taking his guests to luncheon in the resplendent successor to that aristocratic club which the mob fired long ago, never doubts the beneficence of the march of progress which Charles Gould has set in train. But Mrs. Gould knows one price: her husband has passed outside the operation of common human sympathies and all that is softening in human relationships. Old Dr. Monygham knows the wider price:

There is no peace and no rest in the development of material interests. They have their law, and their justice. But it is founded on expediency, and is inhuman; it is without rectitude, without the continuity and the force that can be found only in a moral principle. Mrs. Gould, the time approaches when all that the Gould Concession stands for shall weigh as heavily upon the people as the barbarism, cruelty, and misrule of a few years back.

But although material interests destroy alike Charles Gould and the incorruptible Nostromo; although at the ironic close of the book they are eating into the health of Sulaco as fatally as the bestial tyrant Guzman Bento ever did: yet there is little suggestion of certain security in any other attitude or allegiance. *Nostromo*, beneath the serenity of its powerful art, is a profoundly disillusioned creation. Decoud, a man of honour, education, and intellect, puts his trust entirely in the world of personal relationships. In applying his wits to working out the separatist programme which Sulaco eventually follows, he is actuated only by the hope of winning acceptance as Antonia's suitor. The representative of sceptical intelligence, he is paired with Nostromo in the end with an evident symbolic intent. Neither is rescuing the silver in the service of any large impersonal purpose. But, equally, there is no salvation in abstract ideals. Dr. Monygham's faith had once lain there—in the ideal of the absolute honour of the gentleman. The moment long ago, when that honour deserted him (as he conceived) in Bento's torture chamber, distorted his vision and broke his life. Old Don José Avellanos, Minister to the Courts of England and Spain, wholly disinterested and nobly magnanimous as he is, has become an unpractical old statesman, unaware in a crisis of the difference between action and the concocting of a manifesto. His daughter is on the road to fanaticism. And so on. In all this, beneath the artistic detachment in the interest of which he is developing a pervasively ironic method, Conrad shows himself passionate. It is passion rather than any refined analysis that makes the characters so convincing. It is an answering sustained creative pressure upon every aspect of their world that gives the novel its exceptional integration and force. The radical virtue of vivid realization pervades this fiction. It pervades alike things great and small, central and peripheral. The picture combines, we may almost say, the virtues of impressionist and post-impressionist painting. Mr. Guerard has remarked that, as we make our way into the book, 'Life (as form, color, movement) repeatedly reaches us before any coherent understanding of it'. At the same time, stand at whatever point we choose in Sulaco and look wherever we will, everything is quite solid. There is nothing we could not walk round. Move where we will, we never come upon the sense of a backcloth, of a limit to the illusion. That first conquest of Conrad's, his tremendous descriptive power, which he exploited in his earlier writing in a simple and massively emotive way, is here elevated into the service of sustained and intricate drama. The evocation of the night which Decoud and Nostromo spend on the silver-laden lighter on the Placid Gulf, with the wretched and ill-fated Hirsch cowering somewhere in the bows and the throb of the approaching army transport in their ears, affords one striking instance of the hallucinatory realism which is nowhere this novel's end but which is everywhere its instrument.

Two further particulars evidence the book's deep artistic consideration. One is the interbalance of characters which gives pattern to the whole. Old Don José the retired Ambassador, and Giorgio Viola the former Garibaldino, first inn-keeper and later lighthouse-keeper in Sulaco, are answering studies, set at widely different social levels, in purity of motive in politics, and in all the strength and vulnerability that spring from this. Over against them are set Charles Gould and Nostromo, the master of the mine and the master of the stevedores, the two most dynamic and practically effective men in Sulaco, each ultimately corrupted by the stream of silver that flows down from San Tomé. So with Decoud and Dr. Monygham, with the two women, with the two ruffians in rivalry for the spoils of the province: there is a constant play of similitude and dissimilitude, of affinities and contrasts now strongly and now subtly marked. This becomes one of the most notable structural strengths of the novel. A second and almost equally important characteristic is the movement of time. After a brief introductory chapter setting the physical scene we are taken straight to the critical day upon which the liberal dictator backed by the mine comes bolting over the mountains and all is cast into confusion. The account even of this is given a retrospective tone through the voice of the reminiscent Captain Mitchell. Thus we are confronted at the start with the disastrous failure of what later on we are going to watch being laboriously planned. Again, we are given a good deal of the actual disorders of that time of crisis before beginning to learn much about the Goulds and their mine. And this method is employed throughout. Conrad shuttles to and fro, so that, as we read, we are never for very long far from the crucial few days in which the great cargo of silver is the centre of the action. Furthermore the tempo varies. We are given one important phase of the story directly, moving through it as with the natural and actual effluxion of time. Another comes to us foreshortened, speeded up, refracted, and coloured in Captain Mitchell's talk. Moreover Conrad employs the freedom of forward reference which his plan allows him for the purpose of bringing into interplay fact and expectation, hope and fulfilment. Into a brief aside he will slip information from which we can infer the shape of things to come. Or again, at the end of the book, Captain Mitchell's satisfied evocation of the prosperous recent past of Sulaco is brought hard up against Dr. Monygham's grim judgement on its probable future.

If the Goulds' Costaguana is as vivid as Jim Hawkins's island, it must yet have appeared to many readers in 1904 almost equally remote. Decoud, who carries the modern European civilized consciousness, is infuriated and discouraged by his country's isolation from the real world—by which he means from that civilization:

Imagine an atmosphere of *opéra-bouffe* in which all the comic business of stage statesmen, brigands, etc., etc., all their farcical stealing, intriguing and stabbing is done in dead earnest. It is screamingly funny, the blood flows all the time, and the actors believe themselves to be influencing the fate of the universe.

Take Decoud out of *Nostromo*, invite him to read it, and he would pronounce its author to be an exotic writer—which Conrad still certainly seemed at the turn of the century. Cunninghame Graham, an Anglo-South American, spoke of him as seeing to the heart of the continent. But to Conrad's first readers in the golden age of European liberalism the spectacle must have appeared indeed remote: perpetual uncertainty, insecurity; a state in which the more rational and enlightened elements have no better repository for their hopes than great material interests by which public order is regarded essentially as something favouring private gain; a whole population at the mercy now of one and now of another ruthless dictatorship; proscriptions, expropriations, terrors, dungeons, barbarous cruelties. Yet Conrad was writing his time. Within a decade of the publication of this novel the German armies were once more at the gates of Paris, Louvain and its great library were in ashes, and the *Lusitania* lay beneath those broad waters which had till lately made of Costaguana another world. Within a generation of that again, all the great capitals of Europe but

one had known such days as Conrad's Sulaco knew, remote
between Higuerota and the Placid Gulf.

5

Nostromo is Conrad's largest canvas. His art now contracts—
but, in the first instance, to an effect of extraordinary intensity,
of packed complexity, in *The Secret Agent* (1907). This novel—
like *Lord Jim*, *Nostromo*, and *Victory* first envisaged as a short
story—came to have for him the importance of 'a new departure
in *genre*'. He described it as 'a sustained effort in ironical treatment of a melodramatic subject'. Externally it belongs to that
early phase of the popular 'thriller' in which unscrupulous
diplomats, ruthless revolutionaries, commissioners of police, and
other picturesque persons are represented as involved in espion-
age, counter-espionage, and the contriving or preventing of
acts of political violence. It is territory which can very effectively be brought within the boundaries of serious fiction, and it
was later to be pertinaciously frequented to that end by Mr.
Graham Greene. But if *The Secret Agent* has had an abundant
progeny, it has at least one notable progenitor in *The Princess
Casamassima*. Conrad is far more successful than James in
vividly evoking his underworld of conspiracy and outrage, and
his must be accounted, all in all, much the more successful
novel. But James's attempts the greater compass. Hyacinth
Robinson's implication with revolutionary intrigue contains
the stuff of tragedy. The end of Mr. Verloc, although one of the
greatest scenes in English fiction, belongs—as does the end of
Stevie, if not of Stevie's sister—to a world of savage comedy.
Conrad's whole book is the product of a single disenchanted
vision, and it owns the limitations as well as the strength of this.
We may feel that a disproportionate part of its virtue is in the
sustained ironic tone. We may feel that this tone, like the plu-
rality of consciousnesses through which other of the novels are
filtered to us, is a distancing device in places rendering vehe-
ment real life a little too distant altogether. Certainly concentration upon 'treatment' and 'doing' is growing in Conrad,
perhaps under the influence of James himself. It can eventually
be discerned, far more certainly than with James, as a debilitating factor in his art.

As so often too with James, the theme of this novel came to

Conrad in casual conversation. His own account of this is interesting as making clear certain strong persuasions, if not prejudices, which he brought to its theme:

The subject of *The Secret Agent*—I mean the tale—came to me in the shape of a few words uttered by a friend in a casual conversation about anarchists or rather anarchist activities; how brought about I don't remember now.

I remember, however, remarking on the criminal futility of the whole thing, doctrine, action, mentality; and on the contemptible aspect of the half-crazy pose as of a brazen cheat exploiting the poignant miseries and passionate credulities of a mankind always so tragically eager for self-destruction. That was what made for me its philosophical pretences so unpardonable. Presently, passing to particular instances, we recalled the already old story of the attempt to blow up the Greenwich Observatory; a blood-stained inanity of so fatuous a kind that it was impossible to fathom its origin by any reasonable or even unreasonable process of thought. For perverse unreason has its own logical processes. But that outrage could not be laid hold of mentally in any sort of way, so that one remained faced by the fact of a man blown to bits for nothing even most remotely resembling an idea, anarchistic or other. As to the outer wall of the Observatory it did not show as much as the faintest crack.

I pointed all this out to my friend who remained silent for a while and then remarked in his characteristically casual and omniscient manner: 'Oh, that fellow was half an idiot. His sister committed suicide afterwards.' These were absolutely the only words that passed between us; for extreme surprise at this unexpected piece of information kept me dumb for a moment and he began at once to talk of something else.

More than once in his letters Conrad denies that *The Secret Agent* was written with any social or philosophical intention, and there are indications that to both Galsworthy and Cunninghame Graham he had to defend himself against some suggestions of an inadequately dispassionate scrutiny of the well-springs of anarchism and revolution. It is perhaps true that, politically, Conrad's sympathies are straitened between a liberal's hatred of tyranny on the one hand and on the other an aristocratic contempt and distrust of the underworld of insurgence and demagogy. As much as Yeats—another writer of aristocratic temper emotionally involved with a subjugated people—he distrusts the motives of those who would 'hurl the little streets against the great', and has no love of 'ragged fellows beating pikes for some conspiracy'. And just as James in *The Princess Casamassima*, and more particularly in *The Bostonians*, shows a defective sympathy with the whole idea of political effort, so does Conrad here show a hatred of the face of violence which might well militate against any great perceptiveness in the tracing of its lineaments. And something of such a deficiency intermittently appears, and can be pointed by turning for comparison to Dostoevsky, notably to *The Possessed*. A certain effect of rigidity is pervasive in *The Secret Agent*. It lacks what Mr. Guerard, again, calls Conrad's 'subtle oscillations of condemning judgment and identifying creative sympathy', and this is a heavy price to pay even for a masterpiece of strong emotion controlled and made doubly effective by an unfaltering ironic method. And if the writer of *The Secret Agent* is revolted even to excess before the spectacle of political fanaticism, he admits no traffic with comfortable views of the established order. We are coldly shown a variety of moral systems and persuasions, each in a void, yet together constituting a sort of gravitational field in which one bears blindly but powerfully upon another to this and that effect of disturbance or cataclysm.

The tale which Conrad founded upon the futile attack on the Observatory is simple in itself, and is so described in the subtitle. Mr. Verloc is discovered in comfortable and respectable circumstances. His business—which is miscellaneously in improper wares and pornographical publications—shows no great profits, but as his shop is a rendezvous of anarchists whose secrets he quietly sells to the embassy of a foreign power he is not doing too badly. Moreover in Winnie Verloc he has an excellent wife. Although she has in fact married him only to achieve security for her weak-minded brother Stevie, Mr. Verloc has never been assailed by any suspicion that he is not loved for his own sake. But these modestly enviable circumstances are presently threatened by the unreasonableness of his diplomatic employers, who reproach him with idleness, and demand that he contrive to 'plant' upon his anarchist associates an outrage which shall have the effect of prompting the English authorities to some repressive action. Mr. Verloc naturally sees this requirement as monstrously unfair to himself. But happening to be made aware that Stevie is devoted to him, he employs him for the delivery of a bomb which, exploding prematurely, blows the boy to unidentifiable fragments. All would thus be well but for the fact that Winnie Verloc has most vexatiously sewn Stevie's name and address into his coat. The discovery of this leads to the tracing of the crime. When the truth becomes known to Winnie, and her husband admonishes her for her excessive concern—'Do be reasonable, Winnie. What would it have been if you had lost me?'—she kills him with a carving knife, attempts to flee the country, is robbed and deserted by one of the anarchist coterie, and drowns herself by jumping from the channel steamer.

Conrad's impressionism—his power to create in terms of the immediate reports of the senses—is supreme in this book, which nevertheless is pervasively and consistently coloured by the contemplating mind. From that obsessive maternal devotion of Winnie's for her brother which is the novel's deepest element to the minute concrete particularities of the Verloc world which is its most immediately astonishing achievement, and over the sluggish and narrow, or maimed and fanatical, consciousnesses so convincingly conjured up, Conrad's irony is constantly at play—to the detriment, perhaps, of any adequately even-handed distribution of that 'pity and scorn' which it was his resolve that the writing should sustainedly carry. The unity of tone is indeed extraordinary, and serves to bind into the whole the few episodes which might otherwise be felt as extraneous to the main theme. Thus the journey of Winnie's mother to the almshouse, which has been censured as an inept importation of the Dickensian grotesque, in fact provides relief which yet blends with the predominant colours of the whole. The old lady is exhibited

in the privacy of a four-wheeler, on her way to a charity cottage (one of a row) which by the exiguity of its dimensions and the simplicity of its accommodation, might well have been devised in kindness as a place of training for the still more straitened circumstances of the grave.

This is, as it were, at one end of the sombre palette. At the other is Chief Inspector Heat's examination of Stevie's mortal remains:

'You used a shovel,' he remarked, observing a sprinkling of small gravel, tiny brown bits of bark, and particles of splintered wood as fine as needles.

'Had to in one place,' said the stolid constable. 'I sent a keeper to fetch a spade. When he heard me scraping the ground with it he leaned his forehead against a tree, and was as sick as a dog.'

The Chief Inspector, stooping guardedly over the table, fought down the unpleasant sensation in his throat. The shattering violence of destruction which had made of that body a heap of nameless fragments affected his feelings with a sense of ruthless cruelty, though his reason told him the effect must have been as swift as a flash of lightning. The man, whoever he was, had died instantaneously; and yet it seemed impossible to believe that a human body could have reached that state of disintegration without passing through the pangs of inconceivable agony. No physiologist, and still less of a metaphysician, Chief Inspector Heat rose by the force of sympathy, which is a form of fear, above the vulgar conception of time. Instantaneous! He remembered all he had ever read in popular publications of long and terrifying dreams dreamed in the instant of waking; of the whole past life lived with frightful intensity by a drowning man as his doomed head bobs up, streaming, for the last time. The inexplicable mysteries of conscious existence beset Chief Inspector Heat till he evolved a horrible notion that ages of atrocious pain and mental torture could be contained between two successive winks of an eye. And meantime the Chief Inspector went on peering at the table with a calm face and the slightly anxious attention of an indigent customer bending over what may be called the by-products of a butcher's shop with a view to an inexpensive Sunday dinner.

But it is at its climax that *The Secret Agent* is most remarkable, and the quality of Conrad's writing there can perhaps best be exhibited in a comparison with Hardy. Tess's killing of Alec d'Urberville is sufficiently appalling, and its immediate effectiveness is no doubt enhanced by the picturesque stroke with which it is intimated to us. 'The oblong white ceiling, with this scarlet blot in the midst, had the appearance of a gigantic ace of hearts.' But Hardy does not 'do' his catastrophe as Conrad does. The terrifying scene in which Mr. Verloc, amid his domestic sanctities and from behind the massive insulation of his own self-regarding vision, all-unconsciously and through a long series of mounting tensions drives his wife to her frenzy, is something which Hardy might have desired to achieve, but which he would scarcely have kept within the bounds of art. And had Hardy attempted to work with an equal closeness the span of minutes leading up to d'Urberville's death, it would surely have become painfully apparent that d'Urberville is not a substantial creation at all. Yet *Tess* with all its imperfection is ultimately a greater novel than *The Secret Agent*—perhaps simply because compassion is deeper than pity and indignation nobler than scorn. But Conrad owns artistic resources of which Hardy, in fiction, has no conception.

6

If *The Secret Agent* is sometimes viewed as standing apart from the main body of Conrad's writing, this is perhaps because it does not contain—at least in a position of prominence—any character in a typically Conradian situation. The theme of honour comes through only in muted echoes, as when we are told that 'a man must identify himself with something more tangible than his own personality, and establish his pride somewhere, either in his social position, or in the quality of the work he is obliged to do.' *Under Western Eyes* (1911) opens upon a young Russian of whom it is recorded that 'there was nothing strange in the student Razumov's wish for distinction. A man's real life is that accorded to him in the thoughts of other men by reason of respect or natural love.' And Razumov's story turns wholly upon the old theme of exile and loneliness following upon betrayal, upon ceasing anywhere 'to belong'. Like Jim, Razumov has bad luck. His allegiance is suddenly claimed, on no volition of his own, for a revolutionary cause neither the exalted idealism nor the ruthless violence of which makes any appeal to his own perfectly honourable but wholly egocentric ambition. He betrays a fellow-student, the selfless and high-minded assassin Haldin, only to find that he has himself thereby fallen into the toils of the political police, by whom he is dispatched to Geneva as a spy within the camp of expatriate revolutionaries there. Among these is Haldin's sister, with whom he falls in love and who idolizes him as her dead brother's loyal friend. He is eventually driven to confession, and suffers horrible violence at the hands of the more brutal of those he has been betraying. It is like a story of Dostoevsky's. But for Conrad Dostoevsky was a 'grimacing, haunted creature'—and the title tells us where a difference is meant to lie. The pupil, above all, of Flaubert and Maupassant—of these certainly more than of his English near-contemporaries, in whom he was not, in fact, well-read—Conrad maintained that his own deepest affinity lay with a Latin civilization in the comparison with which such a pervasive nihilism as he distinguished in Dostoevsky sounds 'like some fierce mouthings from prehistoric ages'. It was apparently in order to distance the whole Slavonic spectacle in the interest of this persuasion that he designed to present it only as it came under the observation of an elderly English teacher of languages. Perhaps not much is gained by this. The narrator's is in no sense, as Marlow's frequently is, a growing and changing sensibility in its own right; nor does he enrich or diversify the architecture of the book like Captain Mitchell in *Nostromo*. He comes to us rather as representing an unfulfilled intention, and this is one of several signs of fatigue which *Under Western Eyes* betrays. Yet the highest artistic vigilance is operative throughout the novel. As Conrad first conceived the story, Razumov was to marry Miss Haldin and have a child by her, and it was to be by the likeness of this child to his wife's dead brother that his confession was to be precipitated. This must have presented itself to Conrad as a wonderful psychological notion. He did well, we may think, to abandon it.

The initial plight of Razumov is rendered with great power—although Conrad has plainly less command of a Russian setting than he has of one in Soho—and the close of his story is convincingly horrible. The intermediate stages are less good. Miss Haldin, if compared with such a character as Elena in Turgenev's *On the Eve*, must appear a somewhat featureless idealization. In this she has been preceded by Antonia Avellanos, and she is to be followed by other heroines of even simpler outline. Conrad's art is to lose much of its complexity and subtlety of moral reference, and many of his people are to become too simply good or bad for their place in what remains to the end, in intention, a highly evolved realistic psychological fiction. It is as if some regressive process is setting in and Conrad is increasingly seeing the world coloured by early loyalties and revulsions. There is moreover a marked difference of emphasis and effect between the portraits of revolutionary characters in this and the preceding book. Although those in *The Secret Agent* have much in common each with the other, they yet present a diversity of spectacle which is the product of a vigorously probing and imaginatively abounding mind. Winnie's eventual betrayer, the wholly base Ossipon, 'author of a popular quasi-medical study (in the form of a cheap pamphlet seized promptly by the police) entitled *The Corroding Vices of the Middle Classes*'; the 'Professor', who, a perfect anarchist, walks the streets a living bomb; Michaelis, the martyr gone soft, opening 'his short, thick arms, as if in a pathetically hopeless attempt to embrace a self-regenerated universe': these are portraits overgone by that of the terrorist Karl Yundt:

The knob of his stick and his legs shook together with passion, whilst the trunk, draped in the wings of the havelock, preserved his historic attitude of defiance. He seemed to sniff the tainted air of social cruelty, to strain his ear for its atrocious sounds. There was an extraordinary force of suggestion in this posturing. The all but moribund veteran of dynamite wars had been a great actor in his time—actor on platforms, in secret assemblies, in private interviews. The famous terrorist had never in his life raised personally as much as his little finger against the social edifice. He was no man of action; he was not even an orator of torrential eloquence, sweeping the masses along in the rushing noise and foam of a great enthusiasm. With a more subtle intention, he took the part of an insolent and venomous evoker of sinister impulses which lurk in the blind envy and exasperated vanity of ignorance, in the suffering and misery of poverty, in all the hopeful and noble illusions of righteous anger, pity, and revolt. The shadow of his evil gift clung to him yet like the smell of a deadly drug in an old vial of poison, emptied now, useless, ready to be thrown away upon the rubbish-heap of things that had served their time.

If we feel that all these are presented with some animus—a quality not apparent in the portrait of Mr. Verloc—this yet appears not excessive in the context of pervasive astringency which gives its predominant tone to the novel. Vengeful bitterness is the mainspring of the 'Professor', and murder pacifies its unrest. Yet he is far from out of nature's family, for 'in their own way the most ardent of revolutionaries are perhaps doing no more but seeking for peace in common with the rest of mankind—the peace of soothed vanity, of satisfied appetites, or perhaps of appeased conscience'. Conrad's remains the same scrutiny as it passes from this dangerous criminal to us. But in *Under Western Eyes* the typical revolutionaries are precisely not human; they are 'apes of a sinister jungle', the 'imbecile and atrocious answer' to the 'ferocity and imbecility' of the Tsars. In the portrait of Peter Ivanovitch, in particular, we are made to feel that Conrad's pen trembles as he contemplates a world of 'senseless desperation provoked by senseless tyranny', and that he has his knife in this horrible simulacrum under the impulse of very much the extremity that conquered Winnie

Verloc. Nothing more betrays a scarcely rational element in some of Conrad's responses to Russia than its appearing, from a cancelled passage in the manuscript, that he had some thought of aiming at Tolstoy in aspects of this dreadful portrait.

7

The appeal of *Under Western Eyes* is to a cultivated literary intelligence, and the book could scarcely have achieved any very immediate popular success. *Chance* (1913) is another matter. In it—'thinking of the public', as he said—Conrad has lowered his sights, particularly in the conclusion given to the story. And *Chance* brought him into wide notice at last; at the same time it is the first mature work in which his grip of his theme is less assured than his command over his craft. That theme is of modern knight errantry—there are two parts, respectively entitled 'The Damsel' and 'The Knight'—and Conrad's deeper proposal is evidently to suggest that it is a vocation holding hazards more insidious than the swords of paynims or the breath of dragons. But this intention announces itself very uncertainly and remains largely abortive. The core of the fable is unrealized and gets by only with some assistance from the values of conventional romance. And the creative energy that thus fails of substantial employment at the centre finds exercise in a rich peripheral elaboration and in a formal structure at once complex and masterfully easy. *Chance* was commended by James for adopting 'the way to do a thing that shall make it undergo most doing'—for being, we may interpret, a little more Jacobean than James himself would ever have dared to be:

It literally strikes us that his volume sets in motion more than anything else a drama in which his own system and his combined eccentricities of recital represent the protagonist in face of powers leagued against it, and of which the dénouement gives us the system fighting in triumph, though with its back desperately to the wall, and laying the powers piled up at its feet. This frankly has been *our* spectacle, our suspense and our thrill.

But in fact the morphology of *Chance* is the very opposite of that which James's best work exhibits. On its surface it is concrete, precise, sharp, brilliant; but our glance as it travels inward encounters successive degrees of obscurity ending in something uncommonly like fog. James's surfaces are generalized, intimated, vague; we traverse obscurities which may indeed seem to thicken as we move—yet we come in the end to some moral vista sufficiently clearly lit. Nevertheless the central situation in *Chance* recalls the work of James in this: that it sustains itself only by doing something less than justice to the simple power of intuitive factors in resolving a false emotional situation. Moreover it is in its special fashion essentially a love story. And Conrad is not really greatly moved or very perceptive about love.

Flora de Barral is a victim of evil circumstances including the ruin and disgrace of her worthless father, horrible betrayal by a wicked governess, and much miserable dependence upon vulgar and base relations or insensitive charity. She stirs the chivalry of a sea-captain, Roderick Anthony, who marries her and takes her to sea together with her broken and malignant father, lately released from prison. But Anthony, persuaded that he has been accepted only out of desperation, resolves that the marriage shall be unconsummated. Flora, believing that commiseration rather than love has actuated him, withdraws into her own reserve. This intolerable state of affairs endures through a long period of strain, and is ended only when the crazy de Barral tries to poison his son-in-law. Potentially, Roderick Anthony's story is related to Charles Gould's. It touches the theme—of which Ibsen may have sharpened Conrad's awareness—of the human mischief that may be wrought by an inflexible idealism. The pitfalls before the knight errant are intimated clearly enough. Thus, when it has become clear to Anthony that Flora's existence, even while befriended by his sister and brother-in-law the Fynes, is 'a combination of dreariness and horror', we read:

When he saw the white-faced restless Flora drifting like a lost thing along the road he put his pipe in his pocket and called out 'Good morning, Miss Smith' in a tone of amazing happiness. She, with one foot in life and the other in a nightmare, was at the same time inert and unstable, and very much at the mercy of sudden impulses. She swerved, came distractedly right up to the gate and looking straight into his eyes: 'I am not Miss Smith. That's not my name. Don't call me by it.'

She was shaking as if in a passion. His eyes expressed nothing; he only unlatched the gate in silence, grasped her arm and drew her in. Then closing it with a kick—

'Not your name? That's all one to me. Your name's the least thing about you I care for.' He was leading her firmly away from the gate though she resisted slightly. There was a sort of joy in his eyes which frightened her. 'You are not a princess in disguise', he said with an unexpected laugh she found blood-curdling. 'And that's all I care for. You had better understand that I am not blind and not a fool. And then it's plain for even a fool to see that things have been going hard with you. You are on a lee shore and eating your heart out with worry.'

What seemed most awful to her was the elated light in his eyes, the rapacious smile that would come and go on his lips as if he were gloating over her misery. But her misery was his opportunity and he rejoiced while the tenderest pity seemed to flood his whole being. . . . It was not pity alone, I take it. It was something more spontaneous, perverse and exciting. It gave him the feeling that if only he could get hold of her, no woman would belong to him so completely as this woman.

But Anthony's is a romantic and exalted egotism. 'That ideal conception of one's own personality every man sets up for himself secretly' is as much his mainspring as it is the young captain's in 'The Secret Sharer'. And he is in danger of being rendered insensitive to an actual human situation by his concentration upon the sublime conception of himself. He is the son of a poet:

The inarticulate son had set up a standard for himself with that need for embodying in his conduct the dreams, the passion, the impulses the poet puts into arrangements of verses, which are dearer to him than his own self—and may make his own self appear sublime in the eyes of other people, and even in his own eyes.

But much in the implications of all this goes subsequently unexplored, and we are offered an Anthony progressively in terms of his own vision. The sea to which Conrad has returned in this novel acts as something of a distorting mirror. Anthony becomes simply an exemplification of that element's power to purify and exalt its servants—a power in which Conrad believed by no means less passionately as his own seafaring days retreated into the past. And de Barral, correspondingly, bodies forth Conrad's unslumbering contempt and hatred for the corruption inherent in all subjection to material interests. The two tremendous denunciations he had lately written upon the occasion of the *Titanic* disaster—denunciations of the intolerable degradation of seamanship which he was convinced must accompany the ruthless commercial development of floating luxury

hotels—express the same feeling only more clearly. *Chance* lacks
the dispassionateness, the ubiquitously impartial penetrations of
Nostromo. But it has almost the same vitality of imaginative
creation and complex and assured artistic skill. Marlow we may
sometimes feel to have become a little tiresome. The gnomic
rather than the perceptive now inclines to be his note. But he is
only one element in a highly developed narrative technique
which (more securely than in much of James) is preserved
from declining into a mere architectonic virtuosity by Conrad's
command of convincing minor characters and a richly ironic
subsidiary comedy.

Victory (1915) turns upon the same essential action as does
Chance—the chivalrous rescue of a woman in distress. This
rehandling appears not to have been on account of any conscious dissatisfaction with the first book. Conrad in fact expressed himself as particularly pleased with *Chance*. But *Victory*,
nevertheless, is a stronger, deeper, and simpler novel. Its simplicity, indeed, has been asserted as virtually that of a morality,
and it is surely unique in Conrad's work in closing upon an
explicit moral. Baron Axel Heyst has learned from his father,
a professional philosopher of disillusion, to armour himself in
a species of nihilism or non-attachment. Ironic, cultivated, and
humane, he drifts thus isolated through the mercantile life of
the Malayan Archipelago. Eventually his innate generosity
prompts him to rescue from threatening degradation the young
Englishwoman Lena, a girl of the people, wretchedly employed
in an itinerant orchestra. Retreating with her to the near-
solitude of his island hermitage, he finds that he is without the
capacity to achieve any full personal or spiritual harmony, or to
induce in his mistress any assurance that she can repose with
confidence in his love. Their imperfect relationship is presently
broken in upon by a trio of ruffians intent on robbery. In this
situation too Heyst is disabled by his mingled fastidiousness,
pride, and disdain—and perhaps the more so because the leader
of the desperadoes is himself a gentleman and a nihilist, although
his gentility is disgraced and his nihilism belongs to the pit.
At the crisis of the tale Lena gives her life for Heyst. And
Heyst dies by his own hand after crying out: 'Woe to the man
whose heart has not learned while young to hope, to love—and
to put its trust in life!' The individual can come to know and
so to command himself only through an acceptance of life

expressed through the acknowledgement of human relatedness and love. This is the knowledge which Heyst finally achieves, and it is from his achieving it that the book takes its title. *Victory* is not a novel in which large reaches of experience open out before the exploring imagination. What is given is still given with force, even if often with sharply diminished linguistic skill; the scenes, the people, and—above all—the hour-by-hour and minute-by-minute tensions of the action are evoked with mastery. But Heyst's predicament is the sole urgent interest. It is as if, under the impulsion of this, Conrad has taken up his old Malayan brush and rapidly sketched, in strong colours and bold masses, a sufficient theatre in which to exhibit his protagonist.

8

After *Victory* there is a decline in Conrad's art. *The Arrow of Gold* (1919), *The Rescue* (begun in 1896, concluded in 1919, and published in 1920), and the unfinished *Suspense* (1925) are fatigued performances—the fatigue making itself evident at almost every level, including that of simple command over English idiom and syntax. But *The Rover* (1923), although perhaps accurately described as merely Conradesque, ends strongly, and has moreover curious interest in any attempt finally to establish the well-springs of Conrad's writing. It poured itself, we are told, suddenly and mysteriously into his mind, and what was intended, once more, as a short tale took on alike mass and urgency as he wrote. The story is of the Napoleonic wars and of two patriots, who come to stand symbolically in the relationship of father and son. Young Réal, a lover, must undertake a perilous mission, sailing with faked dispatches which are to be intercepted by the English; caught between this mission and his love, Réal accepts the mission. It is a matter of his own integrity, since 'on emerging from boyhood [he] had laid for himself a rigidly straight line of conduct amongst the unbridled passions and the clamouring falsehoods of revolution'. And the Revolution, which he inwardly loathes, has stretched out a long arm to strike at him. Arlette, the woman with whom he finds himself in love, has a mind marked for life by ghastly experiences in that time of public disorder. The other patriot is old Peyrol, who by a stratagem succeeds in taking Réal's place, and who thus contrives to go to his death serving equally two loyalties.

It has been ingeniously maintained that this story, written in 1920 when Poland was fighting for its national life against the Russians, marks a turning point in Conrad's own spiritual history. Built on the old theme of desertion, guilt, and atonement, it is the first book in which the outcast gets back to his country, and in which he proves himself a good patriot in spite of all. A long conflict has at last been resolved, and Conrad never again writes out of any inner urgency. Of this it must be said that the personal problem, if thus specially present, makes for no special artistic success. Nevertheless such an interpretation does usefully return us at the last to that burden of guilt felt as pervasively lurking in Conrad's work—its undefinable air, as Mr. Pritchett puts it, of having been written in sackcloth and ashes, and of dealing by choice with characters who 'live on the edge of a great anxiety'. But the interest of this is not exhausted when we have examined it in terms of Conrad's private history. Wider considerations, for example, may suggest themselves if we compare briefly the three novelists so far discussed in this volume.

Set beside Hardy, James and Conrad both display themselves as artists of great technical sophistication. They represent a fresh phase in the development of the modern European novel, and in the establishing of its claim to be a major and highly evolved literary form. When John Galsworthy points out in a preface that one of his female characters, whom he is anxious to render enigmatic, is never presented except through the consciousness of one or other of her fellow characters, he is lisping artlessly the ABC of a new language in which both James and Conrad are deeply read, but of which Hardy is largely unaware. Hardy laments the novelist's being necessarily inside the pantomime horse, but James and Conrad get outside the creature's skin at will. Such calculations as control the manipulating of Marlow or Fanny Assingham are substantially beyond Hardy's scope. Yet it is not in technique that Hardy, set over against the others, shows most significantly as belonging to an age of innocence. Rather it is in his attitude to his people and their world. Certain outbreaks of merely stagey villainy apart, Hardy's characters are themselves essentially innocents —for 'evil' is merely a name for the insensate force hovering perpetually behind the iron curtain of determinism and ready to strike out without consciousness that it is doing so. It is only in

Hardy's last two novels—when indeed he is taking his farewell of the form—that we come upon any strong sense of this blind evil as lurking in or working through the hearts and wills of men and women. Alike in James and Conrad the situation is transformed. Their greatest books turn on the horror of betrayal. And James's work, almost as much as Conrad's, exhibits an obscure sense of guilt. In his drawing-rooms (which are no less than symbolical representations of modern European civilization at its peak) it can be as palpable as on Conrad's nightmare river. Here, moreover, we are only at the root of a major growth in contemporary fiction. Of this new sense of a guilt never quite to be localized or pinned down—characteristic of such a representative modern poem as *The Waste Land* as well as of the Novel—sociological and economic explanations are frequently offered. Thus Mr. Stephen Spender, remarking upon the symbolism of the golden bowl, upon the almost crushing wealth possessed by the people of James's later novels, upon the plain fact that it is Milly Theale's millions that are mortal to her, claims that the pervasive sense of guilt of which we are aware is the product of a capitalist culture in its efflorescence and decay. However this may be, there is territory here across which affiliations between James and Conrad can certainly be traced. The gold which destroys Milly and the silver which destroys Nostromo have their abundant analogues in all literature. But the 'great anxiety' upon the edge of which both novelists so often set their people may well be the product of a specifically modern society in which the 'material interests' so distrusted by Dr. Monygham have asserted an unexampled degree of control, with unpredictable consequences for the moral nature of man.

VI · KIPLING

RUDYARD KIPLING was born in Bombay in 1865. His father was an artist and scholar. Through aunts on his mother's side he came early into contact with people distinguished in art and literature. From the miserable Southsea foster-home and the inferior public school which constituted his luckless introduction to life in England he was able to retreat into a world in which William Morris was by courtesy Uncle Topsy and Burne-Jones was in fact Uncle Ned. He paid his debts by becoming one of the greatest writers of his age. But when he was buried in Westminster Abbey in 1936 it was in circumstances the curiosity of which has been remarked by his biographer, Mr. Carrington:

> The last occasion of that kind had been the burial of Hardy who was borne to the grave by an escort of poets and dramatists. Not so was Kipling; his pall-bearers were the Prime Minister, an Admiral, a General, the Master of a Cambridge College, Professor Mackail from Oxford, Sir Fabian Ware, and two old friends, H. A. Gwynne and A. P. Watt; and the congregation consisted of men of action, the men with whom he had spent his life, rather than men of letters.

Almost the whole of Kipling's character and career could be discussed with this for text. His admiration for men of action had been—in his earlier years, at least—sufficiently wide-ranging. It was an admiration for the entire rank and file of those who, selflessly and with little understanding of the material interests they served, maintained an empire through much dust and heat, bringing, where they could, beneficent rule to

> new-caught, sullen peoples,
> Half devil and half child.

In later life, however, Kipling came to move in a society much too narrow for a writer's health. His wife has been much blamed for screening his acquaintances in terms of her own fondness for top people. But it was to the interplay of his own temperament with the literary climate of the nineties that the beginning of his withdrawal into isolation was due. And to his own mind it was precisely *not* a withdrawal. For his whole career is governed by the image of the boy who stuck it out, who was tough enough to have no need of any retreat into the Palace of Art. And his role, like his fame, came to him early. From the turn of the century he was the major creative writer who had a message, who put public and national things first, who upon grave occasions spoke to his fellow countrymen through the medium of *The Times* in poems for which he would accept no fee. These pronouncements were not always wise or temperate in matters of political persuasion. Yet they had, and have, their own impressiveness. When the most famous of them, 'Recessional', prompted his literary agent, A. P. Watt, to speak of the mantle of Milton, there was not too much hyperbole in the claim.

But Milton himself was scarcely more remote from the literary world of the Restoration than was Kipling from the London into which he so dazzlingly broke in the last decade of the nineteenth century. It is no doubt fallacious to regard the Anglo-Indian society in which he had enjoyed his first precocious successes as entirely philistine—although we may here attach less significance than Mr. Carrington does to the fact that 'the best appointments were reserved for men with high academic honours'. Yet at least it was a society not quick to sniff at broad emphatic writing, or to quarrel with the proposition that

> sometimes in a smoking-room, one learns why things were done.

Kipling soon found that literary London was different:

> But I consort with long-haired things
> In velvet collar-rolls,
> Who talk about the Aims of Art,
> And 'theories' and 'goals',
> And moo and coo with womenfolk
> About their blessed souls.

In face of this aestheticism the twenty-three-year-old arrival took on the attitude of a sufficiently confident provincial angry young man:

> But what they call 'psychology'
> Is lack of liver-pill,

And all that blights their tender souls
   Is eating till they're ill,
And their chief way of winning goals
   Consists of sitting still.

It's Oh to meet an Army man,
   Set up, and trimmed and taut,
Who does not spout hashed libraries
   Or think the next man's thought,
And walks as though he owned himself,
   And hogs his bristles short.

As much as any house-master or adjutant Kipling was intolerant of long hair, and throughout his career he was to remain undeviatingly faithful to the ethos underlying that sort of tabu. Viewed unsympathetically, therefore, he is the very type of the artist who lacks faith in the artist's vocation. It is thus that Mr. Edmund Wilson sees him:

> Instead of *becoming* a man of action like Rimbaud, a course which shows a boldness of logic, he fell into the ignominious rôle of the artist who prostrates his art before the achievements of soldiers and merchants, and who is always declaring the supremacy of the 'doer' over the man of ideas.

But we must reflect that Rimbaud's logic shut him up, whereas Kipling's ignominy resulted in the conquest of large new territories by the imagination.

And at least in 1890 his acclaim was so tremendous that the dubieties of a refined criticism simply didn't count. His appeal to a public wider than that commanded by most of the established writers of the period was to be defined by H. G. Wells:

> In the middle nineties this spectacled and moustached little figure with its heavy chin and its general effect of vehement gesticulation, its wild shouts of boyish enthusiasm for effective force, its lyric delight in the sounds and colours, in the very odours of empire, its wonderful discovery of machinery and cotton waste and the under-officer and the engineer, and 'shop' as a poetic dialect, became almost a national symbol. He got hold of us wonderfully, he filled us with tinkling and haunting quotations.

With the fastidious, however, the charm was not to hold, and the young Anglo-Indian journalist who had Henry James at his feet was to end with virtually no writer among his intimates except Rider Haggard, the author of *She* and *King Solomon's Mines*. James's comments, indeed, almost serve to graph the course of Kipling's reputation. In 1890 Kipling is 'the star of the hour'; in 1891 an 'infant monster' and a 'little black demon' with the 'mark of a real vocation' and by no means to be quarrelled with on the score of the primitive element in his subject-matter and his love of low life. In 1892 he has become 'the most complete man of genius (as distinct from fine intelligence) that I have ever known'. But a little earlier than this, again, James speaks of 'the talent enormous, but the brutality even deeper-seated'. And by 1897 he has abandoned his first hope of 'an English Balzac' and taken to a humorous view of Kipling's progress:

He has come down steadily from the simple in subject to the more simple—from the Anglo-Indians to the natives, from the natives to the Tommies, from the Tommies to the quadrupeds, from the quadrupeds to the fish, and from the fish to the engines and screws.

It is clear that in the face of criticism of this sort Kipling enjoyed trailing his coat; 'marine engines and such like' are baldly set down in a letter of 1895 as likely to be his next concern in fiction. And if such themes were not agreeable to aesthetes and intellectuals, no more were aesthetes and intellectuals agreeable to him. When in 1897 one of these—his connexion by marriage, J. W. Mackail—irritated him with a facile enthusiasm for 'Recessional', he replied in a letter through which there sounds his angry impatience with what he judged to be the political irresponsibility of the cultivated classes:

DEAR JACK,—Thank you very much: but all the same, seeing what manner of armed barbarians we are surrounded with, we're about the only power with a glimmer of civilization in us. I've been round with the Channel Fleet for a fortnight and any other breed of white man, with such a weapon to their hand, would have been exploiting the round Earth in their own interests long ago. This is no ideal world but a nest of burglars, alas; and we must protect ourselves against being burgled. . . .

The big smash is coming one of these days, sure enough, but I think we shall pull through not without credit. It will be common people—the 3rd class carriages—that'll save us.

Ever yours,

RUDDY.

And as Kipling's anxieties sharpened he broadened his indictment. In 'The Islanders' of 1902 there is not much praise of the
3rd class carriages; the gentry are told that pheasant-shooting
will be of little use to them 'when the raided coast-towns burn';
it is made clear—by implication and in a superb and famous
line—that the playing-fields of Eton are the very territories that
the next war may be lost on; and any intellectual or academic
person disposed to take pleasure in this castigation of his betters
must pause on finding himself described as 'Arid, aloof,
incurious, unthinking, unthanking, gelt'. Soldiers, sailors,
technicians, and civil servants not too exalted on the scale were
finally the only people having any occasion to regard Kipling
with charity. Thus it was that, while still in his thirties, he
became typed in the regard of many critics as a formidably
talented barbarian, a menacing presence sulking and ful-
minating somewhere just beyond the recognized frontier of
literature, a rhymester and story-teller for the uncultivated and
the young, offensive because prone to debase the currency of
imaginative writing with the impurities of political passion—
and eventually a Nobel prizeman whose services to literature
included providing his sovereign with the novels of Edgar
Wallace. It is recorded that the response of Yeats to an invitation to discuss Kipling's poetry was only a raised hand and the
two words: 'That, no.'

Kipling himself can hardly have been unaffected by this sort
of relegation, by the discrepancy between his status as a national
institution and the contempt in which he was held by persons
claiming authority in literature. When his writing, at least in
prose, finally became compressed, complex, and elliptical, it is
possible that he was prompted to this manner—even if almost
unconsciously—by the desire to show that he could be subtle
when he wanted to be. Recent critics have tended to base their
vindication of his genius upon the later work. But Kipling's
Daemon—of which he often speaks—was perhaps most potent,
after all, when Kipling himself was still the 'little black demon' of
James's fascinated and horrified regard. Certainly it will never
do to write off Kipling as an artist wherever he makes us tingle:

Never the lotos closes, never the wild-fowl wake,
But a soul goes out on the East Wind that died for England's sake—
Man or woman or suckling, mother or bride or maid—
Because on the bones of the English the English Flag is stayed.

Writing of this sort traffics in something sufficiently primitive. It releases strong and perhaps unsuspected emotion, just as may the skirl of bagpipes, a battleship glimpsed on a grey sea, the passing of an actual flag down the street. The effect is, no doubt, commonly ephemeral, and it can be seldom that a poet need soberly ask, with Yeats:

> Did that play of mine send out
> Certain men the English shot?

But Kipling's explicitly patriotic verse is backed by a whole solid world of balladry and of prose fiction in which the same ethos holds. When his only son, John Kipling, was killed at Loos in 1915 he was but one of many thousand boys ruled by a code, fortified by a faith or myth, which Kipling had done as much to form as had all the public schools of England put together. It is a substantial creative achievement, a signal instance of the power of art, whether it be regarded on this side of some frontier of literature or the other.

2

Kipling left the United Services College when he was sixteen —thus missing, we may suppose, at least a full year at the executive end of the canes and cricket-stumps and ground-ashes which seem seldom to have ceased flailing there:

> And they beat on us with rods—
> Faithfully with many rods—
> Daily beat us on with rods,
>   For the love they bore us!

The deprivation was one for which he was later a little prone to make up in fantasy. That he soberly felt deprived of other of the benefits of upper-class education is clear from a letter which he wrote two years later: 'My salaams to Stanley. I'd give something to be in the Sixth at Harrow as he is, with a University Education to follow.' Yet formal education is not everything. Stanley Baldwin was to become a Prime Minister, but it was his cousin Rudyard who polished his best speeches.

Kipling worked for seven years in newspaper offices in India, living for much of the time with his parents. The employment was scarcely exalted. Nor did his father, as the mere curator of a museum, rank high in the rigidly ordered hierarchy of Anglo-Indian society. But John Lockwood Kipling was a man of natural distinction and impressive acquirements, his wife was brilliant, his daughter was a beauty, and his son, although of unpolished manners, had whatever advantage nascent genius gives. The family was taken up by the Viceroy, Lord Dufferin, and to this circumstance is owing something of the wide range of experience, or at least of observation, which is a feature of those prodigal collections of tales—volume, it seemed, crowding upon volume—with which Kipling dazzled England hard upon his return to it at the end of 1889. His dawning celebrity, indeed, had accompanied him across America—so that it had been not quite a nobody who publicly announced, as earnest of much that was to come, his 'great joy' upon observing that the fortifications of San Francisco harbour could be demolished at need by a couple of English gunboats. This was the meteoric, prolific, and readily xenophobic young man who presented himself in London armed with a vivid and strident art very little congruous with the *fin-de-siècle* feeling he found there.

Of the Indian stories those concerning private soldiers are not quite the earliest. But they are the first coherent group with which Kipling startled and held a large public, and sufficiently characteristic to give us a good start. In 'The Taking of Lungtungpen'—apparently a tale with some basis in fact—Private Mulvaney tells of an action against dacoits in Burma. One is captured, and Mulvaney takes him into the jungle and beats him with a cleaning-rod until he tells the whereabouts of his fellows. The small English force strip to swim a stream in the night, and then enter and capture Lungtungpen armed but stark naked. 'We wint into thim, baynit an' butt, shriekin' wid laughin' '—with a resulting death-roll of 'sivinty-foive dacoits besides wounded'. The women of Lungtungpen are naturally alarmed, but the English spend the rest of the day 'playin' wid the Burmese babies—fat, little, brown little divils, as pretty as picturs'. Mulvaney finally boasts that 'they tuk Lungtungpen nakid; an' they'd take St. Pethersburg in their dhrawers!' The hair-raising and the sentimental are deftly blended in this spirited narrative, which is provided with a verse epigraph sufficiently consonant with its tone:

> So we loosed a bloomin' volley,
> An' we made the beggars cut,

> An' when our pouch was emptied out,
> We used the bloomin' butt,
> Ho! My!
> Don't yer come anigh,
> When Tommy is a playin' with the baynit an' the butt.

'On the City Wall', a story set against a communal riot during
Mohurrum, is the same sort of thing without the babies—and
full of batons, gun-butts, dog-whips cracked across writhing
backs, and 'British soldiers . . . stamping, with shouting and
song, upon the toes of Hindu and Mussulman'. For good
measure Kipling provides us with doctrine to match the story:

> If an advance be made all credit is given to the native, while the
> Englishmen stand back and wipe their foreheads. If a failure occurs
> the Englishmen step forward and take the blame. Overmuch
> tenderness of this kind has bred a strong belief among many natives
> that the native is capable of administering the country, and many
> devout Englishmen believe this also, because the theory is stated in
> beautiful English with all the latest political colours.

This confident pronouncement was made by a youth scarcely
come of age. But, politically, the child was father of the man.
Kipling would never have renounced these attitudes and convictions.

Mulvaney and his friends have their lighter moments. In
'The God from the Machine' the Colonel's daughter is saved
from an undesirable elopement with no more violence than is
represented by a native servant's first getting his nose 'smashed
in flat' and then being thrashed by the thwarted ravisher. 'My
Lord the Elephant' tells how Mulvaney restrained and quieted
an elephant which had become enraged through being required
to work in an elephant-battery, and how he later fell in with the
same beast when it was holding up traffic in a pass. The merit
here is all in the vividness and vigour of the evocation—and in
that sort of boldness in claiming to know what it is like to be an
elephant which D. H. Lawrence was later to show in regard to
snakes and tortoises. There is almost nothing that the young
Kipling does not know—his knowingness was from the first a
point of irritation with his critics—unless it be a few of the
minor canons of good taste. In 'The Incarnation of Krishna
Mulvaney'—a tale told with terrific verve—Mulvaney, having
purloined the palanquin of some princess, finds himself intro-

duced into a temple in Benares during a big Queens' Praying.
Successfully impersonating the god, and thus giving the temple
the appearance of being exceptionally under the divine favour,
he is able to extract money from one of the priests and make his
escape. He has overstayed his leave but is let off by the Colonel
since he knows how to 'lick the new batch of recruits into
shape . . . with blarney and the buckle-end of a belt'. The last
accomplishment receives further emphasis in a tale with far more
power to impress and offend, 'His Private Honour'.

This is the story of an ordeal, or rather of a double ordeal.
Private Ortheris is struck by a young officer, Ouless, on parade.
Ouless instantly confesses the act to his captain; Ortheris as
instantly protects Ouless by lying. Each man remains with his
honour to rescue. Ouless, having thought the matter over, takes
Ortheris on a private shooting-expedition. They fight with fists;
Ortheris plasters his adversary but is fairly beaten; and thus the
incident is purged. 'The boy was proven', we read of Ouless in
the last sentence. And Ortheris, the mature soldier, has needed
no proving:

> 'It was your right to get him cashiered if you chose,' I insisted.
> 'My right!' Ortheris answered with deep scorn. 'My right! I ain't
> a recruity to go whinin' about my rights to this an' my rights to
> that, just as if I couldn't look after myself. My rights! 'Strewth
> A'mighty! I'm a man.'

But if Ortheris, as well as being a man, is a public-school boy
under his skin, it is a public-school boy of the decidedly unredeemed sort that we are to meet in *Stalky & Co*. Ortheris
celebrates the restoration of his honour by taking a wretched
Jewish recruit, Samuelson, and rolling him up and down the
verandah—and earlier, when things have been black, he has
relieved his feelings by pitching Samuelson's kit about and
kicking him 'every time that the bewildered creature stooped to
pick anything up'. Ortheris is entitled—if not obliged—to do
this because Samuelson has not yet become a good soldier. The
ethic, which is to run strongly and harshly through much of
Kipling's work, is explicitly stated: 'First a man must suffer,
then he must learn his work, and the self-respect that that
knowledge brings.' In the foreground we have Ortheris who has
learned and Ouless who has been learning; in the background
we are shown the process at its most naked among the new men.

The story has begun with the sentence 'The autumn batch of recruits for the Old Regiment had just been uncarted'—and they are recruits who are about to be taught that 'there is no scorn so complete as that of the old soldier for the new'. 'It is right that this should be so', Kipling adds. And he goes on to describe the recruits' manner of study in terms that we may at first guilelessly suppose to be metaphorical. Thus, 'Learoyd thrashed them methodically one by one, without haste but without slovenliness; and the older soldiers took the remnants from Learoyd and went over them in their own fashion'. But when Mulvaney declares that 'There's the makin's av colonels in that mob if we only go deep enough—wid a belt', and we learn further that 'each old soldier took a new draft and kicked him very severely', while 'the non-commissioned officers had neither eyes nor ears for these accidents', we realize that we are in a world of terrorists as forthright as any that Kipling is going to describe at Westward Ho! or Lord Berners and Mr. Cyril Connolly at a more celebrated school. Moreover we suspect, rightly or wrongly, that Kipling approves—and even with an urgency which makes him, as narrator, a little too active in his own story. The result of the veterans' attentions is that 'the new draft began to stand on their feet and feel that they belonged to a good and honourable service'. It seems that if Samuelson is to be saved, his race must be insulted, his person tortured, and his manhood humiliated.

Here is stiff doctrine—and Kipling repeats it often enough:

> The young recruit is silly—'e thinks o' suicide.
> 'E's lost 'is gutter-devil; 'e 'asn't got 'is pride;
> But day by day they kicks 'im, which 'elps 'im on a bit,
> Till 'e finds 'isself one mornin' with a full an' proper kit.

Yet it is doctrine arrived at, we have to admit, by a mind capable of seeing very clearly. The brutality of the barrack-room is set over against the ruthlessness towards the individual of the whole hierarchy of authority that is an army—or, by an obvious extension, a society. Ouless's act has been little more than a sudden nervous spasm, and it is mere chance that rips Ortheris's tunic and makes the incident observable. Moreover B Company has been hardly dealt with—given too many recruits and then kept at the disagreeable Fort Amara until tempers are frayed beyond any useful disciplinary purpose. But all this is nothing in an inflexible code; old privates may use their boots and belts with impunity, yet an officer who flicks out with his cane can be broken at a word. Greater privilege brings greater hazard. The justice which we are asked to sanction (and we *are* asked to sanction it) is very rough, and there is no appeal from it:

> An' you mustn't swear an' curse, or you'll only catch it worse,
> An' we'll make you soldiers yet!

Its first principle—here declared—is that 'there is a beautiful little ripple in a well-made line of men, exactly like the play of a perfectly-tempered sword'. Or, as it is expressed in 'A Song in Storm':

> The game is more than the player of the game,
> And the ship is more than the crew!

In 'His Private Honour' this justice, such as it is, works. And although it is made to point astringently the remoteness of the narrator's day-dream (being indulged in at the moment Ouless strikes) of an independent India based upon 'such an army as the world had never seen', it is plausibly displayed as compatible not merely with a high sense of personal honour in officer and ranker alike but also with a delicacy of feeling which, paradoxically, Kipling's individual soldiers hardly ever lack.

'His Private Honour' is an impressive performance. Within the same group come four tales which would alone establish Kipling as among the greatest writers of short stories—and the first of them, 'The Man who would be King', must have been written well before his twenty-third birthday. Carefully set in the kind of frame or induction to which he was to give much attention, it tells of two low-class English adventurers possessed by the wild dream of making their way to Kafiristan and there establishing their own empire. In fact they succeed, dominating and drilling whole tribes and achieving quasi-divine status before the determination of the dominant partner to break a vow and take a native wife brings their position crashing down, so that one is hurled to death in a ravine and the other must survive crucifixion before telling the story. The surface narrative is rich, vigorous, and convincing. The deploying of it is already full of a skilled craftsman's subtleties. There is a play of unobtrusive symbols, and a psychological realism so economically

achieved that it serves to give glimpses of the two principal
characters in depth without ever holding up the sheer sustained
excitement of the action. Carnehan and Dravot have more of
nature than do some answering characters in the maturest
Conrad. Nor can Conrad—although so powerful an atmospheric writer—ever give body and sharp actuality to exotic
scenes with the speed and spareness Kipling here achieves.
Moreover, while the lesser symbolisms are designed artifice, we
are aware of the sort of richness that comes from the pressure of
less conscious significances. Dravot's *raj* might be a greater one
in which analogous perils lurk, and the specific occasion of its
downfall reverberates with a fear and horror lying very deep in
Kipling's sexual nature.

In 'The Courting of Dinah Shadd' Mulvaney courts Dinah
and is accepted. He celebrates, flirts with another girl, Judy
Sheehy, and is presently confronted by the two mothers and
their daughters. Almost before we know that this is anything
other than coarse comedy, Judy's mother is pronouncing a
tremendous curse upon Mulvaney, and the story turns perfectly
upon the strong pivot of Dinah's response:

'"Strong you think yourself? May your strength be a curse to
you to dhrive you into the divil's hands against your own will!
Clear-eyed you are? May your eyes see clear evry step av the dark
path you take till the hot cindhers av hell put thim out! May the
ragin' dry thirst in my own ould bones go to you that you shall niver
pass bottle full nor glass empty. God preserve the light av your
onderstandin' to you, my jewel av a bhoy, that ye may niver forget
what you mint to be an' do, whin you're wallowin' in the muck!
May ye see the betther and follow the worse as long as there's
breath in your body; an' may ye die quick in a strange land,
watchin' your death before ut takes you, an' onable to stir hand or
foot!"

'I heard a scufflin' in the room behind, and thin Dinah Shadd's
hand dhropped into mine like a rose-leaf into a muddy road.

'"The half av that I'll take," sez she, "an' more too if I can.
Go home, ye silly talkin' woman,—go home an' confess."

'"Come away, Come away!" sez Judy, pullin' her mother by the
shawl. "'Twas none av Terence's fault. For the love av Mary stop
the talkin'!"

'"An' you!" said ould Mother Sheehy, spinnin' round forninst
Dinah. "Will ye take the half av that man's load? Stand off from
him, Dinah Shadd, before he takes you down too."'

The curse upon Dinah that follows is yet more tremendous, and we need no assurances that it will be fulfilled, since Mrs. Sheehy is now plainly a sibyl:

> 'She pitched forward on her head an' began foamin' at the mouth. Dinah Shadd ran out wid water, an' Judy dhragged the ould woman into the verandah till she sat up.
> ' "I'm old an' forlore," she sez, thremblin' an' cryin', "and 'tis like I say a dale more than I mane." '

This is in essence a *short* story; it has the speed and power of a traditional ballad, with all its active virtue in the extreme concentration of its crisis. It ends with a ballad of Kipling's own, and it has been prefaced with a vivid and bustling description of the manœuvres during which Mulvaney tells his tale. We may doubt here whether the frame enhances the effect. Admirable in itself, it may yet strike us as a display of useless facile vigour when surrounding an action which commands so surely depths of primitive feeling and drives so straight at tragedy.

'Love-o'-Women' also drives at tragedy. The pitch at which it aims is made clear in the opening paragraph:

> The horror, the confusion, and the separation of the murderer from his comrades were all over before I came. There remained only on the barrack-square the blood of man calling from the ground. The hot sun had dried it to a dusky goldbeater's-skin film, cracked lozenge-wise by the heat; and as the wind rose, each lozenge, rising a little, curled up at the edges as if it were a dumb tongue. . . . A knot of soldiers' wives stood by one of the entrances to the married quarters, while inside a woman shrieked and raved with wicked filthy words.

This, once more, is the beginning not of the main tale but of an induction. The main tale is to end with an explicit reference to *Antony and Cleopatra*. If the induction, when we go back to consider its effect, sets us obscurely thinking of *King Lear*, this must be because it works rather after the fashion of the sub-plot in Shakespeare's play. Like causes produce like effects; twice a bullet ends what passion has begun. The major story has the greater depth, but the co-presence of the minor universalizes the theme. Raines, 'a quiet and well-conducted sergeant', shoots one of his own corporals who has seduced his wife; in the gentleman-ranker, Love-o'-Women, enslavement to sex brings a slower and direr nemesis. The syphilis that finally kills him eats no deeper than his remorse over many women and his bitter remorse over one; her, in throwing away whom he had thrown away diamonds and pearls, he discovers at the last in a brothel:

'He lifted up his eyes, slow an' very slow, an' he looked at her long an' very long, an' he tuk his spache betune his teeth wid a wrench that shuk him.

' "I'm dyin', Aigypt—dyin'," he sez. Ay, those were his words, for I remimber the name he called her. He was turnin' the death-colour, but his eyes niver rowled. They were set—set on her. Widout word or warnin' she opened her arms full stretch, an' "Here!" she sez. (Oh, fwhat a golden mericle av a voice ut was!) 'Die here!" she sez; an' Love-o'-Women dhropped forward, an' she hild him up, for she was a fine big woman.'

The woman shoots herself, and is buried with Love-o'-Women in one grave. The closing page of this story, as the narrative fades away to the final marching song, is full of drink, adultery, and strong clear pathos. It is a triumph of its young writer's art.

A similar pathos informs 'On Greenhow Hill', the fourth of these stories, but one less high in colouring and harsh in strength. Here the narrator is Learoyd, a Yorkshireman, who tells how his despair when he knew the girl he loved to be dying led him to enlist. In the eyes of the girl's father and his co-religionists it was an act that courted damnation:

'I went away into the town and knocked up against a recruiting sergeant. The old tales o' th' chapel folk came buzzin' into my head. I was to get away, and this were th' regular road for the likes o' me. I 'listed there and then, took th' Widow's shillin', and had a bunch o' ribbons pinned i' my hat.'

Then he had been admitted to the presence of the dying girl:

'Her eyes were all alive wi' light, and her hair was thick on the pillow round her, but her cheeks were thin—thin to frighten a man that's strong. "Nay, father, yo' mayn't say th' devil's colours. Them ribbons is pretty." An' she held out her hands for th' hat, an' she put all straight as a woman will wi' ribbons. "Nay, but what they're pretty," she says. "Eh, but I'd ha' liked to see thee i' thy red coat, John, for thou was allus my own lad—my very own lad, and none else." '

Without the ribbons the story would be a good one, yet only half as good as it is—and the beginning of our acknowledgement of Kipling as a great writer is in our coming to notice such things as we read. But this simple note, perhaps reminding us a little of Hardy's *Trumpet-Major*, does not sound alone in 'On Greenhow Hill'. There is murderous jealousy in the tale, and it is out of this that Learoyd has won his way to the grim clean work of soldiering in which he is engaged as he tells it.

Kipling's officer-class stories (as they may be called) of this early period are not so good, but a few may be mentioned as characteristic. In 'A Bank Fraud' Reggie Burke, the genial and competent manager of an up-country branch of an Indian bank, is landed with an intolerably inefficient and censorious accountant. Notice of the man's dismissal comes when he is mortally ill, and Burke conceals it from him and pays his salary out of his own pocket till he dies. This is a sentimental tale on a simple gentleman-versus-cad formula which Kipling was never entirely to cease to exploit. 'Only a Subaltern' is decidedly better. 'Thrown Away' is the story of a boy reared under what parents call the 'sheltered-life system'—which Kipling knows is 'not wise'. The boy passes high into Sandhurst, not so high out —and then in India takes things too seriously. (This is unwise too.) He 'fretted over women not worth saddling a pony to call upon', made various mistakes, received a common 'Colonel's wigging', and then got leave to go hunting and in fact shot himself after writing despairing letters to his parents and a girl in England. An apprehensive major and the narrator arrive only in time to bury the body, burn the letters, and put up a story of death by cholera. They are much affected as they do all the right things—including chopping off a lock of the major's hair to send home, since the boy's hair is in no state for exhibition. At the same time they find themselves convulsed with laughter as they work 'at the grotesqueness of the affair'. There is to be much strange laughter in Kipling. 'The Bronckhorst Divorce-Case' is a disagreeable story (and an obscure one if the reader be ignorant of Section 497 of the Indian Penal Code of 1860). Bronckhorst, 'a three-cornered, middle-aged man in the Army', behaves with consistent brutality to his wife and later institutes proceedings 'on the criminal count' against a man called Biel. 'No jury, we knew, would convict a man on the criminal count on native evidence in a land where you can buy a murder-charge, including the corpse, all complete for fifty-four rupees; but Biel did not care to scrape through by the benefit of a doubt.' So a certain Strickland (who will reappear in *Kim*) somehow brings into play his genius for disguise and follows this up by coming into court carrying 'a gut trainer's-whip'. Bronckhorst's false witnesses are intimidated, the case collapses, and 'ten minutes later, Biel was cutting Bronckhorst into ribbons behind the old Court cells, quietly and without scandal'. Then the Bronckhorsts' life settles down much as before. Kipling has no doubt about this—any more than he has about the precise cost of a murder-charge, or what regularly happens 'when the reaction of marriage sets in'. There is a strong antagonism to women in many of these stories. And all hold the same encyclo-pedic assuredness—from the manner in which 'Indian banking is totally distinct from Home work' to the habits of puppies when invited to eat soap. But Kipling was twenty or there-abouts, and perhaps the cleverest man in India. A phase of delusion may be forgiven him. Yet if his was a brilliant mind it was in some ways an obstinately naïve one. 'The Tomb of his Ancestors' is a rather later story, but it exhibits his myth of Anglo-India still in its archetypal simplicity. 'Colonel Lionel Chinn served thirty years and retired. In the Canal his steamer passed the outward-bound troopship, carrying his son eastward to the family duties.' Young Chinn is received with satisfaction by the old regiment. 'No need', the Colonel says, 'to ask the young un's breed. He's a *pukka* Chinn.' As a Chinn young Chinn carries a sort of *mana* which takes him triumphantly through a variety of trying situations, including one in which the chaplain of the regiment goes to work among the natives 'magisterially with a riding-whip'. The myth, of course, is not wholly Kip-ling's. If we turn, for instance, to *Eothen* we find that Kinglake's 'English gentleman among Orientals' exemplifies it in rudi-mentary form.

Of the remaining large number of Indian stories, major or minor, at least a dozen cannot be passed by—most of them because they are so good, and some because they are so sig-nificantly bad. Two introduce what is to be the prolific theme of Kipling's interest in children, and several more his even greater interest in the supernatural. 'Tods' Amendment' has at least some curiosity for the student of Kipling's psychology. 'Every one in Simla knew Tods. . . . He was an utterly fearless young Pagan, about six years old', who 'had honour in the land' and 'ruled justly according to his lights'. Frequenting the Simla

Bazaar, he understands 'the real native—not the hybrid, University-trained mule'. And so when the mere Native Member of Council leads the Viceroy and Government of India astray in a matter of agrarian reform, Tods, having slipped into a dinner-party as the privileged child he is, explains things to the Legal Member—and when the relevant Bill is passed, 'Tods' Amendment' is duly included in it. Here is the germ of *Kim*; the young man who has returned to India is day-dreaming about the small boy who had been banished from it. This holds, too, of 'Wee Willie Winkie', the Colonel's six-year-old son and idol of the regiment, 'child of the Dominant Race', who undauntedly faces the Bad Men and so saves his friend's *fiancée* from being kidnapped. It is a thickly sentimental and revoltingly false little tale. Of the stories with a supernatural element the most powerful is 'The Mark of the Beast', which might have been written to overgo the horror of H. G. Wells's (actually later) *Island of Dr. Moreau*. A drunken Englishman desecrates a temple, is embraced by a leper and rapidly develops all the characteristics of a wolf. Strickland and the narrator capture the leper and torture him for some hours until he agrees to remove the curse. The possessed man then recovers. This is, as the final paragraph thinks to inform us, 'a rather unpleasant story'. One editor to whom it was submitted prophesied, comprehensibly but erroneously, that the author would presently pass into madness and perish. 'The Phantom Rickshaw' is a very early tale— one of the two earliest that Kipling wished to preserve—and is scarcely successful, but it deserves notice as the first work during the creation of which he felt the presence of 'the Personal Daemon of Aristotle and others'. 'The Return of Imray' is a commonplace story into which the supernatural is introduced through the expedient of a psychic dog. The creature has a remote descendant in 'The Dog Hervey', one of the most oblique and obscure of his later stories. 'The Strange Ride of Morrowbie Jukes', the second of the two very early stories of which he approved, deals with horror rather than with the supernatural. Jukes, a civil engineer, rides off in a fever and tumbles into a trap: a horse-shoe enclosure in sandy cliffs fronting a river. It is a place to which are relegated Hindus who have revived after being consigned in some ritual way to the burning *ghat* and who ought therefore to be dead. They live in little caves in extreme destitution, unable to escape since they are hemmed in on the river side by quicksand. Jukes recognizes an old decayed Deccanee Brahmin, once in charge of a branch telegraph-office, who explains things and tries to bully him until Jukes bullies back. He finds the body of another Englishman, who had nearly worked out an escape route and had been killed by the Brahmin. The Brahmin tries to double-cross Jukes, who is then rescued by a servant who has traced him. The climax is muffed and flat, but the description of the terrifying place is effective—and we may reflect that all these stories had to pass with literal-minded readers who knew their setting. This story, again, may afford a comparison with the early H. G. Wells—and elsewhere the two writers share a fascination with violence.

And violence, too, of a jocular cast was from the first a pre-occupation and resource of Kipling's. In 'A Friend's Friend' a guest called Jevon gets drunk and misconducts himself at a ball. 'When the ladies had gone, and some one was calling for songs at the second supper' (these stories are full of interesting sidelights on Anglo-Indian social habits) Jevon is tied up, elaborately smeared and decked with burnt cork, meringue-cream, and gelatine, hung with ham-frills and cutlet-frills, rolled up in a carpet, and sent away in a bullock-cart along with a load of furniture. 'He vanished utterly. . . . Perhaps he died and was thrown into the river.' We may be intended not to take this last conjecture too seriously, but there is often to be something equivocal in the tone of these stories of puni-tive ragging. 'The Judgment of Dungara' tells how a local priest avenges himself upon an intolerant and humourless German missionary and his converts by persuading them to weave garments from Nilgiri Nettle—the result being a sort of comically conceived shirt of Nessus which begins to eat into the converts when they are on show before the Collector and his wife. 'The end of conversion was the fire of the Bad Place—fire that ran through the limbs and gnawed into the bones.' There is an implausible element in the story, since the toxic qualities of the plant would surely have revealed themselves in the process of weaving. But the notion of the converts writhing in a sort of Hell Fire after all is genuinely neat and brutally amusing. A story like this connects on the one hand with a number of short anecdotes of native life, such as 'Dray Wara Yow Dee' and 'Gemini', which are straight confrontations of violence and cruelty, and on the other with later and more elaborately evolved stories which contrive to square a farcical tone with the notion that the joyous inflicting of some painful physical humiliation is being pursued in the interest of moral reform. The classical place here is to be in *Stalky & Co.*

3

A short review of the Indian stories may conclude by returning to more substantial achievements. First, there is 'To be Filed for Reference'. 'In most big cities natives will tell you of two or three *Sahibs*, generally low-caste, who have turned Hindu or Mussulman, and who live more or less as such.' McIntosh Jellaludin seems not to be low-caste. He is, or claims to be, 'an Oxford Man'. 'He was, when sober, a scholar and a gentleman. When drunk, he was rather more of the first than the second.' The narrator is present at his death in extreme squalor and degradation. His last words are 'Not guilty, my Lord!' and he gives the narrator the tattered manuscript of a book which he believes will make him famous. This story is of interest as an early example of one accompanied by verses developing its theme on another level. Here the verses appear to challenge the justice of placing sentient beings in a determined universe:

> By the hoof of the Wild Goat up-tossed
> From the Cliff where She lay in the Sun,
>   Fell the Stone
> To the Tarn where the daylight is lost;
> So She fell from the light of the Sun,
>   And alone.
>
> Now the fall was ordained from the first,
> With the Goat and the Cliff and the Tarn,
>   But the Stone
> Knows only Her life is accursed,
> As She sinks in the depths of the Tarn,
>   And alone.
>
> Oh, Thou who hast builded the World!
> Oh, Thou who hast lighted the Sun!
> Oh, Thou who hast darkened the Tarn!
>   Judge Thou
> The sin of the Stone that was hurled
> By the Goat from the light of the Sun,
> As She sinks in the mire of the Tarn,
>   Even now—even now—even now!

Kipling could not at this time have read the poetry of Hardy,
most of which was still to be written, but he must have known
FitzGerald's *Rubáiyát*. But Kipling's is essentially not a
speculative mind, and this limits, now and later, the scope and
effectiveness of his dealings with the starkest intimations of
experience. 'At the End of the Passage' begins with an elaborate
and effective evocation of the strains endured by Englishmen
whose duties tie them to unbearable places during the rigours
of an Indian summer. Hummil suffers first from insomnia and
then from what appear to be hallucinations. Eventually he is
found dead, and 'in the staring eyes was written terror beyond
the expression of any pen'. But in the eyes—it is intimated—
there can be seen something else as well: the lingering images
of substantial and objective horrors susceptible of record by
a Kodak. This is not a very good way of suggesting that there
can be more to a vision of evil than a disordered liver as sworn
to by the obtuse doctor of 'The Phantom Rickshaw'. And if
as we read the story we happen to think of Conrad's 'Heart of
Darkness' or James's 'The Turn of the Screw' we shall scarcely
feel that Kipling can challenge either on this ground. Yet it
has all Conrad's power—and far more than James's power—
of actually sticking to the skin and pricking at the nerves and
pounding in the head as it evokes the physical conditions prelusive of its dubious mystery. Moreover this story, even if not
wholly successful, has importance as looking forward to one of
Kipling's most mature themes. Hummil has been 'seven fathom
deep in hell' and has there met despair and horror of which
there can be no rational account. That we inhabit a universe
in which this can happen is to remain Kipling's grand problem
long after the tumult and the shouting dies.

A distinguished American critic, Mr. Lionel Trilling, has
declared Kipling to retain some interest at least on account of
his 'effect upon us in that obscure and important part of our
minds where literary feeling and political attitude meet'. This,
as far as it goes, is certainly true, and in 'The Man who Was'
we come upon a story in which this meeting may render the
effect of violent collision. Here we have an English army officer
who, captured by the Russians in the Crimea and for some
unjust reason long held in barbarous captivity as a criminal,
staggers into his old regimental mess in India, the manhood
flogged out of him, to expire after having his identity revealed

in a moment of high drama which is in itself one of the finest
bravura things in Kipling. There is no mischief in the large
improbability of the fable, for the writer realizes his situation
irresistibly. The mischief is rather in an incidental intrusive
chauvinism. We have seen that the basis of Kipling's political
attitude is a just and Miltonic patriotism and a down-to-earth
knowledge, such as he judged dangerously neglected, that
powder had better be kept dry and sentinels vigilant. But a
perversion of this feeling sometimes mars his most vivid imaginative achievements. In 'The Man who Was' we have it
strikingly. For being resolved to give his feelings rein, he goes
about the job with ruthless impetus and resource. Over
against Dirkovitch, the disagreeable Russian guest, is set
Rissaldar Hira Singh, 'the son of a king's son' and a sort of
well-affected Hotspur of a native regiment—and this to effects
so crude that they could appeal, one would suppose, to the
taste only of an inebriated subaltern. Indeed the appeal is not
soldierly at all, and not even masculine. Mr. Trilling remarks,
with some acid truth, that although Kipling makes much to-
do about manliness he is not manly. There is a problem here
which must be deferred. Yet the next two stories to be considered are not without relevance to it.

'Without Benefit of Clergy' tells of a young English civilian
who takes a native mistress by whom he has a son. The couple
are very close to each other in their love, wholly sundered by
culture and situation. The child dies. Cholera comes and the
woman, who will not go away as the white women do, dies in
her turn. It is a searing episode in the man's life and it is over—
over with a special poignancy implicit in the tenuousness,
tension, and intensity of the bond between a man and woman
thus circumstanced. This story—austere and pure except for
a certain characteristic sentimentality in the presentation of the
child—stands in some isolation, reminding us of the very large
tracts of his particular international situation which Kipling's
so abundant art attempts very little survey of. As a study of
sexual passion, it bears a sort of antithetical relationship to the
next story, one of somewhat later date, 'William the Conqueror'.

William is a girl, but perhaps her name tells us that she was
born to live in a man's world, in which duty is the prime
imperative, helpless natives are saved from calamity by white
men driving themselves to the verge of madness, and a wife is

lucky if she gets a 'Steady, Lizzie', admonishingly flung at her over her husband's shoulder. From the first William plays the game, keeping house under primitive conditions for her brother, an impecunious irrigation engineer, through years during which she could have made half a dozen successful matches:

None the less William had enjoyed herself hugely in her four years. Twice she had been nearly drowned while fording a river on horseback; once she had been run away with on a camel; had witnessed a midnight attack of thieves on her brother's camp; had seen justice administered, with long sticks, in the open under trees; could speak Urdu and even rough Punjabi with a fluency that was envied by her seniors; had altogether fallen out of the habit of writing to her aunts in England, or cutting the pages of the English magazines; had been through a very bad cholera year, seeing sights unfit to be told; and had wound up her experiences by six weeks of typhoid fever, during which her head had been shaved; and hoped to keep her twenty-third birthday that September.

When William does find a lover in young Scott it is at an unpropitious season, 'for the famine was sore in the land, and white men were needed'. William manages to go on famine relief too, and when Scott adopts the resourceful plan of feeding to herds of goats rice which the starving natives refuse to eat, thus securing milk with which he supports a growing crèche of babies, she is there to help him:

The Rains fell at last, late, but heavily; and the dry, gashed earth was red mud, and servants killed snakes in the camp. . . . Now the Government decreed that seed-grain should be distributed to the people, as well as advances of money for the purchase of new oxen; and the white men were doubly worked for this new duty, while William skipped from brick to brick laid down on the trampled mud, and dosed her charges with warming medicines that made them rub their little round stomachs; and the milch-goats throve on the rank grass. . . . Scott was taking thirty grains of quinine a day to fight the fever that comes if one works hard in heavy rain. . . . That was the time when eight years of clean living and hard condition told.

There is a moment of supreme test when Scott, passing within five miles of William, does not deviate to visit her, and she says 'It wouldn't be him if he did'. She has her reward when all ends well, and the white men can relax and think of sport and matrimony:

They were picking them up at almost every station now—men and women coming in for the Christmas Week, with racquets, with bundles of polo-sticks, with dear and bruised cricket-bats, with fox-terriers and saddles. . . . Scott was with the bachelors at the far end of the train, where they chaffed him mercilessly about feeding babies and milking goats; but from time to time he would stroll up to William's window, and murmur: 'Good enough, isn't it?' and William would answer with sighs of pure delight: 'Good enough, indeed.' The large open names of the home towns were good to listen to. Umballa, Ludianah, Phillour, Jullundur, they rang like the coming marriage-bells in her ears.

Here again has been the myth of Anglo-India in its entire simplicity—but it has been superbly, one must almost say nobly, celebrated. William and her kind perhaps never quite existed, any more than did their antitypes, the English wives of Mr. Forster's *A Passage to India*. When the climax of William's romance embarrasses Mr. Somerset Maugham he is no doubt right, and this sort of love scene may be as 'adolescent' as he says. Certainly it is without—and seems not to look forward to—those vividly realized sexual excitements which the reader of modern erotic chronicles is supposed to demand and relish. Yet somehow, within the frame of its illusion, it is not the less authentic and moving for being so unutterably wholesome and desperately public-school. When William says 'Good enough, indeed' we are at her feet, and believe that she knows what she is talking about. Yet when *Bakri* Scott marries his William Martyn the faintly equivocal ring of it reminds us that the world of Kipling's admiration is very much a masculine one. And this is to note again that there is something not wholly masculine in his sensibility.

4

Kipling's output of fiction before leaving India was so copious as to be susceptible of distribution into six volumes in the interest of an enterprise called Wheeler's Indian Railway Library, and this already included work as fine as 'The Man who would be King'. But the majority of the best stories so far considered belong to his prodigious first London years, being collected in *Life's Handicap* (1891) and *Many Inventions* (1893). It was natural that his ambition should now turn to the writing of a novel, and the result was *The Light that Failed*. Behind alike the action and the odd bibliographical history of this book there lies a good deal of the pressure of Kipling's private circumstances at the time. His position was not an easy one. In the foster-home of his early childhood and at least in his earlier terms at school his life had been hideous. Thereafter, despite a considerable effect of knocking about through widely ranging experience, it had been essentially sheltered within the 'family square' constituted by his parents and his sister Alice. From the years of his earlier manhood there survive few traces of any emotional involvement outside the walls of this fortress, and all his life he was to be notably dependent on domesticity and family counsel. This applied even to the range of his writing and to the perfecting of his craft. His mother seems to have frowned effectively upon his pursuing too radically his researches into the fast life of Simla; again and again we hear how nothing was fully approved by himself until it had been 'smoked by the Pater'; and he records that his thought of turning novelist was often debated in the family. In London, while continuing to work at very high pressure, he was substantially isolated. His success had been meteoric and had given him the freedom of such literary society as he might find congenial. But in that society there were plenty who were glad to murmur that meteors commonly burn themselves out.

It was now that he made the acquaintance of Wolcott Balestier, a young American who had established himself in England as agent for a New York publisher. Balestier had great power of recommending himself to writers: he had become, for example, like Hugh Walpole, one of Henry James's decorously adored young men. But he was in a hurry, and there is no evidence that his attitude to literary production evinced the high seriousness which in a good publisher is to be desired. He persuaded Kipling to a collaboration, and they produced together *The Naulahka* (1892), a carelessly run-up romance of little merit. It is surprising that Kipling, who had his father's standards of careful craftsmanship and was disposed to guard alike his literary and his personal privacy, should have been drawn into such a project. But there can be no doubt about the explanation. Kipling had become deeply attached to Balestier. And it was an attachment with other than merely literary consequences. When Balestier died suddenly at the end of 1891, Kipling made a lightning return from a visit to his parents in India and married Balestier's sister Caroline—his own senior by three years—eight days after reaching London. Where the emphasis of his affection had first lain is curiously illustrated in a poem, 'The Long Trail', written on the occasion of his departing on the Indian trip. Its valediction was addressed to a 'dear lad', and only upon publication were the words 'dear lass' substituted—inappositely in what is very much a man's poem in tone. For this alteration he perhaps made amends to his friend's shade by appropriating to his memory, as the dedication of *Barrack Room Ballads*, verses accurately described by Mr. Carrington as 'wildly adulatory'. Had Arthur Hallam lived, he would have married Tennyson's sister Emily. There is an odd if imperfect parallel in these histories.

The Light that Failed may be said—although this is a simplification—to exist in two forms the precedence between which is uncertain, but which were given to the world within three months of each other (1890–1). One of these has an ending, commonly admitted as of unbelievable badness, in which the hero and heroine become happily engaged; to the shaping of this there can be little doubt that the commercial instinct of Wolcott Balestier decisively contributed. The other and longer version, declared by Kipling to be the story 'as it was originally conceived by the Writer', is fairly called by Mr. Carrington 'an anti-feminist tract'. And a dramatization, produced in 1903, was to elicit from Kipling's inveterate enemy Max Beerbohm the conjecture that matter which so 'doted on the military' and so abounded in 'cheap cynicism about the female sex' had perhaps been 'fondly created out of the inner consciousness of a female novelist'. But in fact *The Light that Failed* is a painful rather than a merely embarrassing book. Like Lawrence's *Sons and Lovers* it is written out of experiences still bearing hard upon the novelist as he works. And Kipling, who could see so brilliantly both places and people he had known and battles he had never witnessed, has no power to see himself—but only to see a press of his own angers and frustrations and fears. Some expression of these he contrives, and ekes it out with episodes of irrelevant robust *rapportage* surprising in a writer who believes himself to be here following *Manon Lescaut*. Yet the comparison is not quite absurd. It is possible to feel that had Kipling broken through some remaining barrier—or even given adequate time and artistic consideration to his task—he

might have achieved a powerful presentation of the destructiveness of sexual passion.

The story opens virtually in that Southsea House of Desolation which he had already indicted in a horrifying short story,
'Baa, Baa, Black Sheep'. But, instead of a sister, the tormented
small boy, Dick Heldar, has as fellow-victim a girl, Maisie,
unrelated to him and with whom he precociously falls in love.
From this situation—now known also to have autobiographical
substance—we move on abruptly to Dick in young manhood:
an artist who has knocked about the world in the toughest
fashion and has commemorated the fact in his sketch-book:

> The young man produced more sketches. 'Row on a Chinese pig-
> boat,' said he sententiously, showing them one after another.—
> 'Chief mate dirked by a comprador.— Junk ashore off Hakodate.—
> Somali muleteer being flogged.—Star-shell bursting over camp at
> Berbera.— Slave-dhow being chased round Tajurrah Bay.— Soldier
> lying dead in the moonlight outside Suakin,—throat cut by Fuzzies.'

He has some success and celebrates with a party: 'the naked
Zanzibari girls danced furiously by the light of kerosene lamps'.
Like Kipling he comes to London and as with Kipling his
success continues. His toughness continues too. He despises
aesthetes who 'talk about art and the state of their souls'. For
a time—and until pulled up by robust friends who feel that
'he wants the whip-lash'—he toys with a cynical and commercial attitude to his talent. He defeats a rapacious agent by
threat of violence; 'pawing him, as a cat paws a soft hearth-
rug', he says: 'This gray oaf dares to be a thief! I have seen an
Esneh camel-driver have the black hide taken off his body in
strips for stealing half a pound of wet dates, and *he* was as
tough as whipcord. This thing's soft all over—like a woman.'
But upon Dick—arrogant in his chosen world of crack war-
correspondents with outlandish nicknames, the Nilghai, the
Keneu—a woman now turns up: Maisie, herself become an
artist, although not a talented one. His contacts with women
have hitherto not been refined. Their highlight has been represented by 'a sort of Negroid-Jewess-Cuban, with morals to
match', whom he had commemorated on a ship's rotten plates
in brown, green, and black ship's paint—'just three colours and
no chance of getting any more, and the sea outside and unlimited love-making inside, and the fear of death atop of everything else'. Dick, flushed and confident with success, falls in

love with Maisie once more. But Maisie—years before Shaw's Vivie Warren—has become a sort of New Woman; she is capable of loving only the vision of success in her own career. Against this situation (and there is said again to be a direct autobiographical reference) Dick hurls himself and breaks. And then suddenly he is going blind—an inconsequent disaster a little prepared for by a broken head in an early scrap, and also several times symbolically adumbrated at moments of crisis in his story. One of the child Kipling's miseries at Southsea had been a temporary collapse of his sight, and this first eruption of a phobia into his fiction (there are to be others) makes an effect that is powerful enough. Indeed the whole book—which ends, in its tragic form, with the blind man struggling back to war in Egypt and getting killed—is only too powerful, since the power is all put behind the 'lash' that again and again figures in it. Constantly in Kipling—it is what, in favouring circumstances, constitutes his prime genius—there is imaginative penetration to very deep and primitive layers of consciousness. What we are left with here is essentially magical: a fantasy of propitiatory self-punishment. Dick Heldar is a Kipling who has presumed. 'He had suffered. Now he would take toll of the ills of others.' It is what is to animate Beetle in *Stalky & Co.* as he plies the cricket-stump. But here, instead, there is fulfilled the prophecy of the ruined artist Binat at the beginning of the book: 'Monsieur will descend alive into hell, as I have descended.' For the sense of ὕβρις was strong in Kipling. There is a clear line from this poor novel to 'Recessional'.

Whatever the personal crisis behind *The Light that Failed*, it was substantially resolved by Kipling's marriage. Nevertheless the marriage brought troubles of its own. His father described Caroline Balestier as 'a good man spoiled' and Henry James was copious in misgivings over the match with 'poor concentrated Carrie'. She was certainly a strong-minded woman, and there is clearly more than malicious gossip behind the many stories of her husband's extreme submissiveness to her authority. He was already the Apostle of Empire; on a journey through the United States he had comported himself in a manner earning him the nickname 'Johnny Bull'; in return he had been prone to remark 'the American Eagle screaming for all it was worth'; there was therefore something a little strange in the young couple's resolve to build and settle on the Balestier's estate in

Vermont. Kipling managed to like and admire a great deal that
this let him in for. But finally it didn't do. The cook resented the
caps Carrie expected her to wear. The coachman, being English, liveried and lately in the employment of a peer, was ill
regarded. And Kipling, having been threatened with Kip-
lingesque violence by a shiftless but locally endeared brother-
in-law, was foolish enough to hurry off for protection to the
police. This last trouble led to his being publicly ridiculed
in a court of law, and the couple were virtually constrained
to return to England. Carrie, however, did not readily give
in. Another attempt was made, and unfortunately resulted in
an infectious illness which nearly killed Kipling and did kill
his elder daughter. After these misfortunes Kipling altogether
ceased to tolerate Americans who failed in due submissiveness
to a civilization maturer than their own. America, he felt, was
going the wrong way, and he was able to substantiate this impression—not wholly unjustifiably, perhaps, on its particular
occasion—by a visit to the White House during its tenancy by
President Cleveland. It was 'awful; inexpressible; incredible;
a colossal agglomeration of reeking bounders'.

The Kiplings continued to spend more of their time abroad
than was common even among other rich people in the period.
For six or seven years, for instance, they lived more than half
their time in South Africa in a house given them by Cecil
Rhodes. It was comparatively late that Kipling settled down
as a somewhat loudly proclaimed native Englishman. When he
wrote in 1902 of England as 'the most marvellous of all foreign
countries that I have ever been in' there was a profound truth
underlying the joke. One glimpses to the end a hint of inspired
travel journalism in his most 'English' performances.

5

Kipling's production was presently to enter upon a phase
which, because variously nostalgic, it is possible to view as
reflecting a failure in confidence bred of the Vermont episode—
an episode which Mr. Wilson would exhibit as standing in a
fatal series with Southsea and Westward Ho! But it is very easy
to exaggerate anything of the sort. We have still to consider
some stories in *Many Inventions*. *The Day's Work* (1898), largely
written in Vermont, has stories conditioned by his residence

there while at the same time flowing on—as in 1904 *Traffics and Discoveries* is in turn to do—continuously from the preceding volume. Kipling's work falls into its broad phases of development, but to trace it through with chronological exactitude is neither easy nor very advantageous.

He shows during these years an increasing and at times oppressive interest in technical processes and the vocabularies of many crafts. 'Kipling had the darndest mind', a Vermont railwayman said. 'He wanted to know everything about everything, and he never forgot what you told him. He would sit and listen and never stir.' He himself declared that he 'revelled in profligate abundance of detail—not necessarily for publication but for the joy of it'. And this is very true. The disposition represents as much an emotional as an artistic need.

'The Disturber of Traffic', the story of a lighthouse keeper in Flores Straits who goes mad and plays pranks on the vessels seeking to pass, is a good example of this steeping of an anecdote in the language of the particular trade involved:

> The light-frame of the thousand lenses circled on its rollers, and the compressed-air engine that drove it hummed like a bluebottle under a glass. The hand of the indicator on the wall pulsed from mark to mark. Eight pulse-beats timed one half-revolution of the Light; neither more nor less.
>
> Fenwick checked the first few revolutions carefully; he opened the engine's feed-pipe a trifle, looked at the racing governor . . . .

This is in fact about another and merely introductory lighthouse, and Fenwick, its keeper, is simply the narrator of the madman's story. But here as elsewhere the almost religious attention paid to the functioning of machines, as to the lore of professions and trades, is not exclusively a device for enhancing verisimilitude and conviction, or merely a method by which Kipling can show off. We read on:

> He began with a dissertation on pilotage in the Hugli. I had been privileged to know a Hugli pilot intimately. Fenwick had only seen the imposing and masterful breed from a ship's chains, and his intercourse had been cut down to 'Quarter less five', and remarks of a strictly business-like nature. Hereupon he ceased to talk down to me, and became so amazingly technical that I was forced to beg him to explain every other sentence. This set him fully at his ease; and then we spoke as men together, each too interested to think of anything except the subject in hand.

'We spoke as men together.' In Kipling's world a sort of *mystique* attends upon one man's telling another that 'there's reverse currents in the Gulf of Boni' or that, if you are not full-powered, 'it stands to reason you go round by the Ombay Passage'. For what men ought most to respect is the lore and skilled striving of their fellows. And here is the function of the 'frame' which Kipling gives so many of his stories. The thing is not merely, as with Conrad, a distancing and subtilizing device, aesthetically conceived. It is—this of one man's telling a yarn to others —a matter of sacramental implication. In *Something of Myself*, his reticent and posthumously published volume of memoirs, he speaks of what was to him, as a child, 'the loveliest sound in the world—deep-voiced men laughing together over dinner'. The laughter was always to be important to Kipling—but so, we feel, was the depth of the voices. The world of work is the *manly* world—and hence his whole doctrine of work and discipline. Mr. C. S. Lewis has an acute remark here:

> In the last resort I do not think he loves professional brotherhood for the sake of the work; I think he loves work for the sake of professional brotherhood. . . . To belong, to be inside, to be in the know, to be snugly together against the outsiders—that is what really matters.

Mr. Lewis seems disposed to attribute 'a terrible vagueness, a frivolity or scepticism' which he finds at the centre of the doctrine to Kipling's neglecting the fact that 'the spirit of the Inner Ring is morally neutral'. However this may be, there is certainly truth in the conclusion that 'after Kipling there is no excuse for the assumption that all the important things in a man's life happen between the end of one day's work and the beginning of the next'.

The seaman's work is becoming increasingly important with Kipling; of his middle period it is true to say, among other things, that he moves on from the barracks to the engine-room. An engine-room has more gadgets to be happy with. 'The Devil and the Deep Sea' is an anecdote about a crew of English near-pirates who, having been much humiliated after their capture on the pearl-fisheries of a foreign power, eventually repair the wrecked engines of their ship and choose to sail it not to safety but to a spot where it can be scuttled with the certainty of wrecking the gun-boat that originally apprehended them. The theme of revenge can be only too often sovereign with Kipling, but here it is almost played off the stage by the engines. The reader who is prepared to listen in respectful incomprehension to a modicum of talk about piston junk-rings and condenser-columns must rebel when matter of this sort spreads through whole paragraphs. 'Bread upon the Waters', on the other hand, is as the merest and sheerest entertainment beyond praise. It is the tale of a ship's engineer who, unjustly dismissed by his owners, and aided by the guile of another owner, exacts a spectacular revenge by successfully plotting to rescue as a derelict a freighter carrying an exceptionally valuable cargo. It is a tale entirely of the surface. But the surface is that of the Atlantic in dirty weather, and to the landsman, at least, Kipling's conduct of events lacks nothing of the knowledge and confidence that one might expect of Conrad, while being flung on its marine canvas with an impetus and verve such as Conrad seldom achieves.

Some of the later sea stories are unabashed orgies of oafish humour—for example, 'Their Lawful Occasions', a dreadful mixture of music-hall badinage ('You buy an 'am an' see life') and naval knowingness ('Secure tube to ball of diaphragm, clear away securin'-bar, release safety-pin from lockin'-levers'). 'Brugglesmith', perhaps the most celebrated of Kipling's pure buffooneries, begins on shipboard although it ends at Brook Green, Hammersmith. Finally we may note here that Kipling went on from marine engines to railway engines. '·007' is a story treating these as if they were sentient beings. Since written in a very conversational manner, it is disconcertingly reminiscent of a dismal species of composition much required of us in our earlier schooldays. There will always be minds that boggle over the deployment of large and vigorous powers of literary craftsmanship in such enterprises, judging animals that talk to be bad enough, and puff-puffs that do so to be the infantile end. Others find in fantasies of this kind a sort of advanced pantheism with real imaginative substance.

Animals talk in 'A Walking Delegate', a beast fable about a group of Vermont horses with names like Tedda Gabler and Marcus Aurelius Antoninus. They talk with a carefully indicated American accent (this laborious manner of dealing with regional or vulgar speech was something Kipling never abandoned) and their job is to resist, expose, ridicule, and kick

a yellow demagogic horse from Kansas. The Kansas horse is
not given much of a spin: when he strikes an attitude that he
means to be extremely impressive he contrives only to look as
if he has been badly stuffed; he has 'an underhung sneer';
and the language in which he denounces Man the Oppressor
is unengaging:

> The horses o' Kansas are behind me with their multitoodinous
> thunderin' hoofs, an' we say, simply but grandly, that we take our
> stand with all four feet on the inalienable rights of the horse, pure
> and simple,—the high-toned child o' nature, fed by the same wavin'
> grass, cooled by the same ripplin' brook,—yes, an' warmed by the
> same gen'rous sun as falls impartially on the outside an' the *in*side of
> the pampered machine o' the trottin''-track, or the bloated coupé-
> horses o' these yere Eastern cities. Are we not the same flesh and
> blood?

The precise bearing of this melancholy equine prosopopoeia is
not clear, but it seems that the horses are being urged to a
class-war or inter-state war of their own as well as to a general
revolt against their masters. At least, however, Rod—the son
'of a Hambletonian sire and a Morgan dam'—understands how
well-affected quadrupeds should reply:

> There's jest two kind o' horse in the United States—them ez can
> an' will do their work after bein' properly broke an' handled, an'
> them as won't. . . . When a horse comes along an' covers up all his
> talk o' killin' with ripplin' brooks, an' wavin' grass, an' eight quarts
> of oats a day free, *after* killin' his man, don't you be run away with
> by his yap.

'A Walking Delegate' has amusing touches. But its shallowness
and incoherence as an allegorical representation of men in
society appears startlingly as soon as we think to compare it
with George Orwell's *Animal Farm*.

'An Error in the Fourth Dimension' goes back to railway
trains, but for the purpose of evolving a comedy of the international situation. One would be interested to know what Henry
James thought of it. Another authority on Anglo-American
relations, Mr. Wilson, certainly dislikes it—finding 'hateful
caricature' in Wilton Sargent, the hitherto Anglophil son of an
American railroad king, who flags an English express train and
is in consequence taken to be a lunatic. 'There is room for an
infinity of mistakes', Kipling writes, 'when a man begins to

take liberties with his nationality'. Sargent, ironically enough, makes in England much the sort of mistake that Kipling was to make in America two years after writing the story, which thus takes on the colour of a prelude to the Vermont family feud. It is in poor taste, harbours venom, and admits strokes that impair its artistic effectiveness. Sargent's Americanness is posited as an intrinsic inferiority: it is described as 'beginning to ooze out all over' him; his voice, we are told, 'had risen to the high, throaty crow of his breed when they labour under excitement'; and when the narrator realizes that Sargent is going to be taken for mad he is filled with 'pure joy'. All this lacks amenity. Recalling Kipling's idea of a good joke, we may be surprised that his victim gets off without being clapped into a strait-jacket or subjected to some other physical indignity. But as it is, and with all its sins upon it, this is not a story that anyone need turn down as failing to be really funny. Outright physical violence, however, proliferates in 'The Record of Badalia Herodsfoot', a story not intended to amuse, and making a unique and characteristically verisimilar incursion into London's slums. The world of Shaw's Eliza Doolittle and Major Barbara pales before Kipling's evocation. It would be hateful to say that the shattering brutality which provides the background and much of the substance of the story is done with relish, but it is certainly done, and overdone, out of a compulsive interest that is disturbing. Against it is set Badalia, an unsuccessful flower girl retained by some of the local mission folk as an irregular almoner. Knowing her world, and being as courageous and incorruptible as she is unrefined, Badalia justifies her trust—to the extent, eventually, of being battered to death by the husband she has always hoped would return to her: this rather than yield up the few shillings currently in her trust. She dies protecting him:

My 'usband 'e never come a-nigh me these two years . . . 'e never come a-nigh me. . . . A man come and 'it me over the 'ead, an' 'e kicked me, Miss Eva; so it was just the same 's if I had ha' had a 'usband, ain't it? . . . Tom 'e never come a-nigh me for two years, nor I 'aven't seen 'im yet.

If this story is unrestrained upon what may be called the thud-and-crush side of Kipling's interests it is otherwise with its art. We have had Cleopatra in 'Love-o'-Women'. Desdemona makes no overt appearance in 'The Record of Badalia Herodsfoot'.

Three stories of this period, all of the highest accomplishment, touch variously upon the supernatural. In 'The Finest Story in the World' Charlie Mears is a twenty-year-old bank clerk, full of literary aspirations which it is clear that his normal personality and endowments give him no chance of realizing. But presently he brings to the narrator fragments of a story to be called 'The Story of a Ship' which contain matter of a vividness and authenticity inexplicable except on the assumption that his mind in composition has direct access to the experience of men who have manned ships in several ages of the remote past. His inspiration fades out, presumably for good, when he finds a girl and becomes a commonplace young lover. In this we may hear a faint echo of the conclusion, propounded in the immature *Story of the Gadsbys* in 1888, that 'a good man married is a good man marred'. We are scarcely to suppose that Charlie would have become a writer if he had stuck to celibacy. But there does for long lurk in Kipling the feeling which he expressed in a single trenchant line:

He travels the fastest who travels alone.

'The Finest Story in the World' remains one of his most startling *tours de force*. Had Henry James attempted such a theme in one of his tales of the supernatural, Charlie's command of his material would have been merely suggested or intimated; one can imagine James in his notebook deciding at the start that this is the only possible way. But Kipling's attack is not oblique; it is simply head-on. He gives us Charlie's inspired prose (and, for good measure, some inspired verse too) in its *ipsissima verba*. If the mysterious power in Charlie is tied a little too closely to the hypothesis of metempsychosis, this is no doubt partly because of Kipling's nodding acquaintance with Hindu thought. But it is also—as Miss Tompkins, the most thorough and steadily illuminating of Kipling's students, has shown—owing to the story's having an immediate source in Edwin Arnold's *Wonderful Adventures of Phra the Phoenician* (1890). Most essentially, however, Kipling is here drawing, almost for the first time, upon what is to be one of the greatest of his powers: a brilliant historical imagination.

'The Brushwood Boy' is a story of similar strangeness and fascination, but one marred in a significant way. George Cottar is a character exemplary beyond any other that Kipling has drawn. He is the youngest Major in the army; he deserves the V.C.; and he returns, honourable, chaste, and covered in glory, to a home in which everything is laid on: good shooting, faithful old retainers, a proud father, and a mother with whom he talks 'as mother and son should, if there is to be any future for our empire'. There is even a dream girl, and he marries her. Only this is a dream girl of a special sort. She *dreams*. In fact it turns out that for years she has been dreaming, richly and strangely, the identical dreams that George Cottar has been dreaming. There is no rational explanation. And it is just to enhance the extreme strangeness of the thing, we may suspect, that Cottar's achievements are of the copy-book banality that they are, and indeed that the coming together of the girl and himself has the flat wholesomeness (reminiscent of 'William the Conqueror') that it has. But this steep contrast defeats itself. The strength of the story lies in the fact that the writer appears to command Cottar's sleeping as securely as his waking life. The dream scenery is entirely convincing, and we may even be brought to admit its proprietorship by so unlikely seeming a young man as a valid if symbolical dealing with real facts of mind. But we simply cannot imagine a marriage, so evidently posited as of an order wholly suitable and nice, accommodating itself to the oddity of this marriage's setting. Cottar and his wife, were the end to be congruous with the beginning, would have to be taken up by dragons.

Of Kipling's power to exploit what must be called a double vision there is a yet more remarkable instance in 'The Bridge-Builders'. This opens upon what looks like one of his standard celebrations of white devotion and efficiency in India. Findlayson and his assistant Hitchcock have been toiling at a large engineering project, the building of a bridge over the Ganges. Findlayson looks forward to a C.I.E. or even a C.S.I., and already Hitchcock has 'been appointed a magistrate of the third class with whipping powers, for the better government of the community'. As so often in the stories, 'the underlings were not to be trusted': 'Then the native workmen lost their heads with great shoutings, and Hitchcock's right arm was broken by a falling T-plate, and he buttoned it up in his coat and swooned, and came to and directed for four hours. . . .' But presently the Ganges unseasonably comes down in flood, and Findlayson directs emergency measures which are described, as is the whole business of building a bridge, with all Kipling's flamboyant command of technical operations. Then something totally unexpected happens. Findlayson rashly accepts, when exhausted and fasting, some opium pellets from a native foreman; finds himself, when in an hallucinated state, swept down the river and wrecked on an island; and there he seems to witness a synod of the gods of India, their brutish forms perhaps recalled to him by animals which like himself have been carried down stream to this refuge. The Crocodile, Goddess of the Ganges, resents the constraint of Findlayson's bridge. Indra replies that in such a time scale as the gods know the bridge is a thing only of a day. Krishna prophesies a sort of Hindu *Götterdämmerung*. The vision fades as the divinities ponder their own ultimate reality as merely something within the dream of Brahm. The effect of this flooding of the strong practical consciousness of the Englishman with this eruptive matter has something of the same effect as that curious geological vision granted to Hardy's Henry Knight as he clings to the cliff in *A Pair of Blue Eyes*. A whole new plane and dimension of things is brought suddenly into focus. But Kipling's gods are too talkative, and the final effect is diffuse. We are left wondering, too, why the story should close on an inconsequent if characteristic image: that of a human back receiving the discipline of 'two feet of partially untwisted wire-rope'. Yet 'The Bridge-Builders' is an impressive valediction—almost a palinode—to India, the soil of which Kipling had touched for the last time just before his twenty-sixth birthday. When one is building a bridge the 'natives' may be unreliable. But their life is implicated with beliefs and rich in attitudes which make their own chastening call to the Western imagination. And implicit in that call is the assertion that Findlayson and Hitchcock and all their fellows are but valiant dust, and that their achievements must, like our navies, melt away. The conflicting visions (which exist, of course, in any society admitting both mundane interests and transcendental concern) may, in certain circumstances, present themselves as conflicting loyalties.

They do so in Kipling's greatest book. It is only, indeed, in a manner too muted to be grateful to some of his critics. But it is at least a manner wholly consonant with the artistic effects proposed.

6

Whether or not there be irony in the fact, Kipling came nearest to a successful novel in a book for young people—for we lose contact with *Kim* (1901) when we regard this story of an orphan white boy gone native, and using his native cloak of invisibility to become a peerless Secret Service agent, as other than essentially that. For Mr. Wilson, indeed, the story 'deals with the gradual dawning of his consciousness that he is really a Sahib. . . . What the reader tends to expect is that Kim will come eventually to realize that he is delivering into bondage to the British invaders those whom he has always considered his own people, and that a struggle between allegiances will result.' It is true that there is such a dawn of consciousness in Kim, but not quite true that the story 'deals' with it. And an alert grown-up reader will not in fact come to expect what Mr. Wilson supposes, any more than a juvenile reader will. The book would have to open on the note of *The Princess Casamassima*, with Kim a potential Hyacinth Robinson, for any such legitimate expectation to be built up. And Kim is—sheerly and superbly—a boy's dream-boy: the kind who since a toddler has been 'hand in hand with men who led lives stranger than anything Haroun al Raschid dreamed of', whose infant ears are privileged to thrill to such words as 'Warn the Pindi and Peshawur brigades', who at a deliciously early age acquires playthings like 'a mother-of-pearl, nickel-plated, self-extracting ·450 revolver', and who is equally adept at driving calving cows from a mountain hut and Russian emissaries from the forbidden valleys of Chini and Bushahr. Certainly Kim's growing sense of himself as a Sahib is unaccompanied—however reprehensible this may be—by the slightest persuasion that he is an invader bringing bondage. He takes British India for granted. He would agree, if he ever reflected on the matter, with the loyal old native soldier's summary explanation of the Mutiny ('A madness ate into all the Army'). He is in no need of the grave advice of the English officer who introduces him to the Great Game: 'Do not at any time be led to contemn the black men.' Kim derives, evidently enough, from Kipling's own dream childhood. And from Kim's brilliant and engaging knowingness we may say that there had developed the knowingness—brilliant again but entirely engaging no longer —of the young author of *Plain Tales from the Hills*.

Kim himself—it is indicative of his species—has, happily, no future to develop into. At fifteen his colleague Mahbub the horse trader had shot his man and begotten his man. Kim is not quite so precocious. We do not know precisely what he has to remember about the girl at Akrola or the scullion's wife behind the dovecot. But at sixteen, when he leaves us, he has resisted the seductions of the Woman of Shamlegh—not indeed for the distinctly *pukka* reason discovered for him by Mr. Wilson, but simply asking himself how a fellow can follow the Great Game if he is to let himself be pestered by women. Nor has he yet killed anybody, having contented himself, so far, with the very modest ration of violence represented by kicking a single Russian expertly in the groin. No, we cannot imagine Kim a year older. Who would care to read of the boy Tinker grown up and taking over from Sexton Blake, or of Billy Bunter in the City?

But 'all India is full of holy men stammering gospels in strange tongues' and Kim is making the acquaintance of one of these in the moment that we are first making the acquaintance of Kim. Kim becomes the lama's disciple—and also his guardian angel—as the old man wanders India seeking that River of the Arrow in which it has been revealed to him in vision that he may find freedom from the Wheel of Things. The lama's Way, which is the life of contemplation, is thus set directly over against the Great Game, which (although time has dealt hardly with the charm of a Secret Police) is a sufficient symbol of the active life at its most exacting and exciting. The lama sinks back afraid as from sorcery when he sees an English regiment pitching camp. Soldiers, he says, 'follow desire and come to emptiness', and he would not have Kim be one of them. Kim is not tempted—drill and routine make no appeal to him—but it is while at the expensive school where the lama is paying for his education that he makes his first ventures in counter-espionage. We must feel that Kim's employers are not very scrupulous here, and that Kim himself is scarcely so when he stage-manages the lama's final wanderings to the end that the two should be guided to territory attractively furnished with Russians. Kim understands all this ('That worth do I see; and to him my heart is drawn'). The lama, he says, is one part of his bond. But here he is thinking of a personal loyalty, which is something he can understand. At school—he tells the lama—

he was taught that to abstain from action was unbefitting a Sahib; and a Sahib, after all, he is. 'It is too high for me', he growls honestly at the conclusion of his master's most impressive sermon. The conflict in all this is not quite Mr. Wilson's. Nor, such as it is, would the book be advantaged if Kim himself were wrought to some high crisis in terms of it. It is something, we are left to feel, touched in for us rather than for the boy— for us if we ever come back to the book when our years exceed its hero's.

Kim, completed long after Kipling's Indian days were over, is a genial book largely because so richly and nostalgically sympathetic, at once acknowledging and softening that potentially tragic conflict of races and faiths that was British India. But if that was a conflict which was to be, in the end, harmoniously resolved after all, there was certainly little in Kipling's later mind that could have contributed to anything of the sort. Over *Kim* we must suppose the influence of Lockwood Kipling, a wiser and more dispassionate man than his son, with whom it was much discussed during the years of its composition. It was not only to the lama, we feel, that the Keeper of the Lahore Wonder House gave a pair of spectacles. However this may be, Kipling's own brilliant powers of memory and evocation are here enlisted, as too rarely, in what is entirely a labour of love. The result is a book that knits a lavishly achieved picaresque narrative to a central figure who almost brings off the ultimate feat of escaping from the pages in which he is created. Kim is scarcely either a social or a psychological possibility. But he is quite as real as Jim Hawkins, Bevis, or Huckleberry Finn, and is master of a terrain as irresistible as any these know.

7

Kim was published at about the mid-point of a substantial period of years in which it would have been reasonable to regard Kipling as having become primarily a writer for children. *The Jungle Books* (1894 and 1895) are products of the Vermont period. Together with the later *Just So Stories* (1902), they are perhaps best left unburdened with adult appreciation. Their punch lies, no doubt, in their manner of penetrating to genuinely primitive layers of feeling, and we may little have suspected in our nurseries how consistently this was being exploited in the interest of a didactic intention. Mowgli is one of Kim's immediate ancestors; the animal world in which he learns his own variety of the Great Game is somewhat over-staffed with father-figures; and the whole fantasy is open to the charge that, under cover of a seeming-great deal of freedom and wildness, it makes most play with the concept of submission:

> Now these are the Laws of the Jungle, and many and
>   mighty are they;
> But the head and the hoof of the Law and the haunch
>   and the hump is—Obey!

H. G. Wells's *Island of Dr. Moreau*, which has already been mentioned, was published in 1896. Its most alarming moment appears designed to constitute an oblique comment upon the ethic of Kipling's bestiary. But obedience is in itself a neutral quality. Kipling's sense of its right use perhaps appears most clearly in the last of these stories, 'The Miracle of Purun Bhagat'.

Captains Courageous (1897) is a far less interesting book, over-loaded with efficient second-hand descriptive writing, and dedicated to the mild proposition that judicious adventure and moderate hardship benefit spoilt children. *Puck of Pook's Hill* (1906) and *Rewards and Fairies* (1910) are ingeniously instruc-tive books in which Puck appears to a small boy and a small girl and acts as presenter of a succession of characters whose stories constitute a pageant of English history. Here again Kipling's historical sense is often finely at play, and many of the narratives notably approximate the remote and the wonderful. It has been maintained, indeed, that the young men defending Hadrian's wall in the fourth century are a little too like those whose job it was to keep an eye on the Khyber Pass fifteen hundred years later. But a greater historian than Kipling knew what he was about when he spread over the 'polite' Augustus and his contemporaries some colouring from the age of Anne and the Georges, and Kipling's theme of the continuity of life on an English soil is equally well served by the humbler figure of Hobden the Hedger. Moreover, as Miss Tompkins has remarked, the child who reads these books will not have to unlearn anything about human nature. It is to be feared that this is substantially true, too, of a book that is a much more direct expression of Kipling's personality.

Stalky & Co. is the title given to a collection of school stories brought together in 1899. Every now and then throughout his life Kipling added to the Stalky mythology, and it has received further accretions, not overtly fictional, from persons fortunate or unfortunate enough to have been his schoolfellows. It is clear that the United Services College was a horrible place. There is nothing out of the way in this. Much better-reputed schools have often been so. Winchester in the 1870's, as described by an eminent historian, Sir Charles Oman, puts Westward Ho! in the shade. That Kipling was always loyal to his old school, even contriving to describe it in a public speech as 'the best school in England', is very little out of the way either. Such antic piety is common form among the eminent. What has struck his critics as strange, reprehensible, and probably neurotic, is the fact that Kipling seized upon the quite ordinary beastlinesses of the place, joyously inflated them, and then gave them to the world as hugely edifying. Mr. Carrington gravely commemorates this process: 'Kipling put it on record that he wrote the book as a tract, and, on a closer examination, it will be found that the crudities and flippancies of this book, too, conduce to a moral purpose.' Over against this we may set the indignation of Mr. Somerset Maugham:

A more odious picture of school life can seldom have been drawn. With the exception of the headmaster and the chaplain the masters are represented as savage, brutal, narrow-minded and incompetent. The boys, supposedly the sons of gentlemen, were devoid of any decent instincts. To the three lads with whom these stories deal Kipling gave the names of Stalky, Turkey and Beetle. Stalky was the ringleader. He remained Kipling's ideal of the gallant, resourceful, adventurous, high-spirited soldier and gentleman. Beetle was Kipling's portrait of himself. The three of them exercised their humour in practical jokes of a singular nastiness. Kipling has narrated them with immense gusto. . . . It never seems to have occurred to him that the school was third-rate and the boys a rotten lot.

Conceivably this is a little overdrawn. There are, in fact, two elements making up the disconcertingness of the Stalky stories. In the first place, Kipling accepts quite whole-heartedly the theory of ritual suffering. Schoolboys—even quite small ones— may, like other initiates, be both proved and taught by the endurance of pain. And as the world will bring them plenty of suffering that is not their own fault, it may be held a sound preparatory discipline to see that a liberal allowance of pain comes to them in a completely arbitrary and savage way. Kipling's offence here is only that he takes this primitive doctrine out of the Victorian headmaster's study and hands it over, in day-rooms and boot-cupboards, to any lout who has the brute strength or the cunning to propagate it in a practical manner. Anybody who thus goes to work boisterously and joyously is a good chap, and well on the way to becoming a *pukka Sahib* too. In all this Kipling is scarcely being more than coarse-grained and emphatic; the doctrine has just enough harsh truth to disinfect it tolerably as we go along. The second cause of offence is much more genuine and serious. Roughly, it consists in the assumption that when Insiders flog Outsiders there can be no darkness in the Insider's hearts. King Lear may have been justified in speaking of a rascal beadle. But a rascal Beetle is ruled out. Mr. C. S. Lewis has remarked that in the army stories 'we are given to understand that the old soldiers . . . threaten, mock, and thrash the recruits only from the highest possible motives'. So it is here. And yet the majority of the stories about these boys are surely puerile rather than vicious. 'Regulus', written when Kipling was in his forties, has as its subject the beating by the Captain of Games of a friend and study-mate who would have been exempt from this penalty had his First Fifteen Cap arrived in time from the school out-fitter's. In the course of it various other boys are beaten, or witness beatings. ('Babcock yelled loudly as he had many times before.') 'The United Idolaters' is even later; its theme is the nasty-mindedness of a temporary master who thinks that the general spectacle presented by Westward Ho! can be remotely compatible with or conducive to any manifestation of sex; it follows the common formula of an enormous rag followed by prodigious fustigations. ('They lick 'em twice as hard for it as *we'd* dare to', the school chaplain says enviously of the prefects.) These later stories, at least, surely exhibit a Kipling who has drifted much out of the current of his time. That the sort of institution represented was a place of wise and beneficent training, presided over by persons deeply read in the philo-sophy of education, was an idea moribund long before Kipling had finished with Stalky and his friends. It had been dealt something like a death-blow, indeed, at least for younger readers, when Mr. E. M. Forster published *The Longest Journey* in 1907.

8

Kipling's energies and indeed passions were deeply engaged
by the South African War, which he saw as a struggle, often
waged with disgraceful incompetence, against an obscurantist
minority resolved to thwart the essential development of a
continent. He formed a volunteer company, built a drill-hall,
spent happy hours on a rifle-range, and composed for *The
Times* a poem called 'The Old Issue', which would appear to
be a clarion-call to England to resist some dreadful imminent
tyranny, but which is in fact a denunciation of Kruger:

> We shall take our station, dirt beneath his feet,
> While his hired captains jeer us in the street.
>
> Cruel in the shadow, crafty in the sun,
> Far beyond his borders shall his teachings run.
>
> Sloven, sullen, savage, secret, uncontrolled,
> Laying on a new land evil of the old.

At the beginning of 1900 he had taken his family to South
Africa as usual, so that later in the year he was able to write
triumphantly in a letter: 'As you know we went down to South
Africa (Cape Town) for the winter and there happened to be
a bit of a war on, and I had the time of my life.' As *The Light
that Failed* shows, next after the soldier Kipling loved the war
correspondent (whose heyday, indeed, it was) and he could,
when given the chance, himself show as a very ace at the game.
He has only to take up his pen for the right images to come:

We waited, seeing nothing in the emptiness, and hearing only a
faint murmur as of wind along gas-jets, running in and out of the
unconcerned hills.

Then pom-poms opened. . . . Then to the left, almost under us,
a small piece of hanging woodland filled and fumed with our
shrapnel much as a man's moustache fills with cigarette-smoke.

His stories prompted by the war are full of evidences of the
same perfected craft. But they are streaked, too, with a blind
groping malice likely to make them uncomfortable reading
when these campaigns are as distant as Julius Caesar's. In
Traffics and Discoveries (1904) 'A Sahibs' War' is bad and
'The Comprehension of Private Copper' is very much worse—
chiefly because of the really ugly way in which the writer's
mood is palmed off as the villain's: 'You'll be screaming at

a wagon-wheel in an hour.' 'The Captive', although far from dispassionate, is better: virtually a monologue by Laughton O. Zigler, an American inventor who has brought his 'Laughton-Zigler automatic two-inch field-gun, with self-feeding hopper, single oil-cylinder recoil, and ball-bearing gear throughout' into the service of the Boers. He finds the British incompetent. The Boers, he says, 'fought to kill, and, by what I could make out, the British fought to be killed. So both parties were accommodated.' And he is startled at a British general's willingness to prolong the campaigns as 'a first-class dress-parade for Armageddon'—England itself not being big enough for the training of an army. Zigler is permitted to entertain us with an admirably sardonic account of the kind of fighting that is going on, and it must be remarked that, as a mischievous neutral, he is better treated by his creator than others of his kind are going to be on the occasion of a later war. Until that war comes up with us, we can now turn away from Kipling's dealings with the political passions and with 'lesser breeds', whether white or black.

There is one story, however, which is almost a return to his Indian manner, and it is worth noticing. In 'Little Foxes' an enterprising English Governor introduces fox-hunting in an outpost of empire near Ethiopia and promises 'a most un-measurable beating' to any native on whose land earths remain unstopped. Since a beating thus becomes a kind of title-deed, everybody is eager to be beaten, and there is evolved a ritual whereby the Governor confirms claims by inflicting a light switching (with his hunting-crop) on the readily bared shoulders of the Queen's subjects in this part of the world. But at home an English M.P.—represented as very much an outsider at a dinner-party including four Masters of Foxhounds—concerns himself with the matter, and is given, by way of merited ridicule, a grotesque account of the hideous barbarities perpetrated by the Gihon Hunt. He is thought to be powerless, but this is not so. For—the author tells us—there is a 'New Era' overwhelming and bewildering England:

One by one, the Provinces of the Empire were hauled up and baited, hit and held, lashed under the belly, and forced back on their haunches for the amusement of their new masters in the parish of Westminster. One by one they fell away, sore and angry, to compare stripes with each other at the ends of the uneasy earth.

The M.P. arrives in Gihon with large powers of inquiry and a stock of fatuous pamphlets of a liberal complexion which are virtually an invitation to chaos, since they persuade the dismayed natives that all their cherished beatings have been valueless. Fortunately the M.P.'s features strikingly resemble those of a hound which everybody remembers to have gone mad; he is lured into delivering an absurd speech in the course of which he innocently makes reiterated use of a filthy native word; the whole community collapses into that sort of titanic laughter which Kipling so loves to see visited upon cads; finally he loses his temper, furls his umbrella, and uses it to beat—yes, to *beat*—his unfortunate interpreter. It would be priggish to call this other than a gorgeous story. But it throws a spotlight on the sort of gallery to which Kipling was prone to play.

9

Dr. Arnold of Rugby put on record his persuasion that it is permissible and interesting to visit the good poor. Kipling may be said to have felt like this about good Americans, and he makes one gracious enough visit of the kind in 'A Habitation Enforced'. George Chapin, a New York business man of great wealth, has fallen ill in his early thirties, just when 'his hand was outstretched to crumple the Holz and Gunsberg Combine'. With his wife Sophie he wanders Europe in aimless convalescence, feeling that his life is 'finished now'. They are directed however to the Sussex country-side, fall in love with and buy a derelict manor-house, and are eventually, to their deep satisfaction, accepted both by village and county—partly because they are modest and circumspect, but chiefly because Sophie turns out to be descended on her mother's side from an exalted local family. As Miss Tompkins says of George Chapin —with perhaps involuntary felicitousness—his new circumstances 'combine to fix him'. They are represented as elevating him too. 'I could double the value of the place in six months', he begins by saying with regrettable vulgarity; he ends by accepting the dictatorship of dear old rustic Alfred Cloke, who tugs his forelock (we may say) while obstinately maintaining that, in civilization, oak not larch is the right timber for a new foot-bridge. It is hard to know how to receive a story, mediated by a high literary art, the underlying sentiment of which comes

so close to Dornford Yates. But perhaps Henry James, once
more, offers a less undignified point of comparison. Thus
Sophie has her moment of final triumph when, upon the birth
of her son, the great lady of the district makes him a christening
gift of an old family mug. Sophie comments to her husband:

> 'Can't you see that *she* thought that we thought my mother's being
> a Lashmar was one of those things we'd expect the English to find
> out for themselves, and that's impressed her?' She turned the mug
> in her white hands, and sighed happily. '"Wayte awhyle—wayte
> awhyle." That's not a bad motto, George. It's been worth it.'

James might well have made this the core of a story of the
international situation, of the return of the 'dispossessed princes
and wandering heirs'. But his Chapins would not have been so
'fixed' that they ended up virtually all forelock themselves. The
attitude underlying this story derives both from Kipling's personal response to the Vermont episode and from his general
theory of the ordeal. Similar considerations apply to 'My
Son's Wife', a later story to the same *Captains Courageous* formula.
Here the person to be put through it and licked into shape is
Frankwell Midmore, a disagreeable urban aesthete and idea-
monger of indifferent morals (in fact a 'long-haired thing') who
has the good fortune to inherit a small country property. He is
reformed, saved, and happily married as a result of attending
to its routine problems, reading *Handley Cross*, and belatedly
learning to shoot and hunt. One would be inclined to suppose
that a story so grossly calculated to philistine taste and caste
assumptions would affect us rather like a canvas by Sir Alfred
Munnings. Yet 'My Son's Wife' is a very good story indeed.
The full solidity and assurance of Kipling's imagination is
instanced in the creating of Midmore's small rural world. Even
better in this last regard, because unimpaired by social prejudice, is 'Friendly Brook'. Here a couple of rustics, while hedging
and ditching, review the story of Jim Wickenden, whose foster-
daughter Mary was happily preserved to him when the brook
carried away and drowned her undesirable long-lost father.
These Sussex labourers stand up to their neighbours in Hardy.
Once more it is the historical imagination that is at work. And
the pagan feeling which the story comprehends is here not
merely disposed as choric commentary. It is at the heart of the
little action.

We may say in general of Kipling's last effective phase (which we are now approaching) that the deeper he goes the better he is. The historical imagination, operative at a comparatively superficial level, continues, indeed, to produce some striking achievements. In 'The Eye of Allah' a medieval abbot and his guests and subordinates—all, perhaps, a shade too like modern scholars and gentlemen—are confronted with the invention of the microscope and all that the microscope suggests. This story gains its power from seeming to look into the future as well as the past. The abbot's occasion is not the last upon which science will offer men gifts they are unready for. In 'The Church that was at Antioch' New Testament history is seen from the point of view of Roman police officers. 'The Manner of Men' sets itself the modest task of improving upon the penultimate chapter of *The Acts of the Apostles*. The first of these stories has its analogues and perhaps sources, but certainly nobody has ever done the thing better. The second two are at least highly persuasive elaborative performances. 'With the Night Mail' and 'As Easy as A.B.C.' are Wellsian fantasies of the future of aviation, exuberantly done, and in the second instance reinforced by robust anti-popular feeling summed up in some appended verses:

Once there was The People—Terror gave it birth;
Once there was the People and it made a Hell of Earth.
Earth arose and crushed it. Listen, O ye slain!
Once there was The People—it shall never be again!

In some relation to these are certain set fables with a supernal setting, notably 'On the Gate' and 'Uncovenanted Mercies'. In the first, sub-titled 'A Tale of '16', St. Peter and his staff are dealing as best they can with the swarms of war casualties arriving for Judgement. Compassion is the mainspring of Peter's conduct, and a queer fun is extracted from his manipulating in this interest an eschatological machinery which travesties that of an English government department. Yet Kipling's lightness of air in this fable masks—whether felicitously or not—a deep seriousness of intention. When Peter cries out 'Samuel Two, Double Fourteen' the reference is to the words of the Wise Woman of Tekoah. King David has not fetched home again his banished son—but in this he is faulty, for it is otherwise with God: 'For we must needs die, and are as water spilt on the ground, which cannot be gathered up again; neither doth God respect any person; yet doth he devise means, that his banished be not expelled from him.' God's means, in 'On the Gate', is a wily and resourceful administrator who would do equally well if faced with a famine in British India. And here, indeed, is the archetype of Kipling's stories in this kind. The high-ups are remote and incomprehensible, the natural condition of the down-belows is helpless misery, and the in-betweens—whether angels and archangels or Findlaysons and *Bakri* Scotts—manage in a rough-and-ready fashion to see that something sensible is done.

'Uncovenanted Mercies' expands the theme of the ordeal—already several times explored—into that of the breaking strain: a conception in which Miss Tompkins and Mr. Dobrée, followed by others, discern the most interesting final development of Kipling's thought. It has been remarked by Miss Tompkins that in both these stories 'the writer ascribes to the abyss the qualities that he cannot bear it to be without', and that in 'On the Gate', at least, there is 'a great, even excessive, tenderness of sentiment'. But if 'On the Gate' has indeed a touch of softness which makes it inferior to, say, the best of Kafka's fables, 'Uncovenanted Mercies' is so rooted in a realization of human anguish, of 'the accepted hells beneath', as to be in total effect wholly austere and strong. It leads on to the direst of Kipling's poems, 'Hymn to Physical Pain'. We know nothing of his experience of those 'Pains of Hell' which only physical torture can hold at bay. But that it was a powerful experience, we cannot possibly doubt.

Striking as are these fables, with their suggestion of deliberately excogitated symbolical equivalences, we may yet feel that Kipling gets deepest when he starts off with people as they are, and when the heart of his matter beats obscurely up from intuitive sources.

We may begin here with 'Mrs. Bathurst'—one of a score of stories which the straitened literary historian, counting his paragraphs, sighs that he cannot more adequately exhibit. It is one of the first in which critics seriously complain of obscurity—asserting sometimes that Kipling, drawn towards a compressed, elliptical, and gnomic manner, has here begun to prune his writing to the sacrifice of simple intelligibility. It is certainly true that nobody can tell quite what happens to Mrs. Bathurst.

That she is the second of the two charred corpses with which
we are left at the end of the narrative seems not probable,
although Miss Tompkins lends her authority to this supposition.
Originally Mrs. Bathurst kept a pub near Auckland, and she
had no particular beauty. But she did have 'It'. (A large part
of the story's art consists in the manner in which the tragedy
of Vickery, the naval rating whose fragmentarily glimpsed
passion for Mrs. Bathurst drives him to insanity and death, is
filtered to us through minds in which the fatality and ultimate
mystery of sexual obsession are expressed by such vulgar locu-
tions as this.) Kipling has nowhere more elaborately conjured
and wrought an obliquely potent induction than here—one
hazardously and triumphantly graced by the presence of the
egregious Pyecroft, in other stories perhaps the most atrocious
of all his plebeian humorists. It is part of the system of distancing and so concentrating the pity and the terror of the tale.
In 1895 Kipling had mentioned to a correspondent his disinclination to produce stories 'sexual or within hailing distance of
it', even though he had a yearning for 'hard-bottomed unseemly
yarns'. Where he does deal directly with sex, it is either conventionally and romantically, so that nothing much of value is
added to his work, or it is in the key of fear and aversion which
comes through in *The Light that Failed*. When his mind unveils
itself, in fact, it is upon some recess of the psyche where Eros
and Thanatos stand closely linked. 'Mrs. Bathurst' is akin in
feeling to 'Love-o'-Women'. There is to be one other story,
'Mary Postgate', which we shall find explained and excused in
the light of this association.

The frontiers of consciousness, and the breaking in upon it of
the inexplicable and irrational, make the field of many of the
fully mature stories—and we are dealing now with masterpiece
upon masterpiece. If 'Wireless', among the earlier of these, is
one of the less nearly perfect, this is partly because it sets off
from an idea almost too clever to carry. Shaynor is a young
chemist's assistant who, both as a consumptive and in various
superficial regards, a little suggests the figure of Keats. Having
on an inclement night been given an alcoholic drink concocted
from the chemist's stock, he falls into a trance-like state and to
a struggling effort at poetical composition which results in his
arriving at a number of Keats's lines from 'The Eve of St. Agnes'
and elsewhere. Upon his recovering it becomes apparent that

he has never so much as heard of the poet. His situation is thus akin to that of Charlie Mears in 'The Finest Story in the World'. But the special fascination of Shaynor's experience derives from its setting. In another part of the chemist's shop a Marconi enthusiast, scientific in temper yet vividly aware of the mysterious power which he taps, is receiving imperfect messages from a warship through the ether. The story is a little marred by a bout of Kipling's old knowingness—this time, as to just which are the only five purely magical lines in English poetry. And there is perhaps a basic awkwardness in the idea. Shaynor, for example, has a sweetheart called Fanny Brand. But if this is anything to the point—we may ask—why is his own name not Coates or Weeks? Yet the haunting suggestiveness of the queer analogy propounded makes this story unforgettable.

'They' is another story of commerce with the dead. The narrator in the course of a motor-tour comes upon a country-house of great beauty, presided over by a blind woman whose acquaintance he makes. There are children, though they are not hers—happy but elusive children, more often heard than seen. These children turn out to be no longer of the living— a discovery for which we have been prepared, perhaps with indifferent artistic tact, in an introductory poem:

> Shall I that have suffered the children to come to me
>   hold them against their will?

In the end one of the children is revealed as the narrator's daughter, and the tale closes with his rejecting the trespass inherent in this reunion across the grave. For the blind woman, whose love and yearning have drawn to her these children preferring an earthly home to a heaven too grown-up for them, the trespass may be right. For the narrator it would be wrong. Probably few readers who believe that they dislike sentimentality in literature would be drawn by this summary to read 'They'. We have to notice that it springs directly out of poignant personal experience; some years before it was composed Lockwood Kipling had written in a letter: 'The house and garden are full of the lost child and poor Rud told his mother how he saw her when a door opened, when a space was vacant at table, coming out of every green dark corner of the garden.' The story thus precipitated has a good deal wrong with it. Kipling (a contemporary of Jack Tanner, although with views tending

more to Roebuck Ramsden's) makes the narrator a great deal
too busy with his motor-car. The mellow splendour of the
House Beautiful is rather vulgarly overdone ('the miracle of old
oak that must be called the front door'). There are some un-
necessarily cryptic notes which would be better away. But everything goes down before the power and purity of the central feeling.
'They' belongs with the fourteenth-century *Pearl*, with parts of
the Shakespearian *Pericles*, and with the 'Marina' of Mr. Eliot.

Another story in this group, written much later, is 'The Wish
House'. Mrs. Ashcroft, a cook, has heard of a magical means of
taking upon oneself the physical ill of another: it is done by
communicating with a Token through the letter-box of a
Wish House—which can be any house that has stood long
untenanted. Mrs. Ashcroft has acted thus in the interest of
a former lover; and now, as she tells the facts to a friend, her
voluntary wound is known to have turned cancerous. The
situation is so vividly portrayed, and the fusion of magical
persuasion and deep human sympathy so finely realized, that
'The Wish House' may very reasonably be brought forward as
the best story Kipling ever wrote.

But if we are aware almost of a new Kipling in some of these
tales, it is equally evident in others that the old Kipling—indeed
the old Beetle—lives on. In 'The Honours of War', first printed
in 1911, an underbred and intolerably conceited subaltern (he
has had three years at the 'Varsity) has been mercilessly ragged
by his fellows and is bent on creating a public scandal. But the
guile of Stalky (now a Lieutenant-Colonel) and others of like
kidney lures him into accepting the chance of repaying physical
outrage with physical outrage. The men who tied him up in
a sack are tied up in sacks; the whole Mess is delighted; and the
story ends with tears of joy when this almost hopeless outsider
apologizes for all his previous ill-conduct and is saved. To this
sanguine fable there is appended in the edition of 1917 a poem
called 'The Children' and beginning:

> These were our children who died for our lands: they were
>   dear in our sight.
> We have only the memory left of their home-treasured
>   sayings and laughter. . . .

Kipling went on till the end writing stories of which the primary
design is that they should leave us 'weakened by excessive

laughter'. There are risible adventures with motor-cars and bicycles; obnoxious gas-bags get stung by bees; pigs are painted with alarming-looking spots. Sometimes there is violence, related in a jaunty tone but not precisely with a humorous intention. Thus in the late 'The Tie' a certain Haylock— '*not* semitic, but the flower of the Higher Counterjumpery, by Transatlantic out of Top-Hat'—rouses the resentment of an Officers' Mess as a contractor providing bad food. They corner him and smack his face in turn—'just as one smacks a chap who isn't big enough to beat'. Fortunately Haylock is wearing an 'old E.H.W. tie' and this steadies his tormentors and prevents them from going too far. We may judge this story to represent the ultimate working out of the Stalky vein. A more interesting progress is to be noted in two lightly linked stories: 'The Village that Voted the Earth was Flat', written in 1913, and 'Dayspring Mishandled', which was collected in Kipling's final volume of tales, *Limits and Renewals*, in 1932. The first describes how a number of powerful and talented men, working closely together and expending no end of venom, ingenuity, and money, organize the press and the music halls of England to overwhelm an overweening landowner and magistrate with ridicule. It ends with an outbreak of titanic hilarity in the House of Commons. 'Dayspring Mishandled' concerns an even more elaborate practical joke—one represented, indeed, as slowly evolved through years of absorbed labour. Castorley, a competent but pretentious and unpleasing authority on Chaucer, has offended Manallace, and Manallace forges and plants on him a fragment of an unknown Canterbury Tale. Kipling provides us with extracts from this, including words spoken by a girl praying against an undesired marriage:

> Ah Jesu-Moder, pitie my oe peyne.
> Daiespringe mishandeelt cometh nat agayne.

The spelling 'mishandeelt' is supposed to reveal the work of a Dutch copyist, and Kipling piles up ingenuities of this sort in his most overwhelming 'in the know' manner. So far, the story is on familiar lines. But at the end it takes an unexpected turn: Castorley proves to be dying of cancer; exposure of his gullibility would finish him; and his wife, who has perceived the truth, works to have this exposure effected, since she wishes to marry his surgeon, whose mistress she has become. Miss

Tompkins calls this story 'superb' and Mr. Wilson calls it 'strange and poisoned'. It certainly shows that the themes of hatred and revenge which had always so powerfully engaged Kipling's imagination (although in the end, as we shall see, they were to give way before the theme of healing) were implicated in his mind with repressed material involving notions of sexual guilt—material which found, it may be, disguised representation in obsessive fears of physical illness. These considerations bring us at once to his stories dealing with the Kaiser's War.

10

'The Edge of the Evening', published in 1913, is a prelude here. It contrives, at some sacrifice of artistic unity, to be both anti-American and anti-German—the second, perhaps, more deliberately and consciously than the first. Laughton O. Zigler—the central figure of 'The Captive'—has become immensely wealthy, rented the magnificent country-seat of his old friend Captain Mankeltow, now Lord Marshalton, and filled it with acquaintances from Buffalo, Cincinnati, Cleveland, and Chicago:

A party of young folk popped corn beneath a mantelpiece surmounted by a Gainsborough. . . . In a corner half-a-dozen girls examined the glazed tables that held the decorations—English and foreign—of the late Lord Marshalton.
'See heah! Would this be the Ordeh of the Gyartah?' one said, pointing.

Kipling has forgotten his American—but not that here are the lion and the lizard keeping a *pukka* Sahib's courts. And Zigler, as he unrolls 'the bright map of his fortunes across three continents', is made less sympathetic than his subsequent part in the story really requires. For he tells how, returning from his private golf-course one afternoon together with Lord Marshalton, a judge, and the editor of a great newspaper, he discovered a grounded aeroplane in his park. The two men working on it were German spies who instantly attempted to shoot their discoverers—only themselves to be instantly killed: one by Zigler with a golf-club and the other by the judge as the result of a rugger tackle. Zigler in a sense bears a further responsibility, since it is one of his own inventions, the Rush Silencer, that makes technically possible the covert contriving of 'a bird's-eye telephoto-survey of England for military purposes'. But the real villain of the piece, after all, is the British Government, which lets a march be stolen on it in such a vital matter, and would probably—we are told—not even back up three eminent citizens and a friendly foreigner in their startling situation. Fortunately—Zigler continues—he got the plane going again, set its controls, and sent it out over the English Channel with the dead men on board. The whole of this part of the story is very well told. But there is a large improbability about it—one to be matched in a much more dreadful aeroplane story yet to come.

This is 'Mary Postgate', published in 1915. Its climax presents the spectacle of an Englishwoman standing beside an injured German airman, taunting him with a revolver when he begs for water, and exulting when he dies. And as tailpiece the story carries a poem which begins:

> It was not part of their blood,
> It came to them very late
> With long arrears to make good,
> When the English began to hate.

If we declare it reprehensible that the creator of Kim's lama should have written this story and these words, we may be answered that Kipling is taking up a merely objective attitude, and that here is history. In those months the English were hearing many reports of German atrocities, most of them untrue but some of them true enough; they believed other reports, again no doubt in some measure veracious, that Germans habitually sang something called 'The Hymn of Hate' and greeted each other with the words '*Gott straf' England*'. It is very conceivable that such a woman as Miss Postgate might do what she is described as doing. And in the story everything is piled up against her. She is a repressed lady's companion. She has adored her employer's graceless nephew—and received from him, before he is killed while training as an airman, nothing that might serve in a crisis to open her heart to gentleness. ('It's a great pity', she is made to say, 'he didn't die in action after he had killed somebody.') She has just seen the ripped and shredded body of a child whom this German's bomb has killed. And it is as she stands by the garden incinerator,

destroying the books and toys and motoring journals in the
inventory of which Kipling's concretizing imagination has
scored one of its notable triumphs, that her test comes to her.
We cannot take her for a monster, for she is handled with the
most skilled psychological verisimilitude to the end: 'She would
stay where she was till she was entirely satisfied that It was dead
—dead as dear papa in the late 'eighties; aunt Mary in 'eighty-
nine; mamma in 'ninety-one; cousin Dick in 'ninety-five;
Lady McCausland's house maidin 'ninety-nine . . . .' Here is
a small thing that Kipling knows about; this refuge in compulsive enumeration has turned up in nervous crisis before. And
when Miss Postgate goes back to the house it is to luxuriate in
an untimely hot bath and emerge looking—as her employer
remarks—'quite handsome!' She is like a woman to whom there
has come, late in life, some unexpected and deep erotic satisfaction. Strangely enough it is from this dire fact, and from the
stiff improbability of the German airman's appearing where
and when he does, that the story receives its surest imaginative
sanction. Conceivably against Kipling's conscious intention,
the German is not quite real—there is no final thought that
the police or military must be called, the body disposed of—
and this leaves open to us a level of apprehension at which he
is the employer's nephew over again. Life in the shape of a regardless boy has passed a woman by. What we are left contemplating is the murderous ambivalence of the unconscious mind
—and particularly in the female of the species, elsewhere
celebrated by Kipling as more deadly than the male. The
horror and fear and hate in the story are occasioned by Mary,
not by the wicked Germans; and in the appended poem
Kipling is largely putting up a screen between himself and this
fact. Or we may say that his xenophobia has here telescoped
with something yet stronger in him. 'Mary Postgate' and
'Mrs. Bathurst' grow from the same root. So—long ago in
1897—had grown a poem called 'The Vampire', in which
a woman is described as

a rag and a bone and a hank of hair.

When we turn back to 'Swept and Garnished', another war
story, written a little earlier in 1915, and find a loathsome
German woman in bed during an attack of fever, haunted by
the ghosts of French children killed by the German armies, we

are distinguishably on the same territory still. In both cases the effect is quite different from that found in the third story of this group, 'Sea Constables'. The theme, indeed, is a variant on that of 'Mary Postgate'. The person let die is the captain of a neutral ship, clearly American, who has been trying to enrich himself by delivering oil to German submarines through the British blockade. The person who refuses to get him within reach of medical assistance is an English yachtsman, a naval officer for the 'duration', whose duty it has been to shadow him:

> 'I was perfectly polite. I said to him: "Try to be reasonable, sir. If you had got rid of your oil where it was wanted, you'd have condemned lots of people to death just as surely as if you'd drowned 'em.". . . "Then I'm a dead man, Mr. Maddingham," he said. "That's *your* business," I said. "Good afternoon." And I went out.'

'Sea Constables' may be read as if it were a story by Conrad, and its *clou* the moment of stress and exhaustion at which a man's responses to challenge will violate his established personality. 'I was surprised at myself', Maddingham says—and we can hear a Conrad character saying precisely that. Only Maddingham is pleased with himself as well. And it is the induction to the story, in which he and friends similarly employed are vindicating their character as insouciant Sahibs to the accompaniment of some expensive eating and drinking, that renders the 'murderous' effect of which Mr. Wilson will be found to complain. Even so, it is curious that it is upon a merely incidental character—a foreign actress who is 'the latest thing in imported patriotic piece-goods'—that the most powerful jet of really hostile feeling is directed.

II

What has been called the theme of healing makes a tentative appearance in several quite early stories, notably 'At the End of the Passage' and in one or two of the 'Puck' stories, and it emerges strongly in others belonging to the pre-war period. 'The House Surgeon' is about a house casting a mysterious intermittent depression upon all those living in it. This proves to be some species of telepathic disturbance occasioned by the persuasion of a former inmate that her sister committed suicide in it. When this persuasion is proved erroneous the curse lifts.

'In the Same Boat' appears to be the first story actually centring upon a kind of psychotherapy. A man and woman, each suffering from the same morbid condition of recurrent insupportable nightmare, are thrown together through the contrivance of their physicians. They support one another until the situation resolves itself with the discovery that the nightmares reflect alarming experiences to which their mothers were exposed during pregnancy. Time has not treated this story very well. It has a patness and glibness on what must be called its scientific side which looks forward to modern films exploiting popular interest in psychiatry. And although the man and woman go their several ways at the end of the tale, a sort of hovering romantic interest has been developed in—similarly—a rather facile manner. 'The Dog Hervey' trims between psychology and the supernatural, and is violently distorted in the telling because of the pressures that result. The story seems to be this: the middle-aged and unattractive Miss Sichliffe manages to love a very unattractive dog; a phantasm of this dog in consequence presents itself (during *delirium tremens*) to a wealthy man who had once liked her—and does this in coincident circumstances such as to secure that the man shall be reintroduced to her and marry her. As well as its elliptical construction the story holds enough cryptic detail to disturb tidy-minded readers. And just below the confident expertness of the involuted narrative we may feel an obscure anxiety, symbolized—before Hervey's own psychical release—in the creature itself. In fact there is a cat in the story as well as a dog, a cat which Kipling is unwilling to let more than a few inches— nervously retrenched inches—out of its bag. Perhaps none of his other stories so strongly suggests the operation of forces impeding a full and free creation.

Malignant disease and the war neuroses ('shell shock') are presences in nearly all the remaining stories. Neither topic is well calculated to charm the readers of magazines, and something of the decline of Kipling's reputation may be attributable to his so frequenting them. But we must notice, too, the increasing isolation through which he moved during the long final phase of his career. Back in 1900 there had been a happy day upon which Mrs. Kipling had been obliged to refuse simultaneous dinner-invitations from Mrs. Humphry Ward and the Duchess of Sutherland. The rich promise of this was abundantly fulfilled. Kipling had become extremely eminent, and commonly it was only persons equally eminent who were allowed to disturb his privacy. From Vermont onwards there was literally no admission to him except past Carrie's chair. He lived among the spectres of successive political disillusionments, with India and South Africa both wiped from his slate, and with at least an intermittent rancour against the United States as the remaining legacy of his abortive attempt at domestication there. Moreover neither his status as a national landmark nor his family connexions brought him any real access to the corridors of power. He had moved too far from a central conservatism towards a reactionary Right. 'How much foreign influence was there behind the coal-strike?' he had privately demanded of the editor of *The Morning Post* in 1912. The cousin who was so adroitly to handle a similar strike fourteen years later could have had little use for a temperament like Rudyard's, and Rudyard replied with unmitigated contempt for all politicians. He lived on in his Sussex manor house in a loneliness made suddenly calamitous by the death of his son. He was no longer the challenger and questioner of all and sundry, sopping up crafts and attitudes like a sponge. On 'farm walks' it was Mrs. Kipling who discussed barns and crops and ditches with the men. Kipling 'stood by listening and only sometimes making a suggestion'. He went to bed when he was told. To Hugh Walpole he muttered at a luncheon party that 'he'd had friends once and again he'd done more for than for any woman'. Walpole seems to have judged this unfair, since, as a kind of multiple buffer from the world, 'Ma Kipling' did her job superbly. But such an unnatural insulation from the currents of external circumstances, we must suppose, would leave a man like Kipling only the more a prey to endogenous anxieties.

That Kipling felt the need of some contact with a wider humanity than his actual surroundings afforded is perhaps to be discerned in the setting he devised for many of the stories of this phase: that of a Masonic 'Lodge of Instruction'—apparently somewhat irregularly conceived—in war-time and post-war London. The first of these stories, 'In the Interests of the Brethren', simply introduces the narrator, himself a Mason, to the Lodge, and it seems to have had the practical aim of persuading English Freemasonry that it was not adequately meeting the challenge of the time. There emerges from it very clearly the importance which Kipling was prepared to allow to any sort of ritual: 'All Ritual is fortifying. Ritual's a natural necessity for mankind', and 'a Lodge of Instruction is mainly a parade-ground for Ritual'. So we get:

> When the amateurs, rather red and hot, had finished, they demanded an exhibition-working of their bungled ceremony by Regular Brethren of the Lodge. Then I realised for the first time what word-and-gesture-perfect Ritual can be brought to mean. We all applauded, the one-footed Corporal most of all.

The Corporal is important, for it is on war casualties that the interest of the Lodge is chiefly fixed. With nervous cases there is a particular concern, and the beginnings of a system of occupational therapy are being worked out. 'I cured a shell-shocker this spring by giving him our jewels to look after.' In these stories there is to be a great deal of amateur effort of this sort. Thus in 'The Woman in his Life'—and the title has its significance—an ex-officer suffering from delayed shock has his sanity saved by a clever servant, who persuades him to keep a dwarf Aberdeen bitch: the creature, as it happens, is trapped in a tunnel in circumstances obliging her owner to face the same sort of sapper's risks as during the war, and his complete cure is the consequence.

The thing may be sound in principle, but again it is a little pat. And this holds, too, of a more elaborate story, very seriously intended despite an appallingly facetious start, 'Fairy-Kist'. Here there is a war casualty ('one shrapnel peppering, and one gassing, with gangrene') who, after a period in a mental hospital, and when driven out by hallucinatory voices to plant flowers in the open country-side, is involved in a situation which might result in his being convicted of murder. Happily, he is rescued, and has his symptoms relieved, by another band of Kipling's irregular therapists. In 'The Janeites' the therapist is Miss Austen—and it is a story generally accounted unforgivable by those who think it very vulgar to call this eminent novelist by her Christian name. Certain members of an English battery in Flanders make a cult of her, their general proposition being that 'Every dam' thing about Jane is remarkable to a pukka Janeite!' Nothing happens in the story; it ambles along with fun about naming the guns after appropriate characters in the novels, and the like, until finally the battery is destroyed and

most of its members are horribly killed. This is a rather deeper
story than it looks.

The best of the war stories is perhaps 'A Madonna of the
Trenches'. Here again there is some facile pioneering with
abreaction therapy, but the core of the story is supernatural
rather than psychological. What has shattered the lad who
relates it is not the horror of trench-warfare, with the dead
piled up six deep to keep the mud back. It is his glimpse of the
ghost of a woman—she has just died of cancer—and a living
man facing each other in the last extremity of passion. We have
seen that Kipling has little power over sexual feeling at close
range and in detail. But he can bring it almost blindingly in,
and this story ranks with 'Love-o'-Women', 'Mrs. Bathurst', and
'The Wish House'. Set beside it, a good many of these stories
seem unconvincing and contrived. In 'The Miracle of Saint
Jubanus' the cure of a French soldier—'blasted, withered,
dumb, a ghost that gnawed itself'—is ascribed to a fit of im-
moderate laughter occasioned by a ludicrous incident in his
parish church. France, which Kipling loved, deserved a better
story than this one. 'The Tender Achilles' and 'Unprofessional'
are about doctors. In the first we read of Wilkett, a brilliant
research worker badly needed in the newly extended biological
laboratories at St. Peggotty's, where the Great Search after the
cause of cancer is going forward. Wilkett has broken beneath
the strain of operating under impossible conditions at the Front,
and is living weakly in the shelter of his mother. A group of
senior physicians get him on his feet again and back to work by
means of a somewhat obscure stratagem involving a faulty
diagnosis of a physical condition of his own which could not—
they explain—have been made had he himself stuck to his
duty. This story, with its desperate 'inside' air, compares unfavourably with Shaw's *The Doctor's Dilemma*. 'Unprofessional'
is the strangest of all these tales. A group of doctors, one of whom
is wealthy and able to finance the project, explore a neo-
astrological approach to the study and treatment of cancer.
It involves such activities as microscopical examinations with
one eye on the clock, and the taking of compass-bearings before
a patient is placed upon the operating-table. Kipling's interest
in such conceptions was of long standing, and his researches in
the interest of 'Dayspring Mishandled' may have given him a
further hint. Chaucer's Doctor of Physic

> was grounded in astronomye.
> He kepte his pacient a ful greet del
> In houres, by his magik naturel.

Nothing emerges from the story, because nothing could.

But 'The Gardener', another story concerned, in a sense, with both healing and the supernatural, towers above these. Helen Turrell, believed by her neighbours (or perhaps not so believed—for the writing is extraordinarily subtle) to be 'as open as the day' and one who holds 'that scandals are only increased by hushing them up', contrives to bring up her own illegitimate son under the fiction of his being the illegitimate son of her brother: 'So far as she knew herself, she was not, she said, a child-lover, but, for all his faults, she had been very fond of George, and she pointed out that little Michael had his father's mouth to a line; which made something to build upon.' Thus the relation of mother and son is in fact built upon a denial and a lie. Michael is killed at the Front, and after the war she goes to seek his grave in a vast war cemetery. She meets another such pilgrim, whose situation is similar to her own. This woman confesses to her in agony, but Helen cannot bring herself to respond with her own story. Then:

A man knelt behind a line of headstones—evidently a gardener, for he was firming a young plant in the soft earth. She went towards him, her paper in her hand. He rose at her approach and without prelude or salutation asked: 'Who are you looking for?'

'Lieutenant Michael Turrell—my nephew,' said Helen slowly and word for word, as she had many thousands of times in her life.

The man lifted his eyes and looked at her with infinite compassion before he turned from the fresh-sown grass toward the naked black crosses.

'Come with me,' he said, 'and I will show you where your son lies.'

When Helen left the Cemetery she turned for a last look. In the distance she saw the man bending over his young plants; and she went away, supposing him to be the gardener.

Kipling was not a Christian, and he, too, would have had to suppose the man to be the gardener. Yet this conclusion is one of the finest imaginative strokes in his work.

12

Kipling's verse is not so good as his prose. It shows a radical deficiency which may be illustrated at once from the dedication of *Barrack Room Ballads*, the volume with which he made himself a second reputation in 1892:

Beyond the path of the outmost sun through utter darkness hurled—
Farther than ever comet flared or vagrant star-dust swirled—
Live such as fought and sailed and ruled and loved and made our
    world.

They are purged of pride because they died; they know the worth of
    their bays;
They sit at wine with the Maidens Nine and the Gods of the Elder
    Days—
It is their will to serve or be still as fitteth Our Father's praise.

It is like travelling by hovercraft. We are being skimmed along, just out of contact with the actual weight and texture of the words used. For words do not come to Kipling in that sharply fresh interaction alike of their sensuous and their associative components which distinguishes good poetry. In his best verse he has nearly always to make do with being vigorously rhetorical and variously eloquent, and when falling short of this he is seldom very far from a mere jingling and spouting by rote:

> With my *'Pilly-willy-winky-winky-popp!'*
> (Oh, it's any tune that comes into my head!)

Yet Kipling's range will be much obscured if we allow ourselves, without further exploration, to be deafened by his predominant tone. A first reading, or a reconsideration, may usefully begin with some quiet things: 'The Way through the Woods', for example, and 'My Boy Jack', 'A St. Helena Lullaby', 'Buddha at Kamakura', 'Heriot's Ford', 'Mesopotamia 1917', the finely cut 'General Joubert', the enigmatic and haunting 'Gethsemane 1914–18', and 'Rebirth', which might be by Hardy. That Kipling was fond of Horace says something for Westward Ho! that ought to be said. That he wrote some Horatian odes which are a good deal more than pastiche is only one instance of his versatility. And he can use such models creatively. 'The Benefactors' (related to a story with the same title) moves from a classically inspired ironic opening to a brilliantly unexpected conclusion.

Kipling appears never himself to have claimed to be a poet. Yet the claim, when considered by others, is seldom turned down quite flat. George Orwell offered the view that Kipling is 'a good bad poet . . . what Harriet Beecher Stowe was as a novelist'. Mr. Trilling proposes to credit him with poetry of 'low intensity'—and adds that we can fortunately read through the whole of it 'in two evenings, or even in a single very long one'. Mr. Eliot, arguing that poetry was something aside from Kipling's deliberate intentions which did nevertheless sometimes come to him, has pointed to the significant fact that any aspiration to the writing of it is absent from even Kipling's early verse. That such an ambition should be eschewed by a young man of powerful imagination and brilliant literary endowment is indeed remarkable, and we may see in it an impressive vindication of his stature as an artist. He himself knows the worth of his bays, has the born artist's knowledge of what it is not his to attempt. He cannot charge language with that sort of meaning which results in the creation of the great autonomous and self-subsistent things.

But this is not a technical matter. There have been few better technicians than Kipling. The deficiency comes from deep down. His language lacks the particularity and precision of poetry because his thought and feeling lack these qualities too. In verse—for some reason far more than in prose—he remains the young man who started into a rich imaginative creation while equipped with very little that intellect, reflection, and even education may provide. That he has a meagre stock of ideas—and that, while some of these are strong and true, a good many are simply superstitions and prejudices—is something that shows through more sharply in a body of work which could indeed conceivably be perused in a single evening. For the achieving of poetry, Kipling works on too small a basis alike of self-scrutiny and of contemplative habit. Although often strikingly original, he brings us nothing from a unique world. He touches us only on the side of our most common responses— this in every sense. But what territory is his, he commands. There was never a greater master of 'Common tunes that make you choke and blow your nose':

> Land of our Birth, our faith, our pride,
> For whose dear sake our fathers died . . . .

13

Kipling's patriotic verse has some peaks that are unquestioned. 'For All We Have and Are' is adequate to its grave occasion in 1914, and G. K. Chesterton was never more singularly foolish than when he wrote a parody of 'Recessional'. But Kipling's most original work does not lie here. There is plenty of patriotic verse, sometimes xenophobic in tone, in English. When Kipling began to write, what Swinburne called Tennyson's 'strident anti-Gallican cackle' was still sounding. Swinburne, indeed, produced such cackle himself. Believing in 'the worth and weight of poetry in national matters', he had written verse increasingly imperialist in tone from 'The Armada' (1880) onwards; and such a poem as 'The Jubilee' (1887) is not unlike what Kipling was to offer:

> A commonweal arrayed and crowned
> With gold and purple, girt with steel
> At need, that foes must fear or feel,
> We find her, as our fathers found,
> Earth's lordliest commonweal.

The chief difference is that Kipling went easy on the gold and purple. And Tennyson, again, had even set a precedent in 'Riflemen, Form!' for addressing through the columns of *The Times* a clarion call to the nation whenever a favourable martial occasion turned up.

Kipling, having an easy command of generalized eloquence, slipped readily into this—and sometimes less to the effect of sounding a clarion at us than of blowing our own collective trumpet. Surveying the American scene at the age of twenty-three he had demanded: 'How in the world can a white man, a Sahib of Our Blood, stand up and plaster praise on his own country?' Kipling learned to do it himself, and only the more effectively because the praise is mingled with—sometimes even disguised as—much furious reproach and upbraiding. The phrase 'a Sahib of Our Blood', complete with its unblushing capital O, might thump itself out quite appositely in a poem like 'England's Answer':

> Look, I have made ye a place and opened wide the doors,
> That ye may talk together, your Barons and Councillors—
> Wards of the Outer March, Lords of the Lower Seas,
> Ay, talk to your grey mother that bore you on her knees!—
> That ye may talk together, brother to brother's face—
> Thus for the good of your peoples—thus for the Pride of the Race.

Also, we will make promise. So long as The Blood endures,
I shall know that your good is mine: ye shall feel that my strength
   is yours:
In the day of Armageddon, at the last great fight of all,
That Our House stand together and the pillars do not fall.

It bombinates by no means in an inane. It is tied to certain
realities of policy and sentiment. It looks forward to Anzac
and beyond. But it certainly bombinates. And we are still
likely to reflect today that to lend a capital B to 'blood', and
to add for good measure a capital T to the definite article
accompanying it, is to get well on the road to *ein Volk, ein
Reich, ein Führer*. National sentiment and the bonds of kindred
undoubtedly became facile counters with Kipling:

> A Nation spoke to a Nation,
>   A Queen sent word to a Throne:
> 'Daughter am I in my mother's house,
>   But mistress in my own.
>
> The gates are mine to open . . . '.

This is about Canadian tariffs. We build up the impression
that Mothers and Daughters, Brothers and Sisters, are for ever
throwing open gates in Kipling. Often, they might as well
explore avenues and leave no stones unturned. Too much of
this comes to us not as good verse but as a faded and embarrassing parliamentary eloquence.

   The patriotic verse is certainly best when it is admonitory
and minatory rather than celebrative. Kipling had a hard grip
of *Realpolitik* grateful neither to a commercial nation making
its pile nor to a Liberal caste of

> brittle intellectuals
> Who crack beneath a strain.

He is very good at flailing in verse these selfishly preoccupied
or guilelessly well-intentioned people:

> *Ah! What avails the classic bent*
> *And what the cultured word,*
> *Against the undoctored incident*
> *That actually occurred?*

That in the 1660's De Ruyter could show his topsails 'off naked

Chatham' is a circumstance that he feels should interest us; the reasons bear thinking about. Our fathers 'ensured us an heritage', but we need not

> dream that awestruck Time shall save
> Their labour while we sleep.

Sometimes this conviction stirs Kipling to the point at which its expression becomes figurative, oblique, and essentially poetic—as for instance in 'The Dykes':

Far off, the full tide clambers and slips, mouthing and testing all,
Nipping the flanks of the water-gates, baying along the wall;
Turning the shingle, returning the shingle, changing the set of the
    sand . . .
We are too far from the beach, men say, to know how the outworks
    stand.

The finest expression of this theme—in a figure again appropriate to a marine nation—is a late one in 'The Storm Cone' of 1932:

> Stand by! The lull 'twixt blast and blast
> Signals the storm is near, not past;
> And worse than present jeopardy
> May our forlorn to-morrow be.

This may be called Kipling's central public concern. Certain subsidiary doctrines, already familiar from his prose, support it. Notably, there is the doctrine of work. Of nations, as of individuals, it is true that

> 'im that doth not work must surely die.

It is a doctrine expressed succinctly in 'A Song of the English':

> *Keep ye the Law—be swift in all obedience—*
> *Clear the land of evil, drive the road and bridge the ford.*

But here, whereas the second line says something definite, the first proves upon reflection to say nothing at all. Kipling's 'Law', of which he makes us hear so much alike in verse and prose, we have to resign in the end as the invention of a journalist. It has no discoverable provenance or sanction or content, but merely rationalizes an impulse—going back, no doubt, to Westward Ho!—to be among the rulers rather than the ruled.

When Shaw's Tom Broadbent defines morality so engagingly as drawing a line and making other chaps toe it, he has got hold of Kipling's idea as precisely as its nature admits. And when we read 'Tomlinson'—one of the most dazzling of Kipling's earlier and longer performances in verse—we see how this unexamined notion interdigitates with a fierce prejudice against those who, instead of acting promptly upon our instructions, propose to preface any action with a little thinking of their own. And this is allied again with another prejudice of which the personal roots are clear enough. Kipling may have envied his cousin in the Sixth at Harrow. But:

Harrer an' Trinity College! I ought to ha' sent you to sea—
But I stood you an education, an' what have you done for me?
The things I knew was proper you wouldn't thank me to give,
And the things I knew was rotten you said was the way to live.
For you muddled with books and pictures, an' china an' etchin's an' fans,
And your rooms at college was beastly—more like a whore's than a man's . . .
Weak, a liar, and idle, and mean as a collier's whelp.

We shall only conclude that the Master of the 'Mary Gloster' was unlucky in his Harrovian son. But Kipling intends us to conclude something more—and it is a something more that he hasn't really thought about. Why should he, when he has such a facility in hurrying prejudice into verse? A similar conclusion holds of another Old Salt, McAndrew, the 'dour Scots engineer' of 'McAndrew's Hymn', who contrives to see in coupler-flanges, spindle-guides, and connecting-rods both Predestination and 'Law, Orrder, Duty an' Restraint, Obedience, Discipline', and who calls out for a Robbie Burns to celebrate them 'wi' Scotia's noblest speech'. He must strike us as a pulpit bully out of the Kipling family's past, preaching down his own 'slam-bangin'' engines—tail-rods, crank-throws, main eccentrics, and all.

In work like this we are at least in some danger of feeling in the presence of what Keats calls a careless hectorer in proud bad verse. We may connect it—although the coincidence is far from entire—with one of the three main sources of Kipling's craft as criticism commonly distinguishes them: that of popular hymnology. But it is to the other of these sources, those in music-hall song and popular balladry, that what is really the more original part of his work may be traced back. We may consider here 'The Absent-minded Beggar':

When you've shouted 'Rule Britannia', when you've sung 'God
    save the Queen,'
When you've finished killing Kruger with your mouth,
Will you kindly drop a shilling in my little tambourine
For a gentleman in *kharki* ordered South?
He's an absent-minded beggar, and his weaknesses are great—
    But we and Paul must take him as we find him—
He is out on active service, wiping something off a slate—
    And he's left a lot of little things behind him!
Duke's son—cook's son—son of a hundred kings—
    (Fifty thousand horse and foot going to Table Bay!)
Each of 'em doing his country's work
    (and who's to look after their things?)
Pass the hat for your credit's sake,
                and pay—pay—pay!

This was composed for the purpose of raising funds for the dependants of private soldiers fighting in South Africa. There are three further admirable stanzas. They were set to music by Sullivan and, not surprisingly, were soon 'fetching money in a wonderful way'. 'The Absent-minded Beggar Fund' closed at about a quarter of a million pounds, which was a lot of money in 1899. It is a pleasing circumstance that on the day Kipling composed this all-time record in money-spinners by celebrating the casual procreativity of the British Regular Army he received a visit—doubtless preluded on the visitor's part by a good deal of ceremony—from Henry James. The 'infant monster' was discovered doing his stuff. And 'The Absent-minded Beggar' may stand almost as a symbol of the instinctively kinetic and instrumental uses to which Kipling put his verse. He could raise a subscription. He could modify the image of a nation and its destiny as these things existed in the public mind. He could excite and inform the nearer reaches of the imagination in literary and unliterary people alike. Notably, he brought the British Army alive in the minds of people who listened to songs and joined in choruses in the popular theatre. And he did it so well that the achievement was accepted, too, by persons of much more conscious cultivation. It is recorded that David Masson once flourished before his students at Edinburgh the number of the *Scots Observer* containing 'Danny Deever', and cried out: 'Literature at last!' There are few stories more to the credit of Professors of English. And Kipling performed this feat largely by shock tactics:

> Now remember when you're 'acking round a gilded Burma god
>   That 'is eyes is very often precious stones;
> An' if you treat a nigger to a dose o' cleanin'-rod
>   'E's like to show you everything 'e owns.

This is James's 'brutality even deeper-seated'. It is what has startled us in 'His Private Honour' and elsewhere in the prose. Often the impetus of the verse throws into relief, as here, the equivocal nature of Kipling's attitude to violence, and even a certain coarseness in the whole texture of his mind. It is arguable before this whole area of the verse that no Tommies ever talked like that, and that this makes even more irritating Kipling's laborious robbing them of aspirates and endowing them with such vulgar expletives as were then permissible in print. It is even arguable that no Tommies ever *thought* like that. (This is much more doubtful.) Occasionally we may have to concede that the note is false—there is perhaps an example in 'The Return'. Some times, as in 'The Ballad of East and West', it is certainly a highly romantic imagination that is at work. Yet the soldier's fundamental business is not romanticized, and Shaw's Bluntschli himself might approve the second verse of 'The Settler':

> Here, where the senseless bullet fell,
>   And the barren shrapnel burst,
> I will plant a tree, I will dig a well,
>   Against the heat and the thirst.

For the rest, the soldier-poems open out a new and vivid world of the imagination. 'The Ladies' and 'Mandalay' and 'Danny Deever' and 'Fuzzy-Wuzzy' and 'Gunga Din' are all in their different ways splendid achievements.

A different facet of Kipling's verse is presented in those poems—many of them connected with *Puck of Pook's Hill* and *Rewards and Fairies*—in which the theme is the historical continuity of an English consciousness such as, in Kipling's view, must first have grown up in civilized people among the long-service legionaries and established settlers of the Roman Empire. For Kipling as much as for Hardy the English soil has history engraved upon it—quite literally so for the informed and seeing eye:

> And see you, after rain, the trace
> Of mound and ditch and wall?
> O that was a Legion's camping-place,
> When Caesar sailed from Gaul.

This is from 'Puck's Song'. 'A Tree Song' has the same theme, and parts of 'A Charm' might be from a churchyard meditation by Hardy:

> . . . breathe
> Prayer for all who lie beneath.
> Not the great nor well-bespoke,
> But the mere uncounted folk
> Of whose life and death is none
> Report or lamentation.

'The Land', which is set beside 'Friendly Brook' in *A Diversity of Creatures*, is whimsically conceived, yet fit to stand beside the story—a story in which Kipling's imagination is going almost as deep as it ever did. And it is on this territory that he comes nearest to a fully lyrical expression—as in 'Cities and Thrones and Powers':

> Cities and Thrones and Powers
>   Stand in Time's eye,
> Almost as long as flowers,
>   Which daily die:
> But, as new buds put forth
>   To glad new men,
> Out of the spent and unconsidered Earth
>   The Cities rise again.

> This season's Daffodil,
>   She never hears
> What change, what chance, what chill,
>   Cut down last year's:
> But with bold countenance,
>   And knowledge small,
> Esteems her seven days' continuance
>   To be perpetual.

So Time that is o'er-kind
    To all that be,
Ordains us e'en as blind,
    As bold as she:
That in our very death,
    And burial sure,
Shadow to shadow, well-persuaded, saith,
    'See how our works endure!'

Chronology has been almost disregarded in this brief review. And in fact Kipling's verse does not interest us more as Kipling's own maturity grows. There is no equivalent in it to 'The Wish House' or 'The Gardener'. He does, indeed, consider in the verse of his later years a good many hard matters. 'En-Dor' contains the whole of 'They', and 'Hymn of Breaking Strain' expresses the full burden of 'Uncovenanted Mercies' and a good deal else. But his tools remain the same and his medium scarcely enriches or subtilizes itself. In verse there is no earlier and later Kipling, as there is an earlier and later Shakespeare, an earlier and later Eliot.

But there is—working always carefully within his apprehended compass—a dedicated artist. We have noticed Mr. Wilson's speaking of Kipling as one 'who prostrates his art before the achievements of soldiers and merchants'. Anybody disposed to take this notion very far may usefully read 'The Last Rhyme of True Thomas'. It will a little explain why Kipling declined the Order of Merit. And it is quite as good a ballad as W. B. Yeats's *The King's Threshold* is a poetic drama. The two works have an identical theme.

VII · YEATS

I

WILLIAM BUTLER YEATS was born in 1865 in the Dublin suburb of Sandymount. His ancestry lay in the main among prosperous merchants and professional men of the Irish Protestant ascendancy. But his father, John Butler Yeats, who had become a painter, was without skill in managing affairs, so that the poet's family—much like the families of his fellow citizens Shaw and Joyce—was progressively more impoverished as he grew up. So were many of his more distant connexions. Sandymount Castle, a large Gothicized country house, was in the possession of a kinsman, and the young painter J. B. Yeats in his semi-detached villa rejoiced in this spacious connexion. But the kinsman went bankrupt, the grand house was sold, and it is said to have been partly on account of this decline that the painter removed for some years to London. His buoyant hopes of recognition and fortune remained unfulfilled to the end. He would speak nostalgically to his children of lost family splendours, so that the poet's imagination early revolved about the idea of great demesnes and lofty ancestries. William Butler Yeats was one day to celebrate in verse a Butler who had borne arms at the Boyne. But he was unfortunately under a misapprehension as to which side this forebear had fought on, an error making necessary not the least curious of the innumerable revisions of his work. Meanwhile he had decided, with some approximation to truth, that people's social importance may be assumed as being in proportion to the length of their avenues.

As a painter J. B. Yeats was an indecisive perfectionist, who appears to have diverted much of his energy to forming the minds and artistic inclinations of his children, and particularly of the poet, whom he early viewed as requiring unusual solicitude; 'Willy'—he wrote—'is sensitive, intellectual and emotional, very easily rebuffed and continually afraid of being rebuffed so that with him one has to use sensitiveness.' It is possible that the housemaid Kate McDermott, who amused the Yeats children when at table with their elders by prancing on all fours outside the open door with lighted tapers in her hair, had as wise a nurturing instinct. The father's early portraits of his son represent an extreme of aesthetic fragility which does not accord with much that was robust at least in the character of his sitter. Augustus John, depicting successively 'an unshaven, drunken bar-tender' and 'a gypsy grown old in wickedness', was later to redress the balance. But Yeats was frequently to acquiesce in the earlier view of himself. Lady Gregory would send up bowls of soup to coax him into the fatigues of dressing, and in order that his meditations might be undisturbed pile thick with rugs the corridor outside his room at Coole. It was indeed averred by one irreverent visitor that the savour of nourishing invalid broths could sometimes be distinguished as varied by that of solid dishes of bacon and eggs. Here, at least, is that aesthetic withdrawal from life idealized by the Symbolists which finds its complete expression (as Sir Maurice Bowra points out) in des Esseintes, the hero of Huysmans's novel *A Rebours*. Des Esseintes wishes 'to hide himself away, far from the world, in some retreat, where he might deaden the sound of the loud rumbling of inflexible life as one covers the streets with straw for sick people'—and moreover (as Sir Maurice might have added) gives up a plan to visit England after encountering, in an English restaurant in Paris, the mingled aromas of oxtail soup, haddock, beefsteak, and ale.

Like Henry James Senior, but on less adequate economic foundations, J. B. Yeats deprecated practical concern. His constant theme was the disinterestedness that the artist shares with the gentleman. That his son accepted this proposition is evident in a diary entry made in middle age:

Lady Gregory is planting trees; for a year they have taken up much of her time. Her grandson will be fifty years old before they can be cut. We artists, do not we also plant trees and it is only after some fifty years that we are of much value? Every day I notice some new analogy between the long-established life of the well-born and the artists' life. We come from the permanent things and create them, and instead of old blood we have old emotions and we carry in our heads always that form of society aristocracies create now and again for some brief moment at Urbino or Versailles.

But although the elder Yeats would declare that when he was young 'the definition of a gentleman was a man not wholly occupied in getting along', he was at least full of ambition for his son's artistic success. He read poetry to the boy before breakfast, constantly conversed with him on literary topics, and all his life urged with ability and charm the particular theories and the kinds of poetry which he thought it wise that the poet should pursue. He was specially anxious to see him advance in dramatic writing. In his old age he visited New York, found society there agreeable and conversible, and never came home—unless indeed in a mysterious sense, since his son was convinced they were in telepathic communication. Certainly the father kept up, for fourteen years, a constant material correspondence, hortatory and expository. We are even told that he 'frequently consulted soothsayers . . . about his chances of having grandchildren and the probable looks of his daughter-in-law'. At eighty-one this amiably irresponsible man, being constrained to accept amid his uncompleted pictures a small allowance from the poet, reflected that 'at last I shall be able to put aside money-making and acquire skill, as a palmist advised me to do years ago'. When his granddaughter Anne Butler Yeats was born he at once formed the sanguine expectation that she would become 'a famous hostess in Mayfair'. The poet's own hope was not altogether different—although Duke Frederick's Urbino rather than Park Lane is doubtless in the hinterland of his image:

> And may her bridegroom bring her to a house
> Where all's accustomed, ceremonious;
> For arrogance and hatred are the wares
> Peddled in the thoroughfares.
> How but in custom and in ceremony
> Are innocence and beauty born?
> Ceremony's a name for the rich horn,
> And custom for the spreading laurel tree.

Custom and ceremony were to be powerful loadstones with Yeats. He was no Bohemian, and this probably attenuated the influence upon him alike of his father and of his father's artistic acquaintance whether in London or Dublin. All Yeats's accounts of persons of obscure origin or of disordered or eccentric life, although far from lacking either understanding or sympathy, are written at a conscious remove. His sense of

aloofness, of disdain, is often intimated by a constant adjective:
'some'. John F. Taylor is 'born in some country town, the son
of some little watchmaker'. Sir Charles Gavan Duffy's youth
must be imagined 'in some little gaunt Irish town' and associated
with 'the dirty piece of orange-peel in the corner of the stairs
as one climbs up to some newspaper office'. In the revised
'Lamentation of the Old Pensioner'

> lads are making pikes again
> For some conspiracy;

and even Madame Blavatsky is similarly placed when we read
of her persuasion that in the year 1887 'some cycle or other
ended'. Of 'The Tragic Generation' about whom Yeats writes
in *The Trembling of the Veil* (1922) he is strongly attracted only
to Lionel Johnson, whose dram-drinking never abated a regard
for ceremony and custom not inferior to Yeats's own. As a boy
it offended Yeats that in London he became a shabby-genteel
nobody. All his love at this time was for the west of Ireland,
where several branches of his family had been long involved,
though not with any great distinction, in the history of the
region.

Yet family connexion and consequence were of little importance in comparison with another attraction of Sligo. For
it was there that, in boyhood, his imagination was to find its
proper food. It is plain that he was far less at home in the
studio of his clever father, being informatively discoursed to
in praise of Shelley or Keats or Morris, in dispraise of Wordsworth and Tennyson, than he was in the kitchen of a fisherman's
wife with whom his own undistinguished mother was con-
tentedly gossiping about the popular superstitions of the
country-side. On his regular holidays in the west—first from
London and later from Howth near Dublin to which his family
had returned—he went around the cottages seeking stories of the
supernatural. But the supernatural came nearer than this. If the
Yeatses themselves were on the whole disappointingly lacking in
uncanny powers there was no doubt that his mother's people,
both Pollexfens and Middletons, were 'psychic'. A sea-bird
announces the impending death of a Pollexfen; Middletons
hear ghostly smugglers knocking on the drawing-room window.
Yeats inherited—although not so strikingly as he would have
wished—the susceptibility to such abnormal experiences, and in

'Hodos Chameliontos' he declares that his later developed occultist interests were only an inevitable unfolding of what was innate
in him: 'I had not taken up these subjects wilfully, nor through
love of strangeness, nor love of excitement, nor because I found
myself in some experimental circle, but because unaccountable
things had happened even in my childhood, and because of
an ungovernable craving.' As a small child he was reputed to
have seen 'a supernatural bird in the corner of the room',
although no disaster appears to have succeeded. The fairies
tied knots in his little Union flag. The smell of new-mown hay
came to him when far out at sea—the type of a phenomenon
well known to psychologists and to which he was to be variously
subject in later life. He woke up screaming that his terrifying
Pollexfen grandfather had been shipwrecked—which was indeed true, with the consequence that Mr. Pollexfen thereafter
'if asked to read family prayers never read anything but the
shipwreck of Saint Paul'.

Thus visited, the boy not unnaturally began to play at being
a sage and a magician—finding encouragement to the latter
role, we are told, in *The Lay of the Last Minstrel*. As his formal
education was negligible, being impeded alike by his father's
indigence and his own inability to spell, do sums, or study for
even the easiest examinations, there was little to divert him from
applying his mind pertinaciously and passionately to the
problems inherent in supernatural experience. 'That experience
is my obsession' he was to write flatly in *Dramatis Personae*
(1935)—a statement which it is injudicious to discount. And
in *The Trembling of the Veil* there is a familiar passage which
describes his entire dependence, when sixteen or seventeen
and 'in all things Pre-Raphaelite', upon an imaginative world
bearing a strong accent of the supernatural:

I am very religious, and deprived by Huxley and Tyndall, whom I
detested, of the simple-minded religion of my childhood, I had made
a new religion, almost an infallible Church of poetic tradition, of
a fardel of stories, and of personages, and of emotions, inseparable
from their first expression, passed on from generation to generation
by poets and painters with some help from philosophers and theologians. I wished for a world where I could discover this tradition
perpetually, and not in pictures and in poems only, but in tiles
round the chimney-piece and in the hangings that kept out the
draught. I had even created a dogma: 'Because those imaginary

people are created out of the deepest instinct of man, to be his measure and his norm, whatever I can imagine those mouths speaking may be the nearest I can go to truth.' When I listened they seemed always to speak of one thing only: they, their loves, every incident of their lives, were steeped in the supernatural.

The sense in which Yeats was—or at least in which he remained—'very religious' is not easy to determine. When he once or twice speaks of engaging in prayer we are at once conscious of incongruity. Thus while debating with himself the desirability of marriage he records that: 'All last night the darkness was full of writing, now on stone, now on paper, now on parchment, but I could not read it. Were spirits trying to communicate? I prayed a great deal and believe I am doing right.' We feel that such supernatural powers as Yeats acknowledges would be more appropriately conjured or invoked than supplicated. He did indeed on a celebrated occasion invoke the moon on nine successive evenings while staying with his fellow dramatist Edward Martyn at Tulira Castle, with the happy result of being granted the vision of 'a marvellous naked woman shooting an arrow at a star'. But he found his pious Catholic host most unfortunately outraged that these proceedings had been undertaken in the near-vicinity of his own private chapel, and quite unable to accept Yeats's plea that his 'invocations were a form of prayer accompanied by an active desire for a special result, a more conscious exercise perhaps of the human faculties'. And although, taking a phrase of Blake's, he called a collection of his prose pieces *Ideas of Good and Evil* (1903), these are not categories over which he noticeably broods. Among the writers discussed in this book Yeats is in some aspects closest to D. H. Lawrence, to whom only the uncompromisingly orthodox will deny an essentially religious sensibility. But it is with Henry James, a man upon whose capacious mind religion never glimmered, that he shares an interest in ghosts. Yeats's interest of course bulks in his experience immensely larger than does James's. It develops and extends itself through phases which always show some correspondence to the phases of his poetry. And to each poetic place there is commonly an answering place of some substance in his prose.

His first book, *Fairy and Folk Tales of the Irish Peasantry* (1888), is a compilation to which he added some contributions of his own. It represents a preliminary exploration of territories which antiquarian scholarship was then extending in ways the promise of which he was only beginning to realize. The literary tradition to which his father had introduced him was entirely English. J. B. Yeats appears to have had little interest in Celtic mythology, while of excursions into the supernatural he at this time strongly disapproved, so that the poet records it as being in the study of psychical research and mystical philosophy that he first broke away from his father's influence. Yeats had already begun to broaden his esoteric interests, variously stimulated by his early contacts with George Russell (A. E.), his reading of Sinnett's *Esoteric Buddhism*, the first stirrings in Dublin of the Theosophic Movement, and the arrival there of the Brahmin Mohini Chatterji, who gave instruction in Indian philosophy and—incidentally—advised Yeats against prayer. But the main development of the poet's concern here came a little later and was centred in London. His first original writing is based as to substance largely upon readily available Irish material and in style upon English Pre-Raphaelitism.

2

The Wanderings of Oisin (1889), like much of Yeats's early poetry, harks back through Morris to the second generation of romantic poets. In 1885, when concerned with organizing a group of somewhat juvenile sages known as the Dublin Hermetic Society, he consulted his father's friend Professor Edward Dowden on the esoteric significance of *Prometheus Unbound*. Dowden, who was becoming an authority on Shelley rather against his inclination, replied that the drama was simply Godwin's *Political Justice* versified. Yeats, unconvinced, pursued researches of his own. But he must have judged Keats (his father's, and eventually his own, preferred poet) to be equally significant, since *The Wanderings of Oisin* is virtually *Endymion* in an Ossianic setting. Certainly he began with something like Keats's conception of a long poem. In the year in which *Oisin* was published he wrote in a letter to Katharine Tynan:

There is a thicket between three roads, some distance from any of them, in the midst of Howth. I used to spend a great deal of time in that small thicket when at Howth. . . . The thicket gave me my first thought of what a long poem should be. I thought of it as a region into which one should wander from the cares of life. The characters were to be no more real than the shadows that people the Howth thicket. Their mission was to lessen the solitude without destroying its peace.

This is not remote from Keats's well-known letter to Benjamin Bailey:

I have heard Hunt say and I may be asked—why endeavour after a long Poem? To which I should answer—Do not the Lovers of Poetry like to have a little Region to wander in where they may pick and choose, and in which the images are so numerous that many are forgotten and found new in a second Reading: which may be food for a Week's stroll in the Summer?

Oisin's wandering, like Endymion's, are conceived of as allegorical as well as mythological, and Yeats speaks in another letter of symbols in the poem to which he alone has the key. But this element is not obtrusive, nor is the work troubled—as *The Countess Kathleen* is to be troubled—by incongruities referable to the private predicaments of the poet. The mythology itself is insubstantial. We have a sense—which constitutes regularly a limiting condition upon the weight and substance of Yeats's early work—that the relics from which it is being constructed may have been emasculated as well as aestheticized. In any case they seem too fragmentary and discontinuous to admit of the poet's recapturing and exploiting any mythopœic power the material may originally have had. But Yeats does achieve, in his description of the three successive wanderings of the mortal Oisin with Niamh his supernatural bride, a phantasmagoric richness challenging the immature Keats:

> We rode between
> The seaweed-covered pillars; and the green
> And surging phosphorus alone gave light
> On our dark pathway, till a countless flight
> Of moonlit steps glimmered; and left and right
> Dark statues glimmered over the pale tide
> Upon dark thrones. Between the lids of one
> The imaged meteors had flashed and run
> And had disported in the stilly jet.

When we read indeed in the third part, concerning a gigantic race of great beauty sunk in mysterious slumber, that

So long were they sleeping, the owls had builded their nests in their locks

we may feel in the presence of an imagination not very quick
to detect an incursion of the ludicrous.[1] But at least we feel
throughout in the presence of an imagination. Yeats speaks of
his poem as 'a kind of vision' and describes the intense poetic
excitement that went to its slow composition. And although the
hard-won verse imitates Morris nowhere more than in having
a great air of being effortlessly spun, the underlying involvement and travail are in fact conveyed to us. To turn from *The
Wanderings of Oisin* to Tennyson's somewhat similar tour of
fabulous Irish islands in 'The Voyage of Maeldune' is to have
the sense of turning from a kindled to an unkindled mind.

   The Wanderings of Oisin, although essentially a narrative
poem, exhibits in fact embryonic dramatic form, since, following the traditional story, it represents the aged Oisin as recounting his history to a St. Patrick who offers disapproving
comments from time to time. Yeats was thus led to the possibility of essaying a regular poetic drama, and very soon began
work on *The Countess Kathleen*. This was published in 1892. In 1899
a revised version was produced, together with Edward Martyn's
The Heather Field, at the inauguration of the Irish Literary
Theatre. Yeats had come upon the story 'in a London-Irish
newspaper' when working on *Fairy and Folk Tales*. At that time
he had been 'unable to find out the original source'—for which
he would have had to turn to French, a language still very little
known to him. It is the story of a lady who, during a great
famine, sells her soul to the devil in order to redeem the souls
and save the lives of her starving people. From the inception of
his design Yeats associated his heroine with Maud Gonne, a
young woman of majestic beauty, fanatically devoted to Irish
nationalism, whom he had recently met and who was to be
the great love of his life. The parallelism must have become
more striking in his eyes when Miss Gonne did in fact tax both
her wealth and health in the interest of the distressed peasantry
of Donegal. But if the play gains emotional force from the
identification it loses correspondingly in artistic coherence.
Yeats provides his Countess with a poet—Kevin in the first
version and Aleel subsequently—who loves her in vain, and
whose pleadings and exhortations are freely ornamented with
imagery drawn from the newly resurgent Irish mythology. It
is clear that some feeling for a lover might well sharpen the

---

[1] This phrase came to Yeats from his nurse. But she spoke of herons, not owls.

Countess's plight and render it more poignant to us. It is conceivable that the starkly Christian fable might be set with some dramatic effectiveness against a background of lingering pagan faith. But Yeats in a slight play—and all his plays are to be slight—allows himself no scope for integrating such elements with his theme. There is not even much sign that he got far in considering the problem. With tragedy as an imitation of life he was at this time very little concerned. He was set only on fabricating beauty and convinced (as he records in *Reveries over Childhood and Youth*) 'that only ancient things and the stuff of dreams were beautiful'.

> The years like great black oxen tread the world,
> And God the herdsman goads them on behind,
> And I am broken by their passing feet.

It is a far cry from the cloudy and melodious dolour upon which this play ends to the sharp relevance with which, thirty-six years later, he recreates the close of the *Œdipus Rex*:

> All people said,
> 'That is a fortunate man';
> And now what storms are beating on his head!
> Call no man fortunate that is not dead.
> The dead are free from pain.

The blank verse of *The Countess Kathleen* is not wholly derivative. Yet the shadow of the Jacobean age lies over it as over most nineteenth-century poetic drama; lies, for example, over the Countess's last words:

> The storm is in my hair and I must go.

It is the idiom less of a saint than of a heroine in Webster. Yeats is never to take far the problem of appropriate speech. But that he was concerned to find a medium for dramatic expression in general the future was to make evident. The successive revisions of *The Countess Kathleen* were undertaken chiefly in the interest of consistent artistic effect in production. 'Every alteration', Yeats claims, 'was tested by performance.' Thus he sacrificed to this end what is, individually, one of the finest things in the play: that song, 'Who Goes with Fergus?' which James Joyce was to set to music and later (since he regarded it as the best lyric in the world) to represent as challenging the poethood of the Stephen Dedalus of *Ulysses*:

Who will go drive with Fergus now,
And pierce the deep wood's woven shade,
And dance upon the level shore?
Young man, lift up your russet brow,
And lift your tender eyelids, maid,
And brood on hopes and fear no more.

And no more turn aside and brood
Upon love's bitter mystery;
For Fergus rules the brazen cars,
And rules the shadows of the wood,
And the white breast of the dim sea
And all dishevelled wandering stars.

Yeats excised too the song later called 'The Countess Cathleen
in Paradise', substituting another, 'Lift up the white knee',
which seems to have been inspired by a visit to the Russian
Ballet in 1912.

Along with both *The Wanderings of Oisin* and *The Countess
Kathleen* Yeats had published a number of lyrics. The contents of
both volumes, together with a second verse play, *The Land of
Heart's Desire* (acted 1894), appeared in *Poems* (1895), with the
lyrics grouped under two headings, *Crossways* and *The Rose*.
This book is a landmark. After it, fresh influences, both
occult and literary, are at work, and the Celtic twilight of his
own first invention is blended with the answering shades of the
Cabbala and of French symbolism. That the mysterious and
the arcane are sovereign with him is declared in a quatrain
which he inscribed in a copy of *The Countess Kathleen* in 1893:

God loves dim ways of glint and gleam
To please him well my rhyme must be
A dyed and figured mystery,
Thought hid in thought, dream hid in dream.

On God the statement is arbitrary, but to the poetical credo
which follows Yeats never wholly ceased to subscribe. In his
maturity he is to fabricate his own astrology; at the beginning
of *Crossways*, in what had been in fact the epilogue to a juvenile
drama, he denounces astronomers:

Seek, then,
No learning from the starry men,
Who follow with the optic glass
The whirling ways of stars that pass—

> Seek, then, for this is also sooth,
> No word of theirs—the cold star-bane
> Has cloven and rent their hearts in twain,
> And dead is all their human truth.

The poem asserts that the antique world did better, feeding not on grey truth but on dreaming; and that to recapture something of this capacity should be the object of the poet's 'melodious guile'. We may recall that Keats similarly supposed disaster to attend upon knowing the woof and texture of the rainbow. And it is from Keats once more, and once more by way of Morris—dreamer of dreams, born out of his due time—that Yeats derives much of his attitude. An attitude it certainly is, and the first of many. The verse of *Crossways* and *The Rose* evinces, and even depends for something of its charm upon, the paradox of considerable poetic energy devoted to achieving the most languorous-seeming evocations of a large vague melancholy:

> Rose of all Roses, Rose of all the World!
> You, too, have come where the dim tides are hurled
> Upon the wharves of sorrow, and heard ring
> The bell that calls us on; the sweet far thing.
> Beauty grown sad with its eternity
> Made you of us, and of the dim grey sea.

Yeats was later to feel that to 'eternal Beauty wandering on her way' he had given too monotonous a background of Druid twilight, Danaan fruitage, dim tides and star-laden seas. He made many alterations in later years to temper this mannered writing. 'The Man Who Dreamed of Fairyland' is a striking instance of a poem much modified in this way, and 'The Sorrow of Love' is less modified than transformed. That the process of revision sometimes produced what Yeats himself called 'altogether new poems' is perhaps most strikingly instanced in 'The Lamentation of the Old Pensioner', where the essential subject is changed:

> I had a chair at every hearth,
> When no one turned to see,
> With 'Look at that old fellow there,
> And who may he be?'
> And therefore do I wander on,
> And the fret lies on me.

The road-side trees keep murmuring.
Ah, wherefore murmur ye,
As in the old days long gone by,
Green oak and poplar tree?
The well-known faces are all gone
And the fret lies on me.   (1892)

Although I shelter from the rain
Under a broken tree,
My chair was nearest to the fire
In every company
That talked of love or politics,
Ere Time transfigured me.

Though lads are making pikes again
For some conspiracy,
And crazy rascals rage their fill
At human tyranny,
My contemplations are of Time
That has transfigured me.

There's not a woman turns her face
Upon a broken tree,
And yet the beauties that I loved
Are in my memory;
I spit into the face of Time
That has transfigured me.   (1949)

The Rose concludes with an apologia in which Yeats claims
kinship with the national poets of Ireland, even although his
own verse appears to deal with matters remote from Ireland's
current wrongs:

Nor may I less be counted one
With Davis, Mangan, Ferguson,
Because, to him who ponders well,
My rhymes more than their rhyming tell
Of things discovered in the deep,
Where only body's laid asleep.
For the elemental creatures go
About my table to and fro.

Yeats here touches the core of his inspiration. He is indeed a
visionary poet, as he is claiming to be. But his vision is magical,
not mystical. We shall make little of him if we are unable to
believe that the elemental creatures did really go to and fro

about his table. His evident concern for masks and roles, and even for poses; a recurrent tone of scepticism, which is however less genuine than prudential; the unfashionableness of spiritualism; the general critical persuasion that he advances from ectoplasm to bronze; the comparatively small attention paid to his prose: all these have tended to encourage the view that his magic was little more than a picturesque embroidery on his cloak, which must vanish as soon as he went naked. In reality it is part of his mind. In 'Cuchulain's Fight with the Sea' the climax differs significantly from that in Arnold's broadly analogous 'Sohrab and Rustum'. The tragedy is a tragedy not of fate but of magic:

> The Druids took them to their mystery,
> And chaunted for three days

—just as, for nine nights, Yeats had invocated the moon. And the point of awe is not in Cuchulain's killing his son but in the magically induced delusions constraining him to fight with the invulnerable tide.

Magic enters too into *The Land of Heart's Desire*, which was to become one of Yeats's most popular plays, particularly in amateur production. It was written in order that a ten-year-old girl, the niece of a friend, might make a theatrical début in London; she was to play the part of the fairy child who entices the young bride, Mary Bruin, to leave her husband for the Land of the Ever Living. The piece is therefore short, simple, and perhaps a little too pretty. Yeats was later to admit 'some discomfort when the child was theme', to call the whole a vague trifle, and to see in it 'an exaggeration of sentiment and sentimental beauty' which it shared with some of his lyric verse of the same period. Certainly there is this sort of danger inherent in the story. But *The Land of Heart's Desire* is not sentimental in the manner, say, of Barrie's *Mary Rose*, another play about a girl called away by the fairies. It is saved from this by the provenance of the magic, which is here not literary, antiquarian, or in any way esoteric, but draws directly upon a folklore having the feel of living persuasion still.

Popular superstitions in the west of Ireland and elsewhere, such as he had begun collecting in Sligo and Howth when still a boy, are the subject of most of the pieces collected in *The Celtic Twilight* (1893). In his introduction Yeats claims to have written down accurately and candidly much that he has heard and seen, and nothing that he has merely imagined. Such an assertion by a creative writer must always be treated with reserve. It was made by Joyce Cary, for example, as applicable to the whole astonishing field of his fiction. In Yeats's book the simple and apparently unconsidered prose does largely persuade us that here is simply the product of detached if sympathetic listening. In 'Village Ghosts' one would not much suspect the writer of being himself haunted by what he hears: of 'a dead old gentleman', for example, who robs the cabbages of his own garden in the shape of a large rabbit, or of a wicked sea-captain who 'stayed for years inside the plaster of a cottage wall, in the shape of a snipe'.

But if 'the imagination of the people does dwell chiefly upon the fantastic and capricious', nevertheless 'darker powers' may be encountered by stepping only a little out of the way. 'The Sorcerers' describes Yeats as so employing himself in the more sophisticated environment of Dublin occultism. Having 'turned up about eight' upon an evening on which he had arranged to meet a group of sorcerers ('mainly small clerks and the like') he witnessed a ritual which began with the slitting of the throat of a black cock, and in the later course of which he had to resist falling under some evil influence. Yet, although in the main here representing himself only as a reporter of the talk of others, Yeats does not always conceal his own susceptibility to supernatural solicitation. In '*Regina, Regina Pigmeorum, Veni*' he gives a circumstantial account of an encounter and conversation with the Queen of the Forgetful People. It may have been of this essay that Max Beerbohm was thinking when he executed his pleasing drawing of 'Mr. W. B. Yeats presenting Mr. George Moore to the Queen of the Fairies'. Despite its plain style, therefore, *The Celtic Twilight* renders a total effect that is somewhat equivocal. It is an effect from which Yeats's recordings of his traffic with the supernatural is seldom to rise clear. But we have distinguished that traffic as veridical in the sense that he was himself intermittently subject to the challenge of supernatural experiences. We have further to acknowledge that in these experiences lies the matrix of much of his verse—a verse which was eventually to establish him as first among the European poets of his age. Yet very little, if anything, that came to him either in extra-sensory perception or through occultist study appears to have any enduring importance, or much beauty, in itself. It is the mysteriousness of the intimations concerned rather than any real and meaningful coherence to be established among them that brings him to poetry.

3

In 1887 J. B. Yeats had once more moved his family back to London. The poet attended an art school and received some small commissions from editors and publishers. Although he was in no degree cut off from Ireland—it is difficult to keep track of his going to and fro—he now began to make his way in English literary society. He became known to Henley, and to Morris, whose house he frequented. Throughout the early nineties he was absorbing those influences which were to declare themselves in the next phase of his work. Yet of the new forces coming to bear on him the purely literary were perhaps the least important. And the most important was entirely personal. It was the arrival in his life of Miss Gonne, who had presented herself with an introduction from the venerable Irish patriot John O'Leary:

A tall lanky boy with deep-set dark eyes behind glasses, over which a lock of dark hair was constantly falling, to be pushed back impatiently by long sensitive fingers, often stained with paint—dressed in shabby clothes that none noticed (except himself, as he confessed long after)—a tall girl with masses of gold-brown hair and a beauty which made her Paris clothes equally unnoticeable, sat figuratively and sometimes literally, at the feet of a thin elderly man, with eagle eyes, whose unbroken will had turned the outrage of long convict imprisonment into immense dignity. He never spoke of that imprisonment. . . . John O'Leary, the master, and his two favourite disciples, William Butler Yeats and Maud Gonne.

This, as recalled in old age, is Maud Gonne's own picture of the initial situation. She was well aware of what was due alike to her looks and to an ardour of spirit which was to grow fanatical with the years. That she was an intellectual woman is not apparent, and she came to take little interest in Yeats's poetry where it could not be bent to nationalistic purposes. Yet she had her romantic, indeed mystical, side, which recently published papers show as becoming prominent in a later phase of their relationship. Now, although convinced that 'action not books was needed', she responded to the young man's plans 'for a great literary movement for the glory of Ireland'. Some of these were sufficiently visionary. On an island on Lough Kay there was to be a 'Castle of the Heroes' to which, according to Miss Gonne, 'only those who had dedicated their lives to Ireland might penetrate'. In Yeats's mind the castle was designed for larger purposes: it was to be the headquarters of a secret order which should establish 'mysteries like those of Eleusis and Samothrace'. He was encouraged in this conception by A. E., who believed in an imminent Druidic awakening in Ireland. The presiding genius of this was to be neither Yeats nor A. E. himself but a new avatar, on whose present residence in some little white-washed cottage in Donegal or Sligo A. E. had received secure but topographically imprecise supernatural intelligence.

This complex of ideas was of great significance to Yeats:

For ten years to come my most impassioned thought was a vain attempt to find philosophy and to create ritual for that Order. I had an unshakable conviction, arising how or whence I cannot tell, that invisible gates would open as they opened for Blake, as they opened for Swedenborg, as they opened for Boehme, and that this philosophy would find its manuals of devotion in all imaginative literature, and set before Irishmen for special manual an Irish literature which, though made by many minds, would seem the work of a single mind, and turn our places of beauty or legendary association into holy symbols. I did not think this philosophy would be altogether pagan, for it was plain that its symbols must be selected from all those things that had moved men most during many, mainly Christian, centuries.

I thought . . . that I must some day—on that day when the gates began to open—become difficult or obscure.

It is a programme beyond Maud Gonne's scope and concludes on a note ominous for an effective nationalist poetry. But for long Yeats gave himself to her plans. His entire labour for an Irish theatre is in one aspect only a part of his bondage to her. The bondage, moreover, made an immediate impact on his verse. He believed that 'if a man is to write lyric poetry he must be shaped by nature and art to some one out of half a dozen traditional poses, and be lover or saint, sage or sensualist, or mere mocker of all life'. This faith made it inevitable that a barren passion should equip him with a pose or role. That there was something instinctively elective in his long misfortune—something akin, we may think, to Gérard de Nerval's passion for 'Adrienne'—he later came to recognize. In *Dramatis Personae* he gives the affair, dispassionately, its setting in the climate of the nineties:

I was involved in a miserable love affair, that had but for one brief interruption absorbed my thoughts for years past, and would for some years yet. My devotion might as well have been offered to an image in a milliner's window, or to a statue in a museum, but romantic doctrine had reached its extreme development. Dowson was in love with a girl in an Italian restaurant, courted her for two years; at first she was too young, then he too disreputable; she married the waiter and Dowson's life went to wreck.

And he has a grimly funny story depicting the wreckage vividly. It is of Dowson, half drunk, in company with a particularly common harlot at Dieppe, and whispering 'She writes poetry— it is like Browning and Mrs. Browning'. This sort of disaster did not befall Yeats. Indeed his long and difficult relationship with Miss Gonne (although she ought to have abrupted it) reflects a good deal of credit on each. He can have been nothing but uneasy before her more extreme designs—whether for concealing bombs in the coal of British troopships abroad or 'hurling the little streets against the great' at home. She, on the other hand, was sympathetic to many of what others would have called his eccentricities. Although exclaiming with aristocratic disdain that his mystical friends of the Order of the Golden Dawn were 'an awful set', she accepted initiation into several of its grades, reported a decent quota of ghosts and visions, and is displayed as agreeing to accompany him 'for a week or two perhaps to some country place in Ireland to get . . . the forms and gods and spirits and to get some sacred earth for our evocation'.

The Order of the Golden Dawn was a secret society of Christian Cabbalists. Its leader, Liddell Mathers, who became MacGregor Mathers and finally MacGregor before succumbing (it is said) to the lethal enchantments of a rival thaumaturge, cuts a bizarre figure both in the *Autobiographies* and elsewhere. Even if we are impressed by the intellectual credentials of the occult tradition in general, we may feel it difficult to acknowledge as an important source of Yeats's poetry the cardboard

figures and other magical paraphernalia with which this progressively deranged conjurer taught his techniques of reverie
and trance. It is difficult, too, to take seriously Madame
Blavatsky and the theosophists, the more so as the difficulty
is one which Yeats makes it plain that he often shares with us.
He records that this assured and omniscient lady promised him
a bad illness through loss of mesmeric force when he shaved
his beard; and that she instructed a devout follower that the
earth is really shaped like a dumb-bell. Yet there is not the
slightest doubt that an obsessive craving for supernatural
stimulus made Yeats a pertinacious student of magical lores;
that he found confirmation of their significance in his own
recurrent uncanny experiences; and that much of his verse
was to take its origin in the manner in which his mind constructed and associated images within the context of one or
another obscure symbolic system. Moreover it has to be admitted that of the power of the poetry critical sagacity has so
far offered no better explanation than that of the 'unknown
instructors' which Yeats himself would have brought forward.

If we remain surprised by the credence which he extended to
so much seemingly ramshackle supernatural communication,
we may reflect that it was a strong infection of the age. Certainly Yeats was no lonely figure in his own circle. Maud
Gonne and his initially sceptical father both became dabblers.
His uncle George Pollexfen, after a late start, justified his psychic
lineage by making notable progress as an astrologer. 'Diana
Vernon'—it is the name he gives to a cousin of Lionel Johnson
who was his mistress for a year and thereafter a lifelong
correspondent and friend—proved to have clairvoyant powers
when thrown into a trance. Much later his wife, finding him
on their honeymoon troubled by thoughts of another lady,
sought, curiously, to divert him by simulating the power of
automatic writing—and presently found herself in veritable
possession of this perplexing accomplishment, with notable
results. Even Miss Horniman, that prosaically Saxon patroness
of Celtic drama, had her *tarot* pack, as Yeats had himself.
One would suppose that, in an ambience so genially acceptive of
magic, magic secrets would have been hard to keep. When
Yeats in 1901 printed a pamphlet called *Is the Order of R.R. &
A.C. to remain a Magical Order?* the front cover bore the words
'This Essay must not be given to any but Adepti of the Order

of R.R. & A.C.' Yeats took with a Shelleyan seriousness the conceptions of initiation within initiation, and of the final gaining, by very few, or by one, of

> sovereignty and science
> Over those strong and secret things and thoughts
> Which others fear and know not.

And he was disposed to prize an element of secrecy in his poetry. Of *The Wanderings of Oisin* he had written with satisfaction in a letter: 'I have said several things to which I only have the key. The romance is for my readers. They must not even know there is a symbol anywhere. They will not find out.' *Editos esse et non editos*. Yeats is here even more absolute than the young Pico della Mirandolo when he declared of his commentary on Benivieni's *Canzona d'amore* that it was so filled with mysteries that it would be intelligible only to a few. The letter is perhaps too immature to be important. Yet we may set beside it a considered statement made a good deal later: 'All Art that is not mere story-telling, or mere portraiture, is symbolic, and has the purpose of those symbolic talismans which mediaeval magicians made with complex colours and forms, and bade their patients ponder over daily, and guard with holy secrecy.'

Lurking in this there seems to be an element of confusion between the symbols of magic and the symbols of poetry. Poetic symbols are instruments by which one individual conveys to others what could not otherwise be communicated, and they are successful in proportion as they achieve this with the least possible residuum of unintelligible matter. Mallarmé wrote a poem which he failed to understand, but he believed that it was a good poem and he therefore expected Hérédia, although a very different kind of poet, to understand it. But magic symbols, although they can themselves be communicated, exist not for the purpose of communication between individuals but for the invoking of supernatural or infra-personal powers. Historically, our attitude to them is conditioned by their Faustian associations: a vehicle which is dangerous or illicit will take on in addition to its function as a power a secondary function as a cipher or code. The use of magical symbols in poetry is thus a tricky business; and that the poetic and magical impulses may themselves be related makes the territory yet more difficult. The fascination of the difficult is never to lose hold on Yeats. In the nineties it presented itself for study in much of the contemporary poetry of France.

We must beware here of tracing influences in a heavy-footed way. Yeats was in essentials a symbolist poet, pursuing a reality beyond sense, when Baudelaire, Verlaine, and Mallarmé were still no more than names to him. When he did gain some acquaintance with their work he quickly adapted what he found there to purposes radically his own, arriving finally at that concentration and synthesis of magical with aesthetic effect, substantially unlike anything of theirs, which marks a high point of his poetry, and in which much antecedent confusion about the function of his symbols is resolved. In an essay called 'Magic', printed in *The Monthly Review* in 1901, he sets forth these three tenets:

(1) That the borders of our mind are ever shifting, and that many minds can flow into one another, as it were, and create or reveal a single mind, a single energy.

(2) That the borders of our memories are as shifting, and that our memories are a part of one great memory, the memory of Nature herself.

(3) That this great mind and great memory can be evoked by symbols.

The context given here to symbols was not that current in the Rue de Rome, where the affinity between poet and enchanter had the status only of a refined metaphor. But we need not suppose that Yeats, despite his small French, was unable to grasp what Mallarmé and Verlaine were about, even although this came to him, as he acknowledges, through the translations and conversation of Arthur Symons, the first English authority on the subject, who during these formative years had become his intimate friend. He grasped it very well, and for many years he occasionally wrote closely in Mallarmé's manner. But a poem like 'On a Picture of a Black Centaur', which Mr. Edmund Wilson cites as an example of this ability, is not in the main line of Yeats's development of symbolism. We feel that the horrible green parrots, the seven Ephesian topers, and even (although we meet it elsewhere) the old mummy wheat have come together through entirely private associations which must be for ever closed to us, and that our delight—for the poem is delightful—would be purer if we had some chance of discovering just what is going on. What Yeats did most significantly with symbolism was to transport it from France (or from America, if it stems from Poe) to Ireland, and to apply its methods to his already existing materials in Irish mythology. By doing this he made the weakness of that mythology—its fragmentariness and indefiniteness—a positive strength. He made it yield, that is to say, a complex of symbols exhibiting neither the baffling privacy of much French symbolism nor— as with a classical mythology—long-established public associations inappropriate to the feelings and emotions he was concerned to convey. In particular he made the elusiveness and cloudiness of its supernatural elements reflect, far more effectively than anything he could then have found in the sphere of classical mythology, the particular qualities of his own developing occult perceptions. All this constituted the first of several major operations of the highest poetic intelligence which he was to contrive in the course of a development surely unparalleled among the poets, although its like may perhaps be found among the musicians, and is found in the world of Donatello and Rembrandt.

We should, of course, be far from the end of continental influences upon the young Yeats even if we considered in detail the authors of *Poèmes saturniens* and *L'Après-midi d'un faune*. Chief among the saints of the age came Count Philippe Auguste Mathias de Villiers de L'Isle-Adam. He had the advantage of a medieval lineage more authentic than most; one of his comparatively modern ancestors, we are assured, had defended Rhodes for a whole year against 200,000 Turks; and when his Axel declared that our servants will do our living for us the pronouncement had, for Yeats as for others, the attraction of combining quintessentially aristocratic suggestion with an epigrammatic formulation of that current gospel of aesthetic withdrawal already available to any young Englishman or Irishman who had read his Pater. Yeats had enjoyed the advantage of sitting through a performance of *Axel* with Symons murmuring explanations as the play pursued its solemn and hieratic progress to suicide. And if *Axel* became, as Yeats tells us, a sacred book with his circle, it was scarcely esteemed above Huysmans's *A rebours*, whose hero, des Esseintes, Mallarmé himself had honoured by addressing, not in verse indeed but in sufficiently oracular prose.

Of the group of contemporaries who came loosely together

in the Rhymers' Club and who are celebrated in 'The Tragic Generation' (a title conceivably hit upon as analogous to Verlaine's *poètes maudits*) Yeats says: 'We looked consciously to Pater for our philosophy.' Subsequently, he was to feel that 'the ideal of culture expressed by Pater can only create feminine souls'. But if Pater was not a lasting influence—as indeed he could scarcely be with one who instinctively viewed art not as aesthetic delectation but as a means to evoke 'the elemental creatures' and 'call down among us certain disembodied powers' —there is yet a great deal of Pater in the Yeats of the nineties, and particularly in his prose. *The Secret Rose* (1897) is a collection of stories skilfully blending his own invention with the world of folklore and legend already explored in *The Celtic Twilight*. The son of the High-Queen of Ireland grows up with grey hawk's feathers for hair. Supernatural beings of various orders hover in dim landscapes: a great grey man driving swine among the hazels, a worm with a silver crown upon his head, herons that were learned Druids until metamorphosed by St. Patrick, a hare that has leapt magically from a pack of cards, lovers with heart-shaped mirrors instead of hearts. These wonders—many of them encountered by Red Hanrahan, the hedge schoolmaster, a robust and authentically native-seeming figure—are embodied in a highly artificial and inappropriate *fin-de-siècle* prose. This prose Yeats later came to detest, and he persuaded Lady Gregory to assist him in rewriting it in a manner more congruous with 'the life of the people' in Galway. 'Rosa Alchemica' in the same volume and *The Tables of Law: The Adoration of the Magi* (1897) are fantastic and mannered tales, the first two of which appeared originally in *The Savoy*, Symons's short-lived successor to *The Yellow Book*. In 'Rosa Alchemica' we meet a day-dream Yeats, who owns an historic house in Dublin, a Crivelli, a Francesca 'full of ghostly astonishment', tapestries rich with 'the blue and bronze of peacocks', and the works of Shakespeare, Dante, and Milton respectively and symbolically bound in orange, dull red, and blue grey. While living in this aesthetic seclusion, and after publishing a little work on the alchemists which has been in fact 'a fanciful reverie over the transmutation of life into art, and a cry of measureless desire for a world made wholly of essences', the narrator is visited by an old acquaintance, Michael Robartes, who is determined to make him an initiate of the Order of the

Alchemical Rose. The narrator asks why he should not prefer
Calvary to Eleusis, but presently yields to some sort of mesmeric
force and is persuaded to make a railway journey to the west
of Ireland. The temple of the Order proves to be a square
ancient-looking house on the end of a dilapidated pier, and the
two men have to make their way to it through a hostile demon-
stration by pious fishermen—one of these crying out in Gaelic
as they pass: 'Idolaters, idolaters, go down to Hell with your
witches and your devils; go down to Hell that the herrings may
come again into the bay.' For a time the narrator is lodged in
a small room provided with a library of alchemical books, the
prophetical writings of William Blake, and also

many poets and prose writers of every age, but only those who
were a little weary of life, as indeed the greatest have been everywhere, and who cast their imagination to us, as a something they
needed no longer now that they were going up in their fiery chariots.

He is given for study a work expounding the whole principle of
spiritual alchemy, and dealing 'at the outset and at considerable
length with the independent reality of our thoughts'—a doctrine
upon which Yeats's instructor Mohini Chatterji had set emphasis long ago. Later, the narrator's initiation begins in a great
circular room, splendidly and mysteriously decorated. It includes a ritual dance across a mosaic floor upon which there is
a representation of Christ crucified—the initiates desiring 'to
trouble His unity with their multitudinous feet'. But the richness of all this has been visionary only. The narrator presently
awakes to find himself 'lying on a roughly painted floor', flees
from the building just as the fisherfolk break in with the intention of stoning Robartes and his followers to death, and
returns—it is suggested—to orthodox devotion within the
Catholic Church. That the 'transmutation of life into art'
may cradle the disillusionment of an answering transmutation
of art into life is beautifully conveyed in the episode of the
sleeper's awakening, and the whole story is imaginatively more
coherent and successful than either of the two succeeding it.
In 'The Tables of the Law' we meet Owen Aherne (a figure as
mysterious as Robartes, and like him in a shadowy relationship to his creator), who has possessed himself of an esoteric
book including ten antithetical commandments by which it is
asserted that wizards or artists should live—although of such

indeed we are told, with a direct reminiscence of *Axel*, that they are 'elected, not to live, but to reveal that hidden substance of God which is colour and music and softness and a sweet odour'. 'The Adoration of the Magi' contrives to evoke M. Mallarmé, the Phaeacians, St. Brandan, Leda, and Hermes the Shepherd of the Dead; it is a confused performance full of hints of future speculations and future poems. All these stories carry careful Faustian overtones. The Church had showed suspicion of Yeats's work from the beginning—as for example when a Tipperary priest declared that the Introduction to *Fairy and Folk Tales* attributed degraded beliefs to the Irish peasantry. Here lay a serious threat to one who would build up a national literary movement; and to this circumstance we must attribute the tendency of Yeats's amateurs of magic to repent and turn from their alembics to their rosaries. But his underlying intention in these stories, he told O'Leary, was to found 'an aristocratic, esoteric Irish literature'. Such a literature he felt to be totally lacking, whereas there already existed something of a 'literature for the people'. And his present efforts were at least gravely approved by the twenty-year-old James Joyce, whose fondness for the esoteric was already forming. Joyce pronounced 'The Tables of the Law' and 'The Adoration of the Magi' 'work worthy of the great Russian masters'. Yeats, who was always readily impressed by learned persons, even if lately out of school, reprinted the stories at once.

4

In *The Wind Among the Reeds* (1899) is collected the main body of Yeats's lyrical verse written in his early symbolist manner, and beside this volume must be set *The Shadowy Waters*, a verse play published in 1900 and acted in 1904. It was many times revised, but never in a manner to obscure its derivations from a Pre-Raphaelitism exoticized out of de L'Isle-Adam and Maeterlinck—the latter of whom was now the European theatre's sole and tenuous bastion against that Ibsenite drama which, in his distaste, Yeats somewhat rashly equated with the world of Carolus Duran, Bastien-Lepage, Tyndall, and Huxley. This phase of his writing may be regarded as closing with *Ideas of Good and Evil* (1903), a gathering of prose pieces from *The Savoy* and elsewhere.

The greater part of *The Wind Among the Reeds* is given over to lyrics of frustrated love. It is in fact Maud Gonne's book. Yeats tells us indeed that one or two of the poems are addressed to, or concern, 'Diana Vernon'; and in 'The Lover mourns for the Loss of Love' the two women are brought together:

> Pale brows, still hands and dim hair,
> I had a beautiful friend
> And dreamed that the old despair
> Would end in love in the end:
> She looked in my heart one day
> And saw your image was there;
> She has gone weeping away.

It is perhaps significant that, although the burden of this seems clear, the first line is syntactically ambiguous, so that the attributes may—always at the biographical level—be either Diana's or Miss Gonne's. In 'He bids his Beloved be at Peace' Diana has eyes that half-close and hair that falls over his breast; in 'He gives his Beloved certain Rhymes' Miss Gonne has long hair and a pearl-pale hand. In 'He thinks of those who have Spoken Evil of his Beloved' it is clearly Miss Gonne who is bidden to half-close her eyelids and loosen her hair; in 'He reproves the Curlew' he remembers long heavy hair which is presumably Diana's once more, since it has been shaken out over his breast; elsewhere Miss Gonne has cloud-pale eyelids and is required to cover the pale blossoms of her breast with her dim heavy hair. But if the woman desired is insufficiently distinguished from the woman possessed, so is either from much else in the poems. Bridget in 'The Host of the Air' has long dim hair (three times) and other women have hiding hair, hair like shadowy blossom, hair that is a cloud, and hair that is a folded flower—so that if, lucklessly and prompted by Miss Gonne, we recall the poet himself as in trouble with his own 'constantly falling' hair we may feel altogether too much tangled in tresses for our comfort. Moreover tide, dew, fire, the cup of the sea, and a nightgown are all as pale as the ladies who glimmer before, among, or within them. All this is close to the prose of 'Rosa Alchemica', where there is similar talk of 'dreaming with dim eyes and half-closed eyelids', and where, as the narrator dances with an immortal august woman, 'ages seemed to pass, and tempests to awake and perish in the folds of our robes and in her heavy hair'. In the 'slow moving elaborate poems' which Yeats directly associates with 'Rosa Alchemica' there are many other percurrent epithets, most of them to be fairly described as of the fainting sort. They knit perfectly with the long slow fainting rhythms to a total effect which is narrow, hypnoidal, and undeniably beautiful in the manner that the poet designs.

It is doubtful whether an attentive reader, uninstructed by biographers and literary historians, would divine that between this and the preceding collection of Yeats's poems there have arrived a grand passion and a new literary theory. Here first and foremost is the disciple of Rossetti and Morris still, doing what he has been doing before, but doing it very much better. Part of the increased effectiveness does certainly lie in the essentially symbolist technique of exploiting mythological material for the purpose of intimating mood and emotion. But although some of the poems are susceptible in a new degree to esoteric interpretation, the tensions between actual and ideal experience, between natural and supernatural upon which most are built, remain intelligible even when mysterious:

> The host is riding from Knocknarea
> And over the grave of Clooth-na-Bare;
> Caoilte tossing his burning hair,
> And Niamh calling *Away, come away:*
> *Empty your heart of its mortal dream.*

The enchantment of the 'sweet everlasting Voices' is dangerous. By a simple magic it may draw a bride away from her husband, as in 'The Host of the Air', which echoes one of the stories of Hanrahan in *The Secret Rose*. It may make too poignant for bearing the lover's sense of the imperfections amid which mortal love must be laboured, as in 'The Lover tells of the Rose in his Heart', or too poignant the mere burden of mortality:

> The Danaan children laugh, in cradles of wrought gold,
> And clap their hands together, and half close their eyes,
> For they will ride the North when the ger-eagle flies,
> With heavy whitening wings, and a heart fallen cold:
> I kiss my wailing child and press it to my breast,
> And hear the narrow graves calling my child and me.

Pagan and Christian are seldom brought directly into conflict—a matter less of circumspection, perhaps, than of that vague aspiration, encouraged by theosophy, after a syncretism at

least among the symbolisms of religion that led Yeats to conclude that his 'mysteries like those of Eleusis and Samothrace' should yet not 'be altogether pagan', and that 'supreme
art is a traditional statement of certain heroic and religious
truths, passed on from age to age, modified by individual
genius, but never abandoned'. Yet the conflict exists, and closes
this poem:

> O heart the winds have shaken, the unappeasable host
> Is comelier than candles at Mother Mary's feet.

Sometimes we are in wholly ambiguous territory: when, in
'Into the Twilight', we read that 'God stands winding his lonely
horn' the obscurity of the summons is scarcely lightened by the
substitution of 'His' for 'his' after the first printing of the poem.
The most deliberate conflation of symbols occurs in the magnificent 'The Secret Rose', in which the Holy Sepulchre stands
with the wine-vat; the leaves of the inviolate Rose itself enfold
the helms of the Magi; and a legend of Conchubar's vision, amid
'Druid vapour', of the crucifixion of Christ leads into a processional evocation of Cuchulain and Fand and Emer and Fergus, and this in turn into a prophetic close in which there lurk
both the idea of Irish renaissance and the mysticism of A. E.'s
apocalyptic or chiliastic visions. Nothing of Yeats's hitherto has
carried the resonance achieved in this poem.

Significant as are the new influences bearing upon *The Wind
Among the Reeds*, we may yet attribute greater importance to the
sheer hard work which the achieving of its restricted perfections
represents. Yeats was always concerned to insist that at no time
had he found the writing of poetry easy. As a boy he wrote some
verse with facility but with a curious technical backwardness,
so that at eighteen his versification was still at the twelve-year-
old level at which his spelling was to remain for good. When
writing *The Wanderings of Oisin* he could manage only a few
lines a day, even at times when his theme obsessed him. And
he was in his fifties when he wrote: 'Metrical composition is
always very difficult to me, nothing is done upon the first day,
not one rhyme is in its place; and when at last the rhymes begin
to come, the first rough draft of a six-line stanza takes the whole
day.' When he declared, while still a very young man, that he
had broken his life in a mortar for his poems, the extravagance
of the words must be considered in the light of the unending

toil his verse cost him. Mr. Richard Ellmann, who has made
some valuable examinations of manuscript material, shows convincingly the extent of such toil behind 'To his Heart, bidding
it have no Fear', one of the shortest poems in *The Wind Among
the Reeds*. Yeats always composed aloud, and appears to have
got very little assistance from the appearance of his verse on a
page. To the end of his life he remained entirely ignorant of
the notations of prosody, a subject in which poets commonly
take, whether usefully or not, a certain amount of interest.
It has been stated that in his last years he was sometimes betrayed by his purely intuitive procedure into metrical eccentricities so clamant as to require the correction of his friends.
But there may well have been gossip of this sort about Milton—
a sufficiently learned prosodist—when he published *Samson
Agonistes* and *Paradise Regained*.

The Shadowy Waters had been long in Yeats's mind. When
eighteen he had persuaded a Sligo cousin to take him out in
his yacht at midnight, since he wished to discover, in the interest of this drama, 'what sea-birds began to stir before dawn'.
The poem would have been full of observation, he thought,
had he been able to write it when he first planned it. In fact
Yeats, after boyhood, was very little of the naturalist. 'Quite
suddenly', he declares in *Ideas of Good and Evil*, 'I lost the desire
of describing outward things.' Dorothy Wellesley was to record
roundly that he 'hated flowers' and when walking in the country
was almost obsessively inattentive to the face of nature. William
Rothenstein made the same observation. Certainly the birds
that eventually hover around the hero of *The Shadowy Waters*
owe little to ornithology, since they have human faces and are
in fact the souls of the dead making their way to some after-
world unknown. Forgael, while yet living, has taken them as
guide upon a mysterious voyage which, in the first and never-
finished version, was to represent flight from the horror of his
own loneliness. Other mortals are on the same sea; Forgael's
crew seizes a passing galley, slays those on board, and brings
him as prize Queen Dectora, whom he causes to fall beneath
a love-spell. In the original story, known to A. E. and Yeats
when they were still boys together, Forgael realizes this mortal
passion as delusive, unwinds the spell, and resumes his transcendental search alone. In the play as eventually completed, when
Forgael says that he must still follow the souls of the dead,

Dectora casts in her lot with his, and they sail on together in supersensible quest. There is perhaps no invitation to regard their relationship as other than entirely ghostly, but our acquiescence in the pitch of emotion to which the action is finally raised is nevertheless a little qualified by the sense that Forgael is contriving to have it both ways:

Dectora.   We two—this crown—
    I half remember. It has been in my dreams.
    Bend lower, O king, that I may crown you with it.
    O flower of the branch, O bird among the leaves,
    O silver fish that my two hands have taken
    Out of the running stream, O morning star,
    Trembling in the blue heavens like a white fawn
    Upon the misty border of the wood,
    Bend lower, that I may cover you with my hair,
    For we will gaze upon this world no longer.
                        (*The harp begins to burn as if with fire.*)
Forgael (*gathering Dectora's hair about him*).
    Beloved, having dragged the net about us,
    And knitted mesh to mesh, we grow immortal;
    And that old harp awakens of itself
    To cry aloud to the grey birds, and dreams,
    That have had dreams for father, live in us.

While working on the play Yeats wrote of it as 'magical and mystical beyond anything I have done'. It may certainly be described, particularly in its earlier version, as crammed with secondary symbolism. From *Ideas of Good and Evil* we learn that the morning star, the white fawn, and the silver fish of Dectora's last speech all have hidden significance, and a commentator has not been lacking to remark, somewhat proleptically, that Yeats is here designing to give his dialogue archetypal depth. But the primary symbolism at least is lucid, and as a dramatic poem the evolved 'reading' version remains unsurpassed as the sustained lyrical achievement of the 'romantic' Yeats. 'Acting' versions developed independently and not always felicitously. Yeats rejected, indeed, some enterprising suggestions of George Moore's, when Moore, who enjoyed the reputation of one deeply versed in the theatre, was brought in at an early stage to steer him through his difficulties. But later, being persuaded that the play would be more acceptable to a common audience if the less elevated characters spoke some prose, he appears to have licensed Lady Gregory to make the necessary changes. And she, anxious, it may be, to depart as little as possible from Yeats's own words, in places did little more than trouble the metre, so that these passages exhibit in abundance that sort of 'verse fossil' which speculative critics have been fond of finding in some of the prose of Shakespeare. And the ending of the play was abridged for acting, markedly to its detriment.

5

With the turn of the century comes the period of Yeats's close involvement with the Irish dramatic movement. Not only did he found the movement and supply it with some of its most important plays; he administered it tirelessly and with equal courage and address through years of fierce controversy and endless practical difficulty. His initial interest in the idea of a national theatre stems perhaps from his father's advocacy of dramatic poetry and certainly from the notion of its political possibilities that he was eager for a time to share with Maud Gonne. But if patriotic feeling was a mainspring of the movement it was almost equally a brake upon it. Many potential supporters were entirely unresponsive to literary merit, and insistent that only the most idealized representations of Irish nationhood and morality should be presented on the stage. Thus Yeats was to find that, when a company was sent on tour through the country towns, local patriotic committees, consisting in the main of small shopkeepers, expected without question to have the right to cut and rearrange a play before it was presented. In Dublin these elements of political, moral, and religious prejudice, although leading to much misrepresentation and to occasional riots, were probably less discouraging than was mere indifference. It was at a later period and with another drama that the Abbey Theatre achieved secure popular support; and in particular there appears to have been little effective demand for what Yeats himself wished to give. We may find nothing very surprising in this, and he was certainly following the natural bent of his own mind in developing in his later dramatic period what may be called small plays for big houses. One big house was of great importance at the start.

It was in 1896 that he met Lady Gregory, who became not only his constant supporter and collaborator in the theatre, but a patroness and friend with whom he was to spend many summers at Coole Park. We can easily laugh at Yeats (and Bohemian Dublin was to do a lot of laughing) for so obviously rejoicing that Coole was the real thing: the authentically aristocratic equivalent of that fabled Sandymount Castle of his childhood which had been, after all, no more than a glorified citizen's box. But poetry was to flow from Coole, and Augusta Gregory's must be an honoured name among those who have aided genius to its flowering. And Yeats's own name, as it happens, becomes such a fostering one within the same context of the dramatic movement. In 1896 he visited Paris upon some occultist occasion, in which he was not so absorbed as to fail to make the acquaintance of a fellow countryman living on the top floor of his hotel. John Synge had studied Irish at Trinity College, Dublin, and was now studying classical French literature. Yeats recognized his quality at once, and a little later appears to have been the first to discern, and advise upon, Synge's true line of development. Later he was to see his own early struggles against the rancour and philistinism of the Young Ireland school as abundantly rewarded in having paved the way for Synge, 'the greatest dramatic genius' the country ever produced. After Synge's death in 1909 at the age of thirty-seven Yeats set about building him into his private mythology. Synge was perhaps no more a great genius, rich in unfulfilled renown, than Coole was really a great house, or the Gregorys first cousins to the Counts of Montefeltro. But poetry was to flow from Synge too—and moreover his plays quickly came to have an influence over Yeats's own attempts for the theatre. A work like Synge's *In the Shadow of the Glen*, produced in 1903, had a power and authenticity almost inevitably lacking from such plays of peasant life, cast in peasant idiom, as Yeats was drawn into in his collaborations with Lady Gregory. *The Pot of Broth* (acted 1902), although admirably adapting a little folk-tale to the talents of the new theatre's chief comedian, William Fay, shows as entirely trivial when set beside Synge, and made it clear that Yeats, if he was to be preserved from a mere multiplying of such *genre* pieces, must remember that his own essential medium was verse.

Yet that prose and the labours of collaboration were not without reward is shown in *Cathleen ni Houlihan* (acted 1902), the first of the Irish plays, Yeats tells us, 'where dialect was not

used with an exclusively comic intention'. Set near Killala in
1798, during the rumour of a French invasion, it presents a
peasant household from which the eldest son, although about to
be happily and prosperously married, departs at the call of
a poor old woman, Cathleen the daughter of Houlihan, who is
in fact Ireland, oppressed and despoiled, calling upon the devotion of her children. This play is a small masterpiece, with far
more of dramatic substance than some of its successors, and it at
once became famous. Yeats was quickly concerned to deny that
it was a political play of a propagandist kind; he had simply
taken 'thoughts that men had felt, hopes they had died for',
and put them into sincere dramatic form, so that the action
typifies the perpetual struggle between ideal causes and private
hopes and dreams. If it was chiefly anxiety about the patent
granted to the Abbey Theatre that prompted these remarks,
their lurking disingenuousness reflects a real and enduring
uneasiness owned by Yeats in the face of Irish nationalist
politics. He was at least as shrewd as he was mystical, and must
have realized that the forces Maud Gonne wished to unleash
would be as hostile in the end to Coole Park as to Dublin
Castle. Cathleen ni Houlihan, speaking darkly of the too many
strangers in her house, of the loss of her four beautiful green
fields, and of the many a man who had died for love of her, was,
and long remained, a singularly effective symbol; the last report
of her, as the curtain comes down, is indestructibly thrilling.
It is recorded that Yeats once silenced an angry gathering of
offended patriots by saying superbly 'The author of *Cathleen ni
Houlihan* addresses you', and it was with no fanciful questioning
that he wrote in 'The Man and the Echo' in the last months of
his life:

> All that I have said and done,
> Now that I am old and ill,
> Turns into a question till
> I lie awake night after night
> And never get the answers right.
> Did that play of mine send out
> Certain men the English shot?

That it was Lady Gregory who helped him to the country
speech of the play, and so to 'get down out of that high window
of dramatic verse', and that it was Maud Gonne who played
the part of Cathleen, 'magnificently and with weird power', are

facts almost symbolical in themselves. The two women represented for Yeats a parting of the ways. But, in a sense, he had
not himself to choose. In 1903, when lecturing in America, he
received a telegram telling him that Miss Gonne had married—
unhappily, as it turned out—John MacBride, who had led the
Irish Brigade with the Boers, and who was to be one of those
'the English shot' in 1916. Yeats now no longer had the same
incentive as before to approve direct political action.

The origins of *Where There is Nothing* (acted 1904) belong with
the well-documented comedy of George Moore in Ireland. The
two men projected a collaboration (such as they had already
achieved after a fashion in the *Diarmuid and Grania* produced in
the previous year) on an idea which Yeats believed to be right-
fully his, and when Moore maliciously threatened to use it for
a novel of his own Yeats sought to forestall him by calling Lady
Gregory and Douglas Hyde (eminent as the historian of Gaelic
literature) to his aid and writing a five-act prose tragedy in
a fortnight. One would scarcely expect a play thus fabricated
to be either very successful or very serious. Certainly it was
insusceptible of public performance in Ireland. The hero, Paul
Ruttledge, is a country gentleman who joins a band of tinkers,
marries one of their number amid an extensive orgy of beer-
drinking, arraigns and exposes in their hypocrisy the respectable neighbours who come to expostulate with him, enters a
monastery, preaches heresy and destruction to the monks, and is
finally killed by a mob. Joyce might have invoked 'Russian
masters' as appositely before this nihilistic improvisation as
before the prose tales of Robartes and Aherne.

Yeats himself did not judge the result to be other than a bad
play, but its basic idea had significance for him, and he recast
it five years later, again in prose, as *The Unicorn from the Stars*
(acted 1907). Here, although the writing is almost entirely by
Lady Gregory and undeniably monotonous, he believed that his
original intention, that of carrying 'to a more complete realization the central idea of the stories in *The Secret Rose*', was better
achieved. The modern country gentleman has been replaced
by a young coach-builder, Martin Hearne, living early in the
nineteenth century. A man of visionary temperament, he has
fallen into a trance while working upon a gilded lion and unicorn—the sagacious but heterodox priest Father John remarking, rather in the scientific spirit of Mr. Aldous Huxley

investigating such phenomena, that 'the flashing of light upon it would be enough to throw one that had a disposition to it' into such a state, and that 'a ray of sunlight on a pewter vessel' has been known to have a like effect. Martin has at first only an imperfect recollection of the unicorns he has seen, but a chance word from a beggar brings a fuller memory. The unicorns were breaking the world to pieces in obedience to a mysterious command: 'Destroy, destroy, destruction is the life-giver! destroy!' Thus prompted to anarchy, Martin marshals the beggars and announces that they must 'destroy the Law':

> When there were no laws men warred on one another and man to man, not with machines made in towns as they do now, and they grew hard and strong in body. They were altogether alive like Him that made them in His image, like people in that unfallen country. But presently they thought it better to be safe, as if safety mattered or anything but the exaltation of the heart, and to have eyes that danger had made grave and piercing. We must overthrow the laws and banish them.

This determination to 'go out against the world and break it and unmake it . . . to destroy all that can perish' leads Martin to organize a drunken revel as Paul Ruttledge had done, and to burn down 'some big house'. But a further vision, achieved just before he is shot, persuades him that he was mistaken in thus proposing 'to destroy Church and Law', and that the right place for 'the clashing of the swords' is in Heaven:

> I thought the battle was here, and that the joy was to be found here on earth, that all one had to do was to bring again the old wild earth of the stories—but no, it is not here; we shall not come to that joy, that battle, till we have put out the senses, everything that can be seen and handled, as I put out this candle. (*He puts out candle.*) We must put out the whole world as I put out this candle (*puts out another candle*). We must put out the light of the stars and the light of the sun and the light of the moon (*puts out the rest of the candles*), till we have brought everything to nothing once again. I saw in a broken vision, but now all is clear to me. Where there is nothing, where there is nothing—there is God!

In all this Yeats is, among other things, at once acknowledging the attractiveness and denying the legitimacy of Maud Gonne's bombs in the bunkers. Of the play's esoteric significance, and of its symbolism, there may be different opinions. The traditional identification of the unicorn is with Godhead. But in a letter to his sister Elizabeth written probably in 1920 Yeats says of the play's title: 'The truth is that it is a private symbol belonging to my mystical order and nobody knows what it comes from. It is the soul.' And he impresses upon Elizabeth that this information about a play published twelve years before must not be divulged to the profane.

Another play of this period subsequently underwent rewriting. *The Hour Glass* (acted 1903) is a short prose morality in which a Wise Man who has taught entire disbelief in God is visited by an angel and told that he must die unless in an hour's time he can produce a single surviving believer. He tries to coax some expression of faith from his pupils, who suppose that he is only exercising their wits; from his wife, who merely says it is a hard thing to be married to a man of learning; and from his children, who prove to be little parrots unable to do more than repeat his former lessons. Only the Fool, Teigue, has faith, and to him the Wise Man must humble himself in order to receive salvation. Yeats was to explain, in his lecture to the Royal Academy of Sweden on the occasion of his receiving the Nobel Prize, that the play was characteristic of his and Lady Gregory's 'first ambition' to bring 'the imagination and speech of the country, all that poetical tradition descended from the Middle Ages, to the people of the town'. It is certainly concerned for antique effects. The Wise Man talks scraps of Latin like Marlowe's Doctor Faustus, and the Fool inhabits an indeterminate region between *King Lear* and Max Beerbohm's 'Savonarola Brown'. The resulting piece had more homiletic success than artistic distinction—being, Yeats said, 'only too effective, converting a music-hall singer and sending him to mass for six weeks'. As early as 1903 he mentioned his intention, apparently disapproved of by Lady Gregory, of putting certain parts into verse in order 'to lift the "Wise Man's" part out of a slight element of platitude'. The eventual revision as published in *Plays in Prose and Verse* (1922) does rather more than this, removing altogether the Wise Man's opening soliloquy and altering the conclusion so that he no longer receives salvation as a gift from the Fool but submits himself to a destiny rendered supportable by his having come to an intellectual understanding of it. There is a good deal that is forward-looking in the verse and imagery of the revised text. But this, although interesting

in itself, does not cohere very well with the original and still
dominant tone of the piece.

The King's Threshold (produced in 1903 and published in
1904) is a long one-act verse play which makes clear—what
The Countess Kathleen and *The Shadowy Waters* have already
suggested—a disposition in Yeats to make poetry and poethood
an important theme of poetry. 'Bishops, Soldiers, and Makers
of the Law' have constrained King Guaire to demote the poet
Seanchan from membership of his council, and the play opens
upon the King explaining to the poet's pupils whom he has
summoned that Seanchan is determined to vindicate the dignity
of poetry at the cost of his life:

> He has chosen death:
> Refusing to eat or drink, that he may bring
> Disgrace upon me; for there is a custom,
> An old and foolish custom, that if a man
> Be wronged, or think that he is wronged, and starve
> Upon another's threshold till he die,
> The common people, for all time to come,
> Will raise a heavy cry against that threshold,
> Even though it be the King's.

The play resolves itself into a series of interviews between
Seanchan and those who would, through one prompting or
another, turn him from his purpose. When Yeats said that it
was 'constructed rather like a Greek play' he may have been
thinking of the *Prometheus Bound*; but it has its affinity, too, with
the *Antigone*. He was certainly right in judging it the best thing
that he had done so far. The pride of Seanchan is magnificent—
notably when he dismisses his final temptation in the person of
the girl he was to marry:

> If I had eaten when you bid me, sweetheart,
> The kiss of multitudes in times to come
> Had been the poorer.

Equally good are the exchanges with the Monk (which are
venturesomely anti-clerical), and with the Court Chamberlain,
the eternal privileged amateur. Yet there is perhaps some
weakness in Seanchan's position, since if the poetic power be
all that he claims, then it is scarcely

> One of the fragile, mighty things of God,
> That die at an insult

and he himself would do better to continue his service to it undismayed. Yeats appears, indeed, to have been in some uncertainty about the handling of his fable, and in a letter to Arthur Symons in 1905 he sets some emphasis upon how it developed during production:

The King's Threshold has been changed and rehearsed and then changed again and so on, till I have got it as I believe a perfectly articulate stage play. I have learned a great deal about poetry generally in the process, and one thing I am now quite sure of is that all the finest poetry comes logically out of the fundamental action, and that the error of late periods like this is to believe that some things are inherently poetical, and to try and pull them on to the scene at every moment. It is just these seeming inherently poetical things that wear out.

In fact Yeats's changes extended to reversing the whole issue of the action. When we turn back to the text of 1904 we find not a Seanchan who dies and is borne away to a mournful music, but a Seanchan who brings the King literally to his knees. As in the final version, the pupils elect to be hanged rather than see their master submit. But then 'the King comes slowly down the steps' and the play concludes:

King. (*Kneeling down before* Seanchan.)
  Kneel down, kneel down, he has the greater power.
  I give my crown to you.
(*All kneel except* Seanchan, Fedelm *and* Pupils. Seanchan *rises slowly, supported by one of the* Pupils *and by* Fedelm.)
Seanchan.   O crown, O crown,
  It is but right if hands that made the crown
  In the old time should give it when they will.
  O silver trumpets be you lifted up
   (*He lays the crown on the* King's *head.*)
  And cry to the great race that is to come.
  Long-throated swans among the waves of time
  Sing loudly, for beyond the wall of the world
  It waits and it may hear and come to us.
   (*Some of the* Pupils *blow a blast upon their horns.*)

In the text of 1904, moreover, Seanchan has been banished not from the King's council, to which there is no suggestion that he aspires, but merely from his board. Yeats's source for the work (from which, as he not very handsomely expresses it, he has borrowed some ideas for the arrangement of his subject) was

Sancan the Bard, a poor play in bad rhymed verse by Edwin John Ellis, with whom he had collaborated in 1893 in an unsatisfactory edition of Blake. It is from Ellis's play that Yeats's original happy ending comes. That Yeats had doubts about it from the first is suggested by a curious Prologue included in the edition of 1904, 'written for the first production of "The King's Threshold" in Dublin, but not used, as, owing to the smallness of the company, nobody could be spared to speak it'. In this an Old Man, delivering himself of a good deal of whimsical matter in Lady Gregory's vein, says:

I am to say: Some think it would be a finer tale if Seanchan had died at the end of it, and the king had the guilt at his door, for that might have served the poet's cause better in the end. But that is not true, for if he that is in the story but a shadow and an image of poetry had not risen up from the death that threatened him, the ending would not have been true and joyful enough to be put into the voices of players and proclaimed in the mouths of trumpets, and poetry would have been badly served.

However it may be with the action, there can be little doubt that, where the verse is altered, as it frequently is, the alteration is almost always for the better. More questionable is the substitution (as in *The Shadowy Waters*) of prose for verse where less exalted characters speak. It is a relapse upon a convention not at all in consonance with Yeats's own developing feeling about the utterance that may be expected from beggars, zanies, and cripples. The whole subject of Yeats's revisions—as of Henry James's—must lie largely outside the scope of a brief discussion. But *The King's Threshold* will be found a good place for preliminary investigation.

On Baile's Strand is another play written in 1903, produced in 1904, and subsequently much revised; it is, too, another play springing from Yeats's not altogether modest desire 'to hear Greek tragedy spoken with a Dublin accent'. The legend of the king who is drawn unwittingly to slay his own son in combat is one which he had already treated in 'Cuchulain's Fight with the Sea', and which was to haunt Yeats to the end, long after his imagination had ceased much to dwell on Red Branch kings and their like. In Cuchulain—representing, as he said long afterwards, 'creative joy separated from fear'—he doubtless found one enduring *persona*. He was anxious that 'a shadow of something a little proud, barren and restless' should be evident in Frank Fay's playing of the part. And in the evolved form of the piece his growing tendency to conceive the personages of a drama abstractly and in terms of type and antitype is evident alike in the formally contrasted roles of Cuchulain and Conchubar his overlord, and in the Fool and the Blind Man who stand in a deliberately excogitated metaphysical relationship to these. In themselves the Fool and the Blind Man are the best part of the play, so that their preliminary setting of the scene overshadows everything that follows. The prose here is better— good enough, indeed, to make us aware that Yeats's blank verse is not developing altogether promisingly for the theatre. The pervasive literary overtones enhance our impression that this sort of poetic drama has been happening for a long time and is gaining no great freshness from being peopled out of a laboriously revived corpus of legend. Yeats, although he often expressed satisfaction with *On Baile's Strand*, was perhaps conscious of this. He experimented with a Chorus of Women, never to be very well integrated with the whole, who 'sing in a very low voice after the first few words so that the others all but drown their words' a mysterious exorcism in an altogether more nervous measure:

> Those wild hands that have embraced
> All his body can but shove
> At the burning wheel of love
> Till the side of hate comes up.
> Therefore in this ancient cup
> May the sword-blades drink their fill
> Of the home-brew there, until
> They will have for masters none
> But the threshold and hearthstone.

But if the vehicle of the main heroic action is defective this does no more than reflect a basic uncertainty of touch in Yeats's reaching after the core of drama. Thus he was almost certainly quite wrong in judging the end of the play to be 'particularly impressive'. The episode of Cuchulain's encounter with his son, and of the part played by Conchubar's talk of witchcraft in bringing on the tragic denouement, is excellent. But much of what follows is open to a judgement well expressed by J. B. Yeats, who was sometimes an acute critic of his son's work:

The scene between father and son over the duel was the most thrilling and enthralling experience I ever went through. You touched at
the same moment the fountain of joy and tears.

But I maintain that the end won't do—it is not true to nature to
suppose that the fool would not have had thoughts of dinner driven
out of his head by such a sight as a great knight gone mad and
confronting himself with his own fury. Nor do I quite like the hero's
coming on after the fight 'in good spirits' as you say. There would
have been something more than this—as it stands it rather suggests
that the father killed the son as you would a chicken.

Yeats is certainly chargeable, up to this point, with having
much softened and aestheticized the body of harsh strong heroic
legend the relics of which Irish scholarship had been redis-
covering. He must have been conscious of this in approaching
the most famous of all the stories, that of Deirdre and Naoise,
which we may suppose him, too, as having deliberately reserved
for his culminating work in this kind. Out of it he believed, at
one point at least, that he had made 'a great play . . . most
powerful and even sensational'. Synge's version—his last and
uncompleted work, written when he was a dying man—lay in
the future. Synge was to treat the story episodically and in the
spirit of a folk-tale. Yeats is at another extreme. He chooses an
Attic concentration upon the climax of the action, as much of
an Attic spareness and bareness as he can achieve, and a conception of his characters succinctly described by an American
critic as involving 'an overdose of royal blood'. The play is
set in a guest-house in a wood, and opens upon a Chorus of
itinerant musicians who provide a rapid protasis. Long ago
King Conchubar, when already old, had found the infant
Deirdre on a hillside, nursed by a witch, and had brought her
up to be his bride. But the young Naoise carried her off—and
now, upon promise of reconciliation with Conchubar, has
returned with her into the power of the King. Everything is
ominous in the guest-house when the lovers arrive. There is no
welcome, no message from Conchubar, and in the wood outside
dark-faced men with strange barbaric dress and arms keep
guard. Deirdre knows what impends. Naoise opposes to his
own answering knowledge an inflexible aristocratic code: the
King has given his word; they would dishonour him, and themselves, in doubting it. Then the trap is sprung. If Naoise is to
go free, Deirdre must yield to Conchubar, who has prepared

a marriage bed so evilly enchanted that it must in the end make
the girl his willing bride. She is prepared to make the sacrifice,
but Naoise's resistance leads to his murder, and Deirdre by a
stratagem succeeds in killing herself. Her last words to the
musicians as, with a knife concealed in her dress, she goes
behind the curtain where her lover's body lies, show what
models Yeats has in mind:

> Now strike the wire, and sing to it a while,
> Knowing that all is happy, and that you know
> Within what bride-bed I shall lie this night,
> And by what man, and lie close up to him,
> For the bed's narrow, and there outsleep the cock-crow.

And the short concluding episode (in which Lady Gregory
appears to have had a hand) recalls most clearly, perhaps,
the *Agamemnon*. A crowd appears, shouting 'Death to Conchubar!' and the King's dark-faced guards gather round him.
But he motions them regally away and speaks the final words:

> I have no need of weapons,
> There's not a traitor that dare stop my way.
> Howl, if you will; but I, being King, did right
> In choosing her most fitting to be Queen,
> And letting no boy lover take the sway.

Deirdre, played in 1906, was subsequently much revised,
notably in 1922; and Yeats was to speak of it as 'unified' after
he had torn up many manuscripts. The final text shows great
concentration upon a verse that shall be moving without
luxuriance. This is relieved here and there by rhyming measures,
and by two songs, the second of which is particularly beautiful:

> Love is an immoderate thing
>   And can never be content
> Till it dip an ageing wing
>   Where some laughing element
> Leaps and Time's old lanthorn dims.
>   What's the merit in love-play,
> In the tumult of the limbs
>   That dies out before 'tis day,
> Heart on heart, or mouth on mouth,
>   All that mingling of our breath,
> When love-longing is but drouth
>   For the things come after death?

It is true that Yeats is still using as his main medium a blank verse reasonably to be described as pseudo-Elizabethan; and one of the best and most learned of his critics, Mr. T. R. Henn, declares it to be 'lifeless' when set in comparison with Synge's prose. But although Synge's is no doubt one of those uncommon odd achievements that do last, it remains odd. *Deirdre* is a work of very high poetic craft. Its weakness—and it has a radical weakness—lies elsewhere.

In the guest-house a chess-board stands set out, and we learn that

> It is the board
> Where Lugaid Redstripe and that wife of his,
> Who had a seamew's body half the year,
> Played at the chess upon the night they died.

This is ominous in a manner not at all intended by the poet. Very soon we find Naoise and Deirdre less concerned to fight—which is their heroic business, and the more sensibly so since there is incipient revolt against Conchubar in the air—than to settle down at playing Redstripe and his bird-woman in a highly self-conscious manner. This is initially more Naoise's conception of comportment than Deirdre's. Deirdre says:

> Let's out and die,
> Or break away, if the chance favour us.

But Naoise turns to the musicians with a question:

> Had you been there when that man and his queen
> Played at so high a game, could you have found
> An ancient poem for the praise of it?

And Deirdre at once responds to this note:

> O, singing women, set it down in a book,
> That love is all we need, even though it is
> But the last drops we gather up like this;
> And though the drops are all we have known of life,
> For we have been most friendless—praise us for it,
> And praise the double sunset, for naught's lacking
> But a good end to the long, cloudy day.

Neither in poetry nor out of it, surely, does a woman dignify her own and her lover's death by calling it a double sunset and bidding singers set to work. This is the posturing of Shaw's

Ozymandias and Cleopatra-Semiramis in *As Far As Thought Can Reach*. Remotely behind it, indeed—

> Women, if I die,
> If Naoise die this night, how will you praise?
> What words seek out?

—there does lie something of the heroic idea. But it is not to a charade that Sarpedon exhorts Glaucus, nor has he any appearance of cocking an eye at Homer. Yeats's persuasion —recognized by himself as immature—that only ancient things and the stuff of dreams are beautiful perpetually threatens him with a sort of infinite regress of antiquities. In *Deirdre* this almost fatally falsifies the terror and pity of the tragedy.

Yet, whatever the immediate effect of the scene in which the lovers play at chess, it marks an important step in the development of Yeats's thought, since it virtually dramatizes the psychological origin of his doctrine of the Image, of

> Kings that have cried 'I am great Alexander
> Or Caesar come again'.

Moreover it was hard upon the first production of *Deirdre* that he began work on *The Player Queen*, in which he was to endeavour to give expression to the related doctrine of the Mask. 'All happiness', he wrote in his diary in 1909, 'depends on the energy to assume the mask of some other self . . .; all joyous or creative life is a rebirth as something not oneself.' But for long this new matter proved intractable for drama:

> I wasted the best working months of several years in an attempt to write a poetical play where every character became an example of the finding or not finding of what I have called the Antithetical Self; and because passion and not thought makes tragedy, what I made had neither simplicity nor life.

The Player Queen was to finish up, ten years later, not as poetic tragedy but as prose farce—prose farce retaining, nevertheless, the impress of a theory of personality which haunted Yeats, and which was to be most fully—if gnomically—set out in *Per Amica Silentia Lunae* (1918).

6

'Theatre business, management of men' absorbed much of his energy throughout the opening decade of the century, and

combined with other influences, public and private, to bring
about a change of poetic temper first made decisively evident
in *The Green Helmet and Other Poems* (1910, augmented edition
1912) and successively reinforced in *Responsibilities* (1914), *The
Wild Swans at Coole* (1917), and *Michael Robartes and the Dancer*
(1920)—a volume bringing us to the threshold of Yeats's major
creative period in his later fifties and early sixties. *The Green
Helmet* itself, styled 'an heroic farce', presents Cuchulain and
others of his legend enacting, in robustly jangling measures,
a rough-and-tumble version of *Sir Gawain and the Green Knight*.
Produced in 1910, it constitutes a somewhat ambiguous epilogue
to Yeats's series of poetic dramas on antique subjects. Although
Yeats regularly expressed satisfaction with these heroic plays for
the Abbey, there was much in his manner to hint that his professions were accompanied by substantial reserves. His actors
had long practised themselves in peasant roles, so that when they
moved across the stage as kings and princes it was seldom
without some disturbing suggestion of being late-risen from the
people. Yeats was sensitive alike to these insufficiencies and to
an intermittent tendency in his audience to receive rather
tepidly the whole attempt to dig theatrical entertainment out
of the freshly assembled Irish legendary material. He chafed
inwardly—even to the extent, perhaps, of being tempted by
Miss Horniman's exhortation, so boldly defiant of Lady
Gregory and Coole, to abandon 'hole-and-corner Irish ideas'.
And when Mr. Ezra Pound eventually introduced him to the
Nōh drama of Japan he began to lose interest in a popular
audience. When the first of his 'Plays for Dancers' was produced
in Lady Cunard's drawing-room in 1916, and repeated a few
days later in the presence of Queen Alexandra, it became clear
that Yeats had moved a long way from the *milieu* of his first
dramatic inspiration.

Some external events of this period are important. In 1907,
along with Lady Gregory and her son Robert, he visited Italy.
About the same time he became well acquainted with Mr.
Pound, upon whose early verse he had been an influence, and
who now gave him the benefit both of his own inspired rag-bag
of an education and of a general benevolent surveillance which
extended to lessons in fencing. In 1912 he began to take part in
what became known as the Lane controversy. He had known
Hugh Lane as a young picture-dealer, little interested in

literature, since 1901. They had disliked each other. But Lane
was Lady Gregory's nephew, and when the municipal authorities
of Dublin refused to accept the conditions under which Lane
proposed to present the city with his important collection of
modern French paintings, Yeats—who had discovered in himself at the time of the outcry against Synge a very sufficient
flair for bending his poetry to public issues—entered the fray
with notable results. Later, the events of Easter 1916 moved
him deeply and confirmed him in the exercise of this power.
They had too, the private consequence of bringing about the
widowhood of Maud Gonne, who continued still to be the
inspiration of some of his finest verse. The relationship is not
easy to elucidate. In the latter part of 1908 they appear to have
enjoyed a period of intense communion with strongly magical
overtones, but a few weeks later he recorded in his journal that
she had never really understood his plans or nature or ideas.
In August 1916 he visited her in Normandy and spoke again of
marriage. A year later he was again in Normandy, and this
time made a proposal to her adoptive daughter Iseult. In
September he repeated the proposal in the form of an ultimatum. Iseult rejected this, and in October Yeats married Miss
Hyde-Lees, one of a number of eligible young women approved
(some of them better to be described as sponsored) by Lady
Gregory—who had been alarmed by certain embarrassing
consequences which had for a time appeared to threaten Yeats
as the result of an unsatisfactory liaison in which he had involved himself, and who was resolved that now, at fifty-two,
he should settle down. At least he was already a householder,
since he had bought, some years earlier, a ruined tower once
forming part of a Norman castle on former Gregory land at
Ballylee. This he now proposed to re-edify. As a residence it
must be more romantic than commodious, but it brought
beautifully together the aristocratic with the contemplative
idea. And Yeats—thus finding a home at the conclusion of a
series of domestic events not untouched by absurdity—was to
create from it one of the most majestic symbols that modern
poetry can show.

7

His long involvement with a struggling and unpopular
national theatre brought its rewards. It uncovered in him the

underlying toughness which his father had so notably failed to see and declare in his portraits. But also—and much more importantly—his actual listening to what makes, and what fails to make, an impact through the proscenium arch gave a new discipline to his ear. On this, indeed, one must not set excessive emphasis. In Yeats's artistic development at the time, other, and some of them deeper, processes can be sensed as at work. But one is tempted at least to give primacy, among all that can be advanced, to a capacity to hear and develop new rhythms and new idioms. This is already evident in *In the Seven Woods*, a small collection of lyrics which had been published in 1903. The transitional character of the volume appears in the fact that, although carrying the sub-title *Poems chiefly of the Irish Heroic Age*, it includes 'Adam's Curse':

> We sat together at one summer's end,
> That beautiful mild woman, your close friend,
> And you and I, and talked of poetry.
> I said: 'A line will take us hours maybe;
> Yet if it does not seem a moment's thought,
> Our stitching and unstitching has been naught.
> Better go down upon your marrow-bones
> And scrub a kitchen pavement, or break stones
> Like an old pauper, in all kinds of weather;
> For to articulate sweet sounds together
> Is to work harder than all these.'

This poem, although it relapses at the close upon the old generalized melancholy, is more authentically aristocratic than any in what may be called the full-blown Urbino manner; it is in the tradition of Sidney's letters and Shelley's middle style. Technically, what distinguishes it is a new and colloquial syntax. In a number of the poems surrounding it there appears, if only fragmentarily, a radically new rhythmical organization:

> I thought of your beauty, and this arrow,
> Made out of a wild thought, is in my marrow.
> There's no man may look upon her, no man,
> As when newly grown to be a woman,
> Tall and noble but with face and bosom
> Delicate in colour as apple blossom. . . .
>
> O she had not these ways
> When all the wild summer was in her gaze. . . .

> They had hands like claws, and their knees
> Were twisted like the old thorn-trees
> By the waters.

These new effects stand side by side with others long familiar to us:

> I have no happiness in dreaming of Brycelinde,
> Nor Avalon the grass-green hollow, nor Joyous Isle,
> Where one found Lancelot crazed and hid him for a while;
> Nor Uladh, when Naoise had thrown a sail upon the wind;
> Nor lands that seem too dim to be burdens on the heart.

The sentiment, indeed, here would seem to be forward-looking; but again at the close of the poem there is contradiction or relapse:

> To dream of women whose beauty was folded in dismay,
> Even in an old story, is a burden not to be borne.

Yet, whether as too dim or too poignant, Uladh and Naoise are on their way out, and Tara, with its dream-women from the 'dove-grey faery lands', begins to fade behind

> Those topless towers
> Where Helen walked with her boy.

Indeed it is now Helen's image that the thought of Maud Gonne frequently evokes—this not, perhaps, with the highest appropriateness, but at least to august effect. What Yeats is chiefly searching for *is* august effect, 'a haughtier text'. Dublin —'this unmannerly town' in which he has laboured at unrequited tasks—is unfavourably compared with other localities:

> I might have lived,
> And you know well how great the longing has been,
> Where every day my footfall should have lit
> In the green shadow of Ferrara wall;
> Or climbed among the images of the past—
> The unperturbed and courtly images—
> Evening and morning, the steep street of Urbino
> To where the duchess and her people talked.

It is these particular 'images of the past' that he brings shatteringly to bear in the matter of Lane's pictures:

TO A WEALTHY MAN WHO PROMISED A SECOND SUBSCRIPTION TO THE DUBLIN MUNICIPAL GALLERY IF IT WERE PROVED THE PEOPLE WANTED PICTURES

You gave, but will not give again
Until enough of Paudeen's pence
By Biddy's halfpennies have lain
To be 'some sort of evidence',
Before you'll put your guineas down,
That things it were a pride to give
Are what the blind and ignorant town
Imagines best to make it thrive.
What cared Duke Ercole, that bid
His mummers to the market-place,
What th'onion-sellers thought or did
So that his Plautus set the pace
For the Italian comedies?
And Guidobaldo, when he made
That grammar school of courtesies
Where wit and beauty learned their trade
Upon Urbino's windy hill,
Had sent no runners to and fro
That he might learn the shepherds' will.
And when they drove out Cosimo,
Indifferent how the rancour ran,
He gave the hours they had set free
To Michelozzo's latest plan
For the San Marco Library,
Whence turbulent Italy should draw
Delight in Art whose end is peace,
In logic and in natural law
By sucking at the dugs of Greece.

Your open hand but shows our loss,
For he knew better how to live.
Let Paudeens play at pitch and toss,
Look up in the sun's eye and give
What the exultant heart calls good
That some new day may breed the best
Because you gave, not what they would,
But the right twigs for an eagle's nest!

There is a sense in which this is inflated much beyond its occasion. We may hesitate, moreover, to respond to it from a consciousness of how close it brings us in feeling to the Yeats

who was too haughty to seem to recognize in the street other
than his most humble acquaintance. Yet it is magnificent; what
it does, it does better than any English poem before it. And it is
perhaps a sign of the authenticity of the attitude presented that
in the immediately succeeding poem Yeats can get the same
effect of immense elevation from entirely native material:

> Was it for this the wild geese spread
> The grey wing upon every tide;
> For this that all that blood was shed,
> For this Edward Fitzgerald died,
> And Robert Emmet and Wolfe Tone,
> All that delirium of the brave?
> Romantic Ireland's dead and gone,
> It's with O'Leary in the grave.

Joyce's 'Ivy Day in the Committee Room' does not effect a
more startling transmutation of vulgar political sentiment than
does this. And although there is certainly a little too much of
Paudeen, Biddy, and their 'greasy till' in these poems, all have
the same high felicity of expression. Even 'To a Shade', in which
Yeats gratifies his friends by equating Lane quite absurdly with
Parnell, is admirable in this regard.

   In the later political poems, those composed immediately
after the Rising of 1916, Yeats faces a more difficult problem,
and one certainly not to be solved by any recourse to the bravura
manner so successfully employed in the earlier series. The
society into which he had moved was almost solid for Ireland's
participation in the war against Germany. He was himself
opposed to violent revolution, on the score alike of simple instinct, intellectual conviction, and prudent care for the incipi-
ently fanatical woman he loved. Yet at the least he owed the
men of the Rising a palinode. Jealousy had made his pen too
free in contempt of a populace to whom Maud Gonne had, he
thought, given too much. From that populace had now come
a display of desperate courage which he admired. And he
admired more than this, since he saw the self-immolation of at
least some of the rebels as an act of high intellectual clarity:
a perception (to which he gives dramatic force in 'The Rose
Tree') that the violent measures of repression to which the
English authorities would be prompted must in fact finally
bring about the independence of Ireland. Faced with this

delicate situation, Yeats writes with nothing either of the grand manner or of vigorous political engagement. He writes *in propria persona*, with the dignity of personal utterance which he had first captured in those prefatory lines to *Responsibilities* in which he had invoked the Butlers and Armstrongs in whose ancestry he took pride. 'Easter, 1916' begins simply:

> I have met them at close of day
> Coming with vivid faces
> From counter or desk among grey
> Eighteenth-century houses.

On the counter there may well have been a 'greasy till', but these are the men he must now honour. And among them is one whom he had supposed 'a drunken, vainglorious lout', MacBride:

> He had done most bitter wrong
> To some who are near my heart,
> Yet I number him in the song . . . .

Yeats's private concerns take their place with Miltonic confidence in the picture, and the poem passes on through a sombre consideration of the indurating effect of long-continued political passion to a final measured celebration of the rebels:

> We know their dream; enough
> To know they dreamed and are dead;
> And what if excess of love
> Bewildered them till they died?
> I write it out in a verse—
> MacDonagh and MacBride
> And Connolly and Pearse
> Now and in time to be,
> Wherever green is worn,
> Are changed, changed utterly:
> A terrible beauty is born.

The wearing of the green comes in with muted effect, and it was to be some years before Yeats elevated Connolly and Pearse to quasi-mythological status. These poems are not Miltonic in the sense of being any sort of trumpet-call. They are a finely calculated artistic achievement within which there does lurk some small residuum of equivocal effect. Maud Gonne was not pleased with them.

Honouring counter and desk was not to become habitual
with Yeats. In the introductory verses to *Responsibilities*, indeed,
merchants, having been among his own forebears, had been
celebrated along with scholars, the poet's scorn being reserved
for 'hucksters', plainly an inferior caste. But in 'At Galway
Races', a poem of about the same period, he takes satisfaction
in the fact that 'we' had

> horsemen for companions,
> Before the merchant and the clerk
> Breathed on the world with timid breath;

and it was to be a 'horseman' whom he was to summon, in
one of his last poems, to contemplate his epitaph in the churchyard at Drumcliffe. He had noted in about 1909 that his mind
was dwelling 'more and more on ideas of class'; and Maud
Gonne was to declare tartly that, finding himself among the
comfortable and well-fed, he dignified them too indiscrimi-
nately with the appellation of 'distinguished persons'. The
scorn which is the obverse of this facile admiration was to
ramify pretty widely. The scholars who, like the merchants,
are honoured when Yeatses or Butlers, are elsewhere brilliantly
ridiculed as characteristically people of shambling deportment
and impoverished society—and this even though Yeats's
respect for learning had the exaggerated quality sometimes
remarked in those who regard it from afar. He laments that his
own professional occasions have made him 'notorious'. It
cannot be otherwise, since the chance of fame has perished long
ago, along with the 'ancient ceremony' of which it was but
a part. So now

> all my priceless things
> Are but a post the passing dogs defile.

This is indeed to know the dyer's hand and to be a motley to the
view. Yet we must often enough be checked in any disposition
to make fun of this aspect of Yeats's feeling by the overwhelming excellence of the poetry. In 'The Fisherman' the storm of
contempt which reaches its climax in

> The beating down of the wise
> And great Art beaten down

is superbly phrased in itself, and yet more superbly framed

within the vision of the imagined 'wise and simple man' for whom the poet is resolved, before he is old, to write

> one
> Poem maybe as cold
> And passionate as the dawn.[1]

Habitually to lament that 'the weak lay hand on what the strong has done' is doubtless to court great peril of the spirit, and it cannot be said that Yeats escapes entirely undamaged. Sometimes, too, we must feel that his conception of 'ceremony' as the fine flower of life lived amid hereditary possessions and securities holds not a little of the superficial; we are reminded of those graces of entering a box at the opera and making presentations correctly or felicitously which seemed to Henry James—or at least to Lambert Strether—such exquisite fruits of Chad Newsome's residence in Paris. And sometimes—when the 'beating down of the wise' appears to be associated with a reverse suffered by Coole Hall—we may be inclined to think that a laudable loyalty is getting a little out of hand. Yet before Coole too we cease to be amused when we come to 'Upon a House Shaken by the Land Agitation'.

Yeats had heard with dismay of a reduction of rent ordered by the courts, and he confided to his diary the fear that soon 'all must make their living', whereas it is the value of Coole that 'here there has been no compelled labour, no poverty-thwarted impulse'. To his diary, too, he committed at least two prose drafts for a poem suggested by the occasion—of which this is one:

How should the world gain if this house failed, even though a hundred little houses were the better for it, for here power has gone forth, or lingered giving energy, precision; it gives to a far people beneficent rule, and still under its roof loving intellect is sweetened by old memories, of its descents from far off; how should the world be better if the wren's nest flourish and the eagle's house is scattered?

Lady Gregory's husband had been a Governor of Ceylon, which explains the far people who are given beneficent rule: a point which, in the poem ultimately evolved from this note, is only touched in lightly in the antepenultimate line:

> How should the world be luckier if this house,
> Where passion and precision have been one
> Time out of mind, became too ruinous
> To breed the lidless eye that loves the sun?

[1] Yeats records that he copied this phrase from a letter of his father's.

And the sweet laughing eagle thoughts that grow
Where wings have memory of wings, and all
That comes of the best knit to the best? Although
Mean roof-trees were the sturdier for its fall,
How should their luck run high enough to reach
The gifts that govern men, and after these
To gradual Time's last gift, a written speech
Wrought of high laughter, loveliness and ease?

A performance so decidedly a courtier's has need of all the
courtliness the poet can summon, and Yeats's gifts have not
failed him. It is a beautiful and almost splendid poem. Yet
Yeats's feeling for Coole, and for the social order with which he
linked it, makes its most advantageous appearance in poems
where it supports rather than supplies the main theme. This
holds of 'In Memory of Major Robert Gregory', an irregular
elegy occasioned by the death on active service of Lady
Gregory's only son. The manner in which the young man takes
his place in a roll-call of the dead—Lionel Johnson; 'that en-
quiring man John Synge'; old George Pollexfen, 'in muscular
youth well known to Mayo men'—is moving in itself and
brilliantly dissipates any effect of excess in what Yeats has to
record in praise of the latest among them. In the whole range
of his poetry up to 1921—or at least in those categories of it
so far considered—there is perhaps only a single poem quite
certainly finer than this. It is 'A Prayer for my Daughter', in
which Yeats wishes that his child should enjoy moderate
beauty, be trained in courtesy, and live 'rooted in one dear
perpetual place'. But in Ireland, as elsewhere, an old order was
passing. Coole Hall was demolished only a few years after the
death of the poet it had sheltered and instructed.

8

TO BE CARVED ON A STONE AT THOOR BALLYLEE

I, the poet William Yeats,
With old mill boards and sea-green slates,
And smithy work from the Gort forge,
Restored this tower for my wife George;
And may these characters remain
When all is ruin once again.

In closing *Michael Robartes and the Dancer* with these lines Yeats is formally providing his poetry with a new centre. Irish mythology has failed him, and he will henceforth be his own Cuchulain, the focal point in whatever sustaining myth his art discovers. His evolving relationship to his poetry is well expressed when Yeats the diurnal man actually for certain seasons of the year inhabits the tower which Yeats the poet is to adopt as a major organizing symbol. He was one, it must be acknowledged, accepting heavy burdens. He had already his public role, one which had to be sustained in part in a small and malicious society, in an air full of the wit and resentment of lesser men. Yeats had no appearance of endeavouring to elude the consciousness of himself as being what he was: the peer of Keats and Tennyson. Dublin found this unendearing. Equally a strain was his continuing role as the retrospective lover of Maud Gonne. And here an adequate consideration of the term 'role' might lead us—were it not so desperately difficult—towards the heart of his mystery. For what are we to say of a pose so consciously maintained which yet produces in 'The Cold Heaven' as intense an outcrying of love as was ever disciplined by art? And now comes this further commitment—really quite different in kind from what might seem analogous commitments in Wordsworth and Byron—to accept the defining of his own representative character as the principal charge upon his poetic energy. He was by nature extremely conscious of self— and of conflicting selves. He was even constrained to dramatize his uncertainties in a fashion that led to his being frequently indicted of intolerable affectation. A story is told in Oxford (where he lived for some time) of his standing before a pillar-box in an empty street and—without any knowledge of being observed—miming a searing conflict of impulses in the matter of dropping a letter through the slot. And there is a graphic passage in *The Bounty of Sweden* (1925) in which he admits to just this sort of behaviour. He was vividly aware alike of the possibilities and of the perils of being his own artificer. In 1909 he wrote, and in 1926 published, this diary entry:

To oppose the new ill-breeding of Ireland, which may in a few years destroy all that has given Ireland a distinguished name in the world ... I can only set up a secondary or interior personality created out of the tradition of myself, and this personality (alas, only possible to me in my writings) must be always gracious and simple.

This notion, the notion of 'style, personality—deliberately

adopted and therefore a mask', becomes very important to him. He is presently to be writing both verse and prose designed to give it a rational and philosophic basis.

Where enigmatic matter begins to percolate into the still predominantly lucid *Wild Swans at Coole*, it is often Yeats's increasingly intricate sense of himself that is at work. 'The Hawk' may serve as an illustration:

> 'Call down the hawk from the air;
> Let him be hooded or caged
> Till the yellow eye has grown mild,
> For larder and spit are bare,
> The old cook enraged,
> The scullion gone wild.'

> 'I will not be clapped in a hood,
> Nor a cage, nor alight upon wrist,
> Now I have learnt to be proud
> Hovering over the wood
> In the broken mist
> Or tumbling cloud.'

> 'What tumbling cloud did you cleave,
> Yellow-eyed hawk of the mind,
> Last evening? that I, who had sat
> Dumbfounded before a knave,
> Should give to my friend
> A pretence of wit.'

It is a hard poem, and we are not much assisted in interpretation by the discovery of another 'old cook' in a poem yet harder: 'The Black Tower', which is among the very last of Yeats's compositions. If we accept one commentator's suggestion that cook and scullion stand for all that is grossest in man, we may conclude that we are being called upon to admire the hawk as representing the pure intellect's preference for elevated situations, and refusal to concern itself with the mundane business of foraging for the larder. But in *The Trembling of the Veil* Yeats himself gives hawk and cook a somewhat different context. He has been oppressed by a sense that the world is 'now but a bundle of fragments' and that 'Unity of Being' has as its enemy 'abstraction, meaning by abstraction not the distinction but the isolation of occupation, or class or faculty'; and he cites the first verse of the poem as expressing what he means.

Viewed in this light the intractability of the hawk is not admirable, but represents a tendency of the abstracting intellect
inimical to social cohesion. Something of the sort is implicit in
the nearly contemporary *At the Hawk's Well* (acted 1916), the first
of the 'Plays for Dancers', in which a hawk-woman distracts
the young Cuchulain from his search for a magical spring
symbolizing the survival of the integrated values of a heroic age.
The idea is expressed more clearly in 'The Second Coming', a
majestic and alarming poem, without personal reference, in
which 'things fall apart' when 'the falcon cannot hear the
falconer'. But one point of significance in 'The Hawk', whatever
its precise interpretation, is its manifest origin in the poet's
sense of his own inadequate response to some specific and
representative private occasion. He has failed to cope with
a knave, and he has offered a friend what is not good enough;
and the cause of this appears to lie in his having indulged in
debilitating abstract speculation. Yet, largely because the main
effect of the poem is to present the hawk as a creature compact
of energy and pride, and to some extent because the third
verse turns out not to be the rejoinder to the hawk's reply which
the formal structure of the piece would lead us to expect, the
total impression is confused. Yeats is undecided whether to
take satisfaction in the circumstance that (as he expresses it in
an almost immediately succeeding poem) his

> virtues are the definitions
> Of the analytic mind

or to regret the extreme of subjectivity (of which he elsewhere
declares both hawk and swan to be 'natural symbols') the social
consequences of which can prove so disabling. And this is
characteristic. Almost literally, he doesn't know what to make
of himself. From this predicament come both the theory of the
Mask propounded in *Per Amica Silentia Lunae* and the impulse
to withdraw upon an irrational and deterministic view of the
formation of character which prompts him to the composition
of *A Vision*. He is a divided man. Poetry, he says, is bred 'of the
quarrel with ourselves'. 'We sing amid our uncertainty.'

    It is perhaps a not altogether random generalization upon
poets that, when they do not die young, they grow old swiftly
and live long. Mr. T. S. Eliot's precocious discovery of himself
as an aged eagle is well known. Yeats at least consents to reach

his early fifties—indeed to marry and address himself to the business of begetting children—before he adopts a *persona* expressing this doddering-complex. It is in *The Wild Swans at Coole*, a forward-looking volume in many regards, that he paves the way for the enraged and lustful old man who is to be among the most formidable impersonations of his actual later years:

> I am worn out with dreams;
> A weather-worn, marble triton
> Among the streams;
> And all day long I look
> Upon this lady's beauty
> As though I had found in a book
> A pictured beauty,
> Pleased to have filled the eyes
> Or the discerning ears,
> Delighted to be but wise,
> For men improve with the years;
> And yet, and yet,
> Is this my dream, or the truth?
> O would that we had met
> When I had my burning youth!
> But I grow old among dreams,
> A weather-worn, marble triton
> Among the streams.

'Men Improve with the Years' is the ironic title of this poem. Of kindred inspiration is 'The Living Beauty', which appears to have been printed upon approximately the first anniversary of his marriage:

> I bade, because the wick and oil are spent
> And frozen are the channels of the blood,
> My discontented heart to draw content
> From beauty that is cast out of a mould
> In bronze, or that in dazzling marble appears . . . .

There is a group of poems on this theme, the most succinct being 'A Song', with the refrain:

> *O who could have foretold*
> *That the heart grows old?*

and the entirely stark statement:

> I have not lost desire
> But the heart that I had.

Along with this go, in quite a new manner, direct evocations of sexual encounter. Solomon and Sheba are made to behave in a manner that Naoise and Deirdre would have considered highly indecorous:

> Harshness of their desire
> That made them stretch and yawn,
> Pleasure that comes with sleep,
> Shudder that made them one . . . .

The shudder is to recur in 'Leda and the Swan'. And Leda herself—'that sprightly girl trodden by a bird'—here puts in a preliminary appearance in 'His Phoenix', an uncharacteristically gay and gallant love poem. Another prelusive strain is found in a group of poems dealing with beggars: Billy Byrne, who proposes to 'pick a pocket and snug it in a feather-bed'— but not before indulging in a fancy for the sun and moon as 'golden king and silver lady' which has led some critics to credit him with much arcane philosophy; and others who exhibit the 'frenzy' that later naked wretches are regularly to indulge, or who engage in violent dispute, with the robust consequence of 'commingling lice and blood'. 'The Magi' and 'The Dolls'—both in *Responsibilities*—are early examples of poems hinting some esoteric significance, and are designed to stand to one another in a relationship which Yeats does not illuminate very fully in a note appended to the second. At least the Magi are figures in a cyclical vision of history; and the dolls, although undignified, have an advantage over the baby in not being dying animals. The dolls are enraged by the mystery of human birth. The Magi are perpetually drawn to it and perpetually disillusioned.

9

It is in the latter part of *The Wild Swans at Coole*, in poems composed shortly before the publication of the volume in 1917, that we come upon a first cluster of poems enigmatic in a new way. They are contemporaneous with the beginnings of Mrs. Yeats's automatic writing, and are related—although the relation is sometimes in itself perplexing—to the 'explanation of life' which Yeats evolved from a study of the automatic writing, and to which he gave the title of *A Vision*. To what we can make of this work, whether in its first (1925) or drastically revised (1937) form, we are obliged henceforth frequently to appeal, since much that we immediately acknowledge as valuable in the later poetry contains a large admixture of matter that only some understanding of Yeats's elaborate 'system' seems to hold out any hope of rendering fully intelligible. In addressing ourselves to later Yeats it seems necessary to agree with Professor Wind when he is approaching a field of plastic art in which similar problems present themselves: 'Aesthetically speaking, there can be no doubt that the presence of unresolved residues of meaning is an obstacle to the enjoyment of art.' We shall be insufficient students, that is to say, if we accept what is difficult merely as attractive incantation. This has been fully recognized by many who have over the past twenty years written on the poems. Perhaps an opposite danger does exist: that of which Keats was aware when he wrote that in a great poet the sense of beauty overcomes every other consideration and that this must involve him in accepting 'uncertainties, mysteries'. Yeats's attack in *A Vision* upon his own region of uncertainties and mysteries was not very sheerly a poet's, and there are limits to the book's utility in interpreting his poetry.

Yeats's New Astrology—for *A Vision* is essentially that—is not wholly new, since Mrs. Yeats's supernal and unknown instructors have clearly enjoyed more than a nodding acquaintance with earlier instructors, mundane and identifiable, of Yeats's own. It is perhaps because there is a substantial continuity in the esoteric side of his work from the beginning that the new poems make their way with us as quickly as they do. 'Lines Written in Dejection' was composed in 1915, and in it Yeats's sense of himself as at fifty an ageing man—a sense elsewhere expressed in the clear image of the 'weather-worn marble triton'—is more darkly intimated:

> When have I last looked on
> The round green eyes and the long wavering bodies
> Of the dark leopards of the moon?
> All the wild witches, those most noble ladies,
> For all their broom-sticks and their tears,
> Their angry tears, are gone.
> The holy centaurs of the hills are vanished;
> I have nothing but the embittered sun;
> Banished heroic mother moon and vanished,

> And now that I have come to fifty years
> I must endure the timid sun.

On this Mr. Henn comments demurely that 'women have fallen into perspective'. But they have done so, it seems, because the poet has passed out of a lunar and within a solar influence. It is entirely appropriately that Mr. Henn later reconsiders the poem, with its teasing sun–moon, male–female, timid–heroic cross-correspondence, in the context of a system not supposed to have been adumbrated until several years after the poem's composition.

'Ego Dominus Tuus' is another poem that antedates the automatic writing, and, like the prose *Per Amica Silentia Lunae*, to which it was prefixed and is closely related, it supports the hypothesis—to which much other evidence points—that the basis of *A Vision* was forming well before Yeats's marriage, and that the book took its effective origin in speculations about human personality which were themselves prompted by a keen sense of his own internal disharmonies. If one is uncomfortable about oneself there may be solace in the thought that one's disposition has been determined by the stars or merely by the moon. Conflict, as it sharpens, may be fatalistically viewed in terms of antithetical selves involved in a dance which obeys the majestic and imperturbable gyration of celestial objects. 'Ego Dominus Tuus' confines itself to debating, amid august Dantesque associations intimated in the title, the artist's necessary concern with the seeking of an antiself. Dante, because laughed at for his lechery, invented the lover of Beatrice. Keats was constrained to create a happy art, being the deprived and 'coarse-bred son of a livery-stable keeper'. We can only admire the skill that contrives to edge us from these slightly jejune considerations to:

> I call to the mysterious one who yet
> Shall walk the wet sands by the edge of the stream
> And look most like me, being indeed my double,
> And prove of all imaginable things
> The most unlike, being my anti-self,
> And, standing by these characters, disclose
> All that I seek.

That Keats in fact did more than make 'luxuriant song'—that he essayed a far deeper inquisition into the poetic character than

is here attempted—emerges curiously as something of which
Yeats is aware. The passage immediately preceding the introduction of Keats's name will be found to betray by the very
cadence of the verse that Yeats has been pondering 'The Fall
of Hyperion'.

'The Phases of the Moon' takes wider ground, being in fact
a summary exposition of the central system of *A Vision*, a little
relieved of its inherent didactic bleakness by an ingenious and
characteristically equivocal induction. The poet is in his tower
at night, poring over his books in vain. Noticing his lighted
window, Michael Robartes and Owen Aherne pause as they
pass by in the darkness, and discuss the invisible student and his
chances in a somewhat hostile and derogatory way. He has

> chosen this place to live in
> Because, it may be, of the candle-light
> From the far tower where Milton's Platonist
> Sat late, or Shelley's visionary prince. . . .
> And now he seeks in book or manuscript
> What he shall never find.

Yeats has taken on the airs of a sage, but it is Robartes and
Aherne who could, were they not mysteriously ill-disposed,
expound to him the entire lunar mystery. Instead, they expound
it to each other:

> *Aherne.* Sing me the changes of the moon once more. . . .
> *Robartes.* Twenty-and-eight the phases of the moon,
> The full and the moon's dark and all the crescents.
> Twenty-and-eight, and yet but six-and-twenty
> The cradles that a man must needs be rocked in:
> For there's no human life at the full or the dark.

A compressed exposition of the significance of certain of the
phases follows—

> Eleven pass, and then
> Athene takes Achilles by the hair,
> Hector is in the dust, Nietzsche is born,
> Because the hero's crescent is the twelfth—

until eventually we learn that:

> Hunchback and Saint and Fool are the last crescents.

We can hardly feel other than that we are being introduced, by shock tactics, to some singularly arbitrary propositions. In fathering what is in fact his own invention upon characters summoned for the purpose from his own past fiction, Yeats is taking the same sort of evasive action as is represented by the whole frivolous rigmarole of Giraldus and Kusta ben Luka which, in the first edition of *A Vision*, he whimsically spins to account for the book's existence. But at least after reading 'The Phases of the Moon' we recognize that an examination of *A Vision* itself can no longer be deferred.

10

Chaucer's Franklin—in a place which we know to have been familiar to Yeats—has occasion to speak of a work on natural magic:

> Which book spak muchel of the operaciouns,
> Touchinge the eighte and twenty mansiouns
> That longen to the mone, and swich folye.

That to believe in such 'operaciouns' is indeed 'folye' has been the opinion of most educated men for some hundreds of years; we are all more or less in agreement with Shakespeare's Edmund in judging it a poor thing to subscribe to spherical predominance. *A Vision* accepts that predominance, and sees alike the spectacle of universal history and the disposition and progression of individual human beings as ruled by planetary influence. And indeed if we sufficiently juggle with the stars it is not difficult to make ourselves, being represented as their tennis-balls, seem to bounce on intelligible principles. *A Vision*, generated from an anxiety felt by a devotee of magic to find such principles, holds singularly little intellectual persuasiveness. What gives it a certain power—and its considerable utility for the development of Yeats's poetry—is its odd manner of telescoping a traditional astrological determinism with some irregular derivative of the Hegelian dialectic. The Heavens revolve, and a Golden or a Brazen Age returns. But as well as the Great Wheel there are the Gyres, interpreted in terms of which man shows as involved, to some artistically sufficient effect of drama and the dynamic, in a perpetual action of developing and resolving contradictions.

If we are to arrive at some understanding of *A Vision*, however, it is with the 'eighte and twenty mansiouns' of traditional
astrology that we must begin. Or rather it is with these as
Yeats qualifies them:

> Twenty-and-eight, and yet but six-and-twenty
> The cradles that a man must needs be rocked in.

Chaucer and his authorities are innocent of this mysterious
retrenchment. It is at the heart of Yeats's system.

On Yeats's Great Wheel the twenty-eight phases of the moon
are represented as disposed successively in an anti-clockwise
direction:

> As the lunar circle narrows to a crescent and as the crescent
> narrows to a still narrower crescent, the Moon approaches the Sun,
> falls as it were under his influence. . . . They may be coloured gold
> and silver respectively. The first phase is therefore full Sun as it
> were, and the 15th Phase full Moon, while Phases 8 and 22 are half
> Sun and half Moon.

The primary association of each phase is with a representative
type of human personality, and each is so disposed as to be in
direct opposition, across the hub of the Wheel, to its antitype.
But as 'the Sun is objective man and the Moon subjective man,
or more properly the Sun is *primary* man and the Moon *antithetical* man', and as every conceivable human type must represent a mingling of, and tension between, these elements, it
follows that the 1st and 15th phases, representing complete
objectivity and complete subjectivity respectively, have no
human representatives. Solar, objective or primary man, and
lunar, subjective or antithetical man, are only abstractions. If
they are capable of representation, it is only in a realm of
spirits. This is why there are only 26 'cradles' in 'The Phases
of the Moon'.

The grand opposition among the types of personality, then,
is between 12 that are preponderantly objective and 12 that are
preponderantly subjective (terms which Yeats seeks to define
by reference to the then uncompleted *New English Dictionary*),
while the 8th and 22nd phases each represent the special case
of an equilibrium between these elements. In the first edition
of *A Vision* there is an attempt to name individuals exemplifying
the phases. For this enterprise Yeats was not very abundantly
equipped by either historical or biographical study, and the

groupings appear sometimes shrewd and sometimes freakish. Thus under the 24th phase we find 'Queen Victoria, Galsworthy, a certain friend'; the 25th brings together Luther and Newman; the 27th, that of the Saint, is represented by Socrates and Pascal; while the 26th and the 28th, respectively those of the Hunchback and the Fool, are for some reason regarded as insusceptible of exemplification. And since each type confronts its Mask or antitype across the Wheel, the historical personages must have their correspondences. Thus the preponderantly objective Luther and Newman of the 25th phase balance the preponderantly subjective Savonarola and Spinoza of the 11th.

The main purpose of this part of *A Vision* thus exhibits itself as the classification of human types, one type being more, or less, approximated to another in terms of a varying admixture of elements; and the whole essentially classificatory system being lent a certain dynamic quality by the conception of mysteriously pregnant and fateful tensions as existing between type and antitype. But on top of all this come intimidating complications. The Wheel is not merely a collection of mansions within the precincts of which individuals may be born and repose. It is also a route along at least some part of which an individual may be destined to travel—as when, in 'Lines written in Dejection', the poet sees himself making the radical transition from antithetical to primary, from 'heroic mother moon' to 'timid sun'. This represents the first complication. And when, in 'The Phases of the Moon', 'Athene takes Achilles by the hair' and says—or says in Pope's *Iliad*—

> Let great *Achilles*, to the Gods resign'd,
> To reason yield the empire o'er his mind

we apprehend that 'Hector is in the dust, Nietzsche is born', because universal history itself is on the Wheel, and must ineluctably move from phase to phase. This cosmic progress is a second complication, and the involving of the whole system with a theory of reincarnation is a third. Moreover an individual, having during a single lifetime his natural domicile within one phase, may not merely be constrained to a pilgrimage through the others. He may also, at the cosmic level, have to live out his life at some quite discrepant point on the Wheel. A great deal of discomfort may be accounted for in this way. Thus Yeats himself, inhabiting naturally the 17th phase in the good company of Dante and Shelley and being therefore a preponderantly subjective, antithetical, and lunar man, has to put up with living in, or into, cosmic phase 23—which, although honoured at one level by finding its examples in Rembrandt and Synge, is at the other level variously disagreeable, being for instance characterized by the development of physical and economic science.

Yeats had never shown much predisposition towards the exacter disciplines. Geometry, for example, is recorded as being the only branch of mathematical knowledge with which he made much progress at school. There is a lot of geometry in *A Vision*. Some of it cannot have been very seriously intended— or rather seems to evince the Mirandolan tendency, already remarked, to pursue Truth seriously enough, while yet being prepared to unveil the mysterious divinity only behind sufficiently obfuscating screens of one's own devising. Joyce was to make fun in *Finnegans Wake* of some of the cat's-cradle barriers that Yeats spreads across his page. Nevertheless one of the geometrical constructions is of unquestioned importance, since it expresses, more vividly than does the Great Wheel, Yeats's conception of the dynamic forces at play alike in the individual human personality and in the successive and broadly recurrent cycles of universal history. This is the structure of two interpenetrating cones, equal in volume, identical in proportions, and disposed upon a common axis, so that the apex of each is at rest upon the centre of the base of the other. It is a precise figure. If one of the cones is regarded as in principle solar, objective, or primary, and the other as in principle lunar, subjective, or antithetical, it is clear that we have, at the midpoint of the figure, a state of affairs corresponding to the 8th and 22nd phases of the Wheel, where there is an exact balance between the two dispositions. And, according as we move in one direction or the other, we shall find unequal admixtures again corresponding to phases on the Wheel, the 1st and 15th phases representing the bases of the solar and lunar cones respectively. The gyres, if thus regarded, have perhaps a certain novelty which the idea of the Great Wheel lacks. But the image is inert, and would appear to have nothing in particular to recommend it. If, however, the cones be considered rather as notional, being the volumes successively defined by two expanding spirals travelling each as from an apex to a base, the constituting principle of the gyres as Yeats most commonly apprehended them is probably better caught. Movement on a gyre from primary to antithetical or antithetical to primary, although it may again be seen as an individual's destiny, seems now to be chiefly received as a matter of the majestic and epochal movement of history. The expanding spiral is subject to increasing stress as it moves; arrived at one or the other polar extreme—objectivity or subjectivity entire—some gathered centrifugal force destroys it, so that its elements fly apart and an era closes. But instantly the answering gyre begins to unwind, and upon the millennial movement towards sun or moon a millennial movement towards moon or sun succeeds.

This outline of *A Vision*, although it will certainly not satisfy devotees, is perhaps at least tolerably intelligible. Yeats's elaboration of it, which is strenuous, is not always intelligible, and certainly not always relevant to the study of his poetry. The whole work makes rather bleak reading, and even the real imaginative potency of the gyres is not easily distinguishable. It is with some tact that Mr. Henn, in his admirable exposition, provides us with a twopence-coloured version of what in Yeats is penny-plain, presenting these mysterious entities in an illustration suggestive of cloud-capped towers, and even introducing a falcon from 'The Second Coming' as hovering in the top right-hand corner. But nothing is likely to recommend Yeats's chronological speculations to the regard of the historian. Coldly received, his history is nonsense, and his psychology is nonsense, and his 'explanation of life' is nonsense too. Did he himself acknowledge this? To ask the question is to inquire too curiously. He is capable of speaking of the whole intricate contrivance as his 'lunar parable', and as something to be valued simply as affording him 'metaphors for poetry'. That it does indeed afford him such metaphors, and for such poetry, seems to argue that he had at least considerable power to suspend rational disbelief before his fantastic system upon imaginatively appropriate occasions. Moreover we must return to the significance of the two empty cradles. Achievement is impossible where the conditions for conflict are absent; and the system has a real potency in so far as it is an elaboration of Yeats's urgent sense of quest after integration—an integration which he conceives of as always to be sought in some balance or reconciliation of polar opposites. D. H. Lawrence, another representative writer of the century, is haunted by a similar apprehension, and it is the same sense of a divided being that produces the Shem and Shaun of *Finnegans Wake*. Yeats's system, quirky as in its ramifications it becomes, has its roots in his direct experience of his own poethood. His verse, he had come to believe, was best when 'hard and cold', and it became this only when it admitted the stresses that result from balancing Self against all that is Self's antithesis. 'If you are separated from your opposite, you consume yourself away.' It was upon this intuition of Yeats's that Mrs. Yeats's instructors may be said to have seized as the peg upon which to hang the whole dubious texture of their discourse. Moreover the intuition was one to which Yeats found that he could give both wide public application and something like heroic tone:

Nations, races, and individual men are unified by an image, or bundle of images, symbolical or evocative of the state of mind, which is of all states of mind not impossible, the most difficult to that man, race, or nation; because only the greatest obstacle that can be contemplated without despair, rouses the will to full intensity.

The nation most in focus here is doubtless Ireland, and we may arrive at an important constituting element of the whole system if we remember that Ireland was a nation still readily to be thought of as in a state of immaturity. Yeats associates its problems of maturation with his own, which were acute. 'The ignominy of boyhood' and 'the unfinished man and his pain' were very real to him. Indeed, the identity-crisis of adolescence, abnormally prolonged, is a key to his whole manner of taking experience. Every child knows that it must become that thing antithetical to itself, a man; every child experiments, in perplexity and anxiety, with roles suggested from the grown-up world around him: the striving to become such a one or such another is a large part of the business of turning into an adult. Actually, the child's development is indubitably to a great extent genetically determined. The end is already there, but will be made known only when the last page is turned. The child has an intuitive understanding of the fated aspect of his life, but still he reaches out to elect, grasp, unite with some remotely apprehended other self, while all the time he is in fact passing through developmental phases each coming in some essentially predetermined sequence upon the last. To all this the conceptions of the Mask and the Wheel are readily applicable.

But although the system excogitated in *A Vision* has a certain psychological validity, and is for this reason capable of enriching the poetry on many occasions, it seems to be the product of a somewhat depressive and even regressive phase in Yeats's life— one extending over a number of years, and coming to an end when he goes seriously to work on *The Tower*. The poems immediately anterior to that going to work—those closing *The Wild Swans at Coole* and related to the system in terms of direct expository intention—are at least not uniformly successful. Yet the last of them, 'The Double Vision of Michael Robartes', although 'hated' by Mr. Pound, is sufficiently remarkable— and certainly sufficiently difficult—to challenge examination.

Robartes's first vision occurs during the first phase of the moon.

> On the grey rock of Cashel the mind's eye
> Has called up the cold spirits that are born
> When the old moon is vanished from the sky
> And the new still hides her horn.

This is the phase—*A Vision* tells us—of complete objectivity, and also of complete passivity. There being no conflict of primary with antithetical in it, there can be no humanity: 'human life cannot be completely objective'. And we are told, not entirely lucidly:

> Mind has become indifferent to good and evil, to truth and falsehood; body has become undifferentiated, dough-like. . . . Mind and body take whatever shape, accept whatever image is imprinted upon them, transact whatever purpose is imposed upon them, and are indeed the instruments of supernatural manifestation.

And so:

> Under blank eyes and fingers never still
> The particular is pounded till it is man.
> When had I my own will?
> O not since life began.
>
> Constrained, arraigned, baffled, bent and unbent
> By these wire-jointed jaws and limbs of wood,
> Themselves obedient,
> Knowing not evil and good;
>
> Obedient to some hidden magical breath.
> They do not even feel, so abstract are they,
> So dead beyond our death,
> Triumph that we obey.

The image is of a doll controlled by dolls, and it renders the full burden of the determinism inherent in the system. The second vision is seen

> by the moon's light
> Now at its fifteenth night.

This is the answering phase of complete subjectivity, one again beyond the bounds of human life. It is the moment of unity of being:

> Thought and Will are indistinguishable, effort and attainment are indistinguishable. . . . Thought has been pursued, not as a means but as an end—the poem, the painting, the reverie has been sufficient of itself. . . . The being has selected, moulded and remoulded, narrowed its circle of living, been more and more the artist, grown more and more 'distinguished' in all preference. Now contemplation and desire, united into one, inhabit a world where every beloved image has bodily form, and every bodily form is loved. This love knows nothing of desire, for desire implies effort, and though there is still separation from the loved object, love accepts the separation as necessary to its own existence. . . . As all effort has ceased, all thought has become image . . . and every image is separate from every other, for if image were linked to image, the soul would awake from its immovable trance.

In the verses that answer to this elusive thinking it is precisely true that 'all thought has become image':

> On the grey rock of Cashel I suddenly saw
> A Sphinx with woman breast and lion paw,
> A Buddha, hand at rest,
> Hand lifted up that blest;
>
> And right between these two a girl at play
> That, it may be, had danced her life away,
> For now being dead it seemed
> That she of dancing dreamed. . . .
>
> O little did they care who danced between,
> And little she by whom her dance was seen
> So she had outdanced thought.
> Body perfection brought,
>
> For what but eye and ear silence the mind
> With the minute particulars of mankind?
> Mind moved yet seemed to stop
> As 'twere a spinning-top.

> In contemplation had those three so wrought
> Upon a moment, and so stretched it out
> That they, time overthrown,
> Were dead yet flesh and bone.

In a third section we learn that these balanced visions of the 1st and 15th phases have come as a consequence of the poet's being

> caught between the pull
> Of the dark moon and the full.

As the first is a revelation of the fixity of a determined order, so is the second a revelation of the fixity of a perfected order. In the Sphinx, Buddha, and dancing girl we see mind, heart, and creative imagination (which mediates or 'dances' between mind and heart) each in its own achieved and withdrawn completeness. The poet, normally confined within the temporal order (and at a point of decay and imminent destruction intimated in the image of the ruined house with which the poem concludes) is momentarily made aware in his two visions of two absolutes. He calls them, in a reference to the poem made elsewhere, 'the two halves of the soul separate and face to face'. More exactly, they are the two poles between the tensions of which everything recognizably human must move. The first vision cannot be called evil, since Yeats acknowledges what he calls 'abstraction' as a positive towards which man is prompted as a means of liberation from the urgency of the Self. But at least it is formidable; as in Kipling's 'The Bridge Builders', we may be reminded by it of what Hardy's Henry Knight sees as he clings to the cliff. The second vision appears to give a glimpse of something like the divine entelechy. Humanly, neither vision can be called very encouraging. But the poet, since he is concerned to see, gives thanks for both visions, all the same.

II

The Tower, the first of two volumes which were to establish Yeats among the major English poets, appeared in 1928. The same year saw the publication of Lawrence's *Lady Chatterley's Lover*, the melancholic hero of which we shall find condemning as 'a wrong and bitter thing' the bringing of a child into the world, and somewhat drearily entertaining his new-won mistress to his belief, uttered with the largest effect of cosmic implication, that 'there's a bad time coming'. *The Tower* too is drenched in the ominous, and in sending it to Lady Gregory Yeats distinguished 'bitterness' as the quality it had to a point of astonishment. But the 'bad time' view of things he had enunciated, far more impressively than Lawrence's gamekeeper could do, almost a decade before. 'The Second Coming', written in 1919 and included in *Michael Robartes and the Dancer*, appears to have been intended in the first instance to herald universal disintegration only at a remove which Yeats's transcendental calculations then located with tolerable comfort some two hundred years ahead. But if it owes something of its fame, and of the devotion of its innumerable commentators, to the unanticipated promptitude with which something like its horrors were in fact released upon us, it yet remains the most striking of the poems essentially implicated with *A Vision*, and it affords, at the same time, the best introduction to the dominant tone of *The Tower*:

> Turning and turning in the widening gyre
> The falcon cannot hear the falconer;
> Things fall apart; the centre cannot hold;
> Mere anarchy is loosed upon the world,
> The blood-dimmed tide is loosed, and everywhere
> The ceremony of innocence is drowned;
> The best lack all conviction, while the worst
> Are full of passionate intensity.

'Ceremony' is elsewhere Yeats's word for the ordered and traditional aristocratic way of life which he admired. In the first instance, then, he is here rehearsing the theme opened in 'Upon a House Shaken by the Land Agitation'. The 'best' are his friends who were perplexed about the position they should take up before the lawless element in Irish resurgence. The 'worst' are men and women who find in the troubles of the time scope for a violent and bitter destructiveness. In *The Tower* this theme is developed at a deeper level. Thus in 'Ancestral Houses', the splendid opening poem in the sequence 'Meditations in Time of Civil War', Yeats acknowledges that 'the glory of escutcheoned doors' was itself in all its mellow splendour the achievement of 'bitter and violent men'. 'Greatness', 'violence', and 'bitterness' are at play together in the fashioning of every precious and ordered thing, whether in his own country or in the world at large. However wide the historical view attempted (and this is the age of Frobenius, Spengler, Toynbee, and *The Waste Land*) it remains Yeats's instinct to work outwards from the 'blind bitter land' of Ireland: his papers even show the first of the two Byzantium poems being achieved in this way. 'The Second Coming' is a preliminary essay in such imaginative generalization. The magnificently concrete image of the falcon flying out of control represents the progress of the Christian era towards crisis, disintegration, and an explosion of irrational force such as marked its beginning, and which must now be the point from which the new gyre will begin to unwind. The poem continues:

> Surely some revelation is at hand;
> Surely the Second Coming is at hand.
> The Second Coming! Hardly are those words out
> When a vast image out of *Spiritus Mundi*
> Troubles my sight: somewhere in sands of the desert
> A shape with lion body and the head of a man,
> A gaze blank and pitiless as the sun,
> Is moving its slow thighs, while all about it
> Reel shadows of the indignant desert birds.
> The darkness drops again; but now I know
> That twenty centuries of stony sleep
> Were vexed to nightmare by a rocking cradle,
> And what rough beast, its hour come round at last,
> Slouches towards Bethlehem to be born?

The excellence of this is in part the product of a perfected rhetoric, as when the 'vast image out of *Spiritus Mundi*' follows upon the colloquial simplicity of 'Hardly are those words out'. And it depends in part upon what we feel as the authentic if carefully nourished iconogenic power of Yeats's imagination. As in those dreams which it appears incredible that we should have put together from any antecedent experiences, however fugitive, of our own, the shape, as it moves its slow thighs and slouches, goes far to persuade us that we are veritably in the presence of vision. The same power has been made evident in 'The Double Vision of Michael Robartes'. But 'The Second Coming' has a superiority akin to that which we recognize in a painting when the brilliance of immediate sensuous effect is sustained upon a lucid underlying geometry.

Yet the pressure of thought behind the plastic organization of 'The Second Coming', similar though it may be to some highly conceptual and lucid allegorical statement by Dürer, will be found not fully to cohere with what is intelligible in its speculative basis in *A Vision*, or with a good deal else that Yeats has to say elsewhere about the character of the coming crisis of the gyres. The 'rough beast' had been long an image in his mind—associated, it seems, with that notion of 'laughing, ecstatic destruction' the attractiveness of which he had explored in another context in *The Unicorn from the Stars*. But although the destructiveness answers to the unloosing of irrational force which *A Vision* predicts, it is clear that the laughter and the ecstasy imply a regenerative power, and in *A Vision* something of the sort is certainly suggested as attaching to the approaching reversal of historical process predicted. 'The Second Coming', however, appears to presage a peripety unrelievedly dire.

Yeats's vision of the millennial or bimillennial drifts of things takes, in fact, now one and now another colouring as he moves through the later years of his own life. The years of *The Tower* gather up their bitterness in some measure from the decline of Europe through war to war, in larger measure from the public face of Ireland, and in a measure larger still from the sense of some sombre climacteric in his own late maturity. It is from the power with which all this is bound together, and from the continued pertinacious seeking for a role or attitude intellectually adequate and aesthetically satisfying in face of it, that *The Tower* derives its peculiar quality.

Hard upon marriage, Yeats discovered old age. It is for him an ambiguous discovery, since he found that he could give it so triumphantly the character of a find; and its explosiveness is no doubt much an effect of art. Yet he was a man whom an exigent imagination had too long excluded from any fullness of sensual life, and the reality of his feeling of deprivation is attested by the rash Steinach operation to which he was to submit himself in his sixty-ninth year. Confronted by the actual problems of senescence, he appears to have found his magician's equipment an inadequate armoury. It may be said that, Kusta ben Luka having substantially failed him, he is constrained to wonder whether there may be anything in Rabbi ben Ezra. Is it at all conceivable that, at sixty, the best is yet to be? Withdrawal upon the contemplative life is the solution which the wisdom alike of East and West recommends to the ageing man. But the artist—or artist-magician—faces a special difficulty: one which Prospero cut through drastically when he prepared for that withdrawal by drowning his book. Yeats wishes not to do this. He would fain preserve his poethood even when he has passed beyond the interests of an enjoying and suffering humanity.

Here is the theme which he explores, to a strange effect of fusing mystery and brilliant lucidity, in 'Sailing to Byzantium', the first and key poem in *The Tower*:

> That is no country for old men . . .

The impetus given to the poem by its opening word is alone a stroke of genius. The poet is already at sea, with 'whatever is begotten, born, and dies' behind him. But what he is forsaking he has commanded; the 'sensual music' is poignant as it fades. The second stanza poses the problem: the soul must

> louder sing
> For every tatter in its mortal dress,
> Nor is there singing school but studying
> Monuments of its own magnificence.

At least it is a new singing school that must be found, and its masters will be those 'sages standing in God's holy fire' now magnificently evoked from memories of Classe and Ravenna— and recalling, too, the prose of 'Rosa Alchemica' where the poet's imagination contemplates 'the birds of Hera, glittering in the light of the fire as though of Byzantine mosaic'. It is those masters who will gather him into 'the artifice of eternity'. If eternity is itself an artifice the artist may hope in some sense to find it congenial, and to retain his identity there. This gives the transition to the proud and lovely last stanza. The artist will himself pass into the condition of a work of art: a miraculous automaton exempt from time yet celebrating its endless effluxion —singing, without surcease and without pain,

> To lords and ladies of Byzantium
> Of what is past, or passing, or to come.

Golden nightingales may in fact have chirruped in the courts of Byzantine emperors, and in actuality they belong to the trivial world of Fabergé. But Yeats had been sufficiently the pupil of Mallarmé to be fascinated by the notion of Daedalian ingenuity directed to artistic ends, and there are poems in *The Tower*—notably the two songs from the play *The Resurrection*—

which constitute small explicatory paradises. When we read
that

> The Roman Empire stood appalled:
> It dropped the reins of peace and war
> When that fierce virgin and her Star
> Out of the fabulous darkness called

we are near the heart of a labyrinth to the construction of which
there have gone materials drawn from almost the whole range of
Yeats's speculations. It would be rash to claim that the virtue
of these four lines does not reside in part in an unanalysable
element. We do not know, and we may never know, why they
affect us as they do. Yet the poem will be found not of the sort
in which it is inept to seek a fundamental ratiocinative structure.
From now on much of Yeats's poetry is increasingly difficult.
But he was well aware that Homer (although presently to be
described as 'mad as the mist and snow') talks sense, and that
the paralogical achievements of symbolism, with all that they
have added to the resources of poetry, can be no more than
adjuvant in any sustained and major utterance. This perception, which he shares with the other great and traditional poet
of the age, Mr. T. S. Eliot, controls notably the deployment of
his total powers in *The Tower*.

It is a deployment the technique of which certainly extends
to a careful juxtaposition of poem with poem. 'Sailing to
Byzantium' is followed by a sequence of three poems called
collectively 'The Tower'. Here is the actual tower of Ballylee in
its setting of ruined cottage and blackened tree, with its actual
owner shorn of all 'hammered gold and gold enamelling' and
imaged no longer as nightingale but dog—with 'a sort of battered
kettle at the heel'. Decrepit age is down to earth again; there is
no sort of singing school in sight; there is only a second best:

> It seems that I must bid the Muse go pack,
> Choose Plato and Plotinus for a friend.

Yeats has far too vigorous a dramatic sense to make any kind
of grateful stroll out of old age's necessary descent from Helicon
to the Academy, or to accompany it with a pleasant murmuring
of years that bring the philosophic mind. Rather is he going to
be carried down kicking, and his new masters are to find a
rebellious pupil:

> I mock Plotinus' thought
> And cry in Plato's teeth.

The sequence is a record of struggle. 'I am tired', he had written to his friend Olivia Shakespear, 'and in a rage at being old. I am all I ever was and much more but an enemy has bound me and twisted me.' The first poem declares that an imagination still 'excited, passionate, fantastical' must, in its owner's old age, be content to 'deal in abstract things'. But from this the poet's mind immediately sheers away, and the second poem introduces us abruptly into one of those picture-galleries of persons of local legendary fame which Yeats has such skill in animating. There is Mrs. French, whose serving-man brought her an insolent farmer's ears 'in a little covered dish'; Mary Hynes, a Helen whose beauty led to small disaster in 'the great bog of Cloone'; Hanrahan, whose 'horrible splendour of desire' he had celebrated long ago. We are brought back to the relevance of this procession (so remote, we may think, from that in the 'holy fire' of S. Apollinare Nuovo) by a question:

> Did all old men and women, rich and poor,
> Who trod upon these rocks or passed this door,
> Whether in public or in secret rage
> As I do now against old age?

It is the 'old lecher' Hanrahan—whom we may remember as having written a rhyming curse upon old age—that is bidden stay, and in the context of gross sexuality thus preserved (this with a foreshadowing of a later attitude) the poet's mind is left brooding upon a further question:

> Does the imagination dwell the most
> Upon a woman won or woman lost?

It was from a great 'labyrinth'—the word is significantly chosen—that he had turned aside when pride or cowardice prompted him to relinquish Maud Gonne. And pride, it seems, is his last infirmity, since it emerges as the essential problem in the third poem, which is a testament. The poet must—again—climb down. He must 'make' his soul,

> Compelling it to study
> In a learned school,

and he will bequeath his pride, evoked in a series of splendid images, to young men who can still scale the mountains and touch the well-springs of the sensuous life. He himself renounces that life, and even its reflection in art:

> I have prepared my peace
> With learned Italian things
> And the proud stones of Greece,
> Poet's imaginings.

It is commonly in an arrogant cadence that Yeats makes such submissions.

As far back as *The Green Helmet* volume he had meditated on 'the coming of wisdom with time' and looked forward to a phase in which he must 'wither into the truth'. In poem after poem in *The Tower* the wisdom suggests itself as hard-won still. There is more pride than wisdom in 'My Descendants'. The preceding poem, 'My Table', tells us that, among the enviable Japanese, high accomplishment in an art passes through centuries from father to son. But Yeats's own genius, we now learn, is an efflorescence upon which only 'common greenness' is likely to succeed. If this happens, he hopes that his tower will become a roofless ruin. There is said to be an earlier version of the poem in which what is here invoked is a Lear-like curse. In 'A Prayer for my Son' he supposes the child to be menaced by evil spirits who know

> Of some most haughty deed or thought
> That waits upon his future days.

Such attitudes are rather splendid on the page. But one is prompted to hope that their proponent refrained from carrying them to the nursery.

No questioning of this sort need be brought to those poems in which Yeats shows a powerful and appalled response to public events in Ireland. Henry James's sense, in 1914, of having 'to take it all now for what the treacherous years were all the while really making for and meaning' is exactly echoed in 'Nineteen Hundred and Nineteen'. We had come to suppose the rule of law a permanent achievement, and to repose in

> Public opinion ripening for so long
> We thought it would outlive all future days.

But the very bases of civilization have proved no more 'protected from the circle of the moon' than have its merest if most miraculous toys:

> Phidias' famous ivories
> And all the golden grasshoppers and bees.

Other toys—chargers and trumpeters, powder and cannon
and shot—have proved no toys at all:

> Now days are dragon-ridden, the nightmare
> Rides upon sleep: a drunken soldiery
> Can leave the mother, murdered at her door,
> To crawl in her own blood, and go scot-free;
> The night can sweat with terror as before
> We pieced our thoughts into philosophy,
> And planned to bring the world under a rule,
> Who are but weasels fighting in a hole.

Yeats is only too well equipped with cosmic structures in which
his sombre temperament at this time can expatiate at will. His
danger is luxuriance in metaphysical distresses and a facile
fatalism loftily expressed. It is present in this poem:

> So the Platonic Year
> Whirls out new right and wrong,
> Whirls in the old instead;
> All men are dancers and their tread
> Goes to the barbarous clangour of a gong.

But he is now living in a context of actual violence. The mother
has really crawled in her own blood. The mangled remains of
a young soldier have been dragged past Milton's Platonist as
he stands at the door of his tower. And the poet's singing-robes
are the more splendid for having to be gathered veritably
about him against

> Those winds that clamour of approaching night.

12

The bitterness dominating *The Tower*, like the lust and rage
that are to dominate some of the later verse, is in places so
controlled as to render an essentially elegiac effect. In 'The
New Faces', addressed to Lady Gregory at the end of 1912,
this note has already come in. We are listening now to something
deeper than the voice of the courtier:

> If you, that have grown old, were the first dead,
> Neither catalpa-tree nor scented lime
> Should hear my living feet....

'The Wheel', versifying a thought which, in *The Tables of
the Law*, Owen Aherne is made to attribute to Leonardo da

Vinci, achieves the same effect at an impersonal level. But it is
in the sequence 'A Man Young and Old' that the new note
is most plangently sounded. The first statements are directly
personal. The poet's life has been destroyed by a woman nur-
tured 'in beauty's murderous brood' and with a heart of stone.
He has attempted many things since his disillusionment. But
'not a thing is done':

> So like a bit of stone I lie
> Under a broken tree.

'The Empty Cup' we know to be associated with 'Diana
Vernon':

> A crazy man that found a cup,
> When all but dead of thirst,
> Hardly dared to wet his mouth
> Imagining, moon-accursed,
> That another mouthful
> And his beating heart would burst.
> October last I found it too
> But found it dry as bone,
> And for that reason am I crazed
> And my sleep is gone.

'His Memories' achieves its poignancy by making, perhaps,
more free with biographical fact. Long ago 'She who had
brought great Hector down' took her pleasure with the poet—
and now:

> My arms are like the twisted thorn
> And yet there beauty lay.

In the later poems of this volume other 'crazed' figures begin
to slip in: Madge (who has ancestors in Thomas Russell and
Cowper and Wordsworth) and Peter and Peg and Meg. Their
colloquies, which treat of departed sensual joy, are as bare as
bone. Lear has set about peopling his hovel. But this Lear is
going to continue to know a hawk from a hernshaw (and indeed
to be much attracted by both). Despite its sometimes obsessive
implication with the sexual cycle, the elegiac poetry remains
entirely sane, so that its pathos has Virgilian depth and purity.

Two longer poems in *The Tower*, 'Among School Children'
and 'All Souls' Night', are of equal significance here. The
first is a meditation upon time, which has transfigured Yeats
into 'A sixty-year-old smiling public man' fulfilling one of his

functions as a Senator of the Irish Free State by inspecting a convent school. Looking from pupil to pupil, he thinks of Maud Gonne in childhood—or so we may venture to suppose, although Mr. Cleanth Brooks here warns us of 'the perils of biographical bias'. The poet thinks of some incident in the recounting of which she had seemed to draw very close to him in a spiritual communion:

> And thereupon my heart is driven wild:
> She stands before me as a living child.

But his simple duty is to show the children round him that 'There is a comfortable kind of old scarecrow'—which is, after all, what the greatest intellects have become:

> Plato thought nature but a spume that plays
> Upon a ghostly paradigm of things;
> Solider Aristotle played the taws
> Upon the bottom of a king of kings;
> World-famous golden-thighed Pythagoras
> Fingered upon a fiddle-stick or strings
> What a star sang and careless Muses heard:
> Old clothes upon old sticks to scare a bird.

The resplendent evocations are wittily juxtaposed with the fundamental indignity of man. In the image of fustigation neither Alexander nor his tutor cuts an august figure, and in their context 'golden-thighed' Pythagoras also becomes faintly absurd. This lightening of tone at the point of the poem's opening out is finely contrived, rendering the more effective the two deeply contemplative stanzas of its close. The abstractions of philosophy, religion, art 'break hearts' as surely as a revelation of what awaits the individual child would break the heart of the woman in travail, and wisdom lies in the acceptance of life in the concrete, of the irreducible mystery of the universe as the theatre of Being and Becoming alike:

> Labour is blossoming or dancing where
> The body is not bruised to pleasure soul,
> Nor beauty born out of its own despair,
> Nor blear-eyed wisdom out of midnight oil.
> O chestnut-tree, great-rooted blossomer,
> Are you the leaf, the blossom or the bole?
> O body swayed to music, O brightening glance,
> How can we know the dancer from the dance?

'We ought to dance with rapture', D. H. Lawrence was soon to write at the end of *Apocalypse*, 'that we should be alive and in the flesh, and part of the living, incarnate cosmos.' The final thought of Yeats's poem comprehends this—but it comprehends too, we may think, the kind of perception that Tolstoy's Levin arrives at before the close of *Anna Karenina*. Yeats, in fact, is here near the centre of the modern European imagination, and the later poetry is significant because it explores farther reaches of experience always from this firm basis.

And this centrality of imagination, which speaks of a balance and self-possession not altogether accordant with the bitterness so artfully deployed in *The Tower*, appears too in 'All Souls' Night'. The first poem has had as its setting that dignity of public effort which is to be discerned as always salubrious for Yeats. The second, first printed as an epilogue to *A Vision*, is eminently hermetic. We are back with the conjurer who, within sound of the sober Christ Church bell celebrated in the opening line, would, we know, intimate to equally sober academic visitors to his rooms in Oxford that his days were pleasantly diversified by supernatural occurrences of an order commonly associated with spiritualistic seance. The first triumph of the poem is to give both dignity and an entranced actuality to this context:

> Midnight has come, and the great Christ Church Bell
> And many a lesser bell sound through the room;
> And it is All Souls' Night,
> And two long glasses brimmed with muscatel
> Bubble upon the table. A ghost may come;
> For it is a ghost's right,
> His element is so fine
> Being sharpened by his death,
> To drink from the wine-breath
> While our gross palates drink from the whole wine.

The poet has 'a marvellous thing to say . . . though not for sober ear'. He has in fact the whole substance of *A Vision* to communicate, and for this frequentation of the marvellous— we may hazard—the actual people among whom he is now living in Oxford are as useless as their predecessors were to the Scholar Gipsy. So the muscatel stands on the table. And 'Horton's the first I call'.

The poem thus develops in terms of a now familiar resource;

it is another 'private mythology' poem. Horton was an eccentric visionary and indifferent artist for whose *Book of Images* Yeats had written a preface. He has some importance for the study of the poet's iconography, and he is said to have uttered mysterious warnings about a malign influence centred in Mr. Pound. Florence Emery, the second of the summoned shades, had acted in Yeats's plays and experimented in the speaking of his verse to music. A woman of wit and intellect, the creator of Rebecca West in the first English production of *Rosmersholm*, she had been one of that 'awful set' among whom Miss Gonne found herself as a result of joining the Order of the Golden Dawn. Eventually she dedicated her life to teaching in a school in Ceylon, and made some studies in oriental philosophy before dying of cancer. The last shade summoned is Liddell Mathers, the founder of the London section of the Order:

> And I call up MacGregor from the grave,
> For in my first hard springtime we were friends,
> Although of late estranged.
> I thought him half a lunatic, half knave . . . .
>
> He had much industry at setting out,
> Much boisterous courage, before loneliness
> Had driven him crazed . . . .

The nub of the poem is here. Those whom Yeats summons as fit to receive his 'mummy truths' are held in a just, clear, and compassionate regard. All have 'loved strange thought' and gone to some extremity in its pursuit; have gone farther—we may again feel—than Arnold's poor scholar, whose 'retired ground' still commanded 'the line of festal light in Christ-Church hall'. Horton and Mathers and Mrs. Emery, like the astronomer in *Rasselas*, have risked what may succeed upon the prevalence of imagination. But their devotion will in some sense be vindicated (this is the claim implicit in the close of the poem) if Yeats's own mystical studies have issued, in *A Vision*, in substantial truth:

> Such thought—such thought have I that hold it tight
> Till meditation master all its parts,
> Nothing can stay my glance
> Until that glance run in the world's despite
> To where the damned have howled away their hearts,
> And where the blessed dance.

The Dantesque reference is a measure of the seriousness with which Yeats, at least in certain moments of imaginative elevation, took the audacious task of being his own Aquinas.

13

The dominant theme of *The Winding Stair* (1933) is the acceptance of tragic life—an acceptance based upon Stoicism, a defiant sensuality, and an elusive but intense intuition of transcendence. Yeats's letters show that he planned this phase of his work as substantially antithetical to the 'bitter' phase of *The Tower*. He spoke indeed of writing 'amiable verses . . . bird songs of an old man, joy in the passing moment'. And something of this he was to achieve. Yet there is nothing like a simple and definitive movement from one attitude to its opposite. His whole intellectual disposition was attuned to a constant apprehension of antinomies, so that *The Tower* and *The Winding Stair*, even if each has its characteristic emphasis, can be viewed as constituting together a single continuing and shuttle-like debate. To Yeats as a speculative poet no form came more naturally than that of the dialogue. Thus, of the key poems in *The Winding Stair*, the most immediately striking is 'A Dialogue of Self and Soul'. But it is perhaps in 'Byzantium', and in its relationship to the earlier 'Sailing to Byzantium', that we shall find the essential poetic process—one operating through a sifting and resifting of images at a level of subliminal exploration—most characteristically at work. It is a process in which a substantial measure of the unresolved, the obscure, and the random is a necessary by-product. As we read, we have often to consent to being in uncertainties. We shall find ourselves in a similar position when involved with the frequently intricate, turning, and returning progress of D. H. Lawrence's novels.

Both Byzantium poems are concerned with the idea of escape from the Wheel, from that eternal submergence and resubmergence in natural life which is alone what *Magnus Annus* brings:

> Another Troy must rise and set,
> Another lineage feed the crow.

But whereas in 'Sailing to Byzantium' the poet's desire for 'the artifice of eternity' is a passionate cry, 'Byzantium' shows the escape as actually happening, but shows it only as mirrored in an aloof, contemplative, and perhaps unresolved mind. We are treated to an awe-inspiring spectacle of expiation and liberation. But the poet's place is undetermined; indeed he enters the picture only in the obscure second stanza—one which Mr. Henn rightly distinguishes as not properly of the substance of the whole. This reserve in the recording voice is certainly part of the overpowering imaginative effect of 'Byzantium'. But it is correlative with a sense that we don't quite know where things are going. The dolphins in the last stanza, who bear on their backs the purified spirits of the dead, may not be going at all. Some readers certainly see them as arriving; and according as we take this one way or the other, our conception of Byzantium itself must change. That Yeats's own conception of it has changed is clear from the first stanza:

> The unpurged images of day recede;
> The Emperor's drunken soldiery are abed;
> Night resonance recedes, night-walkers' song
> After great cathedral gong;
> A starlit or a moonlit dome disdains
> All that man is,
> All mere complexities,
> The fury and the mire of human veins.

In 'Nineteen Hundred and Nineteen' it is a 'drunken soldiery' that can murder the mother at her door and persuade us that we are 'but weasels fighting in a hole'. Here, then, in the second Byzantium, mire and fury may rule the 'holy city' by day, and what dies away with the night-walkers' song is something deriving from its context the character of a riotous revelry. All this, although it recedes before the approach of darkness and the superhuman, is given a compelling splendour. What follows is best introduced by a note written by Yeats in 1930:

Describe Byzantium as it is *in the system* towards the end of the first Christian millennium. A walking mummy. Flames at the street corners where the soul is purified, birds of hammered gold singing in the golden trees, offering their backs to the wailing dead that they may carry them to paradise.

So we have:

> Before me floats an image, man or shade,
> Shade more than man, more image than a shade;

For Hades' bobbin bound in mummy-cloth
May unwind the winding path;
A mouth that has no moisture and no breath
Breathless mouths may summon;
I hail the superhuman;
I call it death-in-life and life-in-death.

Mr. Henn conjectures that the 'walking mummy' of the prose
note represents the Egyptian element in Byzantine art. But we
see such things in films designed to attract an X Certificate; and
the stanza (which will be found reminiscent, too, of the obscure
demonology of *The Only Jealousy of Emer*, one of Yeats's plays
for dancers) concludes upon an echo of *The Ancient Mariner*
at its closest point of contact with the tradition of Gothic horror.
The 'superhuman' which the poet hails is presently to be
displayed as miraculous liberation from the tyranny of the
flesh. But this is here set at play against the mere horror and
gruesomeness of being dead—and is throughout the poem set
at play, too, against that conception of a high and integrated
sublunary civilization such as Yeats had delighted to suppose
in the historical Byzantium. The golden bird of the third stanza
is no longer, as in 'Sailing to Byzantium', an automaton; it is
scornful, embittered, and implicated with what it seems to
transcend. And the spirits which, in the matchless fourth stanza,
are purified through flame and the ritual dance that always
haunted Yeats's imagination, if not still 'wailing' as they are
represented in the prose note, must yet ride the dolphin's
mire and blood. The final stanza, indeed, if discursively obscure,
is unmistakable in its general effect:

Astraddle on the dolphin's mire and blood,
Spirit after spirit! The smithies break the flood,
The golden smithies of the Emperor!
Marbles of the dancing floor
Break bitter furies of complexity,
Those images that yet
Fresh images beget,
That dolphin-torn, that gong-tormented sea.

That which is 'broken' by the measure of the dance—all that
fury and complexity of natural life which the poet of 'Sailing
to Byzantium' conceived himself as leaving behind him even
though, as automaton, he might continue to sing of it to the
lords and ladies—is not here being whole-heartedly left behind

at all. The declarative statement, indeed, says that it is. But the
poetry brings it thundering in again, with an ecstasy of its own,
in the final lines. If 'Byzantium' is the richer as well as the
harder poem, it is because conflicting impulses are locked in it.
Certainly Yeats never wrote anything more astonishing—a fact
of which our sense grows sharper when we read an early draft:

> I therefore travel towards Byzantium
> Among these sunbrown pleasant mariners
> Another dozen days and we shall come
> Under the jetty and the marble stair. . . .
> But now these pleasant dark-skinned mariners
> Carry me towards that great Byzantium
> Where all is ancient, singing at the oars
> That I may look in the great church's dome
> On gold-embedded saints and emperors
> After the mirroring waters and the foam
> Where the dark drowsy fins a moment rise
> Of fish that carry souls to paradise.

This (which seems anterior to both poems) might be by Morris,
and there seems no reason why it should not amble on indefinitely.
We must eagerly desire the full publication of Yeats's surviving
manuscripts. The available evidence suggests that few poets
have ever travelled farther from the rudeness of their first conceptions.

'A Dialogue of Self and Soul' is the poem which, in *The
Winding Stair*, is set most explicitly over against 'Sailing to
Byzantium' in the earlier volume; and the explicitness is
perhaps the limiting condition upon its excellence. In a letter
to Olivia Shakespear Yeats recorded: 'I am writing a new
tower poem "Sword and Tower", which is a choice of rebirth
rather than deliverance from birth. I make my Japanese sword
and its silk covering my symbol of life.' He goes on to mention
much activity with a cage of canaries, 'a noisy and cantankerous
dinner at a restaurant last night', and some trouble caused at
the Abbey Theatre by a phantom dog: a brief chronicle of the
satisfaction obtainable from life's miscellaneous traffic that is
not without relevance to the poem. In its first part Soul
summons the poet away from the sword and up the winding
stair to a contemplation of the heavens—and particularly
to the moon in the fifteenth phase: 'That quarter where all
thought is done'.

Why should the imagination of a man
Long past his prime remember things that are
Emblematical of love and war?
Think of ancestral night that can,
If but imagination scorn the earth
And intellect its wandering
To this and that and t'other thing,
Deliver from the crime of death and birth.

The second part asserts the Self's rejection of this escape from
eternal recurrence on the Wheel; asserts its content

> to live it all again
> And yet again, if it be life to pitch
> Into the frog-spawn of a blind man's ditch,
> A blind man battering blind men.

In 'On a Political Prisoner', a poem in *Michael Robartes and the
Dancer*, Yeats had employed this imagery of

> Blind and leader of the blind
> Drinking the foul ditch where they lie

as emblematical of the defeat and degradation that await all
involvement with—we may say—the 'noisy and cantankerous'
affair that active life too readily becomes. Now, in this appro-
bative review of the same mess, he steps up the violence of his
expression to a point at which something like bluster is disturbingly within hail; and the note of uncertainty is enhanced by
the succeeding statement that the 'most fecund ditch of all'
awaits the man who woos 'A proud woman not kindred of his
soul', since here we feel that a personal factor is disturbing the
elevated generality of the thought. But the poem recovers
equilibrium in the concluding stanza, where 'Everything we
look upon is blest'. It is the first intimation of that final world
of Yeats's in which Hamlet and Lear are gay. This whole poem,
indeed, is a splendid one. Yet when we compare it with those
poems of Marvell's, essentially slighter, by which it may have
been prompted, the resulting impression is not altogether to
Yeats's advantage. Marvell is not nearly such a great poet.
But when his *Soul* responds to *Pleasure*:

> If things of Sight such Heavens be,
> What Heavens are those we cannot see?

or declares itself

> Here blinded with an Eye; and there
> Deaf with the drumming of an Ear—

we are in contact with thoughts that have haunted the Western imagination far more authentically than has any notion of Gyre or Wheel. When Yeats's Soul says 'Only the dead can be forgiven' we are aware of a gesture of rhetoric. When Marvell's *Soul* answers *Pleasure*'s last enticement to climb to heaven by the way of knowledge with:

> None thither mounts by the degree
> Of Knowledge, but Humility—

we are set before a stair older by far than that at Thoor Ballylee.

Indeed we are becoming aware that Yeats's symbols are traditional for the most part only in the shadowy archetypal sense. They are therefore protean, and more useful to the poet questioning his own divided mind than they are to some of his critics whole-heartedly intent upon systematic interpretation. As Byzantium does not remain, from poem to poem, quite the same Byzantium, so the tower does not remain quite the same tower. Thus in 'Blood and the Moon', which follows the 'Dialogue', the tower no longer answers, as it does in 'The Phases of the Moon', to Samuel Palmer's illustration for *Il Penseroso*: 'an image of mysterious wisdom won by toil'. Now:

> No matter what I said,
> For wisdom is the property of the dead,
> A something incompatible with life; and power,
> Like everything that has the stain of blood,
> A property of the living . . . .

Now the tower dominates the cottages beneath it. For centuries it has been a focus of 'bloody, arrogant power', inhabited by 'Soldier, assassin, executioner'—in fact by those 'bitter and violent men', celebrated in 'Ancestral Houses', whose creative energy has been part of all historical achievement. And although there be 'Odour of blood on the ancestral stair' yet 'the purity of the unclouded moon' purges it of guilt. Here again the symbolism has been modified, the moonlight affording simply something like a view of history *sub specie aeternitatis*, in which every expression of power, secular, intellectual, or imaginative, is to be accepted in the name of life. There is lurking in this new attitude, and in the question whether every modern nation be not 'Half dead at the top', something of that sort of political and social philosophy which was itself presently to deal all but a lethal blow at Europe. But Yeats was no sort of historian or political thinker, and having long romanticized what he conceived of as a ruling aristocracy he was largely vulnerable to authoritarian and totalitarian notions. In 'Blood and the Moon' Mrs. French, Mary Hynes, and Red Hanrahan yield place to Swift, Berkeley, and Burke. And what is significant about Yeats's presentation of these—if anything be really significant apart from the superb poetry in which they are evoked—is their larger-than-life quality. Swift's is a 'sibylline frenzy'. Burke is 'haughtier-headed'. Berkeley is 'God-appointed'. This titanism is very impressive. There emerges from the verses, massively if imprecisely, a picture of eighteenth-century Ireland as akin to the second Byzantium: a place in which a magnificence of actual human struggle and actual historical achievement is at a fecund interplay with transcendental forces:

The strength that gives our blood and state magnanimity of its own
    desire;
Everything that is not God consumed with intellectual fire.

14

The 'intellectual fire' was to flicker—even to flare—on the horizon of Yeats's consciousness to the end. Yet it remains to the end a sort of hypothesis. Despite all that he can clothe it with, it never becomes a commanding vision towards which he moves in singleness of purpose. The main emphasis of *The Winding Stair* continues to lie elsewhere, and is chiefly borne by the two series, 'Words for Music Perhaps' and 'A Woman Young and Old'. The second group, which was the earlier-composed, complements—this time in personative form and with a larger affirming element—that retrospective meditation upon sensual experience which was the subject of 'A Man Young and Old' in *The Tower*. The two series, taken together, may again bring *Lady Chatterley's Lover* to mind. Lawrence's Mellors, despite his superficial role as Connie Chatterley's instructor, is at a dead end with sex, and embodies—inadvertently, perhaps—the paradox that the erotic, in proportion as it becomes compulsive, is a fetter forged upon the essential masculine principle. But for the woman all joy and sorrow may be comprehended within erotic experience. An imaginative writer of adequate intuition is always likely to go about his deepest exploration of sexuality through some *tour de force* of empathy— such as Joyce, for example, attempts in the final section of *Ulysses*. 'A Woman Young and Old' is a tentative essay in this kind. In the sixth poem, 'Chosen', there is some residual and inapposite matter from *A Vision*, and here and there Yeats may be detected as seeking, in this new territory, guidance from older poets. A phrase in 'Parting' tells us at once that he has been reading Jonson. The impact of Donne has perhaps been exaggerated by the historically minded. Yeats's references to him in his letters are few and unimpressive, scarcely extending beyond a reiterated and eccentric interpretation of 'A nocturnall upon S. Lucies day'. Yet Donne certainly lurks in 'A Last Confession':

> What lively lad most pleasured me
> Of all that with me lay?
> I answer that I gave my soul
> And loved in misery,
> But had great pleasure with a lad
> That I loved bodily.

This is driven brutally home:

> Flinging from his arms I laughed
> To think his passion such
> He fancied that I gave a soul
> Did but our bodies touch,
> And laughed upon his breast to think
> Beast gave beast as much.

The soul, however, is to have its day:

> I gave what other women gave
> That stepped out of their clothes,
> But when this soul, its body off,
> Naked to naked goes,
> He it has found shall find therein
> What none other knows. . . .

The lover with whom there was only misery in life is to secure the best bargain in some purified state. 'The Extasie' is being obliquely drawn on here, perhaps not much to the advantage

of what Yeats really has to say. At a later time, admiring the
'boyish body' of an aristocratic and talented young woman who
became his close friend, Yeats was to wish that he 'could be
a girl of nineteen for certain hours' in order that he might feel
this charm 'even more acutely'—and to reflect that 'the Greek
androgynous statue is always the woman in man, never the
man in woman'. He was to come, in fact, to feel the woman in
himself vividly. But Donne, with his entire masculinity and his
muddy logic so disagreeably applied, was, even though admired,
a false light so far as the empathic enterprise was concerned,
and so indeed was Swedenborg, a more lasting influence.

The poems in 'Words for Music Perhaps' are altogether more
remarkable.

15

Yeats spent the winter of 1928–9 at Rapallo, and during this
time experienced some 'exultant weeks' of which many of these
new poems were the product. He was again enjoying the
society of Mr. Pound, and in his circle met the musician George
Antheil, who, some years before, had composed his *Ballet
méchanique*, *Airplane Sonata*, and *Mechanisms*, and had begun an
opera based on the *Cyclops* episode in Joyce's *Ulysses* which was
to be scored for twelve electric pianos. Yeats, who was tone
deaf, attached great importance to Antheil's theories, set him
to compose music for a Cuchulain play, *Fighting the Waves*, and
gave renewed attention to that old problem of speaking verse
to music which he had formerly explored with Florence Farr,
the Mrs. Emery of 'All Souls' Night'. He sometimes referred to
the new poems as 'little mechanical songs', and the prominence
in them of strangely felicitous refrains is to be connected with
this fresh interest. The concluding word of the title finally
given to the group may remind us, however, that an element
of scepticism commonly accompanied his enthusiasms. And
indeed the poems beginning with 'Crazy Jane and the Bishop'
owe nothing of their essence to any casual prompting from
Yeats's immediate environment at this time. The 'exultance'
of those weeks seems to have been due to the discovery of a
fresh significance, pertinent to the problems posed by old age,
inherent in some of the elements of his earliest imagination.
As a youth he may have encountered the Queen of the Forgetful People. But Sligo and Rosses had made him aware too

of common mortals scarcely less remote from any secure human society: tramps and beggars and solitaries who had lived out their lives in disorder and near-destitution. Synge had celebrated them, and behind Synge was Villon. Vagabonds, frenzy-struck, had already appeared in *Responsibilities*. Now, when he saw in a dream 'strange ragged excited people singing in a crowd', he connected them at once with the 'praise of joyous life', raised in defiance of every ravage of circumstance and time, which he sought to assert. Cracked Mary, later more circumspectly named Crazy Jane, the central figure in the most important group of poems here, was suggested in part by such a wanderer, and in part by an old woman living near Coole who combined with love of her flower-garden 'an amazing power of audacious speech' and drunkenness 'of an epic magnificence'.

These poems, although appearing to hold some tenuous reference here and there to anecdotal matter, are not in the nature of a dramatic sequence. Essentially they are songs, and mad songs at that, and we might understand them better if we better understood that twenty-eighth phase in Yeats's system which is the phase of the Fool. The Fool, having no active intelligence,

owns nothing of the exterior world but his mind and body. He is but a straw blown by the wind, with no mind but the wind and no act but a nameless drifting and turning, and is sometimes called 'The Child of God'. At his worst his hands and feet and eyes, his will and his feelings, obey obscure subconscious fantasies, while at his best he would know all wisdom if he could know anything.

This paradox of the Fool is certainly operative in the poems. And when in the first of them the Bishop, who rebukes Jane for living 'like beast and beast' with Jack the Journeyman, cannot hide 'The heron's hunch upon his back', we recall that the Hunchback of the twenty-sixth phase is 'jealous of those that can still feel'. Jane, and Tom the Lunatic who comes later in the series, can still feel, and therefore they command the wisdom that Yeats is concerned to explore:

> Whatever stands in field or flood,
> Bird, beast, fish or man,
> Mare or stallion, cock or hen,
> Stands in God's unchanging eye
> In all the vigour of its blood;
> In that faith I live or die.

Berkeley, of whom Yeats made an earnest if inexpert study, might have been surprised at the slant given to his thought by the poet. It is in the most intense of sensible experiences, that of the act of sex, that we find warrant for a belief in a super-sensible order that endures 'in God's unchanging eye'. With Jane many lovers have succeeded Jack, but had she not been equally broken by the transience of these passions and sustained by their memory, she would have had no visions such as she records in 'Crazy Jane on God':

> That lover of a night
> Came when he would,
> Went in the dawning light
> Whether I would or no;
> Men come, men go;
> *All things remain in God.*
>
> Banners choke the sky;
> Men-at-arms tread;
> Armoured horses neigh
> Where the great battle was
> In the narrow pass:
> *All things remain in God.*
>
> Before their eyes a house
> That from childhood stood
> Uninhabited, ruinous,
> Suddenly lit up
> From door to top:
> *All things remain in God.*
>
> I had wild Jack for a lover;
> Though like a road
> That men pass over
> My body makes no moan
> But sings on:
> *All things remain in God.*

The battle that reveals itself as still raging and the house that blazes into light again: these are now for Yeats recurrent symbols of the transcending of time. Yet time remains a fact, and when Jane declares that 'All could be known or shown' if time were but gone, she gets a dusty answer in the refrain:

> *'That's certainly the case'*, said he.

Jane's courage may be, once more, only the delirium of the brave, and her faith belong with what Yeats calls elsewhere 'all that heroic casuistry, all that assertion of the eternity of what nature declares ephemeral'. In *The Winding Stair* we get farthest from rhetoric and nearest to Yeats's peak of poetry when the response to the problem of transience is purely elegiac, as it is in 'Three Things':

> 'O cruel Death, give three things back,'
> *Sang a bone upon the shore;*
> 'A child found all a child can lack,
> Whether of pleasure or of rest,
> Upon the abundance of my breast':
> *A bone wave-whitened and dried in the wind.*
>
> 'Three dear things that women know,'
> *Sang a bone upon the shore;*
> 'A man if I but held him so
> When my body was alive
> Found all the pleasure that life gave':
> *A bone wave-whitened and dried in the wind.*
>
> 'The third thing that I think of yet,'
> *Sang a bone upon the shore,*
> 'Is that morning when I met
> Face to face my rightful man
> And did after stretch and yawn':
> *A bone wave-whitened and dried in the wind.*

This is the poem that Yeats particularly singles out as being 'praise of joyous life'. It is indeed at once paean and threnody. And perhaps it is his best poem.

Jane, or what Jane stands for, is to remain in Yeats's poetry to the end. But he would not have been Yeats had he been quite whole-hearted about her, or failed sometimes to feel that there might be a promising role for himself even in the Bishop. Jane, after all, was a slut; and while living at Coole during Lady Gregory's last illness in the winter of 1931–2 he came to feel that the slut's language had become 'unendurable' and that he wanted to 'exorcise' her. Indeed, he cannot but have questioned the processes driving him in old age to verse with so harsh an emphasis upon naked sexuality. This appears in a letter to Mrs. Shakespear at the end of 1931:

I have begun a longish poem called 'Wisdom' in the attempt to shake off 'Crazy Jane' and I begin to think I shall take to religion

unless you save me from it. That Chinese book [apparently a gift
from Mrs. Shakespear] has given me something I have long wanted,
a study of meditation that has not come out of the jungle. I distrust
the jungle.

'Wisdom' became the sequence eventually called 'Vacillation'.
Although so placed in *The Winding Stair* as to obscure the fact,
it represents at least tentative second thoughts on Jane, Jack,
Tom, and the 'jungle' they could be viewed as representing.
The first poem in the series begins:

> Between extremities
> Man runs his course.

Yeats had come to feel acutely that in the romantic tradition in
which his own poetry had been cradled the relationship between spiritual and sensual experience was blurred—as it is
blurred, say, in *The Shadowy Waters* when Forgael proceeds on
his supersensible quest with Dectora as fellow voyager. Now he
has been sketching a new mythology in which an intuition of
timelessness is represented as distilling itself out of the very ashes
of lust. The new world was altogether clearer and harder than
the old. Yet, viewed disenchantedly, an old man's obsessional
interest in the sort of *mundus muliebris* represented by Jane
was at least an equivocal thing. Had it validity as a symbolism
of the poet's ultimate acceptance of life and joy? Or must it
be judged a bad case of what Lawrence was calling sex in the
head? Actually we are not made to feel that the issue of Yeats's
vacillations is so very much in doubt, after all. The sequence
constitutes an apology rather than a debate. A letter which preserves an early draft of the seventh and crucial poem acknowledges cheerfully: 'I shall be a sinful man to the end, and think
upon my death-bed of all the nights I wasted in my youth.'
The poem itself 'puts clearly an argument that has gone on in
my head for years'. And, although it is another dialogue, it is
this time a dialogue that is all over in six lines:

> *The Soul.* Seek out reality, leave things that seem.
> *The Heart.* What, be a singer born and lack a theme?
> *The Soul.* Isaiah's coal, what more can man desire?
> *The Heart.* Struck dumb in the simplicity of fire!
> *The Soul.* Look on that fire, salvation walks within.
> *The Heart.* What theme had Homer but original sin?

And upon this there succeeds, as conclusion, the poem beginning:

> Must we part, Von Hügel, though much alike, for we
> Accept the miracles of the saints and honour sanctity?

and ending:

> Homer is my example and his unchristened heart.
> The lion and the honeycomb, what has Scripture said?
> So get you gone, Von Hügel, though with blessings on your
> head.

The symbolism of the honeycomb is clear: it is amid things at once strong and corruptible that the poet must find his 'theme'. But it is when we ask by what title the unrepentant pagan can call down blessings on the head of the Christian mystic that we come to the heart of the argument. For the fourth poem has recorded a mystical experience such as we know did—although very rarely—befall Yeats:

> My fiftieth year had come and gone,
> I sat, a solitary man,
> In a crowded London shop,
> An open book and empty cup
> On the marble table-top.
>
> While on the shop and street I gazed
> My body of a sudden blazed;
> And twenty minutes more or less
> It seemed, so great my happiness,
> That I was blessèd and could bless.

'And twenty minutes more or less . . . .' It is perhaps not fortuitously that this prosaicism carries a Wordsworthian reminiscence. Natural mysticism is being asserted as having the same reach and authority as religious mysticism. The choice of the saint (Yeats says in the letter last quoted) is comedy, and the heroic choice is tragedy; and he himself will 'live tragically'. Just so, we are to feel, Crazy Jane had lived—with Homer, and by all the honey generated in mortality. She had been no more debarred from beatitude thereby than had Yeats himself in the tea-shop. Jane could have given Von Hügel blessing for blessing. *All things remain in God.*

It is only imperfectly that one can thus trace, in a brief

discussion, even the main thread of *The Winding Stair*. And the volume contains perhaps yet more riches by the way than does *The Tower*. 'Coole Park, 1929' and 'Coole Park and Ballylee, 1931' are notable additions to the poems in which Yeats celebrates if not the deepest of his affections at least that one most untouched by bitterness and the 'remorse' of which he came to speak so frequently. They have an exquisite pendant in 'For Anne Gregory'. And nobody sufficiently young when the volume appeared to be acutely sensitive to the power of sheer incantation in poetry is ever likely to forget a word of 'Mad as the Mist and Snow'. When we puzzle over the mysterious importance to Yeats of Alcibiades and Pythagoras, Plotinus and Delacroix, we find one explanation, belonging with the blessed simplicities of poetry, when we unblushingly chant—as Yeats himself chanted—of our shuddering and sighing

> to think
> That even Cicero
> And many-minded Homer were
> *Mad as the mist and snow.*

16

The second phase of Yeats's dramatic activity opens with *At the Hawk's Well* and *The Only Jealousy of Emer*, which were played in 1916 and published five years later, together with *The Dreaming of the Bones* and *Calvary*, as *Four Plays for Dancers*. The group is best approached by way of the introduction which Yeats contributed, also in 1916, to Ezra Pound's *Certain Noble Plays of Japan*.

It is the nobility of the Nōh drama that emerges as its prime attraction for Yeats. Belonging, we are told, to an age of continual war, these Japanese plays had become part of the education of soldiers—of soldiers 'whose natures had as much of Walter Pater as of Achilles', so that they would have understood, had they had the chance, 'the painting of Puvis de Chavannes, the poetry of Mallarmé and Verlaine'. When *Hamlet* was being played for the first time before the London mob, it seems that matters were differently ordered at Kioto. There young nobles and princes, forbidden to attend the popular theatre with its mere mimicry and naturalism, 'were encouraged to witness and to perform in spectacles where speech, music, song, and dance created an image of nobility and strange beauty'. Nōh means 'Accomplishment'—the accomplishment of 'a few cultivated people who understand the literary and mythological allusions and the ancient lyrics quoted in speech or chorus, their discipline, a part of their breeding'. The Japanese theatre, had it much existed as a physical structure, would eminently have evidenced, we are made to feel, 'the glory of escutcheoned doors'. Even now, it seems, 'a player will publish his family tree to prove his skill'. Meditating all this, Yeats has become convinced that 'in the studio and in the drawing-room we can found a true theatre of beauty'. Indeed, he has got some way already. 'I have invented a form of drama, distinguished, indirect, and symbolic, and having no need of mob or press to pay its way—an aristocratic form.' The achievement, however, will necessarily be a restricted one, and he proposes to 'turn to something else' after 'having given enough performances for I hope the pleasure of personal friends and a few score people of good taste'.

A slight preciosity lurks in all this, and the essay is scarcely improved by being written in what may be called consciously Coole prose. When Yeats goes on to commend the use of the mask as a means of obliterating 'the face of some commonplace player, or . . . that face repainted to suit his own vulgar fancy', and declares that in the public theatre the human voice tends to seek 'some new musical sort of roar or scream', we are listening to one in reaction from long toil at the Abbey. And that reaction controls, too, those parts of the essay which are most clearly the work of a high aesthetic intelligence. The road to Kioto looks in places uncommonly like the road back to Clooth-na-Bare and Knocknarea. Yeats records that the Japanese stories remind him at times of Irish legends and beliefs, and he praises their emotion as self-conscious, reminiscent, and steeped in ancient literary associations; their authors 'found their delight in remembering celebrated lovers in the scenery pale passion loves'. The player in his mask 'will appear perhaps like an image seen in reverie by some Orphic worshipper', and the height of his art is found in its disrealizing power, its 'separating strangeness', its recession into some more powerful life, some deep of the mind, by means of images and symbols. 'There is no observation of life, because the poet would set before us all those things which we feel and imagine in silence.'

Movement upon the stage is founded upon the movement of puppets. And 'at the climax instead of the disordered passion of nature there is a dance, a series of positions and movements which may represent a battle, or a marriage, or the pain of a ghost in the Buddhist purgatory'. Although all these newly discovered conventions were made available to Yeats by Mr. Pound in the interest, no doubt, of bringing the older poet up to date (a programme which, in general, Mr. Pound was triumphantly to carry through) Yeats is, at least in part, applying them to old purposes. 'I want', he wrote, 'to create for myself an unpopular theatre and an audience like a secret society. . . . I desire a mysterious art.' This is an attitude as old as *The Wanderings of Oisin*. The element of ritual that is given such prominence in the plays for dancers seems to aim at invoking much the same trance-like responses as the earlier lyrics. Yeats is exploring new ways of assimilating drama, for which he has comparatively little talent, into the condition of lyric, for which he has a great deal.

At the Hawk's Well has a chorus of three musicians, who open and close the play with singing and with the ceremonial unfolding and folding of a cloth, and it was intended that they should accompany or control the movements of the players throughout upon a drum, a zither, and a gong. The plot has the most slender substance. Cuchulain as a young man has heard of a well that confers immortality upon those who drink from it. But it is guarded by a hawk woman, symbol of those forces of abstraction which are inimical to the heroic life. During the moments that the well is replenished she distracts Cuchulain with a magic dance, so that he has to depart to fulfil his variously bitter mortal destiny.

If Yeats, fretted by the Biddys and Paudeens of the Abbey, had looked forward to the production of this difficult experimental piece on his polite drawing-room occasion, he must have been a little disillusioned by the result. He had hoped for the Prime Minister, but it is not recorded that Mr. Asquith turned up. He had hoped for a few pretty ladies, and got a great many—but there was also 'a wretched woman' intent upon describing their clothes for the newspapers. The musicians, he wrote, were the devil. They had not taken kindly, one supposes, to conducting a sort of tattoo. It was clear that the play must not be done again until Henry Ainley, the fashionable actor who had been required to look like 'an archaic Greek statue' in the part of Cuchulain, had been got well out of the way. On the dance of the hawk woman Yeats passes no criticism. He and a real Japanese dancer, Mr. Ito, had evolved it on the basis of much study of real hawks in the London Zoo. It was just three weeks after this aesthetic adventure in Mayfair that the Easter Rising took place in Dublin, and Maud Gonne, the Cathleen ni Houlihan of his most moving play, was widowed by a firing squad.

Yeats's enthusiasm for his new form, however, was not abated, and *The Only Jealousy of Emer*, which is begun and concluded by musicians with the same kind of ritual as before, has not one masked Cuchulain, but two identical masked Cuchulains. The relationship of the Figure of Cuchulain to the Ghost of Cuchulain, though it can be worried out, could never be theatrically intelligible. It represents a distortion of the underlying legend in the interest of a recondite and perhaps deeply personal consideration of the conflicting forms of human love. For this the conventions of the Nōh play are entirely inapposite, and the disharmony of the attempt is emphasized when the taut and splendid introductory song is succeeded in the dialogue portions of the play by a worn and conventional blank verse. Yeats appears to have acknowledged this failure when in the much later prose version of the piece, *Fighting the Waves*, he simplified the design until it became little more than a vehicle for the dancing of Ninette de Valois and the music of Antheil—with a place kept, however, for the opening and closing songs. The latter of these has some claim to be the most obscure of Yeats's lyrics. Yet it appears that he did not want his Nōh plays to be wholly 'mysterious' or wholly remote in circumstance and time. He proposed next to apply the Japanese conventions in a play

where a Sinn Feiner will have a conversation with Judas in the streets of Dublin. Judas is looking for somebody to whom he may betray Christ in order that Christ may proclaim himself King of the Jews. . . . Judas is a ghost, perhaps he is mistaken for the ghost of an old rag-picker by the neighbourhood.

Nothing came of this promising international situation, but the idea of a contemporary setting, and of a meeting with a person or persons presently revealed as ghostly (a common incident in authentic Nōh drama) is carried over into the next achieved play, *The Dreaming of the Bones*, written in 1917. Here, after the musicians have set the scene in some desolate region of western Ireland before dawn, a young man enters and is at once encountered by a stranger and a girl, who both wear heroic masks. The young man says that he is a fugitive from the Easter Rising; there is a colloquy about supernatural matters; and the masked figures presently reveal themselves as the ghosts of Diarmuid and Dervorgilla, lovers accursed in Irish history as having called into their country an invading Norman power. The ghosts may never kiss until one of their own race shall have forgiven them, and this the young fugitive patriot resists a momentary inclination to do. When played at the Abbey in 1931 *The Dreaming of the Bones* was reported by Yeats to have been enthusiastically received—perhaps because of its political power, which he admitted, rather than for the 'ceremonial movements' upon which he set chief store. 'Half round the stage meant a mountain climbed', he reported with satisfaction to Mrs. Shakespear. *The Dreaming of the Bones* is the best of the plays for dancers, but this symbolic mountaineering is the only opportunity for dancing that it affords. *Calvary*, the last of the four plays, presents, more enterprisingly, a dance of the Roman soldiers as they prepare to dice for Christ's cloak at the foot of the Cross. But *Calvary* is a mystery play rather than a Nōh play, and is further distinguished from the others by being substantially involved with the thought of *A Vision*. The soldiers, Yeats explains in a note, represent a form of objectivity lying beyond Christ's help. Judas, associated with the image of the heron that typifies extreme subjectivity, and Lazarus, who knows himself to have been wronged in his summons from the tomb, are types of 'intellectual despair' whom Christ's sympathy is powerless to reach. Christ, we read in *A Vision*, 'being *antithetical* like His age', knew intellectual despair; yet His pity was not for this, but for the common lot. These farther reaches of serious speculation are not, perhaps, very adequately explored in this short piece. But some of the imagery is deeply evocative—and not least in the two refrains: 'God has not died for the white heron' and 'God has not appeared to the birds'. The relationship of this to Mantegna's 'Agony in the Garden' in the National Gallery has been perceived by Mr. Henn. Yeats speaks elsewhere of 'A thoughtless image of Mantegna's

thought', and here he seems to have established image and painting in an effective symbiosis. At least the first educes a new
dimension in the second.

The Player Queen, which had evolved since 1908 through
various painfully achieved prose scenarios towards its intended
condition as a poetic tragedy, was transformed by 1914 into
'a wild comedy, almost a farce, with a tragic background'.
By 1917 it existed as a prose comedy designed for Mrs. Patrick
Campbell, who had acted Deirdre in Dublin. Nothing came of
this project, and the play was eventually produced in London
in 1919. Its excellence and swift lightness as a stage piece must
have surprised those who were aware that the writer had for
years been attempting to embody much abstruse reflection in
successive versions of it. There is a letter written to Edmund
Dulac in 1922 in which Yeats speaks of his recurrent need to
take refuge in fantastical high spirits 'from logic, and passion,
and the love of God and charity to my neighbours and other
exhausting things', and adds that a reading of *The Player Queen*
will help to make this understood. And yet, as so often with
Yeats, there is something equivocal and self-protecting in the
final levity of the play. This becomes clear as soon as we have
considered the action. It is set in an unknown country and at
an undetermined time, and there are two scenes. In the first
a mob of townsmen and countryfolk—Shakespearian mechani-
cals with overtones from Lady Gregory—are on the point of in-
surrection against their Queen, who has never appeared among
them and who is averred to have been detected coupling with
a white unicorn. Septimus, the poet and leading actor of a company of strolling players, is wandering about the town in a state
of droll and good-humoured drunkenness, garrulously denouncing his 'bad wife' Decima, who has disappeared when due to
play before the court. The rumour about the unicorn, 'a most
noble beast, a most religious beast', rouses Septimus to a state
of high indignation, and he proposes to fight anybody who
denies that its chastity is equal to its beauty. An old beggar
appears, calling out for straw upon which he may lie down and
bray; some species of possession prompts him to this whenever
the crown is to change hands; it is believed that the intrusive
spirit is that of the donkey that carried Christ into Jerusalem.
In the second scene, set in the throne-room of the castle, the
Prime Minister rages against the players, who are failing to

get on with a rehearsal of Noah's Deluge. Decima, who has refused to don the mask of Noah's wife or to take the part of any woman older than thirty, is presently discovered hiding under the throne. She learns that Septimus has become the lover of another of the players, Nona, and that a song which he had composed for her had in fact been written on Nona's shoulder in bed, and its metre tapped out up and down Nona's spine. The Queen, whatever her adventures in the mode of Pasiphaë (by whom Yeats perhaps means Europa) and Leda, is a dim person seeking a dim religious vocation. At the crisis of the action she escapes from the ordeal of facing her indignant subjects by having Decima impersonate her on the throne. Decima thus becomes Queen, expels Septimus and his troupe firmly but kindly from the realm, and marries the Prime Minister—although indeed serious commentators upon the fable are obliged to conclude that her future marital engagements will be on the mysteriously significant superequine plane. That Yeats was justified in calling this a 'wild' play will be evident. And it is wildly strewn with the *disjecta membra* of his symbolical intentions. Thus Decima's song—beautiful in whatever circumstances it is represented as having been composed—takes the mind to the rape of Leda, an occasion upon which he had long brooded as crucial in the cyclic movement of history:

'When she was got', my mother sang,
'I heard a seamew cry,
I saw a flake of yellow foam
That dropped upon my thigh.'

How therefore could she help but braid
The gold upon my hair,
And dream that I should carry
The golden top of care?

That the players should be presenting Noah's Deluge holds an answering reverberation. Yeats considered 'the destruction of all things by the flood' to be a symbol, or an instance, of the universal disintegration that succeeds upon a reversal of the gyres. Indeed we may suppose, for good measure, that the palace revolution which substitutes for the outgoing Queen with her pious Christianity the incoming one who can sing

Any bird or brute may rest
An empty head upon my breast

is involved with the same idea. These and numerous other implications undoubtedly enrich the piece for the careful reader. Yet the 'system' with which they are at play is less interesting in itself than is the ambiguity of attitude leading Yeats at once to exploit it in a high poetry and to resolve it in farce. The moon is going strong in *The Player Queen*, but it is to an effect of tumbling things about. There have not been lacking commentators, wedded to that more sober donkey Explication, to reproach Yeats for failing to be wholly serious in this agreeable diversion. That we have to seek elsewhere for the full text of two admirable lyrics preserved only fragmentarily in the final form of the play may perhaps a little justify us in feeling that the abandoning of the proposal for a poetic tragedy represents a lowering of the flag on the poet's part. We may even feel here that malign influence of Mr. Pound so mysteriously foretold by W. T. Horton. But in fact *The Player Queen* as we have it is on a main line of Yeats's development, since his whole mythology achieves its most effective artistic embodiment in poetry that is fragmentary and tragic, 'wild' and gay. *The Cat and the Moon* (acted 1931), a slight play in the Nōh manner, has its place here. It is framed between portions of one of Yeats's most occult songs—in which, however, we are clearly told that

> The sacred moon overhead
> Has taken a new phase.

In the action this new phase is exemplified when the Lame Beggar (the Soul) who has ridden on the back of the Blind Beggar (the Body) himself takes the Saint on his back. Yeats explains in a gloss that here 'the normal man has become one with his opposite'—a reconciliation of self and anti-self reflecting 'a certain great spiritual event which may take place when Primary Tincture . . . supersedes Antithetical'. But this connexion with *A Vision* is insubstantial. *The Cat and the Moon* looks forward to Crazy Jane's world. At the same time it light-heartedly incorporates an ingenious satirical sketch of the association of Edward Martyn and George Moore, respectively 'a holy man' and 'an old lecher'.

Sophocles' King Oedipus and *Sophocles' Oedipus at Colonus* were played at the Abbey Theatre in 1926 and 1927 respectively. Of the first, Yeats had attempted a version as early as 1912, apparently attracted by the bizarre circumstance that the play

had been banned in England as immoral, and also from a feeling
that it had some affinity with the Irish spirit. Of this latter
persuasion Gilbert Murray endeavoured to disabuse him in
a letter of joyous extravagance which may serve to explain how
Shaw had contrived to base upon this eminent scholar—in
old age so austerely sweet and sad—the character of Cusins
in *Major Barbara*. For both plays Yeats wrote the dialogue in
prose, 'with one sole object, that the words should sound natural
and fall in their natural order', his intention being to produce
the 'Plain Man's *Oedipus*'. To the verse choruses he gave more
attention, particularly to those of the *Coloneus*, two of which,
he had been informed, 'are very famous' in the Greek. The
Coloneus is the better done; it is plainly closer to things that Yeats
understood. But when he declares that 'when Oedipus at
Colonus went into the Wood of the Furies he felt the same
creeping in his flesh that an Irish countryman feels in certain
haunted woods in Galway and in Sligo', he is perhaps in contact
only with a limited aspect of the Sophoclean intention. The
peasant is not ἀραῖος, and we may be disposed to pause in brief
appreciation over Yeats's bland statement that at the time of
making his first version he had 'forgotten his Greek'. He was
capable, we know, of saying the same about his Hebrew.

The Resurrection is a short prose play with songs, to the
perfecting of which Yeats appears to have given much attention
over a number of years. Despite its subject, and rather to his
surprise, it proved playable at the Abbey in 1934. The Crucifixion has taken place. In the streets of Jerusalem worshippers
of Dionysus are celebrating orgiastically the festival of their
slain and revivified god. Indoors, in a chamber adjoining that
in which the still-despairing Apostles sit, a Greek, a Hebrew,
and a Syrian discuss first the rumour and then the fact of
Christ's Resurrection. The Hebrew has concluded that Christ
'was nothing more than a man, the best man who ever lived'—
a man who came in some moment of self-delusion and exhaustion to believe himself the Messiah. The Greek cannot conceive
how a man could believe such a thing. The conception of
vicarious atonement is also incomprehensible to him. The gods
are in eternal possession of themselves, and man too does not
surrender his soul. The Greek stands, in fact, for the order and
rationality of an era which the birth of Christianity is bringing
catastrophically to a close. If he is himself a Christian, it is in

an esoteric sense not very clearly explained. No god can enter history, be slain by human hands, and rise again; this to the Greek is foolishness, like the raving of the Asiatic mob outside. If the tomb is empty, it is because only a Phantom has been laid in it. If Jesus enters the room now, it will be as a Phantom may, straight through the wall. To the Syrian, representative of the East, the speculative subtlety thus enlisted to preserve the cracking mould of classical thought is equally foolishness: 'What if there is always something that lies outside knowledge, outside order? What if at the moment when knowledge and order seem complete that something appears? . . . What if the irrational return? What if the circle begin again?' And this happens. The risen Christ enters, and He is flesh and blood. The Greek touches him, screams—something we are made to feel no Greek has ever before been constrained to do—and cries out in the moment of this dire epiphany: 'O Athens, Alexandria, Rome, something has come to destroy you. The heart of a phantom is beating. Man has begun to die. Your words are clear at last, O Heraclitus. God and man die each other's life, live each other's death.' Heraclitus is saying that the human and the divine stand in eternal opposition. But the phrase attracts Yeats, as Mr. Henn has noted, because its cadence suggests a 'correspondence with the characteristic movement of the gyres'. And it is possible to feel, as we read the dialogue portion of *The Resurrection*, that the gyres have shot their bolt. Yeats's thought is itself too evidently on a Wheel and in danger of turning up once too often. To give the Christian story a backdrop of Dionysiac celebrants coupling in the street is easy and vulgar—something that might be expected rather from a boy making his first acquaintance with *The Golden Bough* than from a man long given to mature historical reflection. We cannot imagine it coming from Thomas Hardy. But equally we cannot imagine Hardy producing—say in some chorus in *The Dynasts*—two heights of lyrical expression like those with which Yeats opens and closes this rather jaded play. The second stanza of the closing song appears to have been composed at a remove from the rest, and in fact it modulates into that purely elegiac mode in which so much of his finest later poetry is composed. The first stanza is certainly not less magnificent, but it is more involved with 'ideas' which the history of poetry offers us no encouragement to suppose as likely to be of any very permanent interest:

In pity for man's darkening thought
He walked that room and issued thence
In Galilean turbulence;
The Babylonian starlight brought
A fabulous, formless darkness in;
Odour of blood when Christ was slain
Made all Platonic tolerance vain
And vain all Doric discipline.

Everything that man esteems
Endures a moment or a day:
Love's pleasure drives his love away,
The painter's brush consumes his dreams;
The herald's cry, the soldier's tread
Exhaust his glory and his might:
Whatever flames upon the night
Man's own resinous heart has fed.

17

That *The Words upon the Window-Pane* (acted 1930) stands
somewhat by itself among Yeats's plays is evident in the first
stage-direction, which specifies 'a lodging-house room, an arm-
chair, a little table in front of it, chairs on either side'. It is like
the world of Ibsen, where tables always have chairs, and chairs
tables. The room, however, has its august associations. It is in
a Dublin house which 'in the early part of the eighteenth century belonged to friends of Jonathan Swift, or rather of Stella'.
And Swift and—at least—Stella's rival Vanessa haunt it, so
that their voices, re-enacting a past agony, break in upon the
commonplace spiritualistic seance which constitutes the action
of the piece. We are prepared for this irruption when one of the
characters utters what is a haunting persuasion of Yeats's own:

Some spirits are earth-bound—they think they are still living and
go over and over some action of their past lives, just as we go over
and over some painful thought, except that where they are thought
is reality.... The murderer repeats his murder, the robber his robbery,
the lover his serenade, the soldier hears the trumpet once again.

Yeats had abundant experience to draw upon in evoking the
banal atmosphere in which mediumship usually exercises itself.
When the spirits seem to have departed there is an effective
tailpiece in which a young student questions Mrs. Henderson,

through whose mouth they have spoken, and quickly realizes that she has never so much as heard of Swift. But the power of this is in turn excelled by the hammer-stroke with which the play ends. Mrs. Henderson has collected her fees—she has a sharp eye to them—and is left alone on the stage:

Mrs. Henderson. How tired I am! I'd be the better of a cup of tea. *(She finds the teapot and puts kettle on fire, and then as she crouches down by the hearth suddenly lifts up her hands and counts her fingers, speaking in Swift's voice.)* Five great Ministers that were my friends are gone, ten great Ministers that were my friends are gone. I have not fingers enough to count the great Ministers that were my friends and that are gone. *(She wakes with a start and speaks in her own voice.)* Where did I put that tea-caddy? Ah! there it is. And there should be a cup and saucer. *(She finds the saucer.)* But where's the cup? *(She moves aimlessly about the stage and then, letting the saucer fall and break, speaks in Swift's voice.)* Perish the day on which I was born!

18

On the canvas of Yeats's final plays *The Words upon the Window-Pane* stands out like a stark *repoussoir* harshly imposed upon a remote and formalized landscape. With *The King of the Great Clock Tower* and *A Full Moon in March* we are returned to a further development of the Japanese tradition. The second play, completed at the end of 1934, is a reworking of the first, which had been brought slowly through prose to a completed verse form about a year earlier, only to be crisply characterized by Mr. Pound as 'putrid'. After a preliminary song a Queen is discovered 'stretching and yawning'—which is Yeats's constant symbol of sexual satisfaction, achieved or contemplated. She knows that some 'terrifying man' has come to her court, and we learn that she has pledged herself to whatever man 'best sings his passion' before her. A Swineherd enters to make this attempt, and promises her

> A song—the night of love,
> An ignorant forest and the dung of swine.

His bold speech has aroused her desire, but this—since she is 'crueller than solitude'—prompts her to order his instant decollation. She dances in blood-stained garments, while holding the severed head in her blood-stained hands. And the severed

head sings—or rather a member of the chorus sings on its
behalf:

> I sing a song of Jack and Jill.
> Jill had murdered Jack;
> *The moon shone brightly;*
> Ran up the hill, and round the hill,
> Round the hill and back.
> *A full moon in March.*
>
> Jack had a hollow heart, for Jill
> Had hung his heart on high;
> *The moon shone brightly;*
> Had hung his heart beyond the hill,
> A-twinkle in the sky.
> *A full moon in March.*

Yeats associated the figure of Salome, 'dancing before Herod
and receiving the Prophet's head in her indifferent hands',
with that 'moment before revelation' which had been his
theme in *The Resurrection*. It is doubtless thus that, in the singing head, the Prophet comes to be telescoped with the revived
Dionysus. But Yeats was to admit to Edmund Dulac that he
did not understand how this 'blood symbolism' had laid hold
upon him. There is comparatively little creative energy in the
dialogue parts of the plays; the prose has been worked up into
a blank verse which seems to belong to a past phase of Yeats's
writing; and of *The King of the Great Clock Tower* we read without
surprise in a letter: 'I made up the play that I might write
lyrics out of dramatic experience, all my personal experience
having in some strange way come to an end.' It is as if, in these
mysterious fables, he is setting himself so many arbitrary
starting-points for incantatory and 'mechanical' songs in moods
when other means of provoking them are in abeyance. Most of
the songs have strange refrains. Some of them, like that which
closes *The King of the Great Clock Tower*, could be set by anyone
familiar with the body of Yeats's work in contexts apparently
more apposite than that which the poet has chosen to give them.
When the Queen has finally pressed her lips to the lips of the
head we read:

> *First Attendant.* O, but I saw a solemn sight;
> *Said the rambling, shambling travelling-man;*
> Castle Dargan's ruin all lit,
> Lovely ladies dancing in it.

Second Attendant. What though they danced! Those days are gone,
    Said the wicked, crooked, hawthorn tree;
    Lovely lady or gallant man
    Are blown cold dust or a bit of bone.

First Attendant. O, what is life but a mouthful of air?
    Said the rambling, shambling travelling-man;
    Yet all the lovely things that were
    Live, for I saw them dancing there.
       [The Queen has come down stage and now stands framed in the half-closed curtains.

Second Attendant. Nobody knows what may befall,
    Said the wicked, crooked, hawthorn tree.
    I have stood so long by a gap in the wall
    Maybe I shall not die at all.

                       [The outer curtain descends]

The relevance of this is wild and gnomic. And we should certainly understand it as well if it stood at the end of *Purgatory*, a play yet to come.

The Herne's Egg is a somewhat longer play, notable for incorporating a good deal of metrical experiment aimed—courageously at this late hour, even if not very successfully—at getting away from the worn blank-verse medium upon which Yeats had been continuing to rely. It belongs, like the two preceding plays, to the uncertain period following upon the operation to which he submitted himself in 1934; and he gives an account of its genesis similar to that which he had given for *The King of the Great Clock Tower.* 'I am trusting to this play', he wrote, 'to give me a new mass of thought and feeling, overflowing into lyrics.' He declared it to be 'as wild a play as *Player Queen*, as amusing but more tragedy and philosophic depth'. Of the wildness there can be no question, since what we have is a farcical fantasia upon heroic and mythological themes. Congal King of Connacht and Aedh King of Tara have fought their fiftieth battle against each other, but Congal dies on a kitchen spit and Aedh is killed with a table-leg. Attracta, the priestess of the Great Herne, believes herself to have lain with the bird, and no doubt to an effect as fateful as when Leda lay with the Swan. But this conjunction appears to be a delusion. Congal and six of his men believe themselves to have raped Attracta as punishment for her misdemeanour in substituting a hen's egg for a herne's egg at a banquet. But this sexual achievement may also be delusory, and the only actual coupling in the play is that between two donkeys. Yeats described the piece as 'very Rabelaisian'. That the moon, which presides over the last scene, is required to be 'the moon of comic tradition, a round smiling face', and that one of the donkeys is a toy donkey on wheels, are circumstances seeming to reinforce the possibility of some burlesque intention. One careful critic has declared the play to be 'fully archetypal' and 'an achievement of the utmost subtlety'. The fact of its being, in Yeats's own phrase, 'the strangest wildest thing' that he had ever written is not necessarily incompatible with this. Yet it must be doubtful whether *The Herne's Egg* will ever yield much to metaphysical criticism. And that it is in a form, as Yeats believed, in which esoteric interests could be pushed far 'without endangering the clarity necessary for dramatic effect' is at least equally challenge-able. The play proved, when tested, inpossible to produce.

Yet Yeats had by no means lost contact with the stage. His last public appearance was after the successful production at the Abbey Theatre in August 1938 of his penultimate play, *Purgatory*. The settings were by Anne Yeats, so we have some public knowledge that this daughter of genius a little escaped 'common greenness' after all. It was a production followed by some controversy—an American Jesuit having risen in the Abbey's lecture-hall to suggest, not unreasonably, that the poet's conception of Purgatory was at variance with that of the Roman Catholic Church. But however this may be, and despite weaknesses which we must note, Yeats achieves here a small masterpiece.

There could be no farther cry from the 'theatre of beauty' than this bare dire piece. It is certainly not designed as a means of activating lyrical impulse, as we have seen some of the dramatic pieces of this period to have been. There are no lyrical interludes at all. In this regard the play marks the concluding phase in what Mr. T. S. Eliot has distinguished as Yeats's 'gradual purging out of poetical ornament . . . the most painful part of the labour, so far as the versification goes, of the modern poet who tries to write a play in verse'. In the narrower sense the versification, if to be described without technical preten-sion, must be called one of boldly resolved decasyllabics and octosyllabics in a free interplay and alternation. It is tentative work, a thing in itself sufficiently remarkable from a poet in his seventy-third year. But if the verse is new it is otherwise with the theme. *Purgatory* gives embodiment, in an action of extraordinary concentration, to those ideas about death, expiation, eternal recurrence, an extra-temporal order, which had haunted Yeats throughout his maturity: these are now concentrated round the familiar image of the house that lights up again, the crisis that re-enacts itself for the seeing eye. And here these things are set before us on the stage. The process may be compared to that actualizing of certain of the dominant images of earlier plays which has been remarked in the final work of Shakespeare.

There are only two speaking parts, those of an old man and a boy, father and son, pedlars or tinkers, wandering from hall to cottage, cottage to hall. The scene in which they are discovered is that of 'A ruined house and a bare tree in the background':

Boy. Half-door, hall door,
    Hither and thither day and night,
    Hill or hollow, shouldering this pack,
    Hearing you talk.

Old Man. Study that house.
    I think about its jokes and stories;
    I try to remember what the butler
    Said to a drunken gamekeeper
    In mid-October, but I cannot.
    If I cannot, none living can.
    Where are the jokes and stories of a house,
    Its threshold gone to patch a pig-sty?

The disgraced and burnt-out house is the memorial to a shameful marriage and a crime. Its lady had married a drunken groom who had then profaned her wedding-night and after her early death squandered all—until the only child of the union, grown to sixteen years, had stabbed his father to death and fled. That child is now the old man present on the stage; the boy is his son, sixteen years old. The old man tells the story to the boy:

        She never knew the worst, because
        She died in giving birth to me,
        But now she knows it all, being dead.
        Great people lived and died in this house;

Magistrates, colonels, members of Parliament,
Captains and Governors, and long ago
Men that had fought at Aughrim and the Boyne. . . .
They had loved the trees that he cut down
To pay what he had lost at cards
Or spent on horses, drink and women;
Had loved the house, had loved all
The intricate passages of the house,
But he killed the house; to kill a house
Where great men grew up, married, died,
I here declare a capital offence.

Now the house lives only for

> The souls in Purgatory that come back
> To habitations and familiar spots.

These relive their transgressions not once but many times.
As Crazy Jane knew, *All things remain in God*. And presently,
as for Jane, as with Castle Dargan in *The King of the Great
Clock Tower*, the house lights up for the old man and he sees at a
window his mother as a young girl, waiting for the drunken man
to come to her bridal bed. The boy sees nothing; his father's
distraction seems a good opportunity to steal his purse; there is
a struggle until the window lights up again and both see the
phantom groom 'like some tired beast'. This precipitates the
crisis:

Old Man. That beast there would know nothing, being nothing,
    If I should kill a man under the window
    He would not even turn his head.
                                    [*He stabs the Boy.*
    My father and my son on the same jack-knife!
    That finishes—there—there—there—
            [*He stabs again and again. The window grows dark.*
    'Hush-a-bye baby, thy father's a knight,
    Thy mother a lady, lovely and bright.'
    No, that is something that I read in a book,
    And if I sing it must be to my mother,
    And I lack rhyme.

The limitations of the piece are here apparent in the decline
upon Jacobean reminiscence. And this is sustained in the naïve
explanatory soliloquy hard upon which the play ends:

> Dear mother, the window is dark again,
> But you are in the light because

I finished all that consequence.
I killed that lad because had he grown up
He would have struck a woman's fancy,
Begot, and passed pollution on.
I am a wretched foul old man
And therefore harmless.

Recalling the Nōh audience which understood 'the literary
and mythological allusions and the ancient lyrics quoted', we
cannot suppose that there is anything inadvertent in Lear's
thus appearing with, as it were, his heath in his pocket.
Othello's handkerchief has been shown to make a similar
appearance in *The King of the Great Clock Tower*, as has the
Brutus–Caesar relationship in *The Herne's Egg*. But here at least
we gain a strong impression that the old man cannot at the
end of the play stand on his own feet as a dramatic creation, and
that he is being supplied with some rather formidable crutches.

Yeats's theatre closes upon *The Death of Cuchulain*, a play
finished only a few weeks before his death. He has returned to
blank verse; it is, after all, his only reliable poetic instrument for
heroic drama. The piece is a brief cento of past themes. The
hero accepts the battle to which his mistress Eithne Inguba
treacherously declares that his wife Emer advises him. He is
wounded and it appears to be his destiny to die at the hands of
Aoife, the woman of *At the Hawk's Well* on whom he had
begotten the son he was himself to kill. But in fact his head is
cut off by the Blind Man of *On Baile's Strand*, to whom Maeve
has promised twelve pennies if he will perform the work.
Cuchulain's last words, 'I say it is about to sing', recall the
symbolism of the earlier plays of decollation, in which the
virtues of heroic and imaginative life assert themselves against
some destructive feminine principle. The action closes upon
Emer dancing before conventional representations of the severed
heads of her husband and of six men who have wounded him.
A singer sings a gnomic and perhaps unperfected song, from the
obscurity of which some lines stand out sharply:

What stood in the Post Office
With Pearse and Connolly?
What comes out of the mountain
Where men first shed their blood?
Who thought Cuchulain till it seemed
He stood where they had stood?

We are back with that modern Irish moment in which 'a terrible beauty' was born. It is Yeats's last salute, in lines designed for a public theatre, to the world of Maud Gonne.

19

Yeats's own final world finds expression in two gatherings of lyric poetry which remain for consideration. The first of these appeared initially in 1934 in a volume taking its title from the prose version of *The King of the Great Clock Tower*, and in augmented form a year later in a volume including the verse form of the play and also *A Full Moon in March*—from which the general title is correspondingly drawn. The second and larger gathering, along with *Purgatory* and *The Death of Cuchulain*, was published in its definitive form posthumously in 1940 as *Last Poems and Plays*.

Our early impression of the first volume may be of somewhat scattered, confused, and in places even factitious inspiration. 'Parnell's Funeral' takes its prompting from Maud Gonne's report that a falling star had appeared in clear daylight at the moment the dead leader's body was lowered into the grave. The poem moves by way of a Sicilian coin, Yeats's own successful invoking of the moon at Tulira Castle, and *The Golden Bough* to speculation on what would have happened had Mr. de Valera eaten Parnell's heart. Upon this political and anthropological *mélange* there follow three marching songs with bizarre refrains. These were originally written in the interest of General O'Duffy's version of Italian Fascism. Later, when Yeats had come to distrust the Blue Shirt movement, they were rewritten in a manner that—in his own words—'increased their fantasy, their extravagance, their obscurity, that no party might sing them'. It is fairly certain that no party has.

With the twelve 'Supernatural Songs' we move into very different territory. These poems are felt at once as the product of deep imaginative excitement—'I have never known the dream deeper', Yeats wrote at this time—and some of them, at least, bear out the statement made in the eighth of them:

> A passion-driven exultant man sings out
> Sentences that he has never thought.

Yet, although they make no coherent statement, and present in their central figure, Ribh, the old restless alternation of

Yeatsian poses, primary and antithetical, contemplative sage
and angry old man, each is poetically a work of the utmost
certainty and precision. The first, 'Ribh at the Tomb of Baile
and Aillinn', deserves notice as one of the most perfectly articu-
lated of his lyrics. The path to it from the *Baile and Aillinn* of
1902 must be one of the longest ever trodden by poet. Yet the
connexion is not entirely confined to the common legendary
background. The disguised Aengus, the 'old gaunt crafty one'
who in the early poem gives each lover delusive news of the
other's death and thus secures their happiness 'in his own land
among the dead', is transformed in the late poem into the aged
hermit Ribh, whose wisdom must come to him by the light
which a perception of that happiness kindles for the seeing eye.
Moreover the late poem preserves, faintly but unmistakably
behind the austerity of its cadence, the echo of all that Pre-
Raphaelite beauty through which the young Yeats had passed
with such passionate love:

> And poets found, old writers say,
> A yew-tree where his body lay;
> But a wild apple hid the grass
> With its sweet blossom where hers was.

In 'Ribh at the Tomb of Baile and Aillinn' the yew and the
apple still grow, but beauty has been turned to miracle—the
miracle that, at the end of the first stanza, 'none have heard':

> Because you have found me in the pitch-dark night
> With open book you ask me what I do.
> Mark and digest my tale, carry it afar
> To those that never saw this tonsured head
> Nor heard this voice that ninety years have cracked.
> Of Baile and Aillinn you need not speak,
> All know their tale, all know what leaf and twig,
> What juncture of the apple and the yew,
> Surmount their bones; but speak what none have heard.

Eidetic experiences on the fringe of sleep had long ago persuaded Yeats to consider with attention that identification of
a luminous with a purified condition which he had encountered
in neo-Platonic writing, and Swedenborg's related persuasion
that 'the sexual intercourse of angels is a conflagration of the
whole being'. It is thus that the old Irish lovers become angels in
the second stanza:

The miracle that gave them such a death
Transfigured to pure substance what had once
Been bone and sinew; when such bodies join
There is no touching here, nor touching there,
Nor straining joy, but whole is joined to whole;
For the intercourse of angels is a light
Where for its moment both seem lost, consumed.

From this the aged hermit is at an immense remove. His gaze is not even upon the transcendent conjunction but upon his 'holy book'—such a book as Yeats had toiled over, baffled, in 'The Phases of the Moon'. Yet it is by that transcendence, as also through much abnegation, that Ribh's book is visible to him at all:

Here in the pitch-dark atmosphere above
The trembling of the apple and the yew,
Here on the anniversary of their death,
The anniversary of their first embrace,
Those lovers, purified by tragedy,
Hurry into each other's arms; these eyes,
By water, herb and solitary prayer
Made aquiline, are open to that light.
Though somewhat broken by the leaves, that light
Lies in a circle on the grass; therein
I turn the pages of my holy book.

For the reader familiar with the body of Yeats's poetry there is in this whole poem a richness of implication that places it among his most perfect achievements. And the final three lines are almost in themselves an answer to the charge that his poetic craft is failing him in his last years. If anything is failing him— and we must treat it as an open question to the end—it is his power to hold together, in any sort of intelligible polarity across the hub of the Wheel, sense and spirit, natural and supernatural. The second poem, indeed, declares absolutely that 'Natural and supernatural with the self-same ring are wed'. Yet, although light from a perfecting of love 'lies in a circle on the grass' and makes the holy book a book that can be read, in the fifth poem Ribh seems to deny the ring with an answering absoluteness:

Why should I seek for love or study it?
It is of God and passes human wit.
I study hatred with great diligence.

With diligence, it is true, a dialectic thread can be traced through these poems—or rather several dialectic threads can be so traced, for more than one harmonizing interpretation has been offered by well-equipped inquirers. But nothing of the sort seems for a time possible at the level of simple imaginative impression. We expect—perhaps the expectation is romantic—that the years, whatever they bring of poetry, will bring the resolved philosophic mind, an esemplastic power, at least some single even if it be a narrowed vision. But coherence of this sort we shall not find. There is a cartoon of Max Beerbohm's, 'The Old Pilgrim Comes Home', in which Henry James is represented as approaching and hailing a city built of bits and pieces from all the great capitals of the world. If Yeats were to be correspondingly represented, it would be not the city but the pilgrim who would have to be composite—or rather there would be several Yeatses, and they would be exploring uncertainly convergent paths. In these present poems it is as if beside Ribh the sage, magistral and composed with his illumined book, there stands the Swift of 'Blood and the Moon', 'beating on his breast in sibylline frenzy blind'. Swift might be the *persona* behind the last of the Ribh poems, 'Meru', where man, 'despite his terror',

> cannot cease
> Ravening through century after century,
> Ravening, raging, and uprooting that he may come
> Into the desolation of reality.

This is very much Thomas Hardy's ironic vision of what the human intellect achieves. And here, we may feel, is at least one Yeats who cries it out with a violence that declares a spirit unreconciled and a heart unsatisfied. And so we arrive at his final volume. The sixty-year-old smiling public man is now in his seventies—and certainly we shall not find among his remaining masks the mask of a man looking, as once in that convent school, pleasantly around him. More becoming will be a wild laughter in the throat of death; and indeed to 'laugh in tragic joy' is a proposal on the opening page of *Last Poems*. Part of Yeats's remaining energy goes to a direct exploring of this paradoxical possibility. Part of it must strike us as devoted to a restless, caged prowling over old ground, a fitful trying on of old cloaks and poses. *Last Poems* is an immediately impressive book, but impressive in a disturbing diversity of ways, so that

again we may think to miss in it something of the 'final' quality
we expect. This is delusive, however. For the paths do converge.

20

Yeats somewhere says that creation without toil is a temptation to the artist. From this temptation his own lack of
facility in composition must always have helped to protect
him. But in a group of political poems in his last volume there
is evident both the retrospective impulse operative throughout
and a need to seek a medium for a free and immediate outpouring of sheer energy—a display, above everything, of
increased zest, undiminished vigour. This, no doubt, is a temptation presenting itself particularly to a skilled and ageing man.
The effect has been called strident; yet, of their kind, these
verses are extremely good. Some are inspired by Irish street-
balladry and equipped with refrains that are now crashingly
relevant—

> *The ghost of Roger Casement*
> *Is beating on the door—*

and now of a weirdly effective obliquity:

> What remains to sing about
> But of the death he met
> Stretched under a doorway
> Somewhere off Henry Street;
> They that found him found upon
> The door above his head
> 'Here died the O'Rahilly.
> R.I.P.' writ in blood.
> *How goes the weather?*

The marching songs of the *Full Moon in March* volume have
been rewritten partly to express a deepening disillusion over
political effort and the modern world—'What if there's nothing
up there at the top?'—and partly (and in significant collocation
with this) as if in search for any material of affirmative statement, or merely of affirmative gesture, if no more than gesture
can be contrived. We have viewed Yeats earlier as one who
would only be carried down the hill kicking. Here we meet an
old man, a 'grandfather', who, brought to the gallows,

> kicked before he died,
> He did it out of pride.

Perhaps the essence of *Last Poems* consists in Yeats's determination to kick before he dies—and from the same motive. Long ago
he had written that the aristocratic code requires of a man that
he should come 'proud, open-eyed and laughing to the tomb'.
He is now much concerned with all these attitudes. The reckless
and arrogantly rejoicing use of life is a theme in several further
ballad-like poems which are without political content. These
shade into others in which there is presented, whether persona-
tively or otherwise, the image, already familiar, of the 'wild
old wicked man' and of a world of madness, frenzy, and harsh
sexual experience:

> Go your ways, O go your ways,
> I choose another mark,
> Girls down on the seashore
> Who understand the dark;
> Bawdy talk for the fishermen;
> A dance for the fisher-lads;
> When dark hangs upon the water
> They turn down their beds.
>   *Daybreak and a candle-end.*

This is the retort of one such old reprobate to the pious woman
who refuses him. And his admission that in sensual living he
has chosen a 'second-best' has to be balanced against the opening lines of the poem:

> 'Because I am mad about women
> I am mad about the hills,'
> Said that wild old wicked man
> Who travels where God wills.

Here there lingers Crazy Jane's belief that some transcendental
illumination glimmers on the farther side of her way of life.
Something of this belief serves as a bridge to a markedly contrasting group of poems: 'The Three Bushes' and the six songs
that accompany it.

The sequence began at a level of literary diversion in the
course of Yeats's correspondence with Dorothy Wellesley. It
ended, without ever taking on great compass, in the achieving
of what is almost a new form, a kind of resolved Nōh play.
'The Three Bushes' itself outlines the action in ballad style, and
the succeeding songs represent an element not of choric but of
dramatic lyric. The story may be described as one designed to

give symbolic value to the medieval theme of the 'bed trick'
familiar to us through *All's Well that Ends Well* and *Measure for
Measure*. A lady, acknowledging that her lover must enjoy
love's 'proper food' if he is to continue to sing of love, and
being yet reluctant to yield up her chastity, appeals to her
chambermaid:

> 'So you must lie beside him
> And let him think me there,
> And maybe we are all the same
> Where no candles are,
> And maybe we are all the same
> That strip the body bare.'
> *O my dear, O my dear.*

> But no dogs barked, and midnights chimed,
> And through the chime she'd say,
> 'That was a lucky thought of mine,
> My lover looked so gay';
> But heaved a sigh if the chambermaid
> Looked half asleep all day.
> *O my dear, O my dear.*

Lady and lover die; the chambermaid plants on their graves
two rose trees which intertwine; herself dying, she confesses her
story to a good priest who 'understood her case':

> He bade them take and bury her
> Beside her lady's man,
> And set a rose-tree on her grave,
> And now none living can,
> When they have plucked a rose there,
> Know where its roots began.
> *O my dear, O my dear.*

This is a happy instance of unobtrusive profundity. Beside it,
even Ribh at the tomb of Baile and Aillinn shows like a professor before a blackboard. And the songs rehearse, alike with
a clearer analysis and a nearer perfection, the riddle of soul and
body that has been Yeats's most constant theme. The six lines
of 'The Lover's Song' might be set down here without much
further burdening the page, but they ought not to be taken from
such a context. The ten lines of 'The Chambermaid's First
Song' achieve as full a statement as do the concluding 20,000
words of Joyce's *Ulysses*. It has been made a question why Yeats

should have wound up such a performance with 'The Chamber-maid's Second Song', in which the bareness of phallic image could not have been exceeded by Joyce himsef, and is scarcely equalled by Donne at the end of 'Farewell to Love'. Yet the impulse behind it, as behind other almost equally savage reductions of sex, is one a distinguishing of which is crucial if we are to move freely about in *Last Poems*. Joy and affirmation beyond the farthest frontier of disillusion is Yeats's present vision. That there is a sheerly elegiac road to these states has already been asserted in 'Three Things'. 'The Chambermaid's Second Song' represents a further concentration of the intui-tion informing that poem, and the concentration is achieved through an exercise of the same empathic power that we have remarked in 'A Woman Young and Old'. Had Lawrence, when writing his last novel, been as interested in Connie Chatterley as he was in Lawrence he might have achieved some-thing similar.

Ribh had pondered the paradox that 'Hatred of God may bring the soul to God'. That there is this road too, that there is even a road through frenzy and rage and lust, is a persuasion which some poems intimate with disturbing vehemence. When Yeats names the last two of these passions and asks 'What else have I to spur me into song?' Mr. T. S. Eliot is sufficiently disturbed to suggest that Yeats is here writing not personally but in a representative character. It is a guess hazarded without the benefit of access to Yeats's letters, but in a sense it remains valid even in the face of what has been gathered from them. When, about the time of 'The Three Bushes', Yeats writes to Dorothy Wellesley 'Forgive all this my dear but I have told you that my poetry all comes from rage and lust', and goes on to speak of his 'erotic dreams', we recognize that we are in the presence of something which, if indeed not very pretty in such a correspondence, is less a matter of an old man's frenzy than of an old actor's histrionic instinct. Yeats in looking back over his life—and we come now to a number of poems that are per-sonal and reminiscent—finds much cause for bitterness, rage, and, no doubt, a sort of retrospective sex-in-the-head. There is a disillusion deeper than Dowson's at Dieppe in 'Why should not Old Men be Mad?' which sees in Maud Gonne

> A Helen of social welfare dream,
> Climb on a wagonette to scream.

And there is a different sort of disillusion in the providing, for a poem celebrating his own 'house, wife, daughter, son', the refrain:

> *'What then?' sang Plato's ghost. 'What then?'*

Yet all the negatives of these poems are flung at us with an energy which the poet knows to be itself an instrument of positive force in the seeking of acceptance and reconciliation. Nor are all the poems in this key. Some return to the grand style and proud processional method. 'Beautiful Lofty Things', for example, begins with 'O'Leary's noble head' and the 'beautiful mischievous head' of the poet's father, and ends with

> Maud Gonne at Howth station waiting a train,
> Pallas Athene in that straight back and arrogant head:
> All the Olympians; a thing never known again.

'The Municipal Gallery Revisited' is in the same manner. Yeats once more celebrates Synge and Lady Gregory, and balances the pride of 'We three alone in modern times . . .' against a conclusion that is splendidly generous:

> You that would judge me, do not judge alone
> This book or that, come to this hallowed place
> Where my friends' portraits hang and look thereon;
> Ireland's history in their lineaments trace;
> Think where man's glory most begins and ends,
> And say my glory was I had such friends.

'Are You Content?' is an appeal to 'uncles, aunts, great-uncles or great-aunts' and to 'Sandymount Corbets', Pollexfens, Butlers, and smuggling Middletons generally to judge what the poet has done. Such commemorative and celebrative poems link with others mingling personal record and philosophical consideration, and these in turn link with the final examples of Yeats's 'cosmic' poetry in its pure state. These are the two groups remaining to be chronicled.

'A Bronze Head' recalls, before a bust of the aged Maud Gonne, her earlier form, full 'As though with magnanimity of light', and again finely balances against the burden of emotion thus released a dispassionate meditation upon form and substance—before closing on the historical spectacle of the woman set over against her time: 'Heroic reverie mocked by clown and knave.' Maud Gonne is the centre also of 'The

Circus Animals' Desertion', in which the account of her influence
upon Yeats's art, described both directly and with a succinct
subtlety, once more gives place to larger speculation:

> Those masterful images because complete
> Grew in pure mind, but out of what began?

'The Man and the Echo' is the last and perhaps most haunting
of Yeats's dialogue poems. 'In a cleft that's christened Alt'—
apparently a magical place near Sligo, and here conceived as
a sort of Irish Delphi—the poet cries out amid broken stone
which will presently yield the 'Rocky Voice' of the echo.
What he would be unburdened of is the sense of a life's responsibilities ill-discharged. Night after night he has considered his
past actions:

> And all seems evil until I
> Sleepless would lie down and die.

Echo replies, 'Lie down and die'—and at this the poet instantly
rebels:

> That were to shirk
> The spiritual intellect's great work. . . .
> While man can still his body keep
> Wine or love drug him to sleep,
> Waking he thanks the Lord that he
> Has body and its stupidity,
> But body gone he sleeps no more,
> And till his intellect grows sure
> That all's arranged in one clear view,
> Pursues the thoughts that I pursue,
> Then stands in judgment on his soul,
> And, all work done, dismisses all
> Out of intellect and sight
> And sinks at last into the night.

Echo answers, 'Into the night'. There is no answer to the poet's
final question:

> O Rocky Voice,
> Shall we in that great night rejoice?

But this silence makes no matter, since the mysterious oracle of
Alt—by an odd arrangement of things, we may be disposed to
think—has already uttered unambiguously in 'The Gyres',
the poem with which *Last Poems* opens. This is again in part

recapitulatory. It contemplates once more 'the blood-dimmed tide' of 'The Second Coming' and the 'nightmare' of 'Nineteen Hundred and Nineteen'. In face of the imminent disintegration of our era, however, the command of 'Old Rocky Face' is absolute:

> What matter though numb nightmare ride on top,
> And blood and mire the sensitive body stain?
> What matter? Heave no sigh, let no tear drop,
> A greater, a more gracious time has gone;
> For painted forms or boxes of make-up
> In ancient tombs I sighed, but not again;
> What matter? Out of cavern comes a voice,
> And all it knows is that one word 'Rejoice!'

> Conduct and work grow coarse, and coarse the soul,
> What matter? Those that Rocky Face holds dear,
> Lovers of horses and of women, shall,
> From marble of a broken sepulchre,
> Or dark betwixt the polecat and the owl,
> Or any rich, dark nothing disinter
> The workman, noble and saint, and all things run
> On that unfashionable gyre again.

The burden of 'The Gyres' is repeated in 'Lapis Lazuli', a poem of greater complexity:

> All things fall and are built again,
> And those that build them again are gay.

It cannot be contended that the impressiveness of this is of the logical order. As soon as the poetry ceases to command us we cease to believe that Yeats or anybody else has ever cheered himself up by reflecting on eternal recurrence, reincarnation, or any confused amalgam of them such as the system of *A Vision* represents. Yet when the poetry *is* commanding us we are by no means being cozened by a fiction. When we find in 'Those Images' a peremptory injunction to leave 'the cavern of the mind' and

> Recognise the five
> That make the Muses sing

we need not be confused by the memory that this is 'no country for old men' and its sensual music a delusion. For beyond all the contradiction of the Masks, and constantly in this last book, we are in contact with a hard fact: that Yeats, at one level and another, be it on this pretext or on that, is saying *Yes*. 'To live it all again' is—we must judge—a thing inconceivable, and to feel that one would be content to do so a delirium. But it is at least a delirium of the brave, and the feeling is a metaphor for something not inconceivable: that all things do remain in God, and that everything we look upon is veritably blessed. There is no arguing on this ground, there is only certainty. And fundamentally in his last poem Yeats is not arguing, any more than Lawrence is arguing at that corresponding height of modern English literature reached at the end of Apocalypse—or, for that matter, than Piero is arguing in the bleak chamber at San Sepolcro or Donatello in his final bronzes.

'Under Ben Bulben' was designed by Yeats as his last poem. It ends with his epitaph, and resumes in less than a hundred octosyllabic lines almost everything he has ever said. This inclusiveness neglects neither old prejudices (there are no such things, we want to tell him, as 'Base-born products of base beds') nor old hobby-horses: the persuasion, for example, so dear to the boy who could never manage sums, that 'Measurement began our might'. But there are few finer poetic testaments—and not least so in the manner in which the verses come home at the end and submit to the sobriety of actual historical process:

> Irish poets, learn your trade,
> Sing whatever is well made. . . .
> Sing the lords and ladies gay
> That were beaten into the clay
> Through seven heroic centuries;
> Cast your mind on other days
> That we in coming days may be
> Still the indomitable Irishry.

Yet in 'Cuchulain Comforted' there is a testament in a sense more nearly final still. It was written, we are told, out of a dream, and a prose draft 'dictated at 3 a.m. on 7 Jan. 1939'. Yeats never achieved a more mysterious poem. 'Thought hid in thought, dream hid in dream'—the phrase he had struck out more than forty years before for the sort of poetry he believed to be his—would be a fair description of it. And if explicators despair before 'Cuchulain Comforted', it may be only to an

acknowledging of one truth about poetry in general which
a literary education ought not to drive wholly out of our heads.

Yet that is not a last word. Great poetry can never wholly
disengage itself from religion and philosophy, or stand clear of
what Matthew Arnold called 'the shadows and dreams and
false shows of knowledge'. Yeats's system is as eccentric and
obscure as Blake's. But, as with Blake, it is an integral part of
some of his finest writing: a framework, rather than a scaffolding which may be stripped away. In the climate in which it
matured there was much to encourage a hazardous luxuriance
not in mystery but in mystification. It may be true, as one
severe critic avers, that some of Yeats's most magical effects
are no more than a sort of 'ad libbing' in an incantatory void.
Still, his speculative efforts do represent an ordering, after
a fashion, of such intuitions as lie at the roots of poetry, and
it is necessary that they should be rigorously examined by
scholars equipped for the task. From these roots come the
magnificent exfoliations of his greatest lyrics. *The Chestnut-Tree*
will be a good title for any finally adequate study of the poet:

> O chestnut-tree, great-rooted blossomer,
> Are you the leaf, the blossom or the bole?

Yeats died on 28 January 1939 in a French hotel called the
Idéal Séjour. Nine years later his body was brought to Ireland
and buried at Drumcliffe, County Sligo, in the presence of his
family and of a Minister of the Irish Republic, Maud Gonne's
son.

VIII · JOYCE

I

THE literary historian approaches James Joyce with misgiving. *Ulysses* and *Finnegans Wake* are works so powerfully original that, twenty years after their author's death, they remain a field as much of controversy as of criticism. They have evoked moreover so high a proportion of absurd comment that the statistical chance of escaping ignominy seems not substantial. There is a prodigious baby to cope with, and also oceans of bath water. One must cling to the lusty limbs of the infant while resolutely pulling out the plug.

Absurdity got off to a good start in the twenties, when a group of admirers in Paris established a magazine, *transition*, with the aim of seeking 'a pan-symbolic, pan-linguistic synthesis in the conception of a four-dimensional universe' and acclaiming *Work in Progress* as something like a decisive new stage in the biological evolution of the race. Before these ravings Joyce's own mind may have held some reserve. He was a highly intelligent man with an adequate formal education and a lively interest in the boundaries of sense and nonsense. But in accepting with only a private pinch of salt much extravagant homage and strange exegesis he must have been prompted by prudential considerations rather than by a simple impulse to laugh up his sleeve. It has indeed been suggested that he enjoyed a hoax. What he himself had to say about the derivations of his stream-of-consciousness technique makes a debatable case in point. He declared that he had it from an obscure French novel, *Les Lauriers sont coupés*, written by Édouard Dujardin in 1887. This statement brought Dujardin into such notice as he had never before enjoyed, and in 1930 he delivered several lectures on his forgotten innovation—which had once evoked, he now divulged, the admiration of Huysmans and Mallarmé. It has been claimed that this digging up of Dujardin was a joke, and a joke highly representative of Joyce's cast of mind. Again,

it has been roundly declared that Mr. Stuart Gilbert, when he
believed himself to be getting from Joyce a mass of authentic
information on the extremely elaborate structure of *Ulysses*,
was being fooled in a similar fashion. All this is scarcely
plausible. There was no doubt an element of irony and secret
amusement in Joyce's attitude to his admirers. But if he played
up to them in a manner that seems perplexing now it was
chiefly because he was never in a position to disconcert them.
From the earliest days of his continental exile he had been
obliged to learn—despite a heroic independence in many
matters—that a penniless writer disdainful of popular appeal
must reckon with the foibles and hobbyhorses of patrons.
Moreover, there was the special circumstance of his defective
eyesight and the consequent quite exceptional difficulties standing in the way of the mere physical transmission of a text so
peculiar as *Finnegans Wake*. This was not simply a matter of
money. A great amount of devoted labour by more or less
informed persons was required if the whole project was not to
founder. Joyce probably thought this worth paying for with
a certain amount of embarrassment. He had nothing to fear in
the end, since his achievement must eventually rise clear of
everything surrounding it.

If that achievement has noticeably continued to attract the
attention of imperfectly critical minds the reason must lie in
the ready entrance it appears to afford to recondite researches
and arcane solemnities—to picking around, in fact, in the vast
rag-bag of learning which Joyce's work may be viewed as
constituting. There should be nothing but high praise for high
seriousness in the presence of important literary productions.
But when an astringent American critic speaks of the 'rolling-
along-in-great-delight-with-a-great-work-of-art' school we are
certainly being pointed to something vulnerable in much
discussion of Joyce; to an approach fatally telescoping the
pedantic and the portentous. At least we are reminded of the
necessity of making sure that it is the highly serious in a work
of art that we are ourselves proposing to be highly serious about.
We must be chary of thinking a work significant, simply
in proportion to the amount that can be got out of it. An enormous amount can be got out of *Ulysses*, and an even more
enormous amount out of *Finnegans Wake*, simply because an
enormous amount has been put in. But this is even truer of the

Encyclopaedia Britannica, which is not a highly serious work in the sense with which we are concerned.

Yet Joyce's earliest supporters deserve great respect, for they were in fact championing genius in its perennial struggle with neglect and prejudice. That their advocacy was often woolly and extravagant is unimportant, except perhaps in its tendency to alienate some lively and powerful minds coming a little later to judgement. Joyce has been as resoundingly depreciated as puffed—and certainly to an even larger effect of critical aberration. For at least it begins to be apparent that no estimate of him can hope to hold the field that fails to acknowledge the plain fact of his stature. It is a representative stature. He is the great artificer in English prose in the age of Proust and Gide and Mann. And he attempts more radical innovation than any of these.

In the penultimate section of *Ulysses* Leopold Bloom is described in bed at the end of the day, curled up like a child in the womb. The section ends thus:

Womb?   Weary?
He rests.   He has travelled.

With?
Sindbad the Sailor and Tinbad the Tailor and Jinbad the Jailer and Whinbad the Whaler and Ninbad the Nailer and Finbad the Failer and Binbad the Bailer and Pinbad the Pailer and Mindbad the Mailer and Hinbad the Hailer and Rinbad the Railer and Dinbad the Kailer and Vinbad the Quailer and Linbad the Yailer and Xinbad the Phthailer.

When?
Going to dark bed there was a square round Sinbad the Sailor roc's auk's egg in the night of the bed of all the auks of the rocs of Darkinbad the Brightdayler.

Where?

Here is evidently an odd way of saying that we are all going the same way home; Bloom has travelled as the whole crowd of us must travel. The final question *Where?* is ambiguous and unanswered. If we stress the All-life-in-a-day aspect of *Ulysses* it is a question about futurity, and there is in fact no answer to it on any premisses that Joyce admits. If we think simply of 16 June 1904, then Bloom's journey is from the waking world to the world of dream, and there is a sense in which *Where?* receives its answer in Joyce's next book. Bloom has fallen asleep; we have accompanied him just over the threshold and so gained a preliminary glimpse of the vast territory of the unconscious mind into which we are to be conducted in *Finnegans Wake*. Sindbad the Sailor and Tinbad the Tailor (as well as making the statement 'Bloom = Everyman = Us') constitute a sort of jingling catalogue such as the relaxing mind may spin to itself on the approach of sleep. With Dinbad the Kailer there is a further relaxation, for the effort to get alliteration has been abandoned; and Xinbad the Phthailer has an awkwardness suggesting the point at which the conscious mind gives up altogether. The syntactical obscurity of *a square round Sinbad* and the strange resonance of *Darkinbad the Brightdayler* express the violence done by the unconscious and its queer categories to the logic of waking life.

A positive response to Joyce's writing as a whole depends upon the ability to accept such uses of language as this passage adumbrates. Some readers find it endlessly fascinating. Others declare it boring, and assert Joyce to be simply one who, solemn and wide awake, adds Finbad to Ninbad and Binbad to Finbad till the cows come home; a man compulsively addicted to letting words fool around, and owing his distinction simply to the circumstance that his brain was the most elaborately equipped playground for this frivolous purpose ever to have left a record of itself in literature. Whether Joyce is in fact to be convicted of progressive artistic irresponsibility is a very hard question. But even if he is he remains, at least as a writers' writer, a very important figure indeed.

2

Joyce was born in 1882 in Dublin, where his father was sufficiently prosperous to send him to a fashionable Jesuit boarding school, and sufficiently improvident to be virtually penniless a few years later. Partly because they were Irish, and partly because they were tumbling steadily downhill, it is difficult to place the Joyces tidily in a social class. Virginia Woolf, distressed by the *milieu* of *Ulysses*, concluded—with a revealing absurdity—that its author must be 'a self-taught working man'. Wyndham Lewis made fun of Joyce's fictional *alter ego*, Stephen Dedalus, for his anxiety to appear a gentleman.

Simon Dedalus, in whom Joyce depicts his father, is given to urging the external habits of gentility upon Stephen, and is himself represented as a man of family, with aristocratic airs. But Simon's associates are unrefined, and his own manners and language become more and more plebeian as the record proceeds. (Joyce's fiction, indeed, scarcely appears to do justice to the wit in his father. Presented in old age with Brancusi's 'portrait' of his son, which consists of three parallel lines and a whorl, Mr. Joyce is recorded as having remarked with gravity: 'The boy seems to have changed a good deal.') One gets an impression that the whole family became shabby more pronouncedly than it remained genteel. But class consciousness is not important with Joyce. Priest, artist, citizen are his categories; not gentle and simple.

Nevertheless what may be called the Gissing flavour of his youth—the evident precariousness of his slender degree of privilege, the meanness and cultural poverty of the life around him—affected him deeply, and gave him more than a full share of the arrogance of youth. When his parents took him to Sudermann's *Magda* he told them: 'The subject of the play is genius brèaking out in the home and against the home. You needn't have gone to see it. It's going to happen in your own house.' In public he grew up haughty and aloof, contemptuous of all proposals, whether political or artistic, for the regeneration of his country, proud of his precocious knowledge of contemporary continental literature. Although he seems sometimes to have indulged the notion of English as an alien tongue which can never be native to the Celt, he refused to take part in the fashionable activity of learning a little Irish, and instead made some study of Dano-Norwegian in order to read Ibsen in the original. He renounced the Catholic Church and for a time lived in Paris; and when he returned to his mother's death-bed it was in the uncompromising mood which he later dramatized in Stephen's *non serviam*. In 1904 he again left Ireland, taking with him a girl called Nora Barnacle, whom he married in 1931, being by then less absolute to reject 'the whole present social order' than he represents himself in his first correspondence with her. The elder Joyce disapproved of the connexion but had enough of his son's verbal habit to see promise of fidelity in the lady's name. Miss Barnacle, who had worked in an hotel, was not literary, and she never read

Joyce's books. 'My wife's personality', he was to say wryly, 'is absolutely proof against any influence of mine.' But she had vivacity and humour, and some of her recorded utterances suggest a pungent and independent temper. 'I guess the man's a genius', she said, 'but what a dirty mind he has, hasn't he?' Yet her inability to understand or even tolerate his aims must have been burdensome. 'Why', she demanded when he was in a phase of deep discouragement, 'don't you write sensible books that people can understand?' Mrs. Joyce failed to take any sort of cue from people whom she must have known to be of great weight in Joyce's chosen world—and this although she had found in him a faithful if vagabond husband and a devoted father of two children. To support his family Joyce laboured for many years as a teacher of English in Trieste and Zürich. It was only during his later life—and not quite to the end of that—when benefactions and his first substantial royalties enabled him to live in Paris modestly if with a sporadic improvidence no doubt congruous with the artistic nature, that the threat of destitution ceased to hang over him. He was intemperate, and swiftly distrustful alike in his domestic and his professional relations. In his maturer years his life was darkened by the decline of his only daughter into madness. The record of his struggle to preserve a view of her disease as curable is very moving, and he appears to have been aware that in his last work he was himself wrestling into art the products of irreversible degenerative processes such as were at work in her. He had latterly little interest in literature or affairs: for example, the strangely developing verse of his friend Mr. Ezra Pound and the fresh drift of Europe into war. When the Russians invaded Finland in 1939 he saw the event as in some mysterious correspondence with the publication of *Finnegans Wake*, and he was often irrationally impressed by similar coincidences. There is no record of his having like Yeats (whom alone of his generation he admitted to be a greater writer than himself) made much study of magic. But magical habits were strong in him. He watched the efforts of his friends to guess the title of the *Wake* in the trepidation of a savage who fears to lose his secret name. Yet Joyce appears to have been very sure of his genius and of the creative path it must tread. He resisted the discouragements of poverty, neglect, moral censorship, domestic calamity, and a grave disease of the eyes. After the fall

of France he contrived to return to Zürich, where he died in
1941.

3

The first of Joyce's works to appear in book form was
Chamber Music (1907), a collection of thirty-six short poems.
He had read Elizabethan lyrics with attention and judged them
'dainty'; now he imitated them with a *fin de siècle* care for
elegance which was always to be a significant element in his
writing:

> I would in that sweet bosom be
>   (O sweet it is and fair it is!)
> Where no rude wind might visit me.
>   Because of sad austerities
> I would in that sweet bosom be.
>
> I would be ever in that heart
>   (O soft I knock and soft entreat her!)
> Where only peace might be my part.
>   Austerities were all the sweeter
> So I were ever in that heart.

Nearly all the poems are unchallengeably lyrical; as with the
best of the Elizabethan, each seems to sigh for its accordant
air:

> Who goes amid the green wood
>   With springtide all adorning her?
> Who goes amid the merry green wood
>   To make it merrier?
>
> Who passes in the sunlight
>   By ways that know the light footfall?
> Who passes in the sweet sunlight
>   With mien so virginal?

The stanzas never move stiffly beneath obtrusive garments of
their own mellifluousness, as do those of Yeats's *The Wind
among the Reeds* with which they are in some ways comparable.
They are stripped for marriage to an actual music. Yet if
naked they are scarcely enterprising. One acknowledges in the
writer a notable command of language; one would never guess
that these nice dabblings and paddlings in familiar shallows
preluded some of the farthest voyages ever achieved over the
broad waters of the Word. Nor did Joyce, indeed, ever go

much farther in verse. *Pomes Penyeach*, the self-consciously depreciatory title of a volume diminutive to the point of affectation which he published in 1927, cost a shilling and contained
thirteen 'pomes' (or apples); one of them is called 'Tilly'—a
Dublin word for the extra pour of milk one may get in one's
jug. The verse shows the influence of the Imagists and is the
better—as so much of the century's poetry is the better—for
the writer's acquaintance with Mr. Pound. But the properties
remain grey, wan, pale, frail, and *démodé*—although this, indeed,
serves to render only the more strikingly poignant those verses
evoked by his own children, a son and daughter:

> Wind whines and whines the shingle,
> The crazy pierstakes groan;
> A senile sea numbers each single
> Slimesilvered stone.
>
> From whining wind and colder
> Grey sea I wrap him warm
> And touch his trembling fineboned shoulder
> And boyish arm.
>
> Around us fear, descending
> Darkness of fear above
> And in my heart how deep unending
> Ache of love!

This poem, 'On the Beach at Fontana', was written in 1914.
'A Flower given to my Daughter' belongs to the previous year:

> Frail the white rose and frail are
> Her hands that gave
> Whose soul is sere and paler
> Than time's wan wave.
>
> Rosefrail and fair—yet frailest
> A wonder wild
> In gentle eyes thou veilest,
> My blueveined child.

'Alone' was written in 1916, when *Ulysses* was well under way:

> The moon's greygolden meshes make
> All night a veil,
> The shorelamps in the sleeping lake
> Laburnum tendrils trail.

> The sly reeds whisper to the night
> A name—her name—
> And all my soul is a delight,
> A swoon of shame.

Joyce had disparaged *Chamber Music*, calling it 'a capful of light odes' and declaring that 'all that kind of thing is false'. He even persuaded some of his disciples that the title had been intended to convey what would certainly be a characteristic Joycean play upon words, and went to the trouble of inserting supporting puns into both *Ulysses* and *Finnegans Wake*. Yet twenty years later, when he had become one of the most celebrated writers in Europe, he published this even slighter gathering. He had a wish, it seems, to present himself unequivocally in the character of a poet.

Of poetry when sufficiently broadly defined, all his work was to be full. From Stephen Dedalus's early turnings-over of words—

> A day of dappled seaborne clouds—

on to the last cadences of *Finnegans Wake*—

> There's where.   First.   We pass through grass behush the bush to.
> Whish!   A gull.   Gulls.   Far calls.   Coming, far!   End here.   Us
> then.   Finn, again!   Take. Bussoftlhee, mememormee!   Till thou-
> sendsthee.   Lps.   The keys to.   Given!   A way a lone a last a loved
> a long the

—we hear the poetry plainly; and Joyce's own readings from his work as preserved on gramophone records are astonishing achievements in verbal music. Moreover his prose is 'poetic' in more ways than this. When Stephen is looking out from the Martello tower at the beginning of *Ulysses* we read:

> Woodshadows floated silently by through the morning peace from the stairhead seaward where he gazed. Inshore and farther out the mirror of water whitened, spurned by lightshod hurrying feet. White breast of the dim sea. The twining stresses, two by two. A hand plucking the harpstrings merging their twining chords. Wavewhite wedded words shimmering on the dim tide.

We feel that this is consciously presented as poetry, and that it is challengingly, not fortuitously, that it comes immediately after a quotation from Yeats's 'Who Goes with Fergus?'—

And no more turn aside and brood
Upon love's bitter mystery
For Fergus rules the brazen cars—

and also incorporates half a dozen words from the same lyric.
But if it is chiefly a verbal music still, it yet has other elements.
Joyce is never solely concerned to abstract from language a
mere residuum of melopoeic effect. As in the passage in which
Bloom falls asleep, he manipulates words in all sorts of extra-
logical but linguistically meaningful ways. At its most effective,
his developed prose was to combine musical evocation with a
hitherto unexampled power to play upon the connotations of
words, to telescope and scramble them. Thus in *Finnegans Wake*
there is an invocation to the River Liffey that runs, enchantingly
if profanely, in parody of the Lord's Prayer:

haloed be her eve, her singtime sung, her rill be run, unhemmed as
it is uneven!

Joyce was not a prolific writer of verse, but his peculiar prose
has certainly been responsible for a good deal of modern
poetry, and for some reinterpretation of older poetry as well.

4

Joyce early found himself in difficulties with doubting publishers and timid printers. *Dubliners*, when it appeared in 1914,
contained fifteen sketches or short stories which, nine years
before, he had endeavoured to recommend in the following
terms:

My intention was to write a chapter of the moral history of my
country and I chose Dublin for the scene because the city seemed to
me the centre of paralysis. . . . I have written it for the most part in a
style of scrupulous meanness and with the conviction that he is a very
bold man who dares to alter in the presentment, still more to deform,
whatever he has seen and heard.

This is a little manifesto of naturalism; but its most significant
phrase is 'moral history'. Stephen Dedalus, paraphrasing Flaubert, was to describe the writer as one who 'remains within or
behind or beyond or above his handiwork, invisible, refined
out of existence, indifferent, paring his fingernails' and was to
sketch an aesthetic in consonance with this. Yet when writing

to his brother about *Dubliners* Joyce condemns Maupassant's moral sense as 'rather obtuse'. And it is apparent in the stories that he does not differ from other young writers in having as his chief impulsion a set of powerful emotional responses before the spectacle of fallen humanity—here mostly represented, it seems, by his own relations and their circle. It is urged upon us that almost every aspect of Dublin life is horrifying or pitiful or degraded; that everything is nasty and that nothing nice gets a square deal; and that to the effective asserting of this the artist must bend all his cunning. Joyce will allow no half-measures. His book is about paralysis—both the word and the thing fascinate a small boy on the first page—and paralysis is uncompromisingly asserted as something to make the flesh creep. Each one of the stories cries out against the frustration and squalor of the priest-ridden, pub-besotted, culturally de-composing urban lower-middle-class living it depicts, and aims at exhaling—so Joyce declared—'the odour of ashpits and old weeds and offal'. An elderly priest dies in a state of mental and perhaps moral degeneration, and a small boy to whom he has given some instruction learns from whispering women that the trouble began when he dropped and broke a chalice. Two boys play truant and have a casual encounter with an ineffec-tive pervert. A coarse amorist, to the admiration of a less ac-complished friend, gets money out of a servant girl. A drunken clerk is scolded by a bullying employer and humiliated in a public house; he goes home and flogs a small boy. In another public house a traveller in tea falls down the steps of a lavatory and injures himself. While convalescent he is visited by friends, who talk tediously and ignorantly about ecclesiastical matters, and then endeavour to reform him by taking him to hear a sermon for business men. It is recorded by Joyce's brother that lavatory, bedside, and church in this story are designed in a ludicrous correspondence to Dante's Inferno, Purgatorio, and Paradiso. Such 'correspondences' were to exercise an increasing fascination over Joyce later on.

We may well agree that the style in which incidents like these are recounted should be 'scrupulously mean'. A great part of their effect lies in Joyce's virtuosity here, and particularly in his employment of a mimetic or semi-ventriloquial technique. Thus in a story about a very simple girl we read: 'One time there used to be a field there in which they used to play every evening

with other people's children. Then a man from Belfast bought
the field and built houses in it.' And similarly with the adults.
The quality of their living is defined by the language:

One said that he had seen Mac an hour before in Westmoreland
Street. At this Lenehan said that he had been with Mac the night
before in Egan's. The young man who had seen Mac in Westmoreland Street asked was it true that Mac had won a bit over a billiard
match. Lenehan did not know: he said that Holohan had stood them
drinks in Egan's.

Even an exclamation mark may be made to do this sort of
work: 'Just as they were naming their poisons who should
come in but Higgens!' Higgens, thus acclaimed, is a cipher; he
has not appeared before and will not appear again. Such effects
would be oppressive if unrelieved, and so the texture of the
prose is bound to show inconsistency. The first story, that of
the priest who broke the chalice, begins in a child's words of
one syllable, but presently the priest has a handkerchief which
is 'inefficacious', and he lies 'solemn and copious' in his coffin.
And everywhere the description and evocation have a precision
and economy and sensitiveness which constitute the substance
of the book's style just as the 'scrupulous meanness' constitutes
its ironic surface. For the method is essentially ironic. The
meanness of language has an air of accepting and taking for
granted the meanness of what is described. It is contrived to
expose what it affects to endorse.

A special use of this technique occurs at the end of 'Ivy Day
in the Committee Room'. We are introduced to a group of
canvassers in a Dublin municipal election. They are working
only for the money they hope to get from their candidate,
whom they despise and distrust and would be quite ready to
desert. This, and much more of the degradation of civic and
national life they represent, emerges in their talk. Because Ivy
Day commemorates the anniversary of Parnell's death one of
those present is persuaded to recite an appropriate poem of his
own composition. It begins:

He is dead. Our Uncrowned King is dead.
O, Erin, mourn with grief and woe
For he lies dead whom the fell gang
Of modern hypocrites laid low.

The verses, which continue in a vein of facile patriotic sentiment and factitious indignation, read as if they might have

been picked out of a forgotten nationalist newspaper, but are
a clever fabrication by Joyce himself. The effect achieved is
subtle. The poem is fustian. Its massed clichés and threadbare
poeticisms declare it to belong to the same world of impoverished
feeling conveyed in the preceding conversations. But this is not
quite all. There is a ghost in the poem—the ghost of generous
enthusiasms and of strong and sincere attachment to large
impersonal purposes. We respond both ways, as we are later to
do to analogous outcrops of romantic clichés in the reveries of
Dedalus.

It is in the last and longest story in *Dubliners*, 'The Dead', that
Joyce's stature as a writer first declares itself unmistakably.
Two old ladies and their niece, all obscure figures in the
musical life of Dublin, are giving their annual party, and to this
their nephew Gabriel Conroy, a schoolmaster with literary
tastes, brings his wife Gretta. The party, which is an undistinguished, rather vulgar, but entirely human affair, is described
in great detail. Gabriel takes prescriptively a leading part,
although his superior education and his sensitiveness prevent
his doing it easily, and he makes a speech which we are given
in full. This speech, like the poem in 'Ivy Day in the Committee
Room', is an example of Joyce's deftest double-talk. It is full
of trite and exaggerated sentiment, dwelling on spacious days
gone beyond recall, absent faces, memories the world will not
willingly let die, and so forth. Gabriel is himself aware of its
insincerity as he speaks. But we ourselves are contrastingly
aware that it represents a sincere attempt to perform a duty
and give innocent pleasure. Our attitude to Gabriel remains
sympathetic even while we are being afforded a searching view
of him. After the party he and his wife drive through snow to
the hotel where they are to spend the night. He is full of desire
for her, but she does not respond. Presently he learns that
a song heard at the party has reminded her of a boy, Michael
Furey, of whom he has never heard, and who died long ago
as the result of a passionate vigil he had kept for Gretta when
he was already very ill. Gabriel's realization that he has been
a stranger to what is thus revealed as the deepest experience of
his wife's life now becomes the deepest experience of his:

While he had been full of memories of their secret life together,
full of tenderness and joy and desire, she had been comparing him in
her mind with another. A shameful consciousness of his own person

assailed him. He saw himself as a ludicrous figure, acting as a penny-boy for his aunts, a nervous, well-meaning sentimentalist, orating to vulgarians and idealizing his own clownish lusts, the pitiable fatuous fellow he had caught a glimpse of in the mirror. . . .

Generous tears filled Gabriel's eyes. He had never felt like that himself towards any woman, but he knew that such a feeling must be love. The tears gathered more thickly in his eyes and in the partial darkness he imagined he saw the form of a young man standing under a dripping tree. Other forms were near. His soul had approached that region where dwell the vast hosts of the dead. He was conscious of, but could not apprehend, their wayward and flickering existence. His own identity was fading out into a grey impalpable world: the solid world itself, which these dead had one time reared and lived in, was dissolving and dwindling.

A few light taps upon the pane made him turn to the window. It had begun to snow again. He watched sleepily the flakes, silver and dark, falling obliquely against the lamplight. The time had come for him to set out on his journey westward. Yes, the newspapers were right: snow was general all over Ireland. It was falling on every part of the dark central plain, on the treeless hills, falling softly upon the Bog of Allen and, farther westward, softly falling into the dark mutinous Shannon waves. It was falling, too, upon every part of the lonely churchyard on the hill where Michael Furey lay buried. It lay thickly drifted on the crooked crosses and headstones, on the spears of the little gate, on the barren thorns. His soul swooned slowly as he heard the snow falling faintly through the universe and faintly falling, like the descent of their last end, upon all the living and the dead.

It appears that this great story, while owing something to George Moore's *Vain Fortune*, is implicated not only with three generations of Joyce's family but also with Nora Barnacle, who had been wooed in Galway by a youth called Sonny Bodkin when he was in an advanced stage of consumption. A sister of Nora's—a woman seemingly altogether too simple to elaborate a myth—has recorded the circumstances as being in detail those of Joyce's fiction. That Sonny Bodkin should become Michael Furey may stand as an epitome of the transmuting power evinced in 'The Dead'. The story mingles naturalism and symbolism with a new confidence and richness. Tragic ironies play across it subtly and economically. Its parts are proportioned to each other strangely but with a brilliant effectiveness. And if its artistry looks forward to a great deal in Joyce's subsequent writing, its charity and compassion are qualities to which he was never to allow so free a play again.

5

In 1914 or 1915 Joyce wrote his only dramatic piece, *Exiles*.
Striking as is his lifelong obsession with Dublin and Dubliners,
he was yet determinedly and from the first a European before
he was an Irishman, and he found in Ibsen an international
figure who could be held up to point the contrast with the
provinciality, as he conceived it, of the Irish literary movement.
But *Exiles* is not merely a counterblast, opposing to the theatre
of Yeats and Lady Gregory an aggressively naturalistic dramatic convention. It is the work of a writer who owns a real if
limited temperamental affinity with Ibsen; and it treats, at
once with a bleak painful intensity and a large measure of
obscurity, the characteristic Ibsen theme of a harsh ethical
absolutism at work in a fatally egotistical personality. Richard
Rowan is an Irish writer who has lived abroad for a number
of years with Bertha, a simple and unintellectual girl whom he
has been unable or indisposed to marry. They return with their
eight-year-old son to Dublin, where an old friend, Robert
Hand, is determined that Rowan shall be appointed to a chair
of romance literature. But Hand is also determined to seduce
Bertha. Presently we find, in a scene of neat theatrical surprise,
that Bertha, while passively accepting the successive stages of
this clandestine advance, is regularly reporting its progress to
Rowan. The plot turns upon Rowan's refusal in any degree
to bind, guide, or support Bertha in face of this situation. He
imagines her dead, and says to Hand:

I will reproach myself then for having taken all for myself because I
would not suffer her to give to another what was hers and not mine to
give, because I accepted from her her loyalty and made her life poorer
in love. That is my fear. That I stand between her and any moments
of life that should be hers, between her and you, between her and anyone, between her and anything. I will not do it. I cannot and I will not.

We are shown Bertha presenting again her former passive face
to Hand's eventual wooing, and then the curtain descends at an
ambiguous moment. In the last act Bertha returns to Rowan
with an earnest protestation that she has been true to him. But
he declares that he now has a deep, deep wound of doubt in
his soul, and that this wound tires him. 'He stretches himself
out wearily along the lounge' and the play closes upon Bertha

murmuring a passionate prayer for the return of their earliest days as lovers.

We never see clearly the persons who move through this strange action, and this seems to be because Joyce is incapable of that distancing of the writer's own obsessions and predicaments which dramatic composition demands. There can be no doubt about the closeness of autobiographical reference in the play. Rowan's equivocal complacence, and Bertha's reporting to him upon the progress of Hand's campaign, own, it appears, a substantial correspondence with domestic events in Trieste in 1911 or 1912. And indeed, although artistically a failure, *Exiles* presents the fascinating spectacle of Joyce finding his theme, or of Joyce's theme finding him. All his major characters henceforth are to be viewed primarily in their domestic relations. His subject is essentially the painfulness and difficulty of being a family man. What has been distinguished as the 'usurper theme' throughout his writing is only one aspect of this. And we may notice what is at least an odd parallelism between *Exiles* and *Ulysses*. Richard Rowan never learns what has happened in Robert Hand's cottage. The enigma 'tires' him, and he stretches out 'wearily' on the lounge. Leopold Bloom, on the contrary, has no doubts about the afternoon's exercises in Eccles Street. But he too ends up 'weary'. 'He rests. He has travelled.' Molly Bloom's concluding monologue is rather like a tremendous expansion of Bertha's last speech. And Maggie Earwicker (or Anna Livia Plurabelle) brings *Finnegans Wake* to a close in much the same manner. It is not alone in its clinging to Dublin that the tenacity of Joyce's imagination is exemplified.

6

Joyce's first secure reception in a literary world was due to Mr. Ezra Pound, who in January 1914 read *Dubliners* and the first chapter of a still uncompleted autobiographical novel. He at once arranged for the publication of the novel by instalments in the *Egoist*, an English periodical of the *avant-garde*, and declared it to be by a writer comparable with Hardy, James, and Conrad. Joyce at times regarded his life as one of sustained misfortune, but he did in fact often land surprisingly on his feet. That Mr. Pound's perceptiveness should have pounced as it did was the greatest good luck in the world.

When *A Portrait of the Artist as a Young Man* appeared in book form in 1916, it was at the end of a process of gestation covering many years. Joyce had begun an autobiographical novel while still in his teens. About 1908 he decided to rewrite the book on a smaller scale and different method, and it appears probable that the greater part of the original manuscript material was then destroyed. The only substantial fragment certainly preserved is rather longer than the whole perfected work but corresponds only to the final third of it. This fragment, posthumously published under Joyce's original title of *Stephen Hero*, is of great interest as exhibiting the writer's mind bent earnestly upon the substance of his adolescent experience and scarcely at all upon its artistic manipulation and elaboration. It is the only one of his works self-evidently and at once to rebut Wyndham Lewis's charge that Joyce is a craftsman stimulated only by ways of doing things, and not by things to be done. Although strictly no more than a draft, it thus deserves at least brief consideration as a substantive production.

The fragment begins shortly after Stephen Daedalus has become an undergraduate in the National University. He is not a docile student; his attendance at classes is irregular; he feels that he must 'disentangle his affairs in secrecy'. Various people are described: 'The dean of the college was professor of English, Father Butt. He was reputed the most able man in the college: he was a philosopher and a scholar. He read a series of papers at a total abstinence club to prove that Shakespeare was a Roman Catholic.' Stephen thinks poorly of Father Butt on Shakespeare. He himself is explaining a theory of prosody to his younger brother Maurice, reading the prose of Freeman and Morris, poring over Skeat's etymological dictionary by the hour, picking up from shops or advertisements words which he repeats to himself until they lose all instantaneous meaning, studying Blake and Rimbaud on the values of letters, and even permuting and combining 'the five vowels to construct cries for primitive emotions'. Despite all this he is not a mere aesthete. 'Stephen did not attach himself to art in any spirit of youthful dilettantism but strove to pierce to the significant heart of everything.' But 'no-one would listen to his theories: no-one was interested in art'. Above all he is distinguished from his coarse companions by his uncompromising revolt from the Church. 'He spurned from before him the stale maxims of the

Jesuits and he swore an oath that they should never establish over him an ascendency.' In the young man thus self-described in the first forty pages we glimpse the whole basic structure of Joyce's personality. And although his full endowments have not yet declared themselves, much of the bent which they are to take is already present in this early autobiographical sketch. When we read of Stephen's literary sensibility at play over Dublin's streets and newspapers we are looking forward to the world of Hely's sandwich men, Plasto's high-grade hats, and

> *What is home without*
> *Plumtree's Potted Meat?*
> *Incomplete.*
> *With it an abode of bliss*

—which Leopold Bloom is to judge a silly ad., especially when printed next to obituaries.

Stephen, although represented as of a solitary habit, in fact engages in a great deal of conversation with acquaintances. There is a determined attempt to present these subsidiary characters in their full individuality. Indeed their only common characteristic consists in their all being very much less clever than Stephen, who is baffled and disheartened by their obtuseness even while exploiting it in the interest of argumentative victory. The central episode in the fragment concerns his reading a paper on 'Art and Life' to a college society. There is a précis of the argument, some account of the preliminary opinions of friends, a mordantly rendered interview with the priest from whom leave to read the paper must be obtained, an ironical description of the actual meeting, and a number of sporadic conversations in which Stephen elaborates or clarifies his opinions. A great deal of seriousness attends all this. His aesthetic speculations are clearly intended as the prelude to an act of dedication overriding that sort of dedication to political effort which there was much in his surroundings to urge him to:

He was persuaded that no-one served the generation into which he had been born so well as he who offered it, whether in his art or in his life, the gift of certitude. The programme of the patriots filled him with very reasonable doubts; its articles could obtain no intellectual assent from him . . . and this refusal resulted in a theory of art which was at once severe and liberal. . . . The poet is the intense centre of the life of his age to which he stands in a relation than which none can be more vital.

This is the core not only of *Stephen Hero* but of the greater book that was evolved from it.

Stephen's relations with his family are presented with some humour. There is as yet no attempt to set them in a light of spectacular hardness and intransigence. Even the scene in which Stephen, badgered by the pious Mrs. Daedalus to make his Easter duty, reveals his lapsed condition in a sudden burst of juvenile and blasphemous wit, is rendered with more care for fidelity than for dramatic effect, and ends on a humane note. The incident occurs during the last illness of Stephen's sister Isabel:

—You have not made your Easter duty yet, have you, Stephen?
—Stephen answered that he had not. . . .
—I have made my Easter duty already—on Holy Thursday—but I'm going to the altar in the morning. I am making a novena and I want you to offer up your communion for a special intention of mine—
—What special intention?—
—Well, dear, I'm very much concerned about Isabel. . . . I don't know what to think . . .—
Stephen stuck his spoon angrily through the bottom of the shell and asked was there any more tea.
—There's no more in the pot but I can boil some water in a minute—
—O, never mind—
—It won't be a jiffy—
Stephen allowed the water to be put on as it would give him time to put an end to the conversation. He was much annoyed that his mother should try to wheedle him into conformity by using his sister's health as an argument. He felt that such an attempt dishonoured him and freed from the last dissuasions of considerate piety. His mother put on the water and appeared to be less anxious as if she had expected a blunt refusal. She even ventured on the small talk of religious matrons.
—I must try and get in to town tomorrow in time for High Mass in Marlborough St. Tomorrow is a great feast-day in the Church—
—Why? asked Stephen smiling—
—The Ascension of Our Lord, answered his mother gravely—
—And why is that a great feast-day?—
—Because it was on that day that he showed Himself Divine: he ascended into Heaven—
Stephen began to plaster butter over a crusty heel of the loaf while his features settled into definite hostility:

—Where did he go off?—

—From Mount Olivet, answered his mother reddening under her eyes—

Head first?—

Stephen is pleased with this quip and adds something about balloons:

—Stephen, said his mother, I'm afraid you have lost your faith—

—I'm afraid so too, said Stephen. . . .

Mrs. Daedalus began to cry. Stephen, having eaten and drunk all within his province, rose and went towards the door:

—It's all the fault of those books and the company you keep. Out at all hours of the night instead of in your home, the proper place for you. I'll burn every one of them. I won't have them in the house to corrupt anyone else—

Stephen halted at the door and turned towards his mother who had now broken out into tears:

—If you were a genuine Roman Catholic, mother, you would burn me as well as the books. . . .

—You are ruining yourself body and soul. Now your faith is gone.

—Mother, said Stephen from the threshold, I don't see what you're crying for. I'm young, healthy, happy. What is the crying for?. . . It's too silly.

There is a great deal of nature in this, as well as a determined naturalism. But while the domestic straits and shifts of the family, and Isabel's death and funeral, are described with the same saving sympathy, it is otherwise with Stephen's father. Simon Daedalus—the fallen gentleman, the thriftless and shiftless boon-companion of vulgarians—is perceived with a cold clarity often in the power of rebellious sons but seldom given such merciless expression. In that heightening of familial relationships in which a large part of Joyce's early art consists, and which was eventually to have an obscure and degenerate reflection in *Finnegans Wake*, it is his father who is at once the chief victim and the greatest success.

The remaining theme of some importance in the fragment concerns Stephen's relationship with a girl, Emma Clery, in order to encounter whom he attends Irish classes in which he takes no genuine interest. But although Emma, like almost everybody in *Stephen Hero*, makes a real impact upon us as a personality, there is something a little perfunctory in the representation of Stephen's dealings with her. When she repulses him he rapidly evolves a denigratory theory of sex, and writes off his late infatuation as commonplace and unbalanced. The way is cleared for his advance upon his true goal, and as the narrative breaks off it is discernibly moving to its climax in his definitive discovery of himself as an artist. The Church—with her services, legends, practices, paintings, music, traditions—is dismissed as herself no more than one of the creations of the artistic impulse. In his fresh approach to aesthetic problems Stephen is intensely serious and essentially traditional. He broods over Aquinas's definition of beauty and declares that 'as an artist he had nothing but contempt for a work which had arisen out of any but the most stable mood of the mind'. His final rejection of a fresh chance under Jesuit auspices is in the name of a humanist faith reduced to terms of the utmost simplicity:

Lord Almighty! Look at that beautiful pale sky! Do you feel the cool wind on your face? Listen to our voices here in the porch—not because they are mine or yours but because they are human voices: and doesn't all that tomfoolery fall off you like water off a duck's back?

This is the clear melody that is to be so tremendously orchestrated at the climax of the *Portrait*. And rather earlier, in one of the periodic set reviews of Stephen's progress to intellectual clarity and self-knowledge which are characteristic of the explicit and objective cast of the whole fragment, Joyce arrives at something like a personal creed:

He wished to express his nature freely and fully for the benefit of a society which he would enrich and also for his own benefit, seeing that it was part of his life to do so. It was not part of his life to undertake an extensive alteration of society but he felt the need to express himself such an urgent need, such a real need, that he was determined no conventions of a society, however plausibly mingling pity with its tyranny, should be allowed to stand in his way.

7

Once upon a time and a very good time it was there was a moocow coming down along the road and this moocow that was coming down along the road met a nicens little boy named baby tuckoo....

The opening of the *Portrait* at once announces a drastic change of method. The whole effort of *Stephen Hero* had been towards objectivity. Now our knowledge of Stephen is going to come to us in terms of the shifting play of his immediate consciousness. That consciousness is to be the theatre of whatever drama the book attempts to present, and at the same time a territory sufficiently broad for the exercise of the vigorous naturalism which Joyce has been learning from continental masters. Yet with a quite bare naturalism he is no longer to be content. On the second page we come upon him putting unobtrusively into operation a different sort of machinery:

The Vances lived in number seven. They had a different father and mother. They were Eileen's father and mother. When they were grown up he was going to marry Eileen. He hid under the table. His mother said:—O, Stephen will apologise.
Dante said:
—O, if not, the eagles will come and pull out his eyes.—

> Pull out his eyes,
> Apologise,
> Apologise,
> Pull out his eyes.

The whole *Portrait* is an apologia. At the same time its cardinal assertion is that Stephen will *not* apologize; he awaits the eagles. Joyce's own eyes, moreover, were in actual fact threatened from the first. Presently Stephen as a schoolboy is going to be unjustly punished as a consequence of defective vision. The master who beats him says something suggesting that his guilt is to be seen in his eye. And the complex of ideas thus established remains with Stephen and is several times resumed in *Ulysses* in a manner fully intelligible only to a reader equipped with the relevant memories of the *Portrait*.

This technique of weaving elusive symbolic themes percurrently through the fabric of his writing is something that Joyce is to exploit more and more, and indeed nobody is likely to follow his work to the end who does not find something congenial in a progressive cryptographic idiosyncrasy. Yet the *Portrait* at least is best read—certainly in the first instance—without anxious attention to obscure correspondences. When we are assured by commentators that the final chapter is an allegory of the betrayal, Crucifixion, and Resurrection of Christ, or that 'fried bread and tea become the Eucharist', the momentary effect is surely to throw violently out of perspective the work of art which Joyce has in fact achieved. Conceivably at some level of his mind Joyce entertained the myth of the birth of the hero and was by no means certain that he was not the offspring of a god, and this may have impressed upon the *Portrait* marks which a penetrating genetic analysis will reveal. But we need not suppose that such penetrations are always to elements which we are required to reckon with when considering the finished work. The fact that the analysis of dreams came to interest Joyce, and that he eventually found in the new depth-psychologies matter which he judged useful to him as an artist, is a relevant consideration. And we may agree that, long before he was much interested in Freud and Jung, his Catholic training had familiarized him with the anagogical and typological aspects of medieval literature and art. This might dispose him from the first to work in the same fashion. But that such mechanisms are important—or even consciously employed at all—in the *Portrait* any more than in *Dubliners* seems very doubtful.

If much in the form and treatment of the *Portrait* was, in 1916, challenging and new, its main substance lay well within the territory of the contemporary English novel. As the chronicle of a struggle between religious faith and doubt, it would have had a familiar ring to the readers of Mrs. Humphry Ward's *Robert Elsmere*. As centring in the conflict between a rebellious adolescent and his familial and social background, and as presenting this conflict in a decidedly partisan way, it recalls Samuel Butler's *The Way of All Flesh*. In tracing the development of a young man destined to be an artist, it belongs to a kind of fiction already prolific in England, as on the Continent, and invites comparison in particular with D. H. Lawrence's then recently published *Sons and Lovers*.

Yet nothing of this qualifies significantly the *Portrait*'s large originality. It is as much a landmark in English fiction as is *Joseph Andrews* or *Middlemarch* or *The Way of All Flesh* itself. We have only to think of that fiction's line of representative young men—Roderick Random, Tom Jones, David Copperfield, Arthur Pendennis, Richard Feverel—to realize that Stephen Dedalus (as the name is now spelt) is presented to us with a hitherto unexampled intimacy. It is true that Smollett, Fielding, Dickens, Thackeray, and Meredith would probably consider this to have been achieved at some cost to the vitality of Joyce's novel as a whole. Here, as later in parts of *Ulysses*, we are locked up firmly inside Stephen's head, and there are times when we feel like shouting to be let out. Stephen is aware of other people only as they affect his own interior chemistry, so there is something shadowy—as there was not in *Stephen Hero*—about the subsidiary personages in the book. But the picture is always clear and hard in its exhibition of Stephen's successive predicaments. The imaginative and unathletic small boy, hard-pressed by the narrow orthodoxies and hovering brutalities of a Jesuit boarding-school; his growing realization of his family's drift into squalor, and the pride and arrogance which he progressively summons to his aid; the overwhelming sense of sin into which the severity of Catholic doctrine precipitates him upon the occasion of his untimely sexual initiation; the breaking of his nerve and his phase of anxious and elaborate religious observance; his stumbling but implacable advance, through reverie and through conversation with whatever acquaintances will listen, upon an understanding of the realm of art and his elected place in it; the crisis of his break with Church and family, and the exalting moment of revelation and dedication on the strand: all these are vividly realized and rendered experiences.

The book's essential character can be partly analysed in terms of what Joyce preserves, and what abandons, of his earlier method as evidenced in *Stephen Hero*. What he most notably preserves is the refusal to compose or stage-manage his episodes in the interest of conventional construction. Stephen has to meet this or that issue, or this and that mingling of issues, whether personal or speculative, simply as they come along. Every resolution of a problem is partial and tentative. On the same page that he finally calls out to his own future as the artist in exile, he is wondering how much he really likes the girl he has been courting ineffectively through the greater part of the book, and whether his feeling for her, if examined, may not prove all his other aims astray. What Joyce chiefly abandons in the *Portrait* is that flat and frugal prose, almost artless in itself, out of which he had evolved the highly expressive 'scrupulous meanness' of *Dubliners*. The style of the *Portrait* is rich and resourceful and varied. Vocabulary, syntax, rhythm are so disposed as to accentuate the contours of the underlying emotion. Joyce is beginning to deploy his reserves as a master of imitative form, although his experiments are still all within the received limits of English usage. Only once is this mould broken. Stephen, with his sins of impurity still unconfessed, has heard one of his schoolfellows repeat the act of contrition, and has gone home strained to breaking-point:

He halted on the landing before the door and then, grasping the porcelain knob, opened the door quickly. He waited in fear, his soul pining within him, praying silently that death might not touch his brow as he passed over the threshold, that the fiends that inhabit darkness might not be given power over him. He waited still at the threshold as at the entrance to some dark cave. Faces were there; eyes: they waited and watched.
—We knew perfectly well of course that though it was bound to come to the light he would find considerable difficulty in endeavouring to try to induce himself to try to endeavour to ascertain the spiritual plenipotentiary and so we knew of course perfectly well—
Murmuring faces waited and watched; murmurous voices filled the dark shell of the cave. . . . He told himself calmly that those words had absolutely no sense which had seemed to rise murmurously from the dark.

The words, of course, have sense—an emotional as distinct from a logical sense. Joyce was to end his days listening to such words as they rose 'murmurously from the dark'.

When we come to *Ulysses* we shall find a book which, considered in point of style, is virtually a museum, displaying as in a series of show-cases all the old ways of using English and a great many new ones as well. In the *Portrait* there is a diversity of styles pointing forward to this—but at the same time an overriding impression of unity, since each of the styles reflects one facet of Stephen, who is a highly unified creation. 'He chronicled with patience what he saw,' we are told, 'detaching himself from it and tasting its mortifying flavour in secret.' This Stephen is best represented in some of the conversations. These, as in *Dubliners* and *Stephen Hero*, are based upon an ear and intellect so alert as to combine a maximum of significant statement with a minimum of apparent selection. The early scene in which Stephen's father and Mrs. Riordan quarrel over Parnell during dinner on Christmas Day is Joyce's early masterpiece in this kind. When Stephen ceases to be merely a recording intelligence, and responds actively to the challenge of a world he finds so largely inimical, the style reaches out at

once for weapons and armour. The whole tone becomes an
extension of Stephen's most caustic and arrogant condemna-
tions: of Dublin which has 'shrunk with time to a faint mortal
odour', of Ireland 'the old sow that eats her farrow', of her
church which is 'the scullery-maid of christendom'. But Stephen
himself is 'a priest of the eternal imagination', and he speaks in
cold exalted phrases consonant with the role:

This race and this country and this life produced me, he said. I
shall express myself as I am.

You talk to me of nationality, language, religion. I shall try to fly
by those nets.

I will not serve that in which I no longer believe, whether it call
itself my home, my fatherland, or my church: and I will try to express myself in some mode of life or art as freely as I can and as
wholly as I can, using for my defence the only arms I allow myself to
use—silence, exile, and cunning.

A comparison of this last and celebrated passage with the
corresponding passage in *Stephen Hero* already cited marks the
significant hardening in tone, the new concern with gesture,
characterizing the *Portrait*.

But there is yet another Stephen in the book—the Stephen
who ceaselessly communes with himself on solitary walks about
Dublin. It is here that the complexity of what Joyce attempts
makes the success of the *Portrait* tremble in the balance. There
are always two lights at play on Stephen. In the one he is seen
as veritably possessing the sanctity and strength he claims—for
he has been set aside, not of his own will, to serve an exalted
and impersonal purpose. In the other he is only the eldest of
Simon Dedalus's neglected children, and his aspirations have
the pathos he is one day to discern in his sister Dilly, when she
shyly produces the tattered French grammar she has bought
from a stall. In the one light he is an artist. In the other he is
an adolescent, subject to emotions which may be comically in
excess of their specific precipitating occasions, and to express
which he must reach out for maudlin tags, conventional pos-
tures, phrases and cadences caught up out of books. It is because he must be seen as thus hovering agonizingly between
sublimity and absurdity, hysteria and inspiration, that he is
regularly represented in his solitude as outrageously senti-
mentalizing himself, and as prone to clothe his poignantly felt

nakedness in the faded splendours of a bygone poetic rhetoric. To treat even a single sentence of this as a mere indulgence in fine writing on the author's part is entirely to underestimate the art of the book:

He heard the choir of voices in the kitchen echoed and multiplied through an endless reverberation of the choirs of endless generations of children and heard in all the echoes an echo also of the recurring note of weariness and pain. All seemed weary of life even before entering upon it. And he remembered that Newman had heard this note also in the broken lines of Virgil, *giving utterance, like the voice of Nature herself, to that pain and weariness yet hope of better things which has been the experience of her children in every time.*

The crisis of the *Portrait* is a remarkable and substantial achievement in which this boldly heightened writing is employed with great skill. Stephen's coming to his true vocation is by way of successive sensuous impressions each of which has a sort of trigger action upon forces which have been building themselves up in his mind. The piety which he has evinced since abandoning and repenting his precocious carnal sins has suggested that he is apt for the priesthood, and the question of whether he has indeed a vocation is put to him temperately and wisely by his Jesuit director. His pride and arrogance are brought into play. He is tempted by the thought of secret knowledge and secret power. He is tempted, too, without clearly knowing it, as an artist: 'He had seen himself, a young and silent mannered priest, entering a confessional swiftly, ascending the altarsteps, incensing, genuflecting, accomplishing the vague acts of the priesthood which pleased him by reason of their semblance of reality and of their distance from it.' On the threshold of the college the director gives Stephen his hand 'as if already to a companion in the spiritual life'. But Stephen feels the caress of a mild evening air, sees a group of young men walking with linked arms, hears a drift of music from a concertina: 'Smiling at the trivial air he raised his eyes to the priest's face and, seeing in it a mirthless reflection of the sunken day, detached his hand slowly which had acquiesced faintly in that companionship.' And this impression is reinforced by memories of his schooldays:

His lungs dilated and sank as if he were inhaling a warm moist unsustaining air and he smelt again the moist warm air which hung in the bath in Clongowes above the sluggish turfcoloured water.

Some instinct, waking at these memories, stronger than education
or piety, quickened within him at every near approach to that life,
an instinct subtle and hostile, and armed him against acquiescence.

He realizes that his destiny is to be 'elusive of social or religious
orders' and that he must 'learn his own wisdom apart from
others'. Yet still his mind oscillates. He is entered at the university, and celebrates the occasion with comical portentousness
in an elaborately harmonious reverie. But this in turn brings
to his mind 'a proud cadence from Newman'—'Whose feet
are as the feet of harts and underneath the everlasting arms'—
and 'the pride of that dim image brought back to his mind the
dignity of the office he had refused. . . . The oils of ordination
would never anoint his body. He had refused. Why?' The
answer—the positive answer—comes as he walks on the beach.
It is, in fact, the secular artist's reply to the 'proud cadence' of
Newman: 'He drew forth a phrase from his treasure and spoke
it softly to himself:—A day of dappled seaborne clouds.' This is
Stephen Dedalus's moment of apocalypse. He realizes that he
has created something beautiful. Soon he will be able to write
in his diary the final truth about himself: 'I desire to press in my
arms the loveliness which has not yet come into the world.' It
is only a shallow irony that would remark that this loveliness is
to be represented by Leopold and Molly Bloom. Nor need we,
in the name of sophisticated restraint, shy away from the pitch
of the prose in which this moment—a moment at once of release
and submission—is celebrated:

Where was his boyhood now? Where was the soul that had hung
back from her destiny, to brood alone upon the shame of her wounds
and in her house of squalor and subterfuge to queen it in faded
cerements and in wreaths that withered at the touch? Or where was
he?

He was alone. He was unheeded, happy and near to the wild
heart of life. He was alone and young and wilful and wildhearted,
alone amid a waste of wild air and brackish waters and the sea-
harvest of shells and tangle and veiled grey sunlight and gayclad
lightclad figures of children and girls and voices childish and girlish
in the air. . . .

The whole great hymn of praise and dedication and pride has
still its aspect of precariousness and pathos. Its uncertain basis is
in the earlier Stephen's 'Mother . . . I'm young, healthy, happy.

What is the crying for?' And Stephen Dedalus, in a last analysis, is singing only as his brothers and sisters have been singing a few pages earlier—when that could be detected in their voices which Newman had heard in the broken lines of Virgil. Mr. T. S. Eliot has distinguished Newman and Pater as the masters of the young Joyce's prose. Certainly it is on the two broad currents represented by these writers—the scholastic and the aesthetic, intellect and sensibility—that the *Portrait* alternately floats. When, in the final chapter, Stephen arrives at what his sort of artist must have, a conception of the nature of art, he expresses this to his friend Lynch (who chiefly wants a cigarette and a job at five hundred a year) in the form of two definitions. In these, the two influences which have moulded Stephen's thought speak clearly enough. But the setting could be Joyce's alone. It succinctly expresses his sense of the conditions under which the modern artist must consent to speculate and create:

—If that is rhythm, said Lynch, let me hear what you call beauty; and, please remember, though I did eat a cake of cowdung once, that I admire only beauty.

Stephen raised his cap as if in greeting. Then, blushing slightly, he laid his hand on Lynch's thick tweed sleeve.

—We are right, he said, and the others are wrong. To speak of these things and to try to understand their nature and, having understood it, to try slowly and humbly and constantly to express, to press out again, from the gross earth or what it brings forth, from sound and shape and colour which are the prison gates of our soul, an image of the beauty we have come to understand—that is art.

They had reached the canal bridge and, turning from their course, went on by the trees. A crude grey light, mirrored in the sluggish water, and a smell of wet branches over their heads seemed to war against the course of Stephen's thought.

—But you have not answered my question, said Lynch. What is art? What is the beauty it expresses?

—That was the first definition I gave you, you sleepyheaded wretch, said Stephen, when I began to try to think out the matter for myself. Do you remember the night? Cranly lost his temper and began to talk about Wicklow bacon.

—I remember, said Lynch. He told us about them flaming fat devils of pigs.

—Art, said Stephen, is the human disposition of sensible or intelligible matter for an esthetic end. You remember the pigs and forget that. You are a distressing pair, you and Cranly.

8

Ulysses (1922) begins as if it were a continuation of the *Portrait*, with the thread taken up after the hero's brief absence from Ireland. In fact it represents the amalgamation of such a sequel with a wholly different project which Joyce had entertained during the period of *Dubliners*. 'Ulysses' was to have been the title of a short story descriptive of a day's wandering about Dublin on the part of a certain Mr. Hunter. The ironic association of this personage with the Homeric hero was later enriched through a further association (perhaps by way of Victor Bérard's *The Phoenicians and the Odyssey*) with the Wandering Jew. From this fusion Leopold Bloom was born. But Joyce, having hit upon the characteristically bookish notion of a loosely organized structural correspondence with the *Odyssey*, perceived that he could begin with a *Telemachia*. Here the central figure would still be Stephen Dedalus, who might very aptly be represented as engaged—albeit unconsciously—in the search for a father. Unfortunately Stephen as an imaginative creation has been pretty well exhausted before *Ulysses* begins. Now we find ourselves ratting on him in a way that Joyce does not intend or control. The young man's weariness, his hauteur, his disposition to speak 'quietly', 'coldly', 'bitterly' ('It is a symbol of Irish art. The cracked looking-glass of a servant'), even his dislike of water and presumably of soap: all these are facets of his character bringing us up short, so that we are awkwardly unable to embark upon the broad current of sympathy which his creator—however austerely a 'realist' in profession—evidently designs as an entry into his book. When presently Stephen is shown teaching in a school we are far from questioning his implied unfitness for the task. His mental habit is now represented as almost wholly pedantic, and he would make any schoolboy howl. This impression is intensified in the succeeding section, which presents us with his highly allusive and recondite stream of consciousness as he walks on the strand, and which begins:

Ineluctable modality of the visible: at least that if no more, thought through my eyes. Signatures of all things I am here to read, seaspawn and seawrack, the nearing tide, that rusty boot. Snotgreen, bluesilver, rust: coloured signs. Limits of the diaphane. But he adds: in bodies. Then he was aware of them bodies before of them coloured.

How? By knocking his sconce against them, sure. Go easy. Bald he was and a millionaire, *maestro di color che sanno*. Limit of the diaphane in. Why in? Diaphane, adiaphane.

Part of the obscurity results from Joyce's demand that our consciousness should be steadily at play over the entire surface of his work, so that phrases and associations are intelligible only in the light of others scores or hundreds of pages away. This is a legitimate device, and the extent of its use is a matter of literary tact. The more serious the undertaking, the more vigorous the co-operation we may fairly be expected to bring to it. But so much in Stephen's reverie is resistant to any ready elucidation that we come to wonder whether all this showing off to himself (if that is it) might have been more succinctly accomplished had his creator been less concerned to show off to us. And in fact we are never to be quite safe from boredom in Joyce's company again.

When Mr. Pound (who admired *Ulysses* to the extent of declaring that Yeats had never taken on anything requiring such concentration and condensation) asked for more Dedalus and less Bloom, Joyce declared that Stephen no longer interested him since he had a shape 'that can't be changed'. And we may ourselves feel that Stephen is a Telemachus to whom Ulysses, in the figure of Bloom, comes decidedly to the rescue, so far as the general artistic success of the book is concerned. Whether, within the fable, Bloom ultimately means much to Stephen, or Stephen to Bloom, is a question which has been variously answered by critics. Considered as an action, *Ulysses* ends in obscurity, whether inadvertent or deliberate. But considered as a theatre of novel design, constructed substantially for the exhibition of a comic character of striking vitality and verisimilitude, it is an unchallengeable even if dauntingly laboured success.

Bloom has been written off as a walking cliché, an orthodox comic figure of the simplest outline presented with a vast technical elaboration. It is certainly true that his lifelikeness seems not to proceed from his being very directly observed from the life. He is a highly evolved literary creation. His complexity—for he is complex—is literary. Some aspects of him exist only because a body of Anglo-Irish humour existed; others, only because *Bouvard et Pécuchet* existed. His most important line of derivation is from the mock-heroic tradition. Here is the reason for its being not quite true to say that the *Odyssey* provided Joyce merely with a scaffolding which a reader may disregard. The Homeric correspondences never go deep, but they are regularly exploited to point Bloom's insignificance and ignobility. They are also capable, as in the best mock-heroic, of working the other way, so that Bloom's positive qualities, his representative character, his pathos, all take emphasis from his original. This is one aspect of the elaborate and considered craft with which he is undoubtedly presented to us. Another is to be found in the immense resource and cunning with which the technique of internal monologue, however derived, is developed in his interest. Once more Joyce is far from drawing directly from life. Bloom never stops talking to himself unless he has to talk to somebody else. We are bound to feel that this assiduity in verbalization, although convenient both to his creator and to us who would make his acquaintance, is quite outside nature. Yet Joyce achieves with it a vivid and deep illusion. The content of Bloom's mind, his interests, his responses to stimuli, are depicted with deliberation as very much those of any vulgar, curious, kindly man. To give just that with unexampled fullness is a large part of the idea of the book, and it carries with it the danger of a tedious lack of particularity. Yet we become convinced that Bloom's mind is not quite like any other mind. It is indeed with his mind rather as with his hat. On 16 June 1904 many Dubliners must have been wearing a high-grade hat from Plasto's, but only Bloom can have been wearing a high-grade ha. We suspect a misprint (as we often do) but are in the presence of a device. Bloom's internal idiom, too, is consistently and not too obtrusively idiosyncratic. A traditional literary resource—one exploited alike by the creators of Hamlet and Mr. Jingle—has been deftly transferred to a new theatre, and there deployed with an astonishing inventiveness and abundance.

Bloom admits us more generously to his intimacy than does almost any other figure in fiction. Yet he is a small man; neither nature nor nurture has given him much; his moral being, which is amoebic, and his intellectual interests, which if lively are circumscribed, prove alike unrewarding to exploration on the scale proposed by the book. Thus he comes, despite an attractiveness which is one of Joyce's greatest achievements, within some distance of shooting his bolt with us rather as Stephen has done. His environment threatens to swamp him. He ceases to float upon the current of his creator's abounding imaginative vitality and is felt as battling rather forlornly against it. It is perhaps by way of redressing a balance here that Joyce offers us finally, and so much at large, the figure of Molly Bloom, the sadly faithless Penelope of the story. She is passive and receptive. In the morning she accepts breakfast in bed from the hands of her husband. In the afternoon, again in bed, she entertains the irresistible Blazes Boylan. In the small hours, in bed still, she indulges herself in the enormous erotic reverie with which the book concludes. This celebrated performance takes about two hours to read, is totally without punctuation (although, for some reason, divided into eight gigantic paragraphs), and appears concerned to carry the technique of internal monologue to something near its theoretical limit. And although it leaves Mrs. Bloom much more chargeable than her husband with being an elaborated cliché, it does afford an impressive exhibition as of some vast sprawled and monolithic image of female sexuality. Bloom, contrastingly, is throughout in restless motion. He visits the pork butcher, feeds the cat, attends a funeral, pursues his profession as an advertisement tout, has a row in a pub, misconducts himself on a beach, and so on. His most characteristic motion is a wriggle—through inhospitable doors and past averted shoulders. He remains symbolically, if not very impressively, male.

If the Blooms have anything in common it is a retrospective turn of mind. Characters or events in *Dubliners* frequently recur to them. Bloom, musing in the privy, recalls how, long ago, he used to jot down on his cuff what his wife said when dressing. 'What had Gretta Conroy on?' she had once asked. Bartell d'Arcy, whose singing of *The Lass of Aughrim* called up for Gretta the shade of Michael Furey, has been among Mrs. Bloom's lovers. So has Lenehan, once the admirer of that Corley who wheedled the gold coin from a servant-girl. Mrs. Bloom during her vigil recalls, among numerous other citizens, 'Tom Kernan that drunken little barrelly man that bit his tongue falling down the mens W C drunk in some place or other'. Two of the friends who took Kernan to a retreat for business men join Bloom at the funeral at Glasnevin. And Bloom reflects that his last visit there was for the funeral of Mrs. Sinico—of whose unfortunate end we have read in a short

story called 'A Painful Case'. Simon Dedalus—another of Mrs.
Bloom's bedfellows—is perhaps a little changed, even as his
family is further degraded. In some regards an engaging character, he now speaks with a violent foulness and out of a deep
venom absent from the *Portrait*. All this reminiscence reflects
Joyce's own mind, which we feel to repose in the Dublin of his
youth in a quite extraordinary way. We cannot conceive of him
as setting out, like Proust, in search of a past, or of his mind as
opening suddenly upon it, like Marcel's at the taste of the made-
leine. For he has simply carried the past along with him in his
consciousness—as he carried, it is said, its newspapers and tram-
tickets along with him in his trunks. Nothing would appear less
justified than his fear, expressed in 1907, that Ireland was
rapidly becoming a mist in his brain. The whole drift of biographical investigation is towards showing that every character
and incident in the book is determined, and over-determined, by
memory. He broods like Dante on his fellow citizens—and often
with similar retributive designs. It is not indeed wholly true
that, as Wyndham Lewis avers, his thought was 'of a conventional and fixed order' which remained unchanged since
his early days. *Ulysses* differs from the *Portrait* not merely in
elaboration, display, technical variousness, and virtuosity. It
mirrors deeper responses to the human comedy. But the comedy
is confined to the same stage; the old props are trundled on and
off; we are progressively more aware of an inflexibly willed,
rather desperate, resourcefulness as the inflating and sustaining
principle of the whole. And the resourcefulness is—surely to
a hazardous degree—linguistic and stylistic. *Ulysses* is quite
staggeringly full of language. The stuff comes at us in great
rollers, breakers, eddies and tumbles of spume and spray. It is
exhilarating. It is also rather buffeting, bruising, exhausting
long before the end.

What chiefly stands out from this powerful and battering sea
of words, what saves it from mere flux, is the steep bold contrast
between the content and movement of Stephen's mind and the
content and movement of Bloom's. The speculative intellect
is ceaselessly at work in Stephen, the practical intellect in
Bloom. Stephen's mind hovers, swoops, soars, tumbles in cloud.
Bloom's scurries alertly here and there in endless short proliferations. The image of the Surinam toad, beloved of Coleridge, fits it: ideas sprouting ideas sprouting ideas at a low

but abundantly vital level of cerebral development, and in a consciousness producing nothing so naturally as a platitude, a hoarded unrelated fact, an amiable vulgar day-dream. What is new in Joyce's art here is not so much the technique of internal monologue in itself as its development in the direction of a muted drama which culminates when these two minds finally meet in mutual incomprehension and obscure need. But that technique, prodigally as it is deployed for the exposing to us not only of Bloom, Stephen, and Molly but of such subsidiary characters as the young Patrick Aloysius Dignam and the elderly and very reverend John Conmee, is only the first of Joyce's resources, and in fact shades into a rich variety of other devices. In the Nausicaa episode Bloom's familiar interior monologue alternates not so much with a strictly equivalent interior monologue in Gerty MacDowell as with prose distilling a whole *ethos* of kitchen romance and cheap sentiment. In the Cyclops something like a group consciousness of the Dublin pubs externalizes itself in the narrative of a nameless low-life character. Frequently—and with a growing obtrusiveness as the day wears on—the point of view seems to hover between mind and mind. At the book's climax, the brothel scene, there is a final blending of individual consciousnesses in the interest of phantasmagoric effect. Not only do past and present jostle, so that at the sound of a customer's slapping one of Bella Cohen's young ladies there pops up out of the pianola the Father Dolan who had so unjustly beaten Stephen in the *Portrait*. The boundaries of the waking world go down, and Bloom and Stephen severally experience hallucinations prompted by the other's earlier experience and not by his own. The Nighttown of *Ulysses* is in this aspect a sort of antechamber to *Finnegans Wake*.

In all this Joyce is not aiming at anything that can be defined as psychological fiction. And he is not aiming at the sort of unity traditional in fiction of any sort. His title perhaps obscures this latter point. For we are not being given one whole and completed action, such as is constituted by Aeneas's removing of his gods from Troy to Latium. Rather we are being given simply Troy or Latium itself. *Ulysses* is about Dublin on 16 June 1904. Even the unexampled fullness with which we are admitted to the mind of one of its citizens on that day forms only a part of the design. Bloom, Stephen, and Molly are by any standards great creations in their own right. But Dublin is not conceived of as their background. Rather they are conceived of as the aptest of Dublin's voices for representation on a large scale. And Dublin has other voices as well, which are not necessarily the voices of human beings. The streets and the bars, the cemetery and the newspaper office and the public library: these are capable of something like internal monologue of their own. We shall be bewildered in *Ulysses* if we seek to orientate ourselves always as from the mind of one or another individual character. This or that identifiable consciousness fades out, deliquesces—and this without, as it were, returning us to the author. It is Dublin to which we are attending—attending with all our senses—on these occasions.

9

On a first reading *Ulysses* is likely to strike us as a large-scale improvisation in which a great deal comes off quite brilliantly—but to a final effect of agglomeration before which any summing up, any secure arriving at a right aesthetic total, is singularly hard to achieve. When we turn to Mr. Stuart Gilbert's official guide, and to the writings of later and even more elaborate scholiasts, our first impulse, correspondingly, is to estimate the size of the pinch of salt with which their expositions should be accepted. And we may remember, perhaps, that Joyce once urged a friend not to plan everything ahead, since 'in the writing the good things will come'. The organs, arts, colours, symbols, and what not in terms of which Joyce is declared to have worked are hard to take seriously. But when we turn back attentively to *Ulysses* itself we have presently to admit that, whether to any good purpose or not, all these things are there. Clearly it was with a remarkably true insight into his own mental constitution that the young Joyce took to himself the name of Daedalus. *Ulysses* is a labyrinth, and a labour of quite fantastically pertinacious artifice. Genetically its grand characteristic is the extent to which it has been worked over again and again through a long process of enrichment and elaboration. Joyce's manuscripts, scored with an intricate system of coloured inks and chalks, sometimes suggest the painful pursuit of processes which might have been expedited by the use of an electronic machine. Even set beside the evidence of Flaubert's drafts and sketches, or of those compulsive reworkings of a theme

which at first so surprise the explorer of the scattered remains
of an Old Master's sketchbooks, Joyce's working methods may
appear disconcerting. One good critic speaks of them as 'the
contrivances of Joyce, where insistent will and ingenuity so
largely confess the failure of creative life'. It is certainly true
that many of these contrivances, at least when isolated for
study, appear trivial and even foolish. Take a single example.
At No. 2 Clare Street, Dublin, and in the year 1904, a dental
practice was, it appears, carried on by a certain M. Bloom.
And in the tenth episode of *Ulysses* we read of a minor character that he 'strode past Mr. Bloom's dental windows'. This is
confusing. We hesitate for a moment, wondering whether we
have missed something about the book's hero. But when we
turn to Mr. Gilbert we learn that here is one of many small
confusions or ambiguities or false clues carefully planted in this
section of *Ulysses*. And they are so planted because the section
is designed to evoke, or relate to, those Wandering Rocks
against which Circe warns Odysseus, and in preference to
which Odysseus eventually chooses the route between Scylla
and Charybdis. The Wandering Rocks are bewildering, so into
this part of Joyce's book must come Mr. Bloom, dentist, and
much else. 'Many forms of mistake are illustrated,' Mr. Gilbert
admiringly tells us, 'arising out of inattention, false inference,
optical illusion, malidentification, etc.' Thus: 'Boody Dedalus,
seeing a pot aboil on the range, expects a meal; the pot, however, proves to contain shirts; appearances have deceived her—
a false analogy.'

We may ask ourselves whether, being entertained by a great
writer in this way, we are not perhaps being offered boiled
shirts when we have some legitimate expectation of honest food.
At least, we shall feel, the ingredients of the meal are largely
of the synthetic order—and 'synthetic' indeed is a pejorative
adjective regularly applied to Joyce's art. Yet the analogy may
not be very sound. All art is artifice. The test of the tricks is in
how they come off, not in how they are contrived. Boody finds
shirts where she expects a stew; a small boy hopes to attend
a boxing match, but it turns out to have taken place some
weeks before; and so on. If these things in fact build up into
a designed effect they can be artistically justified. If, on the
other hand, we feel that Joyce is fitting them into his jigsaw for
his entertainment rather than for our delight and instruction,

we shall experience only irritation upon being called on to admire them—as when he feels that he must find a 'correspondence' for the finny tails of the sirens in the *Odyssey*, and is happy when he hits upon that slatternly part of a barmaid's attire which is concealed below the counter. It is in fact hard not to conclude that the elaborative method at times becomes merely mechanical, something that goes on operating by rote rather than upon specific artistic consideration. The lotus-eaters, Homer tells us, consume a flowery food. So in the fifth episode one of the arts drawn upon is botany, and Bloom's reveries are set wandering down a pervasively flowery path. This must strike us as we read as something entirely arbitrary. Joyce has declined to that order of ingenuity which best exercises itself in literary competitions in ninepenny papers.

The elaborative method is certainly not illegitimate in itself, or in any way peculiar to Joyce. Henry James—at least in his later years, when he had gone over to the method of dictating his novels—expanded his texts, and expanded them again, through a succession of drafts. But Joyce carried the technique farther, and in the face of greater difficulties. There are several stories about these difficulties, most of them no doubt *ben trovato*. But there is one which may be cited as not implausible. It is recounted by an American member of the Joyce circle, Robert McAlmon, who had been entrusted with the task of copying the last fifty pages of Mrs. Bloom's monologue:

The next day he gave me the handwritten script, and his handwriting is minute and hen-scrawly; very difficult to decipher. With the script he gave me some four notebooks, and throughout the script were marks in red, yellow, blue, purple and green, referring me to phrases which must be inserted from one of the notebooks. For about three pages I was painstaking, and actually re-typed one page to get the insertions in the right place. After that I thought 'Molly might just as well think this or that a page or two later or not at all', and made the insertions wherever I happened to be typing. Years later upon asking Joyce if he'd noticed that I'd altered the mystic arrangement of Molly's thought, he said that he had, but agreed with my viewpoint. Molly's thoughts were irregular in several ways at best.

Desmond McCarthy found this illuminating. If McAlmon is to be trusted, he declared, it shows that where the inner monologue is concerned it does not matter much what branching association the author follows. The 'if' is perhaps a large one, since McAlmon is scarcely representing himself in a reliable, any more than in an amiable, light. But it is conceivable that Joyce might in fact have considered a random reassorting of Mrs. Bloom's reflections a perfectly logical extension of what he was attempting in this particular part of his book. Mr. Edmund Wilson has said that *Ulysses* 'suffers from an excess of design rather than from a lack of it'. This is true. What is disconcerting is the co-presence, along with all the planning and planting, of a radical rejection of traditional notions of what constitutes discourse. In *Finnegans Wake* this paradox becomes formidable.

Joyce's principles of composition and his use of language may be very well studied in the eleventh episode, the Sirens. 'The language and content', Mr. Gilbert tells us here, 'are throughout handled in a characteristically musical manner.' This puts it mildly. Joyce had indulged ambitions as a singer, and he certainly listened to human speech as a musician listens to music. He could impose upon talk, with all its repetitions of word and phrase, its perpetual variations and disguisings of one and another familiar theme, something like the grammar of music proper. Of the Sirens we are told that the 'technic' is *fuga per canonem*. Evidently enough, it is only metaphorically that one can write a long piece of prose in fugal structure. But even to contrive such a sustained metaphor as the Sirens is an astonishing feat of virtuosity. Small units that do make themselves felt as strikingly musical are combined, recombined, modified, repeated in a manner that does persuasively suggest a substantial and highly organized musical composition. Yet the episode remains recognizably fiction, with fiction's proper life and drama. We are aware of Miss Douce and Miss Kennedy, of Bloom, of Boylan, of the Vice-Regal cavalcade quite as much as we are of the aspect of the piece as musical excursion:

> Yes, bronze from anear, by gold from afar, heard steel from anear, hoofs ring from afar, and heard steelhoofs ringhoof ringsteel. . . .

> By Bachelor's walk jogjaunty jingled Blazes Boylan, bachelor, in sun, in heat, mare's glossy rump atrot, with flick of whip, on bounding tyres: sprawled, warmseated, Boylan impatience, ardentbold. Horn. Have you the? Horn. Have you the? Haw haw horn.

There is an enormous amount to delight us. And the more often we read the more are we aware of a single delight, as in the contemplation of some large and intricate yet unified and significant architectural performance. Yet if there is much to delight us there is something to perplex. And when we investigate this we come to suspect that Joyce is fatally incontinent. He has no idea of where to stop. The provision of an overture at the beginning of this episode is an example. A German critic tells us that these 'two pages of seemingly meaningless text form in reality a carefully thought out composition', the technic being 'an exact transposition of the musical treatment of the *Leitmotif*' by Wagner. But he at once adds what is in effect a contradiction. The Wagnerian *Leitmotif* is complete in itself and aesthetically satisfying, whereas the first two pages of the Sirens, taken by themselves, are neither intelligible nor pleasing. They are not a composition at all, neither are they of the nature of scenario, preliminary sketch, working notes. It is impossible to believe that Joyce first assembled these fifty-eight sentences, phrases, words, fragments of onomatopoeia and then went to work on them. They are merely a selection of what seems particularly to have taken his fancy among the recurrent images and cadences of the piece itself. The musical analogy is here delusory. And there is a good deal in the body of the episode in which the musical correspondences appear forced and even foolish: 'Goulding, a flush struggling in his pale, told Mr. Bloom, face of the night. Si in Ned Lambert's, Dedalus' house, sang *'Twas rank and fame.'* In the succeeding sentence Joyce sorts this out for us with a sort of facetious explicitness: 'He, Mr. Bloom, listened while he, Richie Goulding, told him, Mr. Bloom of the night he, Richie, heard him, Si Dedalus, sing *'Twas rank and fame* in his, Ned Lambert's house.' We are being shown, it must be supposed, what verbal composition would be like if it took on certain of the characteristics of musical composition. At the same time, perhaps, something is being intimated to us about the state of Bloom's consciousness at this moment—as he sits in the Ormond, fretted by the appearance of Boylan, eating his liverslices, listening to Goulding's voice against the background of the impromptu musical entertainment being offered by three other of the patrons of the establishment. In these circumstances, what Goulding has to say comes to him only as a muddle. The words play at leapfrog in his head just as musical phrases can be made to do. But the musical phrases after their leapfrog can remain

music, whereas the words, after theirs, don't remain sense. One
other example may be considered of this queer pedantic transposing:

BLMSTUP

This, we are told by Mr. Gilbert, is a *hollow fifth*, and it is our
business 'instinctively' to supply the *thirds* and so achieve:

BLOOM STOOD UP

It must be admitted that Joyce very often—like the tradesman
in Johnson's poem—'labours for a joke'. And he is even more
liable to run a joke, an amusing idea, to death. For instance,
there is nothing more splendidly spirited in the whole book
than the Cyclops episode. The presentation of Bloom in his
conflict with the Citizen is vividly dramatic. And the basic idea
for the elaborating of this episode is clearly a good one. What is
proposed is the cross-cutting of the demotic speech of the
anonymous narrator with something equally vulgar of another
sort: an inflated, ye olde, pseudo-literary, spuriously heroic, and
romantic commentary. But this element, once admitted, proliferates disastrously (pastiche often has a fatal attraction for
Joyce) and becomes a major impediment. Why must we be
told all about the wedding of Miss Fir Conifer of Pine Valley—
which is attended by personages as diverse as Mrs. Barbara
Lovebirch, Lady Sylvester Elmshade and Miss O Mimosa San,
and which leads to a honeymoon in the Black Forest? The
Citizen, it is true, has called upon the Universe to save the
trees of Ireland for the future men of Ireland on the fair hills of
Eire, O. But it is to be doubted whether he would have done
this but for Statius, Boccaccio, Chaucer, Spenser, and others:
writers who—although they can scarcely have been known to
the Citizen, to Bloom, or to anyone in *Ulysses* other than
Stephen and some of his acquaintances in the public library—
once upon a time thought it right and proper that a major
literary performance should include, as classical epic includes,
a catalogue of trees. So Joyce too feels that he must have this,
as he must have everything else. Hence the intrusion into
Barney Kiernan's pub of Mrs. Maud Mahogany and the rest of
them.

A curious encyclopedism, such as may be found in some
medieval poets, obsesses the author of *Ulysses*. It is this, more
than anything else, that makes the work so hard of final critical

appraisal. When Yeats declared *Ulysses* to be a mad book, later pronounced it a work of genius surpassing in intensity any novel of its time, and finally was unable to finish it so that he found himself reading Trollope instead, he was only rehearsing a common course of feeling before the work's incontinence. Joyce seems, for instance, to feel that his book should contain not only his own sort of English—or rather his own sorts of English in their almost inexhaustible variety—but every other sort of English as well. So he writes one long section, that in which Bloom visits the National Maternity Hospital in Holles Street and meets Stephen, in a succession of parodies tracing the whole evolution of English prose. Some of these are presented out of order. And we are instructed by the commentators that as this evolution of styles is being appropriately exhibited in a context of development from unfertilized ovum to birth, and as, in an embryo, one or another organ may develop prematurely, there is a particular grace in setting the parodies too in an occasional chronological confusion. To assist him in all this, we are told, Joyce kept beside him as he worked an actual diagram of the development of the human foetus. Joyce's mind, we must recognize, is as tortuous and pedantic as it is prodigal and poetic. And again and again its prodigality seems to render very uncertain its sense of measure. Between the longest section of the book, the unparalleled and astounding fantasia of the unconscious, thronged and farced with spectres of preternatural vigour and overpowering horror, which opens in 'the Mabbot street entrance of nighttown'—between this and the contrasting but equally unexampled long slow earthen pulse of Mrs. Bloom's concluding reverie (the first sentence of which, Joyce proudly announced, 'contains 2500 words') there is obviously required some episode of relaxed tension. Joyce provides two such episodes in succession. First, Bloom and Stephen are represented as sitting in a cabmen's shelter, exhausted. This exhaustion is conveyed, on the governing principle of the book, by recourse to an exhausted, a jejune prose, and the contriving of what is best described as a sustained cliché of some twenty thousand words. Next, the two men—casually thrown together but symbolically regarded as in search of each other—make their way to Bloom's kitchen. They are isolated individuals, souls struggling towards some obscure self-realization through and against the recalcitrant medium of matter. This recalcitrant medium Joyce evokes overwhelmingly by a yet longer and denser device: an interminable inexorable catechism, couched almost exclusively in a flat scientific jargon, exhaustively tabulating in purely physical terms every aspect not only of Bloom's present situation but also of the dream-cottage to which he aspires to retire:

What homothetic objects, other than the candlestick, stood on the mantelpiece?

A timepiece of striated Connemara marble, stopped at the hour of 4.46 a.m. on the 21 March 1896, matrimonial gift of Matthew Dillon: a dwarf tree of glacial arborescence under a transparent bellshade, matrimonial gift of Luke and Caroline Doyle: an embalmed owl, matrimonial gift of Alderman John Hooper.

There are more than three hundred such answers to questions, and some of them describe with minute particularity as many as ten or twenty separate objects. Joyce is said to have taken more satisfaction in this part of *Ulysses* than in any other, letting it take pride of place over the Circe episode in his final regard. Certainly it cannot be called idle or even—strangely enough—uniformly boring. There is no reason to suppose that the precise effect at which it aims—a sort of ultimate in objectivity, balancing an ultimate in subjectivity represented by Mrs. Bloom's reverie—could be produced in any more concise way. Yet this massive accumulation, this enormous *stasis*, is presented to us at a point where we suppose ourselves to be moving towards the resolution of a fable. What, we ask, is this resolution? The mountain has laboured. But where is even the mouse?

Stripped and viewed as an action, *Ulysses* reveals itself as being much what it started out to be: a short story in *Dubliners*. We need not suppose that Mr. Hunter's wanderings about Dublin were to have been no more than a small exercise in the picaresque. That was never Joyce's way. Something always happens in his stories. But it is generally a small, muted, problematically or evanescently significant thing. Most characteristically, it is an encounter—an encounter with some circumscribed hinted consequence which is not pursued. And this is the formula of *Ulysses*, the spare skeleton which has been given so much flesh and so many clothes. None of the great elaborative works of literature—Milton's *Paradise Lost*, Goethe's *Faust*, Mann's *Joseph und seine Brüder*—has made do with quite so little.

And these are works which may without absurdity be mentioned here. *Ulysses*, bitterly described by Joyce himself in *Finnegans Wake* as 'an epical forged cheque on the public for his private profit', has been called by Mr. T. S. Eliot 'the most considerable work of imagination in English in our time'. Obviously it must abide the largest questions. Does it assist us to see life steadily and see it whole? Or does it, in a mordant pun of Joyce's own, see life foully—and that with a persistence altogether too compulsive for good sense? It is 'packed with the defeatism and guilt of youth', Mr. Cyril Connolly says— and he adds that 'Narcissus with his pool before him' must be his own image for his first reading of the book. Some find the pool altogether too muddy. *Ulysses*, Mr. E. M. Forster declares, is 'an epic of grubbiness and disillusion'. Certainly much is admitted to it which has not for many centuries figured in the polite literature of the West. Critics, like magistrates, have a good deal concerned themselves with this—Joyce's best critic, Mr. Pound, among them.

But more significant, perhaps, is what this ambitiously comprehensive work excludes. In absorbing, and giving literary expression to, a whole fresh range of psychological perceptions and persuasions invading the European mind in the first decades of the century, Joyce conceivably establishes himself, in Mr. Edmund Wilson's phrase, as 'the great poet of a new phase of the human consciousness'—a phase in consonance with that modern physics and philosophy which reduces everything to terms of 'events', and which teaches that in thinking to see life steadily we only deceive ourselves, since life is never steady itself. But we may feel that, if this be so, human consciousness has kept afloat only by throwing overboard, in a manner that would startle the great poets from Homer onwards, much of its traditional riches. Yet however we judge *Ulysses* at the level of high philosophic consideration we are likely to return to it again and again as fiction. We shall revisit it—Mr. Wilson has said—as we revisit a city, a city animated by a complex inexhaustible life.

10

Finnegans Wake (1939) is one of the strangest books ever to have gained admittance to the sphere of criticism. Joyce himself—although he sometimes declared it to be a joke, and although a doggedly boisterous jocularity gives it much of its distinguishable tone—must have regarded it with great seriousness, since he worked on it for far longer than he worked on *Ulysses*, expending on it oceans of devotion, elaborating prodigious expanses of linguistic virtuosity—and incidentally (it is said) sifting through in its interest some twelve kilos of notes left over from the earlier work. Nevertheless the *Wake* has a much smaller share of the real seriousness of art than *Ulysses* has, and already it seems necessary to find some explanation of the more portentous estimations which have been current ever since the project got under way. We may notice that it was while labouring on the book (which was for long known as *Work in Progress*) that Joyce was finally captured by Joyceans. And the tone set by these has continued to sound in the writing of many professional students. Thus in *A Skeleton Key to 'Finnegans Wake'* Messrs. Campbell and Robinson sometimes write in the language of the cinema trailer. 'Here for the first time', they claim, 'the complex and amazing narrative of Joyce's dream-saga is laid bare.' The *Wake* is a work of 'majestic logic', 'above all else an essay in permanence', 'a mighty allegory of the fall and resurrection of mankind', and 'a prodigious, multifaceted monomyth'. Of the first couple of pages of the book we are told that 'all the literal and allegorical references compressed into these paragraphs would fill many volumes with historical, theological, and literary data'—and that even then 'there would remain to be conquered . . . depths of moral and anagogical implication'. The *Wake* obviously impresses those prone to be impressed by great heaps of the raw material of education. And it gives enormous scope for setting young people to work with dictionaries and encyclopedias. As one authority says: 'The intensive communal reading of *Finnegans Wake* in graduate seminars by students of widely varied linguistic backgrounds, under the direction of Professors Tindall, Levin, and Kelleher, should be highly productive of future scholarship.'

This demotic and polyglotic vision suggests one use for the *Wake*. But the book also looks as if it might help us to answer a famous question. Is Night or Day the more excellent? Milton addressed himself to this in an academic exercise from which derive 'L'Allegro' and 'Il Penseroso'. A hundred years earlier, Michelangelo produced something like a commentary on it for the tomb of the Duke of Nemours. When we enter the

New Sacristy of San Lorenzo and consult our guide-books we learn that we should give more attention to the sculptor's Night than to his Day; it is the most to be admired of the symbolic creations on view. And presently we acquiesce. Day reveals itself at once as a majestic transcendentalizing of the male principle. Night, being flaccid and disturbingly androgynous, is at first something of a problem. But we gladly hail it in the end as the more profound creation—or the more sublime. In this we may be said to be confirming today's fashionable conclusion in a perennial debate about the human mind. And if Night is more excellent than Day, then *Finnegans Wake* ought to be even more excellent than *Ulysses*. For Leopold Bloom and Humphry Chimpden Earwicker are, for our age, representative figures in the disputation; they recline, we may say, on either side of the gigantic monument which Joyce spent his lifetime erecting to himself: a process which a clever Norwegian critic of his work has rather unkindly termed the cultic use of fiction.

For Michelangelo the prime association of Night and Sleep was with Oblivion. Indeed, in one of his poems he makes his Night express this:

> Non veder, no sentir m'è gran ventura;
> Però non me destar, deh! parla basso.

Però non me destar . . . it is simply the notice we may hang outside our door in an hotel: *Please do not disturb*. But for the contemporaries of Joyce the prime association of Night and Sleep is not with Oblivion, grateful or otherwise, but with an enormous realm of mental life, the Unconscious. Day is only the tip of the mind's iceberg. What we are normally aware of is merely a puppet régime and the real orders come from the underground. There—buried deep—is the tail that wags the dog. And it is a tail far longer even than any told of Shem and Shaun.

While *Ulysses*, then, the record of a single day, has some claim to exhaust the exploration of the waking mind, the *Wake*, its companion piece, seems to be correspondingly the record of a single night, and to aim, with equal exhaustiveness, at interpreting the nature and content of the mind asleep. In the regard of many of his contemporaries Joyce is thus stepping up his ambition, like a Renaissance poet consciously proceeding, as he matures, to a literary kind of greater reach and dignity.

'As if sleep', Coleridge somewhere says wonderingly of his dream experiences, 'had a *material* realm.' We do now, in effect, accord sleep a material realm—or at least a very real realm. The dreaming mind, we feel, substantially and extensively *exists*: a vast mental kingdom of the Unconscious with laws other than ours, but which yet bear fatefully upon us; a kingdom hinting at once dire compulsions and strange freedoms. If the *Wake* effectively explores and in some sense exhibits to consciousness that kingdom, then it must necessarily be, whether a successful work of art or not, a philosophical landmark. If it is even a serious and intelligently planned attempt at this it must be of the greatest interest and value. But perhaps we can say only that a serious—or at least a brilliant—idea underlies the *Wake*; that the idea produced a certain limited success; that in the main however it proved not to work; and that something compulsive in Joyce obliged and enabled him to carry on, nevertheless. Sometimes, indeed, we must suspect that we are being confronted with the evidences of an obstinate struggle against madness. Yet the *Wake*, although in a sense a despairing work, is seldom oppressively morbid. Indeed, and against much of our expectation, it is often astonishingly buoyant.

What then was Joyce's brilliant idea, and where did it come from? Already in *Ulysses* he had manipulated language in hitherto unexampled ways to express one or another special state of consciousness. Could he not go farther, and use it to express unconscious states, or at least that queer borderland of the mind which we inhabit in dreams and catch even more fragmentary glimpses of in slips of the tongue and pen? Certain persons in the *Wake* are described as 'yung and easily freudened', and there is an equally ingenious quip about 'the law of the jungerl'. Indeed both Jung and Freud do come largely in—however much, at times, Joyce may have gone out of his way to disclaim interest in them. For example, he may well have been struck by the opening of Freud's essay *On the Psychic Mechanism of Forgetfulness*, published in 1898 and later made the basis of the better-known *Psychopathology of Everyday Life*.

In this work Freud records how he once tried to recall the artist who painted the 'Last Judgment' in the Capella della Madonna di San Brizio at Orvieto, and instead of the right name, *Signorelli*, found himself remembering the names *Botticelli* and *Boltraffio*, both of which he knew instantly to be wrong. He analyses the slip and discovers, after canvassing a whole group of elusive verbal associations, a complicated sense in which it may be viewed as meaningful and purposeful.

It is obvious how this could interest Joyce, who owned a mind constantly disposed, whether voluntarily or involuntarily, to play strange tricks with words. Mr. Wilson declares rather sweepingly in his study of the *Wake* that 'there is actually a special kind of language which people speak in dreams'. And Joyce himself appears explicitly to have believed this. He was concerned, he said, to 'put the language to sleep' and 'to suit the esthetic of the dream . . . where the brain uses the roots of vocables to make others from them which will be capable of naming its phantasms, its allegories, its allusions'. Yet even in speaking of his task in these formidable terms, Joyce is perhaps underestimating the complexity of his endeavour. No doubt there is an element of verbalization intermittently present in almost everybody's dreams, and in exceptional individuals this may be highly developed. And no doubt when our dreams do speak, the Signorelli–Botticelli–Boltraffio machinery is at work. But, on the whole, dreams like ghosts are characteristically disposed to taciturnity, are visual rather than auditory phenomena. It is hard to believe that the *Wake* is written in an actual language at all extensively used at any level of the mind, or at least that Joyce is doing other than base his whole project on a hazardously idiosyncratic and little-diffused mental habit. And in fact we become convinced that he is much more actively engaged than in simply listening in to voices murmuring in the deeps. He is actively imposing upon *language* those sorts of condensation, displacement, and distortion which the mechanisms of dream constantly impose upon *visual images*—impose upon these, we are told, by way of expressing, evading, solving, disguising conflicts. It is, one must repeat, a complex proposal— far more complex than that transposing of language and music which produced BLMSTUP. We need not indeed believe that Joyce regularly begins with complex visual images, analyses them, and then seeks to build up verbal complexes of answering implication. He is evidently not engaged in a steady labour of translation. In a sense he does begin with words; and what is perhaps radically wrong with the *Wake* as any sort of dream is that he ends with them as well. He begins, we may conjecture, from wit in the modern sense of the term—from a power of mind whereby words are constantly starting up in strange distortions and combinations as the result of unconscious processes certainly related to those operative in dreams. Since his methods of composition became, we know, most elaborate, he must have concluded that by working on this faculty, studying it, imitating it, taking its products as prototype material for consciously willed and planned and directed operations he was—whether artistically or philosophically—getting somewhere. He may be described as lured on by the unparalleled opportunities which the fabricating of a dream language to express a dream logic would afford to his own unique logopoeic genius. He believed that if he drove that genius hard, at the same time applying to it a sort of tact or tutelage represented by more or less coherent theories of history and of the imagination, he would achieve a significant work exploring and expressing the essential structure of the unconscious mind as we intermittently become aware of it in sleep. His new book, once more, would be an Anatomy of Night, as *Ulysses* had been an Anatomy of Day.

II

Finnegans Wake (the first word in the title telescopes conclusion and recurrence; the second is both substantive and verb) is succinctly described by one authority as 'probably the dream of H. C. Earwicker, tavern keeper, on a warm evening', and Joyce's intention as being to depict 'the mind of an average citizen of modern Ireland asleep'. Although other authorities disagree, asserting for example that the point of view adopted is omniscient, moving freely from husband to wife to sons and to external points of observation, we may accept this as a good working hypothesis, provided always that we take proper account of Joyce's theory of what is likely to be happening in the sleeping mind of a citizen, average or otherwise. Earwicker's dream, if conducted in terms of a loose synthesis of the main depth-psychologies current in the nineteen-twenties, will be constituted, in the first place, out of the incidents of his waking life during the preceding day or two. Earwicker, because he wants to remain asleep and must therefore avoid a subliminal row, will be busily grabbing these incidents and improvising out of them an allegorical charade in which various more or less illicit impulses in his psyche are allowed an airing in disguise. This is plain sailing, and Joyce's first task is to provide his hero with a setting upon which his dream may handsomely draw. The *Wake* is to be a 'funferal' and it will conduce to this if poor Earwicker, sleeping or waking, has a good deal to contend with. He is conceived then as being, like Bloom, an instinctively respectable man but liable, morally, to unfortunate lapses. Just lately he has had such a lapse in Phoenix Park. It is all very obscure—since it comes to us only through dream this is inevitable—but apparently he was prompted by the sight of two girls, not themselves behaving with complete propriety, to some indecency which, most unfortunately, was observed by three soldiers. 'Whatever it was they threed to make out he thried to two in the Fiendish park', the result has been scandal and difficulty, and one particularly vexatious consequence is Earwicker's having been defeated in a local election. Moreover his misdemeanour in the Park is only one symptom of a difficult time of life at which he appears to have arrived. A phase of sexual involution has set in; his wife is ceasing to have an important place in his erotic life; and at some level of his mind his daughter and even his twin sons are the subjects of incestuous impulses. Earwicker asleep is to be kept tolerably busy.

So far the plan was perhaps not really very promising. However much Joyce achieved a personative treatment, a private element would be bound to remain embarrassingly prominent. And indeed there always seems to be a concealed facet of self-reference in anything he conveys into his book. Thus he confesses in a letter that Vico's philosophy, in a sense basic to the *Wake*, has attracted him owing to circumstances of his own life—and the circumstance he instances is that he, like Vico, is afraid of thunder. It is possible to regard the whole elaboration undergone by the basic idea or situation as a desperate labour of disguise—Joyce having unwarily got on territory he doesn't quite want to face and certainly doesn't want to exhibit. Hence (as perhaps already in minor degree in *Ulysses*) all the overdoing it, hence all the obscurities imposed upon obscurities with which we must struggle if we are really going to tackle the book. But this interpretation we need not pursue. Everything that follows upon the simple proposal to set a Dublin publican dreaming in terms of his own family constellation can be explained as a consequence of the scale upon which Joyce was predisposed to operate. *Ulysses* had set a standard; *Finnegans Wake* had to be a book of apparent larger dimensions than that. For the achieving of this there was available all that is rich and ingenious and resourceful in perfectly common dream. Yet, in a work on a large scale, this would not in itself be an adequate insurance against a somewhat claustrophobic and impoverished effect. Joyce was therefore constrained to enlarge Earwicker's dream, to canvass those deeper levels of the unconscious at which the individual dream has been thought to merge in the collective myth, and at which individual identities may be less substantial and lasting and continuous psychological units than they are upon the surface of life as we know it. As soon as Earwicker's dream is conceived as in consonance with these ideas, a vast liberation seems to result. If his individual unconscious becomes boring it can simply be faded out into some other individual unconscious, since we are free of a level of mental life at which that is quite the thing. Dream and myth mingle; publican and culture hero; father and son and city and hill; mother and daughter and river. The point of view is very much a matter of omniscience, after all.

Subsidiary to this, and introduced for what it seems to promise in the way of a rather necessary cement, is the philosophy of history which Joyce had discovered in an eighteenth-century Italian writer, Giambattista Vico. That history is an affair of recurrent cycles, and that within the cycle certain phases repeat themselves in a fixed order: these are persuasions useful as giving a little intermittent rational backing to the to-and-fro movement (Finn–Finnegan–Earwicker–Finn–Tristram–Diarmuid–Earwicker–Finn and so on) to which Joyce is so massively committing himself. But the *Wake*, in this aspect, does not suggest itself as containing—any more than does Yeats's *A Vision* —a real depth of historical speculation. The notion that it all happens to all of us—Sinbad and Tinbad and Jinbad—clearly holds for Joyce the largest emotional appeal. So perhaps does Schopenhauer's conception of the world as a system of dreams within a dream. At the bottom of the *Wake* is a somewhat Orientally coloured philosophy of deliquescence. Individuals, races, centuries, countries, languages are all conceived as elements within the slowly revolving kaleidoscope which is the book.

For *Finnegans Wake* is, almost literally, a wheel. It begins: 'riverrrun, past Eve and Adam's, from swerve of shore to bend of bay, brings us by a commodious vicus of recirculation back to Howth Castle and Environs.' And it ends: 'A way a lone a last a loved a long the' The last sentence runs straight into the first. Earwicker's dream takes its form from Vico's system—which makes us a typically sidelong introductory bow here at the start in the 'vicus of recirculation' by which is also suggested a pleasant *giro* that may be taken round Dublin bay. And Earwicker is making us his bow here too. 'Howth Castle and Environs' displays initial letters corresponding with his own: only as Earwicker is in one sense a universal figure, the initials may also stand for Haveth Childers Everywhere or Here Comes Everybody. Eve and Adam's is the popular name for a church on the bank of the Liffey, which is the river that is running in the opening word. But as we are already talking about the stream of history, we are no doubt being invited, incidentally, to consider that longer stream's first welling-up in the Garden of Eden. Joyce is said to have declared in a moment of arrogance (which may indeed have been softened by humour) that the demand he made upon his reader was no less than the application of a lifetime. When we go on to the second paragraph we may begin to wonder whether a lifetime will do; whether in fact the conditions of composition which Joyce has accepted and indeed invented allow of his making, to even the most devoted reader, that sort of elaborately rich and controlled communication which seems to be proposed:

Sir Tristram, violer d'amores, fr'over the short sea, had passencore rearrived from North Armorica on this side the scraggy isthmus of Europe Minor to wielderfight his penisolate war: nor had topsawyer's rocks by the stream Oconee exaggerated themselse to Laurens County's gorgios while they went doublin their mumper all the time: nor avoice from afire bellowsed mishe mishe to tauftauf thuartpeatrick: not yet, though venissoon after, had a kidscad buttended a bland old isaac: not yet, though all's fair in vanessy, were sosie sesthers wroth with twone nathandjoe. Rot a peck of pa's malt had Jhem or Shen brewed by arclight and rory end to the regginbrow was to be seen ringsome on the aquaface.

'The first impression', Messrs. Campbell and Robinson say of this in their *Skeleton Key*, 'is one of chaos, unrelieved by any landmark of meaning or recognition.' But this impression they assert to be mistaken, since the passage holds nothing that need shake our faith in Joyce 'as a wielder of the most disciplined logic known to modern letters'. There are, they say later, no nonsense syllables in *Finnegans Wake*.

Let us consider one strand which the *Skeleton Key* helps us to unravel in this second paragraph: a geographical strand. On *Armorica* the *Key* might have cited Milton, whose 'Begirt with British and Armoric knights' certainly gives the prime literary association of the word to English readers. But the *Key* does point out that behind *Armorica* we are required to hear *America*. Then we are required also to identify 'the scraggy isthmus of Europe Minor', to discriminate a geographical as well as a phallic and a biographical reference in *penisolate*, to look up *Oconee* and *Laurens County* in a gazetteer, to detect Joyce's own city in the phrase 'went doublin their mumper', and to let ourselves be led from *in vanessy* to *Inverness* and so to recall Macbeth, who like Earwicker fell into some moral danger as a consequence of an encounter with females. So far, so good. But now, in the context of all this geography, let us pause on the phrase, 'not yet, though venissoon after'. Shall we be adequate Joyceans, we may ask Messrs. Campbell and Robinson, if we are not prompted to think of something like 'not yet, but nevertheless shortly after the extinction of the Venetian republic'? Yet this is presumably all wrong: something to which not even the darkest abysses of Joyce's mind are being moved to point us. *Venissoon* is intended to telescope Swift's Vanessa and the dish of venison which Jacob brought to his father Isaac. Vanessa comes in again in *in vanessy* and Swift comes in in *nathandjoe*. The significance of the telescoping in *venissoon* resides, we suppose, in the fact that, for Joyce, Swift's young woman and Isaac's luckless dinner represent awkwardnesses that do themselves telescope (and do indeed for all of us, it is implied, at some level of the mind telescope): the awkwardness of ambiguous mistress–daughter relationships and the awkwardness of intense father–child–brother relationships. *Venice*—although indeed described by another writer as the eldest child of Liberty—ought not to be there at all. It is there, either because Joyce has failed to notice it (which is not to the credit of the particular power he is cultivating so intensively) or because, although he has, he nevertheless has refused to bother, being content to leave a casually dropped brick in the very portal of

an edifice for which the very largest and severest architectural
claims are to be advanced.¹ If we pause long enough over these
first four paragraphs, considering both what the *Skeleton Key*
says and what it doesn't say, we may conclude that they resemble
a dream, indeed, chiefly in being susceptible of as many interpretations as there are oneirologists at work. And if we admit to
our studies a hundredth part of the very simple sense of fun in
which Joyce himself abounds (and which most of his commentators notably lack), we shall soon find in the whole imprecise-
ness of the communication being achieved the conditions for
a pleasing literary game. Thus the *Skeleton Key* tells us of the
opening sentence that the 'swerve of shore' is 'the coy gesture
of the pretty isle herself which invites the assault of the bay
waters, thus hinting at a Seduction theme which will later
emerge full of import'. It may be so. When a woman rests all
her weight notably on one leg the plastic effect, referred to by
painters and sculptors as a *déhanchement*, is undoubtedly capable
of seduction; and perhaps this is how the 'pretty isle' is behaving—although we remember that it is the water and not the
land that we are required to accept as symbolizing the feminine
principle. But what of the 'bend of bay'? There is one obvious
association here, perhaps beneath the notice of literary history
but certainly not beneath Joyce's. It is to that Bey of Algiers
who, in a well-known English poem, encouragingly addresses
the ladies of his harem—ladies who, like Cleopatra's on the
barge, assuredly made their *bends* adornings. And in bringing in
that Bey and *those déhanchements* we are again being good Joyceans
—better, for the moment, than Messrs. Campbell and Robinson.
If we are really adept, we shall maintain that there is here
a significant adumbration of another theme full of 'import',
and quote the mention, in the section giving the fable of the
Ondt and the Gracehoper, of being 'boundlessly blissfilled in an
allallahbath of houris'. Here may be the Bey once more. But
again, of course, we may be going wrong. And it appears to
be doubtful whether Joyce would have been much disturbed
by the spectacle of our doing so. To write on the principles invented in and for the *Wake* is perhaps to abandon any anxious
care about the minutiae of what one wants to communicate

---

¹ Yet may not Venice suggest Othello, who like Swift was involved with a
younger woman? And may not anyone become competent in Joycean exegesis who
can concatenate sealing wax and ships?

and what one doesn't. At least the method is not to be defended in terms of Messrs. Campbell and Robinson's 'disciplined logic'. It is another American critic, Mr. Hugh Kenner, who gets nearer the heart of the matter:

> It doesn't . . . really matter that we don't, inevitably, catch a fraction of the detailed implications in a passage of *Finnegans Wake*; Joyce is . . . strewing the text so liberally with so many clues . . . that we can afford to miss a great deal and still, within certain limits of indetermination, possess the work.

We can afford, it is to be hoped, both to miss a great deal that is there and to catch a great deal that isn't. For, unless both these conditions hold, *Finnegans Wake* is a failure.

12

But at least on almost any page there is likely to be found some distortion of language which may be described as comprehensibly amusing. As a boy Joyce had been fond of a party game playing upon place names: 'Harold's Cross because Terenure', 'What Chapelizod?' We find the same thing in the *Wake*—with more 'import', no doubt—when Chapelizod is presented as concealing a reference to Iseult. In the section on Shem the Penman, in which Joyce makes fun of himself, *Ulysses* appears as the Blue Book of Eccles, and is described as 'usylessly unreadable'. This is diverting precisely as any other bad pun is diverting. A little later, in a descriptive catalogue of Shem's house, the Haunted Inkbottle, we come on 'once current puns, quashed quotatoes, messes of mottage'—which is the same sort of thing, only better and cleverer. Puns elaborately strung together are similarly diverting in a short-range way. 'Nobirdy aviar soar anywing to eagle it!' suggests a brighter moment, perhaps, on the Light Programme of the B.B.C. 'Was liffe worth leaving?' is an example of verbal wit of a perfectly lucid sort that carries rather farther. It holds both 'Was exile from Dublin too much to pay for what I have achieved or am achieving?' and 'Has life been supportable?' And some of Joyce's casual effects of this sort are almost extravagantly felicitous—as, for example, a little advertisement for the fragment 'Anna Livia Plurabelle' which ends:

> Sheashell ebb music wayriver she flows.

But when we press beyond these superficial diversions we are made aware of a radical dilemma to which Joyce is committed by the whole nature of his linguistic proposal. All this play with words is either contrived or spontaneous. Where it is contrived it must be, so to speak, conjectural: an intellectual artefact modelled upon what is known or conjectured about the dream-processes which the writer is concerned to suggest. In this case Joyce must face Dr. Leavis's criticism that his exhibition of the subconscious is not merely boring but offensively spurious, and Mr. Empson's that it is all, so to speak, happening the wrong way round and therefore lacking in the vitality and interest of right-way-round verbal creation. When, on the other hand, the word-play is spontaneous, it is likely to include a large element of sheer enigma. We don't know what it is driving at, and Joyce doesn't either. This becomes apparent if we go back to Freud's *Signorelli* analysis. There an unconscious mechanism has erupted upon Freud's speech, and the result is something incomprehensible to him until he has made an elaborate professional investigation. The mechanism is so complex, indeed, that the analysis takes some mastering, even after Freud has set it out with his own great clarity and provided an elucidatory diagram. (We can see that *Signorelli* is possibly in for trouble because the Italian *Signor* is associating with the German *Herr* of 'Sir' and the *Her* of *Herzegovina*, both of which have been detected by the analysis as on a black list. But we are puzzled by *Boltraffio*, allowed into consciousness although compounded of *two* black-listed elements; and although we see that Botticelli very neatly telescopes *Bosnia* and *Signorelli*, it is some time before we can be made to understand the logic of its appearance.) Now, when Joyce gets *Botticelli* (so to speak) he simply waits for what comes next and puts it down—at least to the extent to which any element of psychic automatism is a basis of his book. He can have had only the vaguest idea of the unconscious forces at work, and must have been following free associations he didn't know why—until, every now and then, it became necessary to give them a little conscious shove or sifting in the interest of the large vague general design represented by Earwicker, his pub, his family, his lapse in Phoenix Park, his correspondence to Finn, and all the rest of it.

There is much reasonableness in the contention that when we seek the intelligible in *Finnegans Wake* we are seeking what it is not Joyce's serious proposal to provide. The book is massively dream-like, and that is enough. On this aspect of the work Mr. Wilson has a passage so finely persuasive as to demand quotation:

> Joyce has caught the psychology of sleep as no one else has ever caught it, laying hold on states of mind which it is difficult for the waking intellect to re-create, and distinguishing with marvelous delicacy between the different levels of dormant consciousness. There are the relative vividness of events reflected from the day before; the nightmare viscidity and stammering of the heavy slumbers of midnight; the buoyance and self-assertive vitality which gradually emerge from this; the half-waking of the early morning, which lapses back into the rigmaroles of dreams; the awareness, later, of the light outside, with its effects as of the curtain of the eyelids standing between the mind and the day. Through all this, the falling of twilight, the striking of the hours by the clock, the morning fog and its clearing, the bell for early mass, and the rising sun at the window, make themselves felt by the sleeper. With what brilliance they are rendered by Joyce!

This is in itself brilliant, and a product of close reading. But to some it will seem to suggest that *Finnegans Wake* is much more dreamlike, much more deeply and genuinely nocturnal in effect, than in fact it is. 'Earwicker', Mr. Wilson says again, 'is animated in sleep by the principles of both the sexes.' So, we may add, is Michelangelo's Night, precisely; and both figures do in this intimate to us a truth about the human psyche often hinted in dreams. Yet the *Wake*, set over against Michelangelo's figure, suggests itself to us as miles away from its goal. It *ought* to assert the realm of dream. The pervasively protean nature of the characters (if they are to be called that), interchanging roles and lineaments bafflingly but at the bidding, we may concede, of some valid dialectic of the unconscious; the texture of interrelations and interpenetrations spun over the whole, the strong impression of successive strata of consciousness and of depth opening upon depth: all this *ought* to be deeply dream-like. But is it? In what sense is it really true that Joyce has caught the psychology of sleep? Reading the *Wake* certainly isn't remotely like being asleep and dreaming. As Mr. Wilson himself says earlier, it becomes 'the reader's prime preoccupation to puzzle out who the dreamer is and what has been happening to him'. Far more immediately, we may add, it remains the reader's preoccupation to puzzle out as much as he can of the innumerable misadventures being suffered by the words on the page before him. It is an exacting wide-awake business, and we don't behave at all like this in our dreams as we dream them. We are being put much more in the position, surely, of an amateur psychoanalyst to whom there has been presented a mass of dream material recorded in a new notation of unexampled complexity and ingenuity. It is something like that—with indeed this difference once more: that this dream isn't a genuine dream at all. It is a synthetic performance, evolved over a long period of time by a hard-working writer interested in dreams, interested in using dreams and what he has been told about dreams to make something that is not a dream, interested in several mythologies, interested in indecency, interested in getting back at Wyndham Lewis, interested in an eccentric theory of history. Anything approaching the interpreting of a sixteen-year-long synthetic dream of this sort is a tall order.

To think to pursue at any recondite level the 'meaning' or 'secret' of the *Wake* is, in fact, inevitably to fall out with Joyce. For anybody trailing him in this way he is clearly determined to treat as a menace. It is as if we were after him with a warrant in our pocket concerning some serious offence, committed whether in a park or elsewhere, and he were desperately resolved to throw us off the scent at any cost. Even Mr. Levin, the most urbane and professionally competent of his commentators, gives one cry of despair: 'Every sentence is a wilful divagation from the expectations raised by the last.' And Mr. John Crowe Ransom produced a sweeping indictment to the same effect in the year the *Wake* was published:

Operating constantly through this book is the rule which punctually alters the terms of discourse as soon as discourse has started, and brings its effectiveness to an end. . . . Joyce exploits at least two prime devices for obfuscating discourse. One is stream of consciousness, which is prepared to excrete irrelevances in any situation. The other is the verbal device of going from the relevant meaning of the word to the irrelevant meaning, or from the word to the like-sounding words, and then to the words like the like-words; a device that must be open to a literature from the moment when its language possesses a hundred words. . . . Greater love has never been had for the master artist than that of the Joyceans who argue that there is a close logic in Joyce's book, and in its parts.

Mr. Ransom goes on to compare the *Wake* with surrealist painting, which 'seems to intend to render genuine fragments of finished objects, but assembles them in confusion as if to say that these pieces of life will never add up into a whole'. This is at least to find that the *Wake* 'says' something, and if we accept the implication we may agree with a more recent critic who finds 'nowhere a more desolate view of our world and of the sheer emptiness of ourselves and things', a judgement that life is 'only a dream and this dream is always the same—always as absurd, incoherent and futile as a useless and wearying delirium'. Joyce's brother Stanislaus, a dogged and faithful critic, told him that in the *Wake* he had 'escaped from the toils of the priest and the king only to fall under the oppression of a monstrous version of life itself'. But if this sombre way of taking the book doesn't quite correspond to our sense of it, however baffled, we may canvass again the notion that the impulse to interpret or elucidate the *Wake* is a radically wrong impulse; that 'consciousness'—as it is rather obscurely put by yet another critic—'instead of explaining Earwicker's dream material, often makes it more difficult'. Perhaps we ought merely to give ourselves to the book, trusting that the right things will simply happen if we do. The *Skeleton Key* has the undesigned effect of suggesting that there is something in this. Its concern is with 'the progress of Joyce's story'; and it addresses itself, pertinaciously and in the main judiciously, to a disengaging of matter susceptible of logical interpretation. And we are likely to feel that whatever virtue the *Wake* has tends to evaporate before this intellectual approach. Conversely, the *Wake* can certainly in places be fascinating when passively received. Joyce himself once declared, on being asked whether the book was a blending of literature and music, that it was *pure* music. Yet his famous 'Anna Livia Plurabelle' gramophone record is deceptive. There isn't a great deal in the book that is quite like the section he chose for reading: a section, it may be remarked, which is known to have gone through seventeen distinct stages of revision. And when commentators advance the contention that we must simply *listen* to the *Wake* it is this section, with monotonous regularity, that they cite. Substantial parts of the book simply wouldn't read aloud, are not articulatable. And aural reception of almost *any* part is bound to miss an enormous amount of what has been fed into the text for ends presumably significant to the author.

Finnegans Wake, in short, is before everything else a huge printed puzzle—'a maj jong puzzle' in one of Joyce's own uncomfortably depreciatory phrases. Yet it is a puzzle that won't come out, that isn't designed for elucidation. The book is, indeed, shot through and through with evidences of genius, traversed by rich seams of power. One may almost say of it what Goethe said of Marlowe's *Doctor Faustus*: 'How greatly it is all planned!' Yet what actually haunts it is no more than the uneasy ghost of an architectonic power—for somewhere there has been, as Joyce says, 'a freudful mistake' and the whole Daedalian structure is insecure in its very foundations. But the artificer won't give in, and proves almost inexhaustibly resourceful in gathering and implicating the fragments he would shore against his ruin. As the years went by, as the *Wake* slowly grew, accumulative revision became more and more its governing principle. Joyce seldom deleted anything he had written, except in the special sense of so superimposing one verbal invention upon another that the result was a palimpsest in which the earlier intention was hard to discern. The earlier the draft, moreover, the nearer we are to some distinguishable narrative movement. The later the version, the more vividly do we come to feel what it must be like to be a fly on fly-paper.

Mr. Wilson has acutely observed that the *Wake* represents an ageing phase in the constant human subject with which the series of Joyce's books has dealt. Perhaps we must go farther than this and agree that its pages everywhere suggest degenerative processes at work in the mind which has produced them. Certain of Joyce's specific talents are exhibited in hypertrophy, while much that normally evidences intellectual and imaginative power in an artist has disappeared. What remains constant amid this pervasive shifting of mental balance is an unconquerable comic energy.

The more seriously we take *Finnegans Wake* the more depressing, even saddening, does it appear. In this aspect it is very evidently the work of the man who on being asked 'What do you think of the next life?' replied 'I don't think much of this one'. Correspondingly, the more emphasis we set on the *Wake's* ebullient humour, the better the terms on which we shall get with it, and the less shall we be aware of the large surrounding sterilities and atrophies in which Stephen Dedalus is ending. Here is a great comic work which has gone badly wrong. It is almost as if Joyce had taken on a *Joseph und seine Brüder* when he ought to have been writing a *Felix Krull*. For he is old and gay. He is old—older than his years—and, in an arid, mad, despairing sort of way, robustly gay. Sometimes—we learn—he could be heard laughing uproariously as he sat fabricating his strange obsessional and tortured final tongue. 'I write in that way', he told John Eglinton, 'simply because it comes naturally to me to do so, and I don't care if the whole thing crumbles when I have done with it.'

Even so, it is not to be asserted that Joyce in this long last phase is capable only of a weirdly distorted image of boisterous and heartless comedy; that he is essentially the poet of the Ballad of Persse O'Reilly. He is still capable of effects of great poignancy and delicacy: as for example when, in that last paragraph of the book in which Mrs. Earwicker (less and less Mrs. Earwicker and more and more Anna Livia Plurabelle) turns to flow away in deepest resignation to the sea, her cold father, her mad cold father; as when, sharply eruptive upon that wonderful elegiac fall, comes the child's voice: 'Carry me along, taddy, like you done through the toy fair!' We are borne back to what Stephen heard in the voices of his brothers and sisters singing in the kitchen; to what Newman had heard in the broken lines of Virgil. The family constellation provides the basis upon which the whole work at its thickest and most nightmarish, its dirtiest and its most pretentious, rests. But it provides too the basis of those residual effects of lyric and of pathos which, when we come upon them, afford a very necessary relief from the predominant tones of the book. Kevin and Jerry Earwicker, however fantastically Shemmed and Shauned in the course of the *Wake*'s progress, remain actual and even engaging children. Their sister Isobel, however dubious the world that darkens round her in her character as Iseult la Belle, is still the 'blue-veined child' of *Pomes Penyeach*. In the 'half-awake' section (beginning brilliantly: 'What was thaas? Fog was whaas? Too mult sleepth') there is a passage in which the father, looking at his sleeping child, seems to see her at once as she was in infancy and in several relations which may in the future befall her:

night by silentsailing night while infantina Isobel (who will be blushing all day to be, when she growed up one Sunday, Saint Holy and Saint Ivory, when she took the veil, the beautiful presentation nun, so barely twenty, in her pure coif, sister Isobel, and next Sunday,

Mistlemas, when she looked a peach, the beautiful Samaritan, still as beautiful and still in her teens, nurse Saintette Isabelle, with stiff-starched cuffs but on Holiday, Christmas, Easter mornings when she wore a wreath, the wonderful widow of eighteen springs, Madame Isa Veuve La Belle, so sad but lucksome in her boyblue's long black with orange blossoming weeper's veil) for she was the only girl they loved, as she is the queenly pearl you prize, because of the way the night that first we met she is bound to be, methinks, and not in vain, the darling of my heart, sleeping in her april cot, within her singa-chamer, with her greengageflavoured candywhistle duetted to the crazyquilt, Isobel, she is so pretty, truth to tell, wildwood's eyes and primarose hair, quietly, all the woods so wild, in mauves of moss and daphnedews, how all so still she lay, neath of the whitethorn, child of tree, like some losthappy leaf, like blowing flower stilled, as fain would she anon, for soon again 'twill be, win me, woo me, wed me, ah weary me! deeply, now evencalm lay sleeping. . . .

This is delightful. Yet its muted and broken pathos, its tender-ness and sentiment, do not reflect an important current of feeling in *Finnegans Wake*. It is chiefly when the *vis comica* is at work that we feel Joyce as still an imaginative writer of un-impaired vigour. The section commonly known as Shem the Penman is perhaps the best exemplification of this. Its linguistic texture, while fully representative of Joyce's utmost, his termi-nal ingenuity, is sufficiently transpicuous to afford a reasonable view of the goings-on behind it. And these—in a common phrase here to be used with entire accuracy—are painfully funny. Joyce's scornful and jeering representation of himself makes a wonderful comic turn. At the same time it is the work of a man who has lived too much alone with his own daemon. Nothing Joyce wrote comes closer to a cry of pain. Joyce re-corded what is perhaps the final truth about *Finnegans Wake* in a letter to his devoted patroness, Harriet Weaver, written in 1926: 'I know it is no more than a game, but it is a game that I have learned to play in my own way. Children may just as well play as not. The ogre will come in any case.' And eight years later he wrote to the same correspondent: 'Perhaps I shall survive and perhaps the raving madness I write will survive and perhaps it is very funny. One thing is sure, however. *Je suis bien triste.*'

IX · LAWRENCE

I

DAVID HERBERT LAWRENCE was born in 1885 at Eastwood, a mining village near Nottingham. His father was
a miner. It is not altogether easy to assess the social implications of this fact. In many ways the boy had farther to go
than would one similarly circumstanced today. But the advance
of industrialism had only begun to create a working class
formidably insulated within a substantial and absorbing if
impoverished culture of its own. At certain points, moreover,
class barriers were less rigid then than now. There was as yet
no steady trend of legislation threatening the moderately privileged, and a clever boy from the people, although faced with
sufficient social prejudice, had to contend with nobody who
was afraid of him. When Lawrence was referred to by irritated
friends as a bounder or a cad it was commonly—as they realized
upon reflection—on the score of traits not necessarily identifiable with his origins. And as he possessed, in addition to some
facets of character which were indeed disagreeable and even
reprehensible, a personality capable of captivating and stimulating in what seems to have been an almost transcendent
degree, he never had much difficulty in getting where he pleased.
But humble birth, plebeian manners, and irregular education
can never be other than disadvantageous circumstances, and
Lawrence seldom forgot that they had been his.

His childhood carried a heavier burden in the disharmony
of his home. He identified himself with the aspirations of his
mother, which were towards more refinement than colliers
commonly care for, and he hated his father for seeming coarse
and brutal. At the same time his father's life and what it represented had a deep if unacknowledged power over his imagination. When Alvina in *The Lost Girl* meets a collier she feels in
him 'something forever unknowable and inadmissible, something that belonged purely to the underground . . . knowledge

humiliated, subjected, but ponderous and inevitable'. When Gudrun in *Women in Love* meets colliers she hears in their voices 'the voluptuous resonance of darkness, the strong, dangerous underworld, mindless, inhuman'. The connexion of this with much in Lawrence's developed symbolism is evident. When the novels become battle-grounds between conflicting modes of consciousness they are recreating a struggle first dramatized for him in bitter parental quarrels which he had witnessed as a child. The whole of his subsequent life was conditioned by these. Curiously enough he himself clung to the family pattern, making an article of faith of the noisy domestic row, even reproducing his father's stupid violence to the extent of smashing the crockery or throwing a glass of wine in his wife's face.

Lawrence became a school-teacher and wrote poems and two novels; after several troubled love affairs he ran away with, and eventually married, Frieda von Richthofen, the daughter of a Prussian landowner, who had somewhat unaccountably become the wife of a professor of literature in Nottingham. This event was definitive for Lawrence's subsequent career. He was in many ways an unpromising husband. When Miriam in *Sons and Lovers* conjectures that Paul 'would want to be owned, so that he could work', she hits on something very true of Lawrence himself. But if he eminently required thus to be securely possessed he compensated for any resulting sense of dependence by constant noisy assertions of male superiority and by much insistence upon women's itch to exercise, if unchecked, an 'evil, dominating will'. He was insanely jealous of his wife's children by her deserted professor, and from this he derived the general proposition that 'having children is a clutching at the past'. Naturally nomadic, and believing with his Alvina in the maxim 'When in doubt, *move*', he made the circumstance of Frieda's nationality, and some resultant war-time difficulties which were exacerbated by his own injudicious conduct, the occasion of the first of those restless wanderings which were to continue until his death. And the very success of his marriage, by providing one point of absolute assurance and refuge, must have encouraged him to give licence to that instability of emotional response in personal relations which he lightly describes in the Rawdon Lilly of *Aaron's Rod*:

He gave himself away so easily, paid such attention, almost deference to any chance friend. So they all thought: Here is a wise person
who finds me the wonder which I really am. And lo and behold,
after he had given them the trial, and found their inevitable limitations, he departed and ceased to heed their wonderful existence.
Which, to say the least of it, was fraudulent and damnable.

As applied to Lawrence himself this would be charitable. He
did not always 'depart' without Parthian shots which were
'damnable' in a less airy sense than is here suggested.

The strain imposed upon him by the First World War is
described, powerfully if unengagingly, in a long chapter in
Kangaroo called 'The Nightmare'. But he suffered even more
keenly—and he had a most genuine capacity for suffering—
from the near-persecution to which he had been subjected on
moral grounds after the publication of *The Rainbow*. When to
this were added several years of poverty and the first signs of
pulmonary disease, Lawrence had perhaps some reason to feel
that his life was, as he said, a 'savage pilgrimage'. At least it
was full of courage as well as of high accomplishment. 'So long
as you don't feel life's a paltry and a miserable business'—Paul
Morel is made to say to his mother—'the rest doesn't matter,
happiness or unhappiness.' It was on this ground that Lawrence
must have fought his stiffest fight, and it is not difficult to dig
out of his personal history evidence of his occasional near-
defeat. But the strongest element in his constitution, one before
which every flaw and frailty of character and temperament
fades away, was what Katherine Mansfield called 'his eagerness, his passionate eagerness for life'. The last sentence in his
collected letters—letters, incidentally, which are among the
finest in the language—is 'This place no good'. It was a conclusion to which he was constantly coming about one or another
of his camping grounds—for he was as prone to turn against
a city or a countryside or a continent as he was against individuals. But it was a judgement he never passed on the cosmos.
When he died in 1930, at the age of forty-four, it was as a man
who still saw only unquestioned good in the gift of being alive
in the flesh.

When Edmund Chambers, the father of his first love, said
'Work goes like fun when Bert's there' he was in fact touching
upon what was to be the boy's prime endowment as an artist:
intensity of response to the stimulus of the moment. His mind

was in all its important modes of operation highly intuitive.
Like any true priest of the oracle he was in constant travail to
render intelligible and coherent an uprush of obscure and urgent
utterance. One seems to discern in his work no principle of
composition other than that of setting down whatever comes
next into his head. Yet it is known that some of his books were
many times rewritten. His stature depends not merely on his
inspiration, which presented him perpetually with contradic-
tory convictions and bewildering sequences of ideas in brilliant
quasi-logical concatenation, but upon his belief that all this
broken and many-faceted material could be recomposed in
consciousness, so that eventually he should hold out to us in his
hands the perfected crystal of a visionary truth.

Like most oracles Lawrence can be readily misinterpreted
and like most prophets he can be readily mocked. The spectacle
of a man possessed by the 'mystical belief that he was in some
way selected to express truths beyond himself' and baffled by
the constant 'difficulty of finding out what it was that his subconscious or unconscious self really wanted to say' holds an
element of the ridiculous that has been emphasized even by his
most sympathetic and perceptive critic, Richard Aldington.
But Lawrence himself was the first to get going here. Commanding intuition does not exclude high intelligence, and he was
capable of a searching—and often extremely amusing—self-
criticism such as not all more consciously intellectual people
can put in evidence. Bertrand Russell has some clever strokes
against him, as when he says that, during the war, 'he had such
a hatred of mankind that he tended to think both sides must be
right in so far as they hated each other'. But one would be surprised to find Lord Russell walking round himself as Lawrence
succeeds in doing when he creates Rupert Birkin and Rawdon
Lilly and Richard Lovat Somers. Lawrence saw things very
clearly. It is this more than anything else that gives him his
pre-eminence among the writers discussed in the present
volume.

2

The design of *The White Peacock* (1911) is drawn from Lawrence's early novel reading. 'The usual plan', he reported to
Jessie Chambers in his twentieth year, 'is to take two couples
and develop their relationships. Most of George Eliot's are on

that plan. Anyhow, I don't want a plot, I should be bored with it. I shall try two couples for a start.' If his story does not stick closely to this proposal it evolves along equally traditional lines. Lettie Beardsall hesitates between a gentle and a rustic suitor, and devotes some ingenuity to tormenting each. Eventually she turns down George Saxton, the tenant farmer's son, in favour of Leslie Tempest, who is the heir of a mine-owner. It is a choice against nature, and her placid married life will be lived out in the consciousness of this. To George her decision is fatal. He knows that he has lost Lettie not because of the disparity in their conditions but through a defect of his own will; he marries a commonplace girl and after a period of material success takes to drink and is finally shown on the road to ruin. The other love relationship is wispy. George has a sister Emily, a shy farm-house maiden who foreshadows the Miriam of *Sons and Lovers*. Lettie has a brother Cyril, whose mildly urged interest in Emily is ended by her marriage to another. Cyril is passive and girlish. He is also the young Lawrence, an acute observer of people and an impassioned observer of nature. He tells the story.

A novel begun in nonage need not show mature artistic consideration. But *The White Peacock* has faults which even a beginner might have avoided. It casts in the form of first-person narrative an action largely concerned with intimate exchange between characters of whom the narrator is not one, and if Cyril seems unattractive it is partly because he is condemned to set out on so many walks which he must end in the role of Peeping Tom. Sometimes Lawrence has to give up and let omniscience take over. Henry James, who was to give *Sons and Lovers* somewhat ambiguous praise, would certainly have deplored this primitive violation of any rational 'point of view'. But Lawrence was never to have much care for the elementary techniques of the art of fiction. There is another particular in which *The White Peacock* offends against verisimilitude. Its basis is autobiographical, but Lawrence transposes much of it into a social setting of which he has no experience. The Saxtons on their farm are to the life. But the Beardsalls exist uncertainly in their genteel cottage and the Tempests yet more uncertainly in their Hall. The interrelations of these groups, even allowing for the flexibility of Midland society, are unconvincing. Lawrence is to develop a strong, exasperated, and penetrating sense of class-distinction, but is never to see as essential to his art the achieving of a fully realistic surface over the entire extent of his social scene. Thus he pitches unlikely people together in disregard of superficial plausibility and with an instinct only for the larger and sometimes symbolic purposes of his fiction. But in *The White Peacock* he is often simply at sea, and goes ahead in terms of a confident high-spirited guess-work. It is in another sphere that he has already gained a knowledge and authority that are precious to him. The Lawrence behind this book is a youth who exists chiefly in an intense enjoyment of the rural world at his back door. The prose in which he expresses this, taking licence perhaps from Meredith, is very flowery. Nothing that can bloom in a Nottinghamshire hedgerow gets by unremarked. The last bell hangs from the ragged spire of fox-glove. The few pink orchids stand palely by the path; they look wistfully out at the ranks of red-purple bugle whose last flowers, glowing from the top of the bronze column, yearn darkly for the sun. This natural scene is often much poeticized in terms of human metaphor. Winter begins to gather her limbs, to rise, and drift with saddened garments northward; the breast of the hills heaves in a last quick waking sigh and the blue eyes of the waters open bright. Or again:

It was warm in the quarry: there the sunshine seemed to thicken and sweeten; there the little mounds of overgrown waste were aglow with very early dog-violets; there the sparks were coming out on the bits of gorse, and among the stones the coltsfoot plumes were already silvery. Here was spring sitting just awake, unloosening her glittering hair.

It is customary to get poetry out of wild flowers; Lawrence can get it equally out of turnips, heaped in gold beneath the pulper. And he already sees a dramatic poetry inherent in territory where rural and industrial England meet. At evening it is so still in the fields that one hears the tubes of stubble tinkle like dulcimers, and hears too the rhythmic hum of the engines at the distant coal-mine. The mower relinquishes the snaith of his scythe as the last bantles of men are drawn up from the pit. There is a strike, and the struggle is reflected in the woods and warrens as the keeper sets man-traps for poaching colliers.

Yet all this, notably as it is commanded by so young a writer, serves only as background to a story strongly realized and achieved, and to persons promising more of the traditional novel of character than Lawrence's peculiar genius is in fact to allow him to develop. Of a surer significance for the future are two themes which appear only episodically in *The White Peacock*. These issue from a common complex of feeling so deep that Lawrence is never quite to achieve its resolution. Cyril's is a barely adolescent sexuality, and although he is attracted to George's sister Emily he has to be told by her in the end that it is George himself that he has always thought more of than anybody. The relationship between the two youths is indeed an 'almost passionate attachment'. Its celebration in a chapter called 'A Poem of Friendship' has its climax in a bathing episode:

He saw I had forgotten to continue my rubbing, and laughing he took hold of me and began to rub me briskly, as if I were a child, or rather, a woman he loved and did not fear. I left myself quite limply in his hands, and, to get a better grip of me, he put his arm round me and pressed me against him, and the sweetness of the touch of our naked bodies one against the other was superb. It satisfied in some measure the vague, indecipherable yearning of my soul; and it was the same with him. When he had rubbed me all warm, he let me go, and we looked at each other with eyes of still laughter, and our love was perfect for a moment, more perfect than any love I have known since, either for man or woman.

Lawrence was to believe that men 'must go beyond their women' and that their work in the world requires that 'friendship should be a rare, choice, immortal thing, sacred and inviolable as marriage . . . two great creative passions, separate, apart, but complementary'. Friendship, owning this sacramental character, must have its basis in some physical and not merely emotional communion. In the later novels there is to be a long search for the right mode of embodiment for this obscurely excogitated conviction.

But *The White Peacock* holds in the gamekeeper, Annable, a male yet more impressive than George; indeed Annable marks his entry upon the scene by at once felling both George and Cyril to the ground: 'All the world hated him—to the people in the villages he was like a devil of the woods. . . . But he had a great attraction for me; his magnificent physique, his great vigour and vitality, and his swarthy, gloomy face drew me.' Annable has been a gentleman and married to a lady—'a Lady Crystabel, lady in her own right'. But Lady Crystabel got 'souly' and took up with poets, so now Annable is a gamekeeper, with a slattern wife, innumerable children, and a mystical conviction that one must do as the animals do. The gross bestial fecundity of the Annable *ménage* is vividly described, as is his hatred of civilization as 'the painted fungus of rottenness' and of women as 'all vanity and screech and defilement'. Annable and his doctrine alike are portentous and seemingly inexplicable irruptions upon the novel. And Lawrence, as if confounded by something premature in the whole emergence, hastens to bury his invention in a quarry beneath a pile of fallen stone. The description of Annable's funeral, or rather the assertion of living nature amid which the funeral is set, is the high point in the book:

It was a magnificent morning in early spring when I watched among the trees to see the procession come down the hillside. The upper air was woven with the music of the larks, and my whole world thrilled with the conception of summer. The young pale wind-flowers had arisen by the wood-gale, and under the hazels, when perchance the hot sun pushed his way, new little suns dawned, and blazed with real light. There was a certain thrill and quickening everywhere, as a woman must feel when she has conceived. A sallow tree in a favoured spot looked like a pale gold cloud of summer dawn; nearer it had poised a golden, fairy busby on every twig, and was voiced with a hum of bees, like any sacred golden bush, uttering its gladness in the thrilling murmur of bees, and in warm scent. Birds called and flashed on every hand; they made off exultant with streaming strands of grass, or wisps of fleece, plunging into the dark spaces of the wood, and out again into the blue. . . .

Rising and falling and circling round and round, the slow-waving peewits cry and complain, and lift their broad wings in sorrow. They stoop suddenly to the ground, the lapwings, then in another throb of anguish and protest, they swing up again, offering a glistening white breast to the sunlight, to deny it in black shadow, then a glisten of green, and all the time crying and crying in despair.

But the despair of the lapwings is blended with the ecstasy of the spike and the thrush; a boy moves across the field with a black-legged lamb beside him; the daffodils lift their heads and throw back their yellow curls, and on water blue and white and dark-burnished with shadows the swans sail across reflected trees. Amid all this the funeral procession is a small but vividly depicted appearance:

There is a cry in answer to the peewits, echoing louder and stronger the lamentation of the lapwings, a wail which hushes the birds. The men come over the brow of the hill, slowly, with the old squire walking tall and straight in front; six bowed men bearing the coffin on their shoulders, treading heavily and cautiously, under the great weight of the glistening white coffin; six men following behind, ill at ease, waiting their turn for the burden. You can see the red handkerchiefs knotted round their throats, and their shirt-fronts blue and white between the open waistcoats. The coffin is of new unpolished wood, gleaming and glistening in the sunlight; the men who carry it remember all their lives after the smell of new, warm elm-wood.

In all this Lawrence is beginning to speak, and *The White Peacock* certainly holds more of his authentic genius than does his second novel, *The Trespasser* (1912). For *The Trespasser*, although forward-looking in its theme of extreme sexual preoccupation entangled with extreme sexual frustration, is vitiated by an adherence—for the first and last time in his fiction— to current literary fashion, which at this period inclined to Russians in general and Tchekhov in particular. In *Sons and Lovers* (1913) Lawrence returns to ground more native to him. The result is one of the great English novels.

As a rule his novels are to be indifferently constructed, indeed are scarcely in the conventional sense to be constructed at all. *Sons and Lovers* is to some extent an exception. It gives the effect of one whole and completed action, simply because one complete and significant phase of Lawrence's life was closing while he finished it. The history of the book's creating is complicated and extraordinary. He was working on it while his mother, who is in a sense its central figure, was dying in the manner it chronicles. Much of it was composed under the eye of Jessie Chambers, its Miriam; she even supplied written material which went to the building up of her own part in the story. When we consider that the story turns upon the inability of the hero, Paul Morel, to love Miriam as she is prepared to love him—this because of his unresolved fixation upon his mother; that it includes the record of his finding a temporary solution in breaking away into a carnal relationship with another woman, Clara Dawes; that Jessie Chambers appears to have maintained her part in the fashioning of all this almost up to the time of Lawrence's flight to Germany with his future wife Frieda; and that the final version was written in turn under Frieda's eye (Frieda indeed having lately picked up some impression of Freudian psychology, so that she was able, quite at the eleventh hour, to explain to Lawrence the mysteries of the Oedipus complex and consequently what his perplexities had been about): when we consider all this we are bound to agree that there are other ways of achieving major novels than those set forth in Henry James's notebooks. And we must agree—viewing the book against its biographical background—that here is a cathartic effort the courage, speed, and certainty of which are wholly astonishing. Recent, painful, and obscure experience is not merely realized with striking power; it is presented, almost to the end, with a sustained lucidity such as Lawrence is never to surpass.

The book's first and assured strength is as a vivid evocation of one English working-class home at the end of the nineteenth century. The Morels are indeed sufficiently typical. Theirs is the plight of an entire stratum of society at a time when, despite advancing material prosperity, the remorseless pressure of industrial development was creating a proletariat. But as the small-scale mining enterprises of Nottinghamshire give way before the advances of finance capital, and as Eastwood, although still conscious of an untouched country-side at its back door —the brook and the meadows and the old sheep-bridge not 200 yards away—becomes a proliferating sprawl of dwellings for men daily sucked down by their thousands into the great pits, it is upon one intimately realized family that we see the degrading and straitening impact of all this as bearing. The father Walter Morel, with no grip except on the immediate physical facts of life, is helpless. His circumstances brutalize him, so that he bullies, blusters, loses his self-respect, and finds refuge only in drink. But the mother fights. She is strong-minded, rational, and drawn to some larger world of culture and ideas. 'What she liked most of all was an argument on religion or philosophy or politics with some educated man.' Mrs. Morel fights her husband, striving, in fearful, bloody battle, to make moral and religious a nature that is purely sensuous and earthy. The result is a destructive mutual hatred, and the mother turns to her children, living only for their growing up and achieving such ambitions as her limited knowledge is able to conceive for them. One son is thus destroyed. He forces his way to clerical employment in London, and becomes involved with a socially pretentious girl whom he knows to be frivolous and who despises his family. The effort kills him. Then it becomes the turn of Paul, the younger son. He accepts his mission of climbing into the middle class. We see him becoming imbued, as the whole family is imbued, with the narrower manifestations of his mother's set purpose: the quick contempt for those in their circle who are 'common', the anxious pursuit of a superiority expressing itself in careful speech, pleasant tea-things, the dream of a nice house and a little maid. Poor Walter Morel, scorned by the whole family, is much obliterated as the book proceeds. Visitors feel 'the refinement and sang-froid of the household'. Yet the bond with his mother is so strong in Paul chiefly because of the higher qualities in her: courage, self-control, and a quick response to natural beauty which appeals to the artist he is going to be. It is made real and poignant for us in a multitude of small touches, of simple domestic occasions rendered sometimes with a humour which Lawrence is not always to command. Moments of general alleviation, in which the father potters happily at tasks with his children, or of intense jubilation over the purchase of a pretty plate, the discovery of an unsuspected flower in the garden, the acquiring of a cottage at the seaside for a week: these are implicated with the dominant mother-and-son relationship with delicate art. The whole picture of the Morel family is much more than a striking naturalistic success in a new field—Henry James's 'nearer view of commoner things'. It is finely perceptive and deeply compassionate.

The possessive and destructive love of Mrs. Morel is the more terrifying in that it is seen at work in a temperament essentially rational and controlled. For Paul it is the great fascination of Miriam Leivers, the farmer's daughter with whom he forms a friendship in boyhood, that she seems to be at an opposite remove from this. Intense and mystical, exalting even a household task to the plane of a religious trust, Miriam calls him to a kind of worship of nature which he both understands and resists. He is intellectually masterful and takes charge of her education, but at the same time, there is that in him which can meet her on her own ground. In her company 'all his latent mysticism quivered into life'. She asks why she likes one of his sketches as she does:

'Why *do* you?' he asked.
'I don't know. It seems so true.'

'It's because—it's because there is scarcely any shadow in it; it's more shimmery, as if I'd painted the shimmering protoplasm in the leaves and everywhere, and not the stiffness of the shape. That seems dead to me. Only this shimmeriness is the real living. The shape is a dead crust.'

There is a similar passage in one of the fragments preserved from an early draft of the novel, in which the boy, sketching at sunset, sees, feels that 'a pine-trunk's not a tree-trunk, it's a bit of fire'. Paul as he grows up will remain like his creator intensely aware of the bit of fire, the clear flame of life 'for ever flowing, coming God knows how from out of practically nowhere'. And the level at which he and Miriam can meet is what prevents the fulfilment of their love—since it is a level that does, in fact, after all, approximate Miriam's figure to Mrs. Morel's in his mind. Superficially there appears to be a clash of temperaments between Paul and Miriam. 'Her intensity, which would leave no emotion on a normal plane, irritated the youth into a frenzy.' But there is a deeper disharmony. Simple physical contact causes a violent conflict in him. 'He knew, before he could kiss her, he must drive something out of himself.' We get a glimpse of the truth in a scene of passionate affection with his mother:

'You're old, mother, and we're young.'
He only meant that the interests of *her* age were not the interests of his. But he realised the moment he had spoken that he had said the wrong thing.
'Yes, I know it well—I am old. And therefore I may stand aside; I have nothing more to do with you. You only want me to wait on you—the rest is for Miriam.'
He could not bear it. Instinctively he realised that he was life to her. And, after all, she was the chief thing to him, the only supreme thing.
'You know it isn't, mother, you know it isn't!'
She was moved to pity by his cry.
'It looks a great deal like it', she said, half putting aside her despair.
'No, mother—I really *don't* love her. I talk to her, but I want to come home to you.'
He had taken off his collar and tie, and rose, bare-throated, to go to bed. As he stooped to kiss his mother, she threw her arms round his neck, hid her face on his shoulder, and cried, in a whimpering voice, so unlike her own that he writhed in agony:
'I can't bear it. I could let another woman—but not her. She'd leave me no room, not a bit of room——'

And immediately he hated Miriam bitterly.

'And I've never—you know, Paul—I've never had a husband—not really——'

He stroked his mother's hair, and his mouth was on her throat.

'And she exults so in taking you from me—she's not like ordinary girls.'

'Well, I don't love her, mother', he murmured, bowing his head and hiding his eyes on her shoulder in misery. His mother kissed him a long, fervent kiss.

'My boy!' she said, in a voice trembling with passionate love.

Eventually Paul understands that it is the bond with his mother which bars him from other than a merely sensual relationship with a woman. 'She bore him, loved him, kept him, and his love turned back into her, so that he could not be free to go forward with his own life, really love another woman.' He tells her the truth, with the bleak cruelty that is often to startle us in the succeeding novels. 'I never shall meet the right woman while you live.'

Lawrence begins in this part of *Sons and Lovers* his unending task of probing with his pen pain and perplexity which are still the present substance of his life as he probes. He is to be a Joyce, we may say, who never stops writing his *Stephen Hero*. There will always be those who see this as a negation of artistic process, and it certainly brings danger of sorts of confusion inimical to the normal canons of art. When Paul and Miriam at length come together, and the experience is agony to her and disaster to him, bringing 'always the sense of failure and of death', two assertions are to be felt as in conflict in the narrative. Paul's frequent feeling that the incompatibility must be blamed upon Miriam seems to be offered to us as objective truth, particularly in the final stages, where she is represented as simply lacking the strength to take him 'with joy and authority'. But beneath this, as if percolating into the writer's assessment from intuitive sources not yet openly acknowledged, is the sense that it is only the reflex of Paul's disabilities which, for Miriam, makes their physical moment 'a sacrifice in which she felt something like horror'.

There are places other than the central Miriam story in which Lawrence's reliance upon intuitive form commits him to episodes and narrative sequences which seem artistically unsatisfactory. Clara Dawes, the married woman with whom Paul forms a liaison, is a convincing creation, and convincing too is the description of their passion as one in which a law of diminishing returns inevitably works:

And after such an evening they both were very still, having known the immensity of passion. They felt small, half afraid, childish, and wondering, like Adam and Eve when they lost their innocence and realized the magnificence of the power which drove them out of Paradise and across the great night and the great day of humanity. It was for each of them an initiation and a satisfaction. To know their own nothingness, to know the tremendous living flood which carried them always, gave them rest within themselves. If so great a magnificent power could overwhelm them, identify them altogether with itself, so that they knew they were only grains in the tremendous heave that lifted every grass-blade its little height, and every tree, and living thing, then why fret about themselves? They could let themselves be carried by life, and they felt a sort of peace each in the other. . . .

After that the fire slowly went down. He felt more and more that his experience had been impersonal, and not Clara. He loved her. There was a big tenderness, as after a strong emotion they had known together; but it was not she who could keep his soul steady. He had wanted her to be something she could not be.

Impulses of irritation, flashes of hatred, come between them, and the end of the relationship is in sight. 'Gradually, some mechanical effort spoilt their loving, or, when they had splendid moments, they had them separately, and not so satisfactorily. . . . Gradually they began to introduce novelties, to get back some of the feeling of satisfaction. . . . And afterwards each of them was rather ashamed.' All this has its intelligible place. But there is matter of more perplexity built around Baxter Dawes, the husband from whom Clara is separated. At one point Paul goes out of his way to be beaten up by Dawes. Later he is powerfully and mysteriously drawn to him—'the elemental man in each had met'—and this episode is obtruded upon us strangely just at the time that Mrs. Morel's last illness is arriving at its absorbing and harrowing crisis. There is no sign that either Paul or his creator detects a connexion between the suffered beating-up and the fact that Paul believes himself to have been sleeping with Dawes's wife in complete freedom from the sense of guilt with which sexual congress has hitherto been associated in his mind. Lawrence is regularly thus to present situations the relevance of which is left unexplained.

The effect can be aesthetically disturbing. But Lawrence, simply because he is a great artist, has the right to disturb us. *Sons and Lovers* alone would establish him as the foremost English writer of his generation. The book gives a heightened awareness of the actual texture of living, a vivid and veridical picture of passion in its labyrinth, such as no previous English fiction so much as starts to achieve.

3

Lawrence was now of necessity a professional writer, and for the rest of his life he was to be more variously productive than will appear in a study only of the main lines of his development. He wrote a history-book for schools. He several times tried his hand at drama, and *The Widowing of Mrs Holroyd* (acted 1920) and *David* (1926) have merit. As a critic he could be sensitive and perceptive, notably in *Studies in Classic American Literature* (1923); and also somewhat undisciplined, as in the posthumously published 'Study of Thomas Hardy', which discusses Hardy from time to time, but is in the main all over the place. *Psycho-analysis and the Unconscious* (1921) and *Fantasia of the Unconscious* (1922) pursue important speculative interests—the first with lucidity and the second with a kind of cloudy pungency equally difficult either to describe or to forget. He produced, too, a good deal of miscellaneous journalism and—when his work came under moral censorship—polemical writing which sometimes becomes strident while seldom ceasing to be brilliant.

But this is to look ahead. After his elopement he must have been sharply conscious of the desirability of making writing pay. And in projecting a long novel to be called *The Sisters* he may have had in mind the wide popularity achieved in Germany by Thomas Mann's family chronicle, *Buddenbrooks*. But Lawrence quickly came to speak of himself as much in the dark about what he was doing, and *The Rainbow* (1915), the first of the two lightly linked novels into which the attempt developed, although it does traverse several generations, is in essence something entirely different. It was not in Lawrence to do other than go ahead on his own terms, and with sufficient confidence: 'Tell Arnold Bennett that all rules of construction hold good only for novels which are copies of other novels. A book which is not a copy of other books has its own construction, and what he calls faults, he being an old imitator, I call characteristics.'

It is a 'characteristic' of *The Rainbow* that it begins upon one line of development, continues upon another, and finally turns somewhat abruptly back upon itself. The theme of the book is marriage, and marriage considered far less consistently in the wider social relations at first clearly proposed than against the emerging and rapidly dominating background of Lawrence's gospel of the flesh.

The Brangwens have been yeoman farmers for generations. They are men who stay close to the earth, 'feeling the pulse and body of the soil, that opened to their furrow for the grain, and became smooth and supple after their ploughing'. Thus responsive chiefly to the cycle of the seasons, they sit at night by the fire with their brains inert, 'as their blood flowed heavy with the accumulation from the living day'. Their womenfolk are different:

The women looked out from the heated, blind intercourse of farm-life, to the spoken world beyond. They were aware of the lips and the mind of the world speaking and giving utterance, they heard the sound in the distance, and they strained to listen.

It was enough for the men, that the earth heaved and opened its furrow to them, that the wind blew to dry the wet wheat, and set the young ears of corn wheeling freshly round about. . . . But the woman wanted another form of life than this, something that was not blood-intimacy. Her house faced out from the farm-buildings and fields, looked out to the road and the village with church and Hall and the world beyond. She stood to see the far-off world of cities and governments and the active scope of man, the magic land to her, where secrets were made known and desires fulfilled.

The first section of the novel stresses the typical Brangwen woman's designs upon society. The second begins with a description of the changes produced, about 1840, by the opening of new collieries and the constructing of a canal. We may well suppose that we are to be shown the differing impacts of social change in England upon the Brangwen men and the Brangwen women, and that there is being carried over from *Sons and Lovers* the situation in which the man is animal, instinctive, and the woman restlessly seeking betterment, a dimly apprehended wider and finer life. But what is in fact carried over from the earlier book is the technique of using elements from the novel of social observation alike as spring-board for, and relief from, Lawrence's task—made more compulsive by recent experience—

of psycho-sexual analysis. In *The Rainbow* he projects into one couple after another all that intense and often agonizing exploration of marriage of which there is a more directly personal expression in the series of poems he was to call *Look! We Have Come Through!*

The conviction of something saving in the life of the body, something destructive in a denial of the instinctive and the unconscious, already implicit in *The White Peacock*, is rapidly deepening in Lawrence. Thus he wrote early in 1913:

> My great religion is a belief in the blood, the flesh, as being wiser than the intellect. We can go wrong in our minds. But what our blood feels and believes and says, is always true. The intellect is only a bit and a bridle. What do I care about knowledge. All I want is to answer to my blood, direct, without fribbling intervention of mind, or moral, or what-not.

We are here within sight of the Lawrence who offers a revelation. And in *The Rainbow* the way of taking experience predicated at the start as characteristic of the Brangwen men, as contrasted with the Brangwen women, seems for long to dominate the book. The essential theme is the place of human sexual experience in that vast vital continuum which Lawrence feels the universe to be. As soon as sexual feeling is awakened in the women they are prone to find the world of culture, economic independence, social progress very unimportant. Their new life may be one of strained polarities and fierce antagonisms and exhausting abandonments. But in these they sense fulfilment, or the only road to it; these belong to a different order of reality from that which commended itself to Mrs. Morel or Mrs. Lawrence. Thus when an intense relationship has been established between the book's principal heroine, Ursula Brangwen, and her lover, Skrebensky, Ursula is represented as specifically calling into contempt that wider, more mental life which—we have been assured—Brangwen women long for:

> She went about in the sensual sub-consciousness all the time, mocking at the ready-made, artificial daylight of the rest. . . . Her soul mocked at all this pretence. Herself, she kept on pretending. She dressed herself and made herself fine, she attended her lectures and scribbled her notes. But all in a mood of superficial, mocking facility. She understood well enough their two-and-two-make-four tricks. She was as clever as they were. But care!—did she care about

their monkey tricks of knowledge or learning or civic deportment?
She did not care in the least. . . .

She was free as a leopard that sends up its raucous cry in the night.
She had the potent, dark stream of her own blood, she had the
glimmering core of fecundity, she had her mate, her complement,
her sharer in fruition. So, she had all, everything.

The novel echoes the letter's 'What do I care about knowledge'.
Yet we cannot conclude its burden to be that the original
Brangwen women were deluding themselves in seeking to escape
from a life of blood-intimacy only. Ursula's affair with Skrebensky ends in frustration, negation, misery. Again and again we
are shown absorption in a sexual relationship as something
almost beyond the strength of an individual to bear. The intractability of the problem, indeed, renders broadly identical
the experience of the successive generations chronicled, and
the whole structure of the book might seem inept and repetitive
were it not that, here more than anywhere, Lawrence achieves
powerful and abundant objective creation. The characters are
almost without exception people as fully realized as major fiction
can show. The recurrent discovery of the same intensities, conflicts, frustrations is triumphantly carried by this richness and
authenticity of individual life.

The Rainbow, indeed, is the novel in which Lawrence most
consistently achieves a purely dramatic projection of his
problems, and the firm historical tone with which it opens
may reflect his sense of having reached a new and retrospective
relationship at least to important parts of his material. The mid-
nineteenth century Brangwens, it is true, are merely glimpsed,
and when we move on to Tom Brangwen, the young man of
the people who marries in Lydia Lensky a lady and a foreigner
six years his senior, we happen to know that Lawrence must
be writing closely from his own experience. But the effect of distancing remains, and the special circumstances of the case simply
point and clarify the problems inherent in any marriage, and
apparent to Tom at the moment of his engagement:

They were such strangers, they must for ever be such strangers,
that his passion was a clanging torment to him. Such intimacy of
embrace, and such utter foreignness of contact! It was unbearable.
He could not bear to be near her, and know the utter foreignness
between them, know how entirely they were strangers to each other.
He went out into the wind. Big holes were blown into the sky, the

moonlight blew about. Sometimes a high moon, liquid-brilliant, scudded across a hollow space and took cover under electric, brown-iridescent cloud-edges. Then there was a blot of cloud, and shadow. Then somewhere in the night a radiance again, like a vapour. And all the sky was teeming and tearing along, a vast disorder of flying shapes and darkness and ragged fumes of light and a great brown circling halo, then the terror of a moon running liquid-brilliant into the open for a moment, hurting the eyes before she plunged under cover of cloud again.

We have already been told of Tom's parents that, although neighbours from childhood, they had been 'two very separate beings, vitally connected, knowing nothing of each other, yet living in their separate ways from one root'. The chronicle form is thus being used to insist that here is no new situation. What is new is the acute sense of Tom's marriage as taking place under the impulsion of other-than-personal forces; of its implication with those cosmic processes the mystery and terror of which are imaged in the wild night through which he walks back from his wooing. It is this presence of the other-than-personal, it is this implication, that makes his marriage essentially whole and fulfilled. 'The house was finished', we are told in the Biblical language which Lawrence often employs for impressive state-ment, 'and the Lord took up his abode.' But already the lord is a dark lord, and the marriage has to be lived out as a rela-tionship into which almost intolerable tensions are constantly and seemingly senselessly irruptive. 'It was unbearable.' For Lawrence there is never to be a serious bond between man and woman which is not to seem, again and again, just that. Tom and Lydia are a torment to each other. She is 'like a flower that comes above-ground to find a great stone lying above it'. To him she becomes 'like the upper millstone lying on him, crushing him, as sometimes a heavy sky lies on the earth'. Intermittently she lapses from him—pointlessly, at no distin-guishable prompting—and he experiences chaos. Of the truth of all this flux of passion there need be no question. But Law-rence is to give a lot of it, and with a constant extremity of statement which becomes wearing. Sometimes it loses such dignity as it draws from the impression of suffering, vividly con-veyed, so that we are stranded in a world of mere bad tempers and bad manners which is uninteresting and disagreeable. Here in the early chapters of *The Rainbow* the thing is done so well

that we would almost be glad to know that Lawrence is now
doing it once and for all. Yet nearly everything in these early
pages is quite as good. The evocation of Tom Brangwen's boyhood is consummate. So, more remarkably, is that of the exiled
Lydia's early responses to England. Brangwen's courtship and
the episode of his comforting his step-child Anna during her
mother's labour have the depth and gravity of great painting.

The next marriage is an even stormier affair. Anna Lensky
and Brangwen's nephew, Will, pass straight from an unawakened state to a courtship that is violently sensual, and their
honeymoon, a matter of intense withdrawal from the world,
is made a *tour de force* of Lawrence's finest description:

Inside the room was a great steadiness, a core of living eternity.
Only far outside, at the rim, went on the noise and the destruction. Here at the centre the great wheel was motionless, centred
upon itself. Here was a poised, unflawed stillness that was beyond
time, because it remained the same, inexhaustible, unchanging,
unexhausted.

As they lay close together, complete and beyond the touch of time
or change, it was as if they were at the very centre of all the slow
wheeling of space and the rapid agitation of life, deep, deep, inside
them all, at the centre where there is utter radiance, and eternal
being, and the silence absorbed in praise: the steady core of all
movements, the unawakened sleep of all wakefulness. They found
themselves there, and they lay still, in each other's arms; for their
moment they were at the heart of eternity, while time roared far off,
forever far off, towards the rim.

But disharmony lurks in the relationship from the beginning.
Will feels something 'unmanly, recusant' in giving days as well
as nights to love. 'One ought to get up in the morning and
wash oneself and be a decent social being.' Yet when Anna
turns back to society in the modest form of a tea-party, Will at
once swings violently the other way. And thus it goes on 'continually, the recurrence of love and conflict between them'.
Sometimes there is a state of ecstasy, again rendered in the
language of the Bible. Then immediately comes the reaction.
'He felt, somewhere, that she did not respect him. . . . The deep
root of his enmity lay in the fact that she jeered at his soul.'
When she is pregnant she dances naked before another Lord,
and the conflict becomes maniacal:

She found that, in all her outgoings and her incomings, he

prevented her. Gradually she realised that she was being borne down
by him, borne down by the clinging, heavy weight of him, that he
was pulling her down as a leopard clings to a wild cow and exhausts
her and pulls her down. . . .

'What do you do to me?' she cried. 'What beastly thing do you do
to me? You put a horrible pressure on my head, you don't let me
sleep, you don't let me *live*. Every moment of your life you are doing
something to me, something horrible, that destroys me. There is
something horrible in you, something dark and beastly in your will.
What do you want of me? What do you want to do to me?'

All the blood in his body went black and powerful and corrosive as
he heard her. Black and blind with hatred of her he was. He was in
a very black hell, and could not escape.

They visit Lincoln, and what the cathedral means to Will is
finely described. Anna turns upon Will's vision and rends it in
cold cruelty. It is she who is the leopard now. Within limits, we
are able to understand all this conflict in terms of character.
Will, seemingly a gentle youth with a Ruskinian love of churches
and the medieval forms, has a streak of sadism and is often
possessed by an evil spirit which tortures and wracks him.
Anna, although intermittently disposed to tremble in his service, has nursed from childhood a passion for dominance, and
she is assuaged for a time if she can feel that she has 'broken
a little of something in him'. But although their characters are
real, we feel that their characters are largely beside the point.
Lawrence has brought himself hard up against a problem propounded for him by his gospel of the flesh. Here is a marriage
which, sensually, is from the first deeply satisfactory. Yet it is
torn and riven by an incompatibility which seems to well up
from deep unconscious sources, exploiting temperamental and
intellectual differences as mere instruments, and bearing powerfully and often disastrously upon persons who have not very
discernibly equipped themselves with any moderating moral
consciousness or social code. Here—as with so many of Lawrence's problems—it is hard to say whether we are eventually
offered any solution or not. Will Brangwen begins to go away
from home. In a Nottingham music-hall he picks up a strange
girl and makes love to her, only just failing to seduce her in
a public park. He returns home and Anna is at once excited.
'She saw she could not reduce him to what he had been before'
and 'watched him undress as if he were a stranger'. What

follows, and continues to follow, makes all their earlier passionate experience pale. Previously we have been told of Anna that 'at the bottom of her soul, she felt he wanted her to be dark, unnatural' when it was her own persuasion that 'she wanted to be happy, to be natural, like the sunlight and the busy daytime'. Now, to his own initial terror, Will seems to have his way. 'They accepted shame, and were one with it in their most un-licensed pleasures.' Lawrence is frequently to indulge the notion of something mysteriously purifying in 'unnatural acts of sensual voluptuousness'. But nobody could foresee what they lead to here, only a few lines ahead: 'At this time Education was in the forefront as a subject of interest. There was the talk of new Swedish methods, of handwork instruction, and so on. Brang-wen embraced sincerely the idea of handwork in schools.' We remember that amid the first innocent transports of his honey-moon Will felt uneasy at his insulation from the work of the world—a constant feeling of Lawrence's men when absorbed wholly within a marital sphere. Will is here represented as fighting his way to freedom and becoming 'unanimous with the whole of purposive mankind' by plumbing his own sexuality to its last depth. But in the banality of 'handwork in schools' the whole idea is slightly deflated—this with a kind of caution that Lawrence is never to lack. Here, if we like, is simply a mar-riage that burns itself out in a final flare of passion, leaving a husband given to wood-carving with the village boys, and a wife sunk in babies and domestic torpor.

As the book develops, the emphasis of Lawrence's interest shifts steadily in a direction foreshadowed in the provisional title, *The Sisters*, and finally acknowledged in the title of the sequel, *Women in Love*. In the first generation we are brought closer to Tom Brangwen than to his wife Lydia. In the second, Will and Anna are more or less equally explored. In the third, Will's daughter Ursula dominates the novel, and her lover Anton Skrebensky is the least adequately realized of all the major characters. Lawrence's interest, moreover, is increasingly in women *in love*. Although Ursula's childhood is treated at some length in the key, it may be said, of George Eliot's evoca-tions of provincial life, we are likely to feel that her creator is waiting rather impatiently for her to grow up and thus become available for his essential purpose. It is true that the foundations of her character have the appearance of being laid with some

care in her childhood. The bond between father and daughter
is peculiarly close, as if Lawrence were tentatively exploring the
possibility of a variation upon the basic theme of *Sons and Lovers*.
But Ursula's love affair in fact harks back rather to Tom
Brangwen's. Her lover is a kinsman of Lydia Lensky's, and thus
himself, although a subaltern in the British army, of foreign
and aristocratic extraction. In returning to the attempt,
dropped since *The White Peacock*, to introduce a character of
some importance from a class not intimately known to him,
Lawrence runs into trouble which proves catching. The Marsh
Farm loses something of its earlier fine authenticity when we are
told that Tom Brangwen 'seemed to mature into a gentleman-
farmer' and that 'the boys were gentlemen'. High claims have
been made for Lawrence simply as a social historian. But in fact
his interest in men in their classes, communities, and economic
functions is always to be fluctuating and uncertain.

The final action of the novel falls into two phases, punctuated
by the absence of Ursula's lover, Skrebensky, during the South
African War. The initial relationship, entered into when Ursula
is still a schoolgirl, is ominous in terms of Lawrence's emerging
philosophy of love. Its designed contrast with the story of Tom
and Lydia gives a first glimpse of him as a writer less of novels
than of moralities. Skrebensky's impulse is at first merely predatory. He approaches intimacy by way of hints dropped
about the loose living of his fellow-officers. Ursula is excited
and responds. 'This world of passions and lawlessness was
fascinating to her. It seemed to her a splendid recklessness.'
Herself going one better, she shocks the innately conventional
young man by declaring her conviction that it would be right
to make love in a cathedral. Their early kisses are described:
'And he kissed her, asserting his will over her, and she kissed
him back, asserting her deliberate enjoyment of him. Daring
and reckless and dangerous they knew it was, their game, each
playing with fire, not with love.' To assert the will, to seek enjoyment with deliberation, are alike sins to Lawrence. Presently
Ursula really succeeds in continuing this spooning in a church.
The passage moves to an enigmatic close:

And it was good, it was very, very good. She seemed to be filled
with his kiss, filled as if she had drunk strong, glowing sunshine. She
glowed all inside, the sunshine seemed to beat upon her heart underneath, she had drunk so beautifully.

She drew away, and looked at him radiant, exquisitely, glowingly beautiful, and satisfied, but radiant as an illumined cloud.

To him this was bitter, that she was so radiant and satisfied. . . . It was agony to him, seeing her swift and cleancut and virgin. He wanted to kill himself, and throw his detested carcase at her feet.

What the relationship portends for Skrebensky is already implicit in this. It becomes clearer in an episode of violent but still unconsummated passion. Here, for the time, Ursula appears to achieve, what her mother Anna had sometimes striven to achieve, a dominance which we are made to feel as ultimately frustrating and fatal:

So she held him there, the victim, consumed, annihilated. She had triumphed: he was not any more. . . . His triumphant, flaming, overweening heart of the intrinsic male would never beat again. He would be subject now, reciprocal, never the indomitable thing with a core of overweening, unabateable fire. She had abated that fire, she had broken him.

A few pages later we would appear to be told, tentatively and obscurely, why Skrebensky must be broken. He goes to the war, which is a poor thing to do. He is a man orientated towards society in an inadequate and utilitarian way. 'The good of the greatest number was all that mattered. That which was the greatest good for them all, collectively, was the greatest good for the individual.' Because of his holding to this persuasion 'there came over Skrebensky a sort of nullity, which more and more terrified Ursula'. But this theme, with its renewal of social implication, remains undeveloped. In a chapter called 'Shame' Ursula becomes involved, entirely surprisingly, in a Lesbian relationship with a school-teacher. And this, which contains a good deal of inferior writing, is followed by a long, brilliant, but thematically irrelevant account of her own experiences while teaching. Then Skrebensky returns and their relationship is resumed. It is emphasized that Ursula has gained considerable freedom, and that she feels herself to be an explorer. 'Whither to go, how to become oneself?' she had asked as a girl. Now she feels that 'ultimately and finally, she must go on and on, seeking the goal that she knew she did draw nearer to'. It is this determination to explore her own limits that is to take her past Skrebensky and on into the next book.

The new start is as ominous as the old. 'She knew, vaguely,

in the first minute, that they were enemies come together in a truce. Every movement and word of his was alien to her being. . . . She could only feel the dark, heavy fixity of his animal desire.' Yet Skrebensky's is not now merely a calculating lust. 'For him it was life or death. . . . He must give her himself. He must give her the very foundations of himself.' The submerged theme of his being in a close but inadequate relationship with society, one which she cannot accept since it is 'not her road', emerges again with the discovery that he will probably be going to India. 'In her, the antagonism to the social imposition was for the time complete and final.' Yet the physical relation prospers. It is now that he comes to her 'in a superb consummation'.

The crisis of the book has often been judged unsatisfactory or inexplicable. Physical ecstasies—if with the invariable Laurentian flux and reflux—continue for some time, extending themselves over a holiday in London and on the Continent:

> Then, for some reason, she must call in Rouen on the way back to London. He had an instinctive distrust of her desire for the place. But, perversely, she wanted to go there. . . . In Rouen he had the first deadly anguish, the first sense of the death towards which they were wandering.

It reads uncomfortably like deliberate obfuscation. But it is at least clear that Ursula's love for Skrebensky has suddenly become something that must be sustained by the will. Very soon it simply fails at the physical level. There is a last frenzied attempt at love-making and it is all over. Ursula dismisses Skrebensky with the words, 'It is finished. It has been a failure.'

There can be two readings of Lawrence's intention in this ending. We may suppose him to be asserting that physical love must collapse if unsupported by its spiritual and social complements. For Ursula, Skrebensky is fatally of the wrong set. This reveals itself in the falsity of their London trip ('they came to be treated as titled people'), their discussions of India, and so on. The result is a sudden insulation from each other at the simple level of intense physical response. Alternatively, and since Ursula's implication with Skrebensky is essentially, in her own phrase, with 'the undifferentiated man', it may be maintained that their incompatibilities as differentiated social beings cannot be taken as accounting for much, and that we are being shown

something already shown in Will and Anna: antagonism springing from indefinable instinctive sources and arming itself for
purposes of conscious expression with whatever weapons come
to hand. 'Somehow', we read, 'he could not bear it, when she
attacked things. It was as if she were attacking him.' Certainly
when Ursula criticizes Skrebensky's probable social role in
India it is with a brutality incommensurate with the rational
considerations involved. The absoluteness of her revulsion from
him is entirely instinctual and primitive. 'He aroused no fruitful fecundity in her. He seemed added up, finished'—whereas
she knows that her own concern must be with 'the unknown,
the unexplored, the undiscovered'. These terms can be given
only the most nebulous moral or social content. Essentially
they mean that Ursula has come obscurely to the end of an
experience at once deeply satisfying and widely disruptive, and
that she is an appetitive creature still.

We appear, then, to be confronted in *The Rainbow* with a
dramatic spectacle suggesting two conclusions not easily reconciled. According to the first the fulfilment of the individual lies
exclusively in, or at least mysteriously on the farther side of,
intense sexual experience—experience which is, unhappily,
fraught with immense hazard and pain erupting from levels of
the mind virtually outside our conscious control. According to
the second the anarchic element in sexual experience can be
controlled on the basis of social striving, so that our primary need
is to become individuals responsive to each other over a wide
range of feeling liberated and ordered through the creation of
a good society. On the whole it may be said that the novel
orientates itself at the start towards the second of these propositions, is then caught up into a powerful and sustained
assertion of the first, and turns back upon its original course
briefly but with equal power at the very close. In the final paragraphs we leave Ursula, who lately 'went about in the sensual
sub-consciousness all the time', with her mind centred upon the
paramount necessity of some communal regeneration. She looks
out over the colliery district in which she lives, sees it as vile, and
sees in the rainbow a symbol of undefined forces which will in
the future sweep that vileness away:

And the rainbow stood on the earth. She knew that the sordid
people who crept hard-scaled and separate on the face of the world's
corruption were living still, that the rainbow was arched in their

blood and would quiver to life in their spirit, that they would cast off their horny covering of disintegration, that new, clean, naked bodies would issue to a new germination, to a new growth, rising to the light and the wind and the clean rain of heaven. She saw in the rainbow the earth's new architecture, the old, brittle corruption of houses and factories swept away, the world built up in a living fabric of Truth, fitting to the over-arching heaven.

The conviction behind the whole passage is evident. But it comes with some effect of inconsequence, as if here were the fitting conclusion to the novel Lawrence had projected rather than to the perhaps profounder novel he has achieved. But we may say simply that here is a final strong emergence of the theme, carried over from *Sons and Lovers*, of the crippling consequences for intimate and integral human relationships of those degradations of social life which industrialism and all that prompts industrialism has brought about. Certainly Lawrence in this rather unexpected close is acknowledging the unresolved condition of his problems. Despite the truth to experience of Ursula's contempt, when in love, for 'monkey tricks of knowledge or learning or civic deportment', man is very much a social being, after all, and two people retreating upon a sheer and mere sensual intimacy will presently find even that failing them. For if the individual is not to be at the mercy of a single—even if it be the deepest—side of his nature he must have work in the world, associates, friends, scope for social instincts. He must clear himself of wrong approaches to these things if they are not to vitiate his most intimate and passional relationships. All this is to be matter of important consideration in the next book.

4

The claim that *Women in Love* (1920) is the finest and best integrated of Lawrence's major performances is frequently accompanied by the warning that uninitiated readers may find the novel obscure or boring or revolting. Its difficulties are certainly real, and if increased familiarity resolves most of them and sufficiently establishes the nature and interrelationship of the principal themes, yet many passages remain resistant to interpretation. Moreover the steady pitching up of emotional tensions in which Lawrence's art so largely consists seems at times in danger of becoming a device functioning undiscriminatingly. These imperfections make the book vulnerable to attack. Thus:

But the rabbit played a considerable if wholly obscure part in Lawrence's early erotic symbolism. Even as late as *Women in Love* he has a most curious chapter entitled 'Rabbit'. Two adults, a man and a woman, with a child, take a large rabbit to an enclosed court. In its struggles the rabbit scratches them both. They release it, and it bolts round and round the court, 'like a shot out of a gun'. Then it stops abruptly, and begins nibbling. We then find this baffling paragraph: 'There was a queer, faint obscene smile over his face. She looked at him and saw him, and knew that he was initiate as she was initiate. This thwarted her, and contravened her, for the moment.' I must confess I have not the faintest idea where the obscenity lies, nor in what they were 'initiate', nor why she was 'contravened' by it, nor why the contravention was only for a moment. Perhaps it does mean something, but what?

We may reply to Richard Aldington here that the response engendered in the lovers by the struggle with the rabbit points ominously to the direction which their relationship will follow, but we shall probably have to admit that the picture is painted from a dangerously high palette. Thus of the scratch we read: 'The long, shallow red rip seemed torn across his own brain, tearing the surface of his ultimate consciousness, letting through the forever unconscious, unthinkable red ether of the beyond, the obscene beyond.' Related to this violence of expression is that sort of sledge-hammer reiteration of key words and phrases which is perhaps the principal distinguishing characteristic of Lawrence's prose style. In a preface to *Women in Love* he himself defends what he calls 'the continual, slightly modified repetition' on the ground that 'every natural crisis in emotion or passion or understanding comes from this pulsing, frictional to-and-fro which works up to culmination'. It is of course in highly charged erotic passages that the device is most lavishly deployed:

She would touch him. With perfect fine finger-tips of reality she would touch the reality in him, the suave, pure, untranslatable reality of his loins of darkness. To touch, mindlessly in darkness to come in pure touching upon the living reality of him, his suave perfect loins and thighs of darkness, this was her sustaining anticipation.

The particular loins thus anticipated belong to an Inspector of Schools who has just emerged from some prosaic occasion in a post office. They and others are invoked, with a more than Signorelli-like devotion, in the same incantatory way throughout the book. In the first chapter the crowd watching a smart wedding is edified by the sight of the bride gamesomely taking to her heels round the church, and the bridegroom's 'supple, strong loins vanishing in pursuit'. A little later a gentleman, leaning over the side of a boat in the endeavour to retrieve a floating sketch-book for two ladies, 'could feel his position was ridiculous, his loins exposed behind him'. But later when the same gentleman is desperately diving and diving again in the attempt to save his drowning sister, one of the same ladies wants to die because of 'the beauty of the subjection of his loins, white and dimly luminous'. The diving is unsuccessful—but 'the beauty of his dim and luminous loins as he climbed into the boat, his back rounded and soft—ah, this was too much for her, too final a vision'. It is perhaps too much for us also. Yet these repetitions and insistencies cannot simply be written off as incidental faults in taste. They are integral with that part of Lawrence's design which is properly poetic, seeking to strike down into our 'sympathetic consciousness' by methods taking little account of surface realism or of decorum in any sense. The method is never really offensive except when applied to occasions that are inherently trivial: 'She seemed to become soft, subtly to infuse herself into his bones, as if she were passing into him in a black, electric flow. Her being suffused into his veins like a magnetic darkness, and concentrated at the base of his spine like a fearful source of power.' This is from an account of a casual meeting with an amateur prostitute in Bohemian society; it is a vulgar occasion, portentously inflated. When, later in the book, Lawrence comes to describe a sexual encounter of very different significance, one leading to that 'ultimate' marriage with which the whole quest of his novel is concerned, the tension and the imagery are much the same: 'He knew what it was to have the strange and magical current of force in his back and loins, and down his legs, force so perfect that it stayed him immobile. . . . He had a pure and magic control, magical, mystical, a force in darkness, like electricity.' Lawrence is seldom in the narrow sense an erotic writer. Nevertheless his whole design, as pursued throughout his career, requires the felt presence of extreme sexual sensation. For this purpose he elaborates a vocabulary and imagery which, constantly recurred to, exhaust themselves and decline into a jargon. Even so, he cannot fairly be charged with a rash attempt to do something that with words cannot be done. We do better to see in all this a problem of the greatest technical difficulty, the confronting and solving of which is essential to his entire enterprise, and with which he does the best that a great and pertinaciously striving artist can do.

Women in Love has perhaps a better claim than either *Ulysses* or *Finnegans Wake* to be the radically original English novel of its age; it seems likely to hold the same sort of place in literary history, and to own the same greatness, as Richardson's *Clarissa*. Yet in some aspects it is entirely traditional, and the interplay of old and new appears at once in the first chapter. 'The usual plan is to take two couples and develop their relationships.' Lawrence loses no time in again profiting from this early discovery. Ursula Brangwen is still a schoolmistress. Her younger sister Gudrun is an artist, and we are told that she has 'touched the whole pulse of social England'. At present both sisters are living at home, loathing domesticity and very much prepared for anything. We meet them holding a short conversation in which they question the desirability of marriage and child-bearing. Then they walk out and join the crowd watching the wedding of a Miss Crich, daughter of a colliery owner of the district. The eldest son, Gerald Crich, arrives. Gudrun is at once much struck by him:

In his clear northern flesh and his fair hair was a glisten like sunshine refracted through crystals of ice. And he looked so new, unbroached, pure as an arctic thing. . . . A strange transport took possession of her, all her veins were in a paroxysm of violent sensation. 'Good God!' she exclaimed to herself, 'what is this? . . . Am I *really* singled out for him in some way, is there really some pale gold, arctic light that envelopes only us two?'

If the arctic imagery proves to have a function which may be thought of as belonging to the experimental novel, there is something thoroughly traditional about the speed with which this first love-relationship is launched. Nor does Ursula's tarry. A lady called Hermione Roddice, the daughter of 'a Derbyshire Baronet of the old school', arrives. Gudrun knows her, because Gudrun has 'friends among the slack aristocracy that keeps touch with the arts'. And Ursula at least knows Hermione's lover, Rupert Birkin, because he comes to inspect her school. Abruptly we desert the Brangwens for Hermione and learn that her possessive passion for Birkin is so extreme that his not yet having arrived among the guests is an anguish to her, 'a terrible storm . . . beyond death'. If we feel that, after Gudrun's paroxysm, this terrible storm is excessive, we are simply cling-ing—Lawrence might say—to our conventional notions about novels, notions which certainly won't take us unprotesting through the queer flight and capture of the bride that follows. Yet convention reasserts itself in the speed with which Ursula now interests herself in Birkin. Gudrun reports discouragingly that, although he is 'a wonderful chap . . . a marvellous per-sonality', he has the deplorable habit of treating 'any little fool as if she were his greatest consideration', and the sisters agree that this sort of thing is decidedly an insult to superior girls like themselves. They need scarcely have worried, for Birkin is never in fact going to display the commonplace example of good manners thus attributed to him. After the wedding comes a reception at which the Brangwens are not present, and which is chiefly an occasion for our learning more about Gerald Crich. His mother, who appears in some degree crazed, talks cryptically and gloomily to Birkin about her children and declares Gerald, who seems all power and vitality and decision, to be 'the most wanting of them all'. It seems that as a boy Gerald had accidentally killed a brother, and the chapter ends with a conversation, odd at such a time, in which Birkin tells Gerald that Gerald suffers a lurking desire to be murdered. Then:

There was a pause of strange enmity between the two men, that was very near to love. It was always the same between them; always their talk brought them into a deadly nearness of contact, a strange, perilous intimacy which was either hate or love, or both. They parted with apparent unconcern. . . . They had not the faintest belief in deep relationship between men and men, and their disbelief prevented any development of their powerful but suppressed friend-liness.

But Birkin, at least, is soon to be a believer in such a deep rela-tionship. The issue thus introduced claims, still unresolved, the closing sentence of the book.

The main structure is simple. Ursula and Birkin represent a life-theme over against which is set a death-theme in Gudrun and Gerald. Birkin's and Ursula's progress is impeded by the difficulty of Birkin's conception of marriage and, at a more superficial level, by the residual effects of his liaison with Hermione Roddice. Hermione, although a brilliantly cruel portrait from the life, is a highly representative figure in Lawrence's vision of modern society: a frigid woman, insatiably possessive and dominating, with whom every intellectual or emotional occasion is exploited in the interest of an obsessive will. Her attitude to Birkin is soon made clear to Ursula, into whose classroom the two walk, with no great probability, for the purpose, apparently, of exhibiting before a virtual stranger an unmeasured and frightening mutual hatred. Hermione questions the salubrity of the whole educational process. Are the children better for being roused to consciousness? Birkin turns upon her with the fury of a master against an inept apprentice. In asserting that the mind destroys all our spontaneity she is herself merely seeking a mental thrill:

'Spontaneous!' he cried. 'You and spontaneity! You, the most deliberate thing that ever walked or crawled! You'd be verily deliberately spontaneous—that's you. Because you want to have everything in your own volition, your deliberate voluntary consciousness. You want it all in that loathsome little skull of yours, that ought to be cracked like a nut. For you'll be the same till it *is* cracked, like an insect in its skin. If one cracked your skull perhaps one might get a spontaneous, passionate woman out of you, with real sensuality. As it is, what you want is pornography—looking at yourself in mirrors . . . .'

Ursula, very reasonably, feels 'a sense of violation in the air, as if too much was said'. But she is interested and asks Birkin if he really *wants* sensuality. His reply launches the long sequence of exploratory exhortations in which his part in the novel largely consists:

'Yes', he said, 'that and nothing else, at this point. It is a fulfilment —the great dark knowledge you can't have in your head—the dark involuntary being. It is death to one's self—but it is the coming into being of another.'

'But how? How can you have knowledge not in your head?' she asked, quite unable to interpret his phrases.

'In the blood', he answered; 'when the mind and the known world is drowned in darkness—everything must go—there must be the deluge. . . . You've got to lapse out before you can know what sensual reality is.'

There is significance in the qualification 'at this point'. Birkin's notion of a mystical state to be arrived at through sensuality is for long much in need of clarification. His one fixed faith is that he will 'come right' through marriage. But his view of the sexual conduct of what he calls 'ultimate' marriage is going to fluctuate. At one point common passion seems inimical to true sensuality, so that when it grips him he takes to his bed and is ill. At another point it is admissible to be 'suggestive, quite impossible', and Ursula—now his wife—has to come to terms with what is 'bestial' and 'degraded' in his conception of marital relations. In the final resolution Birkin and Ursula are confirmed in the knowledge that love is, at least for persons advanced like themselves, a false ultimate, 'one of the emotions like all the others'.

The urgency of Birkin's quest is quickly revealed as implicated with his sense of pervasive social disintegration around him. He is much at odds with his time and is represented as constantly irritable and intermittently phrenetic. His dislike of the mass of mankind is described as amounting almost to an illness. To Gerald, who is a powerful furtherer of modern industrial society, he expatiates on the need to 'bust' the mould of contemporary life completely. But this active proposal is immediately followed by another. 'The old ideals are dead as nails—nothing there. It seems to me there remains only this perfect union with a woman—sort of ultimate marriage.' Gerald is unimpressed by what may well seem an unathletic proposition. He belongs to another camp, believing that only work, the business of production, holds men together, that society is a mechanism which it is his task to further and exploit, and that the relationship between man and woman is aside from all this. Birkin is infuriated by such talk. He sees 'the perfect good-humoured callousness, even strange, glistening malice, in Gerald, glistening through the plausible ethics of productivity'. Gerald, having 'conceived the pure instrumentality of mankind' and constituted himself, as a great mine-owner, 'the God of the machine', has cut himself off from the deepest sources of life. In doing this he has elected his damnation and death.

Hermione takes up the Brangwens, and the chief characters are thus—by what is again a sufficiently traditional device—brought together in a country-house for leisured discussion. Nobody seems much to enjoy the party. Gudrun inclines to 'silent loathing', Hermione's talk puts Birkin 'in a white fury' and her possessive attitude to him turns Ursula 'stiff all over with resentment'. But the relationship of Birkin with his former mistress is at least brought to what is all but its conclusion. He is consistently brutal to her and eventually makes, in the strangest fashion, a definitive defiance of her 'persistent, almost insane will'. She tracks him to his room, finds him copying a Chinese drawing of geese, and wants to know—it is her whole being to *know*—why he claims to learn more of China from this activity than from extensive reading. He replies:

I know what centres they live from—what they perceive and feel —the hot, stinging centrality of a goose in the flux of cold water and mud—the curious bitter stinging heat of a goose's blood, entering their own blood like an inoculation of corruptive fire—fire of the cold-burning mud—the lotus mystery.

Hermione realizes that Birkin is asserting his determination to feel and 'know' in modes that are meaningless or offensive to her. Her response is described in language which, startling in citation, is entirely in key with the whole developing episode: 'She hated him in a despair that shattered her and broke her down, so that she suffered sheer dissolution like a corpse, and was unconscious of everything save the horrible sickness of dissolution that was taking place within her, body and soul.' At length a crisis comes and Hermione achieves what is described as her 'voluptuous consummation'. She picks up 'a blue, beautiful ball of lapis lazuli' and does her best to knock out her erstwhile lover's brains. Perhaps we recall his earlier agreeable suggestion that her own 'loathsome little skull' might to her advantage 'be cracked like a nut'. Birkin, having in part warded off the blow, leaves the house, climbs a hill, takes his clothes off, and rolls among the flowers.

It is clear that we can make little sense of such episodes in terms either of accepted English country-house life or of any sort of normal human society whatever. Persons habitually living at such a pitch could not long avoid nervous disintegration. Despite the realistic social setting, intermittently well achieved, which Lawrence gives his fable, he has no intention of entertaining us within the confines of the regular novel. The sense in which, in *Women in Love*, he 'takes two couples and develops their relationships' is a very special one, since what is exhibited in the couples is scarcely character in the received acceptation of the term at all, and the relationships developed are less between stable personalities than between forces of the human psyche which, in normal experience, remain virtually quiescent and unacknowledged except in brief periods of emotional crisis. Lawrence's representative people live at the end of abnormally open channels of communication with infra-personal worlds, and through these channels their conscious minds are constantly inundated by potent and mysterious floods. Of this the violence of Lawrence's language is the necessary and effective instrument.

Birkin's first confidences to Ursula appear those of a very sick man. He responds with cold indifference to her claim that she is happy, and his gloom makes her want to cry:

'And why is it', she asked at length, 'that there is no flowering, no dignity of human life now?'

'The whole idea is dead. Humanity itself is dry-rotten, really. . . . I loathe myself as a human being. Humanity is a huge aggregate lie. . . . I wish it was swept away. It could go, and there would be no *absolute* loss, if every human being perished tomorrow. . . . You yourself, don't you find it a beautiful clean thought, a world empty of people, just uninterrupted grass, and a hare sitting up?'

Listening to this, Ursula is at least attracted by the 'pleasant sincerity' of Birkin's voice. Moreover she is aware of 'his wonderful, desirable life-rapidity, the rare quality of an utterly desirable man'. She sees, with some penetration, that 'all the while, in spite of himself, he would have to be trying to save the world'. At the same time, she immediately begins to fight. 'It was a fight to the death between them—or to new life: though in what the conflict lay, no one could say.' No one, perhaps, can quite confidently say yet. Nevertheless Ursula's and Birkin's is the more readily comprehensible of the two main conflicts in the book: necessarily so, since Birkin is the book's most articulate character. In scene after scene with Ursula he hammers away at his doctrine. His obsessional earnestness is always in danger of making him an infuriating and humourless bore—a fact of which he is not without some saving knowledge. When Ursula, with very reasonable coquetry, asks him if he doesn't find her good-looking, we have this:

He looked at her, to see if he felt that she was good-looking.

'I don't *feel* that you're good-looking', he said.

'Not even attractive?' she mocked, bitingly.

He knitted his brows in sudden exasperation.

'Don't you see that it's not a question of visual appreciation in the least', he cried. 'I don't *want* to see you. I've seen plenty of women, I'm sick and weary of seeing them. I want a woman I don't see.'

'I'm sorry I can't oblige you by being invisible', she laughed.

'Yes', he said, 'you are invisible to me, if you don't force me to be visually aware of you. But I don't want to see you or hear you.'

'What did you ask me to tea for, then?' she mocked.

But Birkin presses on, only remarking by the way that he doesn't want any more of her 'meretricious persiflage': 'I want to find you, where you don't know your own existence, the you that your common self denies utterly. . . . What I want is a strange conjunction with you . . . an equilibrium, a pure balance of two single beings:—as the stars balance each other.' Ursula finds this perplexing and alarming, nor is she impressed by an analogy which he seeks to draw with his cat Mino, who at this moment happens to be engaged in bringing a female friend 'into a pure stable equilibrium, a transcendent and abiding *rapport* with the single male'.

A further stage of the relationship is precipitated by the shock of that drowning incident which makes Gerald Crich's loins appear so dim and luminous to Gudrun. The lovers—if they are to be called that—turn to each other in a movement of strong physical passion which somehow constitutes a false step. Ursula, anxious 'to show him she was no shallow prude', takes hold of Birkin and covers his face 'with hard, fierce kisses of passion'.

In spite of his otherness, the old blood beat up in him.

'Not this, not this', he whimpered to himself, as the first perfect mood of softness and sleep-loveliness ebbed back away from the rushing of passion that came up to his limbs and over his face as she drew him. And soon he was a perfect hard flame of passionate desire for her. Yet in the small core of the flame was an unyielding anguish of another thing. But this also was lost; he only wanted her, with an extreme desire that seemed inevitable as death, beyond question.

That they have in fact all but moved down some lethal path is evident in the extremity of the reaction subsequently besetting each. Ursula spends a Sunday evening meditating death as a consummating experience. She has those feelings of imminent physical dissolution to which Laurentian characters on their off-days are so prone. When Birkin calls, looking ill, she feels 'indefinable repulsion'. 'When he was gone Ursula felt such a poignant hatred of him, that all her brain seemed turned into a sharp crystal of fine hatred.' Later, 'when she heard he was ill again, her hatred only intensified itself a few degrees, if that were possible'. Nor does Birkin fare better. He lies 'sick and unmoved, in pure opposition to everything', reflecting on 'the old way of love' as 'a dreadful bondage, a sort of conscription', and of 'marriage, and children, and a life lived together' as repulsive. He believes in 'sex marriage' as some sort of preliminary to 'pure conjunction'. But 'the merging, the clutching, the mingling of love was become madly abhorrent to him', and in this mood he invents a sort of metabiology of sex:

In the old age, before sex was, we were mixed, each one a mixture. The process of singling into individuality resulted into the great polarisation of sex. The womanly drew to one side, the manly to the other. But the separation was imperfect even then. And so our world-cycle passes. There is now to come the new day, when we are beings each of us, fulfilled in difference. The man is pure man, the woman pure woman, they are perfectly polarised. But there is no longer any of the horrible merging, mingling self-abnegation of love. There is only the pure duality of polarisation, each one free from any contamination of the other. In each, the individual is primal, sex is subordinate, but perfectly polarised.

It is not easy to find any coherence between these and other of Birkin's persuasions at this time. Passion is here sanative, or an evolutionary instrument driving through and beyond sex to 'the pure duality of polarisation'. Yet the very occasion of his present illness has been 'the rushing of passion' when Ursula's 'fierce kisses of passion' caused 'the old blood to beat up in him'. Nor is the comprehensible theory of sex enunciated in his sick meditation, aiming as it does at a state in which 'the individual is primal', readily reconcilable with that doctrine of sensuality as 'the great dark knowledge' that is 'death to oneself' which Birkin inaugurated his relations with Ursula by propounding. Birkin's own effort at clarifying his thought is made within a field of imagery which is to be used also in the subsequent analysis of Gerald.

Earlier in the book the two men have examined together a primitive African statuette of a woman in labour, and Birkin has said:

There are centuries and hundreds of centuries of development in a straight line, behind that carving; it is an awful pitch of culture . . . pure culture in sensation, culture in the physical consciousness, really ultimate *physical* consciousness, mindless, utterly sensual. It is so sensual as to be final, supreme.

We recall that, in Ursula's classroom, Birkin had wanted sensuality—'that and nothing else, at this point'—and had talked in terms which would have been highly consonant with approval of this 'mindless' African culture. But he has fallen out of love with these ideas, and no longer seeks to explore in sensual experience 'something deeper, darker, than ordinary life could give'. He seeks 'only gentle communion, no other, no passion now', and in this mood he turns again to the Africans and sees their way as leading to an abyss:

Thousands of years ago, that which was imminent in himself must have taken place in these Africans: the goodness, the holiness, the desire for creation and productive happiness must have lapsed, leaving the single impulse for knowledge in one sort, mindless progressive knowledge through the senses, knowledge arrested and ending in the senses, mystic knowledge in disintegration and dissolution, knowledge such as the beetles have, which live purely within the world of corruption and cold dissolution. . . .

There is a long way we can travel, after the death-break: after that point when the soul in intense suffering breaks, breaks away from its organic hold like a leaf that falls. We fall from the connection with life and hope, we lapse from pure integral being, from creation and liberty, and we fall into the long, long African process of purely sensual understanding, knowledge in the mystery of dissolution.

He realised now that this is a long process—thousands of years it takes, after the death of the creative spirit. He realised that there were great mysteries to be unsealed, sensual, mindless, dreadful mysteries . . . sensual subtle realities far beyond the scope of phallic investigation.

There remained this way, this awful African process, to be fulfilled.

The fascination of such a fulfilment remains: we are certainly not at the end of it for Lawrence, or even for Birkin. But for the present, at least, Birkin sees himself as rejecting it absolutely for 'another way':

There was another way, the way of freedom. There was the paradisal entry into pure, single being, the individual soul taking precedence over love and desire for union, stronger than any pangs of emotion, a lovely state of free proud singleness, which accepted the obligation of the permanent connection with others, and with the other, submits to the yoke and leash of love, but never forfeits its own proud individual singleness, even while it loves and yields.

Here is in fact a more accommodating version of what he has already been preaching to Ursula, and now he asks her to marry him. But she is not disposed to fall into his arms on his conditions:

She was not at all sure that it was this mutual unison in separateness that she wanted. She wanted unspeakable intimacies. . . . She believed that love far surpassed the individual. He said the individual was *more* than love, or than any relationship. For him, the bright, single soul accepted love as one of its conditions, a condition of its own equilibrium. She believed that love was *everything*.

Their next big scene—which is climactic—begins with a quarrel. Birkin is 'angry at the bottom of his soul, and indifferent':

He knew she had a passion for him, really. But it was not finally interesting. There were depths of passion when one became impersonal and indifferent, unemotional. Whereas Ursula was still at the emotional personal level—always so abominably personal. He had taken her as he had never been taken himself. He had taken her at the roots of her darkness and shame—like a demon, laughing over the fountain of mystic corruption which was one of the sources of her being, laughing, shrugging, accepting, accepting finally. As for her, when would she so much go beyond herself as to accept him at the quick of death?

This, with its revived 'African' note and its highly charged allusions to things that seem not in fact at this stage to have happened, is not without perplexity. But presently we come on more comprehensible matter. 'In rather an uneasy voice' Birkin says that he must leave Ursula because he has an appointment with Hermione. Ursula at once calls him a scavenger dog and an eater of corpses. He replies with equal pungency—and feels that he is back where he started, with an Ursula determined to 'absorb, or melt, or merge'. But presently (they are in the country) she brings him a flower, and 'a hot passion of tenderness for her' fills his heart. With this unwontedly wholesome emotion, their union is suddenly triumphant. Only the terms in which it is described are again, in places, perplexing: 'She had thought there was no source deeper than the phallic source. And now, behold, from the smitten rock of the man's body, from the strange marvellous flanks and thighs, deeper, further in mystery than the phallic source, came the floods of ineffable darkness and ineffable riches.' We seem again to be back with those 'mindless, dreadful mysteries, far beyond the phallic cult', which Birkin has sensed in the African fetish, and which he had resolved to reject for 'another way, the way of freedom'. The two conflicting systems which Birkin had then discerned have not in fact been made the subject of an absolute choice. And they may strike us as being now reconciled only at a level of what is becoming rather facile imagery:

> He knew her darkly, with the fullness of dark knowledge. Now she would know him, and he too would be liberated. He would be night-free, like an Egyptian, steadfast in perfectly suspended equilibrium, pure mystic nodality of physical being. They would give each other this star-equilibrium which alone is freedom.

Nevertheless the assertion of the rightness and fullness of the union is splendidly made. Birkin and Ursula have come through. It is true that some problems remain. Ursula acquiesces in the rootlessness which Birkin makes an article of faith ('Pray God, in this world, no', he replies when she asks if they are ever to have a home). But she is disturbed by his conviction that their proposed nomadic freedom should be shared 'with a few other people':

> 'But why?' she insisted. 'Why should you hanker after other people? Why should you need them?'
> This hit him right on the quick. His brows knitted.
> 'Does it end with just our two selves?' he asked, tense.

We have in this an emergent Laurentian theme. Another, related but distinct, immediately follows:

> 'I *know* I want a perfect and complete relationship with you: and we've nearly got it—we really have. But beyond that. *Do* I want a real, ultimate relationship with Gerald? Do I want a final, almost extra-human relationship with him—a relationship in the ultimate of me and him—or don't I?'
> She looked at him for a long time, with strange bright eyes, but she did not answer.

It is a speculation that returns us to the other half of the novel.

Gerald Crich is the child of 'a relationship of utter inter-destruction'. His father has been a benevolent employer, against the bars of whose philanthropy Gerald's mother has beaten her wings like a bird of prey, opposing her husband 'like

one of the great demons of hell'. Gerald has inherited her ruthlessness, and rejects his father's paternalism in favour of a
realistic economic programme which takes hold of the mining
industry and converts it into 'a new and terrible purity'. The
purity is a purity of death, and it is towards death that Gerald,
in his depths, is orientated from the first. From early on we
cannot help feeling that Lawrence has created him to have, so
to speak, the raw end of the thesis. This is perhaps the grand
weakness of *Women in Love*. Nevertheless the sense of Gerald is
finely achieved. It is his story that finally dominates the book.

Partly as a result of his unfortunate heredity, partly because
his determinedly developed social philosophy has given him no
chance, and partly because of simple fatality symbolized in the
circumstance of his having accidentally killed a brother, Gerald's
is a deeply divided nature. He has intelligence and an interest
in ideas, is capable of troubled introspection, and acknowledges
discontent with himself as the efficient, unenslaved week-end
amorist that seems at first to represent the sum of his sexual
nature. But his inner uncertainty, which is made clear by his
mother in almost malevolent speech, is further revealed in the
manner in which his whole life is conducted as a desperate assertion of the will. Thus, witnessed by Ursula and Gudrun, he
implacably forces his Arab mare to face a noisy train at a railway crossing. For Lawrence the horse is always a major symbol
of the instinctual and vital, and the incident broadly defines
Gerald's significance from the first. And from the first the unpropitious nature of his fascination for Gudrun is made clear.
'They were of the same kind, he and she, a sort of diabolic
freemasonry subsisted between them.' The episode of the rabbit
vividly if cryptically enforces this. So, a little earlier, do their
encounters at that oddly nebulous and socially improbable
'water party' which ends with the drowning of Gerald's sister.
Here Ursula and Gudrun go off in a boat by themselves, and in
a retired spot Gudrun is prompted to do some modish Dalcroze
eurhythmics for the benefit of a herd of Gerald's cattle. The
cattle are soon 'breathing heavily with helpless fear and fascination'. Then Gerald turns up unexpectedly along with Birkin.
Birkin starts dancing too; he has unconvincing fits of frolic-
someness from time to time. But Gerald is annoyed, so that
presently Gudrun is feeling 'in her soul an unconquerable
desire for deep violence against him'. She slaps his face:

'You have struck the first blow', he said at last, forcing the words from his lungs, in a voice so soft and low, it sounded like a dream within her, not spoken in the outer air.

'And I shall strike the last', she retorted involuntarily, with confident assurance. He was silent, he did not contradict her.

Birkin at once improves this unfortunate occasion by some lugubrious observations on love. In our time, he says, Aphrodite is the flowering mystery of the death-process; when the stream of synthetic creation lapses, we find ourselves part of the blood of destructive creation; and Gudrun and Gerald belong just there.

It is shortly after this gnomic talk, and when he and Ursula have arrived at an extreme of antagonism, that Birkin finds himself strongly prompted to a close relationship with Gerald. 'Suddenly he saw himself confronted with another problem—the problem of love and eternal conjunction between two men.' He proposes to Gerald that they should swear to love each other 'implicitly, and perfectly, finally, without any possibility of going back on it'. Gerald, although not without pleasure in this proposal, is reserved and shy, and suggests deferring it until he understands it better. Birkin feels sharp disappointment and 'perhaps a touch of contempt'. He at once sees Gerald as doomed, limited, and exhibiting 'a sort of fatal halfness, which to himself seemed wholeness'. The further definition of Gerald's weakness is continued in the strange chapter called 'Gladiatorial'. In this the two men wrestle, naked, in Gerald's library—Birkin having decided that 'one ought to wrestle and strive and be physically close. It makes one sane.' Birkin tells Gerald that he is beautiful—which is more than he ever tells Ursula—and that it is 'a northern kind of beauty, like light refracted from snow'. There is point in this imagery. Then Gerald confesses that he has never loved a woman and Birkin replies bleakly that he is sure this is so. But for the full diagnosis of Gerald's case we have to go back to the moment at which Birkin rejects for himself the 'awful African process' and chooses 'another way, the way of freedom':

We fall from the connection with life and hope, we lapse from pure integral being, from creation and liberty, and we fall into the long, long African process of purely sensual understanding, knowledge in the mystery of dissolution. . . .

There remained this way, this awful African process, to be fulfilled.

It would be done differently by the white races. The white races, having the arctic north behind them, the vast abstraction of ice and snow, would fulfil a mystery of ice-destructive knowledge, snow-abstract annihilation. Whereas the West Africans, controlled by the burning death-abstraction of the Sahara, had been fulfilled in sun destruction, the putrescent mystery of sun-rays.

Was this then all that remained? Was there left now nothing but to break off from the happy creative being, was the time up? Is our day of creative life finished? Does there remain to us only the strange, awful afterwards of the knowledge in dissolution, the African knowledge, but different in us, who are blond and blue-eyed from the north?

Birkin thought of Gerald . . . .

This is at once crucial and surprising. Gerald, who is restlessly intelligent, who has reorganized a large industrial concern, and who from time to time gets adequate satisfaction from sleeping with one woman or another before returning to his absorbing job, seems sufficiently remote from the long African 'process of purely sensual understanding, knowledge in the mystery of dissolution'. And we are tempted to feel—noting in particular the ingenious switch from Africa to the Arctic—that Lawrence, having suddenly decided against 'purely sensual understanding' for his exemplary character, Birkin, is hastening to endow Birkin's antitype, Gerald, with what will now be a fatal leaning that way. Yet there is nothing more considered in the book than the organization of imagery and symbol designed to enforce the explicit statement that the heart of Gerald's mystery lies precisely here:

Birkin thought of Gerald. He was one of these strange white wonderful demons from the north, fulfilled in the destructive frost mystery. And was he fated to pass away in this knowledge, this one process of frost-knowledge, death by perfect cold? Was he a messenger, an omen of the universal dissolution into whiteness and snow?

If Gerald is all will at one level of his being, he is all insulated sensuality at another, so that the only passional relationship he is capable of forming is one of utter dependence upon an object of sensual excitement. We are presumably to understand that, in such a state of dissociation, 'polarity' and 'star-freedom' are impossible; that a man thus maimed must inevitably 'fall from the connection with life and hope . . . lapse from pure integral being, from creation and liberty', and become subject to that 'mystery of dissolution' which is in fact a death-wish. In thus seeing as fatal Gerald's circumscription within 'mindless progressive knowledge through the senses' Lawrence would appear to be turning against that earlier position according to which it is in admitting the 'fribbling intervention of mind' and betraying 'the blood, the flesh' that we go fatally wrong.

Gerald, then, for whatever underlying reason, is the type of the individual incapable of 'any pure relationship with any other soul', or of employing his energies in other than an ultimately destructive because faithless way. 'He would accept the established order in which he did not livingly believe, and then he would retreat to the underworld for his life.' This retreat, and the weakness inherent in it, is made manifest in the manner of his eventually coming to Gudrun's bed. His father falls mortally ill. In the stress of this ordeal Gerald's will cracks, and he knows that he must find reinforcement from outside or 'collapse inwards upon the great dark void which circled at the centre of his soul'. Gudrun has an obscure understanding that the love which, in these circumstances, Gerald professes for her can be only an oppression in the end. She feels 'as if she were caught at last by fate, imprisoned in some horrible and fatal trap'. His father's death brings Gerald 'the ultimate experience of his own nothingness', and when he comes to Gudrun it is clandestinely in her parents' house, and after frenzied nocturnal wandering which results in his bringing the very earth from the dead man's grave into her room. The succeeding episode of consummation stands in direct opposition to that of Birkin and Ursula, which has been celebrated immediately before. Now again we find a rapt description of the physical experience, but with overtones already sounded in the chapter's title, 'Death and Love':

He had come for vindication. She let him hold her in his arms, clasp her close against him. He found in her an infinite relief. Into her he poured all his pent-up darkness and corrosive death, and he was whole again. . . . And she, subject, received him as a vessel filled with his bitter potion of death. She had no power at this crisis to resist. The terrible frictional violence of death filled her, and she received it in an ecstasy of subjection, in throes of acute, violent sensation.

In Sherwood Forest Birkin and Ursula had 'slept the chilly night through under the hood of the car, a night of unbroken sleep . . . they kissed and remembered the magnificence of the night'. In Gudrun's bedroom only Gerald sleeps, and when Gudrun watches him furtively dressing in the morning 'an ache like nausea was upon her: a nausea of him'. Lawrence is faithfully following out his plan of taking two couples and developing their relationships. And now he has something further to say about the relationship between the two men. Birkin reiterates to Gerald his belief in a permanent union between a man and a woman, but he implies that Gerald would be ill advised to attempt this with Gudrun here and now. And, in any case, we have 'got to take down the love-and-marriage ideal from its pedestal'. We want 'something broader', which is to be achieved by seeking 'the *additional* perfect relationship between man and man'—and it is here that Gerald himself had better begin. But Gerald rejects this fresh proposal, saying that he just can't feel that way himself. Instead, he chooses 'the underworld for his life'. Just as Birkin had seen that 'there was another way, the way of freedom' and embraced it, Gerald sees that there is 'the other way' and turns it down:

The other way was to accept Rupert's offer of alliance, to enter into the bond of pure trust and love with the other man, and then subsequently with the woman. If he pledged himself with the man he would later be able to pledge himself with the woman: not merely in legal marriage, but in absolute, mystic marriage.

Yet although, because of 'a numbness upon him', Gerald has to decline this problematical apprenticeship, the two couples keep together. The sisters believe they hate the idea of domesticity, and Birkin believes he hates his native country most immoderately. 'They say the lice crawl off a dying body', he says ('with a glare of bitterness'). 'So I leave England.' They all make their way to a small *Gasthaus* in a snow-bound Alpine valley. Here the final struggle takes place.

Gudrun is oppressed by Gerald's 'constant passion, that was like a doom on him', and at the same time she realizes that with this torturing dependence he can reconcile an easy promiscuity which shows signs of exercising itself almost at once among their fellow-guests. She feels that one of them must triumph over the other and forms a deep resolve to fight him. There is an early and cryptic crisis. Alone with Gerald in her bedroom, she is suddenly nervous, and knows that she is lost if he realizes this. Summoning all her strength, she speaks to him in 'a full, resonant, nonchalant voice, that was forced out with all her remaining self-control' and asks him to perform some trivial task. He carries it out, and the danger is over. It is as if she had suddenly discovered herself to be closeted with a maniac. And she continues desperate. She tries to convince herself, and Ursula, that love is 'the supreme thing'. But Ursula is now fully confirmed in her husband's doctrine, and declares that what we must fulfil comes out of the unknown to us, is something infinitely more than love, and isn't so merely human. At the same time Ursula tells herself that Gudrun's case is that of one who, never having known love, can't get beyond it. There is thus some estrangement between the sisters. And the men have only one more conversation. Birkin asks Gerald if things are all right with him. Gerald replies out of what appears to be a deep uncomprehending despair. He says that there is something final about the position he has arrived at; it withers his consciousness and burns the pith of his mind. In face of this, Birkin makes his last appeal. 'I've loved you, as well as Gudrun, don't forget', he says bitterly. But Gerald is icily irresponsive. Birkin and Ursula leave the *Gasthaus*.

Gerald and Gudrun are abandoned to a conflict that frightens them both. His humiliating need presses upon her 'like a frost, deadening her':

'Are you regretting Ursula?' he asked.
'No, not at all', she said. Then, in a slow mood, she asked:
'How much do you love me?'
He stiffened himself further against her.
'How much do you think I do?' he asked.
'I don't know', she replied.
'But what is your opinion?' he asked.
There was a pause. At length, in the darkness, came her voice, hard and indifferent:
'Very little indeed', she said coldly, almost flippant.
His heart went icy at the sound of her voice.
'Why don't I love you?' he asked, as if admitting the truth of her accusation, yet hating her for it.
'I don't know why you don't—I've been good to you. You were in a *fearful* state when you came to me.'
Her heart was beating to suffocate her, yet she was strong and unrelenting.
'When was I in a fearful state?' he asked.
'When you first came to me. I *had* to take pity on you. But it was never love.'

It was that statement 'It was never love,' which sounded in his ears with madness.

'Why must you repeat it so often, that there is no love?' he said in a voice strangled with rage.

'Well you don't *think* you love, do you?' she asked.

He was silent with cold passion of anger.

'You don't think you *can* love me, do you?' she repeated almost with a sneer.

'No', he said.

'You know you never *have* loved me, don't you?'

'I don't know what you mean by the word "love",' he replied.

'Yes, you do. You know all right that you have never loved me. Have you, do you think?'

'No', he said, prompted by some barren spirit of truthfulness and obstinacy.

'And you never *will* love me', she said finally, 'will you?'

There was a diabolic coldness in her, too much to bear.

'No', he said.

'Then', she replied, 'what have you against me!'

He was silent in cold, frightened rage and despair. 'If only I could kill her', his heart was whispering repeatedly. 'If only I could kill her—I should be free.'

It seemed to him that death was the only severing of this Gordian knot.

'Why do you torture me?' he said.

She flung her arms round his neck.

'Ah, I don't want to torture you', she said pityingly, as if she were comforting a child. The impertinence made his veins go cold, he was insensible. She held her arms round his neck, in a triumph of pity. And her pity for him was as cold as stone, its deepest motive was hate of him, and fear of his power over her, which she must always counterfoil.

'Say you love me', she pleaded. 'Say you love me for ever—won't you—won't you?'

But it was her voice only that coaxed him. Her senses were entirely apart from him, cold and destructive of him. It was her overbearing *will* that insisted.

'Won't you say you'll love me always?' she coaxed. 'Say it, even if it isn't true—say it Gerald, do.'

'I will love you always', he repeated, in real agony, forcing the words out.

She gave him a quick kiss.

'Fancy your actually having said it', she said with a touch of raillery.

He stood as if he had been beaten.

'Try to love me a little more, and to want me a little less', she said, in a half contemptuous, half coaxing tone.

The darkness seemed to be swaying in waves across his mind, great waves of darkness plunging across his mind. It seemed to him he was degraded to the very quick, made of no account.

From this dreadful scene there can be no going back. Gerald's passion becomes 'awful to her, tense and ghastly, and impersonal, like a destruction, ultimate', and he can scarcely ever leave her alone, but follows her like a shadow. Gudrun is in the stronger position, since on her part hatred is tinged with contempt. We are reminded of Ursula's final ruthlessly brutal relationship with Skrebensky in *The Rainbow*. Gudrun gains an ally in an Austrian sculptor called Loerke, who is the only important character to come late into the novel. Loerke is a highly symbolical intruder, and much in his presentation seems strained, pretentious, and destructive of the impressive simplicity of the catastrophe. Some sense of this prompted Lawrence to describe Loerke as 'a mere contingency'; and his essential function appears to be that of showing contemporary living as sharing its death-orientation with contemporary art. Loerke believes that art and the world have nothing to do with each other, and Gudrun agrees—so that Ursula, whether out of her own good sense or as Birkin's pupil, has to tell them that 'the world of art is only the truth about the real world . . . but you are too far gone to see it'. To the false and rubbishing aesthetic prattle between Gudrun and Loerke—'Art and Life were to them the Reality and the Unreality'—an obscure sexual commerce is soon added:

They had a curious game with each other, Gudrun and Loerke, of infinite suggestivity, strange and leering, as if they had some esoteric understanding of life, that they alone were initiated into the fearful central secrets, that the world dared not know. Their whole correspondence was in a strange, barely comprehensible suggestivity, they kindled themselves at the subtle lust of the Egyptians or the Mexicans. . . .

What then, what next? Was it sheer blind force of passion that would satisfy her now? Not this, but the subtle thrills of extreme sensation in reduction. It was an unbroken will reacting against her unbroken will in a myriad subtle thrills of reduction. . . .

Of the last series of subtleties, Gerald was not capable. He could not touch the quick of her. But where his ruder blows could not

penetrate, the fine, insinuating blade of Loerke's insect-like comprehension could. At least, it was time for her now to pass over to the
other, the creature, the final craftsman.

We may be puzzled by a good deal of this. 'Extreme sensation
in reduction' is abracadabra, and the succeeding nakedly
phallic imagery, seeming to make mere erotic technique a point
of reference, comes to us simply as a rhetorical bad habit. It is
certainly misleading in regard to the nature of the radical
insufficiencies underlying the failure of Gerald's and Gudrun's
relationship. However this may be, Gudrun's flaunting of an
intense and esoteric understanding with Loerke drives Gerald
into as great a desperation as it is meant to. 'He was isolated as
if there were a vacuum round his heart, or a sheath of pure
ice.' Soon he is feeling 'what a perfect voluptuous consummation it would be to strangle her'—a phrase that may be a little
cheapened for us if we remember that it was her 'voluptuous
consummation' that Hermione Roddice was to achieve by
hitting Birkin on the head. Gudrun on her part knows that it is
'a fight to the death . . . one slip, and she was lost'. Her ruthlessness sharpens itself. Gerald suggests, without conviction, that
their attempt 'might have come off':

> 'No', she replied. 'You cannot love.'
> 'And you?' he asked.
> Her wide, dark-filled eyes were fixed on him, like two moons of
> darkness.
> 'I couldn't love *you*', she said, with stark cold truth.

In the end Gerald, maddened by an insolent word from Loerke,
knocks him down, just refrains from murdering Gudrun, wanders off into the snow, and is brought back dead next morning.
He has been 'fulfilled in the destructive frost mystery'.

There is something a shade perfunctory about the description
of Gerald's death, and we learn without surprise of an alternative ending in which Lawrence envisaged Gerald's survival and
a further working out of his relationship with Gudrun which
should turn upon her bearing him a son. It would be unjusti-
fiable to say that this uncertainty points to a weakness in *Women
in Love*. When some overwriting is discounted, the last three
chapters will surely appear as impressive as anything that the
modern novel has to show. If the conclusion lacks that sort
of inevitability which we traditionally associate with serious

fiction, we must reflect that this is a quality difficult of achievement with persons deliberately divorced from 'the old stable *ego* of the character'—as Lawrence put it—in favour of 'another *ego* according to whose action the individual is unrecognisable'. But Gerald, who is dead, and Gudrun, who has in effect killed him, have at least enough 'character' in the traditional sense for Birkin and Ursula to return in judgement upon them in the final chapter. The sisters have little to say to each other. Birkin greets Gudrun with the words, 'The end of *this* trip, at any rate'—an instance, surely, of the horrifying brutality to which Lawrence often blithely commits even his exemplary characters. Then:

> Birkin went again to Gerald. He had loved him. And yet he felt chiefly disgust at the inert body lying there. It was so inert, so coldly dead, a carcase, Birkin's bowels seemed to turn to ice. He had to stand and look at the frozen dead body that had been Gerald.
>
> It was the frozen carcase of a dead male. Birkin remembered a rabbit which he had once found frozen like a board on the snow. . . .
>
> He remembered a dead stallion he had seen: a dead mass of maleness, repugnant.

'He had loved him.' This is the theme upon which the novel ends:

> 'I didn't want it to be like this—I didn't want it to be like this', he cried to himself. . . .
>
> Then suddenly he lifted his head, and looked straight at Ursula, with dark, almost vengeful eyes.
>
> 'He should have loved me', he said. 'I offered him.'
>
> She, afraid, white, with mute lips answered:
>
> 'What difference would it have made!'
>
> 'It would', he said. 'It would.'

If Lawrence were interested in tragic effect, the book called *Women in Love* would probably close with these words. But what he is in fact interested in is a problem or complex of problems, and he drops the tone of his conclusion in order to secure that sense of an open question, a territory still awaiting exploration, which is his favourite way of rounding off a novel. Birkin and Ursula return to England:

> 'Did you need Gerald?' she asked one evening.
>
> 'Yes', he said.
>
> 'Aren't I enough for you?' she asked.

'No', he said. 'You are enough for me, as far as a woman is concerned. You are all women to me. But I wanted a man friend, as eternal as you and I are eternal.'

'Why aren't I enough?' she said. 'You are enough for me. I don't want anybody else but you. Why isn't it the same with you?'

'Having you, I can live all my life without anybody else, any other sheer intimacy. But to make it complete, really happy, I wanted eternal union with a man too: another kind of love', he said.

'I don't believe it', she said. 'It's an obstinacy, a theory, a perversity.'

'Well—' he said.

'You can't have two kinds of love. Why should you!'

'It seems as if I can't', he said. 'Yet I wanted it.'

'You can't have it, because it's false, impossible', she said.

'I don't believe that', he answered.

Yeats was to call *Women in Love* 'a beautiful enigmatic book'. There could be no more succinctly just summary.

5

The Lost Girl, begun in 1913 in frank imitation of the 'old imitator' Arnold Bennett, and rewritten and completed later, was published in 1920. With the exception of *The Boy in the Bush* (1924), his rehandling of a story by an Australian acquaintance, Mollie Skinner, *The Lost Girl* is commonly regarded as the least interesting of Lawrence's novels. Yet its heroine, Alvina Houghton, is the most humanly appealing of his women, and her unpredictable progress from the stifling but steadily diminishing securities of her father's drapery establishment in Woodhouse to married life among the destitute *contadini* of the Abruzzi makes an entertaining social comedy upon the peripheries of which hover, felicitously on the whole, authentic Laurentian evocations alike of passion and of place. At the same time, and distinct from a traditional Dickensian humour which has its richest expression in the account of Alvina's tillworshipping and lucklessly venturesome father, there is a muted burlesque such as the creator of Rupert Birkin might be expected to achieve when in a mood of self-criticism. At one point Alvina, attracted by the robust masculinity of a neighbouring plumber, watches him upon his professional occasions, and laughs to herself, 'seeing his tight, well-shaped hindquarters protruding out from under the sink like the wrong end of a dog from a kennel'. Only those who know *Women in Love* can fully appreciate this. Again, although Cicio, Alvina's Italian peasant lover, is soberly in the authentic line of Lawrence's cruel, tender, mindless, and darkly powerful figures of the kind, he is exhibited in some situations of very pleasing absurdity, as when Alvina's duties as a trained midwife take her to the bedside of Mrs. Tuke, and Cicio's passion brings him into the garden below with a mandoline:

'Oh, it's horrible! It's horrible! I don't want it!' cried the woman in travail. Alvina comforted her and reassured her as best she could. And from outside, once more, came the despairing howl of the Neapolitan song, animal and inhuman on the night. . . .
'That *awful* noise! Isn't love the most horrible thing! I think it's horrible. It just does one in, and turns one into a sort of howling animal. I'm howling with one sort of pain, he's howling with another. Two hellish animals howling through the night! I'm not myself, he's not himself. Oh, I think it's horrible. What does he look like, Nurse? Is he beautiful? Is he a great hefty brute?'

Cicio is brought upstairs and is authentically inarticulate:

'Nurse!' cried Effie. 'It's *no use* trying to get a grip on life. You're just at the mercy of *Forces*,' she shrieked angrily. . . . 'I hate life. It's nothing but a mass of forces. *I* am intelligent. Life isn't intelligent. . . .'
'Perhaps life itself is something bigger than intelligence', said Alvina.
'Bigger than intelligence!' shrieked Effie. '*Nothing* is bigger than intelligence. Your man is a hefty brute. His yellow eyes *aren't* intelligent. They're *animal*—'

When Alvina finds herself in Pescocalascio with her animal the subdued self-parody becomes prophetic:

How unspeakably lovely it was, no one could ever tell, the grand, pagan twilight of the valleys, savage, cold, with a sense of ancient gods who knew the right for human sacrifice. It stole away the soul of Alvina. She felt transfigured in it, clairvoyant in another mystery of life. A savage hardness came in her heart. The gods who had demanded human sacrifice were quite right, immutably right. The fierce, savage gods who dipped their lips in blood, these were the true gods.

Alvina is a sensible girl, well brought up by her governess Miss Frost on Congregationalist principles, and she is not always

wholly convincing as a disciple of D. H. Lawrence. What is
wholly convincing—what is really superbly done—is the natural
scene upon which the book closes: the snow peaks and the
scrubby blue-dark foothills, the villages that 'clung like pale
swarms of birds to the far slopes', the ancient savage holes of
houses in which Cicio and his relations live, 'the flowers that
came out and uttered the earth in magical expression'. Lawrence's intense sensibility to the Mediterranean world, mani-
fested throughout his career from the early travel sketches of
Twilight in Italy (1916) to the posthumously published 'The
Man Who Died' (1931), is here first substantially fused with
fiction. But equally rooted in the book is that 'nostalgia of the
repulsive, heavy-footed Midlands' which he was never to out-
grow. He often delighted in describing England in the vocabulary of the morgue—and Alvina, looking back across the
Channel, sees 'ash-grey, corpse-grey cliffs . . . England, like
a long, ash-grey coffin . . . with streaks of snow like cerements'.
But England never even began to die in Lawrence. He remained
English as, among the other great expatriates, only Landor did.

In *Aaron's Rod* (1922) the action again begins in industrial
England and moves to Italy. But whereas there is a real dramatic effectiveness in isolating Alvina on Cicio's remote *podere*
there appears to be no special virtue in taking Aaron Sisson to
Novara, Milan, and Florence. We are made aware of the full
onerousness of Lawrence's commitment to earning a living
largely as a novelist—and as a novelist whose sole essential
concern lies in dramatizing and analysing his own intractable
problems. 'Hammer, hammer, hammer' appears to have been
his prescription for resolving these problems in private life,
and he was only encouraged in the method by having a wife
well able to hammer back. But readers must be rather more
variously entertained. Here Lawrence's resources are not extensive. His command of humour is uncertain. His interest in
character is slight except in one peculiar regard: he enjoys
achieving the portraiture—too often viciously satirical—of his
friends. But chiefly he enjoys his own high command of the
spirit of place. When Aaron passes from Eastwood to London
it is in order that Lawrence may fill out the page with un-
charitable sketches of Bohemian society; when he moves on to
Italy it is because Lawrence is in Italy, and able to alternate
similarly toned sketches of expatriate English and Americans

with striking evocations of Italian cities and the Italian country-
side. Aaron's spiritual progress is not much furthered by all
this. But then it is a progress which would not, in itself, make
up a book.

In terms of Lawrence's early environment, Aaron is an educated man. For three years he was a schoolteacher. This career
he threw up to go into the pit, and the story opens with him as
a prosperous and apparently settled collier, having a wife and
three daughters to whom his attitude seems to be one of good-
humoured if rather unloving tolerance. But in fact he is at a
breaking-point the nature of which he scarcely understands.
There is 'something tense, exasperated to the point of intolerable anger, in his good humoured breast.... There was a hard,
opposing core in him. . . . He recognised it as a secret malady
he suffered from: this strained, unacknowledged opposition to
his surroundings.' The disharmony clearly centres in his relations with his wife, and is surely reflected in the fact—oddly
uncommented upon throughout the book—that he has no
discernible attachment to his children whatever. He leaves
home and, being something of a musician, obtains employment
as a flautist at Covent Garden. This unlikely feat is followed by
others. Aaron goes to Italy, moves freely among titled and
distinguished people, and several times sleeps with a marchesa.
The marchesa, it is true, is only 'an American woman from the
Southern States', and the affair is not a success, anyway.
'Through him went the feeling, "This is not my woman"', and
he acknowledges an intense resentment against her, so that she
is left in very much the same boat as his Eastwood wife. The
episode has little significance for Aaron's story. Seen in the
general context of Lawrence's work, it must appear no more than
one of those routine conquests of high-born ladies by prole-
tarian lovers which it gave him pleasure to invent. We have
writing of the same order of inspiration in that earlier passage
in which Aaron is entertained by a wealthy English industrialist
living in Novara, and more than keeps his end up in a house full
of 'handsome appointments', 'black and white chambermaids',
plump colonels, young Oxford-like majors, and other intimidating paraphernalia of the upper classes. But if some of the
incidental writing is cheap and bad, a great deal is brilliant.
It is the more significant, then, that what we look out for, and,
when they come, acknowledge as the most absorbing parts of

the book, are the places in which Aaron's predicament is by
one means or another subjected to serious analysis. The first of
these occurs in the Novara sequence—and is immediately
followed, characteristically enough, by an episode of luckless
and jeering comedy at the expense of the colonels and majors.
Aaron reflects on his marriage, and ascribes its failure to his
wife's 'terrible, implacable, cunning will'. He reminds himself
that, of two people at a deadlock, there is not one only at fault.
And his own fault has been to concur with practically all men
in accepting the 'sacred life-bearing priority of woman'. He had
thus encouraged his young wife to believe that 'she, as woman,
and particularly as mother, was the first great source of life and
being'; that 'the highest her man could ever know or ever
reach, was to be perfectly enveloped in her all-beneficent love'.
But from this he had withheld himself, convinced that 'his
intrinsic and central aloneness was the very centre of his being'.
Hence their struggle.

At this point Lawrence becomes aware that his musical
collier has achieved an implausibly articulate meditation. So he
continues:

> The inaudible music of his conscious soul conveyed his meaning in
> him quite as clearly as I convey it in words: probably much more
> clearly. But in his own mode only: and it was in his own mode only
> he realised what I must put into words. These words are my own
> affair. His mind was music.
>
> Don't grumble at me then, gentle reader, and swear at me that
> this damned fellow wasn't half clever enough to think all these
> smart things, and realise all these fine-drawn-out subtleties.

In the tone of this there is something ominous for Lawrence's
fiction, and it is to sound more clearly in the succeeding novel,
Kangaroo. 'Chapter follows chapter', we are told there, 'and
nothing doing. . . . If you don't like the novel, don't read it.'
And: 'I hope, dear reader, you like plenty of *conversation* in
a novel: it makes it so much lighter and brisker.' And: 'He
preached, and the record was taken down for this gramophone of a novel.' If we come to this from James or Conrad we
shall probably feel that Lawrence is a novelist who does not
consistently respect his medium. He has moods, certainly, in
which his impatience with artistic contrivance and consideration
is extreme. He grows bad-tempered with art, just as he grew
bad-tempered with people when out of love with them.

Aaron Sisson, however, as if undisturbed by his creator's momentary lack of faith in him as an historical personage, pursues his introspective way. He sees that for him any extreme of self-abandon in love is an act of false behaviour, and that 'to fling down the whole soul in one gesture of finality in love' is 'as much a criminal suicide as to jump off a church-tower'. Even for the woman who demands it, such a complete surrender is fatal. 'She is driven mad by the endless meal of the marriage sacrament, poisoned by the sacred communion which was her goal.' And now he sees, if figuratively, something of the right way of love:

The process should work to a completion, not to some horror of intensification and extremity wherein the soul and body ultimately perish. The completion of the process of love is the arrival at a state of simple, pure self-possession, for man and woman. . . . Two eagles in mid-air, grappling, whirling, coming to their intensification of love-oneness there in mid-air. In mid-air the love consummation. But all the time each lifted on its own wings: each bearing itself up on its own wings at every moment of the mid-air love consummation. That is the splendid love-way.

Lottie Sisson, left forsaken with three children in Eastwood, might make little of this. But then Lottie has not had the benefit of sitting at the feet of genius. And her husband has. For already Aaron has had his first significant encounter with Rawdon Lilly—a character with whom, far more absolutely than with Rupert Birkin, Lawrence walks straight into the theatre of his own fiction. The thing is so nakedly done as to constitute, although fascinating in itself, a further symptom of his relaxing grip upon fully achieved dramatic creation.

Lilly is a writer with a small private income. Believing that 'a new place brings out a new thing in a man', he wanders about—sometimes with his wife and sometimes without. He has no children and is glad of it, although his wife is of another mind. He is small and ugly, but possesses great personal charm, great penetration into character, and 'a certain belief in himself as a saviour'. He has already exercised his talent upon Aaron, whom he has found dejected and very ill in London as the result of having 'given in' to a woman—in a manner, it would seem, prelusive of his almost equally debilitating affair with the marchesa. Lilly restores Aaron to health when the doctor has

failed—this by means of a massaging operation having the
ritual quality which Lawrence likes to ascribe to physical contact between men—and then takes the lead in a curious anti-
phonal commination which the two men pronounce against
wives and mothers. Lilly says that 'When a woman's got her
children, by God, she's a bitch in the manger' and Aaron—
although not without hinted misgiving—says 'Them and their
children be cursed'.

'Men have got to stand up to the fact that manhood is more than
childhood—and then force women to admit it', said Lilly. 'But the
rotten whiners, they're all grovelling before a baby's napkin and a
woman's petticoat.'

'It's a fact', said Aaron. But he glanced at Lilly oddly, as if
suspiciously.

The pace of indoctrination has been a little fast. But the two
agree on the need to 'find two men to stick together, without
feeling criminal, and without cringing, and without betraying
one another' by going 'fawning round some female'. Lilly also
expresses himself about the recently ended Kaiser's War—'the
war was a lie and is a lie and will go on being a lie till somebody
busts it'—and when Aaron rashly disagrees with him on the
subject of poison gas he finds himself abruptly ordered out of
Lilly's flat: 'I *don't* have friends who don't fundamentally agree
with me.' This piece of tyranny introduces another theme which
is to be developed later: that of power, which Lilly sees as
requiring not only a right subjection of woman to man but
a right subjection of man to man as well. Aaron is inclined to
resent the claim implicit in this. 'You believe you know something better than me . . . . Don't you?' Aaron is not, at this
point, willing to obey 'a certain call' which he knows that Lilly
has made upon his soul. Nevertheless Lilly has secured a disciple.
Aaron's journey to Italy is obscurely motivated by his need to
renew the contact, and when his adventure with the marchesa
proves disturbing he openly acknowledges to himself a new
degree of dependence. 'Like a deep burn on his deepest soul,
Lottie. And like a fate which he resented, yet which steadied
him, Lilly.' Sitting 'for long hours among the cypress trees of
Tuscany', he reflects on the precepts with which he has been
provided. 'Lilly told me that a husband cannot be a lover, and
a lover cannot be a husband.' What this works out to is obscure.
The first term of the proposition presumably invalidates his

late attempt at setting up with a mistress. The second makes him useless for the implacable purposes of his wife. But looking down at Florence from Settignano, he remembers that 'the other man was in town, and from this fact he derived his strength'.

At the close of the book the theme of power becomes dominant. Lilly, although amid evasive argument which is said to have marked Lawrence's own dialectic manner, calls for 'a real committal of the life-issue of inferior beings to the responsibility of a superior being'. Aaron feels that he has to choose between the world and Lilly, in whom is something 'incomprehensible' that has dominion over him. Unfortunately, Lilly seems likely to prove elusive. He has already declared that he would have loved the Aztecs and the Red Indians. Now he announces that he would 'very much like to try life in another continent, among another race . . . quite a new life-mode'. He does, however, preach his disciple a final sermon. There are two great dynamic urges in life: love and power. But in the present age of the world the love-urge is in desuetude or corruption and the power-urge is to supervene. What must be asserted is 'dark, living, fructifying power'. As between man and woman, woman must give 'deep, unfathomable free submission' in this new context. And, equally, 'men must submit to the greater soul in a man, for their guidance . . . the deep fathomless submission to the heroic soul in a greater man'. And Aaron is in the end directly charged:

'You, Aaron, you too have the need to submit. You, too, have the need livingly to yield to a more heroic soul, to give yourself. You know you have. And you know it isn't love. It is life-submission. And you know it. But you kick against the pricks. And perhaps you'd rather die than yield. And so, die you must. It is your affair.'

There was a long pause. Then Aaron looked up into Lilly's face. It was dark and remote-seeming. It was like a Byzantine eikon at the moment.

'And whom shall I submit to?' he said.

'Your soul will tell you', replied the other.

On this broad hint, thus portentously delivered, *Aaron's Rod* closes. Wherever we have got to, it is plainly well outside the bounds of any practicable realistic fiction. Suppose Aaron accepts Lilly's *mitte collum*, what are the two to do? They are in Florence for no particular purpose, and Lilly at least is

losing interest in the Norman Douglas-like characters they have
been frequenting and is beginning to think of Aztecs and Red
Indians. Shall Aaron follow him in his search for a new life-
mode? Lawrence was intermittently enthusiastic about an
ideal colony to be called Rananim, where he was to preside over
the corrected lives now of one and now of another chosen few
of his acquaintance. But he never put this dream to the test of
giving it embodiment in his fiction, and *Aaron's Rod* can have
no sequel of that sort. Aaron Sisson is in fact left much in the
air. He has been made the recipient of a stiff dose of Laurentian
wisdom, and there is really no further use for him.

6

Kangaroo (1923) is in some ways the most astonishing of the
novels. Set in an Australia more powerfully and delicately
evoked than by any other writer, and containing much confident analysis of the Australian national character presented
largely in relation to an entirely invented political movement,
it was written in some six weeks of Lawrence's three-months'
sojourn in New South Wales in 1922. The feat becomes more
extraordinary when we learn that, apart from one or two meetings with literary people in Perth, there is virtually no record of
the Lawrences having made in Australia any acquaintances
whatever. They simply spent a day in Sydney and then moved
to a cottage some forty miles down the coast. There Lawrence
invented his characters and wrote his book. It is true that nothing
essentially Australian is at the heart of *Kangaroo*. Lawrence in
his wanderings has simply brought his home problems with
him; he dumps them in the bush, it may be said, and gets on
with the endless job of solving them. But, for a start, what
a bush—seized and held by a total stranger who never, it
seems, travelled as much as twenty miles towards the interior
of the continent!

It seemed so hoary and lost, so unapproachable. The sky was
pure, crystal pure and blue, of a lovely pale blue colour: the air
was wonderful, new and unbreathed: and there were great dis-
tances. But the bush, the grey, charred bush. . . . It was so phantom-
like, so ghostly, with its tall pale trees and many dead trees, like
corpses, partly charred by bush fires: and then the foliage so dark,

like grey-green iron. And then it was so deathly still. Even the few birds seemed to be swamped in silence. Waiting, waiting—the bush seemed to be hoarily waiting . . . .

As they turned south they saw tree-ferns standing on one knobbly leg among the gums, and among the rocks ordinary ferns and small bushes spreading in glades and up sharp hill-slopes. It was virgin bush, and as if unvisited, lost, sombre, with plenty of space, yet spreading grey for miles and miles, in a hollow towards the west. Far in the west, the sky having suddenly cleared, they saw the magical range of the Blue Mountains. And all this hoary space of bush between. The strange, as it were, *invisible* beauty of Australia, which is undeniably there, but which seems to lurk just beyond the range of our white vision. You feel you can't *see*—as if your eyes hadn't the vision in them to correspond with the outside landscape. For the landscape is so unimpressive, like a face with little or no features, a dark face . . . subtle, remote, *formless* beauty more poignant than anything ever experienced before . . . .

But it is wonderful, out of the sombreness of gum-trees, that seem the same, hoary for ever, and that are said to begin to wither from the centre the moment they are mature—out of the hollow bush of gum-trees and silent heaths, all at once, in spring, the most delicate feathery yellow of plumes and plumes and plumes and trees and bushes of wattle, as if angels had flown right down out of the softest gold regions of heaven to settle here, in the Australian bush. And the perfume in all the air that might be heaven, and the unutterable stillness, save for strange bright birds and flocks of parrots, and the motionlessness, save for a stream and butterflies and some small brown bees. Yet, a stillness, and a manlessness, and an elation, the bush flowering at the gates of heaven. . . .

The frail, wonderful Australian spring, coming out of all the gummy hardness and sombreness of the bush.

Yet even this, with its rapt quality as of something from Coleridge's notebooks, pales before the description of beach and ocean, or of the little ocean bungalow, Coo-ee, and its ambience of forlorn and impermanent-seeming human effort and human litter. These have a quality akin to that which Berenson distinguishes in the very greatest painting: a power of feeling out so sensitively to the essentials of a contemplated world that the work of art comes to us in the guise of an immense intensification of our own faculties and our own sense of being alive. And from the habitat Lawrence works towards the fauna: the fish and the birds and the human beings are all intuitively felt as profoundly conditioned by this unique natural scene. 'The great indifference, the darkness of the fern world', is over everything Australian:

The previous world!—the world of the coal age. The lonely, lonely world that had waited, it seemed, since the coal age. These ancient flat-topped tree-ferns, these towsled palms like mops. What was the good of trying to be an alert conscious man here? You couldn't. Drift, drift into a sort of obscurity, backwards into a nameless past, hoary as the country is hoary. Strange old feelings wake in the soul: old, non-human feelings. And an old, old indifference, like a torpor, invades the spirit. An old, saurian torpor. Who wins? ... Would the people waken this ancient land, or would the land put them to sleep, drift them back into the torpid semi-consciousness of the world of the twilight . . . drifted away into the grey pre-world where men didn't have emotions. Where men didn't have emotions and personal consciousness, but were shadowy like trees, and on the whole silent, with numb brains and slow limbs and a great indifference.

This transcendental ecology, although it conflicts almost absurdly with elements in Lawrence's political fable, the personages of which show no trace of the 'aboriginal *sympathetic* apathy . . . the fern-dark indifference' frequently attributed to them, is certainly not less impressive if one happens to know Australia. And the larger ethos of colonial society Lawrence seems to have grasped with uncanny speed and precision. His picture is blurred only by what he projects upon it from the world of his own private preoccupations. Yet these preoccupations cannot be regarded merely as inept intrusions upon a superb travel-book. For they are dealt with in *Kangaroo* with a force and coherence far outweighing the implausibility, within its local setting, of the action which he contrives for their dramatic embodiment.

The preoccupations carry straight on from *Aaron's Rod*, and so, virtually, do the most important characters. Rawdon Lilly has become Richard Lovat Somers, and to the great advantage of the book's clarity he has swallowed Aaron Sisson in the process. Lilly's wife, now Harriet Somers, has advanced into the foreground, and her stature has immensely increased now that she is frankly Frieda Lawrence. The perfectly straight autobiographical quality of *Kangaroo*, which is tempered only by the political fantasy, works entirely to its advantage, and only an extremely pedantic literary criticism could insist that we should read the novel in stern disregard of its context in Lawrence's actual life. Its great triumph as art—apart from the descriptive power already illustrated—lies in the objectivity and humour brought to the character of Somers. It is astonishing that a man possessed by the insane intensities to which Lawrence admits, constantly prone to finding himself 'in a seethe of steady fury, general rage . . . like a woman who is with child by a corrosive fiend', should in fiction hold with so unfaltering a hand the just balance between the world and himself. The note is struck with certainty from the first. Somers, inconsequently landed in a Sydney suburb—'the long street, like a child's drawing, the little square bungalows dot-dot-dot, close together and yet apart, like modern democracy'—and neither happy nor pretending that he is; Somers, tackled by wary but matey neighbours and 'twisting sour smiles of graciousness on his pale, bearded face'; Somers simply starting 'with a rabid desire not to see anything and not to speak one single word to any single body': this and much else gives a portrait of the reluctant traveller that has all the simple fun of Smollett. Somers's attitude is in direct contrast to Harriet's. He starts by hanging back and then gets mixed in. She starts with a gay acceptance of casual acquaintanceship, but remains at bottom remote from, and even hostile to, people whose deep commonness is alien to her. The commonness is for Somers—although indeed he rails against it—one of the emerging charms of the Australian scene. Amid it he is himself superior—a gentleman, we are several times told—yet generously acknowledging himself as also sprung from the people. Particularly grateful to him in the context of his grand problem of dominance in marriage is the colonial relegation of women—not to the nursery indeed, for his neighbour Jack Callcott has the same high-minded determination as himself not to bring children into this inadequate world, but to the kitchen. There is political talk and 'the women seem almost effaced'. At the end they may come 'running in with the sweets, to see if the men didn't want a macaroon'. Yet it is precisely in the man-and-woman relationship that Lawrence exposes Somers to the most searing ridicule. Harriet will not believe in his political adventure or deliver herself over to it. And his esoteric appeals to the altar of the great Hermes, 'the mystery and the lordship of . . . the forward-seeking male' and the like, are met with devastating deflation:

Him, a lord and master! Why, he was not really lord of his own bread and butter; next year they might both be starving. . . . He was so isolated he was hardly a man at all, among men. He had absolutely nothing but her. Among men he was like some unbelievable creature—an emu, for example. Like an emu in the streets or in a railway carriage.

This is faithful, and so is the whole implicit acknowledgement of the absurdity inherent in voluble demands for a deep and wordless submission to the dark priority of the male. Yet here lies the deadly serious topic of the book. Lawrence–Birkin began with the sufficiency of 'ultimate' marriage, and added to it a sense which was no more than marginal and uneasy of the need of some further relationship with a man, and perhaps with a group of disciples or sympathists. Lawrence–Lilly got no further than an intensified feeling of this, with the marriage become distanced and a little uncertain, and the man-and-man relationship advanced into the foreground. Now with Lawrence–Somers the marriage is to the fore again and enduring stiff tests. The man-and-man relationship, although still holding much of its ambiguous quasi-homosexual quality, is generalizing itself into the problem of a man's work among his fellows. But it is this problem that has to be squared with marriage rather than the other way round. Somers's demand for autonomous male activity betrays in its very insistence upon being 'beyond woman' that its dynamism resides in a craving for improved marital status. It has often been remarked how odd is Lawrence's apparent ignoring of the bearing upon the marriage problems he presents of the almost functionless life to which his representative wives are condemned. The narrative will state that Harriet becomes discontented, but no regard is paid to the fact that she has nothing to do except pack and unpack 'a few shawls and cushion-covers and bits of interesting brass or china'. Less frequently noted is the very similar position of Lawrence's representative husbands. Somers, we are told, writes poems, and essays on democracy and kindred topics. But his poems are certainly not dwelt upon, and there is little suggestion that his political interests are informed by serious study or systematic thought. When he converses on such subjects it is in the main equivocally, and with an evident concern less for the issue than for not giving himself away. What of Lawrence has vanished out of Somers, then, is the genius and a power of absorbed and all-absorbing labour such as produced in the space of six weeks a book like *Kangaroo*. Clearly Lawrence feels himself to be legislating not merely for exceptional individuals, and is playing down those aspects of himself which, if obtruded, would present us far too much with the effect of a special case. But, beyond this, there is his essentially unwise and unrealistic persuasion that intimate problems of human relationship are best tackled on a cleared stage. In a way, this is no more than a convention taken over by Lawrence from a kind of highly evolved psychological fiction with which, in general, he had little sympathy. But it means that when work in the world is due to make some sort of symbolical appearance on that stage, it is apt to do so in the guise of something like mere fantasy.

What is fantasy in *Kangaroo* is Somers's finding himself, hard upon arrival in Australia, in demand as a potential leader of contending political movements. His neighbour Jack Callcott, a motor mechanic, proves to be an officer in the Diggers, an imaginary fascist organization which Lawrence has brought in his luggage from Aaron Sisson's Italy. Callcott, who underneath his easy-going Australian regardlessness is a fanatic, is soon embracing Somers with embarrassing fervour. ' "I knew", he said in a broken voice, "that we was mates".' Somers's response is equivocal. He is aware that he will 'never be pals with any man' but at the same time he is attracted. It is as if 'one blood ran warm and rich between them'. He is introduced by Callcott to the leader of the Digger movement, the lawyer Ben Cooley, who goes by the name of Kangaroo. Kangaroo makes a series of mountingly intense appeals for Somers's help, the last of them being from his deathbed after he has been shot in a riot. But these appeals are made always in the name of love. And Somers, amid all his mental confusion, is quite clear that this is wrong. Even when caught to Kangaroo's breast, even although acknowledging a desire to touch him physically, Somers knows that love has become the wrong approach alike to personal and to political relationships. It is a 'white octopus' from which he must free himself. He says that he cannot love Kangaroo. And Kangaroo dies.

Apart from a certain undesigned repulsiveness, Kangaroo has no reality. He is a cock-shy in whom it is intended to embody that theory of willed benevolence as a guiding principle in life which was Lawrence's only notion of Christianity as an historical force. In Somers's resistance, we are back with Lilly's assertion in *Aaron's Rod*: the love-mode is exhausted and the power-mode must be sought and obeyed. This seeking for a radically new source of power Somers calls, again and again, the search for his own Dark God. There is an important statement of the idea in one of his discussions with Kangaroo:

'It means an end of us and what we are, in the first place. And then a re-entry into us of the Great God, who enters us from below, not from above . . . not through the spirit. Enters us from the lower self, the dark self, the phallic self, if you like.'

'Enters us from the phallic self?' snapped Kangaroo sharply.

'Sacredly. The god you can never see or visualise, who stands dark on the threshold of the phallic me.'

'The phallic you, my dear young friend, what is that but love?' Richard shook his head in silence.

'No', he said, in a slow, remote voice. 'I know your love, Kangaroo. Working everything from the spirit, from the head. You work the lower self as an instrument of the spirit. Now it is time for the spirit to leave us again; it is time for the Son of Man to depart, and leave us dark, in front of the unspoken God: who is just beyond the dark threshold of the lower self, my lower self.'

This proposal is to become important in the next novel. Taken in isolation, it seems incoherent and even childish—and when we immediately go on to read that 'in the sacred dark men meet and touch, and it is a great communion' we realize how much of Lawrence's chthonic symbolism comes from the mind of the Eastwood boy who was insufficiently robust for the man's life in the pit. But hard upon these—as we may feel—false profundities, Lawrence is always able to surprise us with magnificence, particularly when he carries Somers away from such colloquies and implicates his resulting mood with a natural scene:

These days Somers, too, was filled with fury. As for loving mankind, or having a fire of love in his heart, it was all rot. He felt almost fierily cold. He liked the sea, the pale sea of green glass that fell in such cold foam. Ice-fiery, fish-burning. He went out on to the low flat rocks at low tide, skirting the deep pock-holes that were full of brilliantly clear water and delicately coloured shells and tiny, crimson anemones. Strangely sea-scooped sharp sea-bitter rock-floor, all wet and sea-savage.

We may be reminded of Stephen Dedalus on his beach—except that here is a meditation entirely without reliance on the bookish. It continues:

And standing at the edge looking at the waves rather terrifying rolling at him, where he stood low and exposed, far out from the sand-banks, and as he watched the gannets gleaming white, then falling with a splash like white sky-arrows into the waves, he wished as he had never wished before that he could be cold, as sea-things are cold, and murderously fierce. To have oneself exultantly ice-cold, not one spark of this wretched warm flesh left, and to have all the terrific, icy energy of a fish. To surge with that cold exultance and passion of a sea thing! . . . To be an isolated swift fish in the big seas, that are bigger than the earth; fierce with cold, cold life, in the watery twilight before sympathy was created to clog us. . . .

Who sets a limit to what a man is? Man is also a fierce and fish-cold devil, in his hour, filled with cold fury of desire to get away from the cloy of human life altogether, not into death, but into that icily self-sufficient vigour of a fish.

Excerpted, such passages are apt to seem fish out of water. Even so, they represent writing utterly beyond any merely prosaic novelist's capacity.

The rejection of Kangaroo declares the need to formulate, out of Somers's or Lawrence's deepest consciousness, something tantamount to a new religion. Somers shrinks from the effort. 'He tried to think of the dark God he declared he served. But he didn't want to.' 'The fair morning seaward world, full of bubbles of life' distracts him. Nevertheless the compulsion is there, and it is closely involved with the theme, now absorbing in the spheres alike of married and of public life, of power and authority. The source of a man's power is his dark God; he will have more or less of natural authority according to the extent of his revelation. It is thus that Somers comes uncompromisingly to condemn democracy, conceived as the expression of egalitarian thought. Men are not brothers; they are leaders and led. To Somers this comes with the force of 'a new fact'. 'All his life he had cherished a beloved ideal of friendship—David and Jonathan.' Now, when this seems actually to offer itself, he no longer wants it. 'Not mates and equality and mingling. Not blood-brotherhood. None of that.' From the Birkin who baffled Gerald Crich with proposals for a sacramental blood-mingling, this is indeed a change. And what is to succeed is still unsure. 'He did not know. Perhaps the thing that the dark races know: that one can still feel in India: the mystery of lordship.'

'Lordship' undoubtedly attracted Lawrence. Yet he is less concerned with the attempt to exercise power than with dis-

tinguishing the sources of it. Somers's strife with Harriet arises
not merely from his turning 'away from their personal human
life of intimacy to this impersonal business of male activity'
and not merely from his further conviction that in this 'one
quality of ultimate maker and breaker' he should be 'woman-
less'. Harriet indeed wants 'to share, to join in, not to be left
out lonely'. But her abundant ridicule, which leaves her at
times just short of being a shrew, proves that her discontent
and impatience proceed less from his wanting to make and
break than from her clear perception that making and breaking
are in fact beyond him. Somers realizes this. It is all very well
to sit drinking beer with an Australian mechanic in a little 'dog-
kennelly' bungalow, solemnly agreeing on the just exclusion of
women from politics. But it is sadly unimpressive, and Harriet
knows it. She would concur in the real thing. 'But she was not,
if she could help it, going to have him setting off on a trip that
led nowhere.' She can believe in his 'personal being', but not at
all in 'the impersonal man, the man that would go beyond'.
Somers as he is lacks the virtue to go beyond. And he concludes that that virtue is something that he, and the world
with him, must gain from a new sort of 'God-passion' yet to
be realized:

Before mankind would accept any man for a king, and before
Harriet would ever accept him, Richard Lovat, as a lord and master,
he, this self-same Richard who was so strong on kingship, must open
the doors of his soul and let in a dark Lord and Master for himself,
the dark god he had sensed outside the door. Let him once truly
submit to the dark majesty, break open his doors to this fearful
god who is master, and enters us from below, the lower doors; let
him once admit a Master, the unspeakable god: and the rest would
happen.

In *Kangaroo* the true face of this Master is not revealed to us,
because it is not revealed to Somers or to Lawrence. One or two
negatives are clear: 'This time not a God scribbling on tablets
of stone or bronze. No everlasting decalogues. No sermons on
mounts, either.' But the positive lineaments remain in the
darkness to which they appear to belong: 'the great dark God,
the ithyphallic, of the first dark religions'.

This announces the coming theme. Lawrence–Somers,
although he 'won't give up the flag of our real civilised consciousness', sets sail for the United States, 'a country that did

not attract him at all, but which seemed to lie next in his line
of destiny'. At least there lay New Mexico; and, beyond that,
Mexico itself. In default of an Egypt of the Pharaohs—which
Lawrence for some reason appears to have regarded as particularly promising, but which had unfortunately not survived for
his inspection—there was the Taos of Mabel Dodge Sterne, that
wealthy correspondent, and protectress of Indians among whom
some sort of approximation to Aztec and similar observances
was said to survive. This hopeful terrain was achieved on 11 September 1922. It was to provide Lawrence with the material for
a novel, a number of short stories, and the most powerfully
evocative of his descriptive books, *Mornings in Mexico* (1927).

7

The Plumed Serpent (1926) may be regarded as Lawrence's
characteristic contribution to the myth of Atlantis; it sets out
to assert the existence of a long-buried wisdom the recovering
of which must marvellously mend the world. At the same time
the intuitive feeling that it is in some larger and deeper communion with the life of the cosmos that salvation lies is given
a new explicitness—and indeed a full ritual embodiment—in
a book which retains familiar features enough: large reliance
upon natural description and upon minor characters sketched
in from acquaintances of the moment. Among the major
characters there is a change of plan. Lawrence himself withdraws a little into the background. And in the foreground we
find somebody very like Lawrence's wife.

Kate Leslie is a mature woman of good family, a divorcée
whose second husband, now for some time dead, was a distinguished Irish rebel. At home she has children of whom she
sometimes thinks with longing, but an inner compulsion or
sense of quest compels her to travel, and even to linger in places
which she finds uncongenial. If she is not a wholly coherent
character it is perhaps because something of Lawrence himself
does after all lurk in her. Sane, generous, humorous, and with
all the makings of a first-rate recording intelligence, she has
moments in which she 'snarls' and 'jeers', is tactless or down-
right rude, and allows her sense of the deadness of Europe to
drive her to Swift-like extremes of hatred. Life, she says, is
a louse lying on its back and kicking; the longer she lives the

more loathsome the human spirit becomes to her; she finds all
personal contacts disgusting; Mexico drives her to a furious
rage. Even in the earlier part of the book she reveals herself as
an apter pupil of D. H. Lawrence than Frieda Lawrence ever
was. This appears in some fine inconsistencies. 'With Joachim'
—Kate says of her second husband—'I came to realise that a
woman like me *can* only love a man who is fighting to *change*
the world.' But later she makes it clear that Joachim's belief
that something useful can be done on the political plane appears
to her puerile, since 'liberty is a rotten old wine-skin'. One
should lead one's own life while letting 'the beastly world of
man come to an end'—a sentiment in which she would have
found support from Rupert Birkin. 'In her vague woman's way'
she has realized that even the gods must be born again, that
unknown gods are needed to put the magic back into life. She
appears even to have done some preliminary reading in order
to facilitate her entry into the action and atmosphere of the
story. The Mexican Indians, she realizes, 'want to be able to
breathe the Great Breath' and are aware that 'behind the
fierce sun the dark eyes of a deeper sun are watching'—perceptions at which she could hardly have arrived without the help
of Mme Blavatsky. Much of this is useful as in part credibi-
lizing the ensuing events. But the initial strength of the novel
lies largely in what Frieda Lawrence has given it, and much of
its later weakness lies in Kate's consenting to be bent to purposes which Frieda would certainly have held out against.

The Mexico to which Kate Leslie comes is in a state of
degeneration and near-chaos. The prime corrupting factor lies
in 'a profound unbelief that was fatal and demonish'. In Central
America Christianity is without virtue. Its rituals, instead of
bracing and enhancing life, merely make men relaxed and
sloppy. The bullfight upon which the book opens symbolizes
the decay of the numinous—for a bullfight is the dead and revolting husk of something once sacred and awful. This Mexico,
'with its great underdrift of squalor and heavy reptile-like evil',
Kate is resolving to get away from, when she is brought into
contact with, and fascinated by, a man who has diagnosed the
evil and is planning a remedy.

Don Ramón Carrasco has certainly been a student of
Lawrence:

It was borne in upon him that the world had gone as far as it could go in the good, gentle, and loving direction, and that anything further in that line meant perversity. So the time had come for the slow, great change to something else—what, he didn't know.

Actually, the change is to come not all that slowly, and Don Ramón does know. Christianity must go, and in its place must be set up a pantheon of the old gods of Mexico, presided over by Quetzalcoatl, the Plumed Serpent. Ramón himself is to be the First Man of Quetzalcoatl, or perhaps the actual fresh manifestation of the God. Already he has disciples who emerge impressively out of lakes, distribute religious tracts and hymn-sheets, announce at tea-parties that it is time for Jesus to go back to the place of the death of the gods, or perform upon drums in an atavic manner in villages. Too long the Indian consciousness has been 'swamped under the stagnant water of the white man's Dead Sea consciousness'. Now it is to be revived, amid a profusion of archaistic ritual, for Indian and white man alike. There are places in which Ramón talks impressively of what he wants, or in which the Men of Quetzalcoatl contrive imaginatively striking demonstrations. But from the first we are likely to feel that a shadow as of mummers and morris-dancing hangs over the revivalists. Ramón specializes in gnomic utterance from which it is sometimes difficult to extract meaning. 'Fourfold is man', he pronounces solemnly. 'But the star is one star. And one man is but one star.' Since he believes that 'the more you save these people from poverty and ignorance, the quicker they will die', he cannot have any economic or educational programme. When, by force of arms or the connivance of the government of the day, he has substituted his idols and their attendant rituals for Christian images and services in some churches, his movement faces a crisis. It has either to decline upon mere poeticizing or to take seriously a primitive religion the gods of which were in fact cruel and blood-soaked beyond most.

That a woman like Kate Leslie should be fascinated by a venture so bizarre as Ramón's is likely enough. That she should involve herself in it believingly is, on the other hand, as unlikely as could be. But here we come upon another character, General Viedma, commonly called Don Cipriano. If Ramón is Lawrence as leader and prophet, Cipriano is Lawrence as master of the darkest wisdom of sex. All the signs assimilate him to this role. He is a pure Indian and thus authentically primitive and of the 'Pan world'. But he has been, oddly enough, to Oxford and has thus a cultivated status which he is content to renounce. 'His education lay like a film of white oil on the black lake of his barbarian consciousness. For this reason, the things he said were hardly interesting at all. Only what he *was*.' He is a 'curious little man, with his odd, inflammable *hauteur* and conceit, something burning inside him, that gave him no peace'. This eminently Laurentian *persona* becomes, in his fashion, fascinated by Kate. And Kate is fascinated by him. Living, even if still misdoubtingly, in the ambience of the Quetzalcoatl imagery, which is nothing if not insistently and heavily phallic, she comes to see in him the mystery of primeval sex and a compelling otherness. 'She could see how different his blood was from hers, dark, blackish, like the blood of lizards among hot black rocks. . . . He was so still, so unnoticing, and the darkness of the nape of his neck was so like invisibility.' Kate is drawn on towards accepting—even accepting a place in—the new pantheon largely through the spell which Cipriano casts upon her. But here there is another factor. Cipriano is Ramón's man, bound to his leader by a bond in the highest degree mystical and impressive. In *The Plumed Serpent*, in fact, the man-and-man relationship is present as an achieved thing at the start, and heterosexual relationship comes in only later and as its complement. This reverses the emphasis of earlier books. Kate has to take it, assuring herself that 'the highest thing this country might produce would be some powerful relationship of man to man'. Those curiously ambiguous physical contacts between men which begin with the bathing episode in *The White Peacock* have their culmination in *The Plumed Serpent*, where Ramón ties up and paws the naked Cipriano to the accompaniment of a great deal of mumbo-jumbo which points rather than masks the pathological basis of the incident. For all Kate's prominence, this is designed as a man-centred book. 'So hear now, you men, and you women of these men', one of Quetzalcoatl's messengers declaims in a market-place. It is part of the status that Kate has to accept.

She marries Cipriano—who has now assumed divinity as Huitzilopochtli—and the ceremony is performed by Ramón as Quetzalcoatl, with abundant recourse to a pseudo-biblical patter presumably invented for the occasion. The marriage appears to be consummated, however—although with Lawrence one can never be sure, so equivocal is his writing—only after a later and striking ceremony. The church previously despoiled of its Christian associations is reopened for the purpose of the new religion, and here Cipriano appears naked, painted in horizontal bars of red and black, with a thin green line running from his mouth and a yellow band from his eyes. Several traitors to the cult are put to death, Cipriano himself stabbing three of them and delivering the bodies to Ramón in order that their blood may be sprinkled on a sacred fire. Cipriano indeed has already taken to personal butchery, but so far, although accompanied by religious allocutions, this has been more in the ordinary way of a Mexican general's business. Kate, having witnessed these more impressive human sacrifices, has gone back to her house 'gloomy and uneasy'. Cipriano follows her as soon as the proceedings are concluded, persuades her to say solemnly that she is the goddess Malintzi, the bride of the living Huitzilopochtli, leads her back to the church, and there possesses her among the idols. 'What do I care if he kills people?' Kate asks herself hard upon this experience. 'His flame is young and clean. He is Huitzilopochtli, and I am Malintzi.'

What is happening to Kate is the more disconcerting in that her creator appears to be unaware of it. The most brutal part of the book—more brutal than the ritual executions—concerns Ramón's wife Carlota, and here Kate is represented as astonishingly insensitive. Carlota, being a devout Catholic absorbed in charitable labours, is horrified by her husband's actions. He in turn is opposed to her charities: 'against her work and against her flow he was in silent, heavy, unchanging opposition.' Carlota, like Hermione Roddice in *Women in Love*, is the type of woman—giving always willed, spiritual love, but incapable of giving herself—against whom bitter sexual anger is invariably directed in Lawrence, and her husband treats her to the same sort of savage analysis that Hermione receives at the hands of Birkin:

> I don't like the love you have for your god: it is an assertion of your own will. I don't like the love you have for me: it is the same. I don't like the love you have for your children. If ever I see in them a spark of desire to be saved from it, I shall do my best to save them.

Carlota's charity is called 'that cruel kindness', and the book's judgement against her appears to be absolute. 'Life', we are

told, 'had done its work on one more human being, quenched
the spontaneous life and left only the will.' At the end of a long
interview between them her husband simply dismisses her with
contempt. He rises and points to the door. ' "Go away", he
said in a low tone, "Go away! I have smelt the smell of your
spirit long enough".' Later, when the desecrated church is
being reopened for the rites of Quetzalcoatl, Carlota makes
a dramatic appearance, beseeching Christ to take her husband's
life now and save his soul. Ramón, dressed up as the god, says
only that the Omnipotent is with him and he serves Omnipo-
tence. Carlota falls down in a convulsion from which she is not
to recover:

> Not a muscle of his face moved. And Kate could see that his heart
> had died in its connection with Carlota, his heart was quite, quite
> dead in him; out of the deathly vacancy he watched his wife. Only
> his brows frowned a little, from his smooth, male forehead. His old
> connections were broken. She could hear him say: *There is no star
> between me and Carlota.*—And how terribly true it was!

This scene too, we learn, makes Kate 'uneasy'. But before
following the dying woman from the church, she 'lingers' to
hear the end of Ramón's recitation of Quetzalcoatl's latest
hymn. The climax of this episode is yet to come. Cipriano
presents himself at Carlota's bedside and reviles her:

> You are glad you kept back the wine of your body and the secret
> oil of your soul? That you gave only the water of your charity? I tell
> you the water of charity, the hissing water of the spirit is bitter at last
> in the mouth and in the breast and in the belly, it puts out the fire.

Carlota calls out successively for the sacrament and for her
children. Cipriano responds each time with frantic vituperation,
ending with the command, 'You stale virgin . . . die and be
a thousand times dead! Do nothing but utterly die!' During
this strange scene, we are told, Kate 'sat by the window, and
laughed a little'. The whole experience does her good. She
departs from it across the lake with Cipriano, who feels 'the
mysterious flower of her woman's femaleness slowly opening to
him. . . . The hardness of self-will was gone.' As for Ramón, he
attends his wife's funeral 'in his white clothes and big hat with
the Quetzalcoatl sign'. Then he marries a young girl who adores
him, and it is the spectacle of this marriage that completes
Kate's education. Regressing or as yet not fully regenerate, she

a scriptural portentousness. In no other does he adopt quite so nagging a technique—as if in this way (to quote his description of the hymn-singing of the Men of Quetzalcoatl) 'by the slow monotony of repetition, the thing would drift darkly into the consciousness of the listeners'. It is significant that he can never quite bring himself to announce the definitive convincing of Kate. To the end she has revulsions in which she sees the religion of Quetzalcoatl and Huitzilopochtli as 'high-flown bunk' and prays to get 'back to simple human people'. But she is far less aware of the absurdity of the enterprise than of its hazardousness. It is not fantasy, because it is a trafficking with something that is really there to be trafficked with. It encourages a playing with the buried mind which may at any time release 'a sudden ferocity, a sudden lust of death rousing incalculable and terrible'. And principally she realizes that to embark on Ramón's experiment means 'a strange, marginless death of her individual self'. The old consciousness declares *The blood is one blood: we are one blood*—and this is a declaration that sweeps away all individualism. 'The blood of the individual is given back to the great blood-being, the god, the nation, the tribe.' Reading this, we feel suddenly close to the mystical and racial side of Hitler's National Socialism, so that it is without surprise that we learn on the following page of an inferior caste of men who 'are slaves, or . . . should be slaves'. Lawrence as a prophet of fascism has been much discussed. In fact, there can be not the slightest doubt that he would have viewed an achieved totalitarian system with horror; and it may well be that what mounted in him as he struggled with *The Plumed Serpent* was less scepticism than a growing apprehension that the dark gods were really there and that they were very much darker than he had reckoned with. That he is reported during his New Mexico period as sometimes giving the impression of insanity at least suggests the degree of his actual implication with his fable. We may suppose in the boy an unacknowledged ambition to go down the pit. But the pit he has now discovered is an abyss in which the individual consciousness of a man must go out for ever. And Lawrence pulls up. His next, his last hero is not small and dark and chthonic. He is large and red-faced and a gamekeeper. And he is famously far from believing that a woman must renounce the seething, frictional, ecstatic Aphrodite of the foam.

8

In his final major work, *Lady Chatterley's Lover* (1928), Lawrence returns to the industrial midlands of England for a setting.
But it is in more than this that we find ourselves back in the
world of *The Rainbow* and *Women in Love*. We are back with the
central theme of these books, unchequered by those subsidiary
absorptions which make them alike so rich and so bewildering.
The theme is sexual fulfilment as an absolute, and its near-
desuetude among us as the effective cause of the ills of modern
society. There is a vicious circle. Only men whose passional
lives are deprived and depraved could be guilty of the horrors
of industrialism, and these horrors make less feasible any attain-
ing by the individual of a healthy passional life. This is not
a field where Lawrence has doubts. By withdrawing and concentrating upon it he achieves a firm and rich novel even in
his phase of declining power.

Connie Reid has been brought up in a polite Bohemian world
in a way that has enabled her to enjoy healthy but unimportant
sexual experience among German students, and she has married
during the war Sir Clifford Chatterley, a mine-owner. After
a month's honeymoon Clifford returns to the front and is
severely wounded, so that he is crippled and rendered impo-
tent. He takes to authorship, and at first Connie loyally helps
him. Although wealthy, he is avid for success and morbidly
sensitive about his writing, which Connie's artist father declares authoritatively to have nothing in it. This story-writing
is scarcely in keeping with the character as it is developed, and
seems to be brought in largely for the sake of lampooning
literary and 'intellectual' society. Clifford's impotence is not
counterbalanced by any warmth of human feeling, but he nevertheless takes the continued validity of his marriage for granted.
He seriously debates with Connie the advisability of her having
a child by some other man in order to provide an heir for the
estate. When she is restless, 'he thought that all that ailed Connie
was that she did not have a baby, automatically bring one
forth, so to speak'. He gives up his story-writing and takes to
managing his mines, quickly becoming fascinated by 'the almost
uncanny cleverness of the modern technical mind'. Connie
finds this terrifying:

But now that Clifford was drifting off to this other weirdness of

industrial activity, becoming almost a *creature*, with a hard, efficient
shell of an exterior and a pulpy interior, one of the amazing crabs
and lobsters of the modern, industrial and financial world, inverte-
brates of the crustacean order, with shells of steel, like machines,
and inner bodies of soft pulp, Connie herself was really completely
stranded.

So she admits a lover. Unfortunately he is just another clever
literary man, and the affair is not a success. Then she becomes
aware of Mellors, Clifford's gamekeeper. She is quickly his
mistress and deeply satisfied. The relationship has its internal
stresses, and raises formidable social difficulties. But the passion generated is irresistible, and the book ends with the lovers
looking forward to permanent union. Clifford degenerates. His
chief cause of grievance is Connie's having connected herself
with one of the lower orders. But he himself has become
emotionally dependent on a middle-aged village woman hired
to tend him. He ends by placing himself in a perversely infantile
relationship to her, even while continuing a master of industry.

It is in the character of Mellors and in the gospel to which he
makes Connie an adherent that the core of the book consists.
There is the same sort of social ambiguity about Mellors as
there is about his remote but authentic ancestor Annable in
The White Peacock. He has had considerable education and even
his phase as a gentleman, since he gained a commission in
India during the war. But the upper classes have disgusted
him, and of his own choice he has returned to the people, who
turn out to be disgusting too. He is solitary and embittered,
horrified by the modern social order and afraid of it, but yet
more horrified and afraid before the memory of his own searing
sexual history. ('You do seem to have had awful experiences of
women', Connie says.) He is living separated from a brutal wife,
and his recollections of his marriage are entirely and obsessively
of its failure as a carnal relationship. In his secluded cottage
he reads books on a wide variety of topics, but his mind scarcely
exists—he certainly refuses to show it existing—except as brooding upon the success or failure of sexual acts. He might be called
the phallic consciousness incarnate—and by 'phallic' (now
more than ever a key word) as opposed to 'sexual' Lawrence
would apparently distinguish passion in its most radical operation, divorced from all those superficial allures which prompt
civilized men to regard one woman rather than another as

desirable. And to 'phallic' Lawrence regularly joins, both in the novel itself and in his references to it, the other keyword 'tenderness'. 'The new relationship', he had assured a correspondent with reference to the drift of the world at large, 'will be some sort of tenderness, sensitive, between men and men and men and women, and not the one up one down, lead on I follow, *ich dien* sort of business'—this last being a cheerful farewell, such as would surely make Rawdon Lilly turn pale, to the 'leader-cum-follower relationship'.

'Tenderness' may be said to be operative in Mellors's first effective encounter with Connie, since we are told that 'compassion flamed in his bowels' at the mere sight of her forlorn condition. But thereafter the conception seems to exist as a very narrow one. 'I believe in being warm-hearted. I believe especially in being warm-hearted in love', he says—and adds something making precisely clear what connotation 'in love' has here to bear. Nor does the more general of these statements come with much conviction in its context. 'I love thee that I can go into thee', he says—and always does his best not to say or imply more than this. Thus, when Connie asks him if he loves her, he replies, 'Dunna ax me nowt now. . . . Let me be. I like thee. I luv thee when tha lies theer. A woman's a lovely thing when——' and there follows a phrase in which the 'when' is again precisely circumscribed and defined. This is the sum-total of Mellors's philosophy, except indeed that he has fits of muttering darkly about the coming disastrousness of things in general:

'There's black days ahead.'

'No!' she protested, clinging to him. 'Why? Why?'

'There's black days coming for us all and for everybody', he repeated with a prophetic gloom.

Mellors is rarely more conversible than this. He guards his privacy so jealously that we almost feel it to be unfair when his creator betrays to us the existence in him of a train of articulate reflection:

It was not woman's fault, nor even love's fault, nor the fault of sex. The fault lay there, out there, in those evil electric lights and diabolical rattlings of engines. There, in the world of the mechanical greedy, greedy mechanism and mechanised greed, sparkling with lights and gushing hot metal and roaring with traffic, there lay the vast evil thing, ready to destroy whatever did not conform.

Mellors believes that in some way he will be hounded down. 'I'm afraid', he tells Connie. 'I'm afraid o' things. . . . Everybody! The lot of 'em.' He laments that he cannot find 'other men to be with . . . to fight side by side with', and he is deeply withdrawn into his bitter privacy when Connie first meets him. His attempts to cling to this, his reluctance to lower his defences again before a woman, have an important effect on the book's atmosphere. Without them, he would be in danger of appearing a mere figure of lurking lust, taking the lady when she offers. As it is, we are sometimes only skirting this. 'It puzzled her, his queer, persistent wanting her, when there was nothing between them, when he never really spoke to her.' Connie's puzzlement might seem naïve. And Mellors certainly runs silence hard. Cipriano in *The Plumed Serpent* pretty well stopped talking to Kate when he married her. It is likely that Mellors will do the same. He seems to believe that there is something impossible or at least indecent in the maintenance of a personal relationship with a man or woman who stands to one in the intensely impersonal relationship of sex.

Mellors's innate melancholy does not permit him readily to project out upon the world anything of the warmth and joy which he experiences at the phallic level. It seems to him 'a wrong and bitter thing to do, to bring a child into this world'. We may be unimpressed by connubial raptures that knit with this conclusion, and judge more sympathetic the simpler Connie, who both finds it 'warm and fulfilling somehow to have a baby' and projects her own reborn condition out upon the world at once. Thus, when Clifford reads to her from some pretentious philosophical work, and, on her being unimpressed, supposes 'a woman doesn't take a supreme pleasure in the life of the mind', she declares, like Lawrence long ago, her belief that the life of the mind is a lesser reality than the life of the body:

He looked at her in wonder.
'The life of the body', he said, 'is just the life of the animals.'
'And that's better than the life of professorial corpses. But it's not true! The human body is only just coming to real life. With the Greeks it gave a lovely flicker, then Plato and Aristotle killed it, and Jesus finished it off. But now the body is coming really to life, it is really rising from the tomb. And it will be a lovely, lovely life in the lovely universe, the life of the human body.'

This passage, which has interest as pointing forward to Lawrence's final important prose achievement, 'The Man Who Died', characteristically gives to a woman character what is most positive and confident in relation to the outer world. Many of Lawrence's men are fanatical believers in this or that, but nearly all are bodeful and pessimistic alike about humanity and their own chances within it. Under the influence of personal happiness his women take bolder views. They are often confident even amid wreckage, as Ursula Brangwen is when she sees the rainbow. Mellors certainly lacks any shadow of communal confidence. Almost on the last page he is left enunciating with gloomy relish that 'There's a bad time coming, boys, there's a bad time coming!' It is Connie who, having absorbed his philosophy, has to coax him into effective belief in it:

'Shall I tell you?' she said, looking into his face. 'Shall I tell you what you have that other men don't have, and that will make the future? Shall I tell you?'

'Tell me then,' he replied.

'It's the courage of your own tenderness, that's what it is: like when you put your hand on my tail and say I've got a pretty tail.'

The grin came flickering on his face.

'That!' he said.

Then he sat thinking.

'Ay!' he said. 'You're right. It's that really. It's that all the way through. I knew it with the men. I had to be in touch with them, physically, and not go back on it. . . . Sex is really only touch, the closest of all touch. And it's touch we're afraid of. We're only half-conscious, and half alive. We've got to come alive and aware. Especially the English have got to get into touch with one another, a bit delicate and a bit tender. It's our crying need.'

A book in which all salvation is thus brought to depend upon the delicacy of an intimate caress inevitably faced Lawrence with one acute problem, at once social, legal, and aesthetic. How was he to describe those sexual encounters in which ultimate mysteries were to be revealed? *The Rainbow* had run into trouble here, and in general he had made do, again and again, with a figurative language sufficiently imprecise to reassure publishers and printers. The effort had often been frenzied and the effect sometimes unfortunate, since the teasing obscurity of the proceedings at critical moments had the consequence of reducing the reader to the condition of a rather poorly catered-for *voyeur*. Lawrence's dealing with the problem now was direct and effective. He simply scrapped the possibility of any immediate normal publication and described in straightforward English whatever came in the way of his narrative—retreating upon his old manner only in the single instance of Mellors's having to vindicate the Laurentian faith in the salubrity of esoteric episodes in otherwise normal sexual relationships. Whether he showed sufficient artistic circumspection in calling (at a late stage in the book's composition) so heavily upon certain words never before brought into literary use is perhaps doubtful. But in general the consequence of the new straightforwardness is extremely happy. It has a bracing influence on the tone and style of the whole book, and has been admirably praised by Yeats in a letter to Olivia Shakespear:

Its description of the sexual act is more detailed than in [Frank] Harris, the language is sometimes that of cabmen and yet the book is all fire. Those two lovers, the gamekeeper and his employer's wife, each separated from their class by their love, and by fate, are poignant in their loneliness, and the coarse language of the one, accepted by both, becomes a forlorn poetry uniting their solitudes, something ancient, humble and terrible.

Lady Chatterley's Lover, despite its having gone through several rewritings, is a masterpiece of vigorous and spontaneous prose. Joyce called it 'lush'. But then *Work in Progress* prompted Lawrence to call Joyce himself 'a clumsy *olla putrida*'.

'Especially the English have got to get into touch with one another.' Partly because of his health and the inclement times of year at which he was inclined to turn up there, but much more because of ramifying personal intolerances, Lawrence in these later years found it impossible to reacclimatize himself in England. Yet *Lady Chatterley's Lover* has all his old control of the English scene. The long description in Chapter XI of Tevershall, the mining town outside which the Chatterleys' house lies, is one of his finest and fieriest pieces of writing, and equally good is the whole social excursus to which it leads. Germany, the Mediterranean, and Central America have sharpened his eyes to what his own race has made of his own country; and he seems to have gained both a clearer view of the English social structure and a more genuinely passionate concern about it. In *The Rainbow* this concern is a matter more of profession than of strong conviction, so that the book has to make an awkward return to the theme in its final paragraphs. In *Women in Love*, although Gerald Crich's damnation is industrial England's damnation, Lawrence has concentrated his entire imaginative power upon the analysis of private, if representative, relations. But in *Lady Chatterley's Lover*, despite the merely negative although sufficiently passionate regard which is all that Mellors can spare for the world around him, the action is felt as issuing from, and steadily conditioned by, a complex society which is masterfully grasped, examined, and judged in a manner sufficiently compatible with the artistic coherence of the whole work. *Lady Chatterley's Lover* first came into notice as a scandalous innovation in English fiction, and this reputation it continued for long to enjoy. But in fact it is essentially traditional, belonging to that second rank of significant English novels in which a too insistent didactic purpose impairs what remains nevertheless a commanding imaginative achievement. The immediate ancestor of *Lady Chatterley's Lover* is *Jude the Obscure*.

9

Some novelists use the short-story form as a painter uses his sketch-book: for the exploring, lightly and on a restricted scale, of themes and situations which may later receive extended treatment. Lawrence seldom, if ever, uses the short story in this way. Such a relationship as that between James's 'Madame de Mauves' and *The Portrait of a Lady* is not to be found in his work. His special power, that of giving dramatic embodiment to attitudes and perceptions which are becoming available only as the narrative proceeds, is found almost exclusively in the novels. The short stories are in general the work of a man who has made up his mind about the problems which his theme presents. He need argue neither with himself nor with us. He need seldom treat in terms of extraneous disquisition issues which are sufficiently digested to be immediately assimilable within the organic fiction. The best of the short stories are more unflawed artistic successes than any of the novels. But they are perhaps never the product of his most creative, because most intently questioning, imagination. It is an index alike of this strength and of this limitation in the short stories that Lawrence himself is seldom obtrusively present. Admittedly, if we possess a full knowledge of the man, we can relate a great deal in the stories to his personal history, and that not always to his advantage. But this is not the same thing as being conscious of the writer roaming free in his fiction—as we should certainly be before *Kangaroo*, for example, even if Lawrence's life were sealed to us.

Only a few of the most representative stories can be discussed. 'Daughters of the Vicar' belongs to the period of *The White Peacock* and *Sons and Lovers*. Like the first of these it is the story of a girl who is attracted to a young man of a class beneath her own. But whereas in *The White Peacock* there is an identification of the narrator with the middle-class point of view, and at the same time a slight sentimental falsification of the simpler world, 'Daughters of the Vicar' is at once unsparingly realistic all round and annihilatingly critical of such of the gentry as it takes within its view. The vicar, his wife, and son-in-law spell death as absolutely as does the socially pretentious girl who, in *Sons and Lovers*, brings destruction upon Paul's brother William. But the story is a product of class consciousness or prejudice only in the sense that Lawrence is convinced of the emotional etiolation and underlying crass materialism of what he takes to be representative upper-class society. As a story of the blighting effect exercised by snobbery and prudential consideration upon young lives brought within their grip, 'Daughters of the Vicar' is entirely traditional. Jane Austen herself (whom Lawrence is somewhere pleased to call 'the mean Jane Austen') might have recorded without censure the marriage of a penurious clergyman's daughter to a respectable rural character, and there is certainly much in the feeling of the story that is prompted by George Eliot and Hardy. Mr. Lindley, dragging on, 'pale and miserable and neutral', in his hostile or indifferent colliery parish; his wife, retreating from mortification and rage to a safe and unlovely invalidism; their elder daughter Mary, bringing herself, out of a sense of family responsibility, to marry the Casaubon-like Mr. Massy, strong in intellect and Christian duty, whose 'body was almost unthinkable': all these are in the main stream of English fiction, as are the pictures of vicarage ('Indoors the heavy pictures hung obscurely on the walls, everything was dingy with gloom') and cottage and season and natural scene. There is perhaps something new, something amounting almost to a new cruelty, in the uncompromisingness with which the plight and passion of the characters is seen—for example, Mr. Massy:

He was unremittingly shy, but perfect in his sense of duty: as far as he could conceive Christianity, he was a perfect Christian. Nothing that he realised he could do for anyone did he leave undone, although he was so incapable of coming into contact with another being that he could not proffer help. . . . His kindness almost frightened Miss Mary. She honoured it so, and yet she shrank from it. For, in it all Mr. Massy seemed to have no sense of any person, any human being whom he was helping: he only realised a kind of mathematical working out, solving of given situations, a calculated well-doing. And it was as if he had accepted the Christian tenets as axioms. His religion consisted in what his scrupulous, abstract mind approved of.

Watching Mr. Massy, Mary's younger sister Louisa 'felt a desire to put him out of existence'. Mary herself, even when 'in the grip of his moral, mental being', feels 'as if her body would rise and fling him aside'. 'His bent little shoulders and rather incomplete face . . . reminded her of an abortion. . . . She knew, vaguely, that she was murdering herself.' It is against this sufficiently persuasive background that Louisa forms her resolution to marry Alfred Durant, the young collier lately returned from the Navy, and that she boldly and beautifully reaches out to take him from across the social gulf they both feel. Their wooing gains poignancy from being set in close association with the death of Alfred's mother, between whom and her son there exists a special relationship which, although palpably imported from *Sons and Lovers*, constitutes an admirable counterpoise to the Lindley family relationships. The Lindleys show up perhaps altogether too badly at the end. But as a whole this story is unflawed, and it contains passages between Louisa and Alfred that no other English writer could approach.

Over against 'Daughters of the Vicar', with its perfect balance of human and social truth, may be set 'St. Mawr', the longest of the tales, and belonging to the period of *The Plumed Serpent*. Good critics have praised it highly, but to some readers it appears pervasively and startlingly false. The opening paragraphs, in which we meet Lou Carrington, have the uneasily jaunty tone that is always ominous in Lawrence. 'Of course she was American: Louisiana family, moved down to Texas.' She has an 'odd little *museau*', a 'quaint air of playing at being well-bred'. She belongs, if anywhere, 'in Rome, among the

artists and the Embassy people'. She has a wealthy mother, Mrs.
Witt, who possesses a 'queer democratic New Orleans sort of
conceit', a 'peculiar look of extreme New Orleans annoyance'
which comes (as does also a 'duskiness') round her 'sharp, well-
bred nose'. And she has as husband a play-boy amateur artist,
Rico, the son of an Australian government official who has
brought off the rather rare feat of becoming a baronet in that
Dominion. 'St. Mawr' is strewn with social solecisms so thickly
as to suggest not so much carelessness and lack of information
as a determination to be awkward. And there is much that is
absurd in the story itself. Lou presents Rico, who is an indifferent
rider, with a dangerous stallion, St. Mawr. Rico rides St. Mawr
in Rotten Row, where Mrs. Witt expresses her contempt alike
of the young man and her environment in general by there
provoking what might be a dangerous accident. Later Rico is
in fact badly injured by St. Mawr, and Lou, who with some
reasonableness prefers St. Mawr to Rico, sends her well-bred
New Orleans mother, during her husband's convalescence, a
series of letters which would do credit to the pen of a spiteful
kitchenmaid. Mrs. Witt, somewhat in the spirit of Mable Dodge
Sterne with Mr. Tony Luhan, makes a proposal of marriage to
her Welsh groom, an entirely improbable character of osten-
tatious racial remoteness. But her application, unlike Mrs.
Sterne's, is unsuccessful, and she and Lou depart for the American South-West. The story closes with Lou's finding deep spiritual satisfaction on what is in fact Lawrence's ranch at Taos.
The natural description which is here brought massively in
makes one of the finest sustained passages that Lawrence ever
achieved.

'St. Mawr' was clearly written in a black period. The symbolism of the stallion is sultry and over-weighted, and there are
long passages of inconsequent near-raving. Lawrence is writing
badly because writing in the absence of any flow of sympathetic
consciousness. Rico is a mere Aunt Sally. Lou, whether deliberately or not, is made almost equally detestable. Mrs. Witt
is basically horrifying and intended to be just that. The whole
tale, which reads much like parody of Lawrence, reads, too,
like something inspired by the fourth book of *Gulliver's Travels*.
St. Mawr himself is offered to us as our only opportunity of
positive response, and in this the creature is given a good deal
too much to carry:

And as he stood there a few yards away from her, his head lifted
and wary, his body full of power and tension, his face slightly averted
from her, she felt a great animal sadness come from him. A strange
animal atmosphere of sadness, that was vague and disseminated
through the air, and made her feel as though she breathed grief.
She breathed it into her breast, as if it were a great sigh down the
ages, that passed into her breast. And she felt a great woe: the woe of
human unworthiness. The race of men judged in the consciousness of
the animals they have subdued, and there found unworthy, ignoble.

Ignoble men, unworthy of the animals they have subjugated, bred
the woe in the spirit of their creatures. St. Mawr, that bright horse,
one of the kings of creation in the order below man, it had been a
fulfilment for him to serve the brave, reckless, perhaps cruel men of
the past. . . .

But now where is the flame of dangerous, forward-pressing nobility
in men? Dead, dead, guttering out in a stink of self-sacrifice whose
feeble light is a light of exhaustion and *laissez-faire*.

And the horse, is he to go on carrying man forward into this?—
this gutter?

No!

The reader, being in his senses, knows that this is nonsense.
Nor does he feel in either Lou or her mother any quality or
achievement at all entitling them to be quite so scornful of their
fellow human beings as they pervasively are. They have willingly
involved themselves with a frivolous society, largely without
social function, and they cannot reasonably complain of a lack
of nobility, bravery, recklessness, or even cruelty around them.
'English village life, with squire and dean in the background',
may be as false and corrupt as Mrs. Witt emphatically declares
it to be, and may further have been of no manner of use to
Lawrence. Yet artistically disposed baronets from Melbourne
and women with well-bred New Orleans noses were of very
little use to him either. 'St. Mawr' makes one feel that both
Lawrence's character and art were apt to deteriorate when his
acquaintance was preponderantly among unstable and deraci-
nated persons.

It is nevertheless not quite true, as a rapid survey of his work
as a whole might tempt us to hazard, that his writing invariably
loses its quality where it fails to keep substantial contact with
the world of his own earlier environment. Some of the most
successful of the short stories—notably 'The White Stocking'
and 'Odour of Chrysanthemums'—keep entirely within that

world. But what is perhaps the best of them all, 'The Captain's Doll', must be called an entirely upper-class story. Lawrence does, however, always seem to need something in the disposition or social situation of his leading characters to which his own response can be warm and positive. In 'St. Mawr' the landscape of Texas or New Mexico, if only because of its complete inconsequence, is an inadequate substitute for anything of the sort. Lawrence's finest scrutiny of life is always marked by reverence, and he is lost when he allows himself insufficient scope for it.

'The Captain's Doll' is as uncompromisingly Laurentian a fable as 'St. Mawr'. But it is good-tempered where 'St. Mawr' is bad-tempered. And what is extreme in its doctrine is so bound up with insights that validate themselves as we read, and is further given so brilliant a dramatic embodiment and so subtly perceived and finely rendered a social setting, that we finish the course ready, so to speak, to buy almost anything. The story is of a man who has made one marriage upon conventional assumptions and is prepared to make a second only on his own. Towards the close of the action he expresses his demands bleakly and, in a sense, outrageously—but, what is too rare in Lawrence, in a manner that never edges hectoringly out at us from within the frame of the illusion. And as Captain Hepburn has the good fortune to fire off his convictions at a woman of exceptional magnanimity, well able both to submit to what is profound in them and to hold her own against absurdity where need be, his story invites the comment that it ends happily as a love story should—this although it is precisely as an anti-love story that it is designed to come home to us. Lawrence never approaches so near Benedick and Beatrice, and this in handling situations which might have landed him with Petruchio and Katherina.

Countess Hannele is a refugee in a German city occupied by English troops, and she earns her living by making dolls. She has made a doll—we are not told in what medium—of Alexander Hepburn, whose mistress she has recently become:

It was a perfect portrait of an officer of a Scottish regiment, slender, delicately made, with a slight, elegant stoop of the shoulders, and close-fitting tartan trousers. The face was beautifully modelled, and a wonderful portrait, dark-skinned, with a little, close-cut, dark moustache, and wide-open dark eyes, and that air of aloofness and perfect diffidence which marks an officer and a gentleman.

Hepburn is amused by the doll, or at least doesn't trouble to

express himself as being anything else. There is something
curiously and insistently absent about him; 'words of reply
seemed to stray out of him . . . but he himself never spoke.'
He puzzles Hannele. She sometimes feels that she can 'ascribe
no meaning to him, none whatever'; but no more than ourselves is she tempted to attribute this aloofness to the caution of
a married man conducting a temporary amour. When Mrs.
Hepburn, having heard disturbing rumours, arrives on the
scene, his attitude becomes comprehensible. Mrs. Hepburn is
a faded and foolish woman, convinced of the romantic quality
of her husband's attachment to her, and delighting to tell how,
on her wedding night, he had knelt down in front of her and
promised, with God's help, to make her life happy. To Hannele
the image of this seems revolting and absurd, and Hepburn
himself sees it as symbolizing the entire falseness of 'love' as the
basis of a permanent relationship between a man and a woman.
When his wife has a fatal accident, he retires to England to
think things out, and also—it is a very Laurentian touch—'out
of duty to see his children', to whom he wishes 'all the well in
the world—everything except any emotional connection with
himself'. Still less, he discovers, does he want anything that can
be called orthodox emotional connexion with another woman:

> Not all the beauties and virtues of woman put together with all
> the gold in the Indies would have tempted him into the business of
> adoration any more. He had gone on his knees once, vowing with
> faltering tones to try and make the adored one happy. And now—
> never again. Never.
> The temptation this time was to be adored. . . . To be god-almighty
> in your own house, with a lovely young thing adoring you, and you
> giving off beams of bright effulgence like a Gloria! Who wouldn't be
> tempted: at the age of forty? And this was why he dallied.
> But in the end he suddenly took the train to Munich.

Hepburn knows that—upon conditions—he will be safe with
Hannele. He finds not her but the doll, exposed in a shop
window. 'It was such a real little *man* that it fairly staggered him.
The oftener he saw it, the more it staggered him. And the more
he hated it.' A painter buys the doll as a property, so that Hepburn in his turn comes to possess a vulgar modernistic still-life,
in which the doll is represented along with two sunflowers and
a poached egg. Then he seeks out Hannele at a lake resort in
the Austrian Tyrol. The sequence of scenes in which the two

be known at all, and in the intuitive acknowledgement of which any serious relationship between individuals must repose. There is all this in the doll, and its significance comes to us in a series of implications which makes it, artistically, perhaps the most successful of Lawrence's symbols.

And now Hepburn is not without positive proposals, and he advances upon them as the two drive back in a noisy car from their mountain trip. That they have to shout absurdly at each other gives edge to the crisis:

'I may as well finish what I have to say', shouted he, his breath blown away.

'Finish then', she screamed, the ends of her scarf flickering behind her.

'When my wife died', he said loudly, 'I knew I couldn't love any more.'

'Oh—h!' she screamed ironically.

'In fact', he shouted, 'I realised that, as far as I was concerned, love was a mistake'.

'*What* was a mistake?' she screamed.

'Love', he bawled.

His mother, a sister, a girl, and then his wife—it has all been a mistake. And then he made the mistake of loving Hannele. He has come back to her. But he doesn't want marriage on a basis of love. He wants it on a basis that he now expresses briefly and—at least as Hannele tries to feel—scandalously. 'I want a sort of patient Griselda. I want to be honoured and obeyed. I don't want love.'

'Honour, and obedience: and the proper physical feelings', he said. 'To me that is marriage. Nothing else.'

'But what are the proper physical feelings but love?' asked Hannele.

'No', he said. 'A woman wants you to adore her, and be in love with her—and I shan't. I will not do it again, if I live a monk for the rest of my days. I will neither adore you nor be in love with you.'

'You won't get a chance, thank you. And what do you call the proper physical feelings, if you are not in love? I think you want something vile.'

'If a woman honours me—absolutely from the bottom of her nature honours me—and obeys me because of that, I take it, my desire for her goes very much deeper than if I was in love with her, or if I adored her. . . . If a woman loves you, she'll make a doll of you. She'll never be satisfied till she's made your doll. And when she's got your doll, that's all she wants. And that's what love means. And so, I won't be loved. And I won't love. I won't have anybody loving me. It is an insult. I feel I've been insulted for forty years: by love, and the women who've loved me. I won't be loved. And I won't love. I'll be honoured and I'll be obeyed: or nothing.'

'Then it'll most probably be nothing', said Hannele sarcastically.

But Hannele is wrong. Within a page of this perhaps perilously near-Shavian dialogue, she has made her submission. She makes it, indeed, not without abjuring Hepburn to refrain, if he can, from being 'a solemn ass'. But it would be a mistake to think that she is proposing any essential reservation, or treating his ideas as prattle, after the manner of Ann Whitefield with Jack Tanner in *Man and Superman*. It is not altogether happily, indeed, that Hepburn has recourse to the terms of the marriage service. This takes us back to *Kangaroo* and to the inescapable element of the ridiculous in a man's holding forth at length to a woman on the propriety of her honouring and obeying him. The insistence, moreover, has no place at the core of Hepburn's contention, which is simply that any absolute possession of, and absolute dedication to, another individual is possible only in a world of illusion, and that the deepest relationship two human beings can achieve consists in a mutual reverence before the utter mystery of human otherness. If we are to be taken away from this to factors differentiating the sexes, as we are in Hepburn's ultimatum, then we may feel that we ought to hear Hannele's side of the case. From Shaw we should certainly have heard it, had it been his genius to work at this level. With Lawrence the exploration has stopped short before it should, since what has halted it is less some necessary artistic terminus than a limitation in the objectivity achieved by the writer. Hepburn realizes that he cannot live merely, or at all, to make another person happy. Like Richard Lovat Somers he must fulfil himself in the world—labouring, as he proposes, to clear virgin land in Africa. But it looks much as if Hannele, although not allowed to love him, *is* going to be required to live to make *him* happy. At least nothing else is remotely sketched for her. There is nothing new in this rather lop-sided aspect of Lawrence's marital philosophy. Indeed there is nothing new at all in the thought of 'The Captain's Doll'. But the thought has never before been so happily recommended and controlled by apt and confident dramatic realization, by a subtlety and complexity of tone, even by a lightness of air, which is as delightful as the jaunty and flippant manner of much of 'St. Mawr' is displeasing.

Two of the stories—and they are the farthest removed from realism—are exceptional in having something of the exploratory quality commonly reserved for the novels. 'The Woman Who Rode Away' was written during a break in the composition of *The Plumed Serpent*, and it formidably presents both us and Lawrence with the naked body of that sinister divinity to the painting and outfitting and hymning of which Don Ramón and his followers give such tiresome and obfuscating attention in the novel. The woman—she has no name—is blonde and American, a 'Californian girl from Berkeley', and she lives with her Dutch husband on a semi-derelict silver mine in the wilds of Mexico. She has two children. But everything around her speaks of death and decay, so that her nerves go wrong. Hearing talk of 'old, old religions and mysteries' surviving among the Indians of a remote valley, she feels it her destiny to seek them out. This she accomplishes. And the Indians, after a long sequence of ritual observances in which she more and more mindlessly concurs, offer her up as a sacrifice to their gods.

This story, which is realized in its natural and barbaric setting with stupendous power, is essentially a fable, and a fable operative in depth. Superficially the woman meets her fate simply as the consequence of a neurotic fugue, and of a special significance her arrival happens to have for the Indians. The barrenness and frustration of her normal life have been very forcefully portrayed, and render credible her rather idle statement that she has come to seek the God of the Indians in place of her own. To that new God, she rashly agrees, she has brought her heart. The meaning of this in the context of her captors' religious persuasions is explained to her by the only one among them who has any Spanish:

'The Indian got weak, and lost his power with the sun, so the white men stole the sun. But they can't keep him—they don't know how. . . . White men don't know what they are doing with the sun, and white women don't know what they do with the moon. The moon she got angry with white women . . . she bites white women—here inside', and he pressed his side. 'The moon, she is angry in a white woman's cave. The Indian can see it. And soon', he added, 'the Indian women get the moon back and keep her quiet in their house. And the Indian men get the sun, and the power over all the world.'

The explanation is explicit without being exactly lucid, and has an inescapable Black Sambo flavour making it the weakest part of the tale. But it sets out at least the exoteric doctrine involved. 'We say, when a white woman sacrifice herself to our gods, then our gods will begin to make the world again, and the white man's gods will fall to pieces.' This is the simple and somewhat factitious magical faith in which the old priest raises his knife at the end. He will 'strike home, accomplish the sacrifice and achieve the power. The mastery that man must hold, and that passes from race to race.' At the same time the white woman appears to be culpable towards humanity and the cosmos in general. 'The white women', we learn further in the Black Sambo prose, 'have driven back the moon in the sky, won't let her come to the sun'—a statement dubiously clarified by the further explanation that 'when the man gets a woman, the sun goes into the cave of the moon'. In this state of affairs, not unnaturally, 'the sun is angry . . . everything in the world gets angrier'. We may feel that, if this statement is true, the author of 'The Woman Who Rode Away' has at times quite done his bit. However that may be, the woman of the story is a 'spoilt white woman' at the start, and later she herself has a significant vision of her own coming 'obliteration':

Her kind of womanhood, intensely personal and individual, was to be obliterated again, and the great primeval symbols were to tower once more over the fallen individual independence of women. The sharpness and the quivering nervous consciousness of the highly-bred white woman was to be destroyed again, womanhood was to be cast once more into the great stream of impersonal sex and impersonal passion.

We have had all this before, and it is hard to resist the feeling that it represents somebody getting 'angrier' as the consequence of a sense of inadequacy and frustration in an obsessively contemplated sexual sphere. We remember that Miriam in *Sons and Lovers* 'quivered' with an intensity of nervous consciousness, that Paul as a sexual being was humiliated by her, and that her physical submission to him held for her the horror of a 'sacrifice'. Here is one more obscure fruit of that seminal trauma.

But 'The Woman Who Rode Away' carries meaning at a deeper level than this. Here the specific mythology cooked up for the Indians has no significance, and the sex of their victim has no significance either. What has significance is the victim's being compelled away from a world which is visibly perishing around her, and accepting the imposition of progressively remote and alien modes of consciousness which in fact, long before her actual immolation, constitute a death of her whole conscious being. On her first night away from home 'she was not sure that she had not heard, during the night, a great crash at the centre of herself, which was the crash of her own death'. Going forward with 'no will of her own', she 'knew she was dead'— and later the reports of her senses are not those which come to anyone living the life we know:

She felt as if all her senses were diffused on the air, that she could distinguish the sound of evening flowers unfolding, and the actual crystal sound of the heavens, as the vast belts of the world-atmosphere slid past one another, and as if the moisture ascending and the moisture descending in the air resounded like some harp in the cosmos. . . .

They had brought her a little female dog, which she called Flora. And once, in the trance of her senses, she felt she *heard* the little dog conceive, in her tiny womb, and begin to be complex, with young. And another day she could hear the vast sound of the earth going round, like some immense arrow-string booming. . . .

This at length became the only state of consciousness she really recognised: this exquisite sense of bleeding out into the higher beauty and harmony of things. Then she could actually hear the great stars in heaven, which she saw through her door, speaking from their motion and brightness, saying things perfectly to the cosmos, as they trod in perfect ripples, like bells on the floor of heaven, passing one another and grouping in the timeless dance, with the spaces of dark between.

The passage sustains itself beyond astonishment, and is the more striking from its juxtaposition with descriptions of actual scenes such as Lawrence quite equals in no other place. But the process of alienation from a known world, if it leads like drug addiction through beauties and harmonies unspeakable, has like drug addiction no bound: 'More and more her ordinary personal consciousness had left her, she had gone into that other state of passional cosmic consciousness, like one who is drugged. The Indians, with their heavily religious natures, had made her succumb to their vision.' She ends by acquiescing in her own annihilation. In this she represents both the individual psyche under stress, turning towards, and eventually overwhelmed by, the anarchic life of the *id*, and the perishing civilization from which she has come, ready to give up and hand over, ripe for the ultimate operation of the death-wish. 'The Woman Who Rode Away' is an altogether more imaginatively potent work than *The Plumed Serpent*, and much more clearly a *Blick ins Chaos*. The second part of *The Plumed Serpent* is not the work of a man who has yet recoiled, as Lawrence does finally recoil, from that glimpse.

On Palm Sunday, 1927, while on a visit to the Etruscan antiquities at Volterra and during an interval in the composition of *Lady Chatterley's Lover*, Lawrence saw in a shop window 'a little white rooster coming out of the egg' and remarked that it suggested a title, 'The Escaped Cock—a Story of the Resurrection'. Three weeks after this equivocal remark he announced that he had finished a story, 'where Jesus gets up and feels very sick about everything, and can't stand the old crowd any more—so cuts out'. The story in its final and augmented form, 'The Man Who Died', goes on to tell how Jesus becomes the lover of a young priestess of Isis, whom he gets with child, and how he then passes on to live in simple acceptance of the phenomenal world—a world 'far more marvellous than any salvation or heaven'. Although bold in conception, 'The Man Who Died' shows nothing of the manner that Lawrence's first flippant description might suggest. The style, aiming at Biblical austerity, gives an effect of rather strained elevation, and both Jesus and the priestess are so conscious of their remove from the common humanity of peasants and slaves around them that they seem to evince an almost Pierfrancescan hauteur, not wholly accordant with the simplicity of the proceeding to which they devote themselves. The Mediterranean world in which the tale is set is the world to which Lawrence has now come to die, and it is evoked in poignant beauty. But the writing has not the power which he still commands in *Lady Chatterley's Lover*, and the story would not be specially remarkable because of it. It would not be very remarkable at all, did its substance comprehend no more than that straight smack at the Christian religion which would seem to have been Lawrence's first, and perhaps to the end only conscious, intention. Much suggests that it is no more than this. Jesus is steadily represented as seeing and acknowledging the error and futility of his ways before that inefficient crucifixion which has given him his second chance. 'A vivid shame' goes through him when he realizes that he has asked his disciples to

love 'with the corpse of love'. He sees how little he was entitled
to 'embrace multitudes'—he who had 'never truly embraced
even one'. He rejoices that now, in his second life, he 'can be
alone, and leave all things to themselves, and the fig-tree may
be barren if it will, and the rich may be rich'. 'A desireless
resoluteness, deeper even than consciousness,' has preserved him
alive, and he now understands that man's sole concern is with
life's sensible surfaces, swept clean of transcendental illusion:

My triumph . . . is that I am not dead. I have outlived my mission,
and know no more of it. It is my triumph. I have survived the day
and the death of my interference, and am still a man. . . .

Now I am risen in my own aloneness, and inherit the earth, since I
lay no claim on it.

'The necessity to live, and even to cry out the triumph of
life', which he sees in the young captive cock which he will set
free, is now a sufficient creed for him. It is this simple vitalism
that evokes the best writing in the story:

The man who had died looked nakedly on life, and saw a vast
resoluteness everywhere flinging itself up in stormy or subtle wave-
crests, foam-tips emerging out of the blue invisible, a black and
orange cock or the green flame-tongues out of the extremes of the
fig-tree. They came forth, these things and creatures of spring,
glowing with desire and with assertion. They came like crests of
foam, out of the blue flood of the invisible desire, out of the vast
invisible sea of strength, and they came coloured and tangible.

So too the priestess comes. It would be to the artistic advantage
of the story that she stayed away. Convinced as Lawrence now
is of his final doctrine of 'tenderness', of 'the soft warm love
which is in touch', he cannot quite bring off the feat of adding to
that story which began in a stable in Bethlehem an epilogue set
in what is virtually the gamekeeper Mellors's hut. That Jesus
should declare his coming together with the priestess to be 'the
great atonement, the being in touch'; that he should say of
'the deep-folded, penetrable rock of the living woman': 'On
this rock I build my life'; that he should cry out 'I am risen!'
when he does: these extremities perhaps witness to Lawrence's
just sense of the impossible strain to which he is subjecting his
material. Yet there is something profoundly ambiguous about
his whole determination thus to rout Christian love by calling
upon Jesus himself to turn, as it were, King's evidence against

it. And it is in this ambiguity (as so often with Lawrence) that there lies the growing-point of the story, the factor taking it perhaps beyond *Lady Chatterley's Lover* with which it is so closely connected. The dead may be left to bury their dead. And Lawrence, in pausing himself to throw a few more sods on Christianity in 'The Man Who Died', is really betraying his intuition that Christianity isn't quite so dead, after all. The man who makes love to the priestess, and who asks himself, from his new detachment, 'From what, and to what, could this infinite whirl be saved?' is still the Man whose head had hung in universal benediction from the Cross. The tale would be pointless if this were not so. Whatever the further experience to which Jesus lets the little boat carry him off at the end of the tale, it will be bound to subsume within itself his antecedent experience alike of the priestess and of 'the old crowd'. With a race, as with an individual, every experience is at once defined and enriched by every antecedent experience, and a Jesus who had not preached the Spirit would not be the Jesus who came to the woman in the Flesh. A culture which actively rejects Christianity must be a culture which Christianity has conditioned, and the 'rejection' is likely to be a term in a dialectic process of some complexity. There is no ground for seeing 'The Man Who Died' as the beginning of some sort of reconciliation with Christianity on Lawrence's part, rendered abortive by his quickly succeeding death. But beneath the plain fable is an element of submerged allegory witnessing to a growth of historical consciousness which might have deepened in subsequent writing.

10

The museums are full of vases. If one looks for the Greek form of elegance and convention, those elegant 'still-unravished brides of quietness', one is disappointed. But get over the strange desire we have for elegant convention, and the vases and dishes of the Etruscans . . . begin to open out like strange flowers, black flowers with all the softness and the rebellion of life against convention, or red-and-black flowers painted with amusing free, bold designs. It is there nearly always in Etruscan things, the naturalness verging on the commonplace, but usually missing it, and often achieving an originality so free and bold, and so fresh, that we, who love convention and things 'reduced to a norm', call it a bastard art, and commonplace.

What Lawrence here says of Etruscan art is in some degree
applicable to his own poetry, the distinguishing qualities of
which are 'naturalness verging on the commonplace' and a
decided disregard of convention. It is expected of a poem, for
example, that it shall have some sort of formal organization
which will not be irrecoverable should it happen to be set down
on the page as prose. But here is 'Wages' so set down:

The wages of work is cash. The wages of cash is want more cash.
The wages of want more cash is vicious competition. The wages of
vicious competition is—the world we live in. The work-cash-want
circle is the viciousest circle that ever turned men into fiends. Earning a wage is a prison occupation and a wage-earner is a sort of gaol-
bird. Earning a salary is a prison overseer's job, a gaoler instead of
a gaol-bird. Living on your income is strolling grandly outside the
prison in terror lest you have to go in. And since the work-prison
covers almost every scrap of the living earth, you stroll up and down
on a narrow beat, about the same as a prisoner taking his exercise.
This is called universal freedom.

Again, convention suggests that the more intimately personal
and confessional the poetry a writer attempts the more essential
to him is some sort of restraining and distancing structure. But
this canon—if it is entitled to be called that—Lawrence entirely
ignores, so that in his most powerful writing we are liable to be
brought up against something altogether more raw and immediate than it is customary to associate with poetic pleasure.
Thus in *Look! We Have Come Through!* (1917)—a series of poems
to which he prefixes an 'Argument' virtually explaining that
they have been occasioned by his running away with a married
woman, who has had to leave her children behind her, and
with whom he has been involved in a conflict of love and hate
—the writing is for the most part in a technique of simple
effusion:

At last, as you stood, your white gown falling from your breasts,
You looked into my eyes, and said: 'But this is joy!'
I acquiesced again.
But the shadow of lying was in your eyes,
The mother in you, fierce as a murderess, glaring to England.
Yearning towards England, towards your young children,
Insisting upon your motherhood, devastating. . . .

Lot's Wife!—Not Wife, but Mother.
I have learned to curse your motherhood,

You pillar of salt accursed.
I have cursed motherhood because of you,
Accursed, base motherhood!

Confronted with this outpouring, we appreciate Bertrand
Russell's joke about being not much prompted to *Look!* in the
manner so peremptorily demanded. The novels often transform
into a medium essentially poetic matter drawn very directly
from Lawrence's private experience; the poems, paradoxically,
seem sometimes the bleak sheer prose of the same thing.
'Lilies in the Fire', 'Scent of Irises', and 'Coldness in Love' are
poignantly moving performances, and 'Last Words to Miriam'
is almost overwhelmingly dreadful—and all of them present,
with far less effect of aesthetic distancing than we feel in *The
Trespasser*, *Sons and Lovers*, or *The Rainbow*, reflections of a shattering experience or series of experiences from the young Lawrence's most intimate life. Nevertheless, when approached with
an open mind, many of the poems do reveal, like the Tuscan
things, 'an originality so free and bold, and so fresh', that formal
criticism is inept before them. And in some the free verse, so
easy to abound in and so hard to master, takes on a subtle
and assured rhythmic organization, so that we have the rare
experience of watching a complex of emotions or feelings
generating its own seemingly inevitable form.

Love Poems and Others (1913) and Amores (1916) belong to the
period culminating in the death of Lawrence's mother and the
writing of *Sons and Lovers*. Some, including several in dialect,
are dramatic and narrative, and present wry or ironic episodes
closely akin to one or two of his earlier short stories. 'Violets',
'Whether or Not', and 'Two Wives' are of this sort. Others,
like 'Love on the Farm', recombine elements familiar to us
from the novels. 'Discord in Childhood' and 'Cherry Robbers'
take us straight to specific places in *Sons and Lovers*. So, more
strikingly, does 'Brooding Grief'. In the novel we read:

Suddenly a piece of paper started near his feet and blew along
down the pavement. He stood still, rigid, with clenched fists, a
flame of agony going over him. And he saw again the sick-room, his
mother, her eyes. Unconsciously he had been with her, in her
company. The swift hop of the paper reminded him she was gone.
But he had been with her. He wanted everything to stand still, so
that he could be with her again.

The poem runs:

> A yellow leaf, from the darkness
> Hops like a frog before me;
> Why should I start and stand still?
>
> I was watching the woman that bore me
> Stretched in the brindled darkness
> Of the sick-room, rigid with will
> To die: and the quick leaf tore me
> Back to this rainy swill
> Of leaves and lamps and the city street mingled before me.

There is a similar relationship between Hardy's 'Midnight on the Great Western' and a passage describing Little Father Time's railway journey in Part Fifth of *Jude the Obscure*; Lawrence is perhaps the more successful in lending his incident poetic effect. Hardy may be noted as the only important literary influence on Lawrence's earlier poetry. 'Lightning' is like one of Hardy's neatest small fatalities:

> I leaned in the darkness to find her lips
>   And claim her utterly in a kiss,
> When the lightning flew across her face
> And I saw her for the flaring space
>   Of a second, like snow that slips
> From a roof, inert with death, weeping 'Not this! Not this!'

Sometimes when Lawrence's rhyming is merely awkward it appears to be an idiosyncrasy of Hardy's that is being imitated.

> Come then under this tree, where the tent-cloths
>   Curtain us in so dark
> That here we're safe from even the ermine moth's
>   Twitching remark.

Lawrence commonly lacks Hardy's power of being utterly bare without falling into banality. The poems prompted by the illness and death of his mother (which continue into the succeeding series in which his marriage is the central theme) are in places wholly prosaic. Others—notably those written at a remove both of time and place—have a purity of sentiment and simplicity of expression before which our criticism is silenced. In 'All Souls' he gives a picture of an Italian village cemetery

on the feast-day, with the candles burning in daylight on the
graves, and goes on, strangely and effectively:

> And my naked body standing on your grave
> Upright towards heaven is burning off to you
> Its flame of life, now and always, till the end.

In 'Everlasting Flowers' he mourns that he cannot bring the
beauty of Lake Garda to his dead mother:

> To you, my little darling,
>   To you, out of Italy.
> For what is loveliness, my love,
>   Save you have it with me! . . .
>
> All the things that are lovely—
>   The things you never knew—
> I wanted to gather them one by one
> And bring them to you.
>
> But never now, my darling,
>   Can I gather the mountain-tips
> From the twilight like half-shut lilies
>   To hold to your lips.
>
> And never the two-winged vessel
>   That sleeps below on the lake
> Can I catch like a moth between my hands
>   For you to take.

It is characteristic of much in the relationship of the poems to
the prose fiction that the effect of these lines is enhanced—and,
in a sense, purged of excess—by our memory of *Sons and Lovers*,
where Mrs. Morel would turn with a girl's happiness and say
'Pretty!' when her son brought her a wild-flower, or a little
plate from a fair.

While many of the early poems are retrospective and
nostalgic—notably those, like 'Letter from Town: On a Grey
Morning in March' and 'The North Country', written while
he was a school-teacher in Croydon—others foreshadow themes
and attitudes which will become increasingly important as he
matures. The first of all, 'The Wild Common', contains in the
line

> But how splendid it is to be substance, here!

the one cardinal article of faith in which Lawrence is to live
and die. In 'Virgin Youth', a poem which he regarded as

important and took much pains in revising, we are introduced
to the phallus with all the covertly auto-erotic solemnity which
Mellors is to lavish on it fifteen years later. 'Tease' is a light
treatment of what is to be a prime Laurentian bogy, the implacable female will. And in the best of the Croydon poems,
'Discipline', Lawrence draws from his experience with his
pupils a first perception of the limitations of love:

I thought that love would do all things, but now I know I am wrong.
There are depths below depths, my darling, where love does not
  belong.
Where the fight that is fight for being is fought throughout the long
Young years, and the old must not win, not even if they love and are
  strong.

Much of the burden of the next group of poems is here contained in the lines:

And there in the dark, my darling, where the roots are entangled
  and fight
Each one for its hold on the concrete darkness, I know that there
In the night where we first have being, before we rise on the light,
We are not lovers, my darling, we fight and we do not spare.

When Lawrence published a collection of his poems in 1928,
he wrote in a preface that he had 'tried to establish a chronological order, because many of the poems are so personal that,
in their fragmentary fashion, they make up a biography of an
emotional and inner life'. And he went on to contend that 'even
the best poetry, when it is at all personal, needs the penumbra
of its own time and place and circumstance to make it full and
whole'; therefore he would 'like to ask the reader of *Look!
We Have Come Through!* to fill in the background of the poems,
as far as possible, with the place, the time, the circumstance'.
The reader, whatever he may think of the general proposition,
has almost no choice in the particular instance. The manner in
which, once more, the poems insistently relate themselves to the
novels and short stories increases our sense that Lawrence's
entire output is a continuous imaginative autobiography. That
'we fight and we do not spare' has been largely documented in
both *The Rainbow* and *Women in Love*. The poems give us the
struggle both in its full fury, presented with what hostile criticism will certainly call hysterical exaggeration, and—as in the
charming and touching 'Spring Morning'—softened by more of

simple affection and shared pleasure than the novels often admit. Fear, suspense, confidence succeed one another:

> Perhaps she will go back to England.
> Perhaps she will go back,
> Perhaps we are parted for ever. . . .

> She has not chosen me finally, she suspends her choice.
> Night folk, Tuatha De Danaan, dark Gods, govern her sleep. . . .

> But now I am full and strong and certain
> With you there firm at the core of me
> Keeping me. . . .

At the core of the poems is a more humanly appealing figure than we often get in the long series of projections from Paul Morel to Alexander Hepburn and Oliver Mellors. Yet the later Laurentian heroes are all struggling in the young lover who is here so evidently just keeping his chin above the desperate waters of marriage. In 'Lady Wife' the injunction—

> Serve now, woman, serve, as a woman should,
> Implicitly.
> Since I must serve and struggle with the imminent
> Mystery—

although without much poetic merit, would be endorsed by Rawdon Lilly. The verses beginning 'She said as well to me' are Lawrence's announcement that he will not be made a doll of. Two poems at the close, 'New Heaven and Earth' and 'Manifesto', sum up what were to be his settled views on marriage. The first looks forward to his final emphasis upon the mystery of touch, and the second enunciates that doctrine of 'two of us, unutterably distinguished, and in unutterable conjunction' about which Ursula Brangwen hears so much from Rupert Birkin. Several of the poems, indeed, are closely involved with *Women in Love*. In the last but one of the series, 'Frost Flowers', we shall scarcely understand why the women should be 'flowers of ice-vivid mortification, thaw-cold, ice-corrupt blossoms', unless we recall the symbolism evolved for Gerald Crich.

The poems in *Look! We Have Come Through!* have in the main the character of personal marginalia accompanying the series of marriage-novels, and their substantive importance is consequently diminished. *Birds, Beasts and Flowers* (1923) is an achievement of a different kind, and of a different order. 'Cypresses', which looks forward to that concern with the

Etruscans which was to constitute the final intellectual and imaginative interest of Lawrence's life, supplies something like a text for the volume:

> For oh, I know, in the dust where we have buried
> The silenced races and all their abominations,
> We have buried so much of the delicate magic of life.

'To the Etruscan'—he was to write—

all was alive; the whole universe lived; and the business of man was himself to live amid it all. He had to draw life into himself, out of the wandering huge vitalities of the world. . . . The whole thing was alive, and had a great soul, or *anima*: and in spite of one great soul, there were myriad roving, lesser souls: every man, every creature and tree and lake and mountain and stream, was animate, had its own peculiar consciousness. And has it to-day.

'And has it to-day.' The aim of *Birds, Beasts and Flowers* is to recover 'much of the delicate magic of life' by feeling out towards some of the 'lesser souls' in creature and tree and flower. It is easy to dismiss some of the resulting poems as fantastic. Since we none of us know what it is like to be an elephant or a mosquito or an amorous tortoise we are the more likely to take on trust a confident assumption of knowledge. But in fact the poems all acknowledge mystery; they penetrate the little way that makes mystery more indubitable and more overpowering:

I have waited with a long rod
And suddenly pulled a gold-and-greenish, lucent fish from below,
And had him fly like a halo round my head,
Lunging in the air on the line.

Unhooked his gorping, water-honey mouth,
And seen his horror-tilted eye,
His red-gold, water-precious, mirror-flat bright eye;
And felt him beat in my hand, with his mucous, leaping life-throb.
And my heart accused itself
Thinking: *I am not the measure of creation.*
This is beyond me, this fish.
His God stands outside my God.

And the gold-and-green pure lacquer-mucus comes off in my hand,
And the red-gold mirror-eye stares and dies,
And the water-suave contour dims.

But not before I have had to know
He was born in front of my sunrise,
Before my day.

Lawrence's creatures are at a farthest remove from being
almost human. Bats are bats:

> Creatures that hang themselves up like an old rag, to sleep;
> And disgustingly upside down.
> Hanging upside down like rows of disgusting old rags
> And grinning in their sleep.

When in Florence he goes into his room and finds a bat flying
round in insane circles, his encounter with it is across a sufficiently acknowledged chasm: 'Let the God who is maker of
bats watch with them in their unclean corners.' 'Snake' and
the sequence of six 'Tortoise' poems are the peak of this series
and constitute, together with a small body of verse written
immediately before his death, Lawrence's permanent contribution to English poetry.

   Pansies (1929), *Nettles* (1930), and the *More Pansies* which
form the greater part of the posthumously published *Last Poems*
(1932) constitute another distinct species of Lawrence's verse.
In a note to the first collection he declares that 'there is a didactic element about prose thoughts which makes them repellent,
slightly bullying. . . . We don't want to be nagged at.' But putting
his own thoughts into free verse has not proved to be any insurance in these regards, for the effect of the whole collection is
narrow, wearisome, and displeasing—this even although many
are pungent and epigrammatic enough and a substantial minority
have the great merit of being true. Those which are angry about
sex are on the whole better than those which are angry about
class, sometimes confronting us in challenging form with one or
another aspect of the hard core of Lawrence's thought:

> To proceed from mental intimacy
> to physical is just messy,
> and really, a nasty violation,
> and the ruin of any decent relation
> between us.

This is given no limiting context; it is a general proposition which we at once see to be consonant with a large part
of Lawrence's fiction; and, as far as the tradition of western

civilization goes, it is straight heresy. There is a great deal of
the bitterness of defeat and departing power in this stretch
of his work. But 'Terra Incognita', which comes near the end of
More Pansies, and which begins 'There are vast realms of consciousness still undreamed of, vast ranges of experience', is not
the work of a wholly defeated man. And almost suddenly, when
death is very close to him, Lawrence's poetry takes on a gravity
and a certainty of accent which speaks of we cannot tell what
hovering reconciling power.

It is Lawrence's leading religious idea, made explicit in the
deeply imaginative *Etruscan Places* (1932), that myths and
personal gods are only the decadence of a previous cosmic
religion: 'From the shadow of the prehistoric world emerge
dying religions that have not yet invented gods or goddesses,
but live by the mystery of the elemental powers in the Universe,
the complex vitalities of what we feebly call Nature.' Cosmic
religion would assert, as in 'The Body of God':

> There is no god
> apart from poppies and the flying fish,
> men singing songs, and women brushing their hair in the sun.

Yet Lawrence is aware of some power that urges the poppy
and the flying fish into being, and to the paradox inherent in this
he addresses himself in the group of poems beginning with
'Demiurge', which in fact constitute a series of meditations on
the being and nature of God. But what Lawrence comes back
to again and again is the earliest of all his doctrinal assertions.
In the beginning was the Flesh:

> They say that reality exists only in the spirit
> that corporal existence is a kind of death
> that pure being is bodiless
> that the idea of the form precedes the form substantial.
>
> But what nonsense it is!
> as if any Mind could have imagined a lobster
> dozing the under-deeps, then reaching out a savage and iron claw!
>
> Even the mind of God can only imagine
> those things that have become themselves.

One does not here feel that Lawrence's thought is getting
deeper. The best of these poems is the lightest in tone, 'Red
Geranium and Godly Mignonette', in which it is pointed out,

among other things, that 'You can't imagine the Holy Ghost
sniffing at cherry-pie heliotrope'.

The very last poems, however, give an impression of a consciousness on the verge of invasion by fresh intuitions. In 'The
Ship of Death', which exists in several versions, the beautifully simple symbols are taken from the Etruscan tombs; in
the penultimate stanza, most movingly, the sepulchral darkness
admits the faint colours of a supersensible dawn. In 'Bavarian
Gentians', of which again there are variant versions, the darkness is entire. It was from Vence, where Lawrence died, that
Christopher Wood wrote, 'My pictures are getting darker and
darker and so black. No black is black enough.' And 'Bavarian
Gentians' has the quality that Wood, in the same year, was
getting on his last canvases:

Reach me a gentian, give me a torch!
Let me guide myself with the blue, forked torch of a flower
Down the darker and darker stairs, where blue is darkened on blue-
ness
Down the way Persephone goes, just now, in first-frosted September.

Here our interest in Lawrence's beliefs is lost in the wonder
that he could write such poetry. In 'Shadows', perhaps his
finest poem, the primary impression is of being in the presence
of a mind at last revealed to itself as innately religious and
glimpsing truth beyond the reach of conceptual statement:

And if, in the changing phases of man's life
I fall in sickness and in misery
my wrists seem broken and my heart seems dead
and strength is gone, and my life
is only the leavings of a life:

and still, among it all, snatches of lovely oblivion, and snatches of
renewal
odd, wintry flowers upon the withered stem, yet new, strange flowers
such as my life has not brought forth before, new blossoms of me:

then I must know that still
I am in the hands of the unknown God,
he is breaking me down to his own oblivion
to send me forth on a new morning, a new man.

Yet this must not incline us to the view that Lawrence, when
dying, makes any sort of submission. Whatever might hint itself

as lying beyond the phenomenal world, his last loyalty is to that acceptance of life which—and it is in itself an unparalleled triumph of the spirit—he thought to discover, when himself sick to death, in dreary Etruscan tombs which most of us are content to give over to conscientious German tourists. It is the sufficient business of a man 'to get into himself more and more of the gleaming vitality of the cosmos'. His last prose work, *Apocalypse* (1931), although in title and theme witnessing to that obstinate tug of Christian imagination which had been with him since his Congregationalist childhood, contains his final witness to the naturalism and vitalism by which he lived. For at the end of it he turns from the 'strange book', and from his own equally strange commentary on it, and says simply what he has always had to say:

For man, the vast marvel is to be alive. For man, as for flower and beast and bird, the supreme triumph is to be most vividly, most perfectly alive. Whatever the unborn and the dead may know, they cannot know the beauty, the marvel of being alive in the flesh. The dead may look after the afterwards. But the magnificent here and now of life in the flesh is ours, and ours alone, and ours only for a time. We ought to dance with rapture that we should be alive and in the flesh, and part of the living, incarnate cosmos. I am part of the sun as my eye is part of me. That I am part of the earth my feet know perfectly, and my blood is part of the sea. My soul knows that I am part of the human race, my soul is an organic part of the great human soul, as my spirit is part of my nation. In my own very self, I am part of my family. There is nothing of me that is alone and absolute except my mind, and we shall find that the mind has no existence by itself, it is only the glitter of the sun on the surface of the waters.

CHRONOLOGICAL TABLE

1880–1941

Date	Public Events	Literature and the Arts	Verse
1880	Gladstone P.M. Land League agitation in Ireland. Bradlaugh debarred from House of Commons.	George Eliot d. Lytton Strachey b. Flaubert d. Apollinaire b. Dostoevsky, *The Brothers Karamazov*. Maupassant, *Boule de suif*. Zola, *Nana*.	Browning, *Dramatic Idyls: Second Series*. Scawen Blunt, *The Love Sonnets of Proteus*.
1881	Second Irish Land Act. Boycotting. Hyndman founds London Democratic Federation. Assassination of Alexander II. De Lesseps begins Panama Canal.	Borrow d. Carlyle d. Disraeli d. L. Abercrombie b. Dostoevsky d. Bartok b. Picasso b. Jowett, trs. Thucydides. Revised Version of the New Testament. *Evening News* started. Flaubert, *Bouvard et Pécuchet*. Ibsen, *Ghosts*.	Kipling, *Schoolboy Lyrics* (privately printed). D. G. Rossetti, *Ballads and Sonnets*. Swinburne, *Mary Stuart*. Wilde, *Poems*.
1882	Phoenix Park murders. Occupation of Egypt. Married Women's Property Act. Garibaldi d. Italy joins Austro-German alliance.	Darwin d. Pusey d. D. G. Rossetti d. James Thomson d. Trollope d. Joyce b. Wyndham Lewis b. James Stephens b. Virginia Woolf b. Emerson d. Longfellow d. Stravinsky b. Whitman, *Specimen Days and Collect*.	Swinburne, *Tristram of Lyonesse*.
1883	Agricultural Holdings Act. Maxim gun produced. Marx d. Mussolini b. Kruger President of South African Republic.	Derwent Coleridge d. Fitzgerald d. Manet d. Turgenev d. Wagner d. Nietzsche, *Also Sprach Zarathustra* (–1885). Von Ranke, *Weltgeschichte* (–1888).	Bridges, *Prometheus the Fire-giver*. Meredith, *Poems and Lyrics of the Joy of Earth*.
1884	Representation of the People Act. Foundation of Fabian Society. Morris and others form Socialist League. St. Gotthard Tunnel opened.	Mark Pattison d. Charles Reade d. Flecker b. Sean O'Casey b. Art Workers' Guild formed. *A New English Dictionary* (–1928). Revised Version of the Old Testament. Huysmans, *A Rebours*. Ibsen, *The Wild Duck*. Twain, *Huckleberry Finn*. Bruckner, Seventh Symphony.	Browning, *Ferishtah's Fancies*. Dixon, *Odes and Eclogues*. Sharp, *Earth's Voices*. De Vere, *Poetical Works*.
1885	Salisbury's first Ministry. Irish Land Bill passed. General Gordon d. at Khartoum. Hertz discovers radio waves. Daimler invents internal combustion engine. Starley markets 'Rover' bicycle.	D. H. Lawrence b. Hugo d. Mauriac b. Ezra Pound b. Laforgue, *Les Complaintes*. Zola, *Germinal*.	Bridges, *Eros and Psyche*. Dobson, *At the Sign of the Lyre*. Stevenson, *A Child's Garden of Verses*. Tennyson, *Tiresias*.

Prose Fiction, General Prose	*Drama (date of acting)*
Disraeli, *Endymion*. Gissing, *Workers in the Dawn*. Hardy, *The Trumpet Major*. James, *Confidence*. Meredith, *The Tragic Comedians*. Shorthouse, *John Inglesant*. Trollope, *The Duke's Children*.	Pinero, *The Money Spinner*.
Butler, *Unconscious Memory*. Swinburne, *A Study of Shakespeare*. Trevelyan, *The Early History of Charles James Fox*.	
Hardy, *A Laodicean*. James, *Washington Square*. *The Portrait of a Lady*. Rutherford, *Autobiography of Mark Rutherford*. Trollope, *Ayala's Angel*. *Dr. Wortle's School*.	Gilbert, *Patience*.
Butler, *Alps and Sanctuaries*. Stevenson, *Virginibus Puerisque*.	
Anstey, *Vice Versa*. Hardy, *Two on a Tower*. Jefferies, *Bevis*. Stevenson, *The New Arabian Nights*.	Jones and Herman, *The Silver King*.
Arnold, *Irish Essays*. Creighton, *History of the Papacy during the Reformation* (–1894). Morris, *Hopes and Fears for Art*. Seeley, *Natural Religion*. Stevenson, *Familiar Studies of Men and Books*.	
Broughton, *Belinda*. Mrs. Ewing, *Jackanapes*. Moore, *A Modern Lover*. Schreiner, *The Story of an African Farm*. Stevenson, *Treasure Island*.	Boucicault, *The Amadan*.
F. H. Bradley, *The Principles of Logic*. Galton, *Inquiries into Human Faculty*. Jefferies, *The Story of My Heart*. Trollope, *Autobiography*.	
Gissing, *The Unclassed*. Shaw, *An Unsocial Socialist* (serial publication).	Gilbert, *Princess Ida*. Jones, *Saints and Sinners*.
Birrell, *Obiter Dicta*. Jefferies, *The Life of the Fields*. Ruskin, *The Art of England*. Toynbee, *The Industrial Revolution*.	
Burton, trs. *The Arabian Nights* (–1888). Haggard, *King Solomon's Mines*. Hudson, *The Purple Land*. Jefferies, *After London*. Mrs. Lynn Linton, *The Autobiography of Christopher Kirkland*. Meredith, *Diana of the Crossways*. Moore, *A Mummer's Wife*. Pater, *Marius the Epicurean*. Rutherford, *Mark Rutherford's Deliverance*.	Pinero, *The Magistrate*.

Date	Public Events	Literature and the Arts	Verse
1885 *(cont.)*	Dilke divorce case. Pasteur introduces inoculation. Indian National Congress founded.		
1886	Gladstone's third Ministry. First Home Rule Bill defeated. Salisbury's second Ministry. Bradlaugh permitted to sit in Commons. Anglo-German agreement on East Africa. Opening of the Rand.	Emily Dickinson d. Ronald Firbank b. Harold Nicolson b. Lennox Robinson b. Siegfried Sassoon b. Charles Williams b. New English Art Club founded. *The Dictionary of National Biography* begun. Ibsen, *Rosmersholm*. Rimbaud, *Les Illuminations* (written 1872–3).	Kipling, *Departmental Ditties* (Lahore). Tennyson, *Locksley Hall Sixty Years After*. Yeats, *Mosada*.
1887	Queen Victoria's Jubilee. First Colonial Conference. Trafalgar Square riots. Irish Crimes Act. Independent Labour Party formed. Berne Convention regulating international copyright.	Jefferies d. Rupert Brooke b. Edwin Muir b. Edith Sitwell b. Laforgue d. Dujardin, *Les Lauriers sont coupés*. Mallarmé, *Poésies*. Strindberg, *The Father*. Sudermann, *Frau Sorge*.	Dixon, *Lyrical Poems*. Meredith, *Ballads and Poems of Tragic Life*. Morris, trs. *The Odyssey*.
1888	Local Government Act. Miners' Federation formed. Dunlop invents pneumatic tire.	Arnold d. Lear d. Maine d. Joyce Cary b. T. S. Eliot b. T. E. Lawrence b. Katherine Mansfield b. Eugene O'Neill b. Evening *Star* begins publication. New Gallery opens. Renan, *Drames philosophiques*. Rodin, 'Burghers of Calais'.	Allingham, *Poetical Works* (–1893). Lang, *Grass of Parnassus*. Meredith, *A Reading of Earth*.
1889	Bright d. London dock strike. Second International founded. Hitler b. Atrocities in Armenia. British South Africa Company chartered.	Allingham d. Browning d. Wilkie Collins d. Hopkins d. Tupper d. Middleton Murry b. Henley, ed. *The Scots Observer*. *A Doll's House* produced in London. Adams, *History of the United States*. Bergson, *Les Données immédiates de la conscience*. Hauptmann, *Vor Sonnenaufgang*. Tolstoy, *The Kreutzer Sonata*.	Blunt, *In Vinculis*. Browning, *Asolando*. Lear, *Nonsense Drolleries*. Swinburne, *Poems and Ballads: Third Series*. Yeats, *The Wanderings of Oisin*.

Prose Fiction, General Prose	Drama (date of acting)
M. Arnold, *Discourses in America*. Dicey, *The Law of the Constitution*. Pattison, *Memoirs*. Ruskin, *Praeterita* (–1889). Whistler, *The Ten o'clock Lecture*.	
Corelli, *A Romance of Two Worlds*. Gissing, *Demos*. Hardy, *The Mayor of Casterbridge*. James, *The Bostonians. The Princess Casamassima*. Jefferies, *Amaryllis at the Fair*. Moore, *A Drama in Muslin*. Shaw, *Cashel Byron's Profession*. Stevenson, *The Strange Case of Dr. Jekyll and Mr. Hyde. Kidnapped*.	Pinero, *The Schoolmistress*.
Gardiner, *History of the Great Civil War* (–1891). Stubbs, *Seven Lectures on the Study of Mediaeval and Modern History*.	
Caine, *The Deemster*. Conan Doyle, *A Study in Scarlet*. Gissing, *Thyrza*. Haggard, *She. Allan Quatermain*. Hardy, *The Woodlanders*. Pater, *Imaginary Portraits*. Rutherford, *The Revolution in Tanner's Lane*. Shaw, *An Unsocial Socialist*.	
Butler, *Luck, or Cunning as the Main Means of Organic Modification?* G. Birkbeck Hill, ed. Boswell's 'Johnson'. F. Darwin, ed. *Life and Letters of Charles Darwin*.	
Barrie, *Auld Licht Idylls. When a Man's Single*. Gissing, *A Life's Morning*. Hardy, *Wessex Tales*. James, *The Reverberator*. Kipling, *Plain Tales from the Hills. Soldiers Three. The Story of the Gadsbys. In Black and White. Under the Deodars. The Phantom 'Rickshaw. Wee Willie Winkie*. Moore, *Confessions of a Young Man*. Mrs. H. Ward, *Robert Elsmere*. Wilde, *The Happy Prince*.	Gilbert, *The Yeomen of the Guard*. Pinero, *Sweet Lavender*.
M. Arnold, *Essays in Criticism: Second Series*. Bryce, *The American Commonwealth*. Butler, *Ex Voto*. Doughty, *Travels in Arabia Deserta*. Yeats, *Fairy and Folk Tales of the Irish Peasantry*.	
Barrie, *A Window in Thrums*. Jerome, *Three Men in a Boat*. Ouida, *Guilderoy*. Stevenson, *The Master of Ballantrae*.	Jones, *The Middleman*.
Booth, *The Life and Labour of the People in London* (–1897). Carpenter, *Civilisation, Its Cause and Cure*. Shaw, ed. *Fabian Essays*. Galton, *Natural Inheritance*. Pater, *Appreciations*.	

Date	Public Events	Literature and the Arts	Verse
1890	Rhodes P.M. of Cape Colony. Parnell divorce case. Tranby Croft case. Baring crisis. Heligoland ceded to Germany. Marey uses roll film in cinematography. Tube railway in London.	Newman d. Van Gogh d. Nijinski b. Kelmscott Press founded. *Daily Graphic* published. Villiers de L'Isle-Adam, *Axel*. E. Dickinson, *Poems*. Ibsen, *Hedda Gabler*. W. James. *Principles of Psychology*.	Bridges, *Shorter Poems* (Books I–IV; Book V, 1894). Kipling, *Departmental Ditties, Barrack Room Ballads and Other Verses* (New York). Stevenson, *Ballads*. Watson, *Wordsworth's Grave*.
1891	Bradlaugh d. Parnell d. Elementary Education Act. Chace Copyright Act, U.S.A. Siberian Railway begun.	Kinglake d. Bulwer Lytton ('Owen Meredith') d. Lowell d. Melville d. Rimbaud d. Foundation of Independent Theatre Society and production of *Ghosts*. *Strand Magazine* begun. D'Annunzio, *L'innocente*. Hofmannsthal, *Poems and Lyrical Dramas* (–1893).	Davidson, *In a Music Hall*. Morris, *Poems by the Way*.
1892	Gladstone's fourth Ministry. First Shop Hours Act. Keir Hardie in Commons.	Freeman d. Manning d. Tennyson d. Richard Aldington b. Ivy Compton-Burnett b. Victoria Sackville-West b. O. Sitwell b. Rebecca West b. Renan d. S. George, *Algabal*. Hauptmann, *Die Weber*. Ibsen, *The Masterbuilder*. Maeterlinck, *Pelléas et Mélisande*. Zola, *La Débâcle*.	*The Book of the Rhymers' Club*. Henley, *Songs of the Sword*. *Lyra Heroica*. Kipling, *Barrack Room Ballads*. Tennyson, *The Death of Oenone*. Yeats, *The Countess Kathleen and Various Legends and Lyrics*.
1893	Lords reject Home Rule Bill. Major coal-miners' strike. First meeting of Independent Labour Party. Shop Hours Act.	Jowett d. J. A. Symonds d. Wilfred Owen b. Herbert Read b. De Maupassant d. Taine d. Gaelic League founded. Dvořák, 'From the New World' Symphony. Tchaikovsky, 'Pathetic' Symphony.	Bridges, ed. *Poets and Poetry of the Century* (incl. G. M. Hopkins). Davidson, *Fleet Street Eclogues*. A. Meynell, *Poems*. De Tabley, *Poems, Dramatic and Lyrical* (–1895). F. Thompson, *Poems*.
1894	Resignation of Gladstone. Rosebery P.M. Harcourt's Death Duties. Anglo-Catholic movement founded. Armenian massacres. Dreyfus trial. Panhard automobile produced.	Froude d. Pater d. C. Rossetti d. Stevenson d. Aldous Huxley b. Charles Morgan b. 'Yellow Book' started. Debussy, *Prélude à l'après-midi d'un Faune*. Emily Dickinson, *Letters*. Renard, *Poil de Carotte*.	A. E., *Homeward: Songs by the Way*. Binyon, *Lyric Poems*. Davidson, *Ballads and Songs*. Watson, *Odes*.

Prose Fiction, General Prose

Drama (date of acting)

Broughton, *Alas!* Crawford, *A Cigarette-maker's Romance.* James, *The Tragic Muse.* Kipling, *The Light that Failed* (two versions). *The Courting of Dinah Shadd.* Morris, *News from Nowhere.* Wilde, *The Picture of Dorian Gray.*

Grundy, *A Pair of Spectacles.* Jones, *Judah.*

Booth, *In Darkest England.* Frazer, *The Golden Bough* (–1915). Stanley, *In Darkest Africa.* Whistler, *The Gentle Art of Making Enemies.*

Barrie, *The Little Minister.* Conan Doyle, *Adventures of Sherlock Holmes.* Gissing, *New Grub Street.* Hardy, *Tess of the D'Urbervilles. A Group of Noble Dames.* John Oliver Hobbes, *Some Emotions and a Moral.* Kipling, *Life's Handicap.* Meredith, *One of Our Conquerors.* Wilde, *Lord Arthur Savile's Crime.*

Pinero, *The Times.* Wilde, *The Duchess of Padua.*

Shaw, *The Quintessence of Ibsenism.* Wilde, *Intentions. The Soul of Man under Socialism.*

Du Maurier, *Peter Ibbetson.* Gissing, *Born in Exile.* Kipling and Balestier, *The Naulahka.* Merriman, *The Slave of the Lamp.* Zangwill, *Children of the Ghetto.*

Barrie, *Walker, London.* Shaw, *Widowers' Houses.* Wilde, *Lady Windermere's Fan.*

Bosanquet, *History of Aesthetic.* Hudson, *The Naturalist in La Plata.* Whymper, *Travels among the Great Andes of the Equator.*

E. F. Benson, *Dodo.* J. O. Hobbes, *A Study in Temptations.* James, *The Private Life.* Kipling, *Many Inventions.* F. A. Steel, *From the Five Rivers.*

Pinero, *The Second Mrs. Tanqueray.* Wilde, *A Woman of No Importance.*

F. H. Bradley, *Appearance and Reality.* Hudson, *Idle Days in Patagonia.* T. H. Huxley, *Evolutions and Ethics.* Pater, *Plato and Platonism.* Yeats, *The Celtic Twilight.*

Du Maurier, *Trilby.* Gissing, *In the Year of Jubilee.* G. and W. B. Grossmith, *The Diary of a Nobody.* Hardy, *Life's Little Ironies.* Hichens, *The Green Carnation.* Hope, *The Dolly Dialogues. The Prisoner of Zenda.* Kipling, *The Jungle Book.* Machen, *The Great God Pan.* Meredith, *Lord Ormont and his Aminta.* Moore, *Esther Waters.* Morris, *The Wood Beyond the World.* Morrison, *Tales of Mean Streets.* Weyman, *Under the Red Robe.*

Shaw, *Arms and the Man.* Yeats, *The Land of Heart's Desire.*

Blatchford, *Merrie England.* Havelock Ellis, *Man and Woman.* Hearn, *Glimpses of Unfamiliar Japan.* B. and S. Webb, *History of Trade Unionism.*

Date	Public Events	Literature and the Arts	Verse
1895	Salisbury's third Ministry. Jameson Raid. London School of Economics founded. Trial of Wilde. Röntgen discovers X-rays. Kiel Canal opened.	T. H. Huxley d. William Gerhardi b. Robert Graves b. L. P. Hartley b. Westminster Cathedral begun. S. Crane, *The Red Badge of Courage*.	Johnson, *Poems*. F. Thompson, *Sister Songs*. J. Thomson, *Poetical Works*. Yeats, *Poems*.
1896	Ashanti campaign. Marconi invents wireless telegraphy. Klondike gold rush.	Du Maurier d. Morris d. Patmore d. Edmund Blunden b. Verlaine d. Austin Poet Laureate. *Daily Mail* founded. National Portrait Gallery opened. Puccini, *La Bohème*. Chekhov, *The Seagull*.	Belloc, *The Bad Child's Book of Beasts*. Mary Coleridge, *Fancy's Following*. Dowson, *Verses*. Housman, *A Shropshire Lad*. Kipling, *The Seven Seas*.
1897	Queen Victoria's Diamond Jubilee. Voluntary Schools Act. Workmen's Compensation Act. Sudan campaign. Ramsay discovers helium.	Henry George d. William Faulkner b. Tree opens Her Majesty's Theatre. Tate Gallery opened. Wallace Collection bequeathed to nation. France, *L'Orme du mail*. Gide, *Les Nourritures terrestres*. W. James, *The Will to Believe*. Mallarmé, *Divagations*.	A. E., *Earth Breath*. Davidson, *New Ballads*. Kipling, 'Recessional'. Newbolt, *Admirals All*. Thompson, *New Poems*.
1898	Gladstone d. Bismarck d. Fashoda crisis. Battle of Omdurman. Spanish-American War. The Curies discover radium.	Beardsley d. Burne-Jones d. Lewis Carroll d. Henry Moore b. Mallarmé d. D'Annunzio, *La città morta*. Rimbaud, *Œuvres*. Zola, *J'accuse*.	Bridges, *Poetical Works* (–1905). Hardy, *Wessex Poems*. Watson, *Collected Poems*. Wilde, *The Ballad of Reading Gaol*.
1899	Boer War. First Hague Conference. Board of Education established.	Elizabeth Bowen b. Noel Coward b. Eric Linklater b. Ernest Hemingway b. Irish Literary Theatre	Bridges, *New Poems*. Davidson, *The Last Ballad*. Kipling, 'The Absent-Minded Beggar'.

Prose Fiction, General Prose	*Drama (date of acting)*
Allen, *The Woman Who Did*. Conrad, *Almayer's Folly*. Corelli, *The Sorrows of Satan*. Grahame, *The Golden Age*. Kipling, *The Second Jungle Book*. Macdonald, *Lilith*. Macleod, *The Mountain Lovers*. Moore, *Celibates*. Wells, *The Time Machine*.	Du Maurier, *Trilby*. James, *Guy Domville*. Pinero, *The Notorious Mrs. Ebbsmith*. Shaw, *Candida*. Wilde, *An Ideal Husband. The Importance of Being Earnest*.
Acton, *A Lecture on the Study of History*. Froude, *English Seamen in the Sixteenth Century*. Nordau, *Degeneration*. Patmore, *The Rod, the Root and the Flower*.	
Conrad, *An Outcast of the Islands*. Hardy, *Jude the Obscure*. Jacobs, *Many Cargoes*. James, *The Other House*. Merrick, *Cynthia*. Morrison, *A Child of the Jago*. Stevenson, *Weir of Hermiston*. Wells, *The Island of Dr. Moreau*.	Jones, *Michael and his Lost Angel*. Wilde, *Salome* (Paris).
Beerbohm, *The Works of Max Beerbohm*. Carpenter, *Love's Coming-of-Age*. Dickinson, *The Greek View of Life*. Ker, *Epic and Romance*. M'Taggart, *Studies in Hegelian Dialectic*.	
Beerbohm, *The Happy Hypocrite*. Gissing, *The Whirlpool*. Hardy, *The Well-Beloved* (serial version 1892). James, *The Spoils of Poynton. What Maisie Knew*. Kipling, *Captains Courageous*. Maugham, *Liza of Lambeth*. Merriman, *In Kedar's Tents*. Wells, *The Invisible Man*. Yeats, *The Tables of the Law: The Adoration of the Magi. The Secret Rose*.	Barrie, *The Little Minister*. Jones, *The Liars*. Shaw, *The Devil's Disciple. The Man of Destiny*.
Meredith, *Essay on Comedy*. Hallam Tennyson, *Alfred Tennyson: A Memoir*. Webb, *Industrial Democracy*.	
Conrad, *The Nigger of the 'Narcissus'. Tales of Unrest*. Galsworthy (John Sinjon), *Jocelyn*. Hewlett, *The Forest Lovers*. James, *In the Cage. The Two Magics*. Kipling, *The Day's Work*. Moore, *Evelyn Innes*. Pett-Ridge, *Mord Em'ly*. Watts-Dunton, *Aylwin*. Wells, *The War of the Worlds*.	Pinero, *Trelawney of the 'Wells'*.
Carpenter, *Angels' Wings*. Winston L. Spencer Churchill, *The Story of the Malakand Field Force*. Cunninghame-Graham, *Mogreb-el-Acksa*. Maitland, *Roman Canon Law in the Church of England*. Shaw, *The Perfect Wagnerite*.	
Gissing, *The Crown of Life*. James, *The Awkward Age*. Kipling, *Stalky and Co.* Maugham, *Orientations*. Nesbit, *The Story of the Treasure Seekers*. Phillpotts, *The*	Martyn, *The Heather Field*. Pinero, *The Gay Lord Quex*. Shaw, *You Never Can Tell*. Wills, *The Only Way*. Yeats, *The Countess Kathleen*.

Date	Public Events	Literature and the Arts	Verse
1899 (cont.)	London Borough Councils created.	founded. Tolstoy, *Resurrection.* Chamberlain, *Foundations of the Nineteenth Century. Action française* appears. Elgar, *Enigma Variations.*	Yeats, *The Wind Among the Reeds.*
1900	Commonwealth of Australia established. Boxer rising. Russian occupation of Manchuria. Annexation of Orange Free State and Transvaal. British Labour Party founded. Trial flight of Zeppelin. Central London Railway opened.	Dowson d. Ruskin d. Wilde d. Sean O'Faoláin b. Stage Society founded. Elgar, *Dream of Gerontius.* Bergson, *Le Rire.* Péguy, *Cahiers* (-1914). Freud, *Die Traumdeutung.* Ibsen, *When We Dead Awaken.* Puccini, *Tosca.*	Brown, *Collected Poems.* Henley, *For England's Sake.*
1901	Queen Victoria d. Accession of King Edward VII. Taff Vale judgement. Planck propounds Quantum theory. First wireless communication between Europe and America.	K. Greenaway d. C. Yonge d. Roy Campbell b. Toulouse-Lautrec d. Chekhov, *The Three Sisters.*	Meredith, *A Reading of Life.* Meynell, *Later Poems.*
1902	Balfour P.M. Rhodes d. End of Boer War. Elementary Education Act. Anglo-Japanese alliance.	Acton d. Butler d. Johnson d. Bret Harte d. Zola d. Debussy, *Pelléas et Mélisande.* Gide, *L'Immoraliste.* W. James, *The Varieties of Religious Experience.* Mann, *Buddenbrooks.* Croce, *Estetica.*	De la Mare, *Songs of Childhood.* Hardy, *Poems of the Past and Present.* Masefield, *Salt-Water Ballads.* Symons, *Poems.*
1903	Salisbury d. Irish Land Purchase Act. Wright brothers' first successful flight. Workers' Educational Association founded.	Gissing d. Henley d. Spencer d. Whistler d. George Orwell (Eric Blair) b. William Plomer b. Evelyn Waugh b. Gauguin d. London, *The Call of the Wild.* Croce founds *La Critica.*	Hardy, *The Dynasts* (-1908). Yeats, *In the Seven Woods.*
1904	Russo-Japanese War. *Entente cordiale* between Britain and France. Pavlov	Christina Rossetti d. Graham Greene b. Rosamund Lehmann b. Cecil Day	A. E., *The Divine Vision.*

Prose Fiction, General Prose	Drama (date of acting)
Human Boy. Q., *The Ship of Stars*. Somerville and Ross, *Some Experiences of an Irish R.M.*	
Beerbohm, *More*. Firth, *The Protectorate*. Inge, *Christian Mysticism*. Kipling, *From Sea to Sea*. Mackail, *Life of William Morris*. Symons, *The Symbolist Movement in Literature*.	
Conrad, *Lord Jim*. James, *The Soft Side*. Onions, *The Compleat Bachelor*. Shaw, *Love among the Artists* (Chicago). Wells, *Love and Mr. Lewisham*.	Jones, *Mrs. Dane's Defence*. Phillips, *Herod*. Shaw, *Captain Brassbound's Conversion*.
Firth, *Oliver Cromwell*. Saintsbury, *A History of Criticism* (–1904).	
Butler, *Erewhon Revisited*. Conrad and Hueffer, *The Inheritors*. Douglas, *The House with the Green Shutters*. James, *The Sacred Fount*. Kipling, *Kim*. Malet, *The History of Sir Richard Calmady*.	Granville-Barker, *The Marrying of Anne Leete*. Pinero, *Iris*.
Belloc, *Robespierre*. Bourn, *The Bettesworth Book*. Gissing, *By the Ionian Sea*. Hudson, *Birds and Man*.	
Bennett, *Anna of the Five Towns*. Conrad, *Youth*. Hudson, *El Ombú*. James, *The Wings of the Dove*. Kipling, *Just So Stories*. Mason, *The Four Feathers*.	Barrie, *Quality Street*. *The Admirable Crichton*. Phillips, *Ulysses*. Shaw, *Mrs. Warren's Profession*. Yeats, *Cathleen ni Houlihan*. *The Pot of Broth*.
Belloc, *The Path to Rome*. Chesterton, *Robert Browning*.	
Butler, *The Way of All Flesh*. Childers, *The Riddle of the Sands*. Conrad, *Typhoon*. Conrad and Hueffer, *Romance*. James, *The Ambassadors*. *The Better Sort*. Merrick, *Conrad in Quest of his Youth*. Merriman, *Barlasch of the Guard*. Moore, *The Untilled Field*.	A. Austin, *Flodden Field*. Kipling, *The Light that Failed*. Maugham, *A Man of Honour*. Synge, *In the Shadow of the Glen*. Yeats, *The Hour Glass* (prose version). *The King's Threshold*. W. Poel produces *Everyman*.
Chambers, *The Mediaeval Stage*. Gissing, *The Private Papers of Henry Ryecroft*. G. E. Moore, *Principia Ethica*. Morley, *Life of Gladstone*. Yeats, *Ideas of Good and Evil*.	
Chesterton, *The Napoleon of Notting Hill*. Conrad, *Nostromo*. Corvo, *Hadrian the Seventh*. De la Mare, *Henry Brocken*. Gissing,	Barrie, *Peter Pan*. Bridges, *Demeter, A Mask*. Granville-Barker and L. Housman, *Prunella*. Shaw, *John Bull's Other Island*. Synge, *Riders*

Date	*Public Events*	*Literature and the Arts*	*Verse*
1904 (*cont.*)	awarded Nobel Prize for Medicine. Panama Canal begun.	Lewis b. Chekhov d. Adams, *Mont-Saint-Michel and Chartres*. Chekhov, *The Cherry Orchard*. More, *Shelburne Essays* (–1921). Puccini, *Madam Butterfly*.	
1905	Campbell-Bannerman P.M. Einstein propounds first principle of Relativity. Mutiny on 'Potemkin'. Sinn Fein Party founded. Militant Women's Suffrage movement begun. Motor buses in London.	Irving d. Macdonald d. H. E. Bates b. Henry Green b. William Empson b. Anthony Powell b. C. P. Snow b. Sartre b. Bliss Carman, *Collected Poems*. 'Die Brücke' group formed in Germany. Sibelius, *Finlandia*. Strauss, *Salome*. Wharton, *The House of Mirth*.	Bentley, *Biography for Beginners*. Dowson, *Poems*. Masefield, *A Mainsail Haul*.
1906	Algeciras Conference. Trade Disputes Act. Thirty Labour members in the Commons. Liberals in power. *Dreadnought* launched. Simplon Tunnel opened. Zuider Zee drainage begun.	Maitland d. Cézanne d. Ibsen d. 'Everyman's Library' started. Upton Sinclair, *The Jungle*.	De la Mare, *Poems*. Doughty, *Dawn in Britain* (–1907).
1907	Territorial and Reserve Forces Act. Third Imperial Conference in London. Second Peace Conference at the Hague. Lumière invents colour photography.	Mary Coleridge d. Francis Thomson d. W. H. Auden b. Christopher Fry b. John Lehmann b. Louis MacNeice b. Adams, *The Education of Henry Adams* (privately printed; pub. 1918). Bergson, *L'Évolution créatrice*. W. James, *Pragmatism*. Rilke, *Neue Gedichte*. Strindberg, *The Ghost Sonata*.	Belloc, *Cautionary Tales*. Binyon, *Attila*. Colum, *Wild Earth*. Flecker, *The Bridge of Fire*. Gibson, *The Stonefolds*. Hodgson, *The Last Blackbird*. Joyce, *Chamber Music*.
1908	Asquith P.M. Old Age pensions introduced.	Ouida (Louise de la Ramée) d. Nigel Balchin	Abercrombie, *Interludes and Poems*. Davidson,

| *Prose Fiction, General Prose* | *Drama (date of acting)* |

Veranilda. Harland, *My Friend Prospero.* Hichens, *The Garden of Allah.* Hudson, *Green Mansions.* James, *The Golden Bowl.* Kipling, *Traffics and Discoveries.* Saki, *Reginald.* Sinclair, *The Divine Fire.* Sturgis, *Belchamber.*

to the Sea. Yeats, *The Shadowy Waters.* *Where there is Nothing. On Baile's Strand.*

A. C. Bradley, *Shakespearean Tragedy.* Spencer, *Autobiography.* Stephen, *English Literature and Society in the Eighteenth Century.* Trevelyan, *England under the Stuarts.*

Forster, *Where Angels Fear to Tread.* M. R. James, *Ghost Stories of an Antiquary.* Moore, *The Lake.* Orczy, *The Scarlet Pimpernel.* Shaw, *The Irrational Knot.* Wells, *Kipps.*

Colum, *The Land.* Granville-Barker, *The Voysey Inheritance.* Lady Gregory, *Kincora. The White Cockade.* Hankin, *The Return of the Prodigal.* Shaw, *Major Barbara. Man and Superman* (Act III, 1907). *The Philanderer.* Synge, *The Well of the Saints.*

Chesterton, *Heretics.* Dickinson, *A Modern Symposium.* James, *English Hours.* Vinogradoff, *Growth of the Manor.* Wilde, *De Profundis.*

Blackwood, *The Empty House.* De Morgan, *Joseph Vance.* Galsworthy, *The Man of Property.* Gissing, *The House of Cobwebs.* Hobbes, *The Dream and the Business.* Kipling, *Puck of Pook's Hill.* Malet, *The Far Horizon.* Wallace, *The Four Just Men.* Wells, *In the Days of the Comet.*

Galsworthy, *The Silver Box.* Lady Gregory, *Hyacinth Halvey. The Gaol Gate. The Canavans.* Hankin, *The Charity that Began at Home.* Shaw, *Caesar and Cleopatra* (New York and Berlin). *The Doctor's Dilemma.* Sutro, *The Fascinating Mr. Vandervelt.* Yeats, *Deirdre.*

Acton, *Lectures on Modern History.* Chesterton, *Charles Dickens.* Conrad, *The Mirror of the Sea.* Lady Gregory, *Gods and Fighting Men.* Moore, *Memoirs of My Dead Life.* Saintsbury, *History of English Prosody* (–1910). B. and S. Webb, *English Local Government* (–1922).

Bennett, *The Grim Smile of the Five Towns.* Conrad, *The Secret Agent.* De Morgan, *Alice-for-Short.* Forster, *The Longest Journey.* Galsworthy, *The Country House.* Q., *The Mayor of Troy.*

Colum, *The Fiddler's House.* Galsworthy, *Joy.* Granville-Barker, *Waste.* Lady Gregory, *Dervorgilla. The Rising of the Moon. The Workhouse Ward.* Masefield, *The Campden Wonder.* Synge, *The Playboy of the Western World.* Yeats, *The Unicorn from the Stars.*

Bell, *The Desert and the Sown.* Bourn, *Memoirs of a Surrey Labourer.* Gosse, *Father and Son.* James, *The American Scene.* Murray, *The Rise of the Greek Epic.* Raleigh, *Shakespeare.* Shaw, *Dramatic Opinions and Essays.* Trevelyan, *Garibaldi's Defence of the Roman Republic.*

Bennett, *The Old Wives' Tale.* Chesterton, *The Man Who was Thursday.* Conrad, *A Set*

James, *The High Bid.* Jerome, *The Passing of the Third Floor Back.* Masefield, *The Tragedy*

Date	Public Events	Literature and the Arts	Verse
1908 (*cont.*)	Children's Act. Mines Eight Hours Act. German Naval Bill.	b. Sardou d. Hueffer (Ford) founds *English Review*. France, *L'Île des pingouins*. Sorel, *Réflexions sur la violence*. Stein, *Three Lives*.	*The Testament of John Davidson*.
1909	Navy Bill. The Lords reject Lloyd George's Budget. Blériot flies Channel. Declaration of London. Copyright Act U.S.A. Model T. Ford first produced.	Davidson d. Meredith d. Swinburne d. Synge d. Stephen Spender b. Gaiety Theatre, Manchester, under Miss Horniman. Diaghileff Ballet in Paris. Futurist Manifesto. Maeterlinck, *L'Oiseau bleu*. Pound, *Personae*. Schönberg, 'Klavierstücke'. *Nouvelle revue française* founded.	Binyon, *England*. Freeman, *Twenty Poems*. Hardy, *Time's Laughingstocks*. Meredith, *Last Poems*. Synge, *Poems and Translations*.
1910	King Edward VII d. Accession of King George V. Dominion of S. Africa established. Industrial unrest. Two General Elections. Japan annexes Korea.	W. James d. Tolstoy d. M. Twain d. First Post-Impressionist exhibition in London. Babbitt, *The New Laocoön*. Pound, *The Spirit of Romance*. Santayana, *Three Philosophical Poets*. Stravinsky, *The Fire Bird*.	Belloc, *Verses*. Flecker, *Thirty-six Poems*. Masefield, *Ballads and Poems*. Yeats, *Poems: Second Series. The Green Helmet and Other Poems*.
1911	Railway and dock strikes. Parliament Act. Imperial Conference. National health insurance introduced. Copyright Act. Amundsen at South Pole. Agadir incident. Franco-Russian military convention.	W. S. Gilbert d. Claudel, *Cinq grandes odes*. Pound, *Canzoni*. 'Der blaue Reiter' group formed. Strauss and Hofmannsthal, *Rosenkavalier*.	Abercrombie, *Emblems of Love. The Sale of St. Thomas*. Brooke, *Poems*. Chesterton, *The Ballad of the White Horse*. Davies, *Songs of Joy*. Flecker, *Forty-two Poems*. Masefield, *The Everlasting Mercy*.
1912	Coal strike. Third Home Rule Bill. Militant Suffrage movement intensified. Loss of the *Titanic*. Balkan War. China proclaimed a Republic.	W. Booth, founder of Salvation Army, d. Lawrence Durell b. Roy Fuller b. William Sansom b. *Georgian Poetry* (–1922). Harriet Monroe founded *Poetry*. Claudel, *L'Annonce faite à Marie*. Pound,	De la Mare, *The Listeners*. Kipling, *Collected Verse*. Masefield, *The Widow in the Bye Street*.

Prose Fiction, General Prose	*Drama (date of acting)*

of Six. Forster, *A Room with a View.* Grahame, *The Wind in the Willows.* H. H. Richardson, *Maurice Guest.* Maugham, *The Explorer.*

of Nan. Robinson, *The Clancy Name.* Shaw, *Getting Married.* Yeats, *The Golden Helmet.*

Belloc, *On Nothing.* Davies, *The Autobiography of a Super-Tramp.*

Belloc, *A Change in the Cabinet.* Buchan, *Prester John.* Kipling, *Actions and Reactions.* Masefield, *Multitude and Solitude.* Walpole, *The Wooden Horse.* Wells, *Tono-Bungay. Ann Veronica.*

Baker, *Chains.* Bottomley, *The Riding to Lithend.* Dunsany, *The Glittering Gate.* Galsworthy, *Strife.* Lady Gregory, *The Image.* Pinero, *Mid-Channel.* Robinson, *The Cross-Roads.* Shaw, *The Shewing-up of Blanco Posnet.* Synge, *The Tinker's Wedding.*

Beerbohm, *Yet Again.* Chesterton, *Tremendous Trifles. George Bernard Shaw.* Harris, *The Man Shakespeare.* James, *Italian Hours.* Kipling, *Abaft the Funnel.* F. Thompson, *Shelley.*

Belloc, *Pongo and the Bull.* Bennett, *Clayhanger.* De la Mare, *The Return.* Forster, *Howard's End.* Galsworthy, *A Motley.* James, *The Finer Grain.* Kipling, *Rewards and Fairies.* Wells, *The History of Mr. Polly.* Wodehouse, *Psmith in the City.*

Barrie, *The Twelve-Pound Look.* Granville-Barker, *The Madras House.* Galsworthy, *Justice.* Lady Gregory, *The Full Moon.* Masefield, *The Tragedy of Pompey the Great.* Lennox Robinson, *Harvest.* Shaw, *Misalliance.* Synge, *Deirdre of the Sorrows.* Yeats, *The Green Helmet.*

Angell, *The Great Illusion.* Belloc, *On Anything.* Hudson, *A Shepherd's Life.* Whitehead and Russell, *Principia Mathematica,* Vol. I.

Beerbohm, *Zuleika Dobson.* Bennett, *The Card.* Hilda Lessways. Beresford, *The Hampdenshire Wonder.* Chesterton, *The Innocence of Father Brown.* Conrad, *Under Western Eyes.* De Morgan, *A Likely Story.* Forster, *The Celestial Omnibus.* Galsworthy, *The Patrician.* James, *The Outcry.* Lawrence, *The White Peacock.* Mansfield, *In a German Pension.* Reid, *The Bracknels* (revised as *Denis Bracknel,* 1947). Saki, *The Chronicles of Clovis.* Walpole, *Mr. Perrin and Mr. Traill.* Mrs. H. Ward, *The Case of Richard Meynell.* Wells, *The New Machiavelli.*

Dunsany, *The Gods of the Mountain.* Ervine, *Mixed Marriage.* Maugham, *Loaves and Fishes.* Shaw, *Fanny's First Play.*

Douglas, *Siren Land.* J. L. and B. Hammond, *The Village Labourer 1760–1832.* Moore, *Hail and Farewell* (–1914). Underhill, *Mysticism.*

Belloc, *The Green Overcoat.* Bentley, *Trent's Last Case.* Conrad, *'Twixt Land and Sea.* Lawrence, *The Trespasser.* Locke, *The Joyous Adventures of Aristide Pujol.* Q., *Hocken and Hunken.* Reid, *Following Darkness* (revised as *Peter Waring,* 1937). Saki, *The Unbearable Bassington.* Stephens, *The Crock of Gold.*

Bennett and Knoblock, *Milestones.* Galsworthy, *The Pigeon. The Eldest Son.* Lady Gregory, *McDonough's Wife.* Houghton, *Hindle Wakes.* Monkhouse, *The Education of Mr. Surrage.* Shaw, *Overruled.* Yeats, *The Hour Glass* (verse).

Date	Public Events	Literature and the Arts	Verse
1912 (cont.)		Ripostes. Schönberg, Pierrot Lunaire. Sorge, Der Bettler. Tagore, trs. Gitanjali.	
1913	Poincaré, President of France. Belgian and French Army Bills. Second and Third Balkan Wars. Marconi scandals. Trades Union Act. Bohr's investigation of the structure of the atom.	Austin d. Bridges Poet Laureate. George Barker b. Benjamin Britten b. Angus Wilson b. Apollinaire, Les Peintres cubistes. Alcools. Alain-Fournier, Le Grand Meaulnes. Freud, Totem und Tabu. Lindsay, General William Booth enters into Heaven. Proust, Du Côté de chez Swann. Stravinsky, Le Sacre du printemps. Mann, Der Tod in Venedig. Unamuno, El Sentimiento trágico de la Vida.	De la Mare, Peacock Pie. Flecker, The Golden Journey to Samarkand. Lawrence, Love Poems and Others. Masefield, The Daffodil Fields. Dauber. Meynell, Collected Poems.
1914	Curragh mutiny. Sarajevo assassination. Buckingham Palace Conference. Outbreak of War. Opening of Panama Canal.	Laurie Lee b. Dylan Thomas b. Peguy d. R. Frost, North of Boston. Hasenclever, Der Sohn. Kaiser, Die Bürger von Calais. Pound, ed. Des Imagistes. Trakl, Gedichte. Little Review (Chicago –1929.)	Blunden, Poems 1913 and 1914. Blunt, Poetical Works. Hardy, Satires of Circumstance. Newbolt, Drake's Drum and Other Songs of the Sea. Yeats, Responsibilities.
1915	Coalition Government under Asquith. Munitions of War Act. National Registration Act. South Wales miners strike. Dardanelles campaign.	Brooke d. Flecker d. Phillips d. Alun Lewis b. Gould Fletcher, Irradiations. Pound, Cathay. Stein, Tender Buttons. 'Dada' movement begun in Zürich.	Aldington, Images, Old and New. Brooke, 1914 and Other Poems. Chesterton, Poems. Flecker, The Old Ships. Monro, Trees. Rosenberg, Youth. E. Sitwell, The Mother.
1916	Lloyd George P.M. Easter Rising in Ireland. National conscription. Battle of Verdun. Battle of Jutland. Communist 'Spartacus group' founded in Berlin. Casement executed.	H. James d. Hector Munro (Saki) d. Philip Toynbee b. Barbusse, Le Feu. Jung, The Psychology of the Unconscious. Kafka, Die Verwandlung, Pound, Lustra. Gaudier-Brzeska. Sandburg, Chicago Poems. Bartok, Der holzgeschnitze Prinz.	Drinkwater, Olton Pools. Graves, Over the Brazier. Huxley, The Burning Wheel. Lawrence, Amores. Masefield, Sonnets and Poems. Mew, The Farmer's Bride. E. and O. Sitwell, Twentieth Century Harlequinade. E. Sitwell, ed. Wheels (–1921).

Prose Fiction, General Prose	Drama (date of acting)
Beerbohm, *A Christmas Garland*. Belloc, *The Servile State*. Butler, *Note-books.* ed. Festing-Jones. Conrad, *Some Reminiscences*. Douglas, *Fountains in the Sand*. Roberts, *The Private Life of Henry Maitland* (i.e. George Gissing). Russell, *The Problems of Philosophy*. Strachey, *Landmarks in French Literature*. Yeats, *The Cutting of an Agate*.	
Cannan, *Round the Corner*. Conrad, *Chance*. Galsworthy, *The Dark Flower*. Jesse, *The Milky Way*. Lawrence, *Sons and Lovers*. Mackenzie, *Sinister Street* (–1914). Sinclair, *The Combined Maze*. Stephens, *Here are Ladies*. Wells, *The Passionate Friends*.	Abercrombie, *Deborah*. Barrie, *The Will*. Chesterton, *Magic*. Ervine, *Jane Clegg*. Galsworthy, *The Fugitive*. Shaw, *Androcles and the Lion*. *Pygmalion* (Berlin).
Chesterton, *The Victorian Age in Literature*. Lady Gregory, *Our Irish Theatre*. James, *A Small Boy and Others*.	
Joyce, *Dubliners*. Lawrence, *The Prussian Officer*. Sinclair, *The Three Sisters*. Wells, *The Wife of Sir Isaac Harman*.	Abercrombie, *The End of the World*. Drinkwater, *Rebellion*. Galsworthy, *The Mob*. Masefield, *Philip the King*.
Bell, *Art*. James, *Notes of a Son and Brother*. *Notes on Novelists*. Scott, *The Architecture of Humanism*. Shaw, *Commonsense about the War*.	
S. Benson, *I Pose*. Buchan, *The Thirty-nine Steps*. Conrad, *Victory*. *Within the Tides*. Ford (Hueffer), *The Good Soldier*. Galsworthy, *The Freelands*. Lawrence, *The Rainbow*. Maugham, *Of Human Bondage*. D. Richardson, *Pointed Roofs* (*Pilgrimage* –1938). Wells, *Boon*. Woolf, *The Voyage Out*.	Bottomley, *King Lear's Wife*. Drinkwater, *The Storm*. Galsworthy, *A Bit o' Love*.
Douglas, *Old Calabria*.	
Buchan, *Greenmantle*. Joyce, *A Portrait of the Artist as a Young Man*. Moore, *The Brook Kerith*. Richardson, *Backwater*. Walpole, *The Dark Forest*. Wells, *Mr. Britling Sees it Through*.	Barrie, *A Kiss for Cinderella*. Drinkwater, *The God of Quiet*. Robinson, *The White-headed Boy*. Yeats, *At the Hawk's Well*. *The Only Jealousy of Emer*.
Lawrence, *Twilight in Italy*. Murry, *Fyodor Dostoevsky*. Quiller-Couch, *On the Art of Writing*. West, *Henry James*. Yeats, *Reveries over Childhood and Youth*.	

Date	Public Events	Literature and the Arts	Verse
1917	Bread-cards in England. Battle of Vimy Ridge. Unrestricted submarine warfare. March and October Revolutions in Russia. U.S.A. enters war. Balfour Declaration on Palestine.	De Morgan d. Edward Thomas d. Degas d. Rodin d. Valéry, *La Jeune Parque*.	Binyon, *For the Fallen*. Bridges, *Ibant Obscuri*. Drinkwater, *Poems 1908–1914*. Eliot, *Prufrock and Other Observations*. Hardy, *Moments of Vision*. Hodgson, *Poems*. Lawrence, *Look! We Have Come Through!* Masefield, *Lollingdon Downs*. Harold Monro, *Strange Meetings*. Sassoon, *The Old Huntsman*. Edward Thomas, *Poems*. Yeats, *The Wild Swans at Coole*.
1918	Zeebrugge raid. Treaty of Brest-Litovsk. Armistice (November). First Women's Suffrage Act. Fisher Education Act.	G. Alexander d. W. Owen d. Aiken, *The Charnel Rose*. Blok, *The Twelve*. Kaiser, *Gas* (–1920). Pirandello, *Il giuoco delle parti*. Spengler, *Der Untergang des Abendlandes* (–1922).	De la Mare, *Motley*. Hopkins, *Poems*, ed. Bridges. Lawrence, *New Poems*. Sassoon, *Counter Attack*. E. Sitwell, *Clown's Houses*. Thomas, *Last Poems*. Turner, *The Dark Fire*.
1919	Lloyd George's second Ministry. Treaty of Versailles. Third Communist International. Alcock and Brown fly Atlantic. First woman M.P. 18th Amendment, U.S.A. (repealed 1933).	Renoir d. *London Mercury* started. S. Anderson, *Winesburg, Ohio*. Babbitt, *Rousseau and Romanticism*. Cabell, *Jurgen*. Mencken, *Prejudices* (–1927). *The American Language* (–1948). Pound, *Quia pauper amavi*. Toller, *Die Wandlung*.	Aldington, *Greek Songs in the Manner of Anacreon*. Hardy, *Collected Poems*. Kipling, *Verse: Inclusive Edition*. Masefield, *Reynard the Fox*. Read, *Naked Warriors*. Waley, *170 Chinese Poems*.
1920	Civil War in Ireland. Home Rule Act. Large-scale strikes. Emergency Powers Act. League of Nations meets.	Mrs. Humphry Ward d. Howells d. S. Lewis, *Main Street*. O'Neill, *The Emperor Jones*. Pound, *Hugh Selwyn Mauberley*.	Blunden, *The Waggoner*. Bridges, *October*. De la Mare, *Poems 1901–1918*. Freeman, *Poems New and Old*. Huxley, *Leda*. Masefield, *Enslaved*. Owen, *Poems*, ed. Sassoon. Pitter, *First Poems*. D. Wellesley, *Poems*. Wolfe, *London Sonnets*. Yeats, *Michael Robartes and the Dancer*.
1921	Irish Free State established. First Indian Parliament meets. Disarmament Conference in Washington.	M. Moore, *Poems*. Pirandello, *Sei personaggi in cerca d'autore*. Toller, *Masse Mensch*.	Baring, *Poems 1914–1919*. De la Mare, *The Veil*. Graves, *The Pier Glass*. Lawrence, *Tortoises*. E. Sitwell, *Troy Park*. S. Sitwell, *Doctor*

Prose Fiction, General Prose	Drama (date of acting)
Conrad, *The Shadow-Line*. Douglas, *South Wind*. Conan Doyle, *His Last Bow*. James, *The Ivory Tower. The Sense of the Past*. Kipling, *A Diversity of Creatures*. McKenna, *Sonia*. Richardson, *Honeycomb*. Swinnerton, *Nocturne*. A. Waugh, *The Loom of Youth*. Wells, *The Soul of a Bishop*. Hammond, *The Town Labourer 1760–1832*. James, *The Middle Years*.	Barrie, *Dear Brutus*. Galsworthy, *The Foundations*. James, *The Outcry*. Masefield, *Good Friday*. Maugham, *Our Betters*.
Lewis, *Tarr*. Mansfield, *Prelude*. Wells, *Joan and Peter*. West, *The Return of the Soldier*. Hudson, *Far Away and Long Ago*, Inge, *The Philosophy of Plotinus*. Pearsall Smith, *Trivia*. Strachey, *Eminent Victorians*. Yeats, *Per Amica Silentia Lunae*.	Drinkwater, *Abraham Lincoln*. Maugham, *Love in a Cottage*. Robinson, *The Lost Leader*.
Beerbohm, *Seven Men*. S. Benson, *Living Alone*. Conrad, *The Arrow of Gold*. Firbank, *Valmouth*. Maugham, *The Moon and Sixpence*. Morgan, *The Gunroom*. Richardson, *The Tunnel. Interim*. Woolf, *Night and Day*. Barbellion, *The Journal of a Disappointed Man*. Blunt, *My Diaries* (–1920). Festing Jones, *Samuel Butler: A Memoir*. Hammond, *The Skilled Labourer 1760–1832*. Inge, *Outspoken Essays*. Keynes, *The Economic Consequences of the Peace*. Moore, *Avowals*. Shackleton, *South*.	Dunsany, *A Night at an Inn*. Joyce, *Exiles* (Munich). Maugham, *Caesar's Wife*. Yeats, *The Player Queen*.
Conrad, *The Rescue*. Galsworthy, *In Chancery*. Huxley, *Limbo*. Lawrence, *Women in Love* (privately printed). *The Lost Girl*. Mansfield, *Bliss and Other Stories*. M. Asquith, *Autobiography* (–1922). Beerbohm, *And Even Now*. Eliot, *The Sacred Wood*. Fry, *Vision and Design*. James, *Letters*, ed. Lubbock. Kipling, *Letters of Travel*. Murry, *The Evolution of an Intellectual*. Wells, *Outline of History*.	Barrie, *Mary Rose*. Dunsany, *The Tents of the Arabs*. Galsworthy, *The Skin Game*. Lawrence, *The Widowing of Mrs. Holroyd*. Shaw, *Heartbreak House* (New York).
Coppard, *Adam and Eve and Pinch-Me*. De la Mare, *Memoirs of a Midget*. Holme, *The Trumpet in the Dust*. Huxley, *Crome Yellow*. Macaulay, *Dangerous Ages*. Moore, *Héloïse and Abélard*. Myers, *The Orissers*. Richardson, *Deadlock*. Woolf, *Monday or Tuesday*.	Archer, *The Green Goddess*. Barrie, *Shall We Join the Ladies?* Dane, *A Bill of Divorcement*. Drinkwater, *Mary Stuart*. Dunsany, *If*. Maugham, *The Circle*. Munro, *At Mrs. Beam's*.

Date	Public Events	Literature and the Arts	Verse
1921 (cont.)			Donne and Gargantua (-1930).
1922	Bonar Law P.M. Stalin General Secretary of Russian Communist Party. Fascist revolution in Italy. Treaty of Rapallo. Kemal Pasha proclaims Turkish Republic.	Scawen Blunt d. Hudson d. Alice Meynell d. Proust d. Eliot, ed. The Criterion (-1939). Cummings, The Enormous Room. S. Lewis, Babbitt. Mauriac, Le Baiser au lépreux. Valéry, Les Charmes. Vaughan Williams, 'Pastoral' Symphony.	Childe, The Gothic Rose. Drinkwater, Preludes. Eliot, The Waste Land. Hardy, Late Lyrics and Earlier. Housman, Last Poems. Harold Monro, Real Property. E. Sitwell, Façade. S. Sitwell, The Hundred and One Harlequins. Yeats, Later Poems.
1923	Baldwin's first Ministry. Union of Soviet Socialist Republics established. German inflation. Hitler, Mein Kampf (-1927). French occupy Ruhr. Dictatorship of Primo de Rivera in Spain. Failure of Hitler's coup d'état in Munich.	Hewlett d. K. Mansfield d. Sarah Bernhardt d. Frost, New Hampshire. Maurois, Ariel. Pirandello, La vita che ti diedi. Rice, The Adding Machine. Rilke, Duineser Elegien. Sonette an Orpheus. W. Stevens, Harmonium. Vaughan Williams, Mass 'in G minor'.	Aldington, Exile. Belloc, Sonnets and Verse. Blunden, To Nature. Davies, Collected Poems. Drinkwater, Collected Poems. Lawrence, Birds, Beasts and Flowers. Masefield, Collected Poems. Meynell, Last Poems. E. Sitwell, Bucolic Comedies.
1924	First Labour Ministry under MacDonald. Dawes Plan for Reparations. Baldwin's second Ministry. Lenin d. Civil War in China.	Conrad d. Duse d. France d. Kafka d. Mann, Der Zauberberg. Breton, Manifeste du Surréalisme.	Campbell, The Flaming Terrapin. Davies, Secrets. De la Mare, Ding Dong Bell. E. Sitwell, The Sleeping Beauty. S. Sitwell, The Thirteenth Caesar. Wolfe, Kensington Gardens. Yeats, The Cat and the Moon and Certain Poems.

Prose Fiction, General Prose	Drama (date of acting)

Douglas, *Alone*. Lawrence, *Psychoanalysis and the Unconscious. Sea and Sardinia*. Lubbock, *The Craft of Fiction*. Strachey, *Queen Victoria*. Tawney, *The Acquisitive Society*.

Bennett, *Mr. Prohack*. Galsworthy, *The Forsyte Saga*. Garnett, *Lady into Fox*. Gerhardi, *Futility*. Huxley, *Mortal Coils*. Joyce, *Ulysses*. Lawrence, *England, My England. Aaron's Rod*. Mansfield, *The Garden Party*. Moore, *In Single Strictness*. V. Sackville-West, *The Heir*. Sinclair, *The Life and Death of Harriet Frean*. Swinnerton, *The Three Lovers*. Walpole, *The Cathedral*. West, *The Judge*. Woolf, *Jacob's Room*.

Colum, *The Grasshopper*. Conrad, *The Secret Agent*. Drinkwater, *Oliver Cromwell*. Galsworthy, *Windows. Loyalties*. Maugham, *East of Suez*. Shaw, *Back to Methuselah* (New York).

Evans, *Palace of Minos* (–1935). Lawrence, *Fantasia of the Unconscious*. Lubbock, *Earlham*. Montague, *Disenchantment*. Murry, *Countries of the Mind. The Problem of Style*. Strachey, *Books and Characters*. Yeats, *The Trembling of the Veil*.

Baring, *A Triangle*. Bennett, *Riceyman Steps*. E. Bowen, *Encounters*. Conrad, *The Rover*. Firbank, *The Flower beneath the Foot*. Huxley, *Antic Hay*. Lawrence, *Kangaroo. The Ladybird*. Macaulay, *Told by an Idiot*. Mansfield, *The Dove's Nest*. Richardson, *Revolving Lights*.

Bottomley, *Gruach*. Coward, *The Young Idea*. Drinkwater, *Robert E. Lee*. Ervine, *Mary, Mary, Quite Contrary*. Flecker, *Hassan*. Granville-Barker, *The Secret Life*. Masefield, *Melloney Holtspur*. O'Casey, *The Shadow of a Gunman*. Shaw, *Saint Joan* (New York).

Archer, *The Old Drama and the New*. Chambers, *The Elizabethan Stage*. Churchill, *The World Crisis* (–1929). Forster, *Pharos and Pharillon*. Huxley, *On the Margin*. Ker, *The Art of Poetry*. Kipling, *The Irish Guards in the Great War*. Lawrence, *Studies in Classic American Literature*.

Ford, *Some Do Not*. Forster, *A Passage to India*. Galsworthy, *The White Monkey*. Huxley, *The Little Mexican*. Kennedy, *The Constant Nymph*. Lawrence and Skinner, *The Boy in the Bush*. Masefield, *Sard Harker*. Mottram, *The Spanish Farm* (–1927). T. F. Powys, *Mark Only*. Sackville-West, *Seducers in Ecuador*. Saki, *The Square Egg*. O. Sitwell, *Triple Fugue*. Webb, *Precious Bane*.

Dukes, *The Man with a Load of Mischief*. Lady Gregory, *The Story brought by Brigit*. Hardy, *The Tragedy of the Queen of Cornwall*. Monkhouse, *The Conquering Hero*. O'Casey, *Juno and the Paycock*.

Beerbohm, *Around Theatres*. Dobrée, *Restoration Comedy*. Eliot, *Homage to John Dryden*. Hulme, *Speculations*, ed. Read. Montague, *The Right Place*. Moore, *Conversations in Ebury Street*. Nicolson, *Byron, the Last Journey*. Richards, *Principles of Literary Criticism*. S. Sitwell, *Southern Baroque Art*.

Date	Public Events	Literature and the Arts	Verse
1925	Coal crisis. Return to Gold Standard. Hindenburg, President of Germany. Locarno Conference. Television demonstrated.	S. Anderson, *Dark Laughter*. Dos Passos, *Manhattan Transfer*. Dreiser, *An American Tragedy*. Fitzgerald, *The Great Gatsby*. Gide, *Les Faux Monnayeurs*. Kafka, *Ein Prozess*.	A. E., *Voices of the Stones*. Binyon, *The Sirens*. Bottomley, *Poems of Thirty Years*. Eliot, *Poems 1909–1925*. Gibson, *I heard a Sailor*. Hardy, *Human Shows*. Day Lewis, *Beechen Vigil*. MacDiarmid, *Sangschaw*. Muir, *First Poems*. E. Sitwell, *Troy Park*.
1926	General Strike. Disarmament Conference. Germany joins, Spain leaves, League of Nations.	Doughty d. Firbank d. Monet d. Rilke d. Faulkner, *Soldiers' Pay*. Hemingway, *The Sun Also Rises*. Jouhandeau, *M. Godeau intime*. Kafka, *Das Schloss*. Pound, *Personae*. Van Vechten, *Nigger Heaven*. Wilder, *The Cabala*.	MacDiarmid, *A Drunk Man Looks at the Thistle*. Read, *Collected Poems*. Sackville-West, *The Land*. Sassoon, *Satirical Poems*. Stephens, *Collected Poems*. Wolfe, *News of the Devil*.
1927	British Broadcasting Corporation Charter. World Economic Conference at Geneva. Trade Disputes and Trade Union Act. Chiang Kai-Shek overthrows Chinese National Government.	Hemingway, *Men without Women*. Lowes, *The Road to Xanadu*. Walton, *Sinfonia Concertante*. First talking film shown.	Chesterton, *Collected Poems*. Graves, *Poems 1914–1926*. Joyce, *Pomes Penyeach*. E. Sitwell, *Rustic Elegies*. O. Sitwell, *England Reclaimed*.

Prose Fiction, General Prose

Compton-Burnett, *Pastors and Masters*. Conrad, *Suspense*. Ford, *No More Parades*. Gerhardi, *The Polyglots*. Hartley, *Simonetta Perkins*. Huxley, *Those Barren Leaves*. Lawrence, *St. Mawr*. Maugham, *The Painted Veil*. O'Flaherty, *The Informer*. Plomer, *Turbolt Wolfe*. Ll. Powys, *Black Laughter*. Richardson, *The Trap*. Wells, *Christina Alberta's Father*. Woolf, *Mrs. Dalloway*.

Belloc, *The Cruise of the Nona*. Graves, *Poetic Unreason*. Huxley, *Along the Road*. Lawrence, *Reflections on the Death of a Porcupine*. Richards, *Science and Poetry*. Scott, *Portrait of Zélide*. Whitehead, *Science and the Modern World*. Woolf, *The Common Reader*. Yeats, *A Vision. The Bounty of Sweden*.

Bates, *The Two Sisters*. Coppard, *The Field of Mustard*. Ford, *A Man Could Stand Up*. Galsworthy, *The Silver Spoon*. Green, *Blindness*. Huxley, *Two or Three Graces*. Kipling, *Debits and Credits*. Lawrence, *The Plumed Serpent*. Montague, *Rough Justice*. O. Sitwell, *Before the Bombardment*. Warner, *Lolly Willowes*. Wells, *The World of William Clissold*. R. Wilson, *Dragon's Blood*.

Abercrombie, *Romanticism*. Guedalla, *Palmerston*. Huxley, *Jesting Pilate*. T. E. Lawrence, *The Seven Pillars of Wisdom*. W. Lewis, *The Art of Being Ruled*. Read, *Reason and Romanticism*. Reid, *Apostate*. S. Sitwell, *All Summer in a Day*. Tawney, *Religion and the Rise of Capitalism*. Yeats, *Estrangement. Autobiographies*.

V. Dobrée, *Your Cuckoo Sings by Kind*. Douglas, *In the Beginning* (Florence). Garnett, *Go She Must!* Jesse, *The Moonraker*. R. Lehmann, *Dusty Answer*. W. Lewis, *The Wild Body*. Myers, *The Near and the Far*. T. F. Powys, *Mr. Weston's Good Wine*. Richardson, *Oberland*. S. Warner, *Mr. Fortune's Maggot*. R. Wilson, *Latterday Symphony*. Woolf, *To the Lighthouse*.

G. Bell, *Letters*. Bridges, *Collected Essays and Papers* (–1930). Dunne, *An Experiment with Time*. Forster, *Aspects of the Novel*. Fry, *Cézanne*. Granville-Barker, *Prefaces to Shakespeare* (–1947). Graves and Riding, *A Survey of Modernist Poetry*. Lawrence, *Mornings in Mexico*. W. Lewis, *Time and Western Man. The Lion and the Fox*. Lucas, *Tragedy*. Mansfield, *Journal*, ed. Murry. Waddell, *The Wandering Scholars*.

Drama (date of acting)

Coward, *Hay Fever*. Lonsdale, *The Last of Mrs Cheyney*. Robinson, *The White Blackbird*.

Galsworthy, *Escape*. O'Casey, *The Plough and the Stars*. Yeats, *The Cat and the Moon*. Sophocles' *King Oedipus*.

Berkeley, *The White Château*. Lawrence, *David*. Maugham, *The Letter*. Yeats, *Sophocles' Oedipus at Colonus*.

Date	Public Events	Literature and the Arts	Verse
1928	Women's Suffrage Act. Local Government Act. Kellogg Pact.	Hardy d. Charlotte Mew d. Ellen Terry d. Brecht, *Die Dreigroschenoper.* Lorca, *Primer romancero gitano.* O'Neill, *Strange Interlude.* Pound, *A Draft of the Cantos 17–27.* Remarque, *Im Westen nichts Neues.*	Binyon, *The Idols.* Davies, *Collected Poems.* Hardy, *Winter Words.* Masefield, *Midsummer Night.* Turner, *New Poems.* Wolfe, *This Blind Rose.* Yeats, *The Tower.*
1929	Macdonald's second Ministry. Collapse of New York Stock Exchange: economic depression begins. Clemenceau d. Stresemann d. Dictatorship in Yugoslavia. Trotsky expelled from Russia. First Soviet Five-Year Plan.	First Malvern Festival. Faulkner, *Sartoris. The Sound and the Fury.* Hemingway, *A Farewell to Arms.* Pirandello, *Lazzaro.* Rice, *Street Scene.* Delius Festival in London.	Bridges, *The Testament of Beauty.* Lawrence, *Pansies.* Day Lewis, *Transitional Poem.* MacNeice, *Blind Fireworks.* E. Sitwell, *Gold Coast Customs.* Yeats, *The Winding Stair* (New York).
1930	Mass unemployment. Gandhi opens civil disobedience campaign. Nazi gains in German elections.	Bridges d. Conan Doyle d. D. H. Lawrence d. Hart Crane, *The Bridge.* Frost, *Collected Poems.* Musil, *Der Mann ohne Eigenschaften* (–1943). St. J. Perse, *Anabasis,* trs.	Abercrombie, *Collected Poems.* Aldington, *A Dream in the Luxemburg.* Auden, *Poems.* Blunden, *Poems 1914–30.* Campbell, *Adamastor.* Eliot, *Ash Wednesday.* Freeman,

Prose Fiction, General Prose

Douglas, *In the Beginning* (London: incomplete). Ford, *Last Post.* Forster, *The Eternal Moment.* Galsworthy, *Swan Song.* Huxley, *Point Counter Point.* Isherwood, *All the Conspirators.* Lawrence, *Lady Chatterley's Lover* (Florence: privately printed). *The Woman Who Rode Away.* W. Lewis, *The Childermass* (Vol. I). Maugham, *Ashenden.* Moore, *A Story-Teller's Holiday.* E. Waugh, *Decline and Fall.* Wells, *Mr. Bletsworthy on Rampole Island.* Woolf, *Orlando.*

Barfield, *Poetic Diction.* Beerbohm, *A Variety of Things.* Bell, *Civilization.* Blunden, *Undertones of War.* Clark, *The Gothic Revival.* Douglas, *Birds and Beasts of the Greek Anthology.* Dunsterville, *Stalky's Reminiscences.* Eddington, *The Nature of the Physical World.* Eliot, *For Lancelot Andrewes.* Ker, *Form and Style in Poetry.* Kipling, *A Book of Words.* Muir, *The Structure of the Novel.* Read, *English Prose Style.* Sassoon, *Memoirs of a Fox-hunting Man.* Shaw, *The Intelligent Woman's Guide to Socialism and Capitalism.* Strachey, *Elizabeth and Essex.* Waugh, *Rossetti.* Yeats, *The Death of Synge.*

Aldington, *Death of a Hero* (London, incomplete; full edition published in Paris, 1930). Compton-Burnett, *Brothers and Sisters.* Galsworthy, *A Modern Comedy.* Garnett, *No Love.* Green, *Living.* Greene, *The Man Within.* Hughes, *A High Wind in Jamaica.* Lawrence, *The Escaped Cock* (privately printed). Linklater, *Poet's Pub.* Masefield, *The Hawbucks.* Moore, *The Brook Kerith.* Morgan, *Portrait in a Mirror.* J. C. Powys, *Wolf Solent.* Priestley, *The Good Companions.* Warner, *The True Heart.* West, *Harriet Hume.*

Cecil, *The Stricken Deer.* Dobrée, *The Lamp and the Lute.* Eliot, *Dante.* Graves, *Goodbye to All That.* Lawrence, *Pornography and Obscenity. The Paintings of D. H. Lawrence* (privately printed). W. Lewis, *Paleface.* V. Meynell, *Alice Meynell.* Namier, *The Structure of Politics at the Accession of George III.* Read, *The Sense of Glory.* Richards, *Practical Criticism.* Woolf, *A Room of One's Own.* Yeats, *A Packet for Ezra Pound.*

Belloc, *The Man Who Made Gold.* Bennett, *Imperial Palace.* Church, *Oliver's Daughter.* Coppard, *Pink Furniture.* Lawrence, *The Virgin and the Gipsy.* W. Lewis, *The Apes of God.* Maugham, *Cakes and Ale.* T. F. Powys, *The White Paternoster.* H. H. Richardson, *The Fortunes of Richard Mahony.* Tomlinson, *All*

Drama (date of acting)

Coward, *This Year of Grace.* O'Casey, *The Silver Tassie.* Sherriff, *Journey's End.* Van Druten, *Young Woodley.*

Coward, *Bitter-Sweet.* Shaw, *The Apple Cart.* Yeats, *Fighting the Waves.*

Besier, *The Barretts of Wimpole Street.* Bridie, *The Anatomist. Tobias and the Angel.* Coward, *Private Lives.* Yeats, *The Words upon the Window Pane.*

Date	Public Events	Literature and the Arts	Verse
1930 (cont.)		Eliot. Pound, *A Draft of XXX Cantos*.	*Last Poems*. Lawrence, *Nettles*. E. Sitwell, *Collected Poems*. Spender, *Twenty Poems*.
1931	Statute of Westminster. Second Indian Conference attended by Gandhi. Revolution in Spain. Austrian *Creditanstalt* fails. Japanese invasion of Manchuria.	Bennett d. Broch, *Die Schlafwandler*. Faulkner, *Sanctuary*. O'Neill, *Mourning Becomes Electra*. Wilson, *Axel's Castle*.	Binyon, *Collected Poems*. Bottrall, *The Loosening*. Campbell, *The Georgiad*. Day Lewis, *From Feathers to Iron*. Sturge Moore, *Poems* (–1933). Read, *The End of a War*.
1932	Disarmament Conference at Geneva. De Valera, Irish Premier. F. D. Roosevelt, President U.S.A.	Lady Gregory d. Harold Monro d. Lytton Strachey d. Stein, *The Autobiography of Alice B. Toklas*.	Auden, *The Orators*. Church, *News from the Mountain*. L. Durrell, *Ten Poems*. Lawrence, *Last Poems*. M. Roberts, ed. *New Signatures*. Yeats, *Words for Music Perhaps*.
1933	Hitler Chancellor of German Reich. Reichstag fire. Germany leaves League. Japanese occupation of North China.	Galsworthy d. George Moore d. Hart Crane, *Collected Poems*. West, *Miss Lonelyhearts*.	Auden, *The Dance of Death*. Barker, *Thirty Preliminary Poems*. Day Lewis, *The Magnetic Mountain*. W. Lewis, *One Way Song*. H. Palmer, *Collected Poems*. M. Roberts, ed. *New Country*.

Prose Fiction, General Prose	Drama (date of acting)

Our Yesterdays. Walpole, *Rogue Herries.* Waugh, *Vile Bodies.* Williams, *War in Heaven.*

Chambers, *Shakespeare: A Study of Facts and Problems.* De la Mare, *Desert Islands.* Empson, *Seven Types of Ambiguity.* Jeans, *The Mysterious Universe.* Lawrence, *A Propos of Lady Chatterley's Lover. Assorted Articles.* Moore, *Conversations in Ebury Street.* Read, *Wordsworth.* Sassoon, *Memoirs of an Infantry Officer.* Trevelyan, *England under Queen Anne* (–1934). Williams, *Poetry at Present.* Wilson Knight, *The Wheel of Fire.*

Aldington, *Stepping Heavenward.* Compton-Burnett, *Men and Wives.* Cronin, *Hatter's Castle.* Galsworthy, *Maid in Waiting.* Greene, *Rumour at Nightfall.* Lawrence, *The Man Who Died.* Linklater, *Juan in America.* Mitchison, *The Corn King and the Spring Queen.* Powell, *Afternoon Men.* Richardson, *Dawn's Left Hand.* Williams, *The Place of the Lion.* Woolf, *The Waves.*

Coward, *Cavalcade.* Huxley, *The World of Light.* Johnston, *The Moon in the Yellow River.* Yeats, *The Dreaming of the Bones. The Cat and the Moon.*

Belloc, *On Translation.* Drinkwater, *Inheritance.* Eliot, *Thoughts after Lambeth.* Granville-Barker, *On Dramatic Method.* Huxley, *Music at Night.* Lawrence, *Apocalypse.* W. Lewis, *Hitler.* MacCarthy, *Portraits.* Murry, *Son of Woman.* Rothenstein, *Men and Memories* (–1932). Strachey, *Portraits in Miniature.*

Bowen, *To the North.* Butts, *Death of Felicity Taverner.* Cary, *Aissa Saved.* Gibbon, *Sunset Song.* Gibbons, *Cold Comfort Farm.* Hartley, *The Killing Bottle.* Huxley, *Brave New World.* Kipling, *Limits and Renewals.* W. Lewis, *Snooty Baronet.* Morgan, *The Fountain.* Powell, *Venusberg.* Waugh, *Black Mischief.*

Maugham, *For Services Rendered.* Pinero, *A Cold June.* Shaw, *Too True to be Good.*

Bennett, *Journals* (–1933). Duff Cooper, *Talleyrand.* Drinkwater, *Discovery.* Eliot, *Selected Essays.* Lawrence, *Etruscan Places. Letters,* ed. Huxley. F. R. Leavis, *New Bearings in English Poetry.* Q. D. Leavis, *Fiction and the Reading Public.* Nicolson, *Public Faces.* Thomas, *Arabia Felix.* Williams, *The English Poetic Mind.*

Aldington, *All Men are Enemies.* Cary, *An American Visitor.* Compton-Burnett, *More Women than Men.* De la Mare, *The Lord Fish.* Dunsany, *The Curse of the Wise Woman.* Galsworthy, *Over the River.* Garnett, *Pocahontas.* Gibbon, *Cloud Howe.* C. S. Lewis, *The Pilgrim's Regress.* J. C. Powys, *A Glastonbury Romance.* Waddell, *Peter Abelard.*

Bridie, *A Sleeping Clergyman.* Coward, *Design for Living.* Eliot, *Sweeney Agonistes.* Maugham, *Sheppey.* Robinson, *Is Life Worth Living?* Shaw, *On the Rocks.*

Date	Public Events	Literature and the Arts	Verse
1933 (cont.)			Sackville-West, *Collected Poems*. E. Sitwell, *Five Variations on a Theme*. Spender, *Poems*. Yeats, *The Winding Stair and Other Poems*. *Collected Poems*.
1934	Anglo-Russian trade agreement. King Alexander of Yugoslavia assassinated. Dolfuss assassinated.	Elgar d. R. Fry d. Pinero d. Pound, *Make It New*. Fitzgerald, *Tender Is the Night*.	MacDiarmid, *Stony Limits*. Muir, *Variations on a Time Theme*. Pitter, *A Mad Lady's Garland*. Sassoon, *Vigils*. Dylan Thomas, *18 Poems*. Turner, *Jack and Jill*. Wellesley, *Poems of Ten Years*. Yeats, *The King of the Great Clock Tower*.
1935	National Government reconstructed under Baldwin. Government of India Act. Germany repudiates military clauses of Versailles Treaty. League applies economic sanctions against Italy.	T. E. Lawrence d. A. E. (George Russell) d. Watson d. M. Anderson, *Winterset*. MacLeish, *Panic*. Pound, *A Draft of Cantos XXXI–XLI*.	Barker, *Poems*. De la Mare, *Poems 1919–1934*. Durrell, *Pied Piper of Lovers*. Empson, *Poems*. Heppenstall, *First Poems*. Day Lewis, *A Time to Dance*. MacNeice, *Poems*. Yeats, *A Full Moon in March*. Young, *The White Blackbird*.
1936	King George V d. Accession and abdication of King Edward VIII. Accession of King George VI. Anglo-Egyptian Treaty. German reoccupation of Rhineland demilitarized zone. Army insurrection under Franco in Spain. Rome–Berlin axis.	Chesterton d. Cunninghame-Graham d. A. E. Housman d. Kipling d. Lorca d. Pirandello d. Surrealist exhibition in London. Djuna Barnes, *Nightwood*. Faulkner, *Absalom, Absalom!* Sandburg, *The People, Yes*. Tate, *Reactionary Essays on Poetry and Ideas*.	Auden, *Look, Stranger!* Eliot, *Collected Poems 1909–1935*. Housman, *More Poems*. Joyce, *Collected Poems*. Pitter, *A Trophy of Arms*. Plomer, *Visiting the Caves*. Roberts, *Poems*. Thomas, *25 Poems*. Yeats, ed. *Oxford Book of Modern Verse, 1892–1935*. Young, *Collected Poems*.

Prose Fiction, General Prose	Drama (date of acting)
Betjeman, *Ghastly Good Taste*. Bryant, *Samuel Pepys* (–1938). Churchill, *Marlborough* (–1938). Eden, *The Tribulations of a Baronet*. Eliot, *The Use of Poetry and the Use of Criticism*. Fleming, *Brazilian Adventure*. Housman, *The Name and Nature of Poetry*. Keynes, *Essays in Biography*. Moore, *A Communication to my Friends*. Murry, *Blake*. Orwell, *Down and Out in Paris and London*. Read, *The Innocent Eye*. E. Sitwell, *The English Eccentrics*. Starkie, *Baudelaire*. Strachey, *Characters and Commentaries*. Whitehead, *Adventures of Ideas*.	
Bowen, *The Cat Jumps*. Corvo, *The Desire and Pursuit of the Whole*. Gibbon, *Grey Granite*. Graves, *I, Claudius*. Greene, *It's a Battlefield*. Orwell, *Burmese Days*. Plomer, *The Invaders*. Waugh, *A Handful of Dust*.	Eliot, *The Rock*. Gow and Greenwood, *Love on the Dole*. Yeats, *The Resurrection. The King of the Great Clock Tower* (prose version).
Bodkin, *Archetypal Patterns in Poetry*. Clark, *The Later Stuarts*. Dobrée, *Modern Prose Style*. Eliot, *After Strange Gods*. Forster, *Goldsworthy Lowes Dickinson*. F. Lawrence, *Not I, But the Wind*. Day Lewis, *A Hope for Poetry*. W. Lewis, *Men without Art*. Neale, *Queen Elizabeth*. Stark, *The Valleys of the Assassins*. Toynbee, *A Study of History* (–1954). Wells, *Experiment in Autobiography*. Young, ed. *Early Victorian England*.	
Compton-Burnett, *A House and its Head*. Garnett, *Beany-Eye*. Greene, *England Made Me*. Hanley, *The Furys*. Isherwood, *Mr. Norris Changes Trains*. Myers, *The Root and the Flower*. Orwell, *A Clergyman's Daughter*. Pritchett, *Nothing Like Leather*. Read, *The Green Child*. Richardson, *Clear Horizon*.	Auden and Isherwood, *The Dog Beneath the Skin*. Eliot, *Murder in the Cathedral*. Shaw, *The Simpleton of the Unexpected Isles*. Williams, *Night Must Fall*.
Aldington, *Artifex*. Empson, *Some Versions of Pastoral*. Fisher, *A History of Europe*. Spender, *The Destructive Element*. Waugh, *Edward Campion*. Dover Wilson, *What Happens in Hamlet*. Yeats, *Dramatis Personae*.	
R. Bates, *The Olive Field*. Huxley, *Eyeless in Gaza*. R. Lehmann, *The Weather in the Streets*. Day Lewis, *The Friendly Tree*. Morgan, *Sparkenbroke*. O'Faoláin, *Bird Alone*. Orwell, *Keep the Aspidistra Flying*. Sassoon, *Sherston's Progress*. Smith, *Novel on Yellow Paper*. Spender, *The Burning Cactus*. Waugh, *Mr. Loveday's Little Outing*. West, *The Thinking Reed*.	Auden and Isherwood, *The Ascent of F6*. Barrie, *The Boy David*. Shaw, *The Millionairess*.
Ayer, *Language, Truth and Logic*. Beresford, *Schooldays with Kipling*. Chesterton, *Autobiography*. Forster, *Abinger Harvest*. Greene,	

Date	Public Events	Literature and the Arts	Verse
1936 (cont.)			
1937	Indian Constitution in force. Chamberlain P.M. Destruction of Guernica. Masaryk d. Japanese take Pekin and Shanghai.	Barrie d. Drinkwater d. Pound, *The Fifth Decad of Cantos*. *Polite Essays*. Y. Winters, *Primitivism and Decadence*.	Barker, *Calamiterror*. Dyment, *Straight or Curly?* O. Sitwell, *Mrs. Kimber*. R. Warner, *Poems*.
1938	Munich Agreement.	Abercrombie d. Ransom, *The World's Body*. Sartre, *La Nausée*. Wilson, *The Triple Thinkers*. Y. Winters, *Maule's Curse*.	Auden, ed. *Oxford Book of Light Verse*. Graves, *Collected Poems 1914–1938*. Day Lewis, *Overtures to Death*. MacNeice, *The Earth Compels*. Masefield, *Collected Poems*. Stephens, *Kings and the Moon*. Williams, *Taliessin through Logres*. Yeats, *New Poems*.
1939	British guarantee to Poland. Franco occupies Madrid. Russo-German non-aggression pact. Emergency Powers Bill. German ultimatum to Poland. Britain, Australia, New Zealand, and France declare war on Germany.	F. M. Ford d. Yeats d. Freud d. Frost, *Collected Poems*. Jünger, *Auf den Marmorklippen*. Steinbeck, *Grapes of Wrath*.	Auden and Isherwood, *Journey to a War*. Campbell, *Flowering Rifle*. Eliot, *Old Possum's Book of Practical Cats*. Fuller, *Poems*. MacNeice, *Autumn Journal*. Ridler, *Poems*. Spender, *The Still Centre*. Thomas, *The Map of Love*. Yeats, *Last Poems and Two Plays* (Dublin). Young, *Speak to the Earth*.

Prose Fiction, General Prose   *Drama (date of acting)*

Journey Without Maps. Huxley, *The Olive Tree.* Kipling, *Something of Myself.* Lawrence, *Phoenix.* C. S. Lewis, *The Allegory of Love.* Stark, *The Southern Gates of Arabia.* Waugh, *War in Abyssinia.* Young, *Victorian England: Portrait of an Age.*

Church, *The Porch.* Compton-Burnett, *Daughters and Sons.* Cronin, *The Citadel.* Isherwood, *Sally Bowles.* Day Lewis, *Starting Point.* W. Lewis, *The Revenge for Love.* R. Warner, *The Wild Goose Chase.* Williams, *Descent into Hell.* Woolf, *The Years.*

Bridie, *Susannah and the Elders.* Fry, *The Boy with a Cart.* Priestley, *Time and the Conways. I Have Been Here Before.*

Auden and MacNeice, *Letters from Iceland.* Caudwell, *Illusion and Reality.* Gogarty, *As I Was Going down Sackville Street.* Huxley, *Ends and Means.* W. Lewis, *Blasting and Bombardiering.* Orwell, *The Road to Wigan Pier.* Potter, *The Muse in Chains.* Rowse, *Sir Richard Grenville of the Revenge.* Trevelyan, *Grey of Falloden.* Yeats, *A Vision* (second version).

Bates, *Spella Ho.* Beckett, *Murphy.* Bowen, *The Death of the Heart.* Cary, *Castle Corner.* Durrell, *The Black Book* (Paris). Greene, *Brighton Rock.* Hughes, *In Hazard.* Isherwood, *Lions and Shadows.* Richardson, *Dimple Hill.* R. Warner, *The Professor.* Waugh, *Scoop.*

Auden and Isherwood, *On the Frontier.* Bridie, *The King of Nowhere.* Ervine, *Robert's Wife.* Morgan, *The Flashing Stream.* Shaw, *Geneva.* Spender, *The Trial of a Judge.* Yeats, *Purgatory.*

Caudwell, *Studies in a Dying Culture.* Connolly, *Enemies of Promise.* Maugham, *The Summing-Up.* Mumford, *The Culture of Cities.* Orwell, *Homage to Catalonia.* Read, *Poetry and Anarchism. Collected Essays in Literary Criticism.* Pearsall Smith, *Unforgotten Years.* Steer, *The Tree of Gernika.* J. Thomas, ed. *The Childhood of Edward Thomas.* West, *The Strange Necessity.*

Cary, *Mister Johnson.* Church, *The Stronghold.* Compton-Burnett, *A Family and a Fortune.* Dunsany, *The Story of Mona Sheehy.* Green, *Party Going.* Heppenstall, *The Blaze of Noon.* Huxley, *After Many a Summer.* Isherwood, *Good-bye to Berlin.* Joyce, *Finnegans Wake.* Orwell, *Coming Up for Air.* Powell, *What's Become of Waring?*

Eliot, *The Family Reunion.* Shaw, '*In Good King Charles's Golden Days*'.

Cecil, *The Young Melbourne.* Eliot, *The Idea of a Christian Society.* Lewis and Tillyard, *The Personal Heresy.* Namier, *In the Margin of History.* O'Casey, *I Knock at the Door.* Wells, *The Fate of Homo Sapiens.* Yeats, *On the Boiler.*

Date	Public Events	Literature and the Arts	Verse
1940	Fall of France and Battle of Britain. Churchill P.M.	Buchan d. W. H. Davies d. Fitzgerald d. Britten, *Sinfonia da Requiem*. Hemingway, *For Whom the Bell Tolls*. Pound, *Cantos LII–LXXI*.	Auden, *Another Time*. Blunden, *Poems 1930–1940*. Davies, *Poems 1940*. Eliot, *East Coker*. Empson, *The Gathering Storm*. Day Lewis, trs. *The Georgics. Poems in Wartime*. Read, *Thirty-five Poems*. E. Sitwell, *Poems New and Old*. S. Sitwell, *Sacred and Profane Love*. Yeats, *Last Poems and Plays*.
1941	Roosevelt signs Lend-Lease Bill. Germans invade Russia. Japanese attack on Pearl Harbour. Britain and U.S.A. declare war on Japan. Germany and Italy declare war on U.S.A.	Joyce d. Walpole d. Virginia Woolf d. Bergson d. Kierkegaard, *The Sickness unto Death* (1848), trs. Lowrie. Ransom, *The New Criticism*. Tate, *Reason in Madness*. Wilson, *The Wound and the Bow*.	Auden, *New Year Letter*. De la Mare, *Bells and Grass*. Eliot, *The Dry Salvages*. Ed. *A Choice of Kipling's Verse*. MacNeice, *Plant and Phantom*. Tiller, *Poems*.

Prose Fiction, General Prose	*Drama (date of acting)*

Cary, *Charley is my Darling*. Greene, *The Power and the Glory*. Koestler, *Darkness at Noon*. Morgan, *The Voyage*. Myers, *The Pool of Vishnu*. Snow, *Strangers and Brothers*. Spender, *The Backward Son*. Thomas, *Portrait of the Artist as a Young Dog*.

Buchan, *Memory-Hold-the-Door*. Gill, *Autobiography*. Muir, *The Story and the Fable*. Orwell, *Inside the Whale*. Read, *Annals of Innocence and Experience*. Reid, *Private Road*. Woolf, *Roger Fry*. Yeats, *Letters on Poetry*.

Cary, *A House of Children*. Compton-Burnett, *Parents and Children*. O. Sitwell, *Open the Door!* P. Toynbee, *A School in Private*. Woolf, *Between the Acts*.

Coward, *Blithe Spirit*. Ervine, *Friends and Relations*. Shiel, *The Summit*.

Huxley, *Grey Eminence*. Masefield, *In the Mill*.

BIBLIOGRAPHY

THOMAS HARDY, 1840–1928

Hardy began his writing career in the 1860's and approximately thirty poems written between 1863 and 1867 exist, though many of them were later revised. In 1867 he wrote *The Poor Man and the Lady*, which was rejected by two publishers. The MS. was later destroyed by Hardy, but not before he had incorporated some of the material in subsequent stories, notably in *An Indiscretion in the Life of an Heiress*. Other sections may have been used in *Desperate Remedies*, *Under the Greenwood Tree*, and *A Pair of Blue Eyes*.

His first published novel was *Desperate Remedies*, issued anonymously in three volumes in 1871. Certain textual revisions were made for an 1874 (New York) edition. An 1889 edition included a prefatory note by Hardy; this appears in an expanded form in the collected editions of his work. *Under the Greenwood Tree* (2 vols., 1872) was also published anonymously. The first of the novels to be serialized was *A Pair of Blue Eyes*; it appeared in *Tinsley's Magazine* between September 1872 and July 1873 and was published in three volumes in 1873. *Far from the Madding Crowd* (2 vols., 1874) had been serialized in the *Cornhill Magazine* (Jan.–Dec. 1874); Hardy undertook some slight revisions for a second edition in 1875 and expanded the 1895 preface for a 1902 edition; in 1882 a dramatization was performed at Liverpool and later ran for 114 performances in London. *The Hand of Ethelberta* (2 vols., 1876) had appeared in *Cornhill* (July 1875–May 1876) and in Sunday issues of the *New York Times* (June 1875–April 1876). *The Return of the Native* (3 vols., 1878) first appeared in *Belgravia* (Jan.–Dec. 1878) and *The Trumpet-Major* (3 vols., 1880) in *Good Words* (Jan.–Dec. 1880).

To launch the European edition, *Harper's New Monthly Magazine* serialized *A Laodicean* (Dec. 1880–Dec. 1881), the parts running a month later in the American edition. A New York (1881) edition was based on the serial text which Hardy revised for book publication (3 vols., 1881). *Two on a Tower* (3 vols., 1882) first appeared in the *Atlantic Monthly* (May–Dec. 1882).

The text was revised for an 1883 edition and further minor revisions were made for a one-volume edition later in the same year. An essay, 'The Dorset Farm Labourer: Past and Present', was published in Dorchester in 1884, and a short story, 'The Romantic Adventures of a Milkmaid', in New York in the same year. Extensive revisions were made in the serial text of *The Mayor of Casterbridge* before it appeared in two volumes in 1886. It had been published in the *Graphic* and in *Harper's Weekly* (Jan.–May 1886). Some of Hardy's revisions were included in an 1886 (New York) edition. In May of the same year *Macmillan's Magazine* and *Harper's Bazar* began a serialization of *The Woodlanders* which ran concurrently in both magazines until April 1887; slight revisions were made before publication in three volumes in 1887. Five stories were collected in *Wessex Tales* (2 vols., 1888). 'Fellow-Townsmen' had been published separately in New York in 1880; all five had previously appeared in magazine form between 1879 and 1888 and minor revisions were made. For the 1895–6 Collected Edition Hardy added a sixth story, 'An Imaginative Woman'; but in the 1912 edition of his works this story was included in *Life's Little Ironies*. *A Group of Noble Dames* (1891) contained ten stories all of which had earlier been published in magazines.

The publishing history of *Tess of the D'Urbervilles* (3 vols., 1891) is complicated. Considerably bowdlerized, the novel was serialized in the *Graphic* and in *Harper's Bazar* (July–Dec. 1891). Unacceptable sections of the book were printed in separate instalments in two other periodicals: the *National Observer* (Edinburgh) printed, in a special literary supplement (Nov. 1891), chapters 10 and 11 under the title 'Saturday Night in Arcady', and the *Fortnightly Review* printed (May 1891) chapter 14 under the title 'The Midnight Baptism, A Study in Christianity'. Minor errors in the text of the first edition were corrected in a revised impression in 1892; and in the same year Hardy wrote a significant preface for a single-volume edition. *Tess* was the first volume in the 1912 Wessex Edition, and Hardy added to this not only a note to his earlier preface but also a 'General Preface to the Novels and Poems'. This definitive text was used in the second serial publication of *Tess* in *John O'London's Weekly* (Oct. 1925–July 1926), for which Hardy wrote a special introductory note. The novel was dramatized by Hardy himself and first performed in New York in March 1897. He

revised his text for a 1924 amateur production and the same
text was used in professional productions of 1925 and 1929 in
London. An opera with music by d'Erlanger and libretto by
Ilica was performed in Naples in 1906 and in London in 1909.
Life's Little Ironies of 1894 contained nine stories, all of which
had appeared in magazine form. *Jude the Obscure* (1896 [1895])
was first serialized, in bowdlerized form, in *Harper's New Monthly
Magazine* (Dec. 1894–Nov. 1895). It was slightly revised for
a 1902 edition. *The Well-Beloved* (1897) was the last of Hardy's
novels to appear in volume form during his lifetime. It had
originally appeared in the *Illustrated London News* and in *Harper's
Bazar* (Oct.–Dec. 1892). The text was revised for the 1897 edition.

Wessex Poems and Other Verses (1898) contained fifty-one poems,
of which four had been previously published. In the Wessex
Edition this volume was combined with *Poems of the Past and
Present* (1902 [1901]), which was slightly revised for a further
impression in the same year. The first part of *The Dynasts* was
published in 1903 [1904], a revised second impression also
appearing in 1904. *The Dynasts, Part Second* was published in
1905 [1906] and *Part Third* in 1908. The three parts appeared as
a single volume in 1910. Certain revisions were made and a
special prologue and epilogue added by Hardy for a production
of selected scenes by H. Granville-Barker in November 1914.
Time's Laughingstocks and Other Verses (1909) contained ninety-
four poems of which twenty-nine had been previously published;
a revised impression was issued in 1910. This volume was combined with *The Dynasts, Part Third,* in the definitive Wessex Edition. *A Changed Man and Other Tales* (1913) contained twelve
stories, all previously published. *Satires of Circumstance* (1914)
contained 107 poems, of which thirty-five had been previously
published; slight revisions were made for a second impression
in 1915, and the volume was combined with *Moments of Vision*
in the Wessex Edition. *Selected Poems* (1916) contained nine
previously unpublished poems, and all except eight of the total
of 120 were included, with other additions, in *Chosen Poems*
(1929). *Moments of Vision and Miscellaneous Verses* (1917) contained 159 poems. A privately printed edition of *The Play of
'Saint George'* (1921) was reprinted with a modernized version
in a 1928 (New York) edition which also includes a letter of
authorization by Hardy. *Late Lyrics and Earlier* (1922) contained
151 poems, twenty-two of them previously published. In the

Wessex Edition of 1926 these poems were included with *The Famous Tragedy of the Queen of Cornwall*, which had appeared in 1923 and in a revised form in 1924. The last of Hardy's books to be published in his lifetime were *Human Shows* (1925), which included twenty-five previously unpublished poems, and *Life and Art* (New York, 1925), a collection of essays, notes, and letters edited by E. Brennecke. At the time of his death Hardy was collecting the 105 poems, spanning sixty years, which comprise *Winter Words* (1928).

The Early Life of Thomas Hardy by Florence Emily Hardy (1928) is actually an autobiography, Mrs. Hardy's work being confined to minor revisions. Portions of Parts I and II were serialized in *The Times* (22–27 Oct. 1928). The same author's *The Later Years of Thomas Hardy* (1930) contains many notes and letters previously published in books and periodicals. Again, with the exception of the four final chapters, the book is a third-person autobiography. The two volumes were reprinted as *The Life of Thomas Hardy, 1840–1928* (1962). *Old Mrs. Chundle* (New York, 1929) is a limited edition of a short story, never published in Hardy's lifetime, which first appeared in the *Ladies' Home Journal* (Feb. 1929). In 1934 there appeared a privately printed edition of *An Indiscretion in the Life of an Heiress*. This adaptation of *The Poor Man and the Lady* was first printed in the *New Quarterly Magazine* in July 1878; a different, presumably unrevised, text appeared in *Harper's Weekly* (New York) in the same month. Other reprints include *The Thieves Who Couldn't Help Sneezing* (Waterville, 1942) and *The Three Wayfarers* (New York, 1943), a facsimile edition of the limited 1893 issue of Hardy's dramatization of his short story 'The Three Wayfarers'. The play was produced in 1893, and a revised text used in an amateur performance in 1926 was published in a limited edition in 1930. The discovery of an unknown novel by Hardy in the files of *The Household* (Boston, Nov. 1892–April 1893) led to the publication in 1952 of *Our Exploits at West Poley*, a 20,000-word tale of rural adventure for boys. C. J. Weber has edited the letters at Colby College in the *Letters of Thomas Hardy* (Waterville, 1954); copious annotation gives the book additional biographical value. Hardy's rather unrewarding notebooks were edited by Evelyn Hardy in 1955 under the title *Thomas Hardy's Notebooks*, and the same editor also introduced five previously unpublished poems by Hardy in the *London Magazine* (Jan. 1956).

Extant MSS. are widely dispersed. The University of Texas has a substantial collection. The British Museum contains the MSS. of *Tess of the D'Urbervilles* and *The Dynasts*, and the Dorset County Museum possesses those of *The Mayor of Casterbridge*, *Under the Greenwood Tree*, *The Woodlanders*, *Satires of Circumstance*, *Late Lyrics and Earlier*, and *The Famous Tragedy of the Queen of Cornwall*. The MS. of *The Trumpet-Major* is in the Royal Library, Windsor. MSS. at other institutions include *Jude the Obscure* and *Time's Laughingstocks* in the Fitzwilliam Museum, Cambridge; *Poems of the Past and Present* in the Bodleian Library, Oxford; *Winter Words* in the Library of the Queen's College, Oxford; *Wessex Poems* in Birmingham City Museum; *Moments of Vision* in the Library of Magdalene College, Cambridge; and *Human Shows* in the Library of Yale University. Other MSS. not in private collections include those of 'On the Western Circuit' in Manchester Public Library, 'For Conscience' Sake' in the Library of Manchester University, and 'A Tragedy of Two Ambitions' in the Rylands Library, Manchester. Letters are to be found at the Dorset County Museum, the Library of Congress, Harvard, Colby College, the New York Public Library, the Pierpont Morgan Library, and the Bodleian Library.

The first collected edition of Hardy's works was the Wessex Novels (16 vols., 1895–6). For this Hardy carefully revised the text of every novel and often retitled chapters. In addition, he added a special preface to each novel. The definitive edition is, however, the Wessex Edition (24 vols., 1912–31), for which Hardy revised his novels for the last time; in general, the verbal changes are not as important as those made for the first collected edition. Brief postscripts were sometimes added to earlier prefaces, and for some novels the preface was rewritten or modified. In a 'General Preface to the Novels and Poems' Hardy explained the classification of his novels into (1) Novels of Character and Environment, (2) Romances and Fantasies, (3) Novels of Ingenuity, (4) Mixed Novels. *Collected Poems* (1919) comprises the five collections of verse published by Hardy. The Mellstock Edition (37 vols., 1919–20) is an edition de luxe of 500 copies. *The Short Stories of Thomas Hardy* (1928) is a reprint of his four volumes of stories. The Library and Pocket Editions are current, but neither (1962) is complete.

There is no major published collection of Hardy's letters, but some have appeared dispersedly in biographies and memoirs of the period.

In 1908 Hardy chose and edited *Select Poems of William Barnes*. He had previously reviewed his fellow Dorset poet's *Poems of Rural Life* in the *New Quarterly Magazine* (Oct. 1879) and he included some of this material in an obituary of Barnes in the *Athenaeum* (Oct. 1886). Part of the 1908 preface also appears in Hardy's preface to 'William Barnes' in *The English Poets*, ed. T. H. Ward, vol. v (1918). *Selected Poems*, ed. G. M. Young (1940), is an admirable selection containing what is still perhaps the best general introduction to Hardy's poetry. The introduction is reprinted in Young's *Last Essays* (1950). J. C. Ransom edited and introduced *Selected Poems* (New York, 1961).

At present there is no really satisfactory biography of Hardy. Despite the significant silences, Mrs. Hardy's two volumes, *The Early Life* and *The Later Years*, are indispensable. Other books are E. Brennecke, *The Life of Thomas Hardy* (New York, 1925) and C. J. Weber, *Hardy of Wessex: His Life and Literary Career* (New York, 1940). E. Hardy's *Thomas Hardy* (1954), the latest critical biography, makes some attempt to show the relationship of the poems to Hardy's personal life. Among the many memoirs and accounts of Hardy are W. Archer, *Real Conversations* (1904), S. M. Ellis, 'Thomas Hardy: Some Personal Recollections' (*Fortnightly Review*, March 1928), V. H. Collins, *Talks with Hardy at Max Gate* (1928), R. Graves, *Goodbye to all That* (1929; rev. ed. 1957), recollections by E. Blunden in *The Great Victorians* (ed. H. J. and H. Massingham, 1932), glimpses of Hardy in his last years in T. E. Lawrence's *Letters* (1938) and *Letters to his Biographers* (1962), lively if not wholly reliable memories by F. M. Ford in *Mightier than the Sword* (1938), and L. Powys, 'Recollections of Thomas Hardy' (*Virginia Quarterly Review* xv, 1939). C. Clemens's *My Chat with Thomas Hardy* (1944) is a record, variously padded out, of a short conversation of 1925 in which Hardy mentions American influences upon him. Later material will be found in C. Holland, *Thomas Hardy's Wessex Scene* (1948), N. Flower, *Just As It Happened* (1950), E. Phillpotts, *From the Angle of 88* (1951), F. A. Hedgcock, 'Reminiscences of Thomas Hardy' (*National and English Review*, 1951), C. J. Weber, *Hardy and the Lady from Madison Square* (Waterville, Maine, 1952), and V. Woolf, *A Writer's Diary* (1953). A very short essay by D. MacCarthy in *Memories* (1953) records Hardy's celebrated remark that, had he known *Tess* was to be such a success, he would have made it 'a *really good book*'. Emma Hardy's *Some Recollections* (ed. E. Hardy and R. Gittings, 1961) has an interesting picture of the early Hardy, and indicates the origins of some of his poems. E. Felkin printed some memories in 'Days with Thomas Hardy' (*Encounter*, 103, 1962).

Many full-length critical studies were published during Hardy's lifetime. The first, and still valuable, is L. Johnson's *The Art of Thomas Hardy* (1894, new ed. with a chapter by J. E. Barton on the poetry, 1923). L. Abercrombie's *Thomas Hardy: A Critical Study* (1912) is an excellent book with much perceptive criticism. H. Lea's *Thomas Hardy's Wessex* (1913) is the best of many books on the Wessex country. Other works of some note are H. Child, *Thomas Hardy* (1916), H. C. Duffin, *Thomas Hardy: A Study of the Wessex Novels* (1916, rev. eds. 1921, 1937), and E. Brennecke, *Thomas Hardy's Universe: A Study of a Poet's Mind* (1924). M. E. Chase's *Thomas Hardy: From Serial to Novel* (Minneapolis, 1927) is a good introduction to a subject of considerable critical interest, as is, after another fashion, G. Salberg's *Thomas Hardys Frauen im Lichte seiner Weltanschauung* (Mulhouse, 1927). G. de Catalogne's *Le Message de Thomas Hardy* (Paris, 1928) is one of a number of French studies published at about the time of Hardy's death. Other books of this period are H. M. Tomlinson, *Thomas Hardy* (1929), P. D'Exideuil, *The Human Pair in the Works of Thomas Hardy* (1930), and F. Olivero, *An Introduction to Hardy* (Turin, 1930).

A. McDowall's *Thomas Hardy: A Critical Study* (1931), the first work to make use of Mrs. Hardy's books, is still one of the best studies of Hardy's prose and poetry. R. A. Firor's *Folkways in Thomas Hardy* (Philadelphia, 1931) is about folklore. Other special studies are L. de Ridder-Barzin, *Le Pessimisme de Thomas Hardy* (Brussels, 1932), A. P. Elliott, *Fatalism in the Works of Thomas Hardy* (Philadelphia, 1935), and A. Colling, *Le Romancier de la fatalité* (Paris, 1938). W. R. Rutland's *Thomas Hardy* (1938; reprinted New York 1962) is informative on the English background and influences; the general studies by H. W. Nevinson

(1941) and E. Blunden (1942) are good; and Lord David Cecil's *Hardy the Novelist* (1943) is outstanding. Recent examinations of the poetry include C. M. Bowra's *The Lyrical Poetry of Thomas Hardy* (Byron Foundation Lecture, Nottingham, 1946, reprinted in *Inspiration and Poetry*, 1955) and J. G. Southworth's somewhat unenthusiastic *The Poetry of Thomas Hardy* (New York, 1947). H. C. Webster's *On a Darkling Plain* (Chicago, 1947) traces the development of Hardy's thought as reflected in his work, and A. J. Guerard's *Thomas Hardy: The Novels and Stories* (1949) is a substantial and penetrating study with occasional perversities. R. A. Scott-James's *Thomas Hardy* (supplement to *British Book News*, 1951) is a critical essay with a select bibliography and an index of short stories. D. Brown's *Thomas Hardy* (1954; rev. ed. 1961) has many good pages on the agricultural background, and S. L. Hynes's *The Pattern of Hardy's Poetry* (Chapel Hill, 1961) is a useful survey.

Studies of individual works are: W. H. Gardner, 'Some Thoughts on *The Mayor of Casterbridge*' (Eng. Assoc. Pamphlet, 77, 1930); A. Chakravarty, *The Dynasts and the Post-War Age in Poetry* (1938); W. G. Bebbington, 'The Original Manuscript of Thomas Hardy's *The Trumpet-Major*' (1948), a short pamphlet with facsimiles; M. O. Roberts, *Tess in the Theatre* (Toronto, 1950), a detailed study, with texts, of the various dramatic versions of *Tess*; J. O. Bailey, *Thomas Hardy and the Cosmic Mind: A New Reading of The Dynasts* (Chapel Hill, 1956); J. Paterson, *The Making of 'The Return of the Native'* (Berkeley, 1960); and D. Brown, *Thomas Hardy: The Mayor of Casterbridge* (1962).

J. M. Murry's *Aspects of Literature* (1920) contains an influential discussion of the poetry. Other books with chapters or sections on Hardy are: M. L. Cazamian, *Le Roman et les idées en Angleterre* (Strasbourg, 1923); I. A. Richards, *Science and Poetry* (1926); B. Dobrée, *The Lamp and the Lute* (1929; the essay is reprinted in *English Critical Essays*, ed. P. M. Jones, 1933); G. R. Elliott, *The Cycle of Modern Poetry* (Princeton, 1929); F. L. Lucas, *Eight Victorian Poets* (1930); V. Woolf, *The Common Reader: Second Series* (1932); F. R. Leavis, *New Bearings in English Poetry* (1932); T. S. Eliot, *After Strange Gods* (1934); D. H. Lawrence, *Phoenix* (1936); R. P. Blackmur, *The Expense of Greatness* (New York, 1940); D. Daiches, *Poetry and the Modern World* (Chicago, 1940); A. Tate, *Reason in Madness* (New York, 1941); E. Muir, *Essays on*

Literature and Society (1949); H. Ellis, *From Marlowe to Shaw*, ed, J. Gawsworth (1950); J. Holloway, *The Victorian Sage* (1953); M. D. Zabel, *Craft and Character in Modern Fiction* (1957); and J. Holloway, 'Hardy's Major Fiction' in *From Jane Austen to Joseph Conrad*, ed. R. Rathburn and M. Steinmann (Minneapolis, 1958; reprinted in *The Charted Mirror*, 1960).

The Thomas Hardy Centennial Issue of *The Southern Review* (vi, 1940) contains some of the best criticism of Hardy's poetry and prose. Essays in journals and periodicals include: M. Roberts, 'The Dramatic Element in Hardy's Poems' (*Queen's Quarterly* li, 1944); J. O. Bailey, 'Hardy's "Imbedded Fossil"' (*Studies in Philology* xlii, 1945) and the same writer's excellent article 'Hardy's "Mephistophelian Visitants"' (*Publications of the Modern Language Association* lxi, 1946); R. W. Stallman, 'Hardy's Hour-Glass Novel' [*The Return of the Native*] (*Sewanee Review* lv, 1947); J. I. M. Stewart, 'The Integrity of Hardy' (*Essays and Studies* N.S. i, 1948); C. Day Lewis, 'The Lyrical Poetry of Thomas Hardy' (*Proceedings of the British Academy* xxxvii, 1951); H. N. Fairchild, 'The Immediate Source of *The Dynasts*' (*PMLA* lxvii, 1952); F. R. Leavis, 'Reality and Sincerity' (*Scrutiny* xix, 1952–3); H. Orel, '*The Dynasts* and *Paradise Lost*' (*South Atlantic Quarterly* lii, 1953); J. A. Cassidy, 'The Original Source of *Dynasts*' (*PMLA* lxix, 1954); C. R. Andersen, 'Time, Space, and Perspective in Thomas Hardy' (*Nineteenth-Century Fiction* ix, 1954); R. Church, 'Thomas Hardy as Revealed in *The Dynasts*' (*Études anglaises* vii, 1954); E. Clifford, 'The Child: the Circus: and "Jude the Obscure"' (*Cambridge Journal* vii, 1954); E. Goodheart, 'Thomas Hardy and the Lyrical Novel' (*Nineteenth-Century Fiction* xii, 1957); M. A. Goldberg, 'Hardy's Double-Visioned Universe' (*Essays in Criticism* vii, 1957); J. H. Raleigh, 'Victorian Morals and the Modern Novel' (*Partisan Review* xxv, 1958); E. Hardy, 'Thomas Hardy's Plots for Five Unpublished Stories' (*London Magazine* v, 1958); D. Perkins, 'Hardy and the Poetry of Isolation' (*English Literary History* xxvi, 1959); E. Clifford, 'Thomas Hardy and the Historians' (*Studies in Philology* lvi, 1959); J. C. Ransom, 'Thomas Hardy's Poems' (*Kenyon Review* xxii, 1960); and R. W. King, 'Verse and Prose Parallels in the Work of Thomas Hardy' (*Review of English Studies* N.S. xiii, 1962).

The standard bibliography is R. L. Purdy's *Thomas Hardy:*

A Bibliographical Study (1954), a masterly and essential guide which includes not only much information about the genesis and publication of individual works but also offers considerable material of biographical value. C. J. Weber's *The First Hundred Years of Thomas Hardy: 1840–1940* (Waterville, 1942) is a useful compilation containing more than 3,000 entries relating to Hardy and his writings. The same editor's *Hardy Music at Colby* (Waterville, 1945) is a check list of settings of Hardy's poems by various composers. B. Yamamoto's *Bibliography of Thomas Hardy in Japan* (Tokyo, 1957) records books by and about Hardy translated into Japanese. A special Hardy number of *Modern Fiction Studies* (vi, Autumn 1960) contains selected lists of books and articles on Hardy.

HENRY JAMES, 1843–1916

L. Edel has identified a story entitled 'A Tragedy of Error' as James's first published work (Feb. 1864) and has reprinted it with a prefatory note (*New England Quarterly* xxix, 1956). During the following ten years James published many stories, articles, and reviews in both English and American periodicals. *A Passionate Pilgrim and Other Tales* (Boston, 1875) was a gathering with some revision of six magazine stories. *Transatlantic Sketches* (Boston, 1875) contained twenty-five travel essays; all had been extensively revised since their appearance in periodicals during 1872–4; some were to be again revised for *Italian Hours* (1909). *Roderick Hudson* was serialized (*Atlantic Monthly* xxv–xxvi, Jan.–Dec. 1875), revised for American book publication (Boston, 1876 [1875]), and considerably altered for the first English edition (3 vols., 1879), the original thirteen chapters being divided into twenty-six. *The American* also appeared in the *Atlantic Monthly* (xxxvii–xxxix, June 1876–May 1877). It was published with some revision in Boston in 1877 and in London (where there had been a pirated version) in 1879. James's dramatization was privately printed in 1891, the year in which the play was produced in Southport and London.

James's first book to be published in England was *French Poets and Novelists* (1878), a collection of twelve essays from periodicals. *Watch and Ward* (*Atlantic Monthly* xxviii, Aug.–Dec. 1871) was issued in volume form with many revisions (Boston, 1878). *The Europeans* (*Atlantic Monthly* xlii, July–Oct. 1878) appeared in two volumes in 1878 with a slightly modified text. 'Daisy Miller' (*Cornhill Magazine* xxxvii–xxxviii, June–July 1878) was published as *Daisy Miller, A Study* (New York, 1879 [1878] ;) a stage version appeared both in the *Atlantic Monthly* (li, Apr.– June 1883) and in volume form (Boston, 1883). *An International Episode* (*Cornhill* xxxviii–xxxix, Dec. 1878–Jan. 1879) was published in New York in 1879, and together with 'Daisy Miller' and 'Four Meetings' (*Scribner's Monthly* xv, Nov. 1877) composed *Daisy Miller and Other Stories* (2 vols., 1879). *The Madonna of the Future and Other Tales* (2 vols., 1879) contained six stories from magazines, of which three had appeared in *A Passionate Pilgrim*. *Confidence* (*Scribner's* xviii–xix, Aug. 1879–Jan. 1880) was heavily revised for book publication (2 vols., 1880 [1879]). *Hawthorne* appeared in 1879; there are slight variations in the first American edition (1880). *The Diary of a Man of Fifty* (New York, 1880), in addition to the title story (which had been published in England in *The Madonna of the Future*), contained 'A Bundle of Letters', originally printed in the *Parisian* (Dec. 1879) and pirated by both English and American firms. *Washington Square* (*Cornhill* xli–xlii, June–Nov. 1880) was published in New York in 1881 [1880]; to the English edition (2 vols., 1881) were added 'The Pension Beaurepas' and 'A Bundle of Letters'.

The *Portrait of a Lady* (*Macmillan's Magazine* xlii–xlv, Oct. 1880–Nov. 1881) was published with slight revisions in three volumes in 1881. *The Siege of London* (Boston, 1883) reprinted three stories. *Portraits of Places* (1883) gathered twenty essays from American periodicals, and *A Little Tour of France* (1884) essays and sketches from the *Atlantic Monthly*. *Tales of Three Cities* (Boston, 1884) comprised 'The Impressions of a Cousin', 'Lady Barberina', and 'A New England Winter', all of which had appeared in the *Century Magazine*. 'The Art of Fiction' was printed in *Longman's Magazine* (iv, 1884), included without authorization in Walter Besant's *The Art of Fiction* (Boston, 1885 [1884]), and later revised for inclusion in *Partial Portraits*. *The Author of Beltraffio* (Boston, 1885) reprinted 'Four Meetings' and four more recent stories. *Stories Revived* (3 vols., 1885) included in revised form some of James's early tales, together with three already collected in *A Passionate Pilgrim*. *The Bostonians* (*Century Magazine* xxix–xxxi, Feb. 1885–Feb. 1886) and *The Princess Casamassima* (*Atlantic Monthly* lvi–lviii, Sept. 1885– Oct. 1886) were both revised for book publication (each in

3 vols., 1886). *Partial Portraits* (1888) reprinted eleven literary essays from magazines. *The Reverberator* (*Macmillan's* lvii–lviii, Feb.–July 1888) was published in book form (2 vols., 1888) with slight textual changes. 'The Aspern Papers' first appeared in the *Atlantic Monthly* (lxi, Mar.–May 1888) and 'Louisa Pallant' and 'The Modern Warning' in *Harper's New Monthly Magazine* (lxxvi and lxxvii, 1888); the three stories were brought together in *The Aspern Papers* (2 vols., 1888). *A London Life* (2 vols., 1889) collected the title story (*Scribner's* iii–iv, June–Sept. 1889) and three others. *The Tragic Muse* (*Atlantic Monthly* lxiii–lxv, Jan. 1889–May 1890) was revised for book publication (2 vols., Boston and New York, 1890). *The Lesson of the Master* (1892) and *The Real Thing and Other Tales* (1893) were further collections of stories from magazines. Six such stories of 1892–3 were published in London as *The Private Life* in 1893. In New York, again in 1893, three of them appeared as *The Private Life* and three as *The Wheel of Time. Picture and Text* (New York, 1893) contained five essays on painters, and a sketch 'After the Play'. *Essays in London and Elsewhere* was another miscellaneous gathering of 1893.

Theatricals (1894) consisted of two comedies: *Tenants* and *Disengaged*. Two further plays, *The Album* and *The Reprobate*, were brought together in *Theatricals: Second Series* (1894). None of these plays had been produced or previously printed. Later collections of stories were *Terminations* (1895) and *Embarrassments* (1896); with the exception of 'The Altar of the Dead' in *Terminations* all had previously appeared. *The Other House* (*Illustrated London News* cix, July–Sept. 1896) was published in two volumes in 1896. *The Old Things* (*Atlantic Monthly* lxxvii, Apr.–June 1896) was revised as *The Spoils of Poynton* (1897). *What Maisie Knew* (*The Chap Book* vi, Jan.–May 1897; abridged version in *New Review* xvi, Feb.–June 1897) was revised for book publication in 1897; discrepancies exist between the first English and American editions. *In the Cage* appeared in 1898. 'The Turn of the Screw' (*Collier's Weekly* xx–xxi, Jan.–Apr. 1898), slightly revised, and 'Covering End', printed for the first time, made up *The Two Magics* (1898). 'Covering End' was later adapted by James as *The High Bid* and performed in Liverpool in March 1908. *The Awkward Age* (*Harper's Weekly* xlii, Oct.–Dec. 1898) was revised for book publication in 1899. *The Soft Side* (1900) contained twelve stories, three printed for the first time. Neither *The Sacred Fount* (New York, 1901) nor

The Wings of the Dove (2 vols., New York, 1902) was serialized. *The Ambassadors* (*North American Review* clxxvi, Jan.–June 1903) was published in 1903 with a revised text and the restoration of chapters 28 and 35 which were omitted from the serial version. In the American edition of 1903, chapters 28 and 29 occurred in reverse order, an error continued in the New York Edition and later editions of the novel; the first American edition with the chapters in their correct order appeared in 1960. *The Better Sort* (1903) consisted of eleven stories, three printed for the first time. *William Wetmore Story and His Friends* was published in 1903 in two volumes and *The Golden Bowl* in New York in 1904 in two volumes.

'The Question of Our Speech' and 'The Lesson of Balzac' were reprinted from magazines under the former title in 1905. *English Hours* (1905), like *Italian Hours* (1909), was a reshuffle of various travel pieces. *The American Scene* (1907) collected from American periodicals essays written after James's first visit to America for over twenty years. *The Finer Grain* (New York, 1910) was the last collection of stories to be published during James's lifetime. *The Outcry* (1911) was based on an unproduced play—later performed by the Stage Society in 1917. *A Small Boy and Others* (New York, 1913) was succeeded by *Notes of a Son and Brother* (New York, 1914) and the posthumously published fragment *The Middle Years* (1917). Some of James's best critical essays were collected in *Notes on Novelists* (1914); all of these had appeared in periodicals between 1894 and 1914 and some were revised for this edition; a short preface by James was not included in the American edition of the same year. The last of his writings to be published in his own lifetime was *The Question of the Mind* [1915], an essay on the war which was later reprinted in two American newspapers as 'The Mind of England at War'.

Two unfinished novels were published in 1917: *The Ivory Tower* and *The Sense of the Past*. 'Gabrielle de Bergerac', an uncollected story which first appeared in the *Atlantic Monthly* (xxvi, Aug. 1870), was published in New York in 1918. Five previously printed essays inspired by the war were published as *Within the Rim and Other Essays* [1919], and seven uncollected early stories were brought together in *Travelling Companions* (New York, 1919). *A Landscape Painter* (New York, 1919) contained four stories dating from the late 1860's which had previously been collected in revised form in *Stories Revived*, but which were here published in their original unrevised state. The unrevised serial texts of five stories were also used in *Master Eustace* (New York, 1920); four of these had been printed in revised form in *Stories Revived* ('Théodolinde' with the new title of 'Rose-Agathe'), and the fifth, 'A Light Man', had been published with many revisions in *Stories by American Authors* (New York, 1884).

Remarkably few MSS. are extant. The largest collection is at Harvard; see *Harvard University Library Notes* iv, March 1942. In addition to the MSS. of plays and many hundreds of letters, the Houghton Library possesses the MSS. of *Confidence*, *The Princess Casamassima*, *En Province* [*A Little Tour in France*], 'Longstaff's Marriage' and 'Crawford's Consistency', the type-scripts of *The Sense of the Past*, *The Ivory Tower*, and *The Middle Years*, and the pages of *The American* and *The Portrait of a Lady* revised for the New York Edition. Part of *The Europeans* is at Yale University Library and 'Four Meetings' at the Huntington Library. Other fragments and letters are to be found at the Library of Congress, University of Texas, Dartmouth College Library, New York Public Library, Buffalo Public Library, and the British Museum. The Brotherton Library of the University of Leeds possesses an extensive collection of letters to Edmund Gosse.

The first attempt at a collected edition took place in 1883 when fourteen volumes of novels and stories were issued, the majority having already appeared in volume form. Late in his career James heavily revised many of his works, particularly the early novels, for the selective *Novels and Tales of Henry James*, the 'New York Edition' (New York, 24 vols., 1907–9; reprinted New York, 1961–). Two posthumous volumes, *The Ivory Tower* and *The Sense of the Past*, were added in 1917. To each of the novels and volumes of stories James wrote a preface, and the prefaces were later included in *The Novels and Stories of Henry James* (35 vols., 1921–3). This edition contained all the fiction published in book form during James's lifetime. A considerable body of stories and *nouvelles* had previously been published as *The Uniform Tales of Henry James* (14 vols., 1915–20). With the exception of 'Glasses', which did not appear in the New York Edition and which was revised by James for this series, the text followed that of the New York Edition. Four volumes of the projected twelve of *The Complete Tales of Henry James* edited by L. Edel appeared in 1962.

The Letters of Henry James, ed. P. Lubbock (2 vols., 1920), is an admirable selection, although with an emphasis on the later correspondence. Later collections of letters are '*A Most Unholy Trade*', *Being Letters on the Drama by Henry James* (Cambridge, Mass., 1923), *Three Letters from Henry James to Joseph Conrad* (1926), *Letters to Walter Berry* (privately printed, Paris, 1928), *Henry James: Letters to A. C. Benson and Auguste Monod*, ed. E. F. Benson (1930), and Elizabeth Robins, *Theatre and Friendship* (1932). A correspondence with Stevenson and several essays are included in *Henry James and Robert Louis Stevenson*, ed. J. Adam Smith (1948). *Selected Letters of Henry James*, ed. L. Edel (New York, 1955), includes over 100 letters, half of the number being published for the first time. *Henry James and H. G. Wells*, ed. L. Edel and G. N. Ray (1958), prints fifty-three of James's letters.

The essential work for the study of James as a dramatist is *The Complete Plays of Henry James*, ed. L. Edel (1949); most of James's plays are here published for the first time. Of dramatic versions by other hands the following have been published: *The Tragic Muse*, adapted by H. Griffith (1927), *Berkeley Square* [*The Sense of the Past*], adapted by J. L. Balderston and J. C. Squire (1928), *The Heiress* [*Washington Square*], adapted by R. and A. Goetz (New York, 1948), *The Innocents* ['The Turn of the Screw'], adapted by W. Archibald (New York, 1950), *Letter from Paris* [*The Reverberator*], adapted by Dodie Smith (1954), *Child of Fortune* [*The Wings of the Dove*], adapted by G. R. Bolton (New York, 1957), and *The Aspern Papers*, adapted by M. Redgrave (1959). An operatic version of 'The Turn of the Screw', by B. Britten and M. Piper, was produced in 1954.

There have been numerous reprints and gatherings—many of them the more useful in that there is no current English edition of James's works. *Views and Reviews* (Boston, 1908) collected early critical essays. *Notes and Reviews*, ed. P. C. La Rose (Cambridge, Mass., 1921), consisted of twenty-five previously uncollected essays written during 1865–6. *The Art of the Novel*, ed. R. P. Blackmur (New York, 1934), reprinted James's eighteen prefaces to the New York Edition. F. O. Matthiessen edited *Stories of Writers and Artists* (New York, 1944), *The American Novels and Stories of Henry James* (New York, 1947), and with K. B. Murdock important unpublished material as *The Notebooks of Henry James* (New York, 1947). *The American Scene*, together with three essays from *Portraits of Places*, has been reprinted with an introduction by W. H. Auden (New York, 1946). *The Portrait of a Lady* appeared in the World's Classics in 1947. *Portraits of Places* was reprinted in New York in 1948. *The Princess Casamassima* and *The Bostonians*, with introductions by L. Trilling, were reprinted in (New York) 1948 and 1952 respectively. In 1948 there was a reprint of *The Tragic Muse*, *The Ambassadors* was issued in Everyman's Library, *The Wings of the Dove* in the Century Library, and *The Other House* in an edition carrying an introduction by L. Edel. In *Henry James: The Scenic Art* (New Brunswick, N.J., 1948) A. Wade assembled a survey of James's views on acting and drama from essays and reviews written between 1872 and 1901. L. Edel edited *The Ghostly Tales of Henry James* (New Brunswick, N.J., 1948 [1949]), *Henry James: The American Essays*, and *Henry James: The Future of the Novel* (both New York, 1956). In 1950 E. Kenton edited *Eight Uncollected Tales* (New Brunswick, N.J.). *The Golden Bowl* has been reprinted with an introduction by R. P. Blackmur (New York, 1952) and *The Sacred Fount* with an introduction by L. Edel (New York, 1953). In 1956 J. L. Sweeney selected and introduced *The Painter's Eye: Notes and Essays on the Pictorial Arts*, and F. W. Dupee brought together *A Small Boy and Others*, *Notes of a Son and Brother*, and *The Middle Years* under the general title of *Autobiography*. *A London Life* was reprinted in New York in 1957, as was *William Wetmore Story and His Friends*. Collections offering certain essays, notes, and reviews for the first time in volume form were *The House of Fiction*, ed. L. Edel (1957), fifteen essays on the novel and specific novelists; *Parisian Sketches*, ed. L. Edel and I. D. Lind (New York, 1957), a reprinting of letters written by James to the *New York Tribune* (1875–6); and *Literary Reviews and Essays on American and French Literature*, ed. A. Mordell (New York, 1957). *Italian Hours* was reprinted in New York in 1959. In 1960 L. Edel introduced American editions of *Watch and Ward*, *The Tragic Muse*, *Guy Domville* (with comments by Shaw, Wells, and Bennett), and *The Ambassadors* (in a revised text). In the same year A. L. Lowe edited *English Hours*.

Still one of the best general introductions to James, L. N. Richardson's *Henry James: Representative Selections* (New York, 1941) contains an introduction and useful bibliographical, biographical, and critical tables. Two substantial collections are *The Great Short Novels of Henry James*, ed. P. Rahv (New York, 1944) and *The Short Stories of Henry James*, ed. C. Fadiman (New York [1945]). There are also *The Art of Fiction and Other Essays*, ed. M. Roberts (New York, 1948) and *The Portable Henry James* ed. M. D. Zabel (New York, 1951). Many selections of short stories have been made; among the more recent are L. Edel's *Selected Fiction* (New York, 1953), G. Hopkins's *Selected Stories* (World's Classics, 1957), and M. D. Zabel's *In the Cage and Other Tales* (New York, 1958). Zabel has also edited *The Art of Travel* (New York, 1958), a collection of writings dealing withAmerica, England, France, and Italy.

In *Henry James: The Untried Years* (1953) and *Henry James: The Conquest of London* (1962), the first two volumes of a projected four-volume biography, L. Edel has traced James's life up to 1884. F. W. Dupee's *Henry James* (New York, 1951; revised and enlarged, 1956) is a good general summary. S. Nowell-Smith's *The Legend of the Master* (1947) brings together much entertaining matter from diverse sources. *The James Family* (New York, 1947), a group biography by F. O. Matthiessen, contains many unpublished letters by James together with selections from his writings and those of his father, brother, and sister. Among many books offering biographical information are Mrs. H. Ward, *A Writer's Recollections* (1918), *The Letters of William James*, ed. H. James (2 vols., Boston, 1920), E. Gosse, *Aspects and Impressions* (1922), T. Bosanquet, *Henry James at Work* (1924), C. H. Grattan, *The Three Jameses: A Family of Minds* (New York, 1932), H. Walpole, *The Apple Trees* [1932], W. Rothenstein, *Men and Memories* (2 vols., 1931–2), D. MacCarthy, *Portraits* (1932), *Alice James: Her Brothers, Her Journal*, ed. A. R. Burr (New York, 1934), H. G. Wells, *Experiment in Autobiography* (2 vols., 1934), E. Wharton, *A Backward Glance* (1934), F. M. Ford, *Mightier than the Sword* (1938), V. Harlow, *Thomas Sergeant Perry* (Durham, N.C., 1950), R. Hart-Davis, *Hugh Walpole* (1952), and L. Woolf, *Sowing* (1960). Articles include: E. S. Nadal, 'Personal Recollections of Henry James' (*Scribner's Magazine* lxviii, 1920); R. Herrick, 'A Visit to

Henry James' (*Yale Review*, N.S. xii, 1923); L. P. Smith, 'Slices of Cake' (*New Statesman* xxv, 5 June 1943); S. Leslie, 'A Note on Henry James' (*Horizon* vii, June 1943); M. Swan, 'Henry James and the Heroic Young Master' (*London Magazine* ii, 1955); H. Brewster, 'Henry James and the Gallo-American' (*Botteghe Oscure* xix, 1957); and G. Keynes, 'Henry James in Cambridge' (*London Magazine* vi, 1959).

E. L. Cary's pioneer *The Novels of Henry James* was published in 1905, F. M. Hueffer's (Ford's) eulogistic *Henry James: A Critical Study* in 1913, and R. West's astringent and perceptive *Henry James* a few months after James's death in 1916. In *The Method of Henry James* (New Haven, 1918; reprinted with a long new introduction, Philadelphia, 1954) J. W. Beach made a valuable study of James's technique. S. B. Liljegren in *American and European in the Works of Henry James* (Lund, 1920) opened the study of James's 'international situation', and in *The Pilgrimage of Henry James* (New York, 1925) V. W. Brooks discussed the related theme of expatriation and its consequences. Later studies were M. Roberts, *Henry James's Criticism* (Cambridge, Mass., 1929), C. P. Kelley, *The Early Development of Henry James* (Urbana, Ill., 1930), L. Edel, *Henry James: Les Années dramatiques* (Paris, 1931), F. O. Matthiessen, *Henry James: The Major Phase* (New York, 1944), and F. W. Dupee's collection of essays by various hands, *The Question of Henry James* (New York, 1945). M. Swan's *Henry James* (supplement to *British Book News*, 1950) is a critical essay with a select bibliography and a useful index of short stories. F. C. Crews in *The Tragedy of Manners* (New Haven, 1957) offers a close discussion of the late novels. Q. Anderson's *The American Henry James* (New Brunswick, N.J., 1957) attempts to discuss James's last novels in terms of his father's Swedenborgian thought. In *The Image of Europe in Henry James* (Dallas, 1958), probably the best development of its subject, C. Wegelin traces the course of the international theme in James's work. A. Holder-Barrell's *The Development of Imagery and Its Functional Significance in Henry James's Novels* (Bern, 1959) is a short monograph; a longer and often stimulating work is R. Poirier's *The Comic Sense of Henry James* (1960), a discussion of the comedy in the early novels. *A Casebook on Henry James's The Turn of the Screw*, ed. G. Willen (New York, 1960), assembles a diversity of interpretations of the story. Of

recent brief introductions to James the best is D. W. Jefferson's
Henry James (1960). *Discovery of a Genius: William Dean Howells
and Henry James*, ed. A. Mordell (New York, 1961) collects articles and reviews by Howells. Other works are J. A. Ward's *The
Imagination of Disaster* (Lincoln, 1961), a study of evil in the
fiction, W. H. Tilley's *The Background of The Princess Casamassima*
(Gainesville, 1961), O. Cargill's compendious *The Novels of Henry
James* (New York, 1961), and D. Krook's *The Ordeal of Consciousness in Henry James* (1962).

The following are representative of the large number of books
containing chapters or sections on James's work: O. Elton,
Modern Studies (1907); W. C. Brownell, *American Prose Masters*
(1909); J. G. Huneker, *Unicorns* (New York, 1917); P. Lubbock,
The Craft of Fiction (1921); H. Read, *The Sense of Glory* (1929;
reprinted in *Collected Essays*, 1953); J. W. Beach, *The Twentieth
Century Novel: Studies in Technique* (New York, 1932); W. Lewis,
Men Without Art (1934); S. Spender, *The Destructive Element*
(1935); A. J. A. Waldock, *James, Joyce and Others* (1937); Y.
Winters, *Maule's Curse* (Norfolk, Conn., [1938]; reprinted in *In
Defense of Reason*, 1960); E. Wilson, *The Triple Thinkers* (New
York, 1938; revised and enlarged, 1948); F. O. Matthiessen,
American Renaissance (New York, 1941); and F. Nuhn, *The Wind
Blew from the East* (New York, 1942). *The Shock of Recognition*, ed.
E. Wilson (New York, 1943), contains two short essays by T. S.
Eliot reprinted from the special issue of the *Little Review* in 1918.
R. E. Spiller et al., *The Literary History of the United States* (vol. ii,
New York, 1948), contains one of the best short accounts of
James, contributed by R. P. Blackmur. There may also be noted:
F. R. Leavis, *The Great Tradition* (1948) and *The Common Pursuit*
(1952); P. Rahv, *Image and Idea* (New York, 1949; revised and
enlarged, 1957); M. Bewley, *The Complex Fate* (1953); C. Feidel-
son, Jr., *Symbolism and American Literature* (Chicago, 1953); Ezra
Pound, *Literary Essays*, ed. T. S. Eliot (1954); R. P. Blackmur,
The Lion and the Honeycomb (New York, 1955); R. Chase, *The
American Novel and its Tradition* (New York, 1957); M. D. Zabel,
Craft and Character in Modern Fiction (New York, 1957); F.
O'Connor, *The Mirror in the Roadway* (1957); V. W. Brooks,
Dream of Arcadia (New York, 1958); M. Bewley, *The Eccentric
Design* (1959); W. Wasserstrom, *Heiress of All the Ages* (Min-
neapolis, 1959); L. Auchinloss, *Reflections of a Jacobite* (Boston,

1961); J. Bayley, *The Characters of Love* (1961); and R. W. Stallman, *The Houses That James Built* ([East Lansing,] Michigan, 1961).

Representative articles on James include: D. MacCarthy, 'Mr Henry James and his Public' (*Independent Review* vi, 1905); essays by T. S. Eliot, E. Pound, and T. Bosanquet in a special Henry James number of the *Little Review* (v, 1918); D. Bethurum, 'Morality and Henry James' (*Sewanee Review* xxxi, 1923); E. Kenton, 'The "Plays" of Henry James' (*Theatre Arts* xxi, 1928); C. Cestre, 'La France dans l'œuvre de Henry James' (*Revue anglo-américaine* x, 1932); L. Edel, 'The Exile of Henry James' (*University of Toronto Quarterly* ii, 1933); essays in the *Hound and Horn* special Henry James issue (vii, 1934); W. C. D. Pacey, 'Henry James and His French Contemporaries' (*American Literature* xiii, 1941); D. Lerner, 'The Influence of Turgenev on Henry James' (*Slavonic Yearbook* xx, 1941); the memorial issue of the *New Republic* (cviii, 13 Feb. 1943); R. Mortimer, 'Henry James' (*Horizon* vii, 1943); *Kenyon Review*, James Centenary issue (v, 1943); E. K. Brown, 'James and Conrad' (*Yale Review* xxxv, 1946); M. Roberts, 'Henry James and the Art of Foreshortening' (*Review of English Studies* xxii, 1946); Q. D. Leavis, 'The Institution of Henry James' (*Scrutiny* xv, 1947); W. H. Auden, 'Henry James and the Artist in America' (*Harper's Magazine* cxcvii, 1948); H. Specker, 'The Change in Emphasis in the Criticism of Henry James' (*English Studies* xxiv, 1948); R. W. Short, 'Some Critical Terms for Henry James' (*PMLA* lxv, 1950) and 'Henry James's World of Images' (ibid. lxviii, 1953); P. N. Furbank, 'Henry James: The Novelist as Actor' (*Essays in Criticism* i, 1951); A. Berland, 'James and Forster: The Morality of Class' (*Cambridge Journal* vi, 1953); M. Allott, 'Symbol and Image in the Later Work of Henry James' (*Essays in Criticism* iii, 1953); G. H. Bantock, 'Morals and Civilization in Henry James' (*Cambridge Journal* vii, 1953); R. L. Gale, 'Freudian Imagery in James's Fiction' (*American Imago* xi, 1954) and 'Art Imagery in James's Fiction' (*American Literature* xxix, 1957) and 'Religious Imagery in James's Fiction' (*Modern Fiction Studies* iii, 1957); C. B. Cox, 'Henry James and Stoicism' (*Essays and Studies* viii, 1955); *Modern Fiction Studies* iii, 1957, and *Nineteenth-Century Fiction* xii, 1957, two special Henry James numbers; R. Wellek, 'Henry James's Literary

Theory and Criticism' (*American Literature* xxx, 1958); P. Buitenhuis, 'Henry James on Hawthorne' (*New England Quarterly* xxxii, 1959); and M. Bell, 'Edith Wharton and Henry James: The Literary Relation' (*PMLA* lxxiv, 1959).

There is a comprehensive and definitive *Bibliography of Henry James* by L. Edel and D. H. Laurence (1957; rev. ed. 1961); it includes James's contributions to books and periodicals, his published letters, translations of his works, and the location of principal manuscripts. L. N. Richardson included in his *Henry James: Representative Selections* (New York, 1941) a table of biographical and critical studies which was reprinted in Dupee's *The Question of Henry James*. E. C. Hamilton and V. R. Dunbar respectively supplemented this list in 'Biographical and Critical Studies of Henry James, 1941–1948' (*American Literature* xx, 1949) and in 'Addenda . . .' (ibid. xxii, 1950). See also R. E. Spiller et al., *Literary History of the United States: Bibliography* (New York, 1948) and *Bibliography Supplement*, ed. R. M. Ludwig (New York, 1959). A very full listing of articles appeared in L. Leary's *Articles on American Literature, 1900–1950* (Durham, N.C., 1954). There is a detailed and perceptive survey by R. E. Spiller of biographical and critical writing on James in *Eight American Authors: A Review of Research and Criticism*, ed. F. Stovall (New York, 1956). In 'Criticism of Henry James: A Selected Checklist with an Index to Studies of Separate Works' (*Modern Fiction Studies* iii, 1957) M. Beebe and W. T. Stafford concentrated on critical writing after 1950.

BERNARD SHAW, 1856–1950

Shaw's first novel, *Immaturity*, written in 1879, was first published in 1930, with a preface dated 1921. *The Irrational Knot* appeared in *Our Corner*, 1885–7, and as a book in 1905. *Love among the Artists* appeared in the same journal, 1887–8, and as a book in Chicago in 1900 and in London in 1914. *Cashel Byron's Profession* was published in 1886, immediately after being serialized in *To-day*, and was subsequently several times revised; a dramatic version, *The Admirable Bashville*, was appended to the edition of 1901. *An Unsocial Socialist*, the last completed novel to be written and the first to reach print, appeared in *To-day* in 1884 and as a book in 1887. In 1887 Shaw began a sixth novel, writing forty-one pages in his small, meticulous hand before abandoning it in the following year. The fragment, published in 1958, may be viewed as looking forward to *The Doctor's Dilemma*.

The first of Shaw's plays to be published was *Widowers' Houses* in 1893. It was substantially revised for its appearance in *Plays, Pleasant and Unpleasant* (2 vols., 1898), which also contained *Mrs. Warren's Profession*, *The Philanderer*, *Arms and the Man*, *Candida*, *The Man of Destiny*, and *You Never Can Tell*. *Mrs. Warren's Profession* was republished by itself, together with a new Apology, in 1903. *The Devil's Disciple*, *Caesar and Cleopatra*, and *Captain Brassbound's Conversion* came out together as *Three Plays for Puritans* in 1901. *Man and Superman* occupied a whole volume in 1903; *Passion, Poison and Petrification*, a burlesque melodrama, appeared in 1905; *John Bull's Other Island*, *Major Barbara*, and *How he lied to her Husband* were published together in 1907. *Press Cuttings* appeared in 1909. *The Doctor's Dilemma*, *Getting Married*, and *The Shewing-up of Blanco Posnet* were published together in 1911; *Misalliance*, *The Dark Lady of the Sonnets*, and *Fanny's First Play* together in 1914; and *Androcles and the Lion*, *Overruled*, and *Pygmalion* together in 1916. *Heartbreak House* appeared in 1919, along with some minor pieces: *Great Catherine*, *O'Flaherty, V.C.*, *The Inca of Perusalem*, *Augustus does his Bit*, and *Annajanska, the Bolshevik Empress*. *Back to Methuselah* was published in 1921; there was a revised edition with a postscript, 'After Twentyfive Years', issued as No. 500 in the World's Classics in 1945. *Saint Joan* was published in 1924. *Translations and Tomfooleries* (1926) contains *Jitta's Atonement*, adapted from the German of S. Trebitsch (Shaw's German translator), together with reprints of *The Admirable Bashville*, *Press Cuttings*, and *Passion, Poison and Petrification*, and with three further trifles: *The Glimpse of Reality*, *The Fascinating Foundling*, and *The Music Cure*. *The Apple Cart* was published in 1930; and *Too True to be Good*, *Village Wooing*, and *On the Rocks* together in 1934. *The Simpleton of the Unexpected Isles* appeared in 1935, and was reprinted along with *The Six of Calais* and *The Millionairess* as *Three New Plays* in 1936. *Cymbeline Refinished* was printed in the *London Mercury* (Feb. 1938). *Geneva* and '*In Good King Charles's Golden Days*' appeared separately in 1939. *Buoyant Billions* was published in 1949, and reprinted in the following year along with *Farfetched Fables* and *Shakes versus Shav*.

In addition to the long prefaces which accompanied the publication of nearly all his plays, Shaw's prose writings are very numerous. His more significant contributions to literary, dramatic, and musical criticism are *The Quintessence of Ibsenism* (1891; completed to the death of Ibsen, 1913); *The Perfect Wagnerite* (1898); *Dramatic Opinions and Essays*, selected from the *Saturday Review* 1895–8 (2 vols., 1907); *The Sanity of Art* (*Liberty*, New York, 1895; English publication 1908); *Music in London*, reprinted from the *World* 1890–4 (3 vols., 1931); *Our Theatre in the Nineties*, a full gathering of his notices in the *Saturday Review* (3 vols., 1932); and *London Music in 1888–9* (1937). Among characteristic minor pieces may be mentioned a preface to W. H. Davies's *Autobiography of a Super-tramp* (1908); contributions to the debate on stage censorship, including *Statement of the Evidence in Chief of George Bernard Shaw before the Joint Committee on Stage Plays* (privately printed 1909); a preface to the second edition of Hall Caine's *White Prophet* (1909); *Brieux: A Preface* (1910); *The Art of Rehearsal* (*Arts League of Service Annual*, 1922); a long introduction to W. Archer's *Three Plays* (1927); and *Shaw's Rules for Directors* (*Theatre Arts* xxxiii, 1949).

Shaw's writings on political, economic, and social questions are voluminous, and range from squibs and pamphlets through fables to compendia. In 1889 he edited *Fabian Essays in Socialism*, contributing to the volume 'The Basis of Socialism: Economic' and 'The Transition to Social Democracy'. Further works in the Fabian interest are *The Impossibilities of Anarchism* (1893), 'The Illusions of Socialism' (in *Forecasts of the Coming Century*, 1897), *Fabianism and the Empire* (1900), *The Commonsense of Municipal Trading* (1904; with new preface, 1908), and *Socialism and Individualism* (with S. Webb and others, 1908). Among later widely ranging writings are *Modern Religion* (a lecture, 1912), *Commonsense about the War* (a supplement to the *New Statesman*, 14 Nov. 1914), *How to Settle the Irish Question* (1917), *Peace Conference Hints* (1919), *Irish Nationalism and Labour Internationalism* (1920), *Ruskin's Politics* (1921), *Imprisonment* (a preface, reprinted 1944, to B. and S. Webb's *English Prisons under Local Government*, 1922), *The League of Nations* (1929), *What I really wrote about the War* (1931), *The Political Madhouse in America*

and nearer Home (a lecture, 1933), and *Shaw on Vivisection* (ed.
G. H. Bowker, 1949). Shaw's feeling on this last subject had
first found expression in *The Dynamitards of Science*, a pamphlet
written in 1900; he expresses kindred humanitarian views in
a preface to *Killing for Sport*, essays by various hands published
in 1915. *Table-Talk of G. B. S.* (1925) reproduces 'conversations
on things in general' with his biographer, A. Henderson. *Shaw
and Chesterton: Do We Agree?* (1928) is based upon a public
debate, with Hilaire Belloc in the chair. *The Intelligent Woman's
Guide to Socialism and Capitalism* (1928), Shaw's most sustained
essay in political writing, was later reissued (Pelican Books,
2 vols., 1937) with two additional chapters as *The Intelligent
Woman's Guide to Socialism, Capitalism, Sovietism and Fascism.
Bernard Shaw and Karl Marx: A Symposium* was published in New
York in 1930. *Pen Portraits and Reviews* appeared in 1931. In
Doctors' Delusions, Crude Criminology and Sham Education (1932)
are collected miscellaneous writings on various themes extending over many years. *The Adventures of the Black Girl in her Search
for God* was published in 1932, and reissued in 1934 with some
lesser tales and fragments. *Everybody's Political What's What?*
(1944) was the last published of Shaw's books in its particular
field. *Shaw Gives Himself Away* (1939), *Sixteen Self Sketches* (1949),
and *Bernard Shaw's Rhyming Picture Guide to Ayot Saint Lawrence*
(1959) are variously interesting. *My dear Dorothea . . . A practical system of moral education for females*, written in 1878 and
declared to be Shaw's 'first serious literary effort', was edited
by S. Winsten in 1956.

The MS. of the *Unfinished Novel* is at the National Library
of Ireland, Dublin, and the original MS. of *Widowers' Houses*,
together with some minor MSS. and corrected typescripts, is
in the Berg Collection at the New York Public Library. Since
Shaw employed shorthand from an early date, much of the
surviving material is in this form. The original shorthand MS. of
Saint Joan is in the British Museum, as is much else. The University of Texas has 17 of Shaw's plays in the original manuscript and 2,550 of his letters. The Lockwood Memorial Library
at Buffalo has 135 letters from Shaw to Mrs. Patrick Campbell.
Diaries which Shaw kept from 1882 until a few years before his
marriage are at the London School of Economics, together with
a transcription by his former secretary, B. Patch. His letters to

Sidney and Beatrice Webb during the years 1891–1945 are among the papers of the Passfield Trust in the Library of the University of London.

The major library edition of Shaw's works is in 33 vols., issued between 1930 and 1938. The standard edition, 36 vols., (1931 continuing) is equally comprehensive. The *Complete Plays* were first published in one volume in 1931, with enlarged editions in 1934 and 1938. The *Prefaces*, together with some additional notes, appeared in one volume in 1934, with an enlarged edition in 1938.

A large collection of Shaw's letters is in preparation. Of published letters there are three important volumes: *Ellen Terry and Bernard Shaw: A Correspondence*, ed. C. St. John (1931), *Correspondence between Shaw and Mrs. Patrick Campbell*, ed. A. Dent (1952), and *Bernard Shaw's Letters to Granville-Barker*, ed. C. B. Purdom (1956). Of minor compass and interest are *Letters from George Bernard Shaw to Miss Alma Murray* (privately printed 1927), *More Letters from George Bernard Shaw to Miss Alma Murray* (two letters of 1888, privately printed 1932), *Florence Farr, Shaw and W. B. Yeats: Letters*, ed. C. Bax (Cuala Press, Dublin, 1941; London, 1946), *Advice to a Young Critic* [letters written mainly to R. Golding Bright] (New York, 1955; London, 1956), and *To a Young Actress: the Letters of B. Shaw to M. Tompkins*, ed. P. Tomkins (1960). Shaw wrote many letters to newspapers and periodicals; a scattering of others has been printed in journals (e.g. R. L. Lowe, 'Two Shaw Letters', *Modern Language Review* liii, 1958); and others, again, have been embodied in books and articles on Shaw, since Shaw was often lavish in communication to those who wrote about him.

Among selections from Shaw's writings may be noted *Selected Passages from the Works of Bernard Shaw*, chosen by Charlotte F. Shaw (1912); *Selected Novels*, ed. A. Zeiger (New York, 1946); *Plays and Players: Selected Essays*, ed. A. C. Ward (World's Classics, 1952); *Selected Prose*, ed. D. Russell (1953), a voluminous gathering with much emphasis on the socialist writings; *Bernard Shaw: A Prose Anthology*, ed. H. M. Burton (1959); *Shaw on Theatre*, ed. E. J. West (1960); *Platform and Pulpit*, ed. D. H. Laurence (New York, 1961); *The Theatre of*

Bernard Shaw (ten plays ed. A. S. Downer, New York, 1961); and *Shaw on Shakespeare*, ed. E. Wilson (1961). *How to Become a Musical Critic*, ed. D. H. Laurence (1961), brings together much early journalism. *The Matter with Ireland*, ed. D. H. Greene and D. H. Laurence (New York, 1962), is a similar gathering.

A. Henderson's *George Bernard Shaw: His Life and Works* (1911) was superseded by the same writer's *Bernard Shaw: Playboy and Prophet* (New York, 1932) and then by his *George Bernard Shaw: Man of the Century* (New York, 1956). These 'authorized' books are diffuse and undistinguished, but invaluable for the vast amount of information somewhat randomly disposed in them. H. Pearson's *Bernard Shaw: His Life and Personality* (1942; supplemented in *G. B. S.: A Postscript*, 1951; the two combined, with additions, 1961) and St. John Ervine's *Bernard Shaw: His Life, Work and Friends* (1956) are more continent works. F. Harris's *Frank Harris on Bernard Shaw: An Unauthorized Biography* (1931) is perhaps to be classified as a biographical work, and has a postscript by Shaw. Books of minor interest include D. Rider, *Adventures with Bernard Shaw* (1929), C. Macmahon Shaw, *Bernard's Brethren* (1939), S. Winsten, *Days with Shaw* (New York, 1949) and *Jesting Apostle* (1956), B. Patch, *Thirty Years with G. B. S.* (1951), H. G. Farmer, *Bernard Shaw's Sister and her Friends* (Leiden, 1959), and A. Chappelow, *Shaw the Villager and Human Being* (1961). F. E. Loewenstein's *Shaw through the Camera* (1948) and *Bernard Shaw* (1952) are both pictorial records, as is M. Shenfield's *Bernard Shaw: A Pictorial Biography* (1962).

The three earliest books of any note on Shaw were by H. L. Mencken (1905), H. Jackson (1907), and G. K. Chesterton (1909; enlarged, 1935). *Le Molière du XXᵉ siècle: Bernard Shaw* (Paris, 1913) by A. F. A. Hamon, the French translator of Shaw's plays, and *Die Quintessenz des Shawismus* by H. Richter, the first of many German discussions, were published in 1913 in Paris and Leipzig respectively; there is an English version (1916) of Hamon's book. J. MacCabe's *George Bernard Shaw* (1914) is an early attempt to disengage the dramatist's thought on speculative questions, and was to have numerous successors. C. Duffin's *The Quintessence of Bernard Shaw* (1920) is a competent expository work; it was reissued in 1939 with additional chapters 'freely emended' by Shaw. J. S. Collis's *Shaw* (1925) is another general survey, again with some notes contributed by Shaw. J. M. Robertson's *Mr. Shaw and the Maid* (1925) is a short polemical work. M. Colbourne's *The Real Shaw* (1930; revised and enlarged in 1939 and 1949), while lively rather than penetrating, is of some interest on the theatrical side; and R. F. Rattray's *Bernard Shaw: A Chronicle and an Introduction* (1934; revised, 1951) has a similar limited utility. E. Strauss in *Shaw: Art and Socialism* (1942) traces Shaw's 'development as a Socialist, as revealed in his dramatic works', and A. West's *A Good Man Fallen among Fabians* (1950) takes similar ground. A. C. Ward's *Bernard Shaw* (supplement to *British Book News*, 1950) is a good introductory essay with a select bibliography and some useful indexes. C. E. M. Joad's *Shaw* (1950), although broadly conceived, is concerned in the main with the dramatist's philosophy. W. Irvine's *The Universe of G. B. S.* (New York, 1949), despite its popular title, is a substantial study with merit. *G. B. S. 90*, edited by S. Winsten (New York, 1949) is a symposium which includes one or two attractive pieces; the same editor has himself produced a number of light books of 'Shavian' interest. D. MacCarthy's *Shaw* (1951), although no more than a collection of theatrical notices, remains perhaps the best critical study of the dramatist. Two much more systematic studies of interest are A. Nethercot's *Men and Supermen* (New York, 1954) and J. B. Kaye's *Bernard Shaw and the Nineteenth-Century Tradition* (Oklahoma, 1958). *A Theatrical Companion to Shaw* (1955) by R. Mander and J. Mitchenson is mainly interesting as a pictorial record of the plays in production.

The following books have notable chapters on Shaw: A. B. Walkley, *Frames of Mind* (1899); A. Dukes, *Modern Dramatists* (1911); C. E. Montague, *Dramatic Values* (1911); Dixon Scott, *Men of Letters* (1916); W. L. Phelps, *Essays on Modern Dramatists* (1921); M. Belgion, *Our Present Philosophy of Life* (1929); E. Wilson, *The Triple Thinkers* (1938; revised and enlarged, 1948); E. R. Bentley, *The Playwright as Thinker* (1946); and J. Huizinga, *Men and Ideas* (1960). *Studies in English Drama presented to Baldwin Maxwell* (Iowa, 1962) contains an excellent essay on *Mrs. Warren's Profession* by G. Bullough.

In journals the following may be noted: D. C. Parker, 'Bernard Shaw as a Musical Critic' (*Opera Magazine*, New

York, June 1915); H. A. Jones, 'Bernard Shaw as a Thinker' (*English Review* xxxvi, xxxvii, 1923); E. Cammaerts, 'Molière and Bernard Shaw' (*Nineteenth Century*, Sept. 1926); J. T. Grein, 'Notes about Bernard Shaw' (*Illustrated London News*, Aug. 1926); A. Maurois, 'Bernard Shaw' (*Revue hebdomadaire*, 16 and 23 March 1935); J. Barzun, 'Shaw in Twilight' (*Kenyon Review* v, 1943); W. Irvine, 'Shaw's Musical Criticism' (*Musical Quarterly* xxxii, 1946); M. Crane, ' "Pygmalion": Bernard Shaw's Dramatic Theory and Practice' (*PMLA* lxvi, 1951); H. Ludeke, 'Some Remarks on Shaw's History Plays' (*English Studies* xxxvi, 1935); C. Shattuck, 'Bernard Shaw's "Bad Quarto" ' (*Journal of English and Germanic Philology* liv, 1955) [a study of the text of *Widowers' Houses*]; A Nun of Stanbrook, 'The Nun and the Dramatist' (*Cornhill*, Summer 1956) [correspondence between Shaw and Dame Laurentia McLachlan]; G. S. Barber, 'Shaw's Contribution to Music Criticism', G. W. Couchman, 'Here was a Caesar: Shaw's Comedy Today', and N. F. O'Donnell, 'Shaw, Bunyan and Puritanism' (all in *PMLA* lxxii, 1957); M. M. Morgan, ' "Back to Methuselah": The Poet and the City' (*Essays and Studies* N.S. xiii, 1960); and N. Annan, 'Shaw the Sociologist' (*Herbert Spencer Lecture*, 1960).

There is no full bibliography. G. H. Wells's *Bibliography of the Books and Pamphlets of George Bernard Shaw* (1928) is useful as far as it goes, and C. L. and V. M. Broad's *Dictionary to the Plays and Novels* (1929) is also worth consulting. M. Holmes's *Some Bibliographical Notes on the Novels of Bernard Shaw* [1929] is an exact work. F. E. Loewenstein's *The History of a Famous Novel* (privately printed, 1946) concerns *An Unsocial Socialist*. The same writer's *Autograph Manuscripts of Shaw* (*Book Handbook* ii, 1947) is scarcely comprehensive. His *Rehearsal Copies of Shaw's Plays* (New York, 1950) serves as an introduction to a subject not yet fully explored.

JOSEPH CONRAD, 1857–1924

'The Black Mate', Conrad's unsuccessful offering to *Tit-Bits*, seems not to have survived in the original version, but a story with the same title was published in the *London Magazine* (1908, privately printed 1922, included in the posthumous

Tales of Hearsay, 1925). *Almayer's Folly* was published in 1895; the text was revised by Conrad in 1916 for the first collected edition of his works. *An Outcast of the Islands* was published in 1896. *The Nigger of the 'Narcissus'* was serialized in the *New Review* (Aug.–Dec. 1897) and published in New York in the same year under the title *The Children of the Sea*; from the serial text, with slight revisions, there was produced an English edition of seven copies for copyright purposes; for the first regular English edition (1898 [1897]) Conrad revised the serial text, and further revisions were made for the Collected Edition of 1921. The preface first appeared in the *New Review* (Dec. 1897) and was privately printed in 1902. Together with a note 'To My Readers in America' it appeared under the title *Joseph Conrad on the Art of Writing* (New York, 1914) and both pieces were then reprinted with the novel in New York in the same year. *Tales of Unrest* (1898) contained five stories written during 1896–7, four of which had previously appeared in magazines and were now slightly revised; the fifth, 'The Return', was printed for the first time. According to Conrad the proofs of the first American edition (1898) were uncorrected by him and differences of text probably existed. This was to be a recurrent situation. Like Conrad's regular revision of serial texts for book publication, it is not further noted.

   Lord Jim was serialized in *Blackwood's Magazine* (Oct. 1899– Nov. 1900) and published in 1900; an edition in 1917 was the first to contain the Author's Note. *The Inheritors*, Conrad's first collaboration with F. M. Hueffer (Ford), was published in New York in 1901. *Youth: a Narrative, and Two Other Stories* ['Heart of Darkness' and 'The End of the Tether'] (1902) had all appeared previously in *Blackwood's*; the last was given a second slight revision for an edition in 1917; and in 1920 the title story was reprinted in *Youth, and Gaspar Ruiz*, with a note to the latter story which has never appeared again. *Typhoon and Other Stories* (1903) contained 'Typhoon' (*Pall Mall Magazine*, Jan.–March 1902; published New York, 1902; first separate English publication 1912), 'Amy Foster' (*Illustrated London News* Dec. 1901), the first printing of 'Falk', and 'Tomorrow' (*Pall Mall Magazine*, Aug. 1902). 'Tomorrow' was adapted by Conrad into a one-act play, *One Day More*, which was performed in June 1905 by the Stage Society; it appeared in the *English Review* (Aug. 1913) and a revised version was privately printed in 1917. *Romance*, the second collaboration with Hueffer, was published in 1903. *Nostromo* was published in 1904 after appearing serially in *T.P.'s Weekly* during the first ten months of that year; an edition of 1918 was the first to contain the seven-page Author's Note; the novel was slightly revised for the first Collected Edition; the Modern Library edition (New York, [1951]) contains a valuable introduction by R. P. Warren. *The Mirror of the Sea, Memories and Impressions* (1906) contained forty-nine sections, the last twelve here printed for the first time. *The Secret Agent* (1907) was previously serialized in *Ridgway's, a Militant Weekly for God and Country* (Oct.–Dec. 1906). *The Secret Agent, Drama in Four Acts*, a later dramatization by Conrad, was privately printed (1921), and in November 1922 performed in London; a limited edition with a revised text appeared in 1923.

Six stories, all previously published, comprise *A Set of Six* (1908). The fourth story, 'The Duel', also appeared in *Forum* (July–Oct. 1908) under the title 'The Point of Honor', and with this title was reissued as a separate publication (New York, 1908). Seven years later Conrad wrote a special introduction for the first American edition of *A Set of Six* (1915); this does not appear in the Collected Edition. *Under Western Eyes* (1911) had appeared simultaneously in the *English Review* and the *North American Review* (Dec. 1910–Oct. 1911); the novel was reissued in New York (1951) with an introduction by M. D. Zabel. *A Personal Record* first appeared as *Some Reminiscences* in the *English Review* (Dec. 1908–June 1909); the first part of this text was published separately in a limited edition (New York, 1908) in order to establish copyright; the *English Review* title and a revised text were used in the first edition (1912), for which Conrad wrote a 'Familiar Preface'. Later in that year the book was issued in New York as *A Personal Record*, and the first English edition with this title appeared in 1916. *'Twixt Land and Sea* (1912) collected from magazines 'A Smile of Fortune', 'The Secret Sharer', and 'Freya of the Seven Isles'. *Chance* (1913) had been serialized in the *New York Herald* (Jan.–June 1912). It was followed by *Within the Tides* (1915), four more stories from magazines: 'The Planter of Malata', 'The Partner', 'The Inn of the Two Witches', and 'Because of the Dollars'. The last had previously been called 'Laughing Anne' and Conrad used this title for his dramatized version, published in a limited edition in 1923. *Victory* was both serialized in *Munsey's Magazine* and published in New York in 1915; to the English edition later that year Conrad added an introductory note; a dramatization by B. M. Hastings was performed in London in 1919. *The Shadow-Line: A Confession* (1917) first appeared in the *English Review* (Sept. 1916–March 1917). *The Arrow of Gold* (New York, 1919) first appeared in *Lloyd's Magazine* (Dec. 1918–Feb. 1920); the text of the first English edition contains corrections not included in the American edition. *The Rescue* (originally *The Rescuer*) first appeared in *Land and Water* (Jan.–July 1919) and was published in New York in 1920; the regular English edition of the same year embodied Conrad's final corrections.

A collection of thirty essays, articles, and reviews made up *Notes on Life and Letters* (1921). *Notes on My Books* (New York, 1921) is a similar miscellany. Conrad's last completed work, *The Rover*, was serialized in the *Pictorial Review* (Sept.–Dec. 1923) and published in New York in the same year. *The Nature of a Crime*, written in collaboration with Hueffer, was serialized in the *English Review* (April–May 1909) under the pseudonym 'Ignatz von Aschendorf'; it was published as a book in 1924. *Laughing Anne, One Day More: Two Plays* with an introduction by John Galsworthy appeared in 1924; to these was added *The Secret Agent* in *Three Plays* (1934). The uncompleted *Suspense* (New York, 1925) had been serialized in *Hutchinson's Magazine* (Feb.– Aug. 1925) and in the *Saturday Review of Literature* (June–Sept. 1925). *Tales of Hearsay* (1925) is a posthumous gathering of stories with an introduction by R. B. Cunninghame Graham. *Notes by Joseph Conrad Written in a Set of His First Editions in the Possession of Richard Curle* was privately printed in 1925. *Last Essays*—all but one previously published—appeared in 1926; the last item, 'The Congo Diary', first printed in *Blue Peter* (Oct. 1925), was issued in a limited edition as *Joseph Conrad's Diary of His Journey up the Valley of the Congo in 1890* (1926). 'The Sisters', an unfinished story begun by Conrad in 1896, was printed in *The Bookman* (New York, Jan. 1928). *Complete Short Stories* appeared in 1933; *Three Plays* in 1934; and *Conrad's Prefaces to his Works*, ed. E. Garnett, in 1937. *The Portable Conrad* (ed. with an introduction by M. D. Zabel) was published in New York in 1947.

The outstanding Conrad collection is that at Yale. Among

the MSS. and typescripts are those of 'The Idiots', 'An Outpost of Progress', 'The Shadow-Line', 'Heart of Darkness', 'The End of the Tether', *Chance*, and sections of other novels. MSS. at the British Museum include those of 'The Rescuer' (the first form of *The Rescue*), 'The Black Mate', and the play *Laughing Anne*. Harvard University Library possesses the MSS. of the 'Up-River Book' (the diary furnishing material for 'Heart of Darkness'), 'Tuan Jim' (the first sketch of *Lord Jim*), and several letters. There is Conrad material in the New York Public Library, the Pierpont Morgan Library, Duke University Library, the University of Texas, Indiana University Library, Dartmouth College Library, the Pan Library at Cracow, and the Narodowa Library at Warsaw.

The first collected edition of Conrad's works was *The Works of Joseph Conrad* (20 vols., 1921–7). For this limited edition Conrad made final slight revisions in the text of some novels and added an Author's Note by way of preface to those works which did not already possess one. *The Works of Joseph Conrad: Uniform Edition* (22 vols., 1923–8) has been reissued, with the omission of *The Inheritors*, as the current *New Collected Edition* (21 vols.). Other collected editions include *The Medallion Edition* (21 vols., 1925) and the current American *Memorial Edition* (21 vols.). There is a Polish edition in 28 volumes (*Pisma zbiorowe Józefa Konrada*, Warsaw, 1928–39).

Five Letters by Joseph Conrad Written to Edward Noble in 1895 was privately printed in 1925. *Joseph Conrad's Letters to His Wife* and *To My Brethren of the Pen* (a reprint of a letter of 1919 to *The Editor*) were both privately printed in 1927. G. J. Aubry's *Joseph Conrad: Life and Letters* (2 vols., New York, 1927) contains a large number of letters, not always reliably transcribed. *Letters from Joseph Conrad, 1895–1924* (Indianapolis, 1928) was edited with an introduction and notes by Edward Garnett. The text and notes of R. Curle's *Letters, Joseph Conrad to Richard Curle* (New York, 1928) were revised by the editor as *Conrad to a Friend, 150 Selected Letters from Joseph Conrad to Richard Curle* (New York, 1928). G. J. Aubry introduced *Lettres françaises* (Paris [1930]). Later collections are *Letters of Joseph Conrad to Marguerite Poradowska 1890–1920*, translated from the French and edited by J. A. Gee and P. J. Sturm (New Haven, 1940) and

W. Blackburn, *Joseph Conrad: Letters to William Blackwood and David S. Meldrum* (Durham, N.C., 1958).

The best and most recent biography is that by J. Baines: *Joseph Conrad* (1960). It supplants G. J. Aubry's *Joseph Conrad: Life and Letters* (2 vols., 1927). Books by Jessie Conrad and F. M. Ford (Hueffer) carry some authority but are to be received with caution. D. Goldring's *The Last Pre-Raphaelite* (1948) gives an account of the Conrad–Hueffer collaboration and quotes some Conrad letters. Other books offering biographical information include J. G. Sutherland, *At Sea with Joseph Conrad* (1922), R. B. Cunninghame Graham, *Redeemed and Other Sketches* (1927), J. Galsworthy, *Castles in Spain* (1927), R. Curle, *The Last Twelve Years of Joseph Conrad* (1928), D. MacCarthy, *Portraits* (1931), W. Rothenstein, *Men and Memories* (2 vols., 1931–2) and *Since Fifty* (1939), H. G. Wells, *Experiment in Autobiography* (2 vols., 1934, J. H. Retinger, *Conrad and his Contemporaries* (1941), R. Hart-Davis, *Hugh Walpole* (1952), and D. Garnett, *The Golden Echo* (1953). G. J. Aubry's *The Sea Dreamer* (1957) is a translation of the writer's *Vie de Conrad* (Paris, 1947) which claims, too boldly, to be a definitive biography. Bertrand Russell recalls Conrad, vividly and mordantly, in *Portraits from Memory* (1956). Memoirs and reminiscences in article form include O. Morrell, 'Joseph Conrad: An Impression' (*Nation* xxv, 1924), S. Zeromski, 'Joseph Conrad' (*Nineteenth Century* ci, 1927), F. N. Doubleday, 'Joseph Conrad as a Friend' (*World Today* lii, 1928), M. Dabrowski, 'An Interview with Joseph Conrad' (*American Scholar* xii, 1944), C. Milosz, 'Joseph Conrad in Polish Eyes' (*Atlantic Monthly* cc, 1957), John Conrad's reminiscences in *Conrad Zywy* (1957), and A. A. Knopf, 'Joseph Conrad: A Footnote to Publishing History' (*Atlantic Monthly* cci, 1958).

Several critical studies of Conrad were published during his lifetime, the pioneer work being R. Curle's *Joseph Conrad* (1914). Others include H. Walpole, *Joseph Conrad* (1916; rev. ed. 1924), and R. M. Stauffer, *Joseph Conrad: His Romantic-Realism* (Boston, 1922). A. Symons, *Notes on Joseph Conrad with some Unpublished Letters* (1925), H. Clifford, *A Talk on Joseph Conrad and His Work* (English Association Pamphlet, Colombo, 1927), and M. David, *Joseph Conrad: l'homme et l'œuvre* (Paris, [1929]) are further early studies. G. Morf's *The Polish Heritage of Joseph Conrad* [1930] traces, with some use of psychoanalytical method, the effects of expatriation in Conrad's works. R. L. Mégroz's *Joseph Conrad's Mind and Method* (1931) reproduces in part the same writer's *A Talk with Joseph Conrad and a Criticism of His Mind and Method* (1926). E. Crankshaw's *Joseph Conrad: Some Aspects of the Art of the Novel* (1936) lays a basis for close study, and J. D. Gordan's *Joseph Conrad: The Making of a Novelist* (Cambridge, Mass., 1940), although it considers only the early novels and stories, is a detailed and valuable examination of the first maturing of Conrad's art. M. C. Bradbrook's *Joseph Conrad: Poland's English Genius* (1941) combines a generous war-time tribute with a scholarly assessment; O. Warner's *Joseph Conrad* (supplement to *British Book News*, 1950) is a short appreciation with a select bibliography and an index of short stories, and his *Joseph Conrad* (1951) is a brief critical and biographical study; D. Hewitt's *Conrad: A Reassessment* (1952) is a good short survey; and P. L. Wiley's *Conrad's Measure of Man* (Madison, Wisconsin, 1954) is an interesting study of the theme of failure in the novels and stories. Several studies were published during or immediately following the centenary year of Conrad's birth: R. F. Haugh, *Joseph Conrad: Discovery in Design* (Norman, Okla., 1957) is a study of plot in twelve works of the middle period; T. J. Moser's *Joseph Conrad: Achievement and Decline* (Cambridge, Mass., 1957) examines Conrad's inability to handle love-themes; and *Conrad Żywy* [*The Living Conrad*] ed. W. Tarnawski (1957) contains studies by various Polish authors as well as English summaries. A. J. Guerard offers much acute criticism in *Conrad the Novelist* (Cambridge, Mass., 1958), particular emphasis being placed upon *Lord Jim* and *Nostromo*. Collections of Conrad criticism are *The Art of Joseph Conrad: A Critical Symposium*, ed. R. W. Stallman (East Lansing, Michigan, 1960) and *Joseph Conrad: Centennial Essays*, ed. L. Krzyzanowski (New York, 1960). Fourteen essays are included in *Conrad's Heart of Darkness and the Critics*, ed. B. Harkness (San Francisco, 1960). The difficulty of establishing a reliable text of Conrad is emphasized by the fact that the editor found it desirable to collate no less than nine printed versions of the story. F. R. Karl's *A Reader's Guide to Joseph Conrad* (1960) affords a general survey.

Henry James's essay 'The Younger Generation' (*TLS*, 19 Mar. and 2 Apr. 1914; revised and enlarged as 'The New

Novel' in *Notes on Novelists*, 1914) is an important landmark in the criticism of Conrad. There are further early discussions in J. G. Huneker, *Ivory Apes and Peacocks* [1915], J. C. Powys, *Suspended Judgments* (New York, 1916), H. L. Mencken, *A Book of Prefaces* (New York, 1917), *Schelling Anniversary Papers* (Philadelphia, 1923), E. Muir, *Latitudes* [1924], V. Woolf, *The Common Reader* (1925; and see the same writer's 'Mr Conrad: A Conversation' in *The Captain's Death Bed*, 1950), E. Shanks, *Second Essays on Literature* (1927), R. Fernandez, *Messages* (1927), E. E. Kellett, *Reconsiderations* (1928), E. Garnett, *Friday Nights: Literary Criticisms and Appreciations* (1929), and T. Mann, *Past Masters and Other Papers* (1933). E. M. Forster has a short essay in *Abinger Harvest* (1936), concluding that Conrad 'is misty in the middle as well as at the edges'; F. R. Leavis, on the other hand, writes a major appreciation in *The Great Tradition* (1948). Other works deserving mention are D. Daiches, *The Novel and the Modern World* (Chicago, 1939; rev. ed., 1960) and I. Simon, *Formes du roman anglais de Dickens à Joyce* (Liège, 1949); discussions of *The Rover*, *Nostromo*, and *Lord Jim* respectively in J. Lehmann, *The Open Night* (1952), A. Kettle, *An Introduction to the English Novel*, vol. ii (1953), and D. Van Ghent, *The English Novel: Form and Function* (New York, 1953); and M. D. Zabel, *Craft and Character in Modern Fiction* (1957). There are good discussions in I. Howe, *Politics and the Novel* (New York, 1957) and G. Hough, *Image and Experience* (1960).

Detailed lists of general essays and articles on specific works published in periodicals will be found in Lohf and Sheehy (*vide infra*). The following are notable: H. Clifford, 'The Genius of Mr. Joseph Conrad' (*North American Review* clxxviii, 1904); J. M. Robertson, 'The Novels of Joseph Conrad' (ibid., ccviii, 1918); S. Gwynn, 'The Novels of Joseph Conrad' (*Edinburgh Review* ccxxxi, 1920); G. H. Clarke, 'Joseph Conrad and his Art' (*Sewanee Review* xxx, 1922); and J. Shand, 'Some Notes on Joseph Conrad' (*Criterion* iii, 1924). *transatlantic review* (ii, 1924) contains a 'Conrad Supplement' with essays by F. M. Ford and E. Hemingway; *Nouvelle revue française* (xxiii, 1924) includes pieces by A. Gide, P. Valéry, E. Jaloux, and A. Maurois; *Mentor* (xiii, 1925) is another Conrad number. Later work includes A. R. Thompson, 'The Humanism of Conrad' (*Sewanee Review* xxxvii, 1929), G. W. Whiting, 'Conrad's Revisions of Six of His

Short Stories' (*PMLA* xlviii, 1933); R. G. Lillard, 'Irony in Hardy and Conrad' (ibid. l, 1935); E. Wagenknecht, ' "Pessimism" in Hardy and Conrad' (*College English* iii, 1942); V. Young, 'Joseph Conrad: Outline for a Reconsideration' (*Hudson Review* ii, 1949); P. Ure, 'Character and Imagination in Conrad' (*Cambridge Journal* iii, 1950); G. H. Bantock, 'The Two "Moralities" of Joseph Conrad' (*Essays in Criticism* iii, 1953); V. Young, 'Lingard's Folly: The Lost Subject' (*Kenyon Review* xv, 1953); C. Benson, 'Conrad's Two Stories of Initiation' (*PMLA* lxix, 1954); M. Mudrick, 'Conrad and the Terms of Modern Criticism' (*Hudson Review* vii, 1954) and 'The Originality of Conrad' (*Hudson Review* xi, 1958); I. Vidan, 'One Source of Conrad's "Nostromo" ' (*Review of English Studies*, N.S. vii, 1956); F. R. Leavis, 'Joseph Conrad' (*Sewanee Review* lxvi, 1958); G. H. Bantock, 'Conrad and Politics' (*English Literary History* xxv, 1958); J. Halverson and I. Watt, 'The Original Nostromo' (*Review of English Studies* N.S. x, 1959); and R. W. Stallman, 'Conrad Criticism Today' (*Sewanee Review* lxvii, 1959).

Modern Fiction Studies, vol. i (1955), is devoted to Conrad, and *The London Magazine* for November 1957 contains a symposium 'Joseph Conrad Today'. Among Polish works accessible in English are L. Krzyzanowski, 'Joseph Conrad: Some Polish Documents' (*The Polish Review* iii, 1958) and P. Mroczkowski, 'The Gnomic Element in Conrad' (*Kwartalnik Neofilologiczny* vi, 1959).

There are several bibliographies of Conrad. T. J. Wise's *A Bibliography of the Writings of Joseph Conrad: 1895–1920* (privately printed 1920) was reissued in the following year with revisions. A more complete descriptive bibliography is the same collector's *A Conrad Library* (privately printed, 1928). G. T. Keating's *A Conrad Memorial Library* (New York, 1929) is an admirable and substantial guide with introductory essays by various authors on each of Conrad's works, together with much incidental biographical information and reproductions of MSS. and photographs. See also 'A Check List of Additions to *A Conrad Memorial Library* 1929–38' compiled by J. T. Babb (*Yale University Library Gazette* xiii, 1938). Other bibliographical works include *The Richard Curle Collection* (New York, 1927), T. J. Wise, *The Ashley Library XI* (privately printed, 1936), and M. Beebe, 'Criticism of Conrad: A Selected Checklist' (*Modern Fiction*

Studies, vol. i, 1955). An enumerative rather than a descriptive bibliography, *Joseph Conrad at Mid-Century: Editions and Studies 1895–1955* by K. A. Lohf and E. Sheehy (Minneapolis, 1957) is a comprehensive guide to the work of, and writings upon, Conrad. It should be supplemented by L. Krzyzanowski's 'Joseph Conrad: A Bibliographical Note' (*The Polish Review* ii, Spring and Summer, 1957) and I. F. Bell and D. Baird, *The English Novel 1578–1956: a Checklist of Twentieth-Century Criticisms* (Denver, 1958).

RUDYARD KIPLING, 1865–1936

Kipling's earliest preserved composition appears to be a poem on the loss of the *Carolina*, written shortly after 1876. He took a step towards publication (since it was produced in two handwritten copies) in *The Scribbler*, a literary venture under the control of the children of Burne-Jones and Morris, which flourished from 1878 to 1880. He edited *The United Services College Chronicle* from June 1881 to July 1882. Many of his contributions have been identified, and he himself reprinted eight of the poems in *Early Verse* (1900). His first book was *Schoolboy Lyrics*, privately printed by his parents in Lahore in 1881. It was followed by *Echoes. By Two Writers* (Lahore, 1884), a volume containing 32 poems ascribed to Kipling and seven ascribed to his sister Beatrice. *Quartette*, the Christmas Annual of the *Civil and Military Gazette* for 1885, was written entirely by Kipling, his parents, and his sister: the 'family square'. *Departmental Ditties* was published in Lahore in 1886, and *Plain Tales from the Hills* (40 stories) in Calcutta in 1888. From this time onwards the record of his publications becomes complicated beyond the possibility of summary exposition. Professional journalism, a popularity which called constantly for new and often varied or augmented editions both of prose and verse, suppressions by the author, piracy and sundry manœuvres designed to defeat it: all these contribute; and all these are competently chronicled and elucidated in the standard bibliographies. What follows is only an outline.

Soldiers Three, The Story of the Gadsbys, In Black and White, Under the Deodars, The Phantom 'Rickshaw, and *Wee Willie Winkie*, each volume containing from four to eight stories, all appeared in the

Indian Railway Library (Allahabad) in 1888. *The Courting of Dinah Shadd* (6 stories) and *Departmental Ditties, Barrack-Room Ballads, and Other Verses* were both published in New York in 1890, as were both the 'happy' and 'unhappy' versions of *The Light that Failed*—the latter being augmented in an English edition of the following year, and subsequently several times revised. *Life's Handicap* (24 stories) appeared in 1891; the augmented (English) edition of *Barrack-Room Ballads*, and Kipling's collaboration with Wolcott Balestier, *The Naulahka*, in 1892; *Many Inventions* (14 stories and 2 poems) in 1893; the two *Jungle Books* in 1894 and 1895; *The Seven Seas*, a new collection of verse, in 1896; *Captains Courageous* in 1897; and *The Day's Work* (12 stories) in 1898. 'Recessional' (first printed in *The Times*, 17 July 1897) was published with three other poems, 'White Horses', 'The Old Issue', and 'The Absent-Minded Beggar', in 1899. *Stalky and Co.* (1899) reprints nine stories from magazines, together with a prefatory poem; in the augmented edition, *The Complete Stalky and Co.* (1929), there are five further stories and one further poem. *From Sea to Sea* (2 vols., New York, 1899) collects, in part from earlier minor collections, a large number of journalistic pieces, mainly of travel. *Kim* appeared in 1901, *Just So Stories* (12 stories and 9 poems) in 1902, *Traffics and Discoveries* (11 stories and 11 poems) in 1904, and *Puck of Pook's Hill* (10 stories and 16 poems) in 1906. *Collected Verse* was published in New York in 1907 and in London in 1912. *Abaft the Funnel* (New York, 1909), a miscellaneous collection of stories, letters, and articles, was authorized by Kipling to counter a quasi-piratical publication of the same non-copyright material earlier in the same year; several other volumes owe their existence to similar occasions.

Actions and Reactions (8 stories and 8 poems) appeared in 1909, *Rewards and Fairies* (11 stories and 23 poems) in 1910, and *A Diversity of Creatures* (12 stories and 13 poems) in 1917. *Rudyard Kipling's Verse: Inclusive Edition* appeared in three volumes in 1919, and with changes and augmentations in 1921, 1927, and 1933; *Letters of Travel* in 1920; *Land and Sea Tales for Boys and Girls* in 1923; *The Irish Guards in the Great War* in two volumes in 1923; and *Debits and Credits* (14 stories and 20 poems) in 1926. *A Book of Words* (1928) is a collection of speeches. *Healing by the Stars* (New York, 1928) is an address to Members of the Royal Society of Medicine. *Thy Servant a Dog* (1930) collects three dog stories. Kipling's last major publication, *Limits and Renewals* (14 stories and 19 poems), appeared in 1932; *Collected Dog Stories* in 1934; and the autobiographical *Something of Myself* posthumously in 1936. A definitive edition of the *Verse* was published in 1940.

There are substantial Kipling collections at Dalhousie University (including 7 titles in MS.) and Texas University (15 titles in MS. and 99 letters). Cornell University has 238 letters and fifteen MSS. or typescripts. The Universities of Columbia, Princeton, Syracuse, and Yale all have MS. material, as have Dartmouth College and Williams College. The Houghton Library at Harvard has letters to Henry James and C. E. Norton, and an early draft of 'Recessional'. The Berg Collection in the New York Public Library has holograph copies of poems and some stories, typescripts with author's autograph corrections, holograph notes for *A Fleet in Being* (dated 1897), several notebooks containing holograph poems, letters among the James B. Pinker Papers, and scattered letters to various correspondents. The Pierpont Morgan Library has the MS. of *Captains Courageous* and 'The Brushwood Boy', twenty letters, and two autograph poems. There is further material in the Carpenter and Chandler Collections (including the MS. of 'William the Conqueror'), and in the Theodore Roosevelt Papers, all in the Library of Congress. Kipling's letters to Cecil Rhodes and Herbert Baker are at Rhodes House, Oxford, and there is further correspondence among the Milner Papers at New College, Oxford.

The first eleven volumes of the Outward Bound Edition were issued in 1897 and the last two in 1937, making thirty-six volumes in all. The Edition de Luxe, begun in the same year, was concluded in thirty-eight volumes in 1938; it does not include *The Irish Guards in the Great War*. The American Trade Edition, in which most of the first American editions of Kipling's works appeared, began in 1898 with *The Day's Work* and concluded in thirty-one volumes with *Limits and Renewals* in 1932. In England, similarly, first publication, from *Stalky and Co.* (1899), was commonly in the Uniform Edition, which concluded in twenty-eight volumes with *Thy Servant a Dog* in 1938. The handsome Bombay Edition in thirty-one volumes is in substance virtually identical with the Uniform Edition. The Sussex Edition (35 vols., 1937–9) embodies Kipling's last revisions and is definitive; its text is followed in the American Burwash Edition (28 vols., 1941). The Library Edition (24 vols., 1949–51) follows the text of the Uniform Edition, but does not contain *From Sea to Sea*, *Songs from Books*, and *A Book of Words*.

There is no substantial published collection of Kipling's letters, but many have appeared dispersedly and may be traced by way of the index in Stewart's *Bibliographical Catalogue*. It was one of Mrs. Kipling's formidable 'rules' for the conduct of her husband's life and affairs that every letter received should be destroyed as soon as answered. She also caused all his personal correspondence to be checked and listed upon dispatch, a regimen which literary biographers are bound to praise. The six letters of the so-called 'Dorian' correspondence, preserved in the Houghton Library and privately printed in 1936, have been proved forgeries, thanks, in part, to these business-like if draconic dispositions.

A Kipling Anthology: Verse and *A Kipling Anthology: Prose* were published in two uniform volumes in 1922. There have been numerous subsequent selections. *A Choice of Kipling's Verse* (1941) has an important introduction by T. S. Eliot, and *A Choice of Kipling's Prose* (1952) has a substantial essay by Somerset Maugham.

Kipling early became an object of biographical interest: a 'Life' was published in New York in 1899 and a 'Biographical Sketch' in London in the same year. He himself came increasingly to prize personal privacy, and in 'The Appeal' he wrote:

> If I have given you delight
> By aught that I have done,
> Let me lie quiet in that night
> Which shall be yours anon:
>
> And for the little, little, span
> The dead are borne in mind,
> Seek not to question other than
> The books I leave behind.

Any authorized biography was thus understandably delayed; it came eventually in C. Carrington's *Rudyard Kipling: His Life and Work* (1955), a capable, sympathetic, and circumspect performance. The possibility of a livelier approach may be glimpsed in Lord Birkenhead's 'Kipling and the Vermont Feud' (*Essays by Divers Hands* xxx, 1960). The same subject has been treated by F. F. van de Water in *Rudyard Kipling's Vermont Feud* (1937). L. C. Dunsterville's *Stalky's Reminiscences* (1928) and G. C. Beresford's *Schooldays with Kipling* (1936) are informative when sifted. H. A. Tapp's *United Services College 1874-1911* (1933) has two unconsciously eloquent photographs opposite page 13. Lady Burne-Jones's *Memorials of Edward Burne-Jones* (2 vols., 1904) has some background interest in a dull way, and the Marchioness of Dufferin and Ava's *Our Viceregal Life in India* (2 vols., 1889) rather more in an august one. Dorothy Ponton's *Rudyard Kipling at Home and at Work* (1953) is a reminiscent sketch by a former secretary. References to Kipling of any substance and interest are not numerous in the anecdotal and familiar writing of the period. But see F. Harris, *Contemporary Portraits: Second Series* (privately printed, 1915) and M. Cohen's *Rider Haggard* (1960).

Early books on Kipling's art are on the whole not critically distinguished, but two of considerable merit appeared in 1915: C. Falls, *Rudyard Kipling: A Critical Study* and J. W. Palmer, *Rudyard Kipling*. There are three interesting French studies: A. Chévrillon, *Rudyard Kipling* (Paris, 1936), R. Escarpit, *Rudyard Kipling: servitudes et grandeurs impériales* (Paris, 1955), and F. Léaud, *La Poétique de Rudyard Kipling* (Paris, 1958). The last is valuable for considering the prose and verse in their interrelation. E. Shanks's *Kipling: A Study in Literature and Political Ideas* (1940) achieves a perceptive examination of the development of Kipling's ideas towards their maturity, and Hilton Brown's *Kipling: A New Appreciation* (1945) is a sensible as well as an enthusiastic book. R. Croft-Cooke's *Rudyard Kipling* (1948) has merit. J. M. S. Tompkins's *The Art of Rudyard Kipling* (1959), an outstanding work, gives only incidental notice to the verse.

A pioneer and balanced appreciation of Kipling's early work appeared in A. Lang's *Essays in Little* (1891). The same year saw the publication of Henry James's introduction to *Mine Own People* (reprinted in *Views and Reviews*, 1908). G. K. Chesterton's

Heretics (1905) has an essay evolving the characteristic paradox that Kipling's imperialism goes along with a lack of patriotism. There is an essay by P. E. More in *Shelburne Essays*, ser. 2 (New York, 1905). Arnold Bennett's review of *Actions and Reactions* (*New Age*, 4 Nov. 1909) is reprinted in *Books and Persons* (1917); it records how Kipling progressively declined in Bennett's estimation, and is in this characteristic of much criticism of the time. In H. Jackson's *The Eighteen Nineties* (1913; revised 1922) there is a good account, on the other hand, of Kipling's impact on his earliest public. Further notable short studies are to be found in Dixon Scott, *Men of Letters* (1916), H. Williams, *Modern English Writers* (1918), and B. Muddiman, *Men of the Nineties* (1920). In 1921 R. Shafer reprinted three reviews by Lionel Johnson, originally written for the *Academy*, under the title *Reviews and Critical Papers*. Vernon Lee in *The Handling of Words* (1923) analysed a short passage from *Kim* and concluded that Kipling is among 'the least disciplined of English writers'. In *Scrutinies by Various Writers*, ed. E. Rickward (1928), R. Graves, although without aberration of this sort, contrived an astringent essay on Kipling as 'the literary aspect of the British Empire'. Two of the best essays, differing widely in point of view, are B. Dobrée's in *The Lamp and the Lute* (1929) and E. Wilson's in *The Wound and the Bow* (New York, 1941). With parts of the latter—it may here be noted—D. H. Hill takes issue in 'Kipling in Vermont' (*Nineteenth-Century Fiction* vii, 1952). Dobrée's later *Rudyard Kipling* (supplement to *British Book News*, 1951) is an authoritative essay together with a select bibliography and an invaluable index to the short stories.

Further interesting discussions will be found in C. Williams, *Poetry at Present* (1930), A. Maurois, 'Kipling' (*Revue hebdomadaire* xliv, 9 and 16 Feb. 1935; translated in *Poets and Prophets*, 1936), and W. L. Renwick, 'Re-reading Kipling' (*Durham University Journal* xxxii, 1940). B. Ford's 'A Case for Kipling?' (*Scrutiny* xi, 1942), in form a review of T. S. Eliot's essay on the verse, is in substance an extreme depreciation. A better-argued case against aspects of Kipling's work is presented by George Orwell in *Critical Essays* (1946). Still better, because showing a full awareness of Kipling's powers, is C. S. Lewis's lecture printed in *Literature and Life: Addresses to the English Association* (1945) and reprinted in *They asked for a Paper* (1962). J. M. S. Tompkins's 'Kipling's Later Tales: the Theme of Healing'

(*Modern Language Review* xlv, 1950) marks a significant turning-point in the criticism of its subject. L. Trilling's essay in *The Liberal Imagination* (1951) is an attempt at reasoned appraisal, in some degree disabled by a fundamental lack of sympathy. Sympathy, indeed, is more in evidence in N. C. Chaudhuri's 'The Finest Story about India—in English' (*Encounter* viii, 1957), a lively essay by a Bengali writer. F. Léaud's 'La Bibliothèque de Rudyard Kipling' (*Études anglaises* xii, 1959) has both biographical and critical interest. Finally, and of great importance, is N. Annan's 'Kipling's Place in the History of Ideas' (*Victorian Studies* iii, 1960).

The standard bibliographical work is F. V. Livingston's *Bibliography of the Works of Rudyard Kipling* (New York, 1927), together with its *Supplement* (Harvard, 1938). The information it contains may be checked and augmented from the yet more comprehensive, if not always well-ordered, *Bibliographical Catalogue* by J. McG. Stewart and A. W. Yeats (Toronto, 1960). *A Summary of the Work of Rudyard Kipling* by L. H. Chandler (New York, The Grolier Club, 1930) serves as a bibliographical list and includes a great deal of the uncollected material. *English Fiction in Transition* (iii, 1960, Nos. 3, 4, and 5) contains a most comprehensive annotated list of writings on Kipling. *The Kipling Journal* (1927 continuing) is published quarterly by the Kipling Society of London. It contains much scattered information, opinion, and discussion. The more recent numbers are the most rewarding; the issue for December, 1954, for example, has an excellent article, 'The Chronology of Stalky and Co.', by R. Lancelyn Green.

WILLIAM BUTLER YEATS, 1865–1939

'Voices', Yeats's first printed work, appeared in the *Dublin University Review* in March 1885. It was later incorporated in 'The Island of Statues' (included in *The Wanderings of Oisin*) and a rewritten version appeared in *Poems* (1895) with the title 'The Cloak, the Boat and the Shoes'. His first published work was *Mosada: A Dramatic Poem* (Dublin, 1886), reprinted from the *Dublin University Review*. It was included along with other poems from periodicals in *The Wanderings of Oisin* (1889).

Fairy and Folk Tales of the Irish Peasantry appeared in 1888. Yeats's only published novel, issued pseudonymously in 1891 as *John Sherman and Dhoya* by Ganconagh, was followed by *The Countess Kathleen and Various Legends and Lyrics* (1892). Revised versions of *The Countess Kathleen* were included in the 1895 and 1899 editions of *Poems*, and a final version was printed separately in 1912. Twenty-six poems, tales, and sketches were published in 1893 as *The Celtic Twilight* (revised and enlarged edition, 1902). *The Land of Heart's Desire* was published in 1894, the year in which it was first acted. *Poems* (1895) contained all the verse, much of it revised, which Yeats then wished to preserve; new and revised editions were issued in 1899, 1901, 1912, and 1927. *The Secret Rose* and *The Tables of the Law: The Adoration of the Magi* appeared in 1897, and *The Wind Among the Reeds* in 1899. *The Shadowy Waters* was published in 1900 after appearing in the *North American Review* for May of that year; there was a revised version in *Poems 1899–1905* (1906) and an acting edition with prose by Lady Gregory was published in 1907 after the production at the Abbey Theatre in 1906; in 1922 a version entirely in verse was included in *Later Poems*.

Two plays were published in 1902: *Cathleen ni Hoolihan* and *Where there is Nothing*; the first had already appeared that year in *Samhain*, as had the second as a supplement to the *United Irishman*; in 1903 *Where there is Nothing* was reissued as volume one of *Plays for an Irish Theatre*. *Ideas of Good and Evil* (1903) reprinted essays from journals. *In the Seven Woods* (Dundrum, 1903), which included *On Baile's Strand*, was the first book to be issued by the Dun Emer (later the Cuala) Press. *The Hour-Glass*, originally printed in the *North American Review*, was published with *Cathleen ni Hoolihan* and *The Pot of Broth* as volume two of *Plays for an Irish Theatre* (New York, 1904); a new version of the play was privately printed in 1914 and then included in *Responsibilities* in the same year. *The King's Threshold* was privately printed in New York in 1904, and with *On Baile's Strand* formed volume three of *Plays for an Irish Theatre* in the same year; new versions of both these plays were included in *Poems 1899–1905* (1906). *Stories of Red Hanrahan* (Dundrum, 1904) was in the main a rewriting of *The Secret Rose*. *The Poetical Works of William B. Yeats* appeared in New York in two volumes in 1906–7; a revised edition of the second volume (New York, 1912) contained new versions of *The Countess Cathleen* and *The*

Land of Heart's Desire. Deirdre was published in 1907 (rev. ed., 1911), as was *Discoveries* (Dundrum), a gathering of recent essays. Two volumes published in New York in 1908 were *The Unicorn from the Stars and Other Plays by William B. Yeats and Lady Gregory*, and *The Golden Helmet*, a prose version of the play later rewritten as *The Green Helmet*.

Poems: Second Series (1909) was followed by *The Green Helmet and Other Poems* (Dundrum, 1910; new edition with additional poems, New York, 1912) and *Synge and the Ireland of his Time* (Dundrum, 1911). Seven previously published plays (some with new notes) were brought together as *Plays for an Irish Theatre* in 1911. *The Cutting of an Agate* (New York, 1912) contained essays and prefaces some of which appeared here for the first time; an English edition of 1919 contained additional material. *Poems Written in Discouragement 1912–1913* (Dundrum, 1913) consisted of five poems later included in *Responsibilities: Poems and a Play* (Dundrum, 1914); most of the contents had previously been printed either in periodicals or in earlier collections; additional poems were included in the 1916 London edition. *Reveries Over Childhood and Youth* was published at Dundrum in 1915. In 1916 appeared *Eight Poems* (previously printed in *Poetry*) and the privately printed *Easter*. With one exception all the poems in *The Wild Swans at Coole* (Dundrum, 1917) had earlier appeared in print; seventeen poems—including *Nine Poems* (privately printed, 1918)—were added to a 1919 London edition. *Per Amica Silentia Lunae* was published in 1918. *Two Plays for Dancers* (Dundrum, 1919) contained *The Dreaming of the Bones* and *The Only Jealousy of Emer*; these were added to *At the Hawk's Well* and *Calvary* to form *Four Plays for Dancers* (1921). *Michael Robartes and the Dancer* (Dundrum, 1920 [1921]) was a collection of poems the majority of which had already appeared in periodicals. *Four Years* (Dundrum, 1921) was included in Yeats's second collection of autobiographical essays, *The Trembling of the Veil* (subscribers' edition, 1922). *Seven Poems and a Fragment* (Dundrum), *The Player Queen*, and *Plays in Prose and Verse* were also published in 1922. *The Cat and the Moon* (Dublin, 1924) consisted of a play and twelve poems, all with one exception previously published. *The Bounty of Sweden* (Dublin, 1925) contained in addition to the title essay Yeats's Nobel Prize address, 'The Irish Dramatic Movement' (published separately in Stockholm, 1924).

Essays and five previously published poems were included in *A Vision* (subscribers' edition, 1925); a new and heavily revised edition containing much additional material was published in 1937, and a 1956 New York edition contained some final revisions. *Estrangement* (Dublin, 1926) consisted of extracts from a diary. The poems in *October Blast* (Dublin, 1927) were reprinted the following year in *The Tower*, which also included poems from *The Cat and the Moon* and *Seven Poems and a Fragment*. Other works published in the late twenties were *Sophocles' King Oedipus* (1928), *The Death of Synge and Other Passages from an Old Diary* (1928), *A Packet for Ezra Pound* (Dublin, 1929), and *The Winding Stair* (New York, 1929), a collection of sixteen poems. 'Three Things', a short poem in the Ariel Series, also appeared in 1929. *Stories of Michael Robartes and his Friends* (Dublin, 1931) contained a play, *The Resurrection*, an earlier version of which had been published in 1927. Poems published in *Words for Music Perhaps* (Dublin, 1932) were added to those in *The Winding Stair* to form *The Winding Stair and Other Poems* (1933). In 1933 the titles of some early poems were altered for inclusion in the *Collected Poems* (New York; revised and enlarged edition, 1950). *Letters to the New Island*, edited by H. Reynolds (Cambridge, Mass., 1934), contained articles written by Yeats between 1888 and 1892 for two Irish-American newspapers. *The Words upon the Window Pane* (Dublin, 1934) was included in *The Collected Plays* (1934; revised and enlarged edition, 1952), as were three of the four plays comprising *Wheels and Butterflies* (1934). Much of the material in *The King of the Great Clock Tower, Commentaries and Poems* (Dublin, 1934) had appeared in periodicals; a new version of the play and some of the poems appeared in *A Full Moon in March* (1935). *Dramatis Personae*, memoirs covering the years 1896 to 1902, was published in Dublin in 1935; a 1936 New York edition contained additional previously published material. The broadcast lecture *Modern Poetry* was published in 1936 and *Nine One-Act Plays* in 1937. Nearly all the essays in *Essays, 1931 to 1936* (Dublin, 1937) had previously appeared in print. *The Herne's Egg* was published in 1938, as was *New Poems* (Dublin).

Last Poems and Two Plays and *On the Boiler* were published in Dublin in 1939; material from these two volumes and from *New Poems* made up *Last Poems and Plays* (1940). Other posthumously published works were *If I Were Four-and-Twenty*

(Dublin, 1940), two essays previously published in 1919 and 1920 respectively; *Pages from a Diary Written in Nineteen Hundred and Thirty* (Dublin, 1944); and *Tribute to Thomas Davis* (1947). The Definitive Edition of *The Poems of W. B. Yeats* (2 vols., 1949) incorporated the author's final revisions. *The Variorum Edition of the Poems* edited by P. Allt and R. K. Alspach was first published in New York in 1957. D. R. Pearce has edited *The Senate Speeches of William Butler Yeats* (Bloomington, Ind., 1960).

Fourteen manuscripts and over 300 letters by Yeats are at the University of Texas. The Lilly Library of Indiana University possesses the late Allan Wade's collection, which includes MSS. and many letters. Trinity College, Dublin, has the MS. of *Mosada*, the National Library of Ireland the MSS. of nineteen plays, and there is some material at the New York Public Library, the Huntington Library, Harvard University, Mills College Library at Oakland, and the British Museum. But the majority of Yeats's manuscripts remain in private hands.

Yeats planned a complete edition of his works, but this has not been achieved so far. *The Collected Works in Verse and Prose* (8 vols., 1908) contained revisions made by Yeats for this edition. Between 1922 and 1926 six volumes were issued in a *Collected Edition of the Works*: *Later Poems* (1922) was a selection of verse often considerably revised from volumes published between 1899 and 1921; *Plays in Prose and Verse* (1922) contained eleven plays and some new notes; in *Plays and Controversies* (1923) *The Countess Cathleen* and *The Land of Heart's Desire* were further revised; *Essays* (1924) included three previously published collections and some new material; *Early Poems and Stories* (1925) contained work published before 1898 with revisions and omissions; and *Autobiographies* (1926) consisted of *Reveries over Childhood and Youth* and *The Trembling of the Veil* with new material. Additional material was added to a New York 1938 edition entitled *Autobiography* and to *Autobiographies* (1955). Other collections of miscellaneous prose are *Mythologies* (1959), and *Essays and Introductions* (1961), which contains Yeats's last revisions and prints for the first time two general essays originally written for a complete edition of the works.

The Letters of W. B. Yeats, admirably edited by A. Wade, appeared in 1954. Other collections of importance are *Letters on Poetry from W. B. Yeats to Dorothy Wellesley* (1940), which are more authentically letters than the title might suggest; *Some Letters from W. B. Yeats to John O'Leary and his Sister*, edited by A. Wade (New York, 1953); *W. B. Yeats and T. Sturge Moore*, edited by U. Bridge (1953); and *Letters to Katharine Tynan*, edited by R. McHugh (Dublin and London, 1953).

A Selection from the Poetry of W. B. Yeats was made by Yeats for a Tauchnitz edition (Leipzig, 1913), and a selection was published in New York in 1921. *Selected Poems: Lyrical and Narrative* (1929) contained a preface by Yeats stating that the early poems were left 'in their original context, for all belong in thought and sentiment to the time when they were first written'. Yeats contributed an introduction and fourteen poems to his selection, *The Oxford Book of Modern Verse 1892-1935* (1936).

The authorized biography is by J. Hone: *W. B. Yeats, 1865–1939* (1942; rev. ed., 1962). R. Ellmann's *Yeats: The Man and the Masks* (New York, 1948) and A. N. Jeffares's *W. B. Yeats: Man and Poet* (1949) both contain unpublished material and attempt to relate the man and his work. Memorial essays were collected in S. Gwynn, ed., *Scattering Branches* (1940). J. Masefield wrote *Some Memories of W. B. Yeats* (Dublin, 1940). M. Gibbon in *The Masterpiece and the Man* (1959) gave a somewhat irked account of Yeats in his last years.

Chapters or sections of biographical interest in books include: G. Moore, *Hail and Farewell* (3 vols., 1911–14); K. Tynan, *Twenty-five Years* (1913) and *The Middle Years* (1916); Lady Gregory, *Our Irish Theatre* (New York, 1913) and *Hugh Lane's Life and Achievement* (1921); W. Rothenstein, *Men and Memories* (2 vols., 1931–2) and *Since Fifty* (1939); A. E., *Song and Its Fountains* (1932); O. St. J. Gogarty, *As I Was Going Down Sackville Street* (1937); M. Gonne MacBride, *A Servant of the Queen* (1938); C. Bax, ed., *Florence Farr, Bernard Shaw and W. B. Yeats* (Dublin, 1941); L. Robinson, *Curtain Up* (1942); J. Hone, ed., *J. B. Yeats: Letters to his Son W. B. Yeats and Others, 1869–1922* (1944); L. Robinson, ed., *Lady Gregory's Journals* (1946); M. Colum, *Life and the Dream* (New York, 1947); M. Beerbohm, *Mainly on the Air* (enlarged edition, 1957); E. Coxhead, *Lady*

Gregory: A Literary Portrait (1961); and L. A. G. Strong, *Green Memory* (1961).

Early studies of Yeats are H. S. Krans, *William Butler Yeats and the Irish Literary Revival* (New York, 1904), F. Reid, *W. B. Yeats: A Critical Study* (1915), and J. M. Hone, *William Butler Yeats: the Poet in Contemporary Ireland* (Dublin and London, 1916). L. MacNeice's *The Poetry of W. B. Yeats* (1941) and V. K. Menon's *The Development of W. B. Yeats* (1942; rev. ed., 1960) are general surveys. More specialized works are J. P. O'Donnell, *Sailing to Byzantium* (Cambridge, Mass., 1939), a study of the late style and symbolism; P. Ure, *Towards a Mythology* (1946), an account of Yeats's use and adaptation of Irish myth; and D. A. Stauffer, *The Golden Nightingale* (New York, 1949). J. Hall and M. Steinmann, eds., *The Permanence of Yeats* (New York, 1950) is a collection of critical essays, and T. R. Henn's *The Lonely Tower* (1950) a learned and valuable examination of some aspects of the poetry. More limited in scope are B. Bjersby, *The Interpretation of the Cuchulain Legend in the Works of W. B. Yeats* (Uppsala, 1950); V. Koch, *W. B. Yeats: The Tragic Phase* (1951), an analysis of thirteen of *Last Poems*; and T. Parkinson, *W. B. Yeats, Self-Critic* (Berkeley, 1951), a study of the early verse in the light of Yeats's own criticism. Two thoroughgoing discussions of Yeats's thought, his symbolism, and its sources, both of which contain unpublished material, are R. Ellmann's *The Identity of Yeats* (1954) and Virginia Moore's *The Unicorn* (New York, 1954). G. S. Fraser's *W. B. Yeats* (*Writers and their Work*, no. 50, 1954; new edition, 1962) is a short introduction to the poetry together with a select bibliography. F. A. C. Wilson's *W. B. Yeats and Tradition* (1958) attempts an elucidation of Yeats's last five plays, and his *Yeats's Iconography* (1960) similarly interprets the *Plays for Dancers* and related poems. J. Unterecker's *A Reader's Guide to William Butler Yeats* (New York, 1959) is useful in the early stages of study. G. Melchiori's *The Whole Mystery of Art* (1960) is a sophisticated and able discussion of Yeats's sources. Other recent works are A. G. Stock's *W. B. Yeats: His Poetry and Thought* (1961), A. N. Jeffares's, *The Poetry of W. B. Yeats* (1961), and J. Stallworthy's important *Between the Lines* (1963).

Representative chapters and sections in books include: W. Archer, *Poets of the Younger Generation* (1902); E. Boyd, *Ireland's*

Literary Renaissance (rev. ed., New York, 1922); E. Wilson, *Axel's Castle* (1931); F. R. Leavis, *New Bearings in English Poetry* (1932, rev. ed. 1950); S. Spender, *The Destructive Element* (1935; see also *The Creative Element*, 1953); A. E., *The Living Torch*, ed. M. Gibbon (1937); D. M. Hoare, *The Works of Morris and Yeats in Relation to Early Saga Literature* (1937); J. Bronowski, *The Poet's Defence* (1939); C. Brooks, *Modern Poetry and the Tradition* (Chapel Hill, 1939; see also *The Well Wrought Urn*, New York, 1947); U. Ellis-Fermor, *The Irish Dramatic Movement* (1939); L. Robinson, ed., *The Irish Theatre* (1939); M. Bowra, *The Heritage of Symbolism* (1943); L. C. Knights, *Explorations* (1946); G. Orwell, *Critical Essays* (1946); R. Peacock, *The Poet in the Theatre* (1946); *English Institute Essays, 1946* (New York, 1947); A. Warren, *Rage for Order* (Chicago, 1948); G. Hough, *The Last Romantics* (1949); L. Robinson, *Ireland's Abbey Theatre* (1951); R. Tschumi, *Thought in Twentieth-Century English Poetry* (1951); R. P. Blackmur, *Language as Gesture* (New York, 1952); A. Ussher, *Three Great Irishmen: Shaw, Yeats, Joyce* (1952); M. Rudd, *Divided Image: A Study of William Blake and W. B. Yeats* (1953); H. H. Watts, *Hound and Quarry* (1953); H. Adams, *Blake and Yeats: The Contrary Vision* (Ithaca, 1955); R. Aldington, *A. E. Housman and W. B. Yeats: Two Lectures* (1955); J. Press, *The Fire and the Fountain* (1955) and *The Chequer'd Shade* (1958); T. R. Henn, *The Harvest of Tragedy* (1956); T. S. Eliot, *On Poetry and Poets* (1957); J. Bayley, *The Romantic Survival* (1957); F. Kermode, *Romantic Image* (1957); A. Alvarez, *The Shaping Spirit* (1958); H. Howarth, *The Irish Writers, 1880–1940* (1958); D. Donoghue, *The Third Voice* (Princeton, 1959); A. MacLeish, *Poetry and Experience* (Boston, 1960); R. Ellmann, ed., *Edwardians and Late Victorians: English Institute Essays 1959* (New York, 1960); and G. Wright, *The Poet in the Poem* (Berkeley, 1960.)

Articles in journals include: A. J. M. Smith, 'Poet Young and Old—W. B. Yeats' (*University of Toronto Quarterly* ix, 1939); *The Arrow*, Summer 1939 (a commemorative number); *Southern Review* vii, Winter 1941 (a Yeats memorial issue); P. Allt, 'Yeats and the Revision of his Early Verse' (*Hermathena* lxiv, 1944 and lxv, 1945); A. N. Jeffares, 'The Byzantine Poems of W. B. Yeats' (*Review of English Studies* xxii, 1946); N. Frye, 'Yeats and the Language of Symbolism' (*University of Toronto Quarterly* xvii, 1947); E. Bentley, 'Yeats as Playwright' (*Kenyon Review* x, 1948);

M. Witt, 'A Competition for Eternity: Yeats's Revisions of his Later Poems' (*PMLA* lxiv, 1949); P. Allt, 'Yeats, Religion and History' (*Sewanee Review* lx, 1952); A. Davenport, 'W. B. Yeats and the Upanishads' (*Review of English Studies* N.S. iii, 1952); F. L. Gwynn, 'Yeats's Byzantium and Its Sources' (*Philological Quarterly* xxxii, 1953); T. R. Henn, 'W. B. Yeats and the Irish Background' (*Yale Review* xlii, 1953); *Irish Writing* xxxi, Summer 1955 (a special Yeats issue); P. Ure, 'Yeats's Supernatural Songs' (*Review of English Studies* N.S. vii, 1956); T. R. Henn, 'The Accent of Yeats's "Last Poems"' (*Essays and Studies* N.S. ix, 1956); A. Thwaite, 'Yeats and the Noh' (*Twentieth Century* clxii, 1957), C. Bradford, 'Yeats's Byzantium Poems: A Study of their Development' (*PMLA* lxxv, 1960); P. Ure, 'Yeats's Christian Mystery Plays' (*Review of English Studies* N.S. xi, 1960); Y. Winters, 'The Poetry of W. B. Yeats' (*Twentieth Century Literature* vi, 1960); T. R. Whitaker, 'The Early Yeats and the Pattern of History' (*PMLA* lxxv, 1960) and 'Yeats's Alembic' (*Sewanee Review* lxviii, 1960); A. Zwerdling, 'W. B. Yeats: Variations on the Visionary Quest' (*University of Toronto Quarterly* xxx, 1960); G. Martin, 'Fine Manners, Liberal Speech: A Note on the Public Poetry of W. B. Yeats' (*Essays in Criticism* xi, 1961); J. R. Moore, 'Yeats as a Last Romantic' (*Virginia Quarterly Review* xxxvii, 1961); T. Parkinson, 'Vestiges of Creation', (*Sewanee Review* lxix, 1961); and M. J. Sidnell, 'Manuscript Versions of Yeats's *The Countess Cathleen*' (*Papers of the Bibliographical Society of America*, 56, 1962).

Earlier bibliographies were superseded by A. Wade's *A Bibliography of the Writings of W. B. Yeats* (1951); a revised edition (1958) contains additional material, an enlarged index, and an appendix on 'Yeats and Broadcasting' by G. Whalley. Two volumes by G. B. Saul, *Prolegomena to the Study of Yeats's Poems* and *Prolegomena to the Study of Yeats's Plays* (Philadelphia, 1957 and 1958), are useful works of reference. See also: A. N. Jeffares, 'An Account of Recent Yeatsiana' (*Hermathena* lxxii, 1948), G. B. Saul, 'Thread to a Labyrinth: A Selective Bibliography in Yeats' (*Bulletin of the New York Public Library* lviii, 1954), and two catalogues of exhibitions held at Trinity College, Dublin, and at the Whitworth Art Gallery, Manchester: *W. B. Yeats: Manuscripts and Printed Books* (Dublin, 1956) and *W. B. Yeats: Images of a Poet* (1961).

JAMES JOYCE, 1882–1941

Joyce's earliest independently printed works were polemical. The first of them, denouncing the betrayers of Parnell, was composed in his ninth year, and printed in 1891 or 1892 at the expense of his father, who sent a copy to the Pope. Of this poem, the title of which appears to have been 'Et Tu, Healy', no copy is known to survive outside the Vatican. But some lines remained in the memory of Stanislaus Joyce, and in these the spirit of the dead leader is likened to an eagle which, from his 'quaint-perched aerie on the crags of Time', looks down on a 'rude din' which 'can trouble him no more'. 'The Day of the Rabblement', an article denouncing the parochial programme of the newly founded Irish Literary Theatre, was rejected by a college magazine on the advice of a Father Henry Browne. Joyce joined forces with another rejected contributor, Francis Skeffington, who had wished to air his views on the academic education of women, and the result was *Two Essays*, privately printed probably in November 1901 (reprinted Minneapolis, 1957). 'The Holy Office', a vigorous and scatological vituperative poem somewhat in the manner of Swift, was designed for the same magazine in 1904, and similarly and inevitably rejected. Joyce caused it to be printed in Pola in the following year and copies to be distributed in Dublin, chiefly among those whom it attacked. 'Gas from a Burner' is a later broadside of the same kind, prompted by a Dublin printer's destruction of a proposed first edition of *Dubliners*. This pasquinade was printed in Trieste in 1912.

Chamber Music appeared in 1907 and *Dubliners* in 1914, both after many discouraging hitches. *A Portrait of the Artist as a Young Man* first appeared in the *Egoist*, London, in twenty-five instalments between February 1914 and September 1915; the first publication in volume form was in New York in 1916. The earlier work from which it was developed survived in part and was edited by T. Spenser in 1944 under the title *Stephen Hero*; a reprint in 1956 contains a further small fragment. *Exiles* was published in 1918 and acted in a German translation in Munich in the following year. There were productions in New York in 1925 and in London in 1926; in Dublin the play appears to have had to await performance until 1948. A later reprint (New York, 1951, London, 1952) includes some 'hitherto unpublished notes by the author, discovered after his death'. These are scarcely elucidatory, and suggest that Joyce's mind did not, in fact, move much like Ibsen's—or, perhaps, any natural-born dramatist's.

The *Little Review*, New York, published serially (April 1918–Dec. 1920) the first thirteen and part of the fourteenth of the eighteen 'episodes' of *Ulysses*; in all twenty-three instalments appeared before publication was stopped in face of action brought by the American Society for the Suppression of Vice. The *Egoist* published three episodes and part of a fourth between January 1919 and December of the same year, when it went out of existence. The complete book was first published in Paris in 1922. The 'Circe' episode was successfully dramatized by M. Barkentin in 1958.

Pomes Penyeach was published in Paris in 1927. *The Joyce Book* (1933) reprints these, each with a musical setting by a different composer. *Collected Poems* (New York, 1936) includes a poem, 'Ecce Puer', first printed in the *New Republic* (30 Nov. 1930).

The first published fragment of what was eventually to be called *Finnegans Wake* appeared as 'From Work in Progress' in the *transatlantic review* (Paris, April 1924) and the second in the *Criterion* (July 1925). *transition* began its regular printings of excerpts in April 1927, and these continued until April–May 1938. Between 1928 and 1930 there were five printings of substantial passages in New York for copyright purposes. 'Anna Livia Plurabelle' was published in New York (1928), 'Tales Told of Shem and Shaun' in Paris (1929), 'Haveth Childers Everywhere' in Paris (1930), 'The Mime of Mick Nick and the Maggies' at The Hague (1934), and 'Storiella as She is Syung' in London (1937). *Finnegans Wake* as a whole appeared in 1939. 'Corrections of Misprints in Finnegans Wake' was published in 1945, and also bound up with the 1946 American printing and the 1946 and 1948 English printings. An interesting attempt by M. Manning to dramatize parts of the work was published as *The Voice of Shem* in 1958 and produced in 1962.

'Ibsen's New Drama' and 'James Clarence Mangan' were private reprintings, both in 1930, of articles which had appeared respectively in the *Fortnightly Review* (April 1900) and *St. Stephen's*, Dublin (May 1902). *Pastimes of James Joyce*, published in New York in 1941 by the Joyce Memorial Fund Committee, contains trivia. *Epiphanies*, edited by O. A. Silverman (University of Buffalo, 1956), consists of twenty-two brief jottings by Joyce, with related passages from the published writings and elsewhere. Joyce's *Critical Writings* were edited by E. Mason and R. Ellmann in 1959.

The most important Joyce collection is at the University of Buffalo; it contains his working library and more than 170 MSS. There are further collections at Yale and at the University of Kansas. S. Joyce's collection is at Cornell, as are the S. Beach and J. Spoerri collections; *The Cornell Joyce Collection, a Catalogue* was published at Cornell in 1961. The original MSS. of *Ulysses* and *Finnegans Wake* are in the Rosenbach Foundation in Philadelphia and the British Museum respectively.

Joyce's *Letters* were edited by S. Gilbert in 1957. They show a somewhat single-minded concentration upon business affairs, but are not without interest and idiosyncrasy. One to his son Giorgio begins 'Dear Oigroig' by way of expressing the writer's sense that 'everything's upside down'.

In 1942 T. S. Eliot published a volume of prose selections from Joyce, together with an essay, under the title *Introducing James Joyce*. *The Portable James Joyce*, a substantial compendium with editorial matter by H. Levin, was published in America in 1947. In the following year it was published in England, with the omission of a bibliographical note, as *The Essential James Joyce*.

The standard biography is that by R. Ellmann, *James Joyce* (New York, 1959), an admirable and indispensable work. Among other books useful for the study of Joyce's life are H. Gorman, *James Joyce: His First Forty Years* (New York, 1924) and *James Joyce: A Definitive Biography* (1941), F. Budgen, *James Joyce and the Making of 'Ulysses'* (1934), S. Joyce, *Recollections of James Joyce by his Brother* (New York, 1950) and *My Brother's Keeper* (1958), M. and P. Colum, *Our Friend James Joyce* (1958), and K. Sullivan, *Joyce among the Jesuits* (New York, 1958), a study of the influence of Joyce's schooling at Clongowes Wood College.

Critical works devoted to Joyce are rapidly becoming numerous. H. Levin's *James Joyce: A Critical Introduction* (1944;

revised, and with an additional chapter, 'Revisiting Joyce', 1960) is the best-considered appreciation yet to have appeared. Other works of a general character, or designed to pursue a specific theme through the body of the writing, are *James Joyce: Two Decades of Criticism*, ed. S. Givens (New York, 1948), L. A. G. Strong, *The Sacred River: An Approach to James Joyce* (1949), P. Hutchins, *James Joyce's Dublin* (1950) and *James Joyce's World* (1957), and W. Y. Tindall, *James Joyce: His Way of Interpreting the Modern World* (New York, 1950). A. Huxley and S. Gilbert's *Joyce the Artificer* (privately printed, 1952) presents reproductions, with brief introductory notes, of two page-proofs of *Ulysses*, two page-proofs of 'Tales Told of Shem and Shaun', and a letter to the printer of a section of *Work in Progress*. K. Smidt's *James Joyce and the Cultic Use of Fiction* (Oslo, 1955) sees Joyce's work as not merely a monument but also an altar to Joyce. D. Hayman's *Joyce et Mallarmé* (2 vols., Paris, 1956) is an exhaustive and refined investigation. H. Kenner's *Dublin's Joyce* (1956), although rebarbative in style, is a work of penetrating critical intelligence. *Joyce: the Man, the Work, the Reputation* by M. Magalaner and R. M. Kain (New York, 1956) is a very long book. J. I. M. Stewart's *James Joyce* (*Writers and their Work*, no. 91, 1957, revised 1960) is a short introduction together with a select bibliography. *Joyce and Aquinas* by W. T. Noon S.J. (Yale, 1957) arrives at judicious if somewhat negative conclusions. L. Gillet's *Claybook for James Joyce* [*Stèle pour James Joyce*] (1958) presents reminiscences and appraisals by a conservative French critic, together with a short dialogue by A. Gide. Four books published in 1959 may be mentioned here: J. M. Morse's *The Sympathetic Alien: Joyce and Catholicism*; W. Y. Tindall's *A Reader's Guide to James Joyce*; M. Magalaner's *Time of Apprenticeship*, a study in the main of *Dubliners* and *Portrait of the Artist*; and M. J. C. Hodgart and M. P. Worthington's *Song in the Works of James Joyce*, an example of the specialized research which Joyce seems endlessly to invite. A. W. Litz's *The Art of James Joyce* (1961) represents scholarship of a different order, and is an important critical study based upon textual analysis. Recent works include W. Y. Tindall, *The Joyce Country* (University Park, Pa., 1960), M. Parr, *James Joyce: The Poetry of Conscience* (Milwaukee, 1962), and R. S. Ryf, *A New Approach to Joyce* (Berkeley, 1962).

Early studies of *Ulysses* include P. J. Smith, *A Key to*

the 'Ulysses' of James Joyce (Chicago, 1927), E. R. Curtius, *James Joyce und sein 'Ulysses'* (Zürich, 1929), and S. Gilbert, *James Joyce's 'Ulysses'* (1930). M. L. Hanley's *Word Index to James Joyce's 'Ulysses'* (Wisconsin, 1937), a work prepared with mechanical aids in the interest of general linguistics, has some utility as a concordance. More recent works are R. M. Kain, *Fabulous Voyager* (Chicago, 1947), R. Loehrich, *The Secret of 'Ulysses'* (1955), W. M. Schutte, *Joyce and Shakespeare: A Study in the Meaning of 'Ulysses'* (Yale, 1957), and S. C. Goldberg, *The Classical Temper* (1961), a well-argued reminder that *Ulysses* is a novel.

The first body of critical writing on *Finnegans Wake*, by S. Beckett and others, appeared as *Our exagmination round his factification for incamination of Work in Progress* (Paris, 1929). *A Skeleton Key to 'Finnegans Wake'* by J. Campbell and H. M. Robinson (1947) is a gallant pioneer attempt at serious elucidation. A. Glasheen's *A Census of 'Finnegans Wake': An Index to the Characters and their Roles* (New York, 1956) is supplemented by the same writer's pleasantly named 'Out of My Census' (*The Analyst* xvii, Northwestern University, 1959). J. S. Atherton's *The Books at the Wake: A Study of Literary Allusions in James Joyce's 'Finnegans Wake'* (1959) is an orderly inquiry, with a particularly interesting chapter on Lewis Carroll, and some sensible observations on Joyce and Mallarmé. F. M. Boldereff's *Reading Finnegans Wake* (Pennsylvania, 1959) is a somewhat eccentrically disposed, but useful, work of exegesis. F. H. Higginson's *Anna Livia Plurabelle: The Making of a Chapter* (Minneapolis, 1960) is a thoroughgoing textual study.

Many books, of which the following are only representative, include chapters or sections on Joyce: E. Pound, *Instigations* (New York, 1920), *Polite Essays* (1937), and *Literary Essays*, ed. T. S. Eliot (1954); E. Muir, *Transition: Essays on Contemporary Literature* (1926); W. Lewis, *Time and Western Man* (1927), a vigorous polemical approach; R. West, *The Strange Necessity* (1928); E. Wilson, *Axel's Castle* (1931) and *The Wound and the Bow* (1942), containing admirable critical accounts of *Ulysses* and *Finnegans Wake* respectively; F. R. Leavis, *For Continuity* (1933); A. J. A. Waldock, *James Joyce and Others* (1937); D. Daiches, *The Novel and the Modern World* (Chicago, 1939; rev. ed., 1960); H. Miller, *The Cosmological Eye* (Norfolk, Conn.,

1939); E. E. Stoll, *From Shakespeare to Joyce* (New York, 1944);
C. Connolly, *The Condemned Playground* (1945); and D. Mac-
Carthy, *Memories* (1953). F. Russell, in *Three Studies in Twentieth-
Century Obscurity* (1954), considers the 'Alexandrian' character of
Joyce's work, with an ingenious comparison with Lycophron.
W. Weidlé, *Les Abeilles d'Aristée* (Paris, 1954), L. Edel, *The Psycho-
logical Novel 1900–1950* (1955), W. Y. Tindall, *The Literary Symbol*
(New York, 1955), and E. Dahlberg and H. Read, *Truth Is More
Sacred* (1961), all contain interesting discussions. *James Joyce's
Scribbledehobble, the ur-workbook for Finnegans Wake*, edited by
T. E. Connolly (Evanton, 1961) reproduces, but does not much
clarify, the largest of the *Finnegans Wake* notebooks in the Lock-
wood Memorial Library, Buffalo.

Essays in journals include Valéry Larbaud, 'James Joyce'
(*Nouvelle revue française*, April 1922; English translation in the
Criterion, Oct. 1922); Marcel Thiébaut, 'Ulysses' (*Revue de Paris*,
15 June 1929); Georges Borach, 'Gespräche mit James Joyce'
(*Die neue Zürcher Zeitung*, 3 May 1931; reprinted in *Omnibus:
Almanach auf das Jahr 1932*, Berlin, 1932); W. Troy, 'Stephen
Dedalus and James Joyce' (*The Nation*, cxxxviii, New York,
14 Feb. 1934) and 'Finnegans Wake' (*Partisan Review* vi, 1939);
J. C. Ransom, 'Finnegans Wake' (*Kenyon Review* i, 1939);
A. John, 'Fragment of an Autobiography XV' (*Horizon* xiii,
1946); G. Melchiori, 'Joyce and the Eighteenth-Century
Novelists' (*English Miscellany* 2, ed. M. Praz, Rome, 1951);
M. J. C. Hodgart, 'Work in Progress' (*The Cambridge Journal*
vi, 1952) and 'The Earliest Section of "Finnegans Wake"'
(*The James Joyce Review* i, 1, New York, Feb. 1957); D. Knight,
'The Reading of "Ulysses"' (*English Literary History*, Mar.
1952); C. J. Jung, '*Ulysses: A Monologue*' (*Nimbus* ii, 1953; first
published in Zürich, 1934); J. Prescott, 'James Joyce's "Stephen
Hero"' (*Journal of English and Germanic Philology*, liii, 1954);
R. Ellmann, 'The Background of "Ulysses"' (*The Kenyon Review*
xvi, 1954) and 'The Limits of Joyce's Naturalism' (*Sewanee
Review* lxiii, 1955); A. Glasheen, '"Finnegans Wake" and the
Girls from Boston, Mass.' [on Joyce's use of Morton Prince's
The Dissociation of a Personality] (*Hudson Review* vii, 1955); W.
Litz, 'The Evolution of Joyce's *Anna Livia Plurabelle*' (*Philo-
logical Quarterly* xxxvi, 1957); F. W. Sternfeld, 'Poetry and
Music: Joyce's "Ulysses"' (*English Institute Essays*, 1957); C.

Hart, 'Notes on the Text of "Finnegans Wake"' (*Journal of English and Germanic Philology* lix, 1960); C. C. Loomis Jr., 'Structure and Sympathy in Joyce's "The Dead"' (*PMLA* lxxv, 1960); R. S. Jackson, 'A Parabolic Reading of James Joyce's "Grace"' (*Modern Language Notes* lxxvi, 1961); B. Benstock, 'The Final Apostasy: James Joyce and "Finnegans Wake"' (*English Literary History* xxviii, 1961); and J. I. Cope, 'The Rhythmic Gesture: Image and Aesthetic in Joyce's "Ulysses"' *English Literary History* xxix, 1962).

Joyce made a phonographic recording from the 'Aeolus' episode of *Ulysses*. It is extremely rare. He made two recordings from 'Anna Livia Plurabelle'. One of these had to be discarded. There are several pressings of the other.

A. D. Parker's *James Joyce: A Bibliography of His Writings, Critical Material and Miscellanea* was published in Boston, Mass. in 1948. There are substantial additions, particularly of critical material, in W. White, 'James Joyce: Addenda to Alan Parker's Bibliography' (*Bibliographical Society of America* xliii, 1949). The standard bibliography now is J. J. Slocum and H. Cahoon, *A Bibliography of James Joyce* (Soho Bibliographies v, 1953). Specialized bibliographies are: J. F. Spoerri, *Finnegans Wake by James Joyce: A Check List* (Evanston, Illinois, 1953), T. E. Connolly, *The Personal Library of James Joyce: A descriptive Bibliography* (Buffalo, 1955) and M. Beebe and W. Litz, 'Criticism of James Joyce' (*Modern Fiction Studies* iv, 1958). The *James Joyce Review*, New York (vol. i, 1, Feb. 1957, and subsequent issues), has printed some useful bibliographical lists, as well as articles of varying merit and some reviews.

DAVID HERBERT LAWRENCE, 1885–1930

Lawrence's first published work, 'A Prelude'—a pseudonymous prize-winning story printed in the *Nottinghamshire Guardian* in December 1907—was reprinted with an introduction by P. B. Wadsworth in 1949. *The White Peacock* (1911) was followed by *The Trespasser* (1912) and by *Love Poems and Others* (1913); some of these poems had appeared in periodicals. *Sons and Lovers* was published in 1913. *The Widowing of Mrs. Holroyd*

(New York, 1914; first performed in Altrincham, 1920) was followed by a collection of twelve short stories, *The Prussian Officer and Other Stories* (1914); the titles and text of some of these were changed after their first appearance in periodicals. *The Rainbow*, published in September 1915, was suppressed two months later and an expurgated edition was published in New York the following year. Certain sections of *Twilight in Italy* (1916), Lawrence's first travel book, were printed in periodicals and revised for book publication. *Amores* was published in 1916 and *Look! We Have Come Through!* in 1917: a recent edition of the latter (Marazion, 1958) includes some poems previously omitted and earlier versions of several others. *New Poems* was published in 1918, and to a 1920 New York edition was added a preface originally printed under the title 'The Poetry of the Present'. *Bay: A Book of Poems* was published in 1919. In 1920 appeared *Touch and Go*, Lawrence's second published play.

Although Lawrence had completed *Women in Love* in 1916 it was not published until 1920, appearing then in a privately printed limited edition issued in New York. *The Lost Girl* was published in the same year: the American edition of 1921 has a slightly different text. *Movements in European History* (1921) was published under the pseudonym Lawrence H. Davison. Other publications of 1921—first issued in New York—were *Psychoanalysis and the Unconscious*, *Tortoises* (later included in the English edition of *Birds, Beasts and Flowers*), and *Sea and Sardinia*, two sections of which were revised after serial publication. *Aaron's Rod*, *Fantasia of the Unconscious*, and *England, My England*, a collection of ten short stories some of which had previously appeared in periodicals and had been revised for this volume, were all published in New York in 1922. *The Ladybird* (1923) also contained 'The Fox' and 'The Captain's Doll'. Some of the essays in *Studies in Classic American Literature* (New York, 1923) first appeared in the *English Review* during 1918 and 1919; they were revised for the book. *Kangaroo* was published in 1923. *Birds, Beasts and Flowers* was published in New York in the same year and reissued in 1930 with prefatory notes to each section. *The Boy in the Bush* (1924) was a collaboration with M. L. Skinner. The English edition of *St. Mawr* (1925) also contained 'The Princess', previously serialized in the *Calendar of Modern Letters* (Mar.–May 1925). *Reflections on the Death of a Porcupine* was published in Philadelphia in 1925; one essay, 'The Crown', had been published in part in *The Signature* in 1915 and was revised for book publication. *The Plumed Serpent, David* (acted 1927), the privately printed *Sun* (an unexpurgated and expanded version was published in Paris, 1928), and *Glad Ghosts* (later included in *The Woman Who Rode Away*) were all published in 1926. The majority of the eight essays in *Mornings in Mexico* (1927) had appeared in periodicals.

In 1928 *Rawdon's Roof* was followed by *The Woman Who Rode Away*, a collection of ten short stories most of which had already appeared in periodicals; an additional story, 'The Man Who Loved Islands', was included in the American edition of the same year. *Lady Chatterley's Lover* was first published in a limited edition (Florence, 1928). A popular edition (Paris, 1929) contained an introductory essay 'My Skirmish with Jolly Roger' (published separately, New York, 1929), later expanded and published posthumously in 1930 as *A Propos of Lady Chatterley's Lover*. An authorized expurgated edition of the novel was published in 1932, but it was not until 1959 that a full text was published in New York. In England, after a celebrated trial, the unexpurgated text was published in 1960. An early version of the novel appeared in New York in 1944 with the title *The First Lady Chatterley*. An intermediate version has been published only in an Italian translation.

Many of Lawrence's early poems were revised for *Collected Poems* (2 vols., 1928). *The Paintings of D. H. Lawrence* (privately printed, 1929) contained a long introduction. *Pansies* was published in 1929; a privately printed limited edition later in the same year contained the author's original preface and fourteen additional poems. *The Escaped Cock* (privately printed, Paris, 1929) was considerably revised and expanded after its initial appearance in *The Forum* (Feb. 1928); in 1931 it was published as *The Man Who Died*. *Pornography and Obscenity*, part of which had appeared in *This Quarter* (July–Sept. 1929) was also published in 1929. A further collection of poems appeared as *Nettles* (1930). In the same year *Assorted Articles* contained essays which had been printed in magazines and newspapers during 1928 and 1929, some of the original titles being changed for book publication. Further publications in 1930 were *The Virgin and the Gipsy* (Florence), 'The Triumph of the Machine' (later included in *Last Poems*), and *Love Among the Haystacks*, a collection of three early pieces with an introduction by D. Garnett.

Apocalypse was published in Florence in 1931. Other posthumous volumes, all published in 1932, were *Last Poems* (Florence) edited by R. Aldington and G. Orioli; *Etruscan Places*, a collection of essays which had appeared in 1927 and 1928 in *Travel* and *World To-day*; and *The Lovely Lady*, a gathering of late stories. Three plays were included in *The Plays of D. H. Lawrence* (1933), and an earlier play, *A Collier's Friday Night*, was published in 1934. Further collections were *The Tales of D. H. Lawrence* (1934), containing most of the shorter fiction published before 1931; *A Modern Lover* (1934), comprising six early tales and the unfinished novel *Mr. Noon*; and the large number of essays and reviews edited by E. D. McDonald as *Phoenix* (1936; reprinted 1961). R. Jeffers wrote a foreword to *Fire and Other Poems* (San Francisco, 1940), and A. Arnold edited early versions of *Studies in Classic American Literature* as *The Symbolic Meaning* (1962).

The outstanding collection of Lawrence manuscripts is at the University of Texas. It contains over one hundred letters and approximately one hundred MSS., including those of *Sons and Lovers*, *The Rainbow*, *Women in Love* (two versions), and an early draft of *Lady Chatterley's Lover*. The New York Public Library also possesses substantial manuscript resources. A large number of letters and an early revised typescript of *The Plumed Serpent* are at Harvard, while Yale has letters, notebooks, MSS. of poems, and a typescript of *Sea and Sardinia*. Other manuscript material is located at the University of Buffalo Library, the Huntington Library, the libraries of the University of California at Berkeley and Los Angeles, Stanford University, the University of Cincinnati, the University of Nottingham, and the British Museum.

A Uniform Pocket Edition of the novels was published in twenty volumes, 1927–34, and a Uniform Edition of the Works in thirty-three volumes, 1936–9. The Phoenix Edition (21 vols., 1954–7) contains the novels, short stories, travel writings, and poems. The presentation of the poems in this last edition would do credit to an irrationality far greater than any attributed to their author, and for a full and reliable text the reader must at present turn to that accompanying the Italian translation by P. Nardi. An edition by V. de S. Pinto and F. W. Roberts is in preparation. By August 1961 there were twenty-two volumes by Lawrence in Penguin Books.

A. Huxley selected and introduced *The Letters of D. H. Lawrence* in 1932. *D. H. Lawrence's Letters to Bertrand Russell* were edited by H. T. Moore (New York, 1948) and *Eight Letters to Rachel Annand Taylor* by M. Ewing (Pasadena, 1956). *The Collected Letters* were edited in two volumes by H. T. Moore in 1961. There are selections of letters by R. Aldington (1950) and D. Trilling (New York, 1958).

R. Aldington edited *Selected Poems* (1934) and *The Spirit of Place* (1935); A. D. Hawkins, *Stories, Essays and Poems* (1939); and D. Trilling, *The Portable D. H. Lawrence* (New York, 1947). Other selections of poems were made by K. Rexroth (New York, 1948), W. E. Williams (1950), and J. Reeves (1951). H. T. Moore edited *Sex, Literature and Censorship* (New York, 1953), a collection of essays with an introduction on Lawrence's struggle with censorship. More recent selections include A. Beal's *Selected Literary Criticism* (1955) and T. R. Barnes's *Selected Poetry and Prose* (1957).

Among biographical works on Lawrence pride of place must be given to Frieda Lawrence's *Not I, But the Wind* (New York, 1934). Two books by H. T. Moore are highly informative: *The Life and Works of D. H. Lawrence* (New York, 1951) and *The Intelligent Heart* (New York, 1955; revised edition, 1960). E. Nehls's three-volume work *D. H. Lawrence: A Composite Biography* (Madison, 1957–9) is a useful source of reference which includes almost everything of biographical value written on Lawrence in addition to much fresh material. Frieda Lawrence's *Memoirs and Correspondence* were edited by E. W. Tedlock in 1961.

Much writing on Lawrence is more or less polemical in tone. N. Douglas's *D. H. Lawrence and Maurice Magnus: A Plea for Better Manners* (Florence, 1924) was included in his *Experiments* (1925). Letters and early work were included in Ada Lawrence's and G. S. Gelder's *Young Lorenzo: The Early Life of D. H. Lawrence* (Florence, 1931); a slightly enlarged version appeared in London the following year as *The Early Life of D. H. Lawrence*. J. M. Murry's *Son of Woman* (1931), described by Aldous Huxley as a 'curious essay in destructive hagiography', was reprinted with a new introduction in 1954. A reply was made by C. Carswell in *The Savage Pilgrimage* (1932); her book was withdrawn after publication and a revised version issued in the same year. M. Dodge Luhan's *Lorenzo in Taos* (New York, 1932) included letters but little else of value. In *Reminiscences of D. H. Lawrence* (1933) J. M. Murry reprinted essays from the *Adelphi* and elsewhere and also defended himself against Mrs. Carswell's strictures. Other memoirs are D. Brett, *Lawrence and Brett: A Friendship* (Philadelphia, 1933), E. and A. Brewster, *D. H. Lawrence: Reminiscences and Correspondence* (1934), and E. T. [Jessie Chambers], *D. H. Lawrence: A Personal Record* (1935). In 1938 K. Merrild recalled Lawrence in Mexico in *A Poet and Two Painters*. A detailed and sympathetic account of Lawrence's life is to be found in P. Nardi's *La Vita di D. H. Lawrence* (Milan, 1947), the introductory volume to a complete Italian translation of Lawrence's works. The early 1950's saw R. Aldington's sympathetic and astringent *Portrait of a Genius, But . . .* (1950); A. West's short biographical and critical study, *D. H. Lawrence* (1950); W. Bynner's *Journey with Genius* (New York, 1951); and H. Corke's brief memoir of Jessie Chambers, *D. H. Lawrence's 'Princess'* (1951). In *Poste Restante: A Lawrence Travel Calendar* (Berkeley, 1956) H. T. Moore produced a short 'geographical biography' with extracts from unpublished letters.

H. J. Seligman's *D. H. Lawrence: An American Interpretation* (New York, 1924) is an early attempt at explicit discussion of the writing. Later pamphlets and books are R. Aldington, *D. H. Lawrence* (Seattle, 1927; English edition slightly revised, 1930), R. West, *D. H. Lawrence* (1930), F. R. Leavis, *D. H. Lawrence* (1930), S. Potter, *D. H. Lawrence* (1930), A. Nin, *D. H. Lawrence: An Unprofessional Study* (Paris, 1932; reprinted London, 1962), F. Carter, *D. H. Lawrence and the Body Mystical* (1932), and H. Corke, *Lawrence and Apocalypse* (1933). These last two books also contain limited biographical information. H. Gregory's *Pilgrim of the Apocalypse* (New York, 1933; reprinted with a new introduction, 1957) includes a survey of the verse. W. Y. Tindall's *D. H. Lawrence and Susan his Cow* (New York, 1939) is a frequently perceptive but basically hostile study of Lawrence's ideas; an answer is attempted by Fr. W. Tiverton [W. R. Jarrett-Kerr] in *D. H. Lawrence and Human Existence* (1951; reissued with a new introduction, 1961), a survey from the viewpoint of Christian theology. K. Young's *D. H. Lawrence* (*Writers and their Work*, no. 31, 1952; rev. ed., 1960) is an introductory essay with a select bibliography and a useful index to the short stories and essays. *The Achievement of D. H. Lawrence* (Norman, Okla., 1953), edited by F. J. Hoffman and H. T. Moore, is a compendium reprinting essays by eighteen writers.

F. R. Leavis's *D. H. Lawrence: Novelist* (1955) is a work of high critical authority, and G. Hough's *The Dark Sun* (1956) is a balanced and judicious survey. Other recent publications are M. Freeman's *D. H. Lawrence: A Basic Study of His Ideas* (Gainesville, Fla., 1955), M. Spilka's *The Love Ethic of D. H. Lawrence* (Bloomington, Ind., 1955), and A. Arnold's *D. H. Lawrence and America* (1958), which has some interesting pages on *Studies in Classic American Literature* but is chiefly valuable for a substantial appendix on Lawrence's reputation in England and America. C. H. Rolph edited *The Trial of Lady Chatterley* (1961); an edition privately printed in the same year includes a reprint from *Hansard* of a debate in the House of Lords on 14 Dec. 1960, notable for a penetrating speech by Lord Hailsham. E. Vivas's *D. H. Lawrence: The Failure and the Triumph of Art* (Evanston, Ill., 1960), a detailed examination of seven major novels, sees a decline in Lawrence's artistic powers; A. Beal's *D. H. Lawrence* (1961) is a short introduction.

Chapters or sections in books include: H. James, *Notes on Novelists* (1914); E. Garnett, *Friday Nights* (1922); E. Muir, *Transition* (1926); B. Dobrée, *The Lamp and the Lute* (1929); W. Lewis, *Paleface* (1929); A. Huxley, *Music at Night* (1931); R. West, *Ending in Earnest* (New York, 1931); G. Hughes, *Imagism and the Imagists* (Stanford, 1931; reprinted, 1960); J. W. Beach, *The Twentieth Century Novel: Studies in Technique* (New York, 1932); F. R. Leavis, *For Continuity* (1933); T. S. Eliot, *After Strange Gods* (1934); A. Maurois, *Prophets and Poets* (New York, 1935); S. Spender, *The Destructive Element* (1935; see also *The Creative Element*, 1953); C. Caudwell, *Studies in a Dying Culture* (1938); H. Miller, *The Wisdom of the Heart* (Norfolk, Conn., 1941); E. Bentley, *A Century of Hero Worship* (Philadelphia, 1944; English edition, *The Cult of the Superman*, 1947); H. Gregory, *The Shield of Achilles* (New York, 1944); D. S. Savage, *The Personal Principle* (1944); W. Phillips and P. Rahv, eds., *The Partisan Reader* (New York, 1946); V. Woolf, *The Moment and Other Essays* (1947); G. H. Bantock, *Freedom and Authority in*

Education (1952); R. P. Blackmur, *Language as Gesture* (New York, 1952); F. R. Leavis, *The Common Pursuit* (1952); S. de Beauvoir, *The Second Sex* (1953); N. A. Scott, *Rehearsals of Discomposure* (New York, 1953); L. Vivante, *A Philosophy of Potentiality* (1955); J. M. Murry, *Love, Freedom and Society* (1957); R. Rees, *Brave Men: A Study of D. H. Lawrence and Simone Weil* (1958); D. Krook, *Three Traditions of Moral Thought* (1959); G. Hough, *Image and Experience* (1960); and E. Dahlberg and H. Read, *Truth is More Sacred* (1961).

Representative essays in periodicals include: L. Trilling, 'D. H. Lawrence: A Neglected Aspect' (*Symposium* i, 1930); A. Malraux, 'Preface to the French Translation of *Lady Chatterley's Lover* (*Criterion* xii, 1933); S. Anderson, 'A Man's Song of Life' (*Virginia Quarterly Review* ix, 1933); J. Wahl, 'Sur D. H. Lawrence' (*Nouvelle revue française*, Jan. 1934); H. Davis, 'The Poetic Genius of D. H. Lawrence' (*University of Toronto Quarterly* iii, 1934); H. Hesse, 'Erinnerung an ein paar Bücher' (*Die Neue Rundschau* lxv, 1934); *The Phoenix*, 1938–40 (a short-lived and idiosyncratic journal which devoted much of its space to Lawrence); E. Vivas, 'Lawrence's Problems' (*Kenyon Review* iii, 1941); W. H. Auden, 'Some Notes on D. H. Lawrence' (*Nation* clxiv, 26 April 1947); and W. Allen, 'Lawrence in Perspective' (*Penguin New Writing* No. 29, 1947). Later articles include J. F. Danby, 'D. H. Lawrence' (*Cambridge Journal* iv, 1951); T. Greene, 'Lawrence and the Quixotic Hero' (*Sewanee Review* lix, 1951); H. Davis, '*Women in Love*: A Corrected Typescript' (*University of Toronto Quarterly* xxvii, 1957); V. de S. Pinto, 'D. H. Lawrence: Letter-Writer and Craftsman in Verse' (*Renaissance and Modern Studies* i, 1957); M. Gindre, 'Points de Vue sur D. H. Lawrence' (*Études anglaises* xi, 1958); M. Engel, 'Lawrence's Short Novels' (*Hudson Review* xi, 1958); K. Widmer, 'D. H. Lawrence and the Art of Nihilism' (*Kenyon Review* xx, 1958); *Modern Fiction Studies* v, 1959 (a special Lawrence issue); R. Hogan, 'D. H. Lawrence and his Critics' (*Essays in Criticism* ix, 1959); R. B. Heilman, 'Nomad, Monads, and the Mystique of the Soma' (*Sewanee Review* lxviii, 1960); A. E. Waterman, 'The Plays of D. H. Lawrence' (*Modern Drama* ii, 1960); V. de S. Pinto, 'Poet Without A Mask' (*Critical Quarterly* iii, 1961); and C. Hassall, 'D. H. Lawrence and the Etruscans' (*Essays by Divers Hands* N.S. xxxi, 1962). See also a series of articles and letters in *Encounter* (Feb. 1961–June 1962) on *Lady Chatterley's Lover* and the trial of 1960.

Until the appearance of the Soho bibliography by F. W. Roberts the standard work is that by E. D. McDonald: *A Bibliography of the Writings of D. H. Lawrence* (Philadelphia, 1925) and *The Writings of D. H. Lawrence 1925–1930: A Bibliographical Supplement* (Philadelphia, 1931). These two volumes should be supplemented by W. White's *D. H. Lawrence: A Checklist 1931–1950* (Detroit, 1950), which also prints a full list of works and articles on Lawrence during these years. More specialized bibliographies are L. C. Powell's catalogue *The Manuscripts of D. H. Lawrence* (Los Angeles, 1937) and the descriptive bibliography by E. W. Tedlock, Jr., *The Frieda Lawrence Collection of D. H. Lawrence Manuscripts* (Albuquerque, N.M., 1948). Catalogues of general interest are those by E. Tannenbaum, *D. H. Lawrence: An Exhibition of First Editions, Manuscripts, Paintings, Letters and Miscellany* (Carbondale, Ill., 1958), and V. de S. Pinto, *D. H. Lawrence after Thirty Years* (Nottingham, 1960). A 'Checklist of Criticism' will be found in the special Lawrence number of *Modern Fiction Studies* (v, 1959).

INDEX

Works by the eight writers discussed are listed under the authors' names: other titles are listed separately in alphabetical order. References to extended discussions are in bold figures. Biographical information is indicated by italics.